# STUDIES ON VOLTAIRE AND THE EIGHTEENTH CENTURY

*SVEC*
2008:

*SVEC*
INDEX

A fully searchable index to over
fifty years of research published in *SVEC*
http://www.voltaire.ox.ac.uk/svec_index

*General editor*
JONATHAN MALLINSON, Trinity College, University of Oxford

*Associate editors*
HUBERT BOST, Ecole Pratique des Hautes Etudes, Paris
DANIEL BREWER, University of Minnesota
SARAH MAZA, Northwestern University

*Advisory panel*
WILDA ANDERSON, Johns Hopkins University
MARC ANDRÉ BERNIER, Université du Québec à Trois-Rivières
NICHOLAS CRONK, Voltaire Foundation
SIMON DAVIES, Queen's University, Belfast
MICHEL DELON, Université de Paris-Sorbonne – Paris IV
JULIA DOUTHWAITE, University of Notre Dame
JENS HÄSELER, Universität Potsdam
MARIAN HOBSON, Queen Mary, University of London
MARK LEDBURY, Sterling and Francine Clark Art Institute
FRANÇOIS MOUREAU, Université de Paris-Sorbonne – Paris IV
MICHAEL O'DEA, Université Lumière – Lyon II
PHILIP STEWART, Duke University
CATHERINE VOLPILHAC-AUGER, ENS Lettres et sciences humaines, Lyon

*Managing editor*
LYN ROBERTS

Manuscripts should be prepared in accordance with the *SVEC* style sheet, available on request and at the Voltaire Foundation website (www.voltaire.ox.ac.uk). One paper copy should be submitted to the *SVEC* general editor at the Voltaire Foundation, 99 Banbury Road, Oxford OX2 6JX, UK; an electronic version, with a summary of about 750 words, should be sent to jonathan.mallinson@trinity.ox.ac.uk.

# Peripheries of the Enlightenment

*Edited by*

RICHARD BUTTERWICK,
SIMON DAVIES

*and*

GABRIEL SÁNCHEZ ESPINOSA

*SVEC*
2008:01

VOLTAIRE FOUNDATION

OXFORD

2008

© 2008 Voltaire Foundation, University of Oxford

ISBN 978 0 7294 0926 1
ISSN 0435-2866

Voltaire Foundation
99 Banbury Road
Oxford OX2 6JX, UK

A catalogue record for this book
is available from the British Library

The correct reference for this volume is
*SVEC* 2008:01

This series is available on annual subscription

For further information about *SVEC*
and other Voltaire Foundation publications see
www.voltaire.ox.ac.uk, or email svec@voltaire.ox.ac.uk

This book is printed on acid-free paper

Typeset and printed in Europe by the Alden Group, Oxfordshire

# Contents

| | |
|---|---|
| Acknowledgements | vii |
| List of abbreviations | ix |
| RICHARD BUTTERWICK<br>Peripheries of the Enlightenment: an introduction | 1 |
| SIMON DAVIES<br>Whither/wither France: Voltaire's view from Ferney | 17 |
| GRAHAM GARGETT<br>French periphery, European centre: eighteenth-century Geneva and its contribution to the Enlightenment | 29 |
| MICHAEL BROWN<br>Was there an Irish Enlightenment? The case of the Anglicans | 49 |
| JOHN ROBERTSON<br>Political economy and the 'feudal system' in Enlightenment Naples: outline of a problem | 65 |
| MARIE-CHRISTINE SKUNCKE<br>Jean-Jacques Rousseau in Swedish eyes around 1760 | 87 |
| ORSOLYA SZAKÁLY<br>Enlightened self-interest: the development of an entrepreneurial culture within the Hungarian elite | 105 |
| MARTIN FITZPATRICK<br>The view from Mount Pleasant: Enlightenment in late-eighteenth-century Liverpool | 119 |
| SIMON BURROWS<br>Grub Street revolutionaries: marginal writers at the Enlightenment's periphery? | 145 |
| ULTÁN GILLEN<br>Varieties of Enlightenment: the Enlightenment and Irish political culture in the age of revolutions | 163 |

*Contents*

GABRIEL SÁNCHEZ ESPINOSA
An *ilustrado* in his province: Jovellanos in Asturias     183

RICHARD BUTTERWICK
Between Anti-Enlightenment and enlightened Catholicism: provincial preachers in late-eighteenth-century Poland-Lithuania     201

SIMON DIXON
'Prosveshchenie': Enlightenment in eighteenth-century Russia     229

FIONA CLARK
The *Gazeta de Literatura de México* and the edge of reason: when is a periphery not a periphery?     251

LYNDA PRATT
Tea and national history? Ann Yearsley, John Thelwall and the late-eighteenth-century provincial English epic     265

PETER HANNS REILL
The Enlightenment from the German periphery: Johann Herder's reinterpretation of the Enlightenment     281

Summaries     289

Bibliography     295

Index     329

# Acknowledgements

This volume of essays, with one exception, originated in papers delivered at a colloquium of the same name at Queen's University Belfast in 2005. The colloquium was the first international event organised by the interdisciplinary Centre for Eighteenth-Century Studies at Queen's (CECS). Participation was by invitation only. We should like to record our gratitude to our speakers for their invigorating and congenial presence. In addition, we should like to thank them for often expanding and reworking their papers in the light of discussions at the colloquium.

The colloquium would not have been possible without the generous financial assistance from Research and Regional Services, headed by Trevor Newsom at Queen's University. Jonathan Mallinson, the general editor of *SVEC*, encouraged the idea of the colloquium from the beginning and we are grateful to him for publishing this resulting themed volume. We also want to record our gratitude to the staff of the Voltaire Foundation, especially Lyn Roberts, for seeing the book safely through the press.

The editors dedicate the volume to the memory of their former colleague at Queen's, Professor Peter Jupp (1940-2006). Peter was a masterly historian of British and Irish government and politics in the long eighteenth century. He was a founder member of CECS. He chaired a session at the colloquium and contributed to it with his customary insight and good humour.

Richard Butterwick<br>
Simon Davies<br>
Gabriel Sánchez Espinosa

# List of abbreviations

D*****  Voltaire, *Correspondence and related documents*, ed. Th. Besterman, in *The Complete works of Voltaire*, vol.85-135 (Geneva, Banbury and Oxford, 1968-1977).

*Encyclopédie*  *Encyclopédie, ou Dictionnaire raisonné des sciences, des arts et des métiers, par une société de gens de lettres*, ed. Denis Diderot and Jean D'Alembert, 17 vols (Paris and Neufchâtel, Briasson, 1751-1765).

*M*  Voltaire, *Œuvres complètes*, ed. Louis Moland, 52 vols (Paris, 1877-1885).

*OCV*  *The Complete works of Voltaire*, ed. Th. Besterman (Oxford, 1968-).

RICHARD BUTTERWICK

# Peripheries of the Enlightenment: an introduction

> Glory to the enlightenment of the current century, which illuminates even the Simbirsk region!
>
> A. A. Petrov to N. M. Karamzin, 11 June 1785[1]

THIS collection is founded on two premises. The first is that the Enlightenment made a significant impact across vast tracts of Eurasia and the Americas. The second is that we can learn at least as much about the Enlightenment from commentators, both favourably and unfavourably disposed towards 'the enlightened eighteenth century', at the spatial and temporal peripheries of the enlightened world, as from its most radical theorists in its early epicentres.

The dissection of the illusory optimism of Enlightenment reason and its indictment as a source of domination and oppression, begun by Max Horkheimer and Theodor Adorno, and continued by Michel Foucault, have proceeded apace in the last two or three decades. These have been conducted on the one hand by postmodernists, post-colonialists and feminists, eager to jettison the yoke of scientific truth and white patriarchal power structures, and on the other by conservatives and neo-Romantics who continue to condemn the Enlightenment as an arrogant and ultimately nihilistic revolt against God and His Truth in the name of rationalism. Jürgen Habermas' message that the 'Enlightenment project' for civil society remains incomplete and is worth pursuing still finds adherents but, in general, the optimistic view of the Enlightenment, still prevalent in the 1960s, has lost ground.[2]

---

1. Nikolai M. Karamzin, *Pis'ma russkogo puteshestvennika*, ed. Iu. M. Lotman, N. A. Marchenko and B. A. Uspenskii (Leningrad, 1984), p.502, quoted and discussed by Simon Dixon, below, p.246.
2. Max Horkheimer and Theodor Adorno, *Dialectic of Enlightenment* (1947; English translation: New York, 1972); Michel Foucault, *Discipline and punish* (New York, 1977); Reinhart Koselleck, *Critique and crisis: the Enlightenment and the pathogenesis of modern society* (1973; English translation: Oxford, 1988); Jürgen Habermas, *The Structural transformation of the public sphere: an inquiry into a category of bourgeois society* (1962; English translation: Cambridge, MA, 1989). A weather vane for recent scholarly preoccupations could be *Progrès et violence au XVIII<sup>e</sup> siècle*, ed. Valérie Cossy and Deirdre Dawson, Etudes internationales sur le dix-huitième siècle 3 (Paris, 2001). Compare Robert Darnton, 'George Washington's false teeth: a civic sermon', in *La Recherche dix-huitiémiste: objets, méthodes et*

A common weakness of philosophers' and theologians' discussions on the legacy of the Enlightenment is an inadequate knowledge of it in its historical context.[3] Yet historians' investigations of that context have yielded a bewildering picture over the last three decades or so. We learn of the darker side of the Enlightenment, its diversities, doubts, perversions and contesters. The Enlightenment has fragmented. But not all scholars have concluded that it will share the fate of Humpty Dumpty. Two approaches dominate attempts to characterise the Enlightenment as a whole, roughly corresponding to a narrower focus on a radical vanguard (or vanguards) and a broader sweep over a moderate or 'mainstream' hinterland (or hinterlands). This dichotomy could be recast as the study of ideas and their most enthusiastic propagators, as opposed to a set of broader cultural trends, firmly located in social and political contexts.

The first approach traditionally concentrated on France, and the *philosophes*: the quartet of Voltaire, Montesquieu, Diderot and the dissonant Rousseau to the fore, with a supporting orchestra led by D'Alembert, Holbach, Helvétius and Condorcet, and a variant played by physiocrats (or *économistes*) such as Quesnay and the elder Mirabeau.[4] This 'High Enlightenment' was counterpointed by Robert Darnton with an Enlightenment 'low-life' of wannabe Voltaires who, frustrated in their ambitions, undermined respect for throne and altar with obscene *libelles* before playing leading roles in the Revolution. Darnton sparked a debate that has now left little of his original thesis untouched. The latest contribution is made here by Simon Burrows, showing how revolution could move writers from the murky margins to the spot-lit centre of literary and political life. By looking at the *libellistes*' exile in England, he also moves the debate beyond France.[5]

It was not in France that the Enlightenment began. The role of the Dutch Republic as a crucible of Enlightenment was long ago recognised by Paul Hazard.[6] A mixture of political and religious exiles (Anglo-Irish Whigs, French Huguenots and Polish anti-Trinitarians) and local disciples

---

*institutions (1945-1995)*, Etudes internationales sur le dix-huitième siècle 1, ed. Michel Delon and Jochen Schlobach (Paris, 1998), p.149-65. See also n.8 below.

3. This applies, for example, to the stimulating discussion hosted by John Paul II, published in Polish translation as *Oświecenie dzisiaj: Rozmowy w Castelgandolfo*, ed. Krzysztof Michalski (Cracow, 1999).

4. See, for instance, Peter Gay, *The Enlightenment: an interpretation*, 2 vols (New York, 1966-1969); Norman Hampson, *The Enlightenment* (London, 1968). Ernst Cassirer, *The Philosophy of the Enlightenment* (1932; English translation: Cambridge, 1953), saw much of eighteenth-century rationalist thought as a necessary preparation for Kant.

5. Robert Darnton, 'The High Enlightenment and the low-life of literature in pre-revolutionary France', *Past and present* 51 (1971), p.81-115. Compare John Lough, 'The French literary underground reconsidered', *SVEC* 329 (1995), p.471-82; *The Darnton debate: books and revolution in the eighteenth century*, ed. Haydn T. Mason (Oxford, 1998). See also Simon Burrows, *Blackmail, scandal, and revolution: London's French libellistes, 1758-1792* (Manchester, 2006).

6. Paul Hazard, *La Crise de la conscience européenne* (Paris, 1935).

of Spinoza found helpful conditions for intellectual combustion in the high degree of religious toleration and low level of centralised political authority of the United Provinces. So, according to Margaret Jacob, from Amsterdam and Utrecht spread Masonic or quasi-Masonic networks. Huguenots based in London played a crucial role in informing francophone Europe of literary and scientific developments in England.[7] More recently Jonathan Israel has, with dazzling erudition, placed Spinoza and his followers centre-stage, downgrading English influences upon the French *philosophes*, among whom Diderot takes pride of place. For Israel, 'the real business was already over' by the 1740s,[8] and 'radical', rather than 'moderate' or 'mainstream' Enlightenment is the key to understanding – and embracing – secular modernity.[9] This view would imply a second, applied wave of 'radical Enlightenment', culminating in the Terror and dechristianisation in France, with a lull in between.[10]

Such a trajectory explicitly contradicts most of the historiography of the Enlightenment over the last quarter of a century, which in the wake of the famous collection edited by Roy Porter and Mikuláš Teich has depicted a widely spread movement, with national, regional, local and even confessional variations, with extensive moderate hinterlands, focused on activity at least as much as ideas. Outside the British Isles and the Dutch Republic, Enlightenment seems to have been at its most intense between the 1740s and 1780s, and even there, enlightened social and cultural initiatives compensated in terms of quantity whatever may have been lacking in terms of radical intellectual quality.[11] The historiography

---

7. Margaret C. Jacob, *The Radical Enlightenment: pantheists, Freemasons and republicans* (London, 1981).

8. Jonathan Israel, *Radical Enlightenment: philosophy and the making of modernity, 1650-1750* (Oxford, 2001), p.7: a conclusion explicitly rejected by Simon Davies below, p.26, n.34, and implicitly by this collection.

9. In his equally impressive second volume, *Enlightenment contested: philosophy, modernity and the emancipation of man, 1670-1752* (Oxford, 2006), Israel accords greater importance to the contest between 'radical' and 'moderate' Enlightenments, while continuing to prioritise the former over the latter, on the grounds of its coherence and cogency, evaluating it as 'inherently superior morally, politically, and intellectually not only to Postmodernist claims but to *all* actual or possible alternatives, no matter how *different*, national and Postcolonial and no matter how illiberal, non-western and traditional' (p.869). This massive work, demanding careful digestion, appeared too late for the contributors to take it into account.

10. See the remarks of Dale K. Van Kley, 'Christianity as casualty and chrysalis of modernity: the problem of dechristianization in the French Revolution', *American historical review* 108 (2003), p.1081-104. The third volume of Israel's trilogy is set 'to continue further the story of the impact of radical thought in the western Atlantic world, centring around the phenomenon of radical and revolutionary philosophy, after 1752 down to and through the American, French and Batavian Revolutions' (*Enlightenment contested*, p.42). The significance of the impact of moderate Enlightenment upon other parts of the Atlantic and Eurasian worlds is thereby diminished *a priori*.

11. *The Enlightenment in national context*, ed. Roy Porter and Mikuláš Teich (Cambridge, 1981). Roy Porter, *Enlightenment: Britain and the creation of the modern world* (Harmondsworth, 2000). Wijnand W. Mijnhardt, 'The Dutch Enlightenment: problems and definitions', in

of the last three decades has also explored the social and institutional contexts in which ideas could be discussed and applied, by women as well as men, much of it summed up in the phrase 'the Republic of Letters'. So we have work on publishers, periodicals, booksellers, as well as work on censors and the clandestine circulation of tracts, in which Robert Darnton has excelled. Much research has also been conducted on the social spaces of discussion, including salons, coffee-houses, taverns and pleasure gardens.[12] Here Habermas' concept of the public sphere ('Öffentlichkeit') has proved immensely useful, despite the faulty chronology of his thesis, and the jettisoning by most historians of his insistence that the public sphere was 'bourgeois', given the number of nobles and clergymen taking part in public discussions of enlightened ideas and policies.[13]

Where attention has focused on the transmission of ideas, it has shown how much was gained, or lost, in translation, and how local circumstances allowed new meanings to be read into texts written elsewhere.[14] Montesquieu's *Esprit des lois*, to take an exceptionally influential and polyvalent example, could be read in England both as a compliment and as a warning, in Germany as a theory of the Teutonic sources of English freedoms, in the newly independent North American states as a prescription for the separation of powers, in Hungary as a justification of the defence of noble liberties, in Russia as a guide to modern jurisprudence, in Poland as a concept of liberty founded on personal security, and in many other ways besides. Even in France, attention has moved to provincial correspondence networks, among men who were far from any desire to turn the world upside-down.[15] The question arises of whether it is possible, or indeed desirable, to isolate the Enlightenment from its influence, and the reaction to it.

---

*Centre(s) et périphérie(s): les Lumières de Belfast à Beijing*, ed. Marie-Christine Skuncke (Paris, 2003), p.169-83. J. G. A. Pocock has proposed multiple Protestant Enlightenments, largely clerical and conservative, in *Barbarism and religion: the Enlightenments of Edward Gibbon, 1737-1764* (Cambridge, 1999). Compare Israel's case against 'diffusionist', 'national' and 'plural' approaches in *Radical Enlightenment*, p.v, 22, and *Enlightenment contested*, p.18-20, 863-65.

12. See, for example, Dena Goodman, *The Republic of Letters: a cultural history of the French Enlightenment* (Ithaca, NY, and London, 1994); Robert Darnton, *The Literary underground of the Old Regime* (Cambridge, MA, 1982); R. Darnton, *The Forbidden bestsellers of pre-Revolutionary France* (New York and London, 1996); Daniel Roche, *France in the Enlightenment* (1993; English translation: Cambridge, MA, 1998). Three syntheses that take the broader and contextual approach are Ulrich im Hof, *The Enlightenment* (1993; English translation: Oxford, 1994); Dorinda Outram, *The Enlightenment* (Cambridge, 1995); Thomas Munck, *The Enlightenment: a comparative social history, 1721-1794* (London, 2000).

13. For a vigorous application of Habermas' theory from an ideologically opposite standpoint, see T. C. W. Blanning, *The Culture of power and the power of culture: Old Regime Europe 1660-1789* (Oxford, 2002).

14. See for example Fania Oz-Salzberger, *Translating the Enlightenment: Scottish civic discourse in eighteenth-century Germany* (Oxford, 1995).

15. L. W. B. Brockliss, *Calvet's web: Enlightenment and the Republic of Letters in eighteenth-century France* (Oxford, 2002).

*Peripheries of the Enlightenment: an introduction*

One response, led by John Robertson, has been to define Enlightenment more strictly in terms of ideas, but with the temporal betterment of humanity, via political economy, at its heart, rather than an assault on Christian belief. The study of human civilisation was the chief preoccupation of enlightened thinkers: a reiteration of the insistence that the Enlightenment was the 'study of man', but the paradigm becomes Scotland, rather than France.[16] Indeed, such intellectual priorities can be found across much of the Euro-Atlantic world during the eighteenth century; according to Wijnand Mijnhardt, 'the French Enlightenment was, instead of the norm, the chief anomaly.'[17]

Another path, pioneered by Barry Nesbit in 1982, and followed by several of the contributors to this volume, is to seek the Enlightenment in eighteenth- and early-nineteenth-century perceptions of the age, not least in the word itself.[18] In Romance languages we speak either of the light itself ('les lumières', 'las luces'), or of an 'ism' ('illuminismo'). But in several languages of northern and eastern Europe we have a process of illumination or elucidation: 'Aufklärung', 'Voorlichting', 'Felvilágosodás', 'Prosveshchenie', 'Oświecenie', 'Upplysning'. These equivalents of Enlightenment, now used as a general characterisation of the (later) eighteenth century, took the lower case in eighteenth-century usages, except, for philological reasons, in German. In his famous essay of 1784, Kant denied that his age was 'enlightened' ('aufgeklärt'), but he did claim that it was an 'age of enlightenment'. Habermas' unfinished project grew out of Kant's answer, just as his idea of 'Öffentlichkeit' did: it was through unfettered public discussion that Enlightenment could spread.[19] Similarly, according to Johann Herder, 'enlightenment ('Aufklärung') is

---

16. See John Robertson, 'The Enlightenment above national context: political economy in eighteenth-century Scotland and Naples', *Historical journal* 40 (1997), p.667-97; J. Robertson, *The Case for the Enlightenment: Scotland and Naples 1680-1760* (Cambridge, 2005); and his essay below.

17. Mijnhardt, 'The Dutch Enlightenment', p.170. Israel, *Enlightenment contested*, p.12, 186-87, 352-56, 367-71, 381-96, 513-19, 862, acknowledges that only in France did 'radical Enlightenment' retain control of the intellectual avant-garde. Britain, the Netherlands, Italy and Germany embraced 'moderate' or 'mainstream Enlightenment'. But was the principal reason the exceptional inability of the French *ancien régime* to adapt itself to 'moderate Enlightenment', the exceptional intellectual cogency of Diderot and his allies, or the exceptional circumstances of the Jansenist attack on the *philosophes* between 1748 and 1752? Compare Israel, *Enlightenment contested*, ch.32-33.

18. H. B. Nisbet, '*Was ist Aufklärung?* The concept of Enlightenment in eighteenth-century Germany', *Journal of European studies* 12 (1982), p.77-95. I have pursued this line in 'What is Enlightenment (*oświecenie*)? Some Polish answers, 1765-1820', *Central Europe* 3:1 (2005), p.19-37. See the essays by Simon Dixon, Orsolya Szakály and Ultán Gillen below.

19. Immanuel Kant, *An Answer to the question 'What is Enlightenment?'* (1784), in I. Kant, *Political writings*, ed. Hans Reiss, 2nd edn (Cambridge, 1991), p.55-61. The essay is reprinted in several collections, including the aptly titled *What is Enlightenment? Eighteenth-century answers and twentieth-century questions*, ed. James Schmidt (Berkeley, CA, 1996).

never an end but always a means. If it becomes the former it is a sign that it has ceased.'[20]

The secondary optical metaphor most often applied to the Enlightenment is diffusion, implying that as light moves away from its source, it becomes not only less bright, but less distinct. Yet a flash of light can be disorienting, even blinding, at its source. Projected, refracted, filtered and focused light can be clearer, and its effects more easily analysed, at a distance – from the peripheries of the illuminated space. But why should the contours of Enlightenment seem clearer when further away from its source(s)? Is it a coincidence that the most famous of all definitions of Enlightenment, Kant's, was written in Königsberg, and published in Berlin in 1784, and not in Amsterdam, London or Paris around 1700? Perhaps it is because at the early epicentres of 'radical Enlightenment', Europe's thinkers did consider problems – ultimately insoluble problems – of universal import. At the peripheries, practical improvements and reforms were required to close the gap with 'enlightened nations' (a frequently employed Polish phrase), and Enlightenment could more easily be understood as a process.

Franco Venturi's labours on the Enlightenment in the Italian peninsula led him to ponder the impact of Enlightenment ideas at the European 'periphery' – for example in Russia, Poland and Hungary – and to sketch out a geography and chronology of the Enlightenment, as it radiated and reflected from country to country. Two parts (in three volumes) of his monumental *Settecento riformatore*, moreover, followed the affairs of almost the entire Euro-Atlantic world between 1768 and 1789 through the prism of enlightened Italian periodicals and commentators. Venturi concluded that 'Enlightenment was born and organised in those places where the contact between a backward world and a modern one was chronologically more abrupt and geographically closer.'[21]

Since then, approaches to the geography of the Enlightenment have become more nuanced (Charles Withers and David Livingstone suggest 'geographies of enlightenment')[22] but the spatial focus of researchers has been enhanced by the growing realisation that much of the Enlightenment's 'study of man' was played out not only in encounters with the 'non-civilised' world beyond Europe, but also in 'Western' encounters

---

20. Johann Herder, *Journal meiner Reise im Jahr 1769: Historisch-Kritische Ausgabe*, ed. Katherina Mommsen (Stuttgart, 1976), p.91, quoted by Peter Hanns Reill below, p.284.

21. Franco Venturi, *Utopia and reform in the Enlightenment* (Cambridge, 1971), p.133. F. Venturi, *Settecento riformatore*, 5 parts, 7 vols (Turin, 1969-1991). See also the translation of parts 3 and 4 by R. Burr Litchfield, *The End of the Old Regime in Europe, 1768-1776: the first crisis* (Princeton, NJ, 1989) and *The End of the Old Regime in Europe, 1776-1789*, 2 vols (Princeton, NJ, 1991).

22. Charles W. J. Withers and David Livingstone, 'Introduction: on geography and Enlightenment', in *Geography and Enlightenment*, ed. D. Livingstone and C. W. J. Withers (Chicago and London, 1999), p.1-28 (p.4).

with the peripheral spaces of 'Eastern' Europe.[23] And, as this collection reiterates, men and women of the peripheries talked back.[24] Fru Nordenflycht's *Defence of Woman*, for example, dedicated to the queen of Sweden, refuted Rousseau's contention (in his *Lettre à D'Alembert*) that women were best suited to 'petits ouvrages' as an unenlightened 'prejudice'.[25]

Commentators and policy-makers at the 'margins' of the enlightened world frequently did acknowledge their peripheral status. 'La masse des lumières est encore infiniment moins répandue ici', admitted King Stanisław August of Poland to his agent in Paris.[26] Sometimes they lamented or warned of peripherality in order to stir their compatriots to greater efforts. The Hungarian baron Miklós Vay wrote of Adam Smith's *Wealth of nations*: 'This outstanding work by the above-mentioned scholar has already been translated by almost all important nations in Europe. And the nations have hugely benefited from this. Why should we fall behind them?'[27] But often they proclaimed that the work of catching up had been accomplished: 'There is only *one* path of education or enlightenment for peoples; they all follow it one after another. Foreigners were more intelligent than Russians: and so it was necessary to borrow from them, to learn, to use their experiences', wrote Nikolai Karamzin, in the past tense.[28] Other writers in the various places studied in this volume sometimes denied peripheral status vehemently.

If responses to perceived social and economic backwardness generally constituted the main body of Enlightenment in practice, then political economy provided its theoretical foundations. In the aforementioned case of Scotland, the Highland line exemplified contact between the backward and the modern at its most 'abrupt', prompting Scottish thinkers to reflect upon the fragility of civilisation. In this collection John Robertson explores the response of Neapolitan political economists to the intractable problem of feudalism, while Orsolya Szakály pursues the entrepreneurial spirit in Hungary. The early Hungarian reception of Adam Smith's *Wealth of nations* exemplifies the discriminate approach to the wider Enlightenment corpus of works, based on almost entirely practical criteria which, she argues, characterised the Hungarian Enlightenment. The primacy of political economy is also endorsed by Ultán Gillen for later eighteenth-century Ireland, while the French physiocrats, filtered through provincial clergymen, provided some of the solutions to backwardness that were

---

23. Larry Wolff, *Inventing Eastern Europe: the map of civilization on the mind of the Enlightenment* (Stanford, CA, 1994).
24. As Darnton agreed, in 'George Washington's false teeth', p.153.
25. See Marie-Christine Skuncke's essay below.
26. Stanisław August to Filippo Mazzei, 21 November 1789, quoted by Richard Butterwick, below, p.210.
27. Miklós Vay to Ferenc Széchényi, 21 November 1791, quoted by Orsolya Szakály, below, p.113.
28. Quoted by Simon Dixon, below, p.237.

proposed in Poland-Lithuania. Catherine the Great eclectically drew on *encyclopédistes*, physiocrats, German cameralists and even the lectures of Adam Smith in the economic sections of her *Nakaz*.[29]

Naples provides an exception to the pattern of the reception of French and Scottish political economists because (as in Scotland) backward circumstances provoked original and central contributions, which in turn were applied elsewhere: witness the interest across Europe in Gaetano Filangieri's *Scienza della legislazione*. If eighteenth-century Naples had long declined into a social and economic periphery of Europe, it was hardly an intellectual periphery of the Enlightenment. In contrast, as Martin Fitzpatrick shows, the undoubted success of commerce in Liverpool led to celebrations of enlightened 'improvements' there, but contemporaries began to worry about the cultural impoverishment of 'money-grubbing Liverpudlian merchants'. Perhaps we have an example of a centre of Enlightenment in practical, economic terms, which was nevertheless on its cultural periphery.[30]

Fiona Clark's essay contains the fullest evaluation in this volume of the theoretical concepts of core (or centre) and periphery in social and cultural studies. Core and periphery are no longer cutting-edge concepts but, thoroughly deconstructed and nuanced, they remain in frequent use. For José Antonio Alzate y Ramírez, Mexico's principal gazetteer, 'there existed multiple centres of authority (geographical, social, and intellectual) with regard to the generation, appropriation and rejection of ideas.'[31] Clark draws on the work of sociologist Edward Shils to argue that core and periphery were and are not merely spatial concepts: they are intricately linked to power relationships and networks within a 'transcendent whole': in this case the Republic of Letters. The 'central value system' in this whole might well be associated with the French *philosophes*, but this was not necessarily so from Alzate's perspective. He sought to legitimise his work as enlightened and useful within the context of the institutional framework for natural sciences in New and metropolitan Spain, institutions which are also considered by Gabriel Sánchez Espinosa.[32]

Peripheries, therefore, can be spatial and temporal but they also relate to the networks between people and institutions, and to hierarchies of values. The Grub Street exiles furnish an example of those marginalised within the enlightened world. The limits of the Enlightenment can be pursued in the ideas themselves – John Robertson writes that 'faced with Neapolitan feudalism, Enlightenment political economy was at the outer reaches of its analytical range.'[33] The infiltration of the Enlightenment

---

29. Isabel de Madariaga, *Russia in the age of Catherine the Great* (New Haven, CT, 1981), p.151-63.
30. Martin Fitzpatrick, below, p.125.
31. Fiona Clark, below, p.252, 257.
32. See Edward Shils, *Center and periphery: essays in macrosociology* (Chicago, IL, 1975).
33. John Robertson, below, p.71.

into the discourse of its critics might also be counted as a periphery of the Enlightenment. So too might media which do not obviously come to mind as characteristic of the 'enlightened age', such as the sermon. Most of the essays here interrogate the applicability of the concept of the periphery to some or all of their own chosen subjects; they show how the locations and natures of the centre and the periphery could shift, and how they could interact with one another. Places and persons could be peripheral in some respects, but central in others. The city-republic of Geneva, the subject of Graham Gargett's essay, lay on the spatial periphery of France but played a far from peripheral role in the Enlightenment, in both French and European contexts.

The collection presents evidence that many enlightened commentators thought in terms of 'nations'. Not only 'nations', or kingdoms, principalities and empires, however, but also regions, provinces and cities could be peripheries, either in relation to their own centres, or to the enlightened world as a whole. Peripheries could have peripheries of their own. The terms 'province' and 'provincial' had particular resonance – they overlap with 'periphery' and 'peripheral' as pejorative concepts but can also convey a sense of place, associated with proud traditions. Provincial writers, for example Ann Yearsley and John Thelwall, sought to shape national debates. Lynda Pratt analyses the relationship between the claims of English provinces to literary and intellectual status, and metropolitan disparagement of provincial efforts – beginning with an attempt to cut the famed Joseph Priestley of Birmingham down to size.

A model process of Enlightenment in a 'periphery' might lead from recognition of the need to catch up with 'enlightened nations' through the formulation and application of practical reforms, to self-confident membership of the enlightened world. 'Nations which were first enlightened now learn together with those which they had taught', pronounced the ex-Jesuit Piotr Świtkowski in 1783.[34] In the Irish and Polish cases, forms of government constituted the principal basis of the claim to be an example to others – albeit dating respectively from near the beginning (1688) and near the end (1791) of the Enlightenment.

Świtkowski's opinion illustrates how the shifting location of peripheries and centres of Enlightenment was discerned by contemporaries as well as historians. Two giants of the Enlightenment thought likewise. Voltaire's fears that his French *patrie* was declining into peripherality, analysed here by Simon Davies, were echoed by Diderot in 1772: 'The sciences, the arts, taste and wisdom climb to the North, and barbarism with its train comes southwards.'[35] Both discerned the rise of the 'North' (only tentatively, as yet, the 'East') where the torch was carried by Frederick, Stanisław August, Gustav and above all, in their view, the great Catherine.

34. Quoted by Richard Butterwick, below, p.209.
35. Quoted by Simon Dixon, below, p.240.

Voltaire and Diderot were international men of letters, philosophy, politics and science, whose gaze and whose fame spanned Eurasia and the Americas. But they were also emotionally attached to their French fatherland. The relationship between cosmopolitanism and patriotism was placed at the heart of the Enlightenment by Franco Venturi.[36] But was true patriotism the defence of political liberty (or liberties), the act of a Brutus confronted by tyranny, or did it lie in proposing and implementing practical improvements for the public or general good? 'Utilidad pública' (a favourite term of Alzate's) and its equivalents included bringing useful knowledge to the attention of the 'public'. Unquestionably the latter definition prevailed in monarchical polities – a case in point being the activity of Gaspar Melchor de Jovellanos when banished to his province of Asturias.[37] The question was fiercely contested, however, under republican or mixed forms of government, notably Geneva, Hungary, Ireland and Poland-Lithuania, just as it had been in the England of the 1730s.[38]

Enlightened patriotism could take various political inflections. Campaigns for greater national independence (of Hungary from Vienna, Ireland from London and, de facto, Poland from St Petersburg) could be linked in various ways to the promotion of domestic 'improvements'. It was argued that unless Magyars, Irishmen and Poles had their own destiny in their hands, all efforts at improvement would yield insignificant results. For some of those who viewed the short-term chances of winning national independence pessimistically, however, even the least spectacular reforms were important, in order that their nations should not fall behind others. These three countries had political cultures that extolled republican or mixed forms of government and esteemed Montesquieu.

The kind of cosmopolitanism to which national loyalties are irrelevant, or at least firmly subordinated to a shared humanity, sits easily with an early, radical, narrowly defined Enlightenment, as well as the concept of the Republic of Letters. Later on, the 'improving' kind of patriotism tended to fit 'backward' peripheral circumstances. But it did not preclude a sense of solidarity with patriots elsewhere – reflected for example in the accounts of foreign affairs in Italian newspapers, which gave Venturi so much material. 'Cosmopolitans of the periphery' are identified by Martin Fitzpatrick. 'Liverpolitans' thought globally and acted locally. So did Alzate in Mexico, and so did many others. With the process that led from recognition of backwardness to pride in achievements we embark on the road to national revivals. Where cultural and linguistic development was at stake, we approach the beginnings of Romanticism and even ethnic

---

36. J. Robertson, 'Franco Venturi's Enlightenment', *Past and present* 137 (1992), p.183-206.

37. See Gabriel Sánchez Espinosa's article below.

38. Compare Christine Gerrard, *The Patriot opposition to Walpole: politics, poetry and national myth, 1725-1742* (Oxford, 1994).

nationalism. The trend was noted by Hazard.[39] As R. J. W. Evans has put it, '*Aufklärung* became first a patriotic and then a national awakening.'[40]

Wales is a case in point. 'The Welsh Enlightenment' does not trip off the lips, yet Evans has sought a later eighteenth-century 'overlap' between Welshmen, such as Richard Price, who partook of and participated in English, British or even European enlightened culture, and those associated with the nascent Welsh national revival. The Cymmrodorion was founded by London-based Welshmen in the 1750s to promote and renew the Welsh language and literature, and by the end of the century topographers stressed the glories of the Welsh countryside and the romantic associations of its history. The revival of evangelical Protestantism, however hostile it was to freethinking, stimulated instruction in the vernacular. Evans has compared the Welsh situation, on the whole advantageously, with other culturally subject peoples: Basques, Bretons, Catalans, Czechs, Finns, Slovaks, Slovenes and Sorbs. Improving Anglophone gentry often took great pride, moreover, in their 'Cambrian' traditions – a similar situation to the Polonophone nobles of the Grand Duchy of Lithuania.[41] In this volume, the 'patriotic' theme of linguistic and literary improvement is noted for Hungary, Spain, Mexico and Russia. It also resonated strongly in Germany and Poland (although the ethnically Lithuanian national revival came so late that attempts to find continuities with the Enlightenment would be highly tenuous). Provincial English poets strove to encapsulate their nation in epic, a form described by Milton as 'doctrinal and exemplary to a Nation'.[42]

Venturi revealingly criticised Jean Fabre's *Stanisłas-Auguste Poniatowski et l'Europe des Lumières* on the grounds that, despite the subtitle, *Etude de cosmopolitisme*, patriotism dominates cosmopolitanism; the nineteenth century the eighteenth.[43] Not coincidentally, Fabre also edited Jean-Jacques Rousseau's *Considérations sur le gouvernement de Pologne*. In this work, completed in 1771, the 'citoyen de Genève' advised the Poles to renounce the trappings of the enlightened world, such as trade, towns, industry and, above all, cosmopolitan polish. Instead they should cultivate an austere republican strain of patriotism, founded in their own language

---

39. P. Hazard, *La Pensée européenne au XVIII<sup>e</sup> siècle: de Montesquieu à Lessing* (Paris, 1946).

40. R. J. W. Evans, 'The origins of Enlightenment in the Habsburg lands', in R. J. W. Evans, *Austria, Hungary, and the Habsburgs: essays on Central Europe, c.1683-1867* (Oxford, 2006), p.36-55 (55). See also R. J. W. Evans, 'Joseph II and nationality in the Habsburg lands', in Evans, *Austria, Hungary, and the Habsburgs*, p.134-46.

41. R. J. W. Evans, 'Was there a Welsh Enlightenment?', in *From medieval to modern Wales: historical essays in honour of Kenneth O. Morgan and Ralph A. Griffiths*, ed. R. R. Davies and Geraint H. Jenkins (Cardiff, 2004), p.142-59. See also *Wales and the Romantic imagination*, ed. Damian Walford Davies and Lynda Pratt (Cardiff, 2007).

42. John Milton, 'The reason of Church government', quoted by Lynda Pratt, below, p.270.

43. Venturi, *The End of the Old Regime in Europe, 1768-1776*, p.174, n.2. Compare Jean Fabre, *Stanisłas-Auguste Poniatowski et l'Europe des Lumières: étude de cosmopolitisme* (Paris and Strasbourg, 1952).

and customs, which, if they could not be preserved or recovered, should be invented. Much of this passionate work reads like a prescription for ethnic nationalism. But in its denunciation of modern, prosperous, enlightened Europe, it also harks back to Rousseau's *Discours sur les sciences et les arts* of 1750. 'Improving' patriots of several countries did not hesitate to refute the first discourse. 'Quel dogme plus absurde et si je l'ose dire plus barbare?' asked the future King Gustav III of Sweden in 1760. For self-consciously 'enlightened' elites confronted with problems that required practical solutions, Rousseau's condemnation of modernity was a frontal assault on their entire programme.[44]

National causes could be provoked as much as inspired by the Enlightenment. The evidence advanced by Simon Dixon for Russia, for example, reveals a critical distance towards France, as well as attempts to evaluate the relative merits of imported fashions and indigenous customs. 'Patriotism' could acquire an Anti-Enlightenment tincture, for example in France during the Seven Years War and in Great Britain during the French Revolutionary and Napoleonic Wars. In the former case, the *philosophes* were denounced for their Anglophilia, Prussophilia and cosmopolitanism; in the latter 'patriots' damned the Jacobins, blamed the *philosophes* and hounded their supporters.[45] These controversies are touched upon by Lynda Pratt, for a period when a sense of the 'romantic' was linked with developing senses of both national and provincial identity.

The question of the Enlightenment's critics is closely linked to that of its peripheries. Swedish resistance to the Enlightenment was highlighted by Tore Frängsmyr in 1981.[46] One theme raised in some essays is the extent to which places where 'the Enlightenment' is generally held to have arrived later resisted or rejected it. The 'peripheral', as we have noted, overlaps with the 'provincial'. The opposition between the 'province' or 'country' and the metropolis (the court and/or the city) has been a familiar theme in European culture (including political culture) since classical antiquity. Metropolitan sophistication is set against rustic simplicity, and vice against virtue. Rousseau, of course, was very much on the side of old-fashioned provincial mores.

Critics were almost invariably inclined to depict the lamentable tendencies of the 'enlightened age' as originating abroad – usually in France, first with the philosophers and later with the Revolution. Advocates of Enlightenment often called for lessons to be learnt in order

---

44. Quoted by Marie-Christine Skuncke, below, p.87. For a subtler 'peripheral' contemporary response to Rousseau's views, especially on the role of women in the upbringing of 'patriots', see R. Butterwick, 'Polite liberty or *l'esprit monarchique*? Stanisław August Poniatowski, Jean-Jacques Rousseau and *politesse* in England', *SVEC* 2003:07, p.249-70.

45. Edmond Dziembowski, *Un Nouveau Patriotisme français, 1750-1770: la France face à la puissance anglaise à l'époque de la guerre de sept ans*, *SVEC* 365 (1998); Linda Colley, *Britons: forging the nation 1707-1837* (New Haven, CT, and London, 1992).

46. Tore Frängsmyr, 'The Enlightenment in Sweden', in *The Enlightenment in national context*, p.164-75 (166-70).

for their own countries to catch up, but tended to advertise their discriminate approaches to borrowing from abroad, and were also likely to proclaim their country's (or province's) own contributions. As a discursive strategy, the use of the adjective 'enlightened' legitimised stances and persons. Those who challenged the usage were obliged to allege its usurpation by a misleading, 'false' Enlightenment – materialist, libertine and egalitarian. According to Ultán Gillen, in Ireland 'most conservatives refused to surrender Enlightenment to their opponents. Instead, they distinguished true Enlightenment from modern or French philosophy.'[47] Montesquieu and Hume, moreover, were generally excepted from their censure – an observation which applies just as well to Polish-Lithuanian clergymen.

The contemporary assessments of the age found throughout this volume testify to a widely held belief that what we might call the enlightened Zeitgeist of the eighteenth century, albeit at different degrees of intensity and pace, spreading into the deepest provincial corners of the Euro-Atlantic world – even the Simbirsk region – was essentially one. Whether the perspective was hostile or supportive, the main tendencies of the 'enlightened age' emerge fairly clearly: Enlightenment connoted a true and rational understanding of the world, critical interrogation of established thought and practices, especially popular 'superstitions', and rationally justified reforms aiming at the improvement of humanity in this world, including religious toleration. But 'the enlightened age' also generated anxieties for religion and morals.

The work of Darrin McMahon and Didier Masseau has raised the possibility that the Enlightenment could have been 'constructed' by its critics before it was appropriated and reconstructed by the French Revolutionaries. In the Irish case, it is claimed that the 'Counter-Enlightenment' was under way even before the seventeenth century had run its course.[48] The evidence presented here points both ways. Critics and enthusiasts of the age ranged across the Euro-Atlantic world as well as throughout the eighteenth century and into the next – from Swift to Karamzin.

Should critics of the Enlightenment be labelled as representatives of Counter-Enlightenment or Anti-Enlightenment? Richard Butterwick makes a case for the latter, at least until the early nineteenth century. While Counter-Enlightenment implies policies aimed at halting and

---

47. Ultán Gillen, below, p.179.
48. Didier Masseau, *Les Ennemis des philosophes: l'antiphilosophie au temps des Lumières* (Paris, 2000); Darrin M. McMahon, *Enemies of the Enlightenment: the French Counter-Enlightenment and the making of modernity* (New York, 2001); *The Irish Enlightenment and Counter-Enlightenment*, ed. David Berman and Patricia O'Riordan, 6 vols (Bristol, 2002). See also B. W. Young, *Religion and Enlightenment in eighteenth-century England* (Oxford, 1998). Compare Bronisław Baczko, 'Enlightenment', in *A Critical dictionary of the French Revolution*, ed. François Furet and Mona Ozouf (English translation: Cambridge, MA, 1988), p.659-68.

reversing Enlightenment, Anti-Enlightenment simply means negation and criticism of an age that considered itself 'enlightened'. The violent language of polemics can lead to the neglect of stances betwixt and between the extremes of radical Enlightenment and apocalyptic Anti-Enlightenment, and evidence of the influence of the methods, priorities, discourses and assumptions of the 'enlightened age' upon some of its severest critics is not hard to find. Peter Hanns Reill shows how the priorities and categories of Enlightenment, understood as a process, carried Johann Herder, one of Isaiah Berlin's exemplars of 'Counter-Enlightenment', to distinctive and original theories, as well as to a critical stance towards the French metropolitan Enlightenment.[49] Herder raises the question of whether outsiders who make critical, original contributions, rather than merely imitate Parisian prototypes, are within or outside the Enlightenment and, if they are within it, whether they inhabit the centre(s) or the peripheries.

The testimony of contemporaries confirms the recent historiographical emphasis on practical improvements in this world, characteristic of a secular mindset, and a move away from transcendental concerns, but certainly not one towards a secularisation based on a separation between Church and State and a consignment of religion to the private realm.[50] Polemics between the godly and the godless, or the obscurantists and the enlightened, sparked considerable 'creative tension' – for example in the space between Paris and Geneva. Divine sanction, moreover, was claimed (and sought) for 'enlightened' policies, such as the British and Polish constitutional revolutions of 1688 and 1791 – as of course it was by French Revolutionaries of various hues.

Michael Brown writes of a 'religious inflection' of Enlightenment,[51] analysing aspects of the thought of Bishop Berkeley and Dean Swift. Not only did the 'enlightened' legitimise themselves by religion, apologists for the clergy legitimised themselves by 'Enlightenment'. The media, methods and criteria of rational, humane, utilitarian Enlightenment, moreover, could be applied to religion itself – for the greater glory of God, of course. It can be tricky to draw the line between what was substantially Enlightenment and what was substantially Christianity; perhaps we should also consider 'enlightened inflections of Christianity'. Richard Butterwick reaches the conclusion that, unlike Catholic Enlightenment, enlightened Catholicism was not necessarily incompatible with Anti-Enlightenment, and so even 'enlightened Anti-Enlightenment'

---

49. Compare Isaiah Berlin, 'The Counter-Enlightenment' (1973), reprinted in I. Berlin, *Against the current: essays in the history of ideas*, ed. Henry Hardy (London, 1997), p.1-24, and I. Berlin, *Three critics of the Enlightenment: Vico, Hamaan, Herder*, ed. Henry Hardy (Princeton, NJ, 2000), p.168-242.

50. See Jonathan Sheehan, 'Enlightenment, religion, and the enigma of secularization: a review essay', *American historical review* 108 (2003), p.1061-80.

51. Michael Brown, below, p.63.

is not a contradiction in terms. Similar arguments might apply to the *Haskalah*, the Jewish Enlightenment, *maskilim*, enlightened Jews, and their critics.[52]

The key question is posed here by Marie-Christine Skuncke: 'whether or not one allows Christian belief to be included into one's definition of Enlightenment', with the crucial rider of whether or not Christian belief is necessarily founded on divine revelation. Without the admission of Christian belief, as Frängsmyr has argued since 1987, it is hard to find anything like a 'Swedish Enlightenment', or indeed much of an Enlightenment anywhere outside France, at least when understood as an intellectual movement. But with a broader definition that takes in reformist praxis and discussion that did not openly challenge Revelation, then much can be encompassed within Enlightenment.[53] The project remains open. Employing a contemporary idiom, Graham Gargett unashamedly advocates an enlightened Christianity, and passes judgement upon some of its eighteenth-century exponents.

For many well-educated eighteenth-century Christians, Enlightenment as applied to religion meant a greater degree of toleration and a purging from worship of the extravagant and irrational, especially when practised by the 'dark and simple common folk'. Popular customs were often stigmatised as 'superstition'.[54] For some of the Genevan clergy, it meant rather more than that – an abandonment of original sin and thus the need for divine incarnation and redemption, the Trinity and the traditional Christian heaven and hell. D'Alembert's notorious article 'Genève' in the *Encyclopédie*, it transpires, was substantially correct. Martin Fitzpatrick's essay underlines the role of 'rational' dissenters in the improving and philanthropic causes of later eighteenth-century England. Despite this, they provoked the ire of Edmund Burke, who linked their rationalism in religion to their endorsement of the French Revolution.

For critics, such so-called 'Enlightenment' was a revolt against mysteries essential to Christian faith, and against divine authority, inspired by sinful urges of the flesh. Beyond France, they gladly drew on French enemies of the *philosophes*. Their jeremiads from before, and at the outset

---

52. See the sweeping comparisons between Catholicism, Protestantism and Judaism in David Sorkin, 'Reform Catholicism and religious Enlightenment', with commentary by T. C. W. Blanning and R. J. W. Evans, *Austrian history yearbook* 30 (1999), p.187-235, as well as D. Sorkin, *Moses Mendelssohn and the religious Enlightenment* (Berkeley, CA, 1996).

53. Marie-Christine Skuncke, 'Was there a Swedish Enlightenment?', in *Norden och Europa 1700-1830: Synvinklar på ömsedigt kulturellt inflytande*, ed. Svavar Sigmundsson (Reykjavik, 2003), p.25-41. See also Derek Beales, 'Christians and *philosophes*: the case of the Austrian Enlightenment', in *History, society and the Churches: essays in honour of Owen Chadwick*, ed. Derek Beales and Geoffrey Best (Cambridge, 1985), p.169-94, reprinted in D. Beales, *Enlightenment and reform in eighteenth-century Europe* (London, 2005), p.60-89; and D. Beales, 'Religion and culture', in *The Eighteenth century*, ed. T. C. W. Blanning, *Short Oxford history of Europe*, 12 vols (Oxford, 2000), vol.8, p.131-77 (133).

54. Bishop Wojciech Skarszewski, quoted by Richard Butterwick, below, p.208.

of, the French Revolution appeared to have been confirmed by its subsequent radicalisation. It is far easier to accommodate such men (and women, such as Hannah More) within the case for a radical, essentially anti-Christian Enlightenment, which found a relatively small number of imitators elsewhere, than it is to accommodate most 'peripheral' voices within it. Most of the thinkers, writers and commentators whose views are considered in these articles fit better into a moderate, broader – yet still self-consciously single – Enlightenment, which (rightly or wrongly) did not consider its precepts and priorities incompatible with Catholic, Protestant or Orthodox Christianity. Even defenders of Anglican confessional supremacy in Ireland could consider themselves enlightened – to their minds an acceptable degree of toleration had been established, and they viewed Roman Catholicism as both superstitious and inherently intolerant.

The multiple viewpoints of this volume allow us to seek out the limits and explore some of the borderlands of the Enlightenment. Needless to say many themes have not been covered here. But among the perspectives included are seven from five empires, kingdoms and republics left out of *The Enlightenment in national context*: Spain, Poland-Lithuania, Ireland, Hungary and Geneva. Where two essays are devoted to one country, as in the cases of Ireland and England, contrasting approaches are employed. The national level of enquiry itself becomes an object of study, and is joined by provincial and urban contexts. Disciplinary boundaries between the histories of literature, religion, science, philosophy, and political and economic thought are crossed. Some essays focus on individuals, others are broader surveys. The Enlightenment is pursued through its contexts, its ideas, its applications, its critics and in the word 'Enlightenment' itself.

Despite the emphasis on local problems and local solutions, France, the traditional centre of the Enlightenment, is rarely beyond the horizon. France was the principal cultural point of reference, by which the 'enlightened age' or 'philosophical century' was judged from its peripheries.[55] Framed by the personification of the Enlightenment, Voltaire, who worried from his peripheral perch that France herself was becoming peripheral, and the Livonian German thinker, Johann Herder, whose typically peripheral quest for Enlightenment in France led him in directions that took him beyond the Enlightenment, this collection seeks to persuade *dix-huitièmistes* that the study of the peripheries of the Enlightenment yields insights about the movement as a whole.

All translations in the following articles are the authors' own unless otherwise stated.

Full bibliographical references are given on the first occurence; thereafter, shortened references are used.

---

55. See, for instance, Teresa Kostkiewiczowa, *Polski wiek świateł: Obszary swoistości* (Wrocław, 2002).

SIMON DAVIES

# Whither/wither France: Voltaire's view from Ferney

FRANÇOIS-MARIE Arouet was an adventurer in a century of adventurers. A polymath who achieved recognition, even distinction, in a diversity of fields, even ones that he did not particularly wish to cultivate (fiction, for example), he helped to create his own myth by the creation and adoption of his invented name, Voltaire, in 1718. His existence has elements of the picaresque, a real Candide, wandering about the physical and intellectual highways and byways of Europe, stimulated and depressed by what he accidentally and deliberately encountered, constantly surprised to be surprised. Of the four great Francophone *philosophes*, Rousseau was Genevan, Montesquieu from near Bordeaux, Diderot from Langres, leaving Voltaire as the only Parisian.[1] Yet Voltaire was to be absent from his home city for almost the last thirty years of his life, if we exclude his fatal return to the capital in 1778. Voltaire thus lived on the geographical periphery of his own country, almost an exile in his fatherland, a wounding experience for someone who was a 'patriotic' Frenchman.

In his youth Voltaire had visited Holland and, of course more significantly, had 'enjoyed' his exile in England from 1726 to 1728. It is not my purpose to expatiate on the multiple consequences of this sojourn which has received comprehensive treatment[2] but rather to suggest its crucial, formative role in the personal development of Voltaire. It is no longer credible to propose that Voltaire came to England as a poet and left a philosopher. Nevertheless, it is true to assert that he believed, or wanted to believe, that he was living in a land of philosophers, that of Locke and Newton in particular.[3] Here was an island, on the margins of Europe, a traditional enemy of France and much despised, yet capable of producing

---

1. In fact Voltaire was born in the village of Chatenay, just outside Paris (René Pomeau, *D'Arouet à Voltaire*, Oxford, 1988, p.20). He nevertheless spent his childhood and youth in the capital.

2. The most comprehensive account remains André Michel Rousseau's *L'Angleterre et Voltaire*, *SVEC* 145-47 (1976). See also Haydn T. Mason, 'Voltaire européen naissant et l'Europe', in *Voltaire en Europe, hommage à Christiane Mervaud*, ed. Michel Delon and Catriona Seth (Oxford, 2000), p.23-31.

3. In the second 'épître dédicatoire' (1736) prefacing *Zaïre*, composed in honour of Fawkener, Voltaire differentiated between the French and English in the penultimate sentence: 'L'art de plaire semble l'art des Français et l'art de penser paraît le vôtre' (*The Complete works of Voltaire*, ed. Th. Besterman, Oxford, 1968-, henceforward *OCV*, vol.8, p.418).

and fostering intellectual giants, an island which had some claims to allowing freedom of religious belief, however blinkered Voltaire may have been in terms of its application. He knew England only from the people he knew and what he read and saw. In 1728 he wrote to Robert Towne in English: 'The *Henriade* has at least in itself a spirit of liberty which is not very common in France: the language of a free nation as yours is the only one that can vigorously express what I have but faintly drawn in my native tongue' (D340). Voltaire's *Lettres philosophiques* (1734) are far from being an objective account of the reality of England; rather, they are a polemical work geared to highlighting the weaknesses of France, charging his native land with being 'insular'.[4] There is a sense that Voltaire is intimating that France is out of date, that the country needs renewal if it is to prosper in the modern world. It can no longer regenerate itself from within, but requires learning from more successful models abroad. The Revocation of the Edict of Nantes (1685) was a disaster in human and economic terms. The ritual burning by the public executioner in France of the *Lettres philosophiques* in 1734 was the official response of the authorities, an action which could be envisaged as validating Voltaire's argument.[5] France was marginalising herself.

The English experience continued to exercise an effect on Voltaire for the rest of his life. Although his mood could swing from optimism to pessimism, from enthusiasm to despair, Voltaire remained in broad terms an Anglophile but not an *anglomane*. The spirit of philosophical enquiry could hardly be damaging the moral fibre or cohesion of the nation when England was on the winning side of the Seven Years War.[6] By 1763 Voltaire had of course set up his own mini-state.

It is from the vantage point of Ferney, that outpost on the border with Switzerland which Voltaire had purchased in 1758 and where he took up permanent residence in 1760, that he monitored the health of the French nation. When he took possession of Ferney, he was not buying a desirable residence with modern conveniences. On the contrary, he felt obliged to undertake extensive renovations, to modernise. In what one may interpret as a symbolic but concrete gesture, he apparently demolished a gibbet which he would presumably have been entitled to employ as the lord of the manor.[7] Archaic procedures should no longer prevail. If the

---

4. Nicholas Cronk has effectively shown that this work was also directed at an English readership as well as highlighting the implications of Voltaire's use of English (Voltaire, *Letters concerning the English nation*, Oxford, 1994, p.vii-xxvii).

5. The ambiguities of this public condemnation are noted by René Pomeau (*D'Arouet à Voltaire*, p.328-29).

6. In October 1759 Voltaire actually held a party at Ferney to mark the capture of Quebec by the English. See André Michel Rousseau, *L'Angleterre et Voltaire*, SVEC 145 (1976), p.232. Edmond Dziembowski asserts: 'L'Angleterre, représentante de la "modernité", a vaincu la France, prisonnière de ses archaïsmes', in *Un Nouveau Patriotisme français 1750-1770*, SVEC 365 (1998), p.138 (cf. p.140).

7. René Pomeau, Christiane Mervaud *et al.*, *De la cour au jardin* (Oxford, 1991), p.353.

physical surroundings left much to be desired, Voltaire was distressed at the plight of the local inhabitants. He paints a sorry, if possibly exaggerated, picture in November 1758: 'la moitié des habitants périt de misère, et l'autre pourrit dans les cachots' (D7946). He set about reinvigorating the agricultural practices. Arguably the most famous man in Europe, at the age of sixty-four, Voltaire wanted to show that he acted in deeds, not merely words. His colony in Ferney, while having no pretensions to being a utopia, could nevertheless exemplify the benefits of a landowner (that is, a ruler) energetically pursuing the welfare of his tenants/subjects. Voltaire made his visitors and numerous correspondents aware of the success of his stewardship. Catholics and Protestants alike could be shown working together, not just in agricultural pursuits but also in the manufacture of watches.[8] This was a society that worked in all senses of that word. From his internal exile on the peripheries of France, the great man was showing the French authorities what could be achieved.[9]

France was not listening. Looking at France from Ferney was not to be a happy experience. It is perhaps a paradox to note that France, which was generally, until recent decades, regarded as the centre of Enlightenment,[10] earned that questionable accolade precisely because the country was not enlightened. Its lack of Enlightenment fostered the thought and careers of its own native detractors, no more so than in the case of Voltaire, who embodied for enlightened Europe the challenges of the new, the sceptical, even the guru. Voltaire the iconoclast achieved iconic status, the writer as media hero, worthy of automatic information and gossip. His one-man think-tank at Ferney was a site of immense curiosity and a necessary stop for select visitors on forms of the Grand Tour. If he could not be viewed in person, Voltaire could at least be contacted by letter at his philosophical headquarters. To be in correspondence with the great man was flattering for young and old, the powerful and the powerless.

Yet the Parisian exile was patently not playing the role of a public relations consultant for France. On the contrary, Voltaire bewailed France's decadence and continuing mismanagement. His campaigns for the rehabilitation of the unjustly executed Calas and his writings on other

8. See my 'Reflections on Voltaire and his idea of colonies', *SVEC* 332 (1995), p.61-69.

9. On 9 January 1771 the enlightened magistrate, Dupaty, who had been exiled from Paris, acknowledged the benefits of Voltaire's peripheral retreat: 'Ce sont ceux qui donnent des fers qui sont dans les fers véritablement. On n'est point en exil où l'on peut penser, sentir et aimer. *Ferney* à ces titres seroit ma patrie', *Correspondence and related documents*, ed. Th. Besterman, in *The Complete works of Voltaire*, vol.85-135 (Geneva, Banbury and Oxford, 1968-1977), D16979.

10. Colin Jones declares 'for most contemporaries, the *lumière* of this *siècle des lumières* shone from France' (*The Great nation: France from Louis XV to Napoleon, 1715-1799*, London, 2002, p.xiii). While his meaning is evident from the context, it would be clearer if the statement referred to Francophone writers.

miscarriages of justice reverberated throughout Europe. His zeal was expended on an ideal of justice, not on personal advancement. Supporting Voltaire's campaigns produced a feel-good factor for those consciously or unconsciously endorsing the Enlightenment project. Some foreign adherents, moreover, were no doubt happy to find France berated by her most famous subject with the consequent erosion of credibility of her centralised authority.

Voltaire could not be chided with living in an ivory tower as he had frequented the corridors of power in his role as royal historiographer, never mind his dealings with Frederick the Great.[11] A pragmatic monarchist who, Ferney apart, did not after all possess his own realm, he had to search for substitute rulers who might enact policies sympathetic to the thrust of his own ideas in the creation of possible worlds. In this he was happy to correspond with a network of crowned heads who might serve as role models.[12] Often he felt that Louis XV was less the *bien aimé*, more the well scorned. Regal Enlightenment came from abroad; such conduct was alien to Louis XV. But might Louis, or at least his advisers, learn something from the practice of his fellow royals? There were enough of them who could be portrayed as, at the very least, attempting to enact enlightened ideas[13] – of these more later. Depicting himself as the 'Don Quichotte des Alpes' (D17653), Voltaire let his writings travel the roads of Europe in his stead. Short compositions, often in verse form, sung the praises of enlightened acts. These ephemeral, seemingly peripheral, pieces were central to Voltaire's campaigns.[14] These were concrete examples of the freedom to think and, crucially, to think in public.

---

11. See Christiane Mervaud, *Voltaire et Frédéric II: une dramaturgie des Lumières, 1736-1778*, SVEC 234 (1985). Derek Beales has recently published a chapter entitled 'Philosophical kingship and enlightened despotism', which deals with Frederick as well as other rulers, in *Enlightenment and reform in eighteenth-century Europe* (London, 2005), p.28-59. In relation to Frederick, Beales writes that 'His example showed [...] that a monarch might himself be hostile to some assumptions of the *ancien régime*, and hence that reform from above was a serious possibility' (p.38).

12. In *La Voix du sage et du peuple* (1750), Voltaire outlined the beneficial effects of an enlightened ruler: 'Ce qui peut arriver de plus heureux aux hommes, c'est que le prince soit philosophe. Le prince philosophe sait que plus la raison fera de progrès dans ses Etats, moins les disputes, les querelles théologiques, l'enthousiasme, la superstition, feront du mal: il encouragera donc les progrès de la raison' (*Œuvres complètes*, ed. Louis Moland, 52 vols, Paris, 1877-1885, henceforward *M*, vol.23, p.470).

13. On 26 June 1765, in a moment of optimism, Voltaire informed Helvétius: 'L'impératrice de Russie, Le Roy de Pologne [...], le Roy de Prusse, vainqueur de la superstitieuse Autriche, bien d'autres princes arborent l'étendard de La Tolérance et de la philosophie. Il s'est fait depuis douze ans une révolution dans les esprits, qui est sensible' (D12660).

14. I have briefly analysed such verse in 'Poetry and propaganda: 1760-1778', in *Voltaire et ses combats*, ed. Ulla Kölving and Christiane Mervaud, 2 vols (Oxford, 1997), vol.1, p.181-88. For an extensive examination of the use of verse, see Gwenaëlle Boucher, 'La poésie philosophique de Voltaire', SVEC 2003:05, p.1-286.

The cluster of poems extolling the virtues of effective kingship was reinforced by the composition of a tragedy which portrayed a ruler challenging superstitious practices and a fanatical priest. This was *Les Lois de Minos* (1771) where the king, Teucer, vanquishes the forces of obscurantism and tradition in the name of justice. While Teucer is clearly meant to point to Stanisław August of Poland and Gustavus III of Sweden, he is equally meant to evoke Louis XV. For once, in Voltaire's view (in this case counter to most philosophic opinion), Louis had demonstrated kingly decisiveness in the Maupeou coup d'état (1771). Voltaire hoped very much that the play would be staged in Paris and Louis would be suitably flattered. Neither happened. His hopes of ending his exile were dashed again.[15]

In the eighteenth century Paris could be envisaged as the microcosm of France; outside Paris, no salvation for the civilised. Yet Voltaire maintained a love/hate relationship with his native city, depending on his mood, depending on his situation.[16] As ever, it may also depend on whom he is addressing, a particular individual or a wider audience. On occasion, one could almost imagine some of his denigratory comments flowing from the pen of Rousseau, as when one encounters his assaults on the frivolity of Parisian existence, perhaps invisibly signing himself, 'Disgusted of Ferney'. His most scathing attack is encapsulated in his *Discours aux Welches* (1764), one of the many *facéties* composed at Ferney.[17] This short acidic work proves to be a devastating demolition of the pretensions of his compatriots, or at least some of them, for whom he utilised the term 'Welches'. While the term 'Welches' seems sometimes to apply to all French people, Voltaire in fact made a crucial distinction. In a letter of 19 May 1764 to a regular and sympathetic correspondent, Damilaville, Voltaire defended his strictures on his compatriots (D11877). Two days later, however, he felt it necessary to clarify his position: 'Les véritables Welches, mon cher frère, sont les *Omer*, les *Chaumeix*, les *Frérons*, les persécuteurs et les calomniateurs. Les philosophes, la bonne compagnie, les artistes, les gens aimables, sont les Français, et c'est à eux de se moquer des Welches' (D11879). By isolating the good French from the

---

15. See my introduction to the play in *OCV*, vol.73, p.1-72; also my chapter, 'Voltaire's *Les Lois de Minos*: text and context', in *The Enterprise of Enlightenment*, ed. Terry Pratt and David McCallum (Bern, 2004), p.245-64.

16. This has been cogently investigated in an unjustly neglected study by Jean Mohsen Fahmy, *Voltaire et Paris*, *SVEC* 195 (1981).

17. André Magnan notes that *Welches* 'Après l'infâme est la plus célèbre invention verbale de Voltaire'. (*Inventaire Voltaire*, ed. Jean Goulemot, André Magnan and Didier Masseau, Paris, 1995, p.1404). On 21 November 1766, the marquise Du Deffand was informed: 'L'assassinat juridique des Calas, et le meurtre du chevalier de La Barre n'ont pas fait honneur aux Welches dans les païs étrangers. Vôtre nation est partagée en deux espèces, l'une de singes oisifs qui se moquent de tout, et l'autre de Tigres qui déchirent' (D13684). It is interesting to note that Voltaire distances himself from the French by employing 'Vôtre nation'.

bad French, Voltaire was emphasising the possibility of change, of enlightening the miscreants.[18]

Let us imagine the French upper classes being addressed in this discourse. Voltaire begins in exclamatory tones: 'O Welches, mes compatriotes'.[19] He thereby associates himself with them, the better to disassociate himself from them. The second paragraph makes the thrust of his denunciation totally unambiguous (p.230):

> Vous avez eu l'honneur, il est vrai, d'être subjugués par Jules César, qui fit pendre tout votre parlement de Vannes, vendit le reste des habitants, fit couper les mains à ceux de Quercy, et vous gouverna ensuite fort doucement. Vous restâtes plus de cinq cents ans sous les lois de l'empire romain; vos druides, qui vous traitaient en esclaves et en bêtes, qui vous brûlaient pieusement dans des paniers d'osier, n'eurent plus le même crédit quand vous devîntes province de l'empire. Mais convenez que vous fûtes toujours un peu barbares.

Any sense of unquestioning superiority on the part of the French, particularly after the humiliation of the Seven Years War, is devastatingly undermined. If this is an appeal to ancient history, what about contemporary France? Things surely must be better. A rhetorical question is employed with withering effect: 'Etes-vous le premier peuple de l'univers pour le commerce et la marine? ... Hélas!' (p.234). Just as the typographic device of suspension points separates the question from 'Hélas', the French, in their Continental isolation, cannot answer. Some things are nevertheless wonderful in France (p.234):

> Vous êtes la seule nation du monde chez qui on achète le droit de juger les hommes, et même de les mener tuer à la guerre.[20] On m'assure que vous faites passer par cinquante mains l'argent du trésor public; et quand il est arrivé à travers toutes ces filières, il se trouve réduit tout au plus au cinquième.
> Vous me répondez que vous réussirez beaucoup à l'opéra-comique; j'en conviens; mais, de bonne foi, votre opéra-comique, ainsi que votre opéra sérieux, ne vous vient-il pas d'Italie?
> Vous avez inventé quelques modes, je l'avoue, quoique vous preniez aujourd'hui presque toutes celles des peuples de Britain; mais n'est-ce pas un Génois qui a découvert la quatrième partie du monde où vous possédez enfin deux ou trois petites îles? N'est-ce pas un Portugais qui vous a ouvert le chemin des Indes orientales, où vous venez de perdre vos pauvres comptoirs?[21]

The diatribe continues with Voltaire pointing out French borrowings, often unacknowledged borrowings, from other nations: 'Je voudrais donc

---

18. Voltaire had learnt from the comte and comtesse d'Argental the great offence that he had caused, of 'quelques Welches affligés' (D11878).

19. *M*, vol.25, p.230.

20. For a subtle analysis of Voltaire's attitude to venality, see William Doyle, 'Voltaire and venality: the ambiguities of an abuse', in *The Secular city*, ed. T. M. Hemming, E. Freeman and D. Meakin (Exeter, 1994), p.102-11.

21. In writing about the squaring of the circle to Sophie Volland in December 1765, Diderot declared: 'Si je ne me trompe, j'aurai fait la seule vraie découverte que les Welsh aient faite' (*Correspondance*, ed. Georges Roth, 16 vols, Paris, 1955-1970, vol.5, p.218).

que, dans vos livres, vous témoignassiez quelquefois un peu de reconnaissance pour vos voisins.'[22] Still worse, however, France is behind the times, much to the detriment of her people. In terms of medical advance, Voltaire reiterates his championing of inoculation. France has carelessly allowed her women and children to perish through obdurate obscurantism (one recalls that Voltaire himself suffered an attack of smallpox in his youth). France may repent that it has not followed 'la pratique des nations plus sages que vous et plus hardies', but such a recognition does not last long, 'le préjugé et la légèreté reprennent chez vous leur empire ordinaire' (p.236). Voltaire apostrophises his nation: 'O premier peuple du monde! Quand serez-vous raisonnable?' (p.236). The exclamatory address is impregnated with irony. It would seem plausible to regard 'raisonnable' as synonymous with enlightened. The subtext is surely that Voltaire would like the French to constitute the world's leading nation, but the country requires help; it is incapable of regenerating itself without outside assistance or examples.

Since Voltaire was a monarchist who dreamt of 'une monarchie sophocratique',[23] he believed in a powerful but not a tyrannical ruler. He found it very useful to point to reigning monarchs as examples. He chose these examples, as is well known, from the geographical north of Europe.[24] I shall leave aside his lengthy and tumultuous relationship with Frederick the Great to comment on four other rulers: Stanisław of Poland, Catherine of Russia, Christian of Denmark and Gustav of Sweden. In addition to praise in private correspondence, Voltaire eulogised their real and potential achievements in a series of texts which were widely disseminated. These were often in verse. Such verses could be circulated in manuscript, sometimes in letters, printed in full or in part in periodicals, printed individually or in collections of Voltaire's works or with the works of others. As ever Voltaire was potentially controversial and eminently marketable.

Voltaire celebrated the election of Stanisław in 1764 with a poem[25] welcoming his accession (one recalls that he was not the candidate approved by the French authorities). In 1767 Voltaire could describe Stanisław in laudatory terms as an 'Ennemi du trouble, zélé pour le bonheur et la gloire de son pays, tolérant par humanité et par principe, religieux sans superstition, citoyen sur le trône, homme éclairé et homme

---

22. Diderot, *Correspondance*, vol.5, p.235. Voltaire told Helvétius that 'Nous ne sommes pas faits en France pour arriver les premiers. Les vérités sont venues d'ailleurs; mais c'est beaucoup de les adopter' (D12660).

23. François Quastana, *Voltaire et l'absolutisme éclairé (1736-1778)* (Aix and Marseille, 2003), p.45.

24. The enlightened contribution from the north is stressed by Voltaire on 6 November 1762: 'la philosophie est presque toujours venue à Paris, des contrées septentrionales; en récompense, Paris leur a toujours envoyé des modes' (D10795).

25. Voltaire, *Sur l'élection du comte Poniatowski au trône de Pologne* (D12062).

d'esprit',[26] assuredly a job description which is eminently suited for Voltaire's conception of regal duties. In a letter sent to D'Alembert on 13 November 1772, Gustavus III of Sweden is admired above all for his 'renonciation solemnelle au pouvoir arbitraire' (D18010). Not long before this letter, Voltaire had penned a poem which begins with approval of the prince's coup d'état in August and ends by underlining the support of his people (l.21-24):

> Qu'un roi ferme et prudent prenne en ses mains les rênes.
> Le peuple avec plaisir reçoit ses douces chaînes;
> Tout change, tout renaît, tout s'anime à sa voix;
> On marche alors sans crainte aux pénibles exploits.[27]

This was a clear statement that the people are happy to be governed by firm leadership. Scandinavia is also to the fore in the praise of Christian, king of Denmark. The latter is commended for an action dear to Voltaire and enlightened thinking: the installation of the freedom of the press. Again he resorted to verse to convey his approval in a poem which was widely diffused despite its author's anxiety (at least ten editions in Voltaire's lifetime). Its opening line says much about the possibilities of kingship: 'Monarque vertueux, quoique né despotique'. Voltaire thus highlights the power of the king but equally the potentiality to discard previous practices and reign well (surely a lesson for Louis XV). He mentions Catherine, Stanisław and Frederick. In unambiguous terms, he proclaims that in Paris 'Sans l'agrément du roi vous ne pouvez penser' (l.32). In a ringing endorsement of Catherine, however, he cries: 'Tu rends ses droits à l'homme, et tu permets qu'on puisse penser' (l.26).[28] A similar sentiment had appeared in Voltaire's epistle to Catherine drafted in early 1771 which had at least six editions. The empress is addressed as someone 'Qui penses en grand homme, et qui permets qu'on pense' (l.3). Voltaire goes on to deny the idea of climatic determinism (l.51-55):

> Ce n'est pas le climat qui fait ce que nous sommes
> Pierre était créateur, il a formé des hommes.
> Tu formes des héros. – Ce sont les souverains
> Qui font le caractère et les mœurs des humains.

---

26. *Essai historique et critique sur les dissensions des Eglises de Pologne*, ed. Daniel Beauvois and Emanuel Rostworowski (*OCV*, vol.63A, p.284).

27. The opening quatrain of the poem is quoted as a conclusion to the informative study by Marie-Christine Skuncke, 'Un prince suédois auteur français: l'éducation de Gustave III, 1756-1762', *SVEC* 296 (1992), p.123-63.

28. The mission of writers and advisers to monarchs is trumpeted in l.131-40: 'Rois! qui brisa les fers dont vous êtes chargés, / Qui put vous affranchir de vos vieux préjugés? / Quelle main favorable à vos grandeurs suprêmes / A du triple bandeau vengé cent diadèmes? / Et qui du fond du puits tirant la vérité, / A su donner une âme au public hébété? / Les livres ont tout fait: et quoi qu'on puisse dire, / Rois! vous n'avez régné que lorsqu'on a su lire. / Soyez reconnaissants, aimez les bons auteurs: / Il ne faut pas du moins vexer vos bienfaiteurs.'

The paramount role of the exemplary sovereign, the *grand homme*, is stressed again almost immediately (l.57-59):

> Les exemples d'un roi
> Feraient oublier Dieu, la nature et la loi.
> Si le prince est un sot, le peuple est sans génie.

These three lines by France's most high-profile author printed for public display strike me as extraordinary. The good king need pay no heed to God,[29] nature or law (the latter presumably to be understood as established practice and customs). Is this to be taken as a lesson for Catholic France? Louis XV is unlikely to take note and is thus in danger of being a 'sot' and the French people 'sans génie'. The ringing climax to the epistle begins with the plea (l.85-86):

> Achève, Catherine, et rends tes ennemis,
> Le Grand Turc, et les sots, éclairés et soumis.

That is to say, do not just conquer them on the battlefields but conquer their minds, win them over to enlightened ideas, destruction should lead to construction.[30] Once again there is the recognition that 'C'est du Nord aujourd'hui que nous vient la lumière' (l.8).[31]

If Voltaire was the pre-eminent exponent of enlightened ideas in France and French the lingua franca of the social and intellectual elite, France herself was not, for progressive minds, a model to follow. Voltaire had praised the contribution of Henri IV to the French nation in *La Henriade*, a frequently republished work on kingship with which he was particularly associated in the minds of his contemporaries. Much as Voltaire might have liked to revive the aesthetic and cultural glories of the Sun King, that age was over and seemed impossible to revive. Voltaire was aware that the political landscape was changing; France's power and prestige

---

29. In the *Epître au roi de Suède, Gustave III* (1771), one reads in lines 24-25: 'Sur les bords du Volga Catherine tient lieu / D'un grave patriarche, ou si l'on veut de Dieu.' Gender issues apart, Voltaire is not talking about divine right monarchy with Catherine as God's representative on earth. This poem was printed at least nine times during Voltaire's lifetime.

30. One should bear in mind that Voltaire was acting as Catherine's spin-doctor in her war against Turkey while France supported the Turks. See among other texts, *Le Tocsin des rois* (*OCV*, vol.73, p.387-409). Simon Dixon reminds us that the 'most enduring symbol' of the empress's role is 'Catherine as enlightened legislator. No more appropriate image could have been chosen to illustrate the frontispiece of the four-language edition of the Nakaz published in 1770' (*Catherine the Great*, Harlow, 2001, p.45).

31. Voltaire had already told Catherine in February 1767, 'Un temps viendra, Madame, je le dis toujours, où toute la lumière nous viendra du nord. Vôtre Majesté Impériale a beau dire, je vous fais étoile, et vous demeurez étoile. Les ténèbres cimmériennes resteront en Espagne, et à la fin même elles se dissiperont... Vous faittes tout le bien que vous pouvez au dedans et au dehors. Les sages feront vôtre apothéose de vôtre vivant; mais vivez longtemps, Madame, cela vaut cent fois mieux que la divinité' (D13996).

were in decline.[32] Voltaire, the global historian, was well aware that history does not stand still. The glory of the king had been exchanged for the glory of the committed writer. The Promised Land needs to be now, not in the hereafter. The prestige of the French language was ebbing, Rivarol's *Discours sur l'universalité de la langue française* (1784) is not as confident a work as it seems. Many enlightened ideas may have been generated in France, yet so often went into print abroad or bore fictitious imprints. In such circumstances, can one deem France the centre of Enlightenment?

From the periphery of Ferney, despite periodic anxieties about his precarious position, Voltaire felt able to speak up in unambiguous terms about the ills of his country. He was well aware that he could not enjoy such freedom in Paris. One recalls that Diderot had to be far more circumspect in his public utterances, leaving many of his radical texts to be discovered by posterity. Indeed, in 1766, Voltaire dreamed of setting up a colony of philosophers in the Prussian territory of Cleves to pursue enlightened projects untrammelled.

I began by stating that Voltaire invented himself. He wanted his country at least partially to reinvent itself.[33] It would do so in an event inconceivable to Voltaire – the French Revolution. Despite appearances to the contrary, Voltaire cared deeply for his native land. The patriarch was engaged in a struggle, an enlightened adventure without spatial or temporal limits.[34] Voltaire saw words as action, and could only point, in a mixture of sorrow and anger, to the deficiencies of his nation. In so doing, he embodied his credo as citizen, as activist, as role model.[35] From the periphery of France, he sought to recreate an enlightened central authority. I shall end by quoting a few lines of verse, not by the prolific Voltaire who was the only major French philosophic writer to use verse in his campaigns, but by W. H. Auden. In a poem published in 1940,

---

32. H. M. Scott notes the increasing influence of Britain and that 'Prussia and Russia were now viewed as the leading continental states, while France and Austria vied for the status of weakest great power', *The Emergence of the eastern powers 1756-1775* (Cambridge, 2001), p.32.

33. France should not abandon her literary traditions. While recognising Shakespeare's genius, Voltaire did not admire his taste. His stance was exemplified in his *Lettre à l'Académie Française*. Haydn Mason opines that 'Far from seeing himself as a subversive firebrand, Voltaire viewed his role in the Letourneur affair as being to defend French values as a true patriot. [...] Voltaire represents himself as the heroic outcast, unappreciated by the country for which he is fighting' ('Voltaire versus Shakespeare: the *Lettre à l'Académie Française* (1776)', *British Journal for eighteenth-century studies* 18:2 (1995), p.173-84 (176).

34. It is difficult to accept Jonathan Israel's pronouncement that 'even before Voltaire came to be widely known, in the 1740s, the real business was already over' (*Radical Enlightenment*, p.7).

35. In his masterly dialogue, *Le Neveu de Rameau*, Diderot has his character, Moi, assert in relation to Voltaire: 'C'est un sublime ouvrage que *Mahomet*, j'aimerais mieux avoir réhabilité la mémoire des Calas', in *Le Neveu de Rameau*, ed. Jean Fabre (Genève, 1963), p.42.

appropriately entitled *Voltaire at Ferney*, he wrote of the campaigning workaholic:

> He'd done his share of weeping for Jerusalem: As a rule
> It was the pleasure-haters who became unjust.
>
> Yet, like a sentinel, he could not sleep. The night was full of wrong,
> Earthquakes and executions. Soon he would be dead,
> And still all over Europe stood the horrible nurses
> Itching to boil their own children. Only his verses
> Perhaps could stop them. He must go on working.

GRAHAM GARGETT

# French periphery, European centre: eighteenth-century Geneva and its contribution to the Enlightenment[1]

IN a sense, it may seem strange to include Geneva in a discussion of peripheries of the Enlightenment for the simple reason that Geneva clearly *was* one of the Protestant capitals of Reformation Europe, if not *the* capital, the home for many years of its most active and militant reformer.[2] In addition, the Reformation is usually thought of as a precursor of the Enlightenment, or – to put things the other way round – the Enlightenment is in some ways at least the intellectual heir of the Reformation. To quote William Barber: 'Whatever its manifold other affinities, the Enlightenment is essentially a child, or if one prefers a younger sister, of Protestantism.'[3] So how could one argue that Calvin's city was on the periphery, when even someone as unsympathetic to Presbyterians as Voltaire[4] paid at least lip service to its continuing importance, in the famous line from his epic poem, *La Henriade*: 'Je ne décide point entre Genève et Rome'?[5]

Yet when one contextualises Geneva's situation in an eighteenth-century perspective, the idea that it was on the periphery is not so silly. Presbyterianism had lost its expansionist dynamism and much of its earlier power and influence by the eighteenth century. True, it was the

1. I have recently given a brief overview of Geneva's role in the eighteenth century in 'Genève au dix-huitième siècle: de la cité de Calvin au foyer des Lumières', in *The City in French writing, the eighteenth-century experience/Ecrire la ville au dix-huitième siècle*, ed. Síofra Pierse (Dublin, 2004), p.136-61. Many aspects of Geneva's intellectual and political life in the eighteenth century are also described in Graham Gargett, *Jacob Vernet, Geneva and the 'philosophes'*, *SVEC* 321 (1994), an intellectual biography of the city's most important contemporary pastor.

2. Calvin arrived in Geneva in the summer of 1536, at the request of Guillaume Farel, who had undertaken the reform of the city's religion. After a period in exile in Strasbourg (1538-1541) Calvin returned to Geneva, where he lived until his death in 1564, playing an important political as well as religious role (Owen Chadwick, *The Reformation*, The Pelican history of the Church 3, Harmondsworth, 1964; reprinted 1970, p.82-96).

3. William H. Barber, 'Voltaire and Quakerism: Enlightenment and the inner light', *SVEC* 24 (1963), p.81-109 (108).

4. For Voltaire's views on, and relations with, Protestants see Graham Gargett, *Voltaire and Protestantism*, *SVEC* 188 (1980), and on Presbyterians in particular, p.57-74.

5. Second canto, line 5, *La Henriade*, ed. O. R. Taylor, in *OCV*, vol.2, p.391. The poem was originally printed in 1723 under the title of *La Ligue*, but the first nine cantos were ready by October 1721 (*La Henriade*, p.37).

established religion in Scotland and in the United Provinces (the official name of the present-day Netherlands or Holland), and it was tolerated in Britain and Ireland. But in France, Geneva's powerful neighbour and arguably the centre of the Enlightenment, Calvinist Christians were struggling to survive after the Revocation of the Edict of Nantes of 1685 had deprived them of their precarious legal existence.[6] Even in Geneva, as we shall see,[7] Calvinism had changed dramatically in nature by about 1720.[8] Geneva, moreover, was a tiny place, a miniature city-state of about 20,000 to 25,000 people, nicknamed 'la parvulissime' by Voltaire.[9] It was dwarfed, surrounded and had for a long time been threatened by its neighbours, Catholic France and Savoy, at that time an independent state extending into present-day Italy, though the tiny city-state was allied to powerful Swiss cantons, in particular Bern. The fact that this Protestant statelet was a Calvinist republic was not a circumstance likely to help it become popular with its Catholic neighbours. Its continued existence was actually a minor miracle in itself, since the duke of Savoy's forces almost took it in a surprise attack, on 12 December 1602, which was heroically and fortuitously repulsed. The attack involved scaling the old city's fortress walls, and the defeat of the attempted *Escalade* became the national day of celebration, a tradition still very much alive today.

So, to all intents and purposes, Geneva may seem of little or no importance in terms of eighteenth-century politics and power-brokering. It is true that Protestant states like Britain and various German principalities maintained friendly relations with it and kept a watchful eye on it, and this no doubt helped to guarantee its continuing existence. The Swiss cantons might also have put up a fight had it been occupied. But France had become, at least in the eyes of the French court, 'le premier allié de Genève', a situation illustrated by the paternalist language used by French representatives in official declarations.[10] From 1679 France maintained a *résident* in Geneva who, though inferior in status to an ambassador,[11] played an extremely influential role.[12] But Geneva's situation was characterised by a series of paradoxes, appropriately personified by its most famous eighteenth-century citizen and writer,

---

6. Except in Alsace, where the French government dutifully respected the Treaty of Westphalia of 1648 which, while ceding the province to France, stipulated that both Lutheranism and Calvinism should remain legal. For the situation of Protestants in France see Geoffrey Adams, *The Huguenots and French opinion 1685-1787* (Waterloo, Ontario, 1991), and Gargett, *Voltaire and Protestantism*, p.250-398.

7. Below, p.35.

8. See Maria-Cristina Pitassi, *De l'orthodoxie aux Lumières: Genève 1670-1737* (Geneva, 1992).

9. See D12899, D13063.

10. See Fabrice Brandli, 'Le résident de France à Genève (1679-1798): institution et pratiques de la diplomatie', *Dix-huitième siècle* 37 (2005), 49-68 (61).

11. Brandli explains the differences: basically, ambassadors were sent only to large and important states ('Le résident de France', p.50-54).

12. See Louis Sordet, *Histoire des résidents de France à Genève* (Geneva, 1854).

Jean-Jacques Rousseau. It is around these paradoxes that this chapter will be articulated.

## i. The 'Genève' article in the *Encyclopédie*

The old opinion retailed by so many textbooks that the publishing of the *Encyclopédie* was one of the key events – if not the key event – of the French Enlightenment really is true as regards the role played by Geneva in the *siècle des Lumières*. Suddenly, this tiny city attracted the attention of the entire continent. Throughout Europe intellectuals and those who could read what was going on sat up and paid notice over the furore, both in France and Geneva, when in volume 7 of the *Encyclopédie*, published in October 1757, there appeared a long, apparently flattering article on Geneva,[13] written by the mathematician, *philosophe*, illegitimate son of Mme de Tencin, and Diderot's co-editor of the *Encyclopédie*, Jean D'Alembert.[14] A few months earlier D'Alembert had been Voltaire's guest and had met several members of the city's *Petit Conseil* (or government), influential pastors like Jacob Vernet, and other members of Genevan society.[15] Voltaire had been living in Geneva since the beginning of 1755, finally settling down after his harrowing departure from Frederick the Great's Prussia.[16] D'Alembert's article contained two extremely provocative and controversial points. In the apparently more serious of these, he praised the clergy of Geneva for their moderate and seemly conduct and their absence of political ambition: 'Le clergé de *Genève* a des mœurs exemplaires. Les ministres vivent dans une grande union; on ne les voit point, comme dans d'autres pays, disputer entre eux avec aigreur sur des matières inintelligibles, se persécuter mutuellement, s'accuser indécemment auprès des magistrats.'[17] Above all, he praised their rational version of Christianity. One important aspect of this, according to him, was that they no longer believed in hell and eternal damnation:

L'enfer, un des points principaux de notre croyance, n'en est pas un aujourd'hui pour plusieurs ministres de *Genève*. Ce serait, selon eux, faire injustice à la Divinité d'imaginer que cet Etre plein de bonté et de justice fût capable de punir nos

---

13. For example, describing Geneva's political system, D'Alembert comments: 'On voit [...] que le gouvernement de *Genève* a tous les avantages et aucun des inconvénients de la démocratie' (*The Encyclopédie of Diderot and D'Alembert*, ed. John Lough, Cambridge, 1954, p.88).

14. The most useful introduction to D'Alembert remains Ronald Grimsley's *Jean d'Alembert (1717-1783)* (Oxford, 1963).

15. For a more detailed treatment of this incident see Raymond Naves, *Voltaire et l'Encyclopédie* (Paris, 1938), p.34-50, and Gargett, *Jacob Vernet*, p.144-51.

16. The standard Voltaire biography is now *Voltaire en son temps*, ed. René Pomeau, 2nd edn, 2 vols (Oxford, 1995). For his arrival and establishment at Geneva see vol.1, p.777-94. For a useful account in English see Theodore Besterman, *Voltaire* (London and Harlow, 1969), p.334-50.

17. Lough, *The Encyclopédie*, p.93-94.

fautes par une éternité de tourments. Ils expliquent le moins mal qu'ils peuvent les passages formels de l'Ecriture qui sont contraires à leur opinion, prétendant qu'il ne faut jamais prendre à la lettre dans les Livres Saints tout ce qui paraît blesser l'humanité et la raison. Ils croient donc qu'il y a des peines dans une autre vie, mais pour un temps.[18]

This alleged change in belief created a major paradox: 'le purgatoire, qui a été une des principales causes de la séparation des Protestants d'avec l'Eglise Romaine, est aujourd'hui la seule peine que plusieurs d'entre eux admettent après la mort: nouveau trait à ajouter à l'histoire des contradictions humaines.'[19] Changes like this meant that, for D'Alembert, an important frontier had been crossed:

Pour tout dire en un mot, plusieurs pasteurs de *Genève* n'ont d'autre religion qu'un socinianisme parfait, rejetant tout ce qu'on appelle *mystères* et s'imaginant que le premier principe d'une religion véritable, est de ne rien proposer à croire qui heurte la raison. Aussi quand on les presse sur la *nécessité* de la révélation, ce dogme si essentiel au christianisme, plusieurs y substituent le terme d'*utilité* qui leur paraît plus doux. En cela, s'ils ne sont pas orthodoxes, ils sont au moins conséquents à leurs principes.[20]

D'Alembert concluded that some of Geneva's pastors were really Christian deists, retaining only a marginal loyalty to traditional doctrines: 'La religion y est presque réduite à l'adoration d'un seul Dieu, du moins chez presque tout ce qui n'est pas peuple; le respect pour Jésus-Christ et pour les Ecritures sont presque la seule chose qui distingue d'un pur déisme le christianisme de *Genève*.'[21] All this may sound like wishful thinking, the self-interested musings of a *philosophe* determined to find what he wanted to see, and one moreover perhaps prompted by his former host Voltaire, but we shall see shortly that D'Alembert did have more than a little justification for his embarrassing praise and that he was personally committed to the opinions expressed here.

In addition, D'Alembert made a further recommendation. Why should Geneva not break with its Calvinist past and allow the presence of a theatre, which would polish and refine the manners and behaviour of its citizens even further? Admittedly, this might seem to pose some problems, D'Alembert conceded, since he knew that people feared 'le goût de parure, de dissipation et de libertinage que les troupes de comédiens répandent parmi la jeunesse'. Yet he refused to take such dangers seriously, asking rhetorically: 'ne serait-il pas possible de remédier à cet inconvénient par des lois sévères et bien exécutées sur la conduite des comédiens?'[22] D'Alembert's answer – a resounding yes – was hardly in doubt. 'Par ce moyen', he insisted,

18. Lough, *The Encyclopédie*, p.94-95.
19. Lough, *The Encyclopédie*, p.95.
20. Lough, *The Encyclopédie*, p.95.
21. Lough, *The Encyclopédie*, p.95-96.
22. Lough, *The Encyclopédie*, p.90.

*Genève aurait des spectacles et des mœurs et jouirait de l'avantage des uns et des autres; les représentations théâtrales formeraient le goût des citoyens et leur donneraient une finesse de tact, une délicatesse de sentiment qu'il est très difficile d'acquérir sans ce secours. La littérature en profiterait sans que le libertinage fît des progrès, et Genève réunirait à la sagesse de Lacédémone la politesse d'Athènes.*[23]

As is well known, these proposals provoked a furious outburst from many groups. First of all, the French Catholic clergy and their representatives were incensed to be portrayed, by implication, as self-interested, meddling, power-hungry and superstitious. In any case, tactically, the 'Genève' article came at a dreadful moment for the *philosophes* and their allies. Reflecting the generally cosmopolitan outlook of the Enlightenment, D'Alembert was indulging in an implied attack on France at a very unpatriotic time, just when the Seven Years War was starting to bite. This major conflict, almost equivalent to a world war, would turn out to be a disaster for France and in particular for its monarchy. But, even worse, 1757 was the year when an attempt to assassinate Louis XV had been made (in January) by Damiens. A decree was promulgated in April threatening authors of subversive literature with the death penalty. D'Alembert himself abandoned his editorship of the *Encyclopédie* in January 1758, but the permission to publish it was in any case revoked. It was left to the other editor, Diderot, to bring out the rest of the *Dictionnaire* in a semi-clandestine way over the next few years. As if all this were not enough, 1758 was also marked by the publication of another controversial work, the materialist tract, *De l'esprit*, by Helvétius, whose mother was a lady-in-waiting to the queen, and who, as a tax farmer, was both immensely rich and – in every way except in his philosophical opinions – a model member of the establishment.[24] It really did seem to the panicky authorities that subversion, irreligion and republicanism were infiltrating everywhere.

For his part, Jean-Jacques Rousseau felt impelled to refute D'Alembert's ideas on the civilising effect of the theatre, and his *Lettre à D'Alembert sur les spectacles*, also written in 1758, is of course one of the most famous texts dating from the period of the French Enlightenment. Nationalistic, anti-French circles in Geneva rallied to support Rousseau.[25] Most of these were made up of members of the Genevan bourgeoisie, who, as we shall see, were struggling to extend their minimal political rights. So an event in literary history had both political and social implications and, though they concerned a tiny city, they reached an extremely wide audience. At

23. Lough, *The Encyclopédie*, p.90.
24. See D. W. Smith, *Helvétius: a study in persecution* (Oxford, 1965), p.11-12.
25. See the wildly enthusiastic letters by Antoine-Jacques Roustan (*Correspondance complète de Jean-Jacques Rousseau*, ed. R. A. Leigh, Geneva, Banbury and Oxford, 1965-1995, letter 724, 3 November 1758), Paul Moultou (Leigh, *Correspondance*, letter 733, *c.*3 November 1758) and Daniel Rochement, who declared: 'S'il y a encore quelque étincelle d'Esprit Patriotique, de vertu male, et d'amour de la liberté, elle doit s'allumer au feu de vos discours' (Leigh, *Correspondance*, letter 732, *c.*10 November 1758).

the same time, the clergy of Geneva were not much happier than their Catholic colleagues in France about D'Alembert's remarks, since his doubtful compliment of 'unorthodoxy' or 'liberalism' was extremely embarrassing to them. They therefore set up a committee, composed of clergy and laymen, chaired by the famous doctor Théodore Tronchin, which produced a refutation; this was couched in such questionable terms, however, that, if anything, it made matters worse. The document stated that:

> Le terme de *respect pour J.C. & pour l'Ecriture*, nous paroissant de beaucoup trop foible, où trop équivoque, pour exprimer la nature, & l'étendüe de nos sentimens à cet Egard; nous disons que c'est avec Foi avec une Vénération religieuse avec une entière soumission d'Esprit & de Cœur, qu'il faut écouter ce Divin Maître, & le St. Esprit parlant dans les Ecritures.[26]

One did not have to be a *philosophe* or a fellow traveller to feel that this statement was hardly adequate. The outspoken Protestant enemy of Voltaire, La Beaumelle, exclaimed in a letter to Maupertuis dated 14 March 1758: 'Vous avez sans doute vu la déclaration du Clergé de Geneve sur l'accusation de socinianisme faite par d'Alembert dans le dictionnaire. Cette pièce est l'opprobre de Geneve. Les pasteurs & professeurs se défendent d'être sociniens par un bavardage de 4 pages que tout socinien peut signer. Dalembert a beau jeu.'[27] A few weeks later he went even further, repeating and amplifying his opinion while assuring the same correspondent of his independence and good faith:

> Vous me croyez plein des préjugés de ma secte; je vous assure que je ne suis d'aucune. [...] J'ai été des premiers à condamner comme artificieuse la déclaration de nos chers pasteurs de Geneve. Lisez la. Elle revient à ceci: *L'encyclopédie dit que nous sommes sociniens: elle a menti: car nous le sommes.* Pourquoi si Geneve a changé de créance sur la religion, ne faut-il pas le dire dans un dictionnaire? Il seroit singulier que l'on ne pût pas dire qu'un homme de catolique est devenu mahométan, dès que cet homme l'est devenu. Cela ne peut raisonablement déplaire ni à cet homme ni à un tiers. J'étois un peu socinien genevois. Mais je ne veux plus l'être, puisque c'est une religion qu'on n'ose avouer. Peu importe qu'un clergé soit hérétique. Mais il importe infiniment qu'il ne soit pas menteur.[28]

La Beaumelle was well placed to make such remarks, since not only had he studied in Geneva, but he was also a dogged Huguenot who was determined to support his coreligionists, a man whose outspokenness led to his being imprisoned for several years.[29] His comments focus attention

---

26. Geneva, Archives d'Etat, *Registres de la Compagnie des pasteurs*, R28, p.78; quoted in Gargett, *Jacob Vernet*, p.149, n.79.

27. D7682a (14 March 1758).

28. D7740a (5 April 1758).

29. The essential study is Claude Lauriol, *La Beaumelle: un protestant cévenol entre Montesquieu et Voltaire* (Paris, 1978). See also *Correspondance générale de La Beaumelle*, ed. Hubert Bost, Claude Lauriol and Hubert Angliviel de La Beaumelle (Oxford, Voltaire Foundation, 2005-).

on an extremely important topic, 'liberal' or 'enlightened' Protestantism, its role in the Enlightenment and its connection with the *philosophes*. Here, as in other areas, Geneva played a key part, and this contribution is personified by the city's most influential pastor in the mid eighteenth century, Jacob Vernet.

## ii. Jacob Vernet

Vernet's life and career exemplify the link between theology, politics and culture in eighteenth-century Geneva. Born in 1689, Vernet studied with the great Jean-Alphonse Turrettini, a liberal, rationalising theologian who paradoxically reversed the work of his father, François, chief architect of the arch-orthodox *Formula consensus* of 1675. This was abandoned in 1706. During the 1720s Vernet worked as a preceptor in Paris, frequenting erudite Catholic circles and also making the acquaintance of Tournemine and Fontenelle.[30] His first major work was the *Traité de la vérité de la religion chrétienne*, based on Turrettini's lectures, a situation clearly acknowledged in the subtitle, *tiré du latin de M. J.-ALPHONSE TURRETIN, professeur en théologie et en histoire ecclésiastique à Genève*. As the magnum opus proceeded, however, and as the second edition succeeded the first and the *Traité* became more and more Vernet's own, its theological 'liberalism' increased.[31] Book 1, in particular, originally entitled *De la nécessité de la Révélation*, was renamed *De la grande utilité d'une Révélation*, a change which took place in 1749 and which caused considerable controversy:[32] it is to this that D'Alembert refers transparently in his 'Genève' article.[33] Elsewhere in his work, notably the *Instruction chrétienne*, Vernet's teaching confirmed yet again the basic accuracy of D'Alembert's comments.[34] The eternity of hell is questioned in the clearest possible way. To the question: 'Quelle sera la durée de ces peines?' is given the answer:

---

30. For this stage of Vernet's career see Gargett, *Jacob Vernet*, p.1-19. Father René-Joseph Tournemine had been one of Voltaire's distinguished teachers at the Collège de Louis-le-Grand.

31. For the *Traité*, see Gargett, *Jacob Vernet*, p.54-66. N.-C. Falletti, *Jacob Vernet, théologien genevois (1698-1789)* (Geneva, 1885), has a useful 'appendice bibliographique' (p.115-17) devoted to the different volumes and editions of the work. I quote the subtitle here from the first volume of the first edition, published in Geneva in 1730; in 1745 and 1747 the wording changed to 'tiré principalement', then to 'tiré en partie', in later volumes.

32. See Gargett, *Jacob Vernet*, p.63-64. In particular, Vernet was attacked by Jean-Baptiste Tollot (see *Mercure suisse*, November 1748, p.487, and March 1749, p.232-36).

33. Further proof comes from the private correspondence of the Genevan councillor Jean Du Pan who, writing to his friend Abram Freudenreich in Bern about D'Alembert's article, comments: 'il [D'Alembert] ajoute [...] que quand on [...] presse [nos ministres] sur la *nécessité de la revelation*, ils conviennent de son *utilité* seulement', adding in brackets: 'c'est le Vernet' (Geneva, Bibliothèque Publique et Universitaire, MS Suppl.1540, f.140-41).

34. The *Instruction* had three editions during Vernet's lifetime (1751-1754, 1756 and 1771): see Gargett, *Jacob Vernet*, p.90-98.

Nous ne pouvons dire autre chose sinon que l'Evangile nous le dépeint comme étant sans fin. Il est vrai que le mot d'éternel ou de perpétuel ne s'entend quelquefois que d'une durée longue & indéfinie. Il est vrai aussi que cette perpétuité peut regarder particulièrement les peines privatives, qui consistent à être déchus sans retour d'un degré de bonheur auquel d'autres parviennent.[35]

In addition, Vernet no longer accepts original sin and has evidently abandoned any belief in the Trinity.[36] Years after the original furore, D'Alembert insisted, with specific reference to Vernet, that 'la distance est grande de ce qui est *nécessaire*, à ce qui est simplement *utile*'.[37] His other comments were equally damning and just as clearly targeted Vernet:

Il seroit à souhaiter que les Pasteurs de Geneve eussent expliqué [...] l'idée précise qu'ils attachent au mot *éternel*. On sait que plusieurs Ecrivains Protestans ont entendu par ce mot, non pas *ce qui ne finira jamais*, mais *ce qui doit durer très-longtems*. C'est ainsi qu'ils expliquent les passages de l'Ecriture où se trouve le mot *éternel*. On sent donc combien il étoit nécessaire que les ministres de Geneve levassent l'équivoque. Une ligne auroit suffi pour cela.[38]

This theological controversy and its consequences continued to dog Jacob Vernet throughout his long life.

But it was not only in the area of theology that Vernet had the misfortune to create hostility. Despite his clerical calling, he had a very worldly desire to seek contact with the celebrities of the literary world. This began with Fontenelle but, in 1733, Vernet met Voltaire in Paris. The pair carried on a spasmodic correspondence and, for several years, Vernet had excellent relations with Voltaire, becoming self-appointed editor of a Geneva edition of the *Essai sur les mœurs*, Voltaire's huge panoramic history from Charlemagne to the time of Louis XIV.[39] At first Vernet received high praise from the author, with Voltaire going as far as to call him 'un des plus savants hommes de l'Europe'.[40] Once Voltaire arrived in Geneva, however, the situation changed, almost from the outset. Vernet rather tactlessly urged Voltaire to respect the city's religion (see D6146), the two fell out over Voltaire's determination to organise theatrical performances and, by the early 1760s, Vernet had become one of Voltaire's *bêtes noires*, vilified and tormented in a series of pamphlets

---

35. Jacob Vernet, *Instruction chrétienne*, 2nd edn, 5 vols (Geneva, Henri-Albert Gosse & Comp., 1756), vol.2, book 8, ch.13, p.138, quoted in Gargett, *Jacob Vernet*, p.95-96. Vernet, moreover, also commented: 'nous savons que DIEU est si équitable, si bon & si sage pour les régler [i.e. les peines] & les diversifier selon que chacun le mérite, que jamais on ne doit rien apréhender de trop sévère de sa part' (p.139). D'Alembert's article almost echoes this: see above, p.31-32.

36. See Falletti, *Jacob Vernet*, p.64-68; Gargett, *Jacob Vernet*, p.452-56.

37. Jean D'Alembert, *Mélanges de littérature, d'histoire, et de philosophie*, 5 vols (Amsterdam, Zacharie Chatelain & fils, 1763-1767), vol.5, p.590, note f.

38. D'Alembert, *Mélanges*, vol.5, p.586-87, note c.

39. For the early relations between Vernet and Voltaire see Gargett, *Jacob Vernet*, p.35-40, 66-69, 100-102.

40. In a letter to his niece, Mme Denis (D6577, 17 February 1754).

and brochures and playing a major part in Voltaire's mock epic poem, *La Guerre civile de Genève*.[41]

Even before these incidents and before the *Encyclopédie* article, Vernet – and through him, Geneva – had played a vital role in intellectual history. In the late 1740s Montesquieu had some difficulty in finding a suitable place to publish *De l'esprit des lois*, and through a contact in Paris, he eventually decided on Geneva.[42] In consequence, he sought what he called 'un habile correcteur', basically a conscientious proof-reader, and Vernet was the person approached. As things turned out, he became de facto editor, changing the structure of the book, presuming to make a whole set of recommendations to Montesquieu, even – to the author's understandable irritation – amending his French.[43] Worse still, Vernet gave little attention to actual correction of the text and in consequence the first edition was riddled with errors. Understandably, Montesquieu was livid, referring bitterly to 'l'*Esprit des Loix* qui a été estropié à Genève',[44] though he preserved appearances with Vernet.[45] Whatever the problems, Geneva was thus the place where another seminal Enlightenment event had occurred.

In addition to Montesquieu and Voltaire, Vernet also had an important relationship with Rousseau. When the latter wished in 1754 to be re-admitted to the Genevan church, it was to Vernet that he turned for advice, receiving a warm and friendly welcome. For several years the two remained on cordial terms, both in particular being hostile to any attempt to establish a theatre in Geneva.[46] But Vernet was clearly of a domineering frame of mind and, as with Voltaire, he tried to 'direct' Rousseau's conduct, irritatingly providing unwelcome advice when none was sought.[47] The apparent alliance between the two men was in any case shattered by the climactic events of 1762, when the publication of *Emile* and the *Contrat social* set Rousseau at odds not only with the French authorities but also with those of his native Geneva. Vernet seems to have

---

41. See Gargett, *Jacob Vernet*, p.103-331, 370-442. For *La Guerre civile de Genève* see Gargett, *Jacob Vernet*, p.407-411, and *La Guerre civile de Genève, ou les Amours de Robert Covelle: poème héroïque avec des notes instructives*, ed. John Renwick (*OCV*, vol.63A, *1767:I*, p.1-152). One of the most wounding attacks occurred in the *Dialogues chrétiens* of 1760, which I consider to have been only partly composed by Voltaire: see Gargett, *Jacob Vernet*, p.174-97 and 225-60.

42. See Gargett, *Jacob Vernet*, p.73-87; 'Jacob Vernet éditeur de Montesquieu: la première édition de *L'Esprit des lois*', *Revue d'histoire littéraire de la France* 90 (1990), p.890-900; Louis Desgraves, *Montesquieu* (Paris, 1981), p.331-43.

43. This at least was what Montesquieu's friend Guasco claimed: see François Gébelin, 'La publication de l'*Esprit des lois*', *Revue des bibliothèques* 34 (1924), p.125-58 (130).

44. Letter to Domville of 4 March 1749, in *Œuvres complètes de Montesquieu*, ed. André Masson, 3 vols (Paris, 1950-1955), vol.3, letter 465; see also letters 453 and 473.

45. See Masson, *Œuvres complètes de Montesquieu*, vol.3, letters 550, 585 and 699, and Gargett, *Jacob Vernet*, p.87.

46. See Gargett, *Jacob Vernet*, p.151-65, 332-36.

47. Gargett, *Jacob Vernet*, p.335-42.

been the author of a secret report to the Genevan authorities identifying the 'heretical' parts of Rousseau's work.[48] Thereafter Rousseau accused Vernet and his pastoral colleagues of bad faith and hypocrisy in terms just as energetic as those used by Voltaire, particularly in the *Lettres de la montagne* of 1764. The attacks on Vernet by Rousseau and Voltaire certainly brought him notoriety throughout Europe, though this was hardly the type that he had sought.

## iii. Rousseau and Genevan politics

Nowadays we are all familiar with the term 'cultural politics', a concept which is vital in many situations of conflict around the world and which, self-evidently, almost always has a real political connection: the political significance of cultural manifestations such as Orange parades in Northern Ireland would be an all too obvious example. Both the theatre and religion were political as well as cultural issues in eighteenth-century Geneva. The cultural confrontation not actually begun but certainly heightened by D'Alembert's article steadily broadened out into a full-scale political clash over the next few years. In addition, the fact that Rousseau and Voltaire were both involved meant that this dispute would attract the attention of the wider world outside Calvin's city. The influential role played by England in the thinking and writings of Montesquieu, Voltaire and also many other French writers is a commonplace of Enlightenment studies, but Rousseau, on the contrary, had little time for England or representative government. In the *Contrat social* he remarks: 'Le peuple Anglois pense être libre; il se trompe fort, il ne l'est que durant l'élection des membres du Parlement; sitôt qu'ils sont élus, il est esclave, il n'est rien.'[49]

It has been argued that Rousseau was more influenced by the political life of his own city.[50] Until the 1530s, Geneva had been under the sway of its bishop, but once the Reformation attracted support there, the bishop voluntarily left the city in 1536 accompanied by many of his supporters — no doubt he expected to return, though that never happened.[51] Instead,

---

48. Gargett, *Jacob Vernet*, p.348-52, and Leigh, *Correspondance*, appendix 295.

49. *Du Contrat social*, bk 3, ch.15, in J.-J. Rousseau, *Œuvres complètes*, ed. Bernard Gagnebin and Marcel Raymond, 4 vols (Paris, 1964), vol.3, p.430. In his *Considérations sur le gouvernement de Pologne*, Rousseau goes even further, observing sarcastically: 'je ne puis qu'admirer la négligence, l'incurie, et j'ose dire la stupidité de la Nation Angloise, qui, après avoir armé ses députés de la suprême puissance, n'y ajoûte aucun frein pour régler l'usage qu'ils en pourront faire pendant sept ans entiers que dure leur commission' (*Œuvres complètes*, vol.3, p.979).

50. See Helena Rosenblatt, *Rousseau and Geneva: from the First discourse to the Social contract, 1749-1762* (Cambridge, 1997); Michel Launay, *Jean-Jacques Rousseau, écrivain politique (1712-1762)* (Grenoble, 1971).

51. See Jane Ceitac, *Voltaire et l'affaire des Natifs: un aspect de la carrière humanitaire du patriarche de Ferney* (Geneva, 1956), p.14-15.

the General Council of Citizens and Burghers, or *Bourgeois*, met and voted to adopt the Reformation. Geneva became a republic, Calvin arrived and helped not only to reform the city's religion, but also its political institutions.[52] In the mid 1550s, distinctions between the various groups or classes of Genevans seem to have been somewhat indistinct but, as time went on, they were increasingly codified – to the advantage of the richer and more influential inhabitants. The main impetus for this was the influx of large numbers of French Protestant refugees at various stages of the sixteenth century, especially after the Revocation of the Edict of Nantes in 1685; according to Herbert Lüthy, 3000 to 4000 French Protestants settled in Geneva, representing around a fifth of its population in 1711.[53] A considerable number of the more wealthy incomers were allowed to buy bourgeois status, causing a great deal of resentment, since they had used their wealth and connections to arrogate to themselves a position which many native Genevans could not achieve. As George-Louis Le Sage commented, in a letter apparently addressed to La Beaumelle at some time in 1751: 'Les natifs voient avec chagrin que cinq cent nouveaux bourgeois etrangers, d'une naissance souvent equivoque, sont plus favorisez que les natifs. Que l'on n'a jamais doné la bourgeoisie à un natif. Et que depuis cinquante ans, l'on a reçu plus de six cent bourgeois, dont il y a à peine cinquante natifs.'[54] Here, clearly, was one of the seeds of the interclass conflict which would affect Geneva so powerfully in the late Enlightenment.

Many Genevans were indeed completely disenfranchised. By the late seventeenth and in the eighteenth century, only two classes of male Genevans had the right to vote, the *citoyens* and the *bourgeois*, and of the former, only a relatively small group of patrician families could hold office in the city's executive or government, the *Petit Conseil*. A 'citizen' was a Genevan born in the city of parents already belonging to this class; a *bourgeois* was someone born in the city to parents already belonging to this class or someone who had bought *lettres de bourgeoisie*. The total number of *citoyens* and *bourgeois* was at the most around 1500, probably closer to 1300. They were considerably outnumbered by the other classes in the city: the *natifs*, Genevans born in the city but not members of the two privileged classes; the *habitants*, outsiders who had paid for the privilege of

---

52. See Léopold Micheli, *Les Institutions municipales de Genève au XV<sup>e</sup> siècle* (Geneva, 1912), and Marc-Edouard Chenevrière, *La Pensée politique de Calvin* (Paris and Geneva, 1937), who emphasises Calvin's suspicion of democracy (p.195).

53. Herbert Lüthy, *La Banque protestante en France de la Révocation de l'Edit de Nantes à la Révolution*, 2 vols (Paris, 1959-1961), vol.1, p.38. See also Pierre Bertrand, *Genève et la Révocation de l'Edit de Nantes* (Geneva, 1935).

54. I am grateful to Claude Lauriol, who communicated the text of this letter to me. He feels that it was written by one 'Ch. Lesage'. This text, however, would appear to be the one given a slightly different attribution by André Gür: see his 'Un précédent à la condamnation du *Contrat social*: l'affaire George-Louis Le Sage (1752)', *Bulletin de la société d'histoire et d'archéologie de Genève* 14 (1968), p.77-94.

residing in Geneva (children born to them there became *natifs*); and the *sujets*, outsiders who could not afford to pay to reside in the city but whose presence there was tolerated.[55] Most of the *natifs* were artisans or manual workers so although some, like Rousseau's father, were both artisans and *bourgeois* or citizens, generally they represented the city's lower or working class, the *bourgeoisie* and most of the *citoyens* roughly corresponding to a middle class, whereas the upper class, 'les princes manqués' as they were called in a 1760s pamphlet,[56] consisted of a restricted group of patrician families. The eighteenth century saw periodic political disturbances, which became more intractable as time went on. The *bourgeoisie* sought to extend and defend the powers of the General Council, most of whose functions had been devolved to the *Petit Conseil*'s twenty-five members or the Council of Two Hundred. Jean-Jacques Rousseau became the great symbol and – for a while – de facto leader, *in absentia*, of this group of *bourgeois* radicals: for a few years he really did function like a party leader in exile. Trouble really started in 1763, when he renounced his Genevan citizenship, and protests by several hundred fellow citizens took place over several months. And, surprisingly in many ways, the champion of the lower-class *natifs*, after a certain amount of toing and froing, was that gentleman of the king's bedchamber and former darling of Geneva's patrician families, M. de Voltaire. Voltaire seems to have been genuinely taken by the naive candour and earnest good intentions of the *natif* leaders, especially Georges Auzière. In 1766, at the beginning of an external mediation, Voltaire helped them compose documents and to formulate very reasonable and gradualist proposals which were rejected out of hand by the *Petit Conseil*, thereby stirring up more trouble for the future.[57] Voltaire in addition was scolded by the French government, whose chief negotiator, the chevalier de Beauteville, ambassador to the Swiss cantons, was incensed by his meddling and dismissed him as senile in a letter to the duc de Choiseul, de facto prime minister of France.[58]

55. Michel Launay, 'Jean-Jacques Rousseau, écrivain politique', in *Au siècle des Lumières* (Moscow, Ecole pratique des hautes études et Institut d'histoire universelle de l'Académie des sciences de l'U.R.S.S., 1970), p.77-136 (99).

56. *Les Princes manqués: lettre d'un citoyen à J.-J. Rousseau, du 29 mars 1765, se débitent à Carouge à la même enseigne que les Lettres de la campagne*: see Emile Rivoire, *Bibliographie historique de Genève au XVIII$^e$ siècle, vol.1 (1701-1792)* (Geneva, 1897), no.820 and 821, p.129-30.

57. See Voltaire's correspondence for the early months of 1766, especially D13240, D13247, D13248, D13260, D13262, D13263, D13274, D13279, D13282, D13286, D13298, D13305, D13282. See also Pomeau, *Voltaire en son temps*, vol.2, p.261-63; Peter Gay, *Voltaire's politics: the poet as realist* (New York, 1965), p.220-38; *Mémoires de Isaac Cornuaud, sur Genève et la Révolution de 1770 à 1795*, ed. Emilie Cherbuliez (Geneva, 1912), ch.1.

58. 'Je ne veux pas excuser M. de Voltaire; mais permettés, Monsieur le Duc, que je vous représente qu'il a près de 73 ans. Sa conduite également absurde et ridicule est plus digne de compassion que de colère. Elle fait sentir avec regret que l'auteur de la Henriade s'évanouit chaque jour. Il est dans une affliction et un égarement inexprimables' (D13282, 2 May 1766).

So tiny Geneva, through class divisions exacerbated by political inequality and cultural disagreements, prompted intervention by both Catholic France and two major Protestant Swiss cantons, Bern and Zurich. There had been political disturbances in 1707 and 1708, and between 1734 and 1738, the latter series prompting this external 'mediation', as it was called. Then, as described earlier, the troubles began again in the 1760s and a strong light was shone on this peripheral little republic. It was a strong light because of the quite intricate involvement of those literary giants of their day, Jean-Jacques Rousseau and Voltaire. Rousseau's supporters accused Voltaire and his friends of a covert campaign against Rousseau, and there were fierce attacks on the Frenchman.[59] Although the attacks were verbal, Voltaire clearly no longer felt at home in Geneva, and as early as 1759 transferred his residence from 'Les Délices', his house in the environs of Geneva, to Ferney, just over the frontier. After the failed mediation of 1766, the troubles continued, leading to the exiling of some opposition figures and further disturbances in the early 1780s which forced a certain democratisation of the city's political structures. In particular, the *bourgeoisie* was substantially extended.

## iv. Conclusion

For a city of its minuscule size Geneva played an extraordinary role in the eighteenth century. Its Academy was justly famous. Various German princes and princelings received their education in the city, among them Prince Frederick of Hesse-Cassel, the hereditary prince of Saxe-Gotha, and the counts of Schaumburg-Lippe.[60] Geneva produced a legal mind of the highest quality, Jean-Jacques Burlamaqui, known and respected throughout Europe, whose *Principes du droit naturel* and *Principes du droit politique* appeared in 1747 and 1751 respectively.[61] It was an important centre for banking and finance, the most famous institution in this area being the Thellusson bank, though even Jacob Vernet's brother, Isaac, established in Paris, was a millionaire.[62] Geneva was also a centre for

---

59. In particular Charles Pictet accused him of having solicited the condemnation of Rousseau's works in Geneva (see D10523, 22 June 1762) and was deprived of membership of the Conseil des Deux-Cents and ordered to apologise.

60. All these were pupils of Jacob Vernet: see Gargett, *Jacob Vernet*, p.43, 91, n.121.

61. See Rosenblatt, *Rousseau and Geneva*, p.96-99, 154-55, 188-89. Born into a patrician family, Burlamaqui (1694-1748) was a disciple of Jean Barbeyrac. Professor of natural and civil law at Geneva's Academy from 1723 onwards, Burlamaqui had a low opinion of democracy.

62. See Lüthy, *La Banque protestante*, vol.2, p.219-31. Brandli ('Le résident de France', p.56-57) emphasises the comparative poverty of France's representatives at Geneva: when the baron de Montpéroux died in 1765 he was worth 18,889 *livres* and 8 *sols*, with debts of 27,771 *livres*; his Genevan counterpart at Versailles, Isaac Thellusson, left around 2,230,000 *livres tournois*.

scientific networking – although men like Jean Jallabert and Charles Bonnet are hardly major names in the history of science, they contributed in a significant way to the diffusion and dissemination of scientific ideas.[63] Towards the end of the Enlightenment, Geneva did produce a great man of science, the botanist Augustin-Pyramus de Candolle.[64] And all this is without mentioning the role of Geneva's printers: Huguetan, Philibert, Pellet, Barrillot and above all the Cramer brothers, not only Voltaire's favourite printers but – in the case of Gabriel – also his friend and confidant.[65] It is no surprise that, according to Geisendorf, this was the 'second great era of Genevan printing',[66] second only to the era of the Reformation. For a city of some 20,000 to 25,000 people all this is truly astonishing. And Geneva's story does not end with the Enlightenment: Necker would become a crucial figure at the beginning of the French Revolution[67] and, quite apart from that, with Rousseau and Mme de Staël, Geneva was also one of the midwives of the Romantic movement. The nineteenth and twentieth centuries saw it acquire a reputation as a centre of international diplomacy and peacemaking, with the city becoming the seat of many international organisations, perhaps most importantly of the International Red Cross.

How can we explain Geneva's *rayonnement* during the Enlightenment? In a short chapter it seems impossible to do more than to hazard a few guesses. Clearly, the fact that Rousseau was born in Geneva and that Voltaire came to live there must be one of the most vital factors, if not the most. But there was also the creative tension generated by the clash between this Protestant city and its great Catholic neighbour, France, between such opposing histories, traditions and cultures, mediated differently from in previous times during this more enlightened, marginally less bellicose and confrontational age. The continuing heritage of the past ensured too that Genevans would continue to look to Protestant territories like Germany and Britain: when Jacob Vernet defended himself

63. See Ellen McNiven Hine, *Jean-Jacques Dortous de Mairan and the Geneva connection: scientific networking in the eighteenth century*, SVEC 340 (1996); Renato G. Mazzolini and Shirley A. Roe, *Science against the unbelievers: the correspondence of Bonnet and Needham, 1760-1780*, SVEC 243 (1986); and, more recently, *Deux astronomes genevois dans la Russie de Catherine II: journaux de voyage en Laponie russe de Jean-Louis Pictet et Jacques-André Mallet pour observer le passage de Vénus devant le disque solaire, 1768-1769*, ed. Jean-Daniel Candaux et al. (Geneva, 2005).

64. See Augustin-Pyramus de Candolle, *Mémoires et souvenirs (1778-1841)*, ed. Jean-Daniel Candaux and Jean-Marc Drouin (Geneva and Paris, 2004).

65. See the enormous number of letters from him and to him in Voltaire's correspondence. See also Lucien Cramer, *Une Famille genevoise, les Cramer: leurs relations avec Voltaire, Rousseau et Benjamin Franklin-Bache* (Geneva, 1952); Andrew Brown and Ulla Kölving, 'Voltaire and Cramer?', in *Le Siècle de Voltaire: hommage à René Pomeau*, ed. Christiane Mervaud and Sylvain Menant, 2 vols (Oxford, 1987), p.149-83.

66. P.-F. Geisendorf, 'Quelques notes sur une maison d'édition genevoise du XVIIIe siècle: les Barrillot', *Genava* 22 (1924), p.203-10 (204).

67. For a recent study illustrating this see Léonard Burnand, *Necker et l'opinion publique* (Paris, 2004).

against Voltaire and D'Alembert, he entitled his work *Lettres critiques d'un voyageur anglais*, and he had visited England, Germany and Holland, as well as Italy and France. But the same Jacob Vernet also – like a number of fellow Genevans – showed a great openness to Italian culture and antiquities: he and his mentor, Jean-Alphonse Turrettini, helped the Italian radical exile, Pietro Giannone, when he sought refuge in Geneva in 1736.[68] This surely is true cosmopolitanism. Perhaps Geneva's geographical position gives the final clue. On the periphery of not just France, but also Switzerland, Italy and the German-speaking world, it did actually find itself at a type of centre. Rather like today's Strasbourg, on the periphery of France, but close to the centre of Europe, or at least of the old Europe. One thing, however, is sure amid the speculation: no other city of its size played such a dynamic, controversial and fruitful role as tiny Geneva in the eighteenth century's era of Enlightenment.

Yet, despite the multiplicity of Geneva's contributions to the various fields of intellectual endeavour, the two most important were plainly politics and religion. Politics, because of the more than parochial implications of the political disturbances described a little earlier and because of Rousseau, although, as I have tried to show, the two were inextricably connected. Of these two important areas, however, it is the debate around religion which seems to me – in a wider perspective – to have made the greater contribution and still to have more to say to the modern world. As already observed, Rousseau's political thought was inspired and nourished by the political history and contemporary ambience of his native city. The point is easily made and should not therefore be laboured. Despite the lengthy explanations in the *Contrat social* as to how, during the Roman Republic, vast numbers of citizens were assembled together at the time of elections, the 'volonté générale' or 'general will' is transparently associated with the decisions made by the *Conseil Général* of some 1300 souls who met once a year in the Geneva of the *ancien régime*. The special meanings given by Rousseau in his famous text to terms like 'prince' and 'souverain' become more immediately comprehensible when seen against the background of his tiny republic. One of the most anachronistic aspects of his analysis, his dismissal of representative government,[69] also becomes more easily understandable in this perspective. Yet, despite its unworkable and anachronistic elements, no one could deny the universal importance of the *Contrat social* for the late Enlightenment as a whole,[70] and beyond that for the development of

68. See Gargett, *Jacob Vernet*, p.179-86. Vernet had also been asked as a young man, in 1728, to become part of the editorial team of a new journal, the *Bibliothèque italique*.
69. Referred to above, p.38.
70. A further irony is that, by emphasising that the social contract will only work properly if every single member of the state feels a personal stake in it, Rousseau actually defends the political rights of the *natifs*, who as a group hated him (see D13240), since he was associated with their enemies, the *représentants* (a synonym for *bourgeois*).

political thought *per se*. Indeed, Bernard Gagnebin testifies to its influence in certain twentieth-century milieux:

> De nombreux hommes politiques africains ou asiatiques de langue française se sont mis à lire Rousseau, au moment où leurs pays accédaient à l'indépendance. D'éminents hommes d'Etat vietnamiens, guinéens, sénégalais, etc., ont affirmé que leurs carrières avaient été orientées vers la politique par la lecture des œuvres de Rousseau. Fidel Castro n'a-t-il pas déclaré [...] à un journaliste français que Jean-Jacques avait été son maître et qu'il avait combattu Battista avec le *Contrat social* dans sa poche![71]

Generally, though, it would be difficult to argue for the continuing relevance of the *Contrat social* at any more than a rhetorical level.[72]

I feel that Geneva's 'liberal' or 'enlightened' religion, however, does retain a wider relevance. Firstly, in several ways, liberal pastors were quite close to certain *philosophes*. By this I mean that doctrinally they had evolved from the traditional ideas of not only their own denomination but of the Christian religion in general. Men like Jacob Vernet and Jacob Vernes no longer believed in the Trinity; or the traditional doctrine of hell and eternal damnation; or in original sin; or, in the case of Vernet, in the seven days of Creation.[73] They remained sincerely attached to the person of Jesus Christ, but they certainly interpreted the New Testament and the Bible as a whole – at least to some extent – in metaphorical terms. In other words, they wished to update its significance for themselves and their contemporaries. They still, however, saw themselves as loyal Christians, and those common positions they shared with the *philosophes* had been reached from an opposite starting point and were still viewed in a completely different perspective.[74] But this brings us to a second point.

The 'modernisation' carried out by such 'enlightened' clergy was surely far-sighted, prefiguring the attitudes of modern-day Christians, of all

---

71. Rousseau, *Œuvres complètes*, vol.3, p.xxvi.

72. One thinks of the famous opening line of book 1, chapter 1: 'L'homme est né libre, et par-tout il est dans les fers' (Rousseau, *Œuvres complètes*, vol.3, p.351). This might seem far from the political reality of eighteenth-century Geneva, but such was the language of the time, as can be seen in the formulation of the *natifs*' demands (see D13240); it may of course also reflect Rousseau's childhood reading.

73. See Falletti, *Jacob Vernet*, p.64. The days were doubtless 'des périodes très inégales, comme l'indique le contexte, et comme nous autorise à le penser le sens même du mot hébreu, qui n'a rien de rigoureux'.

74. For a discussion of the relations between Voltaire and five pastors (three from Geneva: Vernet, Vernes and Moultou; one from Bern, Elie Bertrand; one from the pays de Vaud, François-Louis Allamand) see Gargett, *Voltaire and Protestantism*, p.173-205. The overlap between the respective positions of Voltaire and his correspondents is sometimes intriguing. On 19 August 1768 (D15180) Voltaire apparently argues that Christianity will not disappear, while Vernes seems to think the opposite: 'Le christianisme, dites vous, est aboli chez tous les honnêtes gens; oui, le christianisme de Constantin, le christianisme des pères; mais le christianisme de Jesu subsistera.'

those indeed who are not to be classified as rigid 'fundamentalists'.[75] The problem is, quite simply, that men like Vernet publicly denied beliefs that they had already published in theological works, and they were therefore taxed, by Voltaire and D'Alembert in particular, with hypocrisy, an accusation which seems totally justified. What would be thought nowadays of a religious leader who preached or taught one thing yet who, in his writings or conduct, was seen to believe another? Admittedly, as I have often been told, there may have been social or economic reasons which caused this attitude.[76] Of course there were. Self-evidently. Anyone can see that it would have been very inconvenient and highly embarrassing for Jacob Vernet to be found to be a neo-Socinian when he was – to all intents and purposes – the leading theologian in eighteenth-century Geneva. Elsewhere, 'enlightened' Protestants were more forthright or braver about declaring their real beliefs. In Ireland, Jean-Pierre Droz, though a Presbyterian clergyman like Vernet, made a point of expressing unorthodox opinions in his periodical, *A Literary journal*.[77] When Samuel Clarke had made clear his theological modernism in England a couple of generations earlier, in his *Scripture doctrine of the Trinity* (1712), he had been censured by Convocation and his ecclesiastical career had been blighted.[78] But is self-interest any justification for hypocrisy? The answer, especially when one is speaking of a religious leader, should hardly need to be given. If writers like Voltaire have often been accused of hypocrisy, why should Vernet and his ilk escape the same charge, especially when it is so obviously true? Voltaire was living in the contemporary equivalent of a police state and there is therefore surely some justification for his lying, subterfuge and ironical side-stepping of the truth. As the publication of the *Lettres philosophiques* and later episodes illustrated, despite his attempts to remain safe, Voltaire did actually risk punishment and persecution. I can see no similar excuse for the pastors of Geneva when, in 1767, asked

75. By this I do not of course mean that all modern Christians apart from fundamentalists reject the Trinity, or original sin and so on; I mean that they all, to some extent, understand at least parts of the Bible in metaphorical terms.

76. However, the distinguished historian, E.-G. Léonard, reacts similarly in his discussion of the various explanations for the Reformation: 'l'élimination, dans la recherche des motifs de la Réforme, de ceux qui ne porteraient que sur telle classe et telle région et la constatation qu'elle intéressa tous les pays et tous les milieux obligent à lui reconnaître des causes valables pour tous les hommes. De ces causes générales aucune n'est plus universelle que le sentiment religieux.[...] Aussi bien est-il naturel de chercher à une révolution religieuse des motifs spécifiquement religieux', *Histoire générale du protestantisme*, 3 vols (Paris, 1961-1964), vol.1, p.9-10.

77. See Graham Gargett, 'Jean-Pierre Droz, *A Literary journal*, and francophone influence on the "Irish Enlightenment"', in *France–Ireland: anatomy of a relationship: studies in history, literature and politics*, ed. Eamon Maher and Grace Neville (Frankfurt, Berlin, New York and Oxford, 2004), p.177-90.

78. Gargett, *Voltaire and Protestantism*, p.427. Clarke also refused to accept any ecclesiastical preferment which involved subscription to the thirty-nine articles, in other words an affirmation of orthodoxy (see Norman Sykes, *Church and state in England in the 18th century*, Cambridge, 1934, p.141, n.2).

by their persecuted coreligionists in France to state clearly that public worship was of a vital necessity for Protestants, they refused point blank – twice! (one cannot help remembering a certain biblical parallel) – to do so.[79] Three chapters of Jacob Vernet's *Instruction chrétienne* were actually entitled: 'De la nécessité d'un Culte extérieur & public', 'De la profession franche & publique que nous devons faire du Christianisme' and 'Des raisons qui nous obligent à ne point dissimuler nôtre Religion & à tout souffrir plutôt que d'être hypocrites'.[80] But does that excuse him and his colleagues for such a craven refusal to say what they thought was true? I find it impossible to think that it does. Of course, it would have been inconvenient. It would have caused political difficulties with the *Petit Conseil* and the French *résident*. Yet that is hardly the point. Voltaire and other *philosophes*, despite their frequent equivocations and ironic falsehoods, were closer to playing the role of martyrs for the truth than were those 'liberal' or 'enlightened' pastors of eighteenth-century Geneva.

Such hypocrisy was arguably a very bad beginning for the development of this particular strand of 'enlightened', 'liberal' or 'modernised' Christianity. It enabled some Protestant historians after the nineteenth-century *réveil* (evangelical revival) to keep very quiet about their predecessors – in actual fact to pretend that the *philosophes* had been telling downright lies and that nothing of the sort had ever happened.[81] Others, on the contrary, saw in these 'liberal' pastors the forerunners of a modern theology which would liberate Protestantism from the straightjacket of 'orthodoxy' or traditionalism.[82]

The position of pastors like Vernet, however, was surely dangerous. Can a new beginning really be based on equivocation and the refusal to answer direct questions? Everyone knows exactly what the beliefs of fundamentalists were or are, both during the Enlightenment and now, however unreasonable or repugnant they might appear. If there was, or is, to be any alternative between fundamentalist religion and atheism, should

---

79. The question had been put by the representative of the *églises du désert* in Paris, Court de Gébelin, in October 1766; it was repeated and debated again on 21 November 1766 (Geneva, registers of the *Compagnie des pasteurs*, R30, p.96, and R30, p.113-14). Gébelin's approach occurred because the duc de Richelieu had claimed that public worship was not necessary for Protestants (Joseph Dedieu, *Histoire politique des protestants français (1715-1794)*, 2 vols., Paris, 1925, vol.2, p.107; Gargett, *Jacob Vernet*, p.526-27).

80. Vernet, *Instruction chrétienne*, vol.3, book 2, chapters 15, 16 and 17 (p.192-201, 201-207 and 208-21).

81. See Jean-Pierre Gaberel, *Voltaire et les Genevois* (Paris and Geneva, 1857), p.2-3, 82-84, 157-61. See also Charles Coquerel's reference to 'ces débats, peu intéressants', in other words doctrinal arguments among French Protestants of the Enlightenment (*Histoire des églises du désert*, 2 vols, Paris, 1841, vol.2, p.376), and his defence of Moultou (vol.2, p.340). Some, like Léon Maury (*Le Réveil religieux dans l'église réformée à Genève et en France (1810-1850)*, Paris, 1892) and Daniel Benoît (*L'Etat religieux du protestantisme français dans la seconde moitié du XVIIIe siècle*, Montauban, 1909), decried those whom they considered as lukewarm or unfaithful Christians.

82. See, for example, Louis Vallette, *L'Eglise de Genève à la fin du XVIIIe siècle* (Geneva, 1892), and J.-E. Cellerier, *L'Académie de Genève* (Geneva, 1872), p.51ff.

it not be reasonable to expect 'enlightened' Christians, both now and in the eighteenth century, to say and write what they actually believe?[83] Geneva played a vital role in the French Enlightenment, in many ways. In particular, it focused attention on 'enlightened' Christianity, but to my mind its pastors' refusal to admit what they really believed obscured their real contribution. In one way, however, Geneva's pastors can perhaps be criticised no more than certain *philosophes*, including Voltaire. In apparently thinking that there was an elite which could deal with truths beyond the grasp of the masses, both were surely committing the same intellectual 'crime'[84] and sinning against what should have been one of the fundamental preoccupations of both Christianity and the more secular *Lumières*, what would nowadays be called transparency, in other words honesty and clarity. In the last analysis, were both not to some extent betraying the Enlightenment and associating themselves, at least in this area, with what the Germans call its dark side?[85]

83. Some may find my argument anachronistic, but I would refer them to the comments by La Beaumelle quoted earlier.
84. I use this term in the sense of the French expression, 'le crime des bien-pensants'.
85. I am thinking of the term 'Die Dunkle Aufklärung', whose English equivalent would be 'Counter-Enlightenment'.

MICHAEL BROWN

# Was there an Irish Enlightenment? The case of the Anglicans

According to the historiography, the Irish Enlightenment does not exist. As A. T. Q. Stewart has pointed out of Enlightenment scholars, 'It is almost as if authors inhabiting so rarefied an intellectual atmosphere dread some kind of devaluation if they mention the homeland of [...] Berkeley, Toland, Swift and Hutcheson.' Indicative of this neglect is the famous collection edited by Roy Porter and Mikuláš Teich on *The Enlightenment in national context* wherein Ireland was absented from the countries chosen for attention. Indeed, Ireland is noted as an absentee in the preface.[1] 'Nor', however, as Stewart then bewails 'do the Irish take much interest in the Enlightenment; they prefer to remember the Age of the Protestant Ascendancy, the penal laws and the 1798 Rebellion.'[2] Thus, a reader as sensitive as Toby Barnard has written of how 'something akin to the Enlightenment, but more practical than speculative flourished among the Protestants who crowded into the Irish capital.'[3]

What is the explanation for this gap? Is it just that the Irish Enlightenment is neglected because it never existed, failing to develop in the strange climate of Europe's most westerly island? Stewart thinks not, clearly identifying two reasons for this strange absence. One is that for Enlightenment scholars a peripheral case, such as Ireland, seems to hold little attraction. And indeed, by virtually any definition of the centre – geographic location, strategic importance, economic power or cultural influence – Ireland seems to languish on the western periphery of Europe. Secondly historians of the country have traditionally been reluctant to dwell on Ireland's similarities with mainland Britain or with Continental Europe, preferring to concentrate on its resemblance to the imperial dominions, notably America. In so doing, they claim a kind of

---

1. *The Enlightenment in national context*, ed. Porter and Teich, p.viii.
2. A. T. Q. Stewart, *The Shape of Irish history* (Belfast, 2001), p.110.
3. Toby Barnard, *The Kingdom of Ireland, 1641-1760* (Basingstoke, 2004), p.11. Alexander Murdoch, writes 'No one has written of an Irish Enlightenment', yet proposes that 'The Anglo-Irish Ascendancy [culture] of scientific enquiry and the expansion of the culture of print in Dublin and Belfast in particular fit into the model of Enlightenment activity anywhere in the European world, from the colonies of the Western hemisphere to the Russian Empire to the east, and involved another elite rethinking its culture and questioning the nature of authority, knowledge and political economy', *British history, 1660-1832: national identity and local culture* (Basingstoke, 2001), p.102, 103.

particularity for Irish development as an internal European colony, but the Irish Enlightenment suffers from neglect as a result.

In identifying an Irish Enlightenment two things are necessary. Firstly the movement must be something more than 'the Enlightenment in Ireland', the transfusion of ideas from abroad into the country. Thus although it has become clear that the Enlightenment was imported, for this to indicate more than intellectual curiosity or commercial opportunism the books had to have fed a home-grown and self-consciously Irish version of the movement.[4] Secondly the indigenous variant must be enlightened in form and content and not just a reaction to developments elsewhere. It is partly this that complicates David Berman's attempt to identify an Irish Enlightenment. Berman has offered a Counter-Enlightenment, a reactive movement divided between right- and left-wing readers of the English thinker John Locke.[5] This has led to the subsidiary complication that in Berman's view, Ireland experienced a Counter-Enlightenment largely before the Continent had experience of a recognisable Enlightenment.

Yet Berman is right to identify a spectrum of thought within Anglican Ireland in the period from 1690 to 1730. To understand the form and character of the Irish Enlightenment, however, it is necessary to comprehend both what the Enlightenment constituted and how Irish conditions placed it under particular stresses which resulted in a distinctive slant on and contribution to the international movement. To the first of these elements, the nature of the Enlightenment itself, we now briefly turn.

## i. The nature of the Enlightenment

I wish to propose that the essential philosophical assumption of the Enlightenment was that the human being, not a divine creator, is the basic unit of analysis. In this, it draws inspiration from the reductive scepticism of Descartes, stripping away the accretions of experience and received wisdom to a primary and irreducible core, 'I think, therefore I am.' From this kernel of knowledge the world is then reconstructed, either through rationalist deductions or from the inductive ordering of experience. And it is as a result of this option regarding method that the Enlightenment contains a spectrum of approaches with empirical

---

4. *Ireland and the French Enlightenment, 1700-1800* (Basingstoke, 1999), ed. Graham Gargett and Geraldine Sheridan; Graham Gargett, 'Voltaire's *Lettres philosophiques* in eighteenth-century Ireland', *Eighteenth-century Ireland* 14 (1999), p.77-98; Máire Kennedy, *French books in eighteenth-century Ireland*, SVEC 2001:07; Geraldine Sheridan, 'Warring translations: Prévost's *Doyen de Killerine* in the Irish press', *Eighteenth-century Ireland* 14 (1999), p.99-115.

5. David Berman, *Berkeley and Irish philosophy* (London, 2005), p.1-173. See also his entries in *The Dictionary of Irish philosophers*, ed. Thomas Doody (Bristol, 2004).

and rationalist strands, which centralised either a posteriori or a priori thought processes when constructing philosophical systems. And, on its fringes, resided speculative free thought, which subverted and dissolved all assertions of orthodoxy. So too there were varying levels of commitment to the Enlightenment project. The movement had its activists, its enthusiastic publicists, its coffee-house advocates and its private sympathisers.

The idea of a spectrum of methodologies emerging from a primary philosophical assumption appears to me to carry with it three distinct positive merits.[6] Firstly it has at its heart a philosophical idea, retaining the sense that the Enlightenment was primarily an intellectual rather than a social or cultural phenomenon, in as much as it constitutes a set of intellectual resources with which historical actors interpreted their experiences and co-ordinated their responses. Secondly the primary intellectual assumption that man is the unit of analysis avoids turning the Enlightenment into a checklist of political (and often politically correct) stances concerning particular issues. Too often the Enlightenment is studied, not on its own terms, but for the value it is perceived to contain as the progenitor of a liberal, tolerant, secular, cosmopolitan modernity. While the broad thrust of this meta-narrative may initially appear convincing, it fractures and fragments under any kind of close scrutiny, corroding confidence in the value of the category. Voltaire was ambivalent in his relationship to democracy, flirting with ideas of enlightened absolutism during his time in Prussia, and showed little tolerance towards the Jews. And in William Robertson the Scottish Enlightenment found a staunch defender of religious faith and the moral superiority of the British constitution. These opinions and attitudes need to be comprehended within our more general understanding of these figures, not treated as unfortunate falls from grace or embarrassing personal peccadilloes. Thirdly the idea of a methodological spectrum enables the Enlightenment to generate debate within itself – allowing for what Peter Gay described as the bickering within the Enlightenment family – while sustaining its shared origin in the revolution towards philosophy and away from theology: towards a science of man and away from a poetics of the divine.[7]

---

6. A rather different spectrum, which prioritises the positive content of philosophical schemes over methodologies is offered in J. Israel, *Radical Enlightenment*, passim, but see for instance, p.11: 'Hence Europe's war of philosophies during the Early Enlightenment down to 1750 was never confined to the intellectual sphere and was never anywhere a straightforward two-way contest between traditionalists and *moderni*. Rather, the rivalry between moderate mainstream and radical fringe was always as much an integral part of the drama as that between the moderate Enlightenment and conservative opposition.'

7. The metaphor of 'quarrelsome family' is used in Peter Gay, *The Party of humanity: studies in the French Enlightenment* (London, 1964), p.262, and P. Gay, *The Enlightenment: an interpretation, vol.1: the rise of modern paganism* (New York, 1966), p.x.

Finally, alongside the initial philosophical assumption, and the concomitant spectrum of methodological assumptions, a third element of the Enlightenment must be recalled, namely, a social environment in which the resulting ideas and proposals are explored, interrogated and tested. In other words, sense can be made of the emergence of the public sphere and Republic of Letters, a world of salons and coffee-houses, clubs, associations and societies. In this environment, in the civil society of the eighteenth century (defined as those places where unrelated individuals associate for shared apolitical, non-commercial, secular ends), the methods could be applied, discoveries disseminated, theses contested and arguments voiced. The social history of the Enlightenment as uncovered in work as diverse as Anne Goldgar's treatment of the Huguenot communities in the Low Countries, Dena Goodman's study of the salon culture of France, Jürgen Habermas' formulation of the public sphere in England, D. D. McElroy's charting of the constellation of Scottish club-life and Margaret Jacob's tracing of European Freemasonry can be comprehended as the social context and consequence of debates engendered by the new methods.[8]

## ii. The context of the Irish Anglican Enlightenment

Having proposed a threefold understanding of the European Enlightenment – a primary assumption, a spectrum of methods and a social environment wherein the debate was conducted – I wish to consider how this formulation might configure a specific manifestation of the movement: that found in Ireland from 1690 to 1730. While the Enlightenment had a significant influence over the shaping of both the Catholic and Presbyterian communities on the island, for the purposes of the current discussion, attention will focus on the Enlightenment's development within the dominant confession, that of the Church of Ireland, for it is this Enlightenment that is most commonly hinted at in the scholarship, as we have seen, and it is the movement David Berman has done most to excavate.[9]

First of all, to understand the purchase which the Enlightenment's primary ideal – that the existence of man and not of God was the starting point for systematic thought about the nature of existence – might have for Anglican thinkers in Ireland in this period we must recall the political

---

8. Anne Goldgar, *Impolite learning: conduct and community in the Republic of Letters, 1680-1750* (London, 1995); D. Goodman, *The Republic of Letters*; J. Habermas, *The Structural transformation*; D. D. McElroy, *Scotland's age of improvement: a survey of eighteenth-century literary clubs and societies* (Washington State, 1969); Margaret C. Jacob, *Living the Enlightenment: Freemasonry and politics in eighteenth-century Europe* (Oxford, 1991).

9. The Catholic and Presbyterian Enlightenments in Ireland took on rather different forms, caused by the rather different conundrums circumstance raised for these communities.

circumstances in which the country found itself. In 1690 and 1691 Ireland experienced one of the most devastating conflicts to occur on its shores, and arguably the only conflagration there to hold significance for the European balance of power.[10] Occasionally recalled in England as a bloodless revolution, the battles induced by William III's decision to remove James II and VII from the throne actually occurred in Ireland. There the campaigns were immensely destructive of life and property. Two battles, the Boyne and Aughrim, saw casualties on a scale normally associated with conflict on the European mainland in the early modern period. And the defeat of the Jacobite forces ensured the completion of a profound re-allocation of land with William's supporters confirming the transfer of estates from Catholic to Protestant control inaugurated by James VI and I with the Plantation of Ulster and continued during Oliver Cromwell's reign in the 1650s. And this in turn reveals the sectarian nature of the contest, as it was understood in Ireland. William's victory ensured and underscored a Protestant hegemony, which was given legislative expression in an array of anti-Catholic measures: the penal code. In this, the War of the Two Kings was a war of religion, and it brought extraordinary suffering upon the country.

For the Anglican community, which constituted perhaps as little as 10 per cent of the country's population, the outcome was positive and suggested, as many of the clergy of the Church of Ireland articulated, that their regime enjoyed divine favour. Providentialism was a common thread in many sermons celebrating William's coming to power.[11] More pertinent here is that some Anglicans, in the light of such an unlikely victory, rested their belief upon the benevolence of the deity, and worried that any alteration in the foundations of faith from a trust in the Lord might lead to his displeasure and the dilapidation and destruction of this Irish city of God.

## iii. Jonathan Swift and the continuation of traditional modes of thought

The finest and most celebrated exponent of the essentially unenlightened position was Jonathan Swift. A splenetic opponent of Presbyterianism and an upholder of the penal code's legitimacy, in the few writings that dwell explicitly on the positive content of his religious understanding, we find

---

10. A useful military history of the conflict is to be found in J. G. Simms, *Jacobite Ireland, 1685-1691* (Dublin, 2000). For a recent treatment of the general British crisis, see Tim Harris, *Revolution: the great crisis of the British monarchy, 1685-1720* (London, 2006).

11. For overviews of this response see S. J. Connolly, 'The Glorious Revolution in Irish Protestant political thinking', in *Political ideas in eighteenth-century Ireland*, ed. S. J. Connolly (Dublin, 2000), p.27-63; Robert Eccleshall, 'The political ideas of Anglican Ireland in the 1690s', in *Political discourse in seventeenth- and eighteenth-century Ireland*, ed. D. George Boyse, Robert Eccleshall and Vincent Geoghegan (Basingstoke, 2001), 62-80.

him to be a proponent of fideism – arguing for the inscrutability of God and the primacy of faith over reason and experience. And in the extravagant masterpieces *A Tale of a tub* (1704) and *Gulliver's travels* (1726) Swift takes to task those perfidious meddlers who foolishly secure knowledge on the shaky grounds of human understanding. As Swift writes in the *Tale*:

> What man in the natural state or course of thinking did ever conceive it in his power to reduce the notions of all mankind exactly to the same length, and breath, and height of his own? Yet this is the first humble and civil design of all innovators in the empire of reason [...] now I would gladly be informed, how it is possible to account for such imaginations as these, in particular men without recourse to my *phenomenon of vapours*, ascending from the lower faculties to overshadow the brain, and thence distilling into conceptions for which the narrowness of our mother tongue has not yet assigned any other name besides that of *madness* or *phrenzy*.[12]

Ironically through these writings we can, by default, conceive of an argument for an Irish Enlightenment, for while Swift condemns and satirises those who dismiss faith as unreasonable, his anxiety is revealing. He clearly thinks the Enlightenment exists and that it poses a profound threat to religious faith by destroying man's sense of moral unworthiness. For Swift the Enlightenment is characterised by intellectual presumption and ontological hubris. And in the person of Gulliver he explicitly attacks the primary assumption that underpins all enlightened thought. Whereas for an enlightened thinker knowledge begins with the individual, Swift uses his fictional traveller to highlight how unreliable human beings are as a means of measurement. Gulliver is in turn too big, too small, too physical and too intellectual for his surrounds. He is notoriously unreliable as a narrator and his personality eventually disintegrates under the weight of experience he garners on his voyages:

> My wife and family received me with great surprise and joy, because they concluded me certainly dead; but I must freely confess the sight of them filled me only with hatred, disgust and contempt, and the more by reflecting on the near alliance I had to them. [...] As soon as I entered the house, my wife took me in her arms and kissed me, at which having not been used to the touch of that odious animal for so many years, I fell into a swoon for almost an hour. At the time I am writing it is five years since my last return to England. During the first year I could not endure my wife or children in my presence, the very smell of them was intolerable; much less could I suffer them to eat in the same room. To this hour they dare not presume to touch my bread, or drink out of the same cup, neither was I ever able to let one of them take me by the hand.[13]

Indeed Jonathan Swift revealed an attack on pride, implicit in the Enlightenment project, to be the central moral purpose of his fable in

---

12. Jonathan Swift, *A Tale of a tub* in J. Swift, *Major works*, ed. Angus Ross and David Wooley (Oxford, 2003), p.141-42.
13. J. Swift, *Gulliver's travels*, ed. Robert Demaria Jr (London, 2001), p.265-66.

the final passage of the book. Note the list, which avails of comparison to highlight the perceived identity of respectable and reproachful professions:

> My reconcilement to the *Yahoo* kind in general might not be so difficult, if they would be content with those vices and follies only, which nature hath entitled them to. I am not in the least provoked at the sight of a lawyer, a pickpocket, a colonel, a fool, a lord, a suborner, an attorney, a traitor or the like: this is all according to the due course of things: But when I behold a lump of deformity, and diseases both in body and mind, smitten with *pride* it immediately breaks all the measures of my patience; neither shall I ever be able to comprehend how such an animal and such a vice could tally together.[14]

In place of the Enlightenment trust in humanity, Swift inserted a fideistic God, observing for example, in his sermon on the Trinity: 'this union and distinction [of the three elements of the Trinity] are a mystery and utterly unknown to mankind. This is enough for any good Christian to believe on this great article, without inquiring any farther: And this can be contrary to no man's reason, although the knowledge of it is hid from him.'[15] Scripture was therefore not answerable to man's humble faculty of reason, for the divine purpose might not be fully exposed in the Bible, and thus was above, not encompassed by, the rigours of philosophy. As Swift informed the congregation: 'It is impossible for us to determine for what reasons God thought fit to communicate some things to us in part, and leave some part a mystery. But so it is in fact.'[16] God was therefore inscrutable to human reason, existing beyond the rules of ordinary existence.[17] He chose only to supply occasional glimmerings of his purpose and of the world to come. This fideism, presupposing the inability of man to comprehend the divine nature through an act of reason, produced in Swift the deep pessimism over human pride evidenced in his ironic creative productions. It also forced a retreat from speculative thought, advocating instead a pragmatic religion of ritualistic observance, the support of polite social norms and the pursuit of economic improvement. As Michael DePorte notes, 'Swift talks about God as the ultimate authority for doctrines of imperative social importance, about crimes against social order being crimes against God, but about individual relationship to God he says remarkably little. Indeed, there is a

---

14. Swift, *Gulliver's travels*, p.271.
15. Jonathan Swift, 'On the Trinity', in *Irish tracts 1720-1723 and sermons*, in *The Works of Jonathan Swift*, ed. Herbert Davis and Louis Landa (Oxford, 1968), p.162.
16. Swift, 'On the Trinity', p.162.
17. 'What comes across most strongly in Swift's references to God is a sense of his remoteness and unknowability', Michael DePorte, 'Swift, God and power', in *Walking Naboth's vineyard: new studies in Swift*, ed. Christopher Fox and Brenda Tooley (Notre Dame, IN, 1995), p.73-97 (89).

great deal in Swift's writings to suggest that he found the whole matter of a personal relationship with God disquieting.'[18]

## iv. William Molyneux and the empirical Enlightenment

The venom and energy Swift brought to bear in attacking the arrogance of Gulliverian man suggests that the targets were by no means wholly fictive, or negligible. And, indeed, among his community, the Anglicans of Ireland, we can find articulate exponents of a very different vision of the world. In particular, many Anglicans were left uneasy, not reassured, by the precarious nature of William's military victories, and sought to found Anglican legitimacy in something other than the power of faith. Most frequently recourse was taken to the empirical method of enlightened investigation; a trend which in fact predates the Williamite wars and which was in part prompted by the conundrums of Cromwellian intervention and the Restoration of the Stuarts. Thus, Robert Boyle engaged in groundbreaking experimentation in the 1660s and 1670s in London's Royal Society, while William Petty acted as the first president of the Dublin Philosophical Society, founded in 1684.[19] Under this umbrella a number of dons of Ireland's sole university, Trinity College, Dublin, and a disparate array of amateur intellectuals (including some Catholics) conducted experiments on a range of fields from optics and ballistics to geography and anatomy.[20] Narcissus Marsh, the archbishop of Dublin and long-time member, described the first meeting of the revived society after the Revolution as follows, in an entry from his diary dating 26 April 1693:

This evening at six of the clock, we met at the Provost's lodgings in Trinity College Dublin in order to the renewal of our Philosophical meeting, where Sir Richard Cox (one of the justices of the king's bench) read a geographical description of the city and county of Derry, being part of a geographical description of the whole kingdom of Ireland, that is designed to be perfected by him wherein will also be contained a natural history of Ireland, containing the most remarkable things therein to be found, that are the products of nature, upon his reading this essay he was admitted fellow of this society together with Dr John Vesey, lord archbishop of Tuam, Francis Roberts Esq, young son to the earl of

---

18. DePorte, 'Swift, God and power', p.88. This connection between fideism and a pragmatic faith is clearly identified in Christopher Fauske, *Jonathan Swift and the Church of Ireland* (Dublin, 2002), p.63-73, 110.

19. On Boyle, see Simon Schaffer and Stephen Shapin, *Leviathan and the airpump: Hobbes, Boyle and the experimental life* (Princeton, NJ, 1985), and Stephen Shapin, *A Social history of truth: civility and science in seventeenth-century England* (London, 1994). On the Dublin Philosophical Society see K. T. Hoppen, 'Early science in Ireland: a study of the Dublin Philosophical Society, 1683-1709', MA dissertation, University College Dublin, 1963.

20. One member, Mark Baggot, was a Roman Catholic, and hence debarred from attending higher education in Ireland (he was to have his lands in County Carlow confiscated by the Williamite administration in the wake of the Revolution), while another, John Baynard, converted to Catholicism during the reign of James II.

Radnor, some time lord lieutenant of Ireland. O Lord, grant that in studying thy works we may also study to promote thy glory (which is the true end of all our studies) and prosper, O Lord, our undertaking, for thy name's sake.[21]

The Society continued to meet sporadically until the early 1700s, by which time the group had lost impetus and focus.

The political subtext behind this commitment to empirical investigation of the natural world is revealed in the person of an original participant of the Society, William Molyneux. In his 1698 tract in favour of Irish constitutional independence, *The Case of Ireland [...] stated*, he utilised historical evidence proffered by ancient charters and acts of Parliament to show how the English had never militarily conquered Ireland. He displayed, moreover, how the country had been constituted as a separate kingdom under the reign of King John and, in a far from fully accomplished attempt to prove a negative, argued that Ireland had never been subjected to English legislation without its parliament having granted explicit, prior permission. The use of a legal rhetoric – the book is composed as though Molyneux were marshalling an argument at the bar – was a literary support to his contention that in Ireland the normal rules of governance pertained. Ireland was no barbaric, irredeemable backwater, but a typical kingdom, just like England.

Thus, the pamphlet abounded with quotation – much of it left in its original Latin, inferring both a learned readership and an erudite author – and with lengthy lists of legislation. For example, in defence of his assertion that Ireland had explicitly enacted that English legislation which did hold sway in Ireland, he compiled the following history of due process:

In the 21$^{st}$ of Henry the 8$^{th}$, an Act was made in England making it a felony in a servant that runneth away with his masters or mistresses goods. This Act was not received in Ireland till it was enacted by a parliament held here in the 33$^{rd}$ of Henry the 8$^{th}$. C.5. See. 1.

In the 21$^{st}$ of Henry VIII. C. 19. there was a law made in England, that all Lords might distrain on the Lords of them holden, and make their avowry not naming the tenant, but the land. But this was not of force in Ireland till enacted here in the 33$^{rd}$ of Henry VIII. C. 1. Ses. 1.

An Act was made in England, anno 31, Henry VIII, that joint tenants in commons should be compelled to make partition as coparceners were compellable at Common Law. But this Act was not received in Ireland till enacted here, An. 33. Henry VIII. C.10.[22]

The full list ran to some seventeen items in this instance, and the repetition of form and structure in its compilation added to this analysis a bludgeoning effect that demanded agreement from the reader. In other

---

21. *Scholar bishop: the recollections and diary of Narcissus Marsh, 1628-1696*, ed. Ray Gillespie (Cork, 2003), p.50.
22. William Molyneux, *The Case of Ireland's being bound by acts of Parliament in England, stated* (1698), ed. J. G. Simms (Dublin, 1977), p.68.

words, the evidence was compiled in such a way as to command assent, building up the appearance of a deep and broad empirical case, grounded on particular practical legal examples.

Yet Molyneux also availed of the language of natural law when his argument was in danger of falling into gaps in the historical record. Towards the end of the tract, for example, he opined, in a central philosophical assertion that underpinned his entire case and made sense of his empirical treatment of Irish legislative case history:

> All men are by nature in a state of equality, in respect of jurisdiction or dominion: this I take to be a principle in it self so evident, that it stands in need of little proof. Tis not to be conceived that creatures of the same species and rank, promiscuously born to all the same advantages of nature, and the use of the same faculties, should be subordinate and subject one to another; these to this or that of the same kind. On this equality in nature is founded that right which all men claim, of being free from all subjection to positive laws, till by their own consent they give up their freedom by entering into civil societies for the common benefit of all the members thereof. And on this consent depends the obligation of all Humane laws; insomuch that without it, by the unanimous opinion of all jurists, no sanctions are of any force.[23]

Molyneux managed to converge the two registers, however, for the evidence was consciously compiled to reveal a general truth about the circumstance of the country: it reveals a law of nations, if not of nature. And in his conviction that the natural law is not suspended in Ireland, he buttressed his normalisation of the country. In other words, Molyneux's politics of knowledge lends itself to a defence of Ireland's constitutional independence without, and Protestant supremacy within, for both are products of historical development. Instead of Anglican supremacy being a gift of God, therefore, he positioned it as a temporal fact, a result of the evolution of society over time. Protestant legitimacy emerges from the nature of things.

This empirical argument in favour of Protestant success did not satisfy all the Anglican intelligentsia, however. In particular, despite occasional indications that he was tempted by the method, notably in his participation in the Dublin Philosophical Society and in his accounts of natural phenomena (in particular an eruption of Mount Vesuvius which he witnessed in April 1717), it failed to convince the bishop of Cloyne, George Berkeley.[24] Instead, he turned to rationalist methods to defend Anglican supremacy.

---

23. Molyneux, *The Case of Ireland*, p.117.
24. *Philosophical transactions*, October 1717, p.354, reproduced in *The Works of George Berkeley*, ed. A. A. Luce and T. E. Jessop, 9 vols (Nendel, 1979), vol.4, p.247-50.

## v. George Berkeley and the rational Enlightenment

As A. A. Luce insightfully observed, when reading Berkeley you think he is building a house, and find that he has built a church.[25] The whole of his intellectual endeavour was directed to defending faith from within the Enlightenment's terrain. He used enlightened methods for a divine purpose, building his chapel from the deductive tools of rationalism.[26] The thrust of his assault was brilliant in its simplicity of conception. It was Berkeley's contention that if you assumed that the human being was the primary unit of analysis, so long as you were true to the logic of the argument, the existence of God became a necessary and unavoidable conclusion. At its simplest, the unwilled nature of many of our ideas argued for the existence of external spirits, and the complexity and benevolence of the world further contended for the existence of a divine creative force: 'The supreme being which excites those ideas in our mind', he wrote in the 1710 text, *Principles of human knowledge*, 'is not marked out and limited to our view by any finite collection sensible of ideas, as human agents are by their size, complexion, limbs and motion.'[27] In a central, if lengthy, passage towards the conclusion of this treatise, he placed the top-stone on his remarkable philosophical construction:

But though there be some things which convince us, human agents are concerned in producing them; yet it is evident to every one, that those things which are called the works of nature, that is, the far greater part of the ideas or sensations perceived by us, are not produced by, or dependent on the wills of men. There is therefore some other spirit that causes them, since it is repugnant that they should subsist by themselves. [...] But if we attentively consider the constant regularity, order, and concatenation of natural things, the surprising magnificence, beauty, and perfection of the larger, and the exquisite contrivance of the smaller parts of the creation, together with the exact harmony and correspondence of the whole, but above all the never enough admired laws of pain and pleasure, and the instincts or natural inclinations, appetites and passions of animals; I say if we consider all these things, and at the same time attend to the meaning and import of the attributes, one eternal, infinitely wise, good and perfect, we shall clearly perceive that they belong to the aforesaid spirit, *who works all in all*, and *by whom all things consist*.

Hence it is evident that God is known as certainly and immediately as any other mind or spirit whatsoever, distinct from ourselves. We may even assert that the existence of God is far more evidently perceived than the existence of men; because the effects of nature are infinitely more numerous and considerable than those of human agents [...] we need only open our eyes to see the sovereign Lord

---

25. A. A. Luce, cited in David Berman, *George Berkeley: idealism and the man* (Oxford, 1996), p.v.

26. The debt he owed to Malebranche is crucial here, for Berkeley's ingestion of the Christianised Cartesianism of his precursor offered him immense sustenance in his polemical battles. See A. A. Luce, *Berkeley and Malebranche: a study in the origins of Berkeley's thought* (Oxford, 1967).

27. George Berkeley, *Principles of human knowledge*, in G. Berkeley, *Philosophical works*, ed. Michael R. Ayers (London, 1993), p.111.

of all things with a more full and clear view, than we do any of our fellow creatures.[28]

Those who denied such a truth were deceitful or conceited.

It is for this reason that Berkeley rejected the sermon and the theological tract in favour of the essay form and the formal philosophical treatise. And it is why he targeted the freethinkers, assailing them throughout his work, deriding them as 'minute philosophers', unable to see the bigger, divine picture. Indeed a middle period study by Berkeley, published in 1732, entitled *Alciphron, or the Minute philosopher* was subtitled 'an apology for the Christian religion against those who are called free thinkers' and was structured as a series of refutations of their systems. So too the earlier *Three dialogues* of 1713 were written 'in opposition to sceptics and atheists'. Trapped by their perceptions of reality, they were incapable of seeing through the glass darkly and perceiving the spiritual enabling power that ordained and sustained the very existence they extolled as sufficient. God became, in Berkeley's hands, a necessary cause.

## vi. The existence of free thought

Certainly the energy and fire of Berkeley's prose gained greatly from his fear that the freethinkers posed an internal threat to Anglicanism as coherent and dangerous as Jacobitism posed to the political order. And nor were the freethinkers a figment of Berkeley's vivid imagination. His close friend and colleague in the ill-fated Bermuda project, Robert Clayton, bishop of Clogher, was openly to declare himself an Arian, denying the divinity of Christ in *An Essay on spirit* (1750). Rather than understanding Jesus as the direct and complete manifestation of God and hence as sharing his nature and substance, Clayton understood Christ to be an envoy doing the bidding of God, at once more spiritual in kind than man and more material than the divine power itself. Jesus thereby became, as Clayton termed it, 'a secondary essence': 'And as that secondary essence was by the Jews called the Image of God, so is the Lord Jesus Christ called in the language of the New Testament "The image of the invisible God": that is the visible image, or delegated representative in power of the invisible God.'[29] He followed up this anonymous tract with a speech delivered to the House of Lords arguing for the removal of the Nicean and Athanasian creeds from the liturgy.[30] His campaign culminated when he placed his name on the third volume of his *Vindication of the*

28. Berkeley, *Principles*, p.148-49.
29. Robert Clayton, *An Essay on spirit* (Dublin, 1750), reprinted in *The Irish Enlightenment and Counter-Enlightenment*, ed. D. Berman and P. O'Riordan, vol.6, p.103, quoting col.1, l.15.
30. Robert Clayton, *The Bishop of Clogher's speech made in the House of Lords, in Ireland* (Dublin, 1757), reprinted in *The Irish Enlightenment and Counter-Enlightenment*, ed. D. Berman and P. O'Riordan, vol.4.

*histories of the Old and New Testaments*, published in 1757, when he once again outlined his thesis that 'Christ was the same person with the great Archangel Michael, who was the guardian angel of Israel.'[31]

Yet, despite the idiosyncratic nature of his faith, Clayton fell into a tradition of sorts; one that identified the political liberty inaugurated in 1688 with a wider intellectual freedom that could query spiritual authority wherever its source lay. It began with John Toland's *Christianity not mysterious* (1696), also condemned by the orthodox minds of the Irish parliament, and encompassed the heretical member of parliament for Eniscorthy, John Asgill, who was expelled from the House of Commons in 1703 for writing a pamphlet which argued that death was not obligatory for Christians, and the subversive playfulness of Peter Lens, head of the secretive Blasters, denounced by Berkeley in a speech at College Green.[32]

The existence of the Blasters, or of the sexually adventurous Hell Fire Clubs, highlights how the Anglican Enlightenment, which produced work expressive of the full spectrum of thought – from scholastic certainties to freethinking speculations – forged social and cultural institutions to sustain itself. An infant public sphere can be broadly dated to the period from 1730 to 1780 when coffee-houses opened, assembly halls were built, newspapers and literary magazines were published and clubs and societies were founded. Alongside the Freemasons arose religious fraternities such as the Knights of St Patrick, and organisations for the exercise of polite sociability and patriotic improvement. Civil society was briefly to flourish in the vexed political and religious landscape of Ireland.

## vii. The Enlightenment and Ireland

As noted above, that there was an Enlightenment in Ireland does not necessarily imply that there was an Irish Enlightenment. For that to exist it must be shown that the country produced a particular addition to enlightened thought, suggested by and redolent of the particular circumstance of the country. What the Anglican Enlightenment delineated briefly above suggests is that this did occur. The complex relationship between confessional identity and political status led Irish thinkers to tease out the relationship between the Enlightenment and religion in a distinctive manner. In particular, the encounter between the Enlightenment

---

31. Robert Clayton, *A Vindication of the histories of the Old and New Testament, part III, containing some observations on the nature of angels and the scriptural account of the fall and redemption of mankind* (Dublin, George Faulkner, 1757), p.189.

32. John Asgill, *An Argument proving, that according to the covenant of eternal life revealed in the Scriptures, man may be translated from hence into that eternal life, without passing through death* (1700; London, 1715); on Toland see Justin Champion, *Republican learning: John Toland and the crisis of Christian culture, 1696-1722* (Manchester, 2003); on Peter Lens see George C. Caffentzis, 'Why did Berkeley's bank fail? Money and libertinism in eighteenth-century Ireland', *Eighteenth-century Ireland* 12 (1997), p.100-15.

and Ireland's political crisis – between Berkeley and the Volcano – suggests that Enlightenment was not intrinsically opposed to faith, and Berkeley, Molyneux and others could defend the orthodoxies of confessional life while availing of Enlightenment methodologies. Religious faith could be buttressed by enlightened assumptions and approaches. God and man could engage in fruitful dialogue, not just contentious argument.

What then does the existence of an Irish Enlightenment tell us about Ireland? At first sight it seems to support the view that Ireland was closely related to wider European models of society and politics. Just as France and Germany experienced Enlightenment, so did Ireland. Yet the character of the Irish Enlightenment reveals that to be a rather limited conclusion, for although the Enlightenment was shared with other European countries, its concern for issues of faith reveals rather than hides the rickety structure of Protestant power that had been erected in the wake of the Williamite wars. There was little confidence that the systems of privilege and patronage – both secular and religious – that had been installed were potent enough to sustain themselves in the face of a Catholic military threat. That Ireland's ruling elite suffered a profound lack of confidence in the legitimacy of its rule (the penal code being an expression of fear as much as a declaration of power) indicated the country was as much a subversively colonial society as it was an orthodox *ancien régime*.

## viii. Enlightenment in the periphery

To conclude, what then does the case of Ireland tell us of the Enlightenment in the periphery? Five points arise. First of all, and this is an observation that requires more elucidation than can be offered here, the idea of a periphery is highly subjective. The Anglicans of Ireland in the period 1690 to 1730 considered themselves to be vibrant participants in a wider British polity, in an international Protestant faith-community and in a European-wide and highly sophisticated commercial civilisation. If anyone was to be thought of as peripheral in Ireland, they would have pointed towards the 'mere Irish', the Gaelic community that had been finally usurped in the Williamite wars. As for the Gaelic community themselves, they sustained a sophisticated poetic culture, participated in an international faith, Catholicism, and forged distinctive intellectual links with numerous European powers through a network of Irish Colleges. They would equally have denied any accusation of living on the periphery.

Secondly it is important to note that the peripheral status of the Anglican community was in no way the defining quality of its members' lived experience. Certainly, they were in many ways peripheral to British political life, let alone the European balance of power; except that is for the heady, desperate days of 1690 and 1691, when the battles fought on their estates had repercussions for the dynamics of French–English and Catholic–Protestant relations. So, while their fate and condition were soon returned to obscurity, their peripheral status was not essential, and they clearly thought they could participate as equals on the great stage of the European Enlightenment, just as they had acted within the passion play of international politics.

Thirdly the definition of periphery itself must in one sense at least remain open. While work on the impact of the French Enlightenment in Ireland has identified a deep debt to French thinkers among the Irish cultural elite, this in no way precludes the possibility that ideas drawn from foreign shores might be altered and recast in the light of local demands.[33] That the ideas came from a centre did not make them sacrosanct. Where they failed to meet the demands of the peripheral condition, or to survive the rigours imposed by local conundrums, the peripheral communities could, and did, generate ideas of their own or play distinctive variations on general themes.

Thus, and this is my fourth observation, in the religious inflection which enlightened discourse took on in Ireland we can see something of the modulations within the movement as a whole. Therein, the peripheral variation found in Ireland testifies to the Enlightenment's multiplicity as much as the foundational idea that humanity is the basic unit of analysis argues for its essential unity.

Finally, in the person of Swift, the Irish Enlightenment's particular history illustrates how resistance to the Enlightenment's fundamental assumptions could result in extraordinary creativity. We must remember the Enlightenment held no monopoly on intellectual life anywhere in Europe, but expressed a position (or sequence of methods) within a range of assumptions and approaches to questions about the nature of existence. Most of Europe's intellectual elite remained wedded to scholastic modes of thought and were decidedly unenlightened in their mental outlook.[34] In other words, the Enlightenment itself was peripheral to the mainstream of intellectual life in eighteenth-century Europe.

---

33. See for example the polemical misattribution of Voltaire's essay to Montesquieu as a result of local political concerns, detailed in Tim Conway and Graham Gargett, 'Voltaire's *La Voix du sage et du peuple* in Ireland, or enlightened anticlericalism in two jurisdictions', *Eighteenth-century Ireland* 20 (2005), p.79-90.

34. This is the force of J. C. D. Clark's thesis in *English society 1660-1832: religion, ideology and politics during the ancien régime* (Cambridge, 2000), but parallels can be found elsewhere.

JOHN ROBERTSON

# Political economy and the 'feudal system' in Enlightenment Naples: outline of a problem

THE kingdom of Naples may have been on Europe's geographical 'periphery', but it hardly belongs on the periphery of the Enlightenment. Throughout the eighteenth century its intellectual life remained open to the main intellectual currents in Europe at the time, both those emanating directly from France, and those which came through France from Britain and the United Provinces. From Pietro Giannone and Giambattista Vico, the great figures of the immediate pre-Enlightenment in the early decades of the century, to Ferdinando Galiani and Antonio Genovesi, who launched the Enlightenment in Naples in the 1750s, to Gaetano Filangieri and Francesco Mario Pagano in the last quarter of the century, the leading Neapolitan thinkers were alert and responsive to the preoccupations of their European contemporaries. They shared the same interests: the study of human nature and human sociability, political economy, and the history of societies and civilisations. And in pursuing these interests, they were committed to the same objective of human betterment on this earth (whether or not they also believed, as most of them affirmed they did, in another life to come). Contrary to what is sometimes still repeated in Anglophone scholarship, moreover, the Neapolitan philosophers were by no means isolated from their own society. They were sufficiently numerous, and sufficiently connected, to form a critical mass of men of letters, whose activities were supported by local patrons and the wider Republic of Letters. As a group they were conscious and supportive of each other (which is not to say that they agreed with each other), and conscious too of belonging to a wider European intellectual movement with the same interests and objectives. Crucially, they were also committed to publicising their ideas, to addressing a wider 'public', and to forming 'public opinion'. These conditions for participation in the Enlightenment were by no means met everywhere in Europe, but they were clearly present in Naples.[1]

1. There is no general overview of the Enlightenment in Naples. But it is amply documented in several volumes of F. Venturi, *Settecento riformatore*, vols.1, 2 and 5 part i (Turin, 1969, 1976, 1987); and in Giuseppe Galasso, *La Filosofia in soccorso de' governi: la cultura napoletana del settecento* (Naples, 1989); in English, see: *Naples in the eighteenth century: the birth and death of a nation state*, ed. Girolamo Imbruglia (Cambridge, 2000); Robertson, *The Case for the Enlightenment*.

There is nevertheless a sense in which the kingdom of Naples stood at the extremities, if not the periphery, of Enlightenment Europe. For at the heart of Neapolitan society and government lay a set of relations, known as the 'feudal system', whose strength and longevity were by then quite unusual, and which confronted Enlightenment thinkers with one of the severest challenges they faced anywhere. Variously characterised as 'il governo feudale', 'la feudalità' and 'il sistema feudale', this was an institution entrenched in the economic, social and political structures of the kingdom. It was as old as the kingdom, and integral to its construction.[2] The Normans who had seized control of southern Italy and carved out a kingdom for themselves in the eleventh and twelfth centuries did so by establishing and enforcing feudal relations, distributing land in fiefs in return for military service. But it was the succession of dynasties – Swabian, Angevin and Aragonese – which ruled, or claimed to rule, the kingdom that embedded the system ever deeper in its structure. Often insecure, these had made a series of concessions to the baronage in order to shore up their position. These included allowing fiefs to become hereditary, exemption from military service by payment of the 'adoa' and, most critical, the sale or grant to the nobility of the exercise of royal jurisdiction in their fiefs. By these concessions, ratified and extended in the sixteenth and seventeenth centuries by the Spanish monarchy, the Crown ensured the existence of a system of feudal relations which had few parallels elsewhere in Europe. But feudal government persisted because it was also in the Crown's interest. Its concessions did not leave the Crown powerless. Feudal lordship gave the ruler leverage: the confiscated fiefs of defeated rebels were a valuable source of patronage, and the Crown continued to exercise the right of 'devolution', whereby in the absence of a qualified heir, a fief reverted to the Crown, to be re-granted or, increasingly, sold, to the benefit of the treasury.

Several features of this system need emphasis. One of the most obvious is the extent to which it shaped the character of the Neapolitan nobility.[3] Although it resembled nobilities elsewhere in the Italian peninsula in that the highest noble status was associated with membership of one of the five

2. Historical reconstruction of the feudal system in the kingdom of Naples began in the late Enlightenment, culminating in David Winspeare, *Storia degli abusi feudali* (Naples, 1811), especially p.xi-xv, 26-99. Recent outlines of the history of the 'regno' which emphasise the prominence and persistence of feudal relations include: Giuseppe Galasso, *Il Mezzogiorno nella storia d'Italia* (Florence, 1977), and Tommaso Astarita, *Between salt water and holy water: a history of southern Italy* (New York and London, 2005).

3. On the Neapolitan nobility: Claudio Donati, 'The Italian nobilities in the seventeenth and eighteenth centuries', in *The European nobilities in the seventeenth and eighteenth centuries*, vol.1: *Western Europe*, ed. H. M. Scott (London and New York, 1995), p.237-68; Maria Antonietta Visceglia, 'Un groupe social ambigu: organisation, stratégies et représentations de la noblesse napolitaine XVI-XVIII[e] siècles', *Annales ESC* 48 (1993), p.819-51; T. Astarita, *The Continuity of feudal power: the Caracciolo of Brienza in Spanish Naples* (Cambridge, 1992).

'seggi', or quarters, of the city of Naples, the real strength of the southern Italian nobility lay in their fiefs. A small proportion of the total population of the south (about 1 per cent), the nobility possessed over 75 per cent of the land of the kingdom in fiefs. Two-thirds of the population, it has been calculated, were thus subject to feudal jurisdiction.[4] When joined to the importance attached to family connection, this reliance on feudal landholding ensured a stubbornly patrimonial approach to their possessions. Once a holding of fiefs had been acquired (usually in the first two generations), a family's priority was to retain the patrimony by deploying the usual array of defensive measures, including primogeniture, 'fideicommissa' (entails) and marriage alliances. The defence of feudal power was abetted by geography: the remoteness of many inland fiefs, high in the Apennines, cut off by rudimentary communications and endemic banditry, encouraged a concentration on the exercise of social authority at the expense of economic initiative. The nobility certainly needed an income to support their consumption when in the city; but enforcement of feudal rights was a surer means of securing it than investment in economic improvement and commercial agriculture. That the share of the noble income directly derived from 'feudal' rents and dues increased over the eighteenth century might have suggested the underlying potential of agricultural investment; in practice, at least until late in the century, it tended to reinforce patrimonial priorities.[5]

Perhaps the most intractable features of Neapolitan feudalism stemmed from its character as a system of rights and obligations. For feudal property was not the direct ownership of land, so much as a series of rights to the use of certain categories of land, to a share of the produce of land farmed by others, and to the processing and transport of that produce. Feudal income typically included the 'terragio', usually 10 per cent of the harvest from land within the feudal domain, fees payable for the services of the lord's mills and ovens, charges for hunting and fishing, occasional levies due on occasions such as the marriage of a female member of the lord's family, and the fines payable for offences committed under feudal jurisdiction. There were also feudal leases, by 'censo', or emphyteusis, with rent payable in kind.[6] When to these rights were added the exercise of royal criminal jurisdiction and the collecting of royal taxes, widely enjoyed by the feudal nobility as a result of royal concessions in the centuries before 1700, the balance of power in rural society was weighted

4. Anna Maria Rao, 'The feudal question, judicial systems, and the Enlightenment', in *Naples in the eighteenth century*, ed. G. Imbruglia, p.95-117, especially p.100; Giovanni Muto, 'The structure of aristocratic patrimonies in the kingdom of Naples: management strategies and regional economic development: 16th-18th centuries', in *European aristocracies and colonial elites: patrimonial management strategies and economic development 15th-18th centuries*, ed. P. Janssens and B. Yun-Casalilla (Aldershot, 2005), p.115-133, especially p.119-21.
5. Muto, 'The structure of aristocratic patrimonies', p.124-31.
6. Astarita, *The Continuity of feudal power*, p.37-40, 82-87.

even more heavily in favour of the nobility. The only bodies capable of resisting the nobility were the 'università', the communal authorities, which were usually composed of richer peasants and traders, and were responsible for the community's demesne land and pasture. But their resistance had been overcome in the seventeenth century, and in the eighteenth the lords were secure in their enjoyment of rising feudal income.[7]

Such a system naturally required the support of lawyers. Naples was famous for the quality of its legal education and the number of its lawyers, and feudal litigation was the bread and butter of many of them. The advocates with the highest reputation (and highest earnings) were those 'in primaria', who were employed by the great nobility. Some nobles kept whole retinues of lawyers in their service, besides making regular, open payments to judges.[8] It is true that the Spanish policy of entrusting more and more of the kingdom's administration to jurists, who came to form a new nobility of the robe, the 'togati', provoked occasional noble resistance; but a common interest in the feudal system was far stronger.[9] Until the very end of the eighteenth century the social objective of most jurists was to join the ranks of the nobility themselves, by the purchase of one or more fiefs of their own.[10]

Another distinctive feature of Neapolitan feudalism was its historic association with the power of the Catholic Church. The papacy's claim that the Normans had been granted the kingdom in return for homage gave the highest possible sanction to the principles of feudal social and political organisation. Subsequently the Church acquired extensive landholdings of its own alongside those of the nobility, often by grants in mortmain. The scale of ecclesiastical landholding was liable to exaggeration by observers: the Scotsman Gilbert Burnet, visiting Naples in 1685, thought that the Church possessed above half the land in the kingdom.[11] But even if the holdings of the Church were much less than those of the

---

7. Rosario Villari, *Mezzogiorno e contadini nell'età moderna* (Bari, 1961), p.118-57, and Astarita, *The Continuity of feudal power*, p.146-55, for contrasting interpretations of this conflict and its outcomes.

8. Rao, 'The feudal question', p.96-98, for estimates of numbers of lawyers in eighteenth-century Naples: for noble employment of lawyers, Anna Maria Rao, 'La questione feudale nell'età tanucciana', *Archivio Storico per la Sicilia Orientale* 84:2-3 (1988), special number on *Bernardo Tanucci: la corte, il paese 1730-1780*, p.77-162, especially p.87-89.

9. On the 'respublica dei togati' and noble resistance: Raffaele Ajello, *Una Società anomala: il programma e la sconfitta della nobiltà napoletana in due memoriali cinquecenteschi* (Naples, 1996); Pier Luigi Rovito, *Respublica dei togati: giuristi e società nella Napoli del Seicento* (Naples, 1981).

10. A. M. Rao, *L'"Amaro della feudalità": la devoluzione di Arnone e la questione feudale a Napoli alla fine del' 700* (Naples, 1984), p.291-97.

11. Gilbert Burnet, *Some letters containing an account of what seemed most remarkable in Switzerland, Italy &c* (Amsterdam, Abraham Acher, 1686): 'The fourth letter, from Rome 8 December 1685', p.192. Although an exaggeration in the kingdom of Naples, such a proportion was not unknown in Catholic Europe.

feudal nobility, the outlook of ecclesiastical landowners was likewise patrimonial, and indifferent to investment.

If the Crown were ever to strengthen its government of the kingdom, therefore, it would have to be at the expense of those who controlled its resources and who had taken over much of the Crown's jurisdiction at local level – the feudal nobility and, to a lesser extent, the Church. Not surprisingly, the jurists who worked for the Crown found it easier to begin by attacking the latter. Until the 1780s the Church and its landholding represented the principal target of reformers. Powerful historical support for this approach had been provided by Pietro Giannone's *Civil history* of the kingdom, published in 1723.[12] A fierce clerical reaction had forced Giannone into exile, but his perspective was widely shared by his fellow jurists, and they encouraged the reassertion of civil authority over the Church by the newly independent monarchy of Carlo Borbone (the future Charles III of Spain) after 1734. The policy was particularly associated with the Bourbon monarchy's longest-serving minister, Bernardo Tanucci. Papal pressure on the new king limited Tanucci's early initiatives to restrict clerical immunity, but he kept ecclesiastical property in his sights, and took his opportunity after the famine of 1764. Expelling the Jesuits from the kingdom in 1767, he proposed a division of their land to the benefit of smallholders rather than large landowners; he also ended the practice of mortmain, blocking the further acquisition of property by the Church. The policy survived Tanucci's fall in 1776: a fresh (if no more successful) attempt was made to expropriate ecclesiastical property and divide it among smallholders after the Calabrian earthquake of 1784.[13]

Attacking the nobility was politically riskier, and Tanucci proceeded cautiously. A first attempt to limit feudal jurisdiction had to be withdrawn six years later. Until the 1760s Tanucci concentrated on strengthening the provincial courts and encouraging their judges to resist or override feudal jurisdiction. After the famine his language became more radical, as he denounced the barons' jurisdictions as so many little monarchies. Policy eventually followed suit: in 1774 the barons' courts were obliged to make their decisions consistent with the laws of the kingdom. An opportunity for a different line of attack also emerged in the 1770s. Demographic failure within the nobility meant that an increasing number of fiefs 'devolved' back to the Crown. Tanucci's advice was to retain the fiefs and manage them directly as royal demesne, exercising the jurisdiction and collecting the income for the Crown. His objective was political, not economic. He would reinforce a 're feudatorio', a feudal

---

12. Pietro Giannone, *Storia civile del regno di Napoli*, 4 vols (Naples, Niccolò Naso, 1723).
13. Elivira Chiosi, 'Il regno dal 1734 al 1799', in *Storia del Mezzogiorno, vol.4: il regno dagli Angioini ai Borboni*, ed. Giuseppe Galasso and Rosario Romeo (Naples, 1986), p.373-467 (393-96, 430-33, 447-53).

king, the better to break the power and connections of the barons in the provinces, not to encourage a new attitude towards agriculture.[14]

With Tanucci's fall, however, financial pressure encouraged a return to the policy of selling the devolved fiefs for the immediate benefit of the exchequer, and debate turned to the conditions to be attached to such sales. The Crown's jurists remained keen to assert its authority, seeking to limit the powers of jurisdiction accompanying the land; some favoured dividing the devolved fiefs and selling them in smaller portions, rather than to existing or aspirant nobility. Yet, however committed they were to strengthening the Crown, the jurists did not contemplate the abolition of feudalism as a legal entity. On the contrary, their strategy presupposed its continued existence, as they sought to exploit the leverage which the right of 'devolution' had always, in principle, given the king as feudal overlord. To exercise its leverage, moreover, the Crown had frequently to turn to the courts. Like any other feudal right, 'devolution' was inherently contestable: there was almost always scope for a relative of the extinguished family to claim to be within the permitted degrees of lineage, and to succeed to the fief instead of the Crown. Even at its most assertive, therefore, the late-eighteenth-century Bourbon monarchy confined itself to reform within the centuries-old structure of feudal relations with its nobility.[15]

Such was the 'feudal system' which the Neapolitan political economists found themselves confronting in the 1780s. A thick and heavily encrusted carapace that pressed on almost every dimension of economic, social and political life in the countryside, it represented an obstacle not only to economic initiative, but to any coherent economic analysis of the kingdom's predicament. In the rest of this essay, I shall examine the terms on which the confrontation between political economy and feudalism took place. As we shall see, it was a confrontation shaped both by long-standing assumptions about the economic resources and prospects of the kingdom, and by a particular choice of – mainly French – texts of political economy to supply the appropriate analytical models. It was also informed by the adoption, from the 1770s, of a historical perspective on feudalism which owed much to contemporary Scottish historians, as well as to Vico. Although the terms of the confrontation have previously been reviewed by others,[16] a key problem remains unexplored. It seems that the feudal system presented the Neapolitans with a challenge with which their political economy struggled to cope. I shall go no further here than to outline this as a problem for further investigation, but the hypothesis I wish to advance is

---

14. Rao, 'La questione feudale', p.127-62.

15. Rao, *L"Amaro della feudalità'*, p.39-43, and 'The feudal question', p.101-15 – authoritative studies on the efforts to reform feudal property.

16. In addition to the works of Rao, already cited, see the earlier survey by Pasquale Villani, 'Il dibattito sulla feudalità nel regno di Napoli dal Genovesi al Canosa', in *Saggi e ricerche sul Settecento*, ed. E. Sestan (Naples, 1968), p.252-331.

that when faced with Neapolitan feudalism, Enlightenment political economy was at the outer reaches of its analytical range.

A perception of the peninsula as economically backward was fundamental to the genesis of Enlightenment in Italy from early in the eighteenth century. Even if they had no reason to regard themselves as peripheral to the intellectual life of Europe, the Italians were painfully aware that the economic centre of gravity had shifted away from their country, to cities and nations of the north, at least a century earlier. No longer was the Mediterranean the most important arena of European commerce; indeed it was no longer under Italian maritime control. As for Italian products, they were competitive neither on price nor on quality. Italy had fallen behind, and the prospectus of the Enlightenment was embraced the more eagerly because it offered to address the problem, and identify the remedies. Although Naples had never enjoyed the economic success and reputation of Venice or Genoa, or of Florence and Milan, the city itself had been the largest in Europe in 1600, and was still the third largest in the eighteenth century, while the kingdom was thought of as naturally fertile, with an agricultural potential only waiting to be released. By 1700, moreover, Neapolitan frustration was compounded by the belief that there was an obvious explanation for the kingdom's predicament. For the past two centuries of Spanish rule, it was observed, Naples had been 'un regno governato in provincia', a kingdom governed as a province, whose resources had been diverted to the defence of the ailing Spanish monarchy.[17] It was the lack of political independence which had held Naples back, costing the kingdom, and indeed the rest of Italy, its former pre-eminence.

Though the Spanish were finally evicted by the Austrian Habsburgs in 1707, this was simply to substitute one viceroyalty for another. Debate over the kingdom's predicament continued, but was focused by Giannone on the Church rather than the economy. It returned to the economy only when the long-standing wish for independence was granted, quite unexpectedly, by Carlo Borbone, who seized the kingdom from the Austrians in 1734 in fulfilment of the dynastic ambitions of his mother, Elizabeth Farnese. Independence might have been none of their own doing, but Neapolitans now had to take responsibility for their conviction that it was the key to realising the kingdom's economic potential. The debate which had begun in manuscript memoranda and pamphlets during the period of the Spanish Succession crisis was resumed. By 1740 a choice of economic visions was available.

One was offered by a leading voice in the earlier debate, Paolo Mattia Doria. Previously Doria had focused on the consequences of being

17. Paolo Mattia Doria, *Massime del governo spagnolo a Napoli*, ed. G. Galasso and V. Conti (Naples, 1973); set in context in Robertson, *The Case for the Enlightenment*, p.184-98.

'governed as a province'. Now he offered a version of Fénelon's vision of a virtuous agrarian economy: self-sufficient, reliant on its own produce and manufactures, and trading with other countries only in necessary rather than superfluous, 'luxury' goods. Those who read his work (again it circulated in manuscript) were also left in no doubt of Doria's underlying philosophical allegiances: denouncing Epicureanism and scepticism, he railed against those who permitted self-interest to triumph over virtue.[18] But, although not without sympathisers, Doria was unable to prevent Neapolitans being offered precisely the alternative he feared: a modern, Epicurean political economy.

The agents of this option were Celestino Galiani, a native of the kingdom who had established himself as a leading theologian in Rome before returning to take up the direction of the University of Naples, and Bartolomeo Intieri, a Tuscan who had forged a career as an agronomist and estate manager. Having previously collaborated on the Florentine edition of Gassendi's *Opera omnia* (1727), these two now discovered a political economist of Epicurean persuasion, Jean-François Melon, author of the *Essai politique sur le commerce* (1734, with a second, expanded, edition in 1736). The attractions of Melon's 'golden book' were twofold. In the first place, it was published and controversial: it set an example of the sort of public discussion of economic affairs which Intieri believed was urgently needed in Naples. Secondly it explicitly addressed the circumstances of an agricultural country. One of Melon's insights was crucial. The great advantage of a fertile, agricultural economy, its capacity to produce in abundance, was also its vulnerability: abundance lowered the price of grain, removed the incentive to producers and exposed the country's inhabitants to famine. Here, Intieri believed, was the key to the economic predicament of Naples.[19]

Melon had also offered clear-cut remedies. First and foremost, an agricultural country should permit the free export of grain. It should also foster the development of manufactures, including luxury manufactures, as an incentive to agricultural producers; Melon was keen on mechanisation and specialisation, and dismissive of critics of luxury. To promote such internal exchange, the government should develop its systems of credit, to facilitate 'circulation'. But Melon was not simply an economic

18. Paolo Mattia Doria, 'Del commercio del regno di Napoli [...] lettera [...] diretta al Signor D. Francesco Ventura, degnissimo Presidente del Magistrato di Commercio, Napoli, 2 Aprile dell'anno 1740', in *Il Pensiero civile di Paolo Mattia Doria negli scritti inediti*, ed. Enrico Vidal (Milan, 1953), p.161-206; 'Il politico alla moda di mente adeguata e prattica' (1739-1740), printed as an appendix to Vittorio Conti, *Paolo Mattia Doria: dalla repubblica dei togati alla repubblica dei notabili* (Florence, 1978), p.130-259; 'Il commercio mercantile' (also 1739-1740), in *Manoscritti Napoletani di Paolo Mattia Doria*, vol.4, ed. Pasquale di Fabrizio (Galatina, 1981), p.277-410.

19. See the letters of Intieri to Celestino Galiani between November 1738 and April 1739: MSS held in the Società Napoletana per la Storia Patria (Naples): collocazione xxxi.A.7: 'Galiani, Celestino: Corrispondenza vol.7', f.19, 27-28, 29-30, 31-34, 36-37, 40.

liberal: he explicitly envisaged an agricultural economy as maintaining a 'balance', both internally and externally. Internally there should be a balance between the countryside and the capital city: sixteen in twenty of the inhabitants of France, he thought, were agriculturalists, and he took this to be exemplary. He also advocated a balance between liberty and protection in foreign trade, not to achieve a 'balance of trade' as such, but to protect manufactures which added value to domestic primary goods.[20]

Two young Neapolitans were chosen by Galiani and Intieri to apply Melon's principles to the kingdom. One was Galiani's nephew, Ferdinando. His precocious early work on money, *Della moneta* (1751), was in considerable part a defence of Melon's controversial treatment of money and credit.[21] But the younger Galiani was not, at this stage, much interested in his native kingdom, and Intieri therefore turned instead to another, Antonio Genovesi, for whom he created an entirely new chair at the University, in 'mechanics and the elements of commerce'.

Genovesi duly did as Intieri expected, and applied Melon's principles to the kingdom.[22] He advocated free trade in grain, and the breaking of the 'Annona', the monopoly by which a grain supply was secured for the city of Naples at the expense of producers and the rest of the kingdom. He also advocated the development of internal manufactures, and the tolerance of a degree of luxury as a necessary incentive to agricultural producers. In addition to circulation, he underlined the need to remedy the appalling lack of internal communications within the kingdom, and urged the removal of the many tolls which impeded such trade as there was. Though Genovesi was by no means the first to identify the problem (which had exercised Doria no less), the disproportionate size and consumption of resources by the city of Naples was an obvious subject for the principle of internal balance: it was imperative to diffuse manufacturing through the provinces.

But Genovesi did not stop at Melon. He familiarised himself with more recent French economic writing, and with the works produced by the circle of Vincent de Gournay in particular. Recognising the purpose of

---

20. In the later edition of Jean-François Melon, *Essai politique sur le commerce* (1734; Amsterdam, François Changuion, 1754). On Melon's significance, István Hont, *Jealousy of trade: international competition and the nation-state in historical perspective* (Cambridge, MA, 2005), p.30-33; and in the Neapolitan context, Robertson, *The Case for the Enlightenment*, p.342-45.

21. Ferdinando Galiani, *Della moneta libri v* (1751), in *Opere di Ferdinando Galiani*, ed. Furio Diaz and Luciano Guerci, *Illuministi italiani* 6 (Milan and Naples, 1975); Venturi, *Settecento riformatore*, vol.1: *da Muratori a Beccaria*, p.490-504.

22. See the repeated invocations of Melon as the first to establish the principles of commerce: Antonio Genovesi, *Discorso sopra il vero fine delle lettere e delle scienze* (1753), in *Antonio Genovesi: scritti economici*, ed. Maria Luisa Perna, 2 vols (Naples, 1984), p.29-30; 'Elementi del commercio' (lectures c.1756 to 1758), and *Delle lezioni di commercio, o sia d'economia civile* (Naples, 1765-1767; 2nd edn 1768-1770), in the new edition by Maria Luisa Perna, *Antonio Genovesi: Delle Lezioni di commercio o sia di economia civile, con Elementi del commercio* (Naples, 2005), p.6-7, 268, and specifically on the danger of abundance in the kingdom, p.537-38.

Gournay's programme of publication of economic works, he edited an Italian translation, from the French translation by Gournay and Butel-Dumont, of John Cary's 1695 *Essay on the State of England*.[23] Here and in other similar edited republications, Genovesi demonstrated an openness to English political economy absent in Melon. One aspect of this was a willingness to think seriously, though not uncritically, about the reasons for English manufacturing and commercial success at the expense of both France and the Italian states. Another was Genovesi's appreciation of both the technical and the social basis of English agricultural success. Not only had the English experimented with new techniques and crops; English farmers had demonstrated that a willingness to innovate was fostered by landholding on terms which combined security of tenure with the opportunity for profit.[24] Applying this lesson to the kingdom, Genovesi realised that it would require no less than a major redistribution of landholding, out of the hands of the Church and the barons, and into those of small cultivators. As things stood, Genovesi alleged, two-thirds of the land of the kingdom were held by the Church, and a further two-ninths by the baronage. It was, he admitted, no longer feasible to redistribute land by an agrarian law; but it should be possible to dismantle the systems of mortmain and 'fideicommissa' by which the Church and the barons respectively prevented the division and alienation of their holdings. The better to promote smallholding cultivation, the barons should also be encouraged, or obliged, to divide and either sell or lease their lands on a long-term basis, known as 'censo'.[25]

In developing this analysis, which took him beyond the ground covered by Melon, Genovesi was turning to face what we have seen were the deep complexities of landholding in southern Italy. Confronted by such complexity, Genovesi went only so far. In the context of his economic writings as a whole, his remarks on landholding, however radical in implication, were brief and general. They are also remarkable for the language they did not use: that of feudalism. Genovesi knew and alluded to the history of the introduction of feudal tenure into the kingdom under the Normans;[26]

---

23. *Storia del commercio della Gran Bretagna, scritta da John Cary, tradotta de Pietro Genovesi, con un ragionamento sul commercio in universale, e alcune annotazioni riguardanti l'economia del nostro regno di Antonio Genovesi* (Naples, 1757-1758), in M. L. Perna, *Antonio Genovesi: scritti economici*, p.111-865. On Genovesi's use of Cary, see Sophus A. Reinert, 'Blaming the Medici: footnotes, falsification, and the fate of the "English model" in eighteenth-century Italy', *History of European ideas* 32:4 (2006), special issue on *Commerce and morality in eighteenth-century Italy*, ed. Koen Stapelbroek, p.430-55, especially p.435-41.

24. *L'Agricoltore sperimentato di Cosimo Trinci: appendice: idea del nuovo metodo di agricoltura inglese dell'abate Genovesi*, in M. L. Perna, *Antonio Genovesi: scritti economici*, p.1101-24; M. L. Perna, *Antonio Genovesi: Lezioni di commercio*, part 1, ch.4, p.319.

25. Antonio Genovesi, 'Prefazione' to Trinci, *L'Agricoltore sperimentato*, in M. L. Perna, *Antonio Genovesi: scritti economici*, p.881-84; M. L. Perna, *Antonio Genovesi: Lezioni di commercio*, part 1, ch.11, p.448-49.

26. M. L. Perna, *Antonio Genovesi: Lezioni di commercio*, part 1a, ch.19, p.556-57, ch.22, p.610-11.

but he attempted no direct attack on feudal tenure as a 'system'. Its absence is underlined by the attempt of his pupil Giuseppe Maria Galanti to suggest the opposite. In his *Elogio Storico* of his teacher, published in 1772, Galanti suggested that Genovesi had once alluded ironically to a certain 'monstrous government' celebrated by the count of Boulainvilliers as 'a masterpiece of the human spirit'. Glossing this reference in a note, Galanti observed that Genovesi attributed the squalor and poverty of the provinces to the prevalence of 'feudal laws' and mortmain. But if we turn to the work in question, Genovesi's preface to his edition of *L'Agricoltore sperimentato* by Cosimo Trinci, we find no such passage, or reference to Boulainvilliers.[27] It was Galanti and his contemporaries, not Genovesi, who were to open this new front in the campaign to advance Enlightenment in the kingdom of Naples.

They did so in the decade after Genovesi's death (in 1769), in a changing political and intellectual context. Tanucci's juristic approach to reform, focused on restricting the exercise of feudal jurisdiction and the reintegration of devolved fiefs within the royal demesne, was replaced by an apparently greater openness on the part of at least some ministers to an economic approach. In 1782 this was given institutional recognition by the establishment of a new Supremo Consiglio delle Finanze. The new council was granted powers over all the tribunals whose jurisdictions covered economic affairs, and was also charged with sending visitors into the provinces to report on the state of agriculture and commerce, and the deficiencies of government. Its establishment appeared to signal a new willingness to work with the economists: Ferdinando Galiani was appointed its secretary, and Galanti's recently published report on his travels in his native Molise was taken as a model of the kind of report the Supremo Consiglio wished to receive. Specific initiatives followed, including incentives for the cultivation of unused land, and an attempt to limit the abuses of the 'contratto alla voce', a form of credit advanced to producers who then lost all opportunity to benefit from higher selling prices.[28]

Intellectually, meanwhile, there had been fresh developments in France, encouraging a focus on the distribution of property, and on the 'feudal question' in particular. The latter was the subject of a widely read pamphlet by Pierre-François Boncerf in 1776, denouncing the 'inconveniences' of feudalism.[29] Meanwhile physiocracy had brought the issue

27. Giuseppe Maria Galanti, *Elogio storico del Signor Abate Antonio Genovesi* (Naples, 1772), p.110-11 and note; Genovesi, 'Prefazione' to *L'Agricoltore sperimentato*, in M. L. Perna, *Antonio Genovesi: scritti economici*, p.881-84.

28. Chiosi, 'Il regno dal 1734 al 1799', p.437-39. On the 'contratto alla voce', see the lucid account by Patrick Chorley, *Oil, silk, and Enlightenment: economic problems in XVIIIth-century Naples* (Naples, 1965), p.83-98.

29. Pierre-François Boncerf, *Les Inconvénients des droits féodeaux* (London, 1776); J. Q. C. Mackrell, *The Attack on 'feudalism' in eighteenth-century France* (London and Toronto, 1973).

of property to the fore within economic analysis. Both an economic and a political theory, physiocracy's renewed endorsement of agriculture as the sole source of wealth was underpinned by a strict concept of property right in land, itself based on an idea of 'natural order'.

French physiocratic writings themselves do not seem to have been widely read (or at least referred to) by Neapolitans.[30] An obvious explanation is that the senior and most intelligent of the Neapolitan economists, Ferdinando Galiani, had subjected the physiocratic case for complete free trade in grain to withering criticism in his *Dialogues sur le commerce des bleds* (1770). But one may also wonder how accessible key physiocratic concepts were to the Neapolitan economists. Quesnay's clear distinction between 'agricultural' and 'commercial' economies would strike a familiar, promising note; much less intuitive would have been the concepts of 'produit net' and 'impôt unique' (the related propositions that the only source of wealth in an economy was the net product of agriculture and that there should be a single tax levied on landowners), or the distinction between 'avances foncières' (capital in the form of property in land) and 'avances' of seed and equipment (the capital held by prosperous but non-landowning 'fermiers'). Recent scholarship has emphasised the inwardness of physiocratic thinking, the extent to which it was a response to specific French circumstances and issues: the debate over a 'noblesse commerçante', the need to accommodate economic freedom within an unequal society of orders, the idea of government as a 'despotisme légal', even Quesnay's ambition to construct a theodicy which would restore justice by inverting the 'unnatural and retrograde' order of modern economic relations.[31] These were not concerns of which the Neapolitans seem to have been aware. It is perhaps unsurprising, therefore, that Melon's work was apparently still in demand in Naples. An annotated Italian translation of his *Essai politique sur le commerce* was produced by another of Genovesi's pupils, Francesco Longano, in 1778, and a new translation, with fresh notes, was published as late as 1795.[32]

In due course the new generation of Neapolitan economists did find a substitute for Melon in the Swiss philosopher and economic writer, Georg-Ludwig Schmid d'Avenstein, whose *Principes de la législation*

30. Lucio Villari, 'Note sulla fisiocrazia e sugli economisti napoletani del '700', in *Saggi e ricerche sul Settecento*, ed. E. Sestan (Naples, 1968), p.224-51.
31. T. J. Hochstrasser, 'Physiocracy and the politics of *laissez-faire*', in *The Cambridge history of eighteenth-century political thought*, ed. Mark Goldie and Robert Wokler (Cambridge, 2006), p.419-42; Philippe Steiner, 'Les propriétaires dans la philosophie économique', and Catherine Larrère, 'Une philosophie de la propriété: les physiocrates entre droit naturel et économie', both in *Studi settecenteschi* 24 (2004), *Fisiocrazia e proprietà terriera*, special number ed. Maria Albertone, p.23-47, 49-70; Michael Sonenscher, 'Physiocracy as a theodicy', *History of political thought* 23 (2002), p.326-39.
32. J.-F. Melon, *Saggio politico sul commercio, tradotto dal Francese colle annotazioni dell' Ab. Longano*, 2 vols (Naples, Vincenzo Flauto, 1778); *Saggio politico sul commercio del Signor Melon, tradotto dal Francese, nuova edizione con note* (Naples, Nicola Russo, 1795).

*universelle* (1776) deployed many of the ideas of physiocracy. In fact, Schmid was adapting physiocracy to a context and purposes of his own: a defence of the feasibility of pursuing agrarian self-sufficiency in the Swiss canton of Bern. But Schmid's work was immediately picked up and reviewed in Italian journals, and an Italian translation was published in Siena as early as 1777; the translation was re-issued in Naples in 1791, edited by Francesco Saverio Salfi, and dedicated to Giuseppe Palmieri.[33] Read by the Neapolitans in French or in Italian, the *Principes* appeared to offer a congenial compendium of the new French arguments. The foundation of civil society was property in one's person and goods: without the security of enjoying the fruits of his labour, man would not have the incentive to cultivate the earth and produce a surplus beyond subsistence. Land was the sole source of wealth, and the class of its proprietors the most important in the state. Schmid reproduced the core physiocrat economic doctrines: the concept of 'produit net', the doctrine of the 'impôt unique' and the vital importance of 'anticipations' (capital). But he also put more emphasis than the original physiocrats on manufactures, to the extent of offering a qualified defence of luxury: manufactures enlarge the internal market by producing more goods for consumption, thereby increasing incentives to agricultural production. This would have chimed with the existing convictions of Neapolitan economists. Even more interesting would have been Schmid's remarks on 'il governo feudale', as a system of laws incompatible with the private ownership of land. Feudal government was a product of 'barbarous times', but too many nations which had freed themselves from its 'gothic fetters' had nevertheless allowed their nobilities to cling to the abusive rights they derived from it. These now prevented the circulation of property and the raising of credit, while the precariousness of feudal succession removed the incentive to improve the land. Schmid was particularly critical of primogeniture, arguing that equitable inheritance should be adopted as a means of spreading the enjoyment of property.[34]

With the help of Schmid d'Avenstein, the new generation of Neapolitan economists were in a position to take the discussion of the problem of feudal landholding further than Genovesi had attempted to do. Although Galanti had identified the target as early as 1772, the standard-bearer of the assault now unleashed was a younger and more daring thinker,

---

33. Georg-Ludwig Schmid d'Avenstein, *Principes de la législation universelle* (Amsterdam, Marc-Michel Rey, 1776); Italian translation: *Principj della legislazione universale* [...] *ed in questa prima edizione Napoletana rivedute e corretta sull'originale, ed accresciuta di più note dell'autore medesimo non ancora pubblicate*, 4 vols (Naples, Michele Stasi, 1791). On these editions: Franco Venturi, 'Su alcune pagine di antologia', *Rivista storica Italiana* 71 (1959), p.321-25.

34. Schmid d'Avenstein, *Principj della legislazione universale*, vol.1, bk 3, 'Della proprietà e della libertà', especially chapters 1, 7-10; on 'il governo feudale', p.255-73. For an overview and interpretation of Schmid's work as more than a summary of physiocracy, see Vieri Becagli, 'Georg-Ludwig Schmid d'Avenstein e i suoi *Principes de la législation universelle*: oltre la fisiocrazia', in *Studi settecenteschi* 24 (2004), p.215-52.

Gaetano Filangieri. Filangieri's *Scienza della legislazione* (published in five volumes between 1780 and 1785, with a posthumous sixth volume in 1791) was the inspiration of the late Neapolitan Enlightenment. The work was explicitly presented as a radicalising of Montesquieu's insight into the potential of legislation as a vehicle of reform. It was not the 'spirit' of the (existing) laws which Filangieri would elucidate, but the 'rules' which should inform new legislation. Such legislation must be the work of a sovereign power, but not of a despot (there is no trace in Filangieri of the idea of 'despotisme légal'): the sovereign should be the agent of public opinion, which is itself the expression of the ultimate sovereignty of the people, as informed and guided by philosophers.[35]

For all the universal ambition of the *Scienza della legislazione*, however, the kingdom of Naples was never far from its author's mind, and through his analysis, as its *filo rosso*, ran the problem of feudalism. As much as anyone, Filangieri defined the terms of the problem, which he variously denominated as 'la feudalità', 'il sistema de' feudi', 'la gran macchina de' feudi' or 'l'antico sistema feudale'. As a jurist, Filangieri recognised feudalism as a system of jurisdiction, but he also recognised and analysed it as a system of economic and social power over the land and those who worked on it. Throughout Europe, agriculture, and hence both population growth and the increase of wealth, had been held back by the pattern of landownership. A small number of proprietors owned land while an 'immense number' were left property-less, and among those who owned land, great proprietors predominated over small. On top of which Filangieri (following Genovesi) estimated that two-thirds of landed property was in the hands of ecclesiastics. Not only did such large landowners have no incentive to improve their agriculture, but the land itself was prevented by its inalienability from being sold to those who did.[36]

Denunciation was accompanied by a series of recommendations which would lead to the dismantling of the system. Not only entails but the principle of primogeniture and the possibility of female succession in the main line in preference to collateral males should be barred, to facilitate the division and distribution of large concentrations of land hitherto held by a single family. When a fief 'devolved' back on the Crown as a result of a family's failure to produce an heir, the land should be sold as 'allodial' property, rather than directly administered by the Crown itself. Common

---

35. Gaetano Filangieri, *La Scienza della legislazione*, 6 vols (Naples, 1780-1785, 1791), in the recent edition directed by Vincenzo Ferrone, 7 vols (Venice, Centro di Studi sull'illuminismo 'Giovanni Stiffone', 2003-2004), vol.1, 'Delle regole generali della scienza legislativa', ed. Antonio Trampus, p.11-46, 78-85: 'Introduzione', and ch.7; vol.5, 'Delle leggi che riguardano l'educazione, i costumi e l'istruzione pubblica', ed. Paolo Bianchini, p.359-65: ch.52, 'Della libertà della stampa'.

36. *Scienza della legislazione*, vol.1, ed. A. Trampus, p.12, 'Introduzione'; vol.2, 'Delle leggi politiche ed economiche', ed. Maria Teresa Silvestrini, p.23-55, compare p.235-37: ch.2-5, p.34.

or 'demesne' land should also be parcelled up to permit its enclosure and individual cultivation.[37] Finally all feudal jurisdictions should be abolished, and the barons compensated with a grant of absolute property in at least some of the land previously held on feudal terms.[38]

Filangieri's programme for the destruction of feudalism was supported by elements of a theory of political economy. Much of this was familiar from Genovesi and Melon. There should be free trade in agricultural produce, and cultivators should have the incentive of manufactured goods to purchase. The excessive concentration of wealth in the capital, itself one of the baneful consequences of Neapolitan feudalism, should be cut back, and resources redirected to the provinces.[39] But there were new recommendations as well, most notably for a single tax on landed property. Here Filangieri seems to have drawn directly on Schmid d'Avenstein, for an argument which presupposed the possibility of clear-cut ownership of land.[40] Although Filangieri allowed that barons might become landowners, he clearly hoped that the outcome of his proposals, combined with his economic prescriptions, would be a much broader distribution of wealth and property, and especially of property in land, across the kingdom and between its classes.[41]

In launching this assault, Filangieri was actively seconded by Galanti and several others. Galanti in particular undertook two major intellectual initiatives in the anti-feudal cause. One was to develop a historical account of the origins and progress of feudalism, regarded as a social system as well as a form of jurisdiction. For this he prepared by wide reading of other Enlightenment historians, notably the Scots David Hume and William Robertson, whose works he also published, in whole or in part, in Italian translations.[42] What the Scots taught Galanti was that feudal government and laws had been the product of a specific, 'barbarous' phase in the history of European nations after the fall of the Roman Empire. It was therefore pointless for rulers and jurists to seek to restore the system, in the hope that it might recover its original purity and validity. On the contrary, the advent of commerce had rendered feudal government and laws archaic, their survival an obstacle to future

---

37. *Scienza della legislazione*, vol.2, ed. M. T. Silvestrini, p.45-49.

38. *Scienza della legislazione*, vol.3, 'Delle leggi criminali, parte prima', ed. Francesco Toschi Vespasiani, p.159-84: ch.17-18.

39. *Scienza della legislazione*, vol.2, ed. M. T. Silvestrini, p.84-128: ch.10-14.

40. Filangieri's debt to Schmid for his treatment of taxation is identified and annotated in *La Scienza della legislazione*, vol.2, ed. M. T. Silvestrini, p.198, 201, 207, 221, 224: ch.27-32. The discussion on luxury in ch.37 seems also to have drawn on Schmid, vol.2, p.249-52. See also Maria Teresa Silvestrini, 'Free trade, feudal remnants and international equilibrium in Gaetano Filangieri's *Science of legislation*', *History of European ideas* 32 (2006), p.502-24, especially p.515-18.

41. *Scienza della legislazione*, vol.2, ed. M. T. Silvestrini, p.235-45: ch.34-36.

42. On Galanti's editorial and publishing initiatives, see Maria Luisa Perna, 'Giuseppe Galanti editore', in *Miscellanea Walter Maturi* (Turin, 1966), p.221-58.

progress.[43] Another historical perspective to inform this discussion was that of Vico, whose identification of early Roman forms of landholding with fiefs was adapted and extended by Francesco Mario Pagano, in his remarkable *Saggi politici: de' principii, progressi e decadenza delle società* (1783-1785, second edition 1791-1792). 'Aristocratic feudal government', Pagano argued, was characteristic of all barbarian nations, not simply those of the Middle Ages. Even more strongly, the implication was that its survival in the kingdom of Naples, which the jurists took for granted, was an extraordinary historical aberration.[44]

Galanti's second major contribution to the attack on feudalism was to undertake detailed surveys of agricultural conditions in the kingdom. His *Descrizione dello stato antico ed attuale del contado di Molise* (1781) set the standard, establishing the value of such surveys; with the initial encouragement of the Supremo Consiglio, he went on to compile a more comprehensive *Nuova descrizione storica e geografica delle Sicilie* (1786-1794).[45] He was joined in this enterprise by two others, Francesco Longano, the translator of Melon, who wrote reports on his journeys through the Molise and the Capitanata, and Domenico Grimaldi, writing on the rural economy of Calabria Ultra.[46] Together these works demonstrated why the shibboleth of the kingdom's natural fertility was not enough: an ignorant, impoverished peasantry must be taught and enabled to cultivate properly. To teach them would require the creation of agricultural societies or academies on the British model: Galanti particularly recommended the improving societies of Dublin and Edinburgh.[47] To enable the peasantry

43. Giuseppe Maria Galanti, *Descrizione dello stato antico ed attuale del contado di Molise, con un saggio storico sulla costituzione del Regno*, 2 vols (Naples, Società Letteraria e Tipografica, 1781), vol.1, ch.4-9; For a similar historical perspective on the problem, Melchiorre Delfico, 'Memoria per la vendita de' beni dello stato d'Atri' (1788), reprinted in Rao, *L'"Amaro della feudalità"*, p.349-67, especially p.349-52. See also, p.229-37, Rao's acute comments on the significance of this historical perspective, compared with that adopted by the jurists; and G. Galasso, 'Galanti: storiografia e riformismo nell' analisi dell'ultimo feudalesimo', in *La Filosofia in soccorso de' governi*, p.485-506.

44. Francesco Mario Pagano, *Saggi politici: de' principii, progressi e decadenza delle società*, 2nd edn (Naples, 1791-1792), in the edition by Luigi and Laura Salvetti Firpo (Naples, 1993), p.224-41, 397. Also in the first edition: *De' saggi politici, vol.2: del civile corso delle nazioni* (Naples, 1785), p.249-63, two concluding chapters devoted to a 'Generale prospetto della storia del regno', not included in the second edition.

45. Even so, Galanti never completed the work: G. M. Galanti, *Nuova descrizione storica e geografica delle Sicilie*, 5 vols (1786-1794), modern edition by F. Assante and D. Demarco, 2 vols (Naples, 1969).

46. Longano's two reports, published in 1788 and 1790 respectively, are reprinted as Francesco Longano, *Viaggi per lo regno di Napoli*, ed. with a vigorous introduction by Giulio Gentile (Naples, 2002). Longano differed from Galanti and Delfico, however, in holding that 'il sistema feudale non è di sua natura vizioso', but had degenerated from its original, wise purpose: p.169-70. Domenico Grimaldi, *Saggio di economia campestre per la Calabria Ultra* (Naples, 1770), with an extract in *Riformatori napoletani, Illuministi italiani* 5, ed. Franco Venturi (Milan and Naples, 1962), p.431-55.

47. Galanti, *Elogio storico*, p.154; *Descrizione*, vol.2, p.92-95; another to refer admiringly to examples of agricultural societies elsewhere was Domenico Grimaldi, *Piano di riforma per*

to apply the new techniques, however, required something more radical: creating a substantial class of peasant farmers who held their land as property. This could be done, Galanti suggested, at the expense of the common rights of the communities. Galanti also recommended the replacement of the existing system of advance purchase from producers, the 'contratto alla voce', which prevented the peasantry from reaping the benefits of free trade in agricultural produce, and the introduction of a single tax on land (a proposal for which he explicitly cited Schmid). Together these should consolidate the emergence of a new class of small- to medium-scale, property-owning cultivators.[48]

By the end of the 1780s the anti-feudal crusade seemed at last to have been taken up by the government itself, acting through the Supremo Consiglio delle Finanze. In 1787 the membership of the council had been afforced by leading economists, including Filangieri (even if he was too ill to serve, and died within a year) and Giuseppe Palmieri. There were two major policy initiatives. In 1791 the council took the decision to sell fiefs which 'devolved' to the Crown as 'allodial' land, thereby abolishing the land's feudal status, and the levies and jurisdiction which had attached to that status. Domenico Gennaro, duca di Cantalupo, an uncompromising reformer, was charged with the policy's implementation. Within a year the Crown found itself facing a test case, the contested devolution of the fief of Arnone, near Capua. The second initiative, which also came to a head in 1792 with the issue of a general edict, was to facilitate the division and enclosure of the demesne lands of rural communities. But neither initiative was easy to carry through. The Crown's lawyers who tackled the jurisdictional issues did not have the same goals as the economists. They were not necessarily averse to the division of the fiefs, to create smaller holdings, but they opposed the economists on the fundamental point of principle, the sale of the land as allodial, that is private, property. Justifying their position as upholding the Crown's authority and maximising its revenues, the jurists continued to defend feudal landholding as integral to the character of the Neapolitan monarchy. For their part, both barons and rural communities resisted the initiatives, though they also found ways to take advantage, frustrating the economists' hopes of creating a new class of smaller landowners.[49]

*la pubblica economia delle provincie del regno di Napoli, e per l'agricoltura delle due Sicilie* (Naples, Giuseppe-Maria Porcelli, 1780), p.lvi-lxii. The reference to the improving societies of Dublin and Edinburgh was repeated by the 1795 translator of Melon, who attributed the idea to Palmieri: *Saggio politico sul commercio del Signor Melon*, p.92-93 note a.

48. Galanti, *Descrizione*, vol.2, p.59-124; the reference to Schmid on taxation is on p.83.

49. On the debate over the anti-feudal initiatives of the 1790s, Rao, *L'"Amaro della feudalità'*, passim. On the parallel initiative to divide and enclose the common lands of the 'università': Gabriella Corona, *Demani ed individualismo agrario nel regno di Napoli* (Naples, 1995). For a fresh account of royal policy, emphasising its coherence and purpose in the 1780s and 1790s, see John A. Davis, *Naples and Napoleon: southern Italy and the European revolutions 1780-1860* (Oxford, 2006), part 1, 'Absolutist Naples', especially p.54-70.

*John Robertson*

It is not the predictable clash of interests which concerns me here, however. Rather, it is the relation between the economists' expectations for the economic development of the kingdom and their assault on the feudal system in the name of private property in land. So far, I have emphasised the univocal character of their arguments, the congruity between the thinking of Galanti, Filangieri and others, and the consistency with which they adapted the arguments of Schmid d'Avenstein. But there was one economist whose support for the Galanti–Filangieri case against feudalism was significantly qualified, Giuseppe Palmieri.

Hitherto mentioned only in passing, Palmieri was none the less a central figure in the Neapolitan debate. Summoned from his native Puglia to Naples in 1787, at the age of sixty-six, Palmieri was appointed to the Supremo Consiglio delle Finanze alongside Filangieri. In 1791 he was appointed director of finance, and played a leading role in preparing the decree of that year on the sale of devolved fiefs as allodial land. While in Naples, he took advantage of the opportunity to publish four works of political economy: *Riflessioni sulla pubblica felicità relativamente al Regno di Napoli* (1787), *Pensieri economici relativi al Regno di Napoli* (1789), *Osservazioni in varii articoli riguardanti la pubblica economia* (1790) and *Della ricchezza nazionale* (1792). He was also the dedicatee of the 1791 Neapolitan edition of the Italian translation of Schmid's *Principes*. By comparison with Filangieri, Galanti and even Longano, Palmieri has received little attention from historians.[50] Yet he engaged with the full spectrum of issues discussed in Neapolitan economic thinking. On many issues he reinforced the consensus deriving from Genovesi. He endorsed the view that an agricultural nation must make that sector its priority by adopting free trade in grain and promoting new techniques. Like Genovesi he held up the example of English agriculture. English leases, he observed, proved that smaller tenant farmers could thrive provided they had unimpeded access to the market.[51] He too underlined the importance of diffusing knowledge of agriculture through 'patriotic societies'.[52] Palmieri was also at one with the consensus in urging the encouragement of manufactures for the internal market, as an incentive to agricultural producers. Other issues he addressed included external commerce, criticising Schmid d'Avenstein's restrictive view of its benefits, luxury, about which he shared the reservations of many later eighteenth-century economists, and the disproportionate size of the city of Naples.[53] Starting from this

---

50. Franco Venturi's 'Nota introduttiva' to the selection from Palmieri's writings in *Riformatori napoletani*, p.1087-1113, remains the essential starting point.
51. Giuseppe Palmieri, *Riflessioni sulla pubblica felicità relativamente al regno di Napoli* (Naples, the brothers Raimondi, 1787; 2nd edn 1788), p.101-103.
52. G. Palmieri, *Osservazioni su varj articoli riguardanti il pubblica economia* (Naples, Vincenzo Flauto and Michele Stasi, 1790), p.145; *Della ricchezza nazionale* (Naples, Vincenzo Flauto and Michele Stasi, 1792), p.81.
53. Palmieri, *Riflessioni sulla pubblica felicità*, p.144-79, 201-11.

common ground, however, Palmieri found key arguments of his fellow economists to be unconvincing.

In particular, he questioned the shibboleths of the anti-feudal economists. Rhetorically, he asked in 1789 whether 'l'anarchia feudale' now existed, and answered his own question by declaring it 'for the most part, a phantom'.[54] Substantively, he challenged two key propositions of the anti-feudal case. He denied that large-scale landholding by the nobility was the problem, to be resolved by the division of fiefs and communal demesne lands among small proprietors. The issue was not the scale of landholding, but whether the proprietors could provide the 'spese di anticipazione' (literally, 'costs of anticipation', that is, capital) and could purchase the labour required to cultivate efficiently. It was true that many great proprietors, both lay and ecclesiastical, had the means to invest in better cultivation, but put the goods of today before those of tomorrow. But so did the peasantry and the 'bracciali' (agricultural labourers), the indolence of the latter in particular being evident in their inclination to shorten the working day to the minimum possible. In their abject condition, a wider distribution of the land was in itself no remedy. The poor would be better off as tenants and labourers of those with funds to invest.[55] If this was to use a physiocratic doctrine against Galanti and Filangieri, Palmieri's second challenge had the opposite tendency. He questioned the preference of Schmid and his Neapolitan followers for a single direct tax on landowners. Although Palmieri understood the distinction between gross and net product, he feared that a tax which fell only on landowners would add to their costs, competing in particular with saving for 'the costs of anticipations'. Moreover, he objected, the information required to raise such a tax did not exist in the kingdom. In the absence of an accurate and universal census of the land, the single tax would be impossible to implement. As it was, proprietors in much of the kingdom had no way of calculating their 'net product'.[56] Palmieri endorsed the principle of private property right as the basis for increasing private and national wealth,[57] but in the kingdom of Naples what counted as property could not be taken for granted.

Palmieri's questioning of his fellow economists has not been judged very sympathetically, at the time or since. In letters to Delfico in 1791 and 1792 an infuriated Cantalupo accused Palmieri of inconsistency, of deferring to the jurists in contradiction of his own arguments. Since Palmieri had already published his reservations over key elements in the reformers' strategy, the inconsistency, if there was one, was with his support for the

---

54. G. Palmieri, *Pensieri economici relativi al regno di Napoli* (Naples, Vincenzo Flauto, 1789), p.140n.
55. Palmieri, *Riflessioni sulla pubblica felicità*, p.80-104; *Pensieri economici*, p.120-38; *Osservazioni*, p.133-35.
56. Palmieri, *Riflessioni sulla pubblica felicità*, p.216-46; *Osservazioni*, p.155-56.
57. Palmieri, *Pensieri economici*, p.120-21.

1791 decree, not with what he had written.[58] Modern historians have categorised him as a defender of the class interests of the nobility to which he belonged; with more evidence, it has been pointed out that feudalism was still very far from a 'phantom' in the kingdom of Naples in the late eighteenth century.[59] Yet this criticism too may miss Palmieri's point. If nothing else, his rhetorical deflation of the feudal problem pointed up the extent to which responsibility for the failings of Neapolitan agriculture was now being attributed to the 'feudal system'.

Palmieri's substantive differences with his fellow economists, moreover, had identified potentially important weaknesses in their arguments. Their reduction of the problem to one of scale and distribution of landownership was an oversimplification. The conviction that agricultural improvement was best entrusted to small proprietors flew in the face of the present poverty and disinclination to work of the southern peasantry. The latter simply did not have the capital required for agricultural improvement. Galanti and Filangieri had also muddled the issues of scale and ownership, failing to recognise the key roles played by small- to medium-scale tenant farmers, whether in the English example or in Quesnay's ideal of the 'fermier'. Even more questionable was the assumption of property right as a given. It was very doubtful whether the concept of property in land, whose acceptance was the prerequisite of replacing feudal rights, would be understood in much of the kingdom – and whether those who worked the land would welcome it if it were offered. (Filangieri's strategy, it will be remembered, depended on winning the support of public opinion, and not on imposition by a 'despotisme légal', an idea which the Neapolitan monarchy was anyway in no position to implement.) In short, the critique of feudalism was diverting attention from the crucial economic need for investment, while taking for granted a change in the understanding of property right which was most unlikely to win immediate acceptance.

Palmieri's economic thinking and the significance of his intervention in the Neapolitan debate need more extended scrutiny than they have received here. Although he certainly irritated his reforming colleagues, Palmieri does not seem to have provoked them into responding to his objections. But at least he had identified a problem. The insight that feudal relations had been constitutive of 'barbarous' societies, in the Middle Ages and even in antiquity, may have inspired the historical thinking of Galanti, Filangieri and Pagano, yielding in the work of Pagano in particular one of the most sophisticated historical philosophies

---

58. Cantalupo's letters are quoted by Venturi in his 'Nota introduttiva', *Riformatori napoletani*, p.1110-11; see also Rao, *L'"Amaro della feudalità'*, p.75-76, who notes that Palmieri expressed himself in favour of selling Crown property rather than managing it directly. (See Palmieri, *Osservazioni*, p.45.) The key issues, however, were whether devolved fiefs should be sold as free property, and whether small purchasers were to be favoured.

59. Rao, 'The feudal question', p.100.

of the late Enlightenment. The desire to observe and catalogue the consequences of feudalism may likewise have inspired the provincial surveys of Galanti, Longano and Grimaldi, which provide such detailed, compelling descriptions of the poverty of the kingdom. But on the evidence outlined here, the energy devoted to the assault on the feudal system in these histories and surveys cannot disguise the analytical difficulties in which Neapolitan economists found themselves when they sought to identify the conditions for its replacement.

In the event, the system of fiefs was abolished in the kingdom of Naples shortly afterwards, during the *decennio* of French rule between 1806 and 1815; it would not be re-established by the Bourbons following their restoration. The outcome of abolition, however, hardly corresponded to the expectations of the economists. What emerged in the first half of the nineteenth century was not a society of small proprietors, but an agrarian economy dominated by a few latifundists, who accumulated great tracts of land by a combination of purchase, foreclosure and usurpation, and then held them together by an informal but rigorous family strategy of primogeniture and entail. By the second half of the century, the backwardness of the south of Italy had become an explicitly posed 'Question', discussion of which accorded a prominent place to the deficiencies of latifundism. Not surprisingly, even the most sympathetic of historians has conceded that the nineteenth-century kingdom of Naples belonged to the 'periphery' of Europe.[60] What has been argued here is that even if the Neapolitans were far from 'peripheral' to the Enlightenment in the eighteenth century, there is, nevertheless, a sense in which they encountered in the feudal system a social and political reality at the margin, or extremity, of European experience, and found the resources of Enlightenment political economy inadequate to the task of its comprehension.

It may be that the Neapolitans made the wrong choice of political economy in preferring French, 'agrarian' models of development to the tougher medicine of competitive international commerce set out in David Hume's *Political discourses* and Adam Smith's *Wealth of nations*.[61] Ever since Intieri spotted the interest of Melon's *Essai politique sur le commerce*, and passed his enthusiasm on to Galiani and Genovesi, the Neapolitan economists had believed that they had good reasons to suppose that an agrarian model better fitted the circumstances of the kingdom; not the least of these was that it seemed to offer an alternative to acceptance of

---

60. Marta Petrusewicz, *Latifundium: moral economy and material life in a European periphery* (Ann Arbor, MI, 1996); and the same author's *Come il meridione divenne una questione: rappresentazioni del sud prima e dopo il quarantotto* (Catanzaro, 1998).

61. This is an implication of István Hont's compelling argument, 'Jealousy of trade: an introduction', in his *Jealousy of trade*, p.1-156, especially p.68-77, 99-123. In fact the first Italian translation of the *Wealth of nations* was published in Naples in 1790: *Ricerche sulla natura, e le cagioni della ricchezza delle nazioni, del Signor Smith*, 5 vols (Naples, Giuseppe Policarpo Merande, 1790-1791). But it was appreciated for its historical rather than its economic analysis.

long-term economic subordination to the already established commercial powers. But if this is to their credit, it is still hard to avoid the conclusion that the critique of the feudal system exposed the limitations of political economy in Naples after Genovesi. To explain how the feudal system, in the peculiarly well-entrenched form it took in Naples, was to be subverted, its critics needed a better economic theory than they were able to deploy. Above all, they needed a political economy which faced and engaged with the problems of property right in the kingdom.

MARIE-CHRISTINE SKUNCKE

# Jean-Jacques Rousseau in Swedish eyes around 1760[1]

IN 1760 a fourteen-year old boy in Sweden bluntly dismissed Jean-Jacques Rousseau's contention that sciences and arts had led to a corruption of manners: 'Mais quel dogme plus absurde et si je l'ose dire plus barbare que celui de Monsieur Rousseau de Genève?'. The adolescent was the Swedish crown prince Gustav, later King Gustav III (1746-1792), and he was writing to his governor, Baron Carl Fredrik Scheffer.[2] His reaction reflects the predominant attitude among contemporary Swedes towards 'Monsieur Rousseau de Genève': rejection.

This article will deal with the early reception of Rousseau in Sweden. The Swedish realm, including present-day Sweden and Finland, undoubtedly belonged to the geographical periphery of Europe. The question of Sweden and the Enlightenment is a much vexed one. Swedish elites in the second half of the eighteenth century perceived themselves as 'upplysta', the Swedish equivalent of 'enlightenened'. The Frenchman Jaucourt described Sweden as 'une nation du Nord des plus éclairées' in his article 'Suède' in the *Encyclopédie* (1765). Among present-day Swedish scholars, however, a fierce polemic has raged for the last decades as to whether or not there existed a Swedish Enlightenment, a Swedish 'Upplysning'.[3]

As for Jean-Jacques Rousseau, a man of paradoxes, he appears both as a major figure of Enlightenment and one of its main critics. In the 1750s and early 1760s, he became known in Sweden as the author of the two discourses and the *Lettre à D'Alembert*. Swedish elites – in the university world, at court, among publicists and writers – mostly dismissed his ideas. How did they argue, and how can we interpret their reactions? Underlying these questions is the assumption that reception studies should not be restricted to charting 'influences' from a centre, perceived as active, to

1. My warm thanks for valuable help in preparing this study are due to Professor Simon Davies, Belfast, Professor Peter Hanns Reill, UCLA, and Professor Bo Bennich-Björkman and Dr Krister Östlund, Uppsala.
2. Prince Gustav to Carl Fredrik Scheffer, 3 February 1760, in *Gustave III par ses lettres*, ed. Gunnar von Proschwitz (Stockholm and Paris, 1986), p.26. See Skuncke, 'Un prince suédois', p.155. A prince's governor had the overall responsibility for his studies, whereas the tutors did the actual teaching.
3. 'Suède', *Encyclopédie*, vol.15, p.623. For a survey of the debate over the Swedish Enlightenment, see Skuncke, 'Was there a Swedish Enlightenment?'

peripheries perceived as passive receivers. It is more fruitful to discuss matters in terms of 'uses', 'dialogue' and 'debate'. As Robert Darnton notes about the French Enlightenment, 'the foreigners talked back.'[4]

My main focus will be on just a few years, 1759 to 1762, when a number of Swedish texts were written about the citizen of Geneva. While also presenting a few earlier texts from the mid 1750s, I shall refrain from exploring the period after 1762. The publication of the *Nouvelle Héloïse* in 1761 and *Emile* (and to some extent the *Contrat social*) in 1762 led to changed attitudes among Swedish readers and to a new phase in the Swedish reception of Rousseau. I shall concentrate on texts explicitly or implicitly dealing with Rousseau's ideas. Rather than attempting to give a full picture of the reception of Rousseau in Sweden, I wish to analyse Swedish reactions at a specific time, in a specific context.[5] To readers not familiar with Swedish history, a short background may be useful.

## i. Sweden around 1760 – an enlightened nation?

Sweden around 1760 played a secondary role in international politics – it had lost its status as a great European power after the death of Charles XII – yet this was a kingdom with an original political system. During the period known as the age of liberty (1720-1772), political power was concentrated in Parliament, the Diet or 'Riksdag', whereas the king's power was strictly limited. The Riksdag included not three but four estates: the nobility, the clergy, the burghers and also the peasantry. Two parties, the Hats and the Caps, competed within the Riksdag, and in practice power rested with the ruling party. The Hats, an alliance between big entrepreneurs, high-ranking civil servants and military officers, had defeated their opponents in 1738 and 1739 and managed to hold sway for over two and a half decades, until 1765. The Cap party traditionally had its base among old aristocratic landowning families; in the 1760s, radical members from new groups, such as lower clergy and small entrepreneurs, were playing an increasing role.[6]

---

4. Darnton, 'George Washington's false teeth, p.153.

5. As far as I am aware, there exists no systematic study of the reception of Rousseau in Sweden. Sten Lindroth gives a short survey of the period 1750-1772 in his *Svensk lärdomshistoria: Frihetstiden* (Stockholm, 1978), p.510-14. Martin Lamm studied the 'first Swedish Rousseauism' in *Upplysningstidens romantik*, vol.1 (Stockholm, 1918), ch.4; on negative reactions to Rousseau, p.248-53. On the early reception of Rousseau in Europe, see Raymond Trousson, *Jean-Jacques Rousseau jugé par ses contemporains: du Discours sur les sciences et les arts aux Confessions* (Paris, 2000), and references on the website http://rousseaustudies.free.fr (Bibliographie de la réception de Rousseau).

6. See Michael F. Metcalf, 'Parliamentary sovereignty and royal reaction, 1719-1809', in *The Riksdag: a history of the Swedish parliament*, ed. M. F. Metcalf (Stockholm and New York, 1987), p.109-64; Michael Roberts, *The Age of liberty: Sweden 1719-1772* (Cambridge, 1986); Skuncke, 'Press and political culture in Sweden at the end of the age of liberty', in *Enlightenment, revolution and the periodical press*, ed. Hans-Jürgen Lüsebrink and Jeremy D. Popkin, *SVEC* 2004:06, p.81-86.

## Jean-Jacques Rousseau in Swedish eyes around 1760

For the Hat leaders, Sweden's future lay in developing science and technology in order to boost the country's economy, especially in manufacturing. The Hats promoted scientific research and launched new institutions. The Royal Academy of Sciences was created in Stockholm in 1739 just after the Hats had come to power; among its founders were the botanist Linnaeus, aged thirty-two, and one of the party leaders, Count Anders Johan von Höpken, aged twenty-seven. In order to investigate the kingdom's natural and human resources, Linnaeus and his disciples went on systematic journeys through various Swedish provinces. The voyages of Linnaeus' disciples to other continents are well known; the Royal Academy of Sciences developed a fruitful collaboration with the Swedish East India Company. At the University of Uppsala, a chair of economics (*œconomia publica*) was established in 1741 with Anders Berch as its first holder. A national office for statistics, the first in Europe, was created in 1749: Tabellverket, the Office of Tables.[7]

There was a belief among leading Hats that scientific progress and rational reforms would lead to a better society. One meets instances of what we would now call 'social engineering'.[8] As plans were made for a reform of the school system, a Hat bishop, Johan Browallius from Åbo (in Finnish: Turku) in Finland, suggested a system of aptitude tests for boys whereby each individual would end up in the right place in the mechanism of society (this plan was not carried out).[9] The promoters of the new office for statistics, as Karin Johannisson has shown, believed in the blessings of 'political arithmetic': 'quantitative analysis was enthusiastically linked to the national welfare programme.'[10]

The mid eighteenth century, thus, was a period of strong institutional support for the sciences in Sweden, and it became a golden age for the natural sciences, with names of international renown like Linnaeus, the physicist Celsius, the astronomer Wargentin, the mineralogist Wallerius and others. As far as natural sciences are concerned, Sweden was far from peripheral: it belonged to the European forefront. An important feature of Swedish intellectual life in this period is that there existed, as a rule, no opposition between science and official religion. On the contrary, the two went hand in hand. For Linnaeus, the harmonious order which he uncovered in Creation proved the goodness of the Creator – the doctrine

---

7. For a comprehensive survey in Swedish see Lindroth, *Svensk lärdomshistoria*. For articles in English, see Tore Frängsmyr and others in *Science in Sweden: the Royal Swedish Academy of Sciences 1739-1989*, ed. T. Frängsmyr (Canton, MA, 1989).

8. See Karin Johannisson, *Det mätbara samhället: Statistik och samhällsdröm i 1700-talets Europa* (Stockholm, 1988), p.185.

9. See M.-C. Skuncke, *Gustaf III – Det offentliga barnet: en prins retoriska och politiska fostran* (Stockholm, 1993), p.134.

10. Johannisson, *Det mätbara samhället*, p.213. Also Johannisson, 'Society in numbers: the debate over quantification in 18th-century political economy', in *The Quantifying spirit in the 18th century*, ed. T. Frängsmyr *et al.* (Berkeley, CA, Los Angeles, CA, and Oxford, 1990), p.353-61.

known as physico-theology.[11] Lutheran parish priests became involved in the practical work of Enlightenment, for example encouraging peasants to inoculate their children against smallpox.[12]

Could mid-eighteenth-century Sweden be described as an 'enlightened' nation? Jaucourt, as we have seen, called Sweden 'une nation du Nord des plus éclairées' in the *Encyclopédie*. He was referring to the Swedish political system, with limited royal power and peasant participation in the Riksdag. In our time, the late Sten Lindroth, professor of the history of ideas at Uppsala, claimed that the natural scientists of the age of liberty were the true champions of Enlightenment in Sweden. This view has been challenged by Tore Frängsmyr, professor of the history of science at the same university, in his book *Sökandet efter Upplysningen (The Search for Enlightenment)* published in 1993. Frängsmyr defines Enlightenment as an intellectual movement, radical, rationalist and anti-Christian; the term 'Upplysningen', 'the Enlightenment', should be reserved for the movement of the *philosophes* in France, or for movements in other countries, inspired by, or parallel to the French one. The Swedish natural scientists of the age of liberty, who were generally good Christians and obedient citizens, do not fit into this definition. Tore Frängsmyr's interpretation, which leaves hardly any room at all for a Swedish Enlightenment, sparked off a heated debate among Swedish eighteenth-century scholars.[13]

The core of the question, I would argue, is whether or not one allows Christian belief to be included into one's definition of Enlightenment. For scholars who view Enlightenment as fundamentally anti-Christian, or at least as questioning religious revelation, Sweden has very little to offer in the way of Enlightenment. If, however, like the Dutch historian Wijnand Mijnhardt, one chooses a definition which gives room for moderate Christian reformers, a case can be made for speaking of Swedish variants of the Enlightenment throughout the eighteenth century.[14] The belief in science and progress among political and intellectual elites in the mid eighteenth century could be seen as a Swedish example of the 'Enlightenment project'.

Around 1760, at any rate, members of the Swedish elites had no qualms about describing themselves as enlightened. The adjective

---

11. See Lindroth, *Svensk lärdomshistoria*, p.217-28.
12. See Carin Bergström, *Lantprästen: Prästens funktion i det agrara samhället 1720-1800* (Stockholm, 1991), p.105.
13. Lindroth, *Svensk lärdomshistoria*, p.510. T. Frängsmyr, *Sökandet efter Upplysningen* (Höganäs, 1993), p.6, 65, 91-111; revised edn (Stockholm, 2006); French translation by Jean-François and Marianne Battail, *A la recherche des Lumières: une perspective suédoise* (Bordeaux, 1999). See Skuncke, 'Was there a Swedish Enlightenment?' (with detailed references).
14. Mijnhardt, 'The Dutch Enlightenment', p.183. Skuncke, 'Was there a Swedish Enlightenment?', p.32-36. On Protestant Enlightenment see Pasi Ihalainen, *Protestant nations redefined* (Leiden and Boston, 2005).

'upplyst', 'enlightened', had strong positive connotations and a fairly vague denotation, somewhat like 'democratic' in our days.[15] For many Swedes who encountered the citizen of Geneva, it was clear that Enlightenment was on their side, not his.

## ii. Early rejection: a Latin dissertation and a German–Swedish review

For an early Swedish reaction, let us turn to the University of Uppsala. In December 1754 the student Petrus (Pehr) Svedelius defended a Latin dissertation refuting Rousseau's first discourse, *An studia litterarum contulerint ad emendationem morum?* (approximately: *Whether the arts and sciences have contributed to improving manners*).[16] The public examination, 'disputatio', was presided over by Professor Johan Ihre, holder of the prestigious chair in eloquence and politics, the leading figure of the Faculty of Arts at the time. He was born in 1707, the same year as his Uppsala colleague Linnaeus. Petrus Svedelius was twenty-two years old, the son of a prominent churchman in the provincial town of Västerås.[17]

Latin was still the normal language for Swedish academic dissertations, except for the new discipline of economics. Eighteenth-century neo-Latin was not an antiquated language but a functional instrument for scientific communication.[18] As regards the authorship of the dissertation, it is probable that, following a frequent practice at the time, it was not written by the student – the 'respondent' Petrus Svedelius – but by the professor, Johan Ihre; the student's task was to defend the theses in the dissertation against an 'opponent'. Even when Ihre's students did write their dissertations themselves, the professor's influence was strong. Boundaries between professorships were elastic in the eighteenth century, and Ihre's actual field of research was Nordic philology. He worked on the ancient Gothic language of the Silver Bible in the Uppsala University Library, on Old Swedish and Old Icelandic.[19] Considering Ihre's research focus, it is

---

15. See Frängsmyr, *Sökandet efter Upplysningen*, on the terms 'Upplysning' and 'upplyst', p.67-71.

16. Johannes Ihre (praes.) / Petrus Svedelius (resp.), *Dissertatio in quaestionem, an studia litterarum contulerint ad emendationem morum?* (Arosiae [= Västerås], n.d.). See Lamm, *Upplysningstidens romantik*, p.251, and Lindroth, *Svensk lärdomshistoria*, p.511. My warm thanks are due to Dr Krister Östlund, Uppsala, for invaluable assistance in helping me to understand the Latin.

17. On Johan Ihre (1707-1780), see Krister Östlund, *Johan Ihre on the origins and history of the runes: three Latin dissertations from the mid-18th century* (Uppsala, 2000), p.20-26. Petrus (Pehr) Svedelius (1732-1805) became professor at Uppsala; see Claes Annerstedt, *Uppsala universitets historia*, 3 vols (Uppsala and Stockholm, 1914), vol.3, part 2, p.80, 90-91.

18. See Hans Helander, *Neo-Latin literature in Sweden in the period 1620-1720* (Uppsala, 2004), and Östlund, *Johan Ihre*.

19. Östlund, *Johan Ihre*, p.14-19, 21-23, 362.

understandable that the refutation of the first discourse concentrated on Rousseau's use of historical argument.

The author must have had access to the first edition of the discourse, and he also refers to a collection of answers from critics and replies by Rousseau, published in Gotha: the *Recueil de toutes les pièces qui ont été publiées à l'occasion du discours de M. J. J. Rousseau* from 1753, the year before the dissertation was submitted.[20] Ihre begins by conceding the 'eloquence' and 'sharp intellect' of the citizen of Geneva, but states that this philosopher is, or at least seems to be, alien to philosophy.[21] The arts and sciences do not, the author contends, corrupt manners, even if they do not always improve manners as they ought to do. His line of argument is to dissociate the two factors between which Rousseau established a causal relationship, 'studia litterarum' on the one hand and 'mores' on the other. He does so through a historical examination of various ancient peoples.

Rousseau's way of characterising ancient peoples does not stand scholarly scrutiny, Ihre argues. The Egyptians for example were both learned and virtuous, as we find from Herodotus, Diodorus and others. Rousseau's description of the Ethiopians, the Greeks and the Romans are equally invalid.[22] The author pays special attention to the Scythians, whom Rousseau praised as being primitive and virtuous. In fact, the Scythians consisted of several peoples. One of these, the 'Massagetes', who practised cannibalism, were far from being virtuous. But a large group among the Scythians were the 'Nomads', and these were not only virtuous but held learning in high esteem.[23] The author's concern for the Scythians is natural, as these had played a prominent role in national Swedish historiography since the sixteenth century: according to the 'Gothic' tradition, the noble Scythians in olden times migrated from areas round the Caspian Sea and the Black Sea and settled in Scandinavia.[24]

One people whom Rousseau did not mention were the Vikings, the ancestors of the Swedes. The author describes them as unmitigated barbarians: among the Vikings, 'no way of life was more honourable than that of thieves and pirates, killing a human being was held as a sport, and it sometimes also happened that wives were burnt together with their dead husband', and so on. The author dismisses the primitive Vikings as criminals. Earlier, he takes sides against the cruel Spartans for the affable, mild and humane Athenians.[25] Virtue, in his eyes, is on the side of

---

20. Ihre / Svedelius, *Dissertatio*, p.2.

21. Ihre / Svedelius, *Dissertatio*, p.1 ('id ipsum tanta cum eloquentia & ingenii tanto acumine praestitit'; 'Est autem, vel esse saltem videtur, hic Philosophus a Philosophia tam alienus').

22. Ihre / Svedelius, *Dissertatio*, p.6-8, 11-16.

23. Ihre / Svedelius, *Dissertatio*, p.8-11.

24. See Lindroth, *Svensk lärdomshistoria*, p.668-69; on 'Gothic' historiography, see Helander, *Neo-Latin literature in Sweden*, p.401-408.

25. Ihre / Svedelius, *Dissertatio*, p.17 ('nulla vitae ratio erat honestior, quam latronum piratarumque, ludus habebatur, hominem occidere, modo interdiu [misprint for

civilisation. The dissertation ends with a pious and patriotic exhortation: we should be intent on the preservation of divine wisdom, and we should do our utmost to let sciences and arts flourish in our fatherland.

Swedish readers outside Uppsala were informed of the dissertation in the Swedish journal *Lärda Tidningar* (*Learned news*), published by Lars Salvius in Stockholm; the reviewer does not appear to have direct acquaintance with Rousseau's first discourse.[26] Meanwhile, a new Swedish journal was launched in Stockholm in the autumn of 1755, the monthly *Den Swänska Mercurius* (*The Swedish Mercury*). Unlike *Lärda Tidningar*, which concentrated on news from the Swedish learned world, the new venture focused on intellectual news from abroad. The editor was Carl Christoffer Gjörwell, a man of inexhaustible enthusiasm and initiative; aged only twenty-four, he was embarking on a long and prolific career as a publicist. The new journal mostly consisted of articles translated from the German- and the French-language press – in many cases from the German *Göttingische Anzeigen von gelehrten Sachen* – often with added comments by Gjörwell. For Swedish readers from the middling orders without access to the foreign press, the journal must have opened new intellectual horizons.[27]

In June 1756 Gjörwell's *Den Swänska Mercurius* contained an article under the heading 'Amsterdam': 'Here [in Amsterdam], a volume of 332 pages in large octavo was published last year', it began.[28] The book was Rousseau's second discourse, on the origins of inequality, a more challenging work than the first discourse, since Rousseau explicitly put the Christian revelation in brackets in his introduction. Although Gjörwell does not mention his source, the article is an adaptation of the review in the *Göttingische Anzeigen* five months earlier, in January 1756.[29] The German reviewer made ironical comments, but Gjörwell sharpens the criticism and the result is a scathing dismissal; whether or not Gjörwell had actually seen Rousseau's book, we do not know, but the author's ideas must have appeared absurd to him. In Gjörwell's version, more than half of the text deals with the first part of the discourse, about man in the state of nature. Rousseau's vision of 'l'homme sauvage' is caricatured in a

'interdum'] fiebat, uxores cum viro mortuo comburebantur'); reference p.19 to Dalin's *Svea Rikes Historia*. On Sparta and Athens, see p.12-14.

26. *Lärda Tidningar* 13 (1756), p.50-52.

27. On *Den Swänska Mercurius* and Gjörwell (1731-1811) see Otto Sylwan, *Svenska pressens historia till statshvälfningen 1772* (Lund, 1896), p.205-33, and Ingemar Oscarsson, 'Med tryckfrihet som tidig tradition (1732-1809)', in *Den svenska pressens historia*, ed. Karl Erik Gustafsson and Per Rydén, 5 vols (Stockholm, 2000-2003), vol.1, p.114-16.

28. *Den Swänska Mercurius* (1755-1756), p.733-36 ('Här utkom förl[idet] år på 332 s. i st[or] 8').

29. *Göttingische Anzeigen von gelehrten Sachen* (5 January 1756), p.21-23, see Sylwan, *Svenska pressens historia*, p.227. Compare Trousson, 'J.-J. Rousseau et son œuvre dans la presse périodique allemande de 1750 à 1800', I, *Dix-huitième siècle*, 1969, p.298-99, and Peter-Eckhard Knabe, *Die Rezeption der französischen Aufklärung in den 'Göttingischen gelehrten Anzeigen' (1739-1779)* (Frankfurt am Main, 1978), p.207-208.

vein reminiscent of Voltaire's famous letter from 1755 ('Il prend envie de marcher à quatre pattes quand on lit votre ouvrage'[30]). In an added parenthesis, Gjörwell suggests that the right place for a 'Rousseauvian human being' would be the lunatic asylum at Danviken near Stockholm (the Swedish equivalent of Bedlam).

The second part of the discourse, about the transition from the state of nature to civilisation and the rise of inequality, is given only a brief outline, with Gjörwell's comment that the rest of the content and the consequences of Rousseau's principles must be self-evident (implying that they are absurd and pernicious). The discourse is 'an obvious proof of how a sane human being has divested himself, as it were, of his nature, and fallen into a kind of delirium'. Gjörwell hints, in an added conclusion, that the book is irreligious, lacking both 'reason' and 'reverence for the word of God'.[31] All in all, the review conveyed the impression that the author was insane and his work contrary to reason, morals and religion, the latter a crucial point as Gjörwell belonged to the Moravian brethren.

### iii. Baron Scheffer, Professor Linnaeus and Prince Gustav against Jean-Jacques

By 1760 Rousseau was becoming a well-known figure among educated Swedes. In 1759 Gjörwell, reviewing the *Lettre à D'Alembert* in *Den Swänska Mercurius*, called him 'one of our famous writers'.[32] The following year, the historian Olof von Dalin did not find it necessary to mention Rousseau's name when he defended the value of sciences and arts in the preface to the latest volume of his history of the Swedish realm, *Svea Rikes Historia*; the readers would understand who was targeted.[33] In the years 1759 and 1760, three prominent Swedes categorically rejected the Rousseau of the discourses in a group of interrelated texts. They belonged to the court and, once again, to the University of Uppsala.

In April 1759 Baron Carl Fredrik Scheffer set out to refute the first discourse.[34] Unlike the academic Ihre and the publicist Gjörwell, Scheffer belonged to the very highest society. A leading member of the Hat party, he had been Swedish minister in Paris – a springboard for a political

---

30. Voltaire to Rousseau, [30 August 1755], D6451.
31. *Den Swänska Mercurius*, p.736 ('et uppenbart bewis, huru en klok menniskja afklädt sig liksom sin natur, och fallit i et slags yra. Här har intet förnuft, mindre wördnad för Guds ord, fört pennan och styrt tankarne').
32. *Den Swänska Mercurius* (July-September 1759), p.295 ('kan räknas bland wåra namnkunniga Skribenter').
33. Olof von Dalin, *Svea Rikes Historia*, 3 parts in 4 vols (Stockholm, Lars Salvius, 1747-1761). Part 3, vol. 1 (1760), 'Företal'. Compare Lamm, *Upplysningstidens romantik*, p.249.
34. On Carl Fredrik Scheffer (1715-1786), see Göran Nilzén's article in *Svenskt biografiskt lexikon* (Stockholm, 1918-), vol.31, 2001, p.520-26, with detailed references; since 2001, Charlotta Wolff, *Vänskap och makt: den svenska politiska eliten och upplysningstidens Frankrike* (Helsingfors, 2005).

career in eighteenth-century Sweden[35] – before becoming a member of the Swedish government, the 'Council'. In 1756 a bitter conflict opposed the Riksdag, dominated by the Hats, and the royal couple, Queen Lovisa Ulrika, the sister of Frederick the Great, and King Adolf Frederick. One of the crucial points was the education of the crown prince, the ten-year-old Gustav. The Riksdag, which superintended the prince's education according to the constitution, replaced the child's teachers with loyal Hat supporters against the will of his parents. Scheffer became the prince's governor, a prestigious and highly responsible position. During his years in Paris, Scheffer had built a wide network of relations. Back in Sweden, he corresponded in exquisite French with Mme Du Deffand, Fréron, Hénault, D'Alembert and others. He had a keen interest in the political and economic debates of the time and introduced the French physiocrats into Sweden.

Scheffer's refutation of Rousseau's first discourse is an autograph manuscript dated '19 avril 1759' and kept at the National Archives in Stockholm (twenty-one pages in folio).[36] The language is French, the natural means of communication for European aristocratic elites. Scheffer's text does not appear to have been published. One may wonder why he chose to write a systematic refutation of Rousseau's discourse. With his intellectual appetite, he probably wanted to make up his mind about one of the major questions of the day. This was all the more important considering his mandate as the crown prince's governor. If Rousseau was right, it was pointless for a monarch to protect arts and sciences, contrary to the received opinion. By refuting Rousseau, Scheffer clarified his own position as a basis for his teaching. On the following day, 20 April 1759, he wrote a lengthy comment on Helvétius' controversial *De l'esprit*.[37]

He has just re-read Rousseau's famous discourse, Scheffer says in his introduction, and he has also read with utmost care the objections of his opponents and Rousseau's subsequent replies. (He does not, however, indicate which editions he used.) The subject is of paramount importance to every good citizen ('tout bon citoyen'). What is at stake is the attitude of sovereigns towards sciences and arts, and the possibility of enlightening human beings, 'eclairer les hommes'. At first, Scheffer concedes, he was seduced by 'l'eloquence du citoyen de Geneve', but on closer scrutiny he found that the discourse and Rousseau's subsequent replies are full of contradictions: 'J'ai trouvé le pour et le contre etablis et soutenus partout.'[38]

---

35. See Wolff, *Vänskap och makt*, p.122-23.
36. Stockholm, Riksarkivet, untitled manuscript in Schefferska samlingen, C. F. Scheffer, vol.1, f.68-78. Mentioned in Carl Fredrik Scheffer, *Lettres particulières à Carl Gustaf Tessin 1744-1752*, ed. Jan Heidner (Stockholm, 1982), p.37, and Skuncke, *Gustaf III*, p.189.
37. Schefferska samlingen, C. F. Scheffer, vol.1, f.79-81; see also Skuncke, *Gustaf III*, p.189.
38. Schefferska samlingen, C. F. Scheffer, vol.1, f.68-69.

Against Rousseau's discourse, Scheffer uses logical argument. One strategy is to expose Rousseau's internal contradictions by giving an opposite series of quotations: the author attacks sciences and 'savants' in a number of passages, but in other places he speaks well of these same sciences and of 'genies sublimes'.[39] Another strategy is to question the causal relationship between sciences and arts on the one hand and corruption on the other. This relationship should be discussed on two levels: on the one hand, the effects that sciences must always produce ('[l']effet] qu'elles doivent toujours produire'), and on the other hand the effects that they have actually produced in history ('l'effet que les sciences ont réellement produit').[40]

As regards the first, philosophical level, Scheffer develops an optimistic view. True science (as opposed to false science – 'fausses sciences', 'fausses lumieres') necessarily leads to moral good: 'Les sciences ne sont autre chose que l'enchainement des verités. Plus l'esprit se remplit de verités, plus il devient facile à la volonté de se determiner au bien, puisqu'elle ne se determine jamais au mal que par defaut de lumieres.'[41] Regarding the second, historical level, Scheffer maintains that the fact that two things have existed at the same time does not entail that one is the cause of the other. Like the 1754 dissertation, Scheffer's refutation dissociates sciences and arts from corruption.

Besides logical argument, Scheffer invokes a metaphysical argument, the goodness of the Creator, the benevolence of Divine Providence:

Mais un argument plus fort contre M. R[ousseau] et que je n'ai point trouvé allegué par ses adversaires, est ce me semble celui que fournit la bonté de l'etre supreme pour la creature qu'il aime et qu'il veut rendre heureuse autant que le peut comporter sa nature imparfaite et bornée. Nous voyons cette bonté infinie manifestée dans toute l'oeconomie phisique et morale de ce monde.[42]

The Creator, who has given to human beings a fundamental desire for acquiring knowledge, cannot have introduced a germ of corruption into that very desire. Scheffer rejects Rousseau from an optimistic stance: man's desire for knowledge is part of the divine world order. Like many Swedish contemporaries, Scheffer believes both in the blessings of science and in Providence.

Let us move forward in time, five months after Scheffer wrote his refutation. On 25 September 1759 the royal family came to the University of Uppsala on an official visit. King Adolf Frederick and Queen Lovisa Ulrika were there, together with Prince Gustav, aged thirteen, and his little sister Sofia Albertina. Baron Scheffer accompanied his disciple. They were received by the vice-chancellor ('Rector'), who was none other, that

---

39. Schefferska samlingen, C. F. Scheffer, vol.1, f.69-71.
40. Schefferska samlingen, C. F. Scheffer, vol.1, f.72r.
41. Schefferska samlingen, C. F. Scheffer, vol.1, f.72.
42. Schefferska samlingen, C. F. Scheffer, vol.1, f.76.

half-year, than Professor Linnaeus. The morning was spent in one of the main lecture rooms. Linnaeus delivered a grand speech to his royal guests, followed by a 'disputation' where the professor of poetry, Carl Aurivillius, and a twelve-year-old baron defended a set of theses against five opponents.[43]

The vice-chancellor's speech was a vindication of the sciences, and the theses debated at the 'disputation' concerned the value of the sciences and, in particular, of letters. Though Rousseau's name was not mentioned, his criticism was clearly an important target in both the speech and the theses. It is likely that there had been some concerting between the university and the court about the choice of subjects, and that these were settled on with a pedagogical purpose, for the benefit of the crown prince. The language, at Uppsala, would normally have been Latin, as we saw in the case of the 1754 dissertation. For the queen and probably also the king, both of them German, French would have been a natural language. In this case, the scholars used the vernacular Swedish.

Linnaeus' speech is a magnificent piece of oratory. It was printed in large folio format, in an elaborate typography reminiscent of poetry. The speech is a panegyric, indeed a double panegyric, extolling both the sciences and the royal family. At the same time, it is a polemical text putting forth two contentions: sciences are necessary in human society (contrary to what Rousseau claimed in his first discourse), and enlightened rulers protect the sciences. Regarding the first point, Linnaeus enumerates, in several series of anaphoras, the benefits of the different sciences – languages, economics, history, politics, morals, law and so on, fourteen disciplines in all – and the negative consequences where sciences are absent. The anaphoras are emphasised by the typographical layout.

A master of the Swedish language, Linnaeus skilfully uses imagery. One central metaphor is light – sciences – versus darkness – ignorance. 'Sciences enlighten ['uplysa'] us in our whole life', he claims:

SCIENCES are a light, which is as little noticed by those that dwell in it, as it gleams splendidly for those that wander in darkness.
A Human Being, without education, left to himself, is more like a Guenon Monkey than the image of God.
Wild Peoples, Barbarians and Hottentots, are distinct from us only through Sciences; just as a thorny, sour crab is distinct from a tasty reinette only through culture.[44]

---

43. On the visit, see *Den Swänska Mercurius* (October 1759), p.116-18, and Skuncke, *Gustaf III*, p.213-14. For the speech, see Carl Linnaeus, *Tal, vid Deras Kongl. Majesteters Höga Närvaro [...] den 25 Septemb. 1759* (Uppsala, n.d.); modern edition in *Poetiskt och prosaiskt: texter från svenskt 1600- och 1700-tal*, ed. Lars and Carina Burman (Lund, 1992), p.264-72. The theses defended are printed separately in Uppsala [1759], Carl Aurivillius (praes.) / Carl Eduard Taube (resp.), and also in *Den Swänska Mercurius* (above), p.117-18.
44. Linnaeus' speech, introduction: 'Vettenskaper uplysa oss i all vår lefnad'. 'VETTENSKAPER äro ett ljus, som så litet märkes af dem däruti vistas, som det härligen glimmar för dem, som vandra i mörkret. En Menniska, utan upfostran, lämnad sig sielf,

The second and third sentences are implicitly directed against Rousseau's depiction of primitive man in the second discourse. What sets 'us', that is civilised Europeans, apart from 'wild peoples' is sciences. Here Linnaeus uses another central metaphor: culture. From his experience as a botanist he draws the vivid image of the sour wild apple as opposed to the tasty, cultivated reinette apple. In our days, Linnaeus has come under attack from post-colonial scholarship. Mary Louise Pratt, in her book *Imperial eyes*, sees him as a white, imperialist and racist writer.[45] It is perhaps a little unfair to make him responsible for the crimes of subsequent generations. But he certainly believed in the superiority of European civilisation.

The speech was delivered by the head of the University of Uppsala to the Swedish royal family. True, the king had little actual power in Sweden, yet he represented the state; above all, the crown prince was there, and it was important to inculcate in him the right attitude towards learning and universities. The speech is a plea for royal support: a gracious sovereign's protection is as necessary to the sciences as the sun to the peasant's harvest. If the crown prince wants to be remembered by posterity, he should promote sciences and aid those who cultivate them.

Back in Stockholm after his visit to Uppsala, Prince Gustav resumed his studies. Since Scheffer had taken over as governor, his education was strongly French-oriented. One central exercise was letter-writing in French. Scheffer asked questions about morals, politics, history and so on, and every Sunday the boy had to write a letter in answer; Gustav reluctantly complied.[46] On 2 February 1760 Scheffer made him discuss 'les différentes causes qui déterminent & qui créent, pour ainsi dire, les mœurs des hommes'. The teacher mentioned different theories, among them Montesquieu's views on the influence of climate and Rousseau's assertion on the effects of sciences and arts. He omitted the writers' names – they should be obvious to Gustav – and referred to Rousseau as '[u]n autre [écrivain], plus éloquent que Philosophe'.[47] The phrase echoes a criticism in King Stanisław Leszczyński's answer to the first discourse, which Scheffer had undoubtedly read: 'S'il avoit parlé moins en Orateur & plus en Philosophe'.[48] Rousseau is a man of outstanding eloquence but

---

liknar mer en Markatta än Guds beläte. / Ville Folkslager, Barbarer och Hottentotter, skilljas ifrån oss endast med Vettenskaper; liksom en taggig Sur-appel skiljes ifrån en smakelig Renette, endast genom cultur' (typographical layout as in the English translation).

45. Mary Louise Pratt, *Imperial eyes: travel writing and transculturation* (London and New York, 1992), p.24-37. On Linnaeus' anthropology see Gunnar Broberg, *Homo sapiens L. Studier i Carl von Linnés naturuppfattning och människolära* (Uppsala, 1975). See also Lisbet Koerner, *Linnaeus: nature and nation* (Cambridge, MA, 1999).

46. Skuncke, 'Un prince suédois', p.130-37, 153-58.

47. [Carl Fredrik Scheffer], *Commerce épistolaire entre un jeune prince et son gouverneur* (Stockholm, 1771), p.278.

48. 'Réponse au discours qui a remporté le prix de l'Académie de Dijon, par le Roi Stanislas [Leszczyński]', in *Recueil de toutes les pièces qui ont été publiées à l'occasion du discours de M. J. J. Rousseau*, 2 vols (Gotha, 1753), vol.1, p.78.

the substance of his writings is questionable – this view often recurs in Sweden, in the 1754 dissertation, in Scheffer's refutation from 1759 and in Gjörwell's review of the *Lettre à D'Alembert* that same year.

Gustav answered on the next day, 3 February, and the lines on Rousseau are a rhetorical flourish: 'Mais quel dogme plus absurde et si je l'ose dire plus barbare que celui de Monsieur Rousseau de Genève? Quoi! les lettres et les sciences rendraient-elles l'homme moins vertueux? Est-il possible d'admettre un système qui nous replongerait, s'il était adopté, dans notre première barbarie? Tant d'autres écrivains ont réfuté ce système qu'il est inutile de m'y arrêter.'[49] The prince dismisses Rousseau with three rhetorical questions and the exclamation 'Quoi!', conveying indignation. The argument is that Rousseau's system would plunge us back into our primeval barbaric condition, and that so many other writers have refuted it that it is not worth dwelling on. The pupil's blunt rejection – 'absurde', 'barbare' – is far from the governor's careful analysis. Both as an adolescent and as an adult, Gustav himself could be characterised as 'plus éloquent que philosophe'.

In his letter to Scheffer two weeks later, on 17 February, the prince took the initiative to discuss Rousseau's *Lettre à D'Alembert*. It hardly ever happened that Gustav himself suggested a theme to his teacher, but the question of the theatre's *raison d'être* was of vital concern to him; he had a passion for the stage and had already written several plays in French. Against Rousseau, the prince defends the moral value of the theatre, arguing in the traditional way that plays entertain us at the same time as they lead us to virtue and make us hate vice. He takes Corneille as an example: 'Quand on voit la belle tragédie de *Cinna*, on ne peut qu'être touché de la grandeur d'âme d'Auguste, on est extasié. Du moins pour moi, j'aurais voulu être dans le même cas pour avoir pu faire la même action.'[50] Scheffer, who hardly shared his disciple's enthusiasm for the stage, proposed in his answer that love be banned in plays, since 'l'amour sur le Théâtre' leads young people to 'sensibilité' or to 'galanterie'.[51]

The letters which the adolescent grudgingly wrote turned out to be a useful political instrument some ten years later, when Gustav became king after his father's sudden death and a fierce power struggle raged in Sweden. Scheffer's correspondence with Gustav from the years 1759 and 1760 was published in Stockholm in 1771, in a bilingual French–Swedish edition. Other editions followed in Greifswald, Leipzig and Venice, presenting to European opinion the image of an enlightened young prince, acquainted with the *philosophes*.[52]

---

49. Proschwitz, *Gustave III par ses lettres*, p.26 (see above n.2). The editor, G. von Proschwitz, has corrected and modernised Gustav's erratic spelling.
50. Proschwitz, *Gustave III par ses lettres*, p.27.
51. Scheffer, *Commerce épistolaire*, p.304 (1 March 1760).
52. Skuncke, 'Un prince suédois', p.157-58.

Scheffer had left his post as governor when the prince came of age in March 1762, but he went on writing to his former pupil, informing him of the latest developments in the French literary world. In July 1762, he tells Gustav of the turmoil caused by the publication of *Emile*. The Parlement in Paris has condemned the work and the author has been forced to leave France in order to escape pursuit. As a result of this affair, the book's price has risen from 18 to 30 livres. Scheffer has not yet seen it, but he finds the *Parlement*'s condemnation of *Emile* 'très juste, si les principes en sont tels que l'Avocat General les a depeints'.[53]

## iv. An advocate of Rousseau in Gothenburg

While the early Rousseau was rejected at the Swedish court and at the ancient university of Uppsala, he found an advocate in Gothenburg, the second city of the kingdom, a port with lively trade relations, the seat of the Swedish East India Company. In May and June 1759, the newspaper *Götheborgska Magasinet* contained a sympathetic account of Rousseau's second discourse, in stark contrast to the review in Gjörwell's journal three years earlier.[54] A brand-new venture, the Gothenburg paper was edited by Johan Rosén, a versatile personality; he was a learned scholar, a clergyman in the official church, a follower of Swedenborg and a publicist of strong and independent views. His weekly focused on matters of local concern – commercial news, articles on herring fisheries – but it also proved receptive to international novelties. The presentation of Rousseau's discourse was followed that year by an appreciative account of Helvétius' *De l'esprit*.[55]

Rousseau's second discourse was presented in three consecutive issues of the newspaper. The introduction suggests that readers who esteem 'the well-known Rousseau' are morally good, whereas his detractors are depraved: 'a Book, which honours its Author in the minds of all sincere persons; but makes him hateful to those who do not have enough heart to look into their own [heart], and who shrink from the picture because of the hideous pattern that plagues their conscience'.[56] For the first time, the language of sensibility ('sincere', 'heart') resounds in a Swedish presentation of Rousseau.

Rosén devotes his second issue to man in the state of nature, dwelling on the question of primitive language, and adding a presentation of

---

53. Scheffer to Gustav, 5 July 1762, Uppsala University Library, MS F 514.
54. *Götheborgska Magasinet* (1759), no.21-23. See Sylwan, *Svenska pressens historia*, p.349.
55. On J. Rosén (1726-1773) and *Götheborgska Magasinet*, see Sylwan, *Svenska pressens historia*, p.343-60, and Oscarsson, 'Med tryckfrihet som tidig tradition', p.130-31. On Helvétius, see *Götheborgska Magasinet* (1759), no.37-39.
56. No.21, p.167: 'en Bok, som hedrar Författaren i alla upriktigas tankar; men gör honom förhatelig hos dem, som ej äga hjerta nog, at se in i sit eget, och derföre sky målningen, för det ohyggeliga mönstret, som qwäljer deras samwete.'

species at the borderline between apes and humans, like the Pongos who had been described by the traveller Battel and were mentioned by Rousseau. Contrary to Gjörwell, Rosén, in his third issue, gives a substantial account of the transition from the state of nature to civilisation, emphasising the keywords 'inequality' ('olikhet') and 'equality' ('jämlikheten') with boldface in the text. Rosén's anthropological discussion is conveyed in a vivid and fluent Swedish style, without any high-flown philosophical pretensions. Intent both on instructing and entertaining his readers, he proves an excellent populariser.

## v. Fru Nordenflycht's vindication of Woman

The most original Swedish reaction to the early Rousseau came from a noblewoman, Hedvig Charlotta Nordenflycht. In 1762 she published a long poem entitled 'Fruentimrets försvar, emot J. J. Rousseau, medborgare i Genève' ('The defence of Woman against J. J. Rousseau, citizen of Geneva').[57] Fru Nordenflycht was Sweden's leading woman poet, an indomitable lady. She issued collections of her own poems under the transparent pen-name 'the Shepherdess of the North' at a time when Swedish poets seldom published their works in book form. She was the central figure in a circle of writers which included men from the high aristocracy, younger than herself, the counts Creutz and Gyllenborg (she belonged to the lesser nobility). She had a passionate interest in intellectual argument and corresponded with learned men in Europe such as Albrecht von Haller, who reviewed her poems in the *Göttingische Zeitungen*. An ardent feminist, she argued that the Hat party's proposals for educational reform should also include girls.[58]

Fru Nordenflycht's first encounter with Rousseau had been favourable. In 1756 she wrote to Albrecht von Haller about the second discourse, a work that interested her all the more since she herself, she claimed, had expressed similar thoughts two years before Rousseau in one of her own poems.[59] In 1759, however, she read Rousseau's *Lettre à D'Alembert* and found the following footnote: 'Les femmes, en général, n'aiment aucun art, ne se connoissent à aucun, et n'ont aucun Génie. Elles peuvent reussir aux

---

57. In Hedvig Charlotta Nordenflycht, *Witterhets Arbeten*, 2 vols (1762; facsimile edition, Stockholm, 1992).
58. On Hedvig Charlotta Nordenflycht (1718-1763), see Sven G. Hansson, *Satir och kvinnokamp i Hedvig Charlotta Nordenflychts diktning* (Stockholm, 1991), Torkel Stålmarck, *Hedvig Charlotta Nordenflycht – Ett porträtt* (Stockholm, 1997), Ann Öhrberg, *Vittra fruntimmer: Författarroll och retorik hos frihetstidens kvinnliga författare* (Hedemora, 2001). The poet Gustaf Fredrik Gyllenborg is often presented as a follower of Rousseau (e.g. Lamm, *Upplysningstidens romantik*, p.274-308), but as Sten Högnäs has shown there is no proof of any direct influence from Rousseau on the early Gyllenborg: S. Högnäs, *Människans nöjen och elände: Gyllenborg och upplysningen* (Lund, 1988), p.144-47, 163.
59. T. Stålmarck, 'Hedvig Charlotta Nordenflychts brev till Albrecht von Haller och Johan Arckenholtz', *Samlaren* 1959 (16 January 1756), p.106-21 (111-12).

101

petits ouvrages [...]. Mais ce feu celeste qui échauffe et embrase l'ame, ce génie qui consume et dévore, cette brulante éloquence, ces transports sublimes qui portent leurs ravissemens jusqu'au fond des cœurs, manqueront toujours aux écrits des femmes.'[60] As a woman writer, Nordenflycht was infuriated. She wrote to Haller on 29 July 1759: 'je suis un peu piquée contre un de vos Compatriotes monsieur. c'est le celebre Rousseau. il a traité le sexe sans menagement dans sa lettre contre le Theatre. et je suis assez hardi pour l'oser combatre un jour dans ma langue.' Indeed, she set out to refute Rousseau. Her 'Defence of Woman', dedicated to Queen Lovisa Ulrika, was the opening poem in a collection published by her circle of writers. It has been analysed in a recent thesis by Ann Öhrberg.[61]

The poem is written in Swedish alexandrines, with a preface in prose where she appeals to 'enlightened and impartial minds' for support. A central argument in both the letter to Haller and the poem is that Rousseau's view of woman is a result of prejudice. The French term for prejudice, 'préjugé', was a keyword for the *philosophes*. Nordenflycht contends that her own fight against prejudice parallels that of Socrates, of Galileo and of Helvétius – the latter a particularly bold assertion considering Helvétius' controversial status. Nordenflycht enlists her own combat against Rousseau in the cause of the French *philosophes*: she shares their battle against 'les préjugés' ('prejugéer').[62]

Rousseau restricted women's intellectual capacity to 'small' tasks. Nordenflycht's answer is surprisingly modern. What she says, paraphrased in present-day terms, is that woman's current condition results not from her biological nature but from unjust social norms, from unfair power relations between the sexes. Man's predominance has its probable origin 'in the strength of the body, the law of fists, and violence'. But physical superiority does not entail a superiority of the mind. The present 'silliness' of women is due to mistaken education.[63] Nordenflycht develops her argument with powerful pathos. She claims that 'Woman, like Man, is a full human being', and that both are entitled to the same 'human right', in Swedish 'menskjo-rätt' (this is the first recorded use of the word in the Swedish language). She uses metaphors for woman's restricted condition, the stopped-up water-spring that cannot flow, the eagle with broken wings that cannot soar.[64]

---

60. Jean-Jacques Rousseau, *Œuvres complètes*, ed. Bernard Gagnebin and Marcel Raymond, 5 vols, Pléiade edn (Paris, 1995), vol.5, p.94.
61. Stålmarck, 'Hedvig Charlotta Nordenflychts brev', p.114 (original spelling and capitalisation). See Hansson, *Satir och kvinnokamp*, p.96-102, Öhrberg, *Vittra fruntimmer*, p.258-74.
62. Nordenflycht, *Witterhets Arbeten*, p.5 ('uplysta och opartiska sinnen'), p.18-19 (prejudice); see Öhrberg, *Vittra fruntimmer*, p.262.
63. Nordenflycht, *Witterhets Arbeten*, p.16 ('i kroppens kraft i näfrätt och i våld'), p.17.
64. Nordenflycht, *Witterhets Arbeten*, p.14 ('Quinnan liksom Man fullkomlig menskja är'), 15 ('menskjo-rätt'), 17-18 (water-spring, eagle); see Öhrberg, *Vittra fruntimmer*, p.270-73.

After this general discussion, Nordenflycht moves on to examples. Against the citizen of Geneva, she summons a whole army of outstanding women, from Sappho to Mme de Sévigné, Mme du Châtelet and Queen Lovisa Ulrika, in the feminist tradition of the *gynaeceum* (a catalogue of illustrious women).[65] Nordenflycht had hoped to have her poem translated into French, but she died the following year, in 1763, and her audience was limited to Swedish-speaking readers.[66]

## vi. Conclusion

In Stockholm and in Uppsala, between 1754 and 1762, we have found two systematic refutations of Rousseau's first discourse, a scathing review of the second discourse, an implicit rejection of the discourses in an official speech and a refutation of Rousseau's views on women. That Prince Gustav dismissed 'Monsieur Rousseau de Genève' was what his teacher expected of him. Writers like Scheffer, Linnaeus and Nordenflycht rejected Rousseau because his theories posed a fundamental threat to what they considered to be 'Enlightenment'. Rousseau's attacks on civilisation collided head-on with the dominant ideology in mid-eighteenth-century Sweden, an optimistic belief in the blessings of scientific progress, which might be described as a Swedish variant of the 'Enlightenment project' at the north-eastern periphery of Europe.

Rosén's sympathetic review of the second discourse in Gothenburg in 1759 heralds a new approach to Rousseau. In the late eighteenth century, as he became known as the author of *Emile* and the *Nouvelle Héloïse*, Swedish reactions turned enthusiastic.[67] As the cult of nature and sensibility spread under Gustav III's reign in the 1770s and 1780s, a young generation of literary rebels hailed him as one of their heroes. Rousseau's educational views became a source of inspiration. A black boy from the West Indies, Badin, is said to have been brought up at Lovisa Ulrika's court according to the principles in *Emile*. Breast-feeding became fashionable among Swedish ladies in the late eighteenth century. In a long-term perspective, Rousseau's pedagogical theories seem to have exerted considerable influence, direct or indirect, on Swedish educational ideals up to the present day. But that story remains to be explored.

65. Nordenflycht, *Witterhets Arbeten*, p.20-54; see Öhrberg, *Vittra fruntimmer*, p.267-68.
66. Hansson, *Satir och kvinnokamp*, p.103.
67. The change in Swedish reactions to Rousseau between 1762 and around 1780 deserves a study of its own.

ORSOLYA SZAKÁLY

# Enlightened self-interest: the development of an entrepreneurial culture within the Hungarian elite

THE period between 1711 and 1765 was relatively peaceful in the history of Hungary. Calm and increasing prosperity rested on a compromise between the Hungarian estates and the Habsburg rulers. Ever since the Habsburg dynasty acquired the lands of Saint Stephen (which included the kingdoms of Hungary and Croatia) in the early sixteenth century, Hungary had been a constituent part of the Habsburg monarchy. Its status within that monarchy, however, was contested. The Viennese central authorities viewed it as one of the numerous Habsburg provinces while the Hungarian estates[1] considered it as an autonomous entity within the Habsburg monarchy. They regarded it as a country united with the rest of the monarchy only through the person of the monarch. The Hungarian estates successfully hung on to this interpretation throughout the 150 turbulent years of the Ottoman occupation of central Hungary. During this period the Habsburgs' authority extended only to a narrow crescent of western and northern Hungary. This was a costly exercise for the Habsburgs who financed the defence of so-called Royal Hungary, because the revenues from the rump of Hungary could not cover the enormous sums consumed by warfare.[2] When the Ottomans were finally driven out of Hungary in the course of the 1680s and 1690s, the Viennese authorities strove to break the power of the estates and make Hungary pull its weight within the monarchy. The consequence was a revolt on a massive scale that ended in compromise in 1711. The resulting draw restored and consolidated the Habsburgs' royal power in Hungary. It also obliged them, however, to respect the extensive privileges of the estates. These extensive privileges included the right to political representation at diets, the right to decide the level of tax and the number of recruits the Habsburgs were allowed to collect from the territory of Hungary and also

---

1. The estates were dominated by the higher echelons of the nobility. In theory the Hungarian nobility that made up around 4.5 per cent of the population was one and undivided, and encompassed the aristocracy as well as the untitled nobility. In the present chapter I use the expression 'noble enterprise' to mean the economic activity of both aristocrats and untitled nobles.
2. Géza Pálffy, *A tizenhatodik század története*, Magyar Századok (Budapest, 2000), particularly p.70-76.

the tax exemption of the nobility. It also left intact the system of noble counties ('vármegyerendszer') as the lower tier of administration. It meant that local noble officials supervised (or sabotaged if they chose to) the execution of royal decrees, including those relating to tax collection and recruitment. As a result of this settlement, the government in Vienna continuously complained about Hungary's proportionally small share of the fiscal burden of the monarchy.[3]

Conflict between the Hungarian political elite and the Habsburg central authorities was rekindled by the advent of enlightened absolutism in the monarchy. The enlightened experiment was kick-started by the shock of Silesia's loss to upstart Prussia and the Habsburgs' inability to regain that rich province in the War of the Austrian Succession (1740-1748). By the 1760s enlightened reforms yielded results in the Habsburg hereditary provinces inasmuch as they successfully undermined the provincial estates' grip on finances and made resource mobilisation easier for Vienna. Hungary, however, was exempted from the early phase of this reform initiative. It was another fiasco in war, this time the disappointment of the Seven Years War (1756-1763) that turned Maria Theresa's attention to Hungary and its underutilised assets. The new phase of confrontation between ruler and the Hungarian estates, which culminated in the unrest of 1789-1790, started at the diet of 1764-1765. It was then that the Habsburg government attempted to increase Hungary's contribution to the monarchy's budget. The estates flatly refused this design and insisted on their traditional privileges and on the preservation of the old order. This in turn ushered in a quarter of a century of Habsburg rule in Hungary through decrees between 1765 and 1790. Enlightenment in Hungary has to be viewed against this backdrop.

What was actually meant by Enlightenment in Hungary is difficult to define. The secondary literature on the second half of the eighteenth century uses it as a chronological descriptor and talks about the 'Age of Enlightenment' which spans the period roughly between the late 1760s and late 1810s, but without tackling its content.[4] It is clear, however, from the contemporary discourse that the word 'Enlightenment' was used in the French sense of 'seeing clearly' and was seen as a weapon against superstition, which was identified as the main cause of Hungary's relative backwardness within Europe. Superstition, however, referred in this case to outdated practices rather than to religious orthodoxy. Here is just one of the many examples, translated from Ferenc Kazinczy's bombastic Hungarian:

---

3. For an excellent book on Hungary within the Habsburg monarchy in the late eighteenth century, see Éva H. Balázs, *Hungary and the Habsburgs, 1765-1800: an experiment in enlightened absolutism* (Budapest, 1997).

4. One of the recent examples concentrating on the Hungarian literature of the 'Age of Enlightenment' is Ferenc Bíró, *A felvilágosodás korának magyar irodalma* (Budapest, 1994).

Still darkness reigns, my dear friend! Now, when small sources of light appear at a few places it seems to me that the darkness of the caves is even blacker than it was when our whole horizon was in twilight. But it makes me even more resolute in my determination to wrest the bloody dagger from the hand of superstition and unmask its terrible face. Voltaire, Rousseau, Helvetius, the philosopher who resided in Sanssouci and Masonry provide me with my shield, just as the gods did when they were preparing Perseus for his task of freeing Andromeda. My only fear is to be overzealous in my task and hence to decrease my chances of success.[5]

It must be said that in Hungary this discourse was employed in at least three languages: Latin, which was the official language of the country until 1844; German, the language of the central authorities of the monarchy and, between 1785 and 1790, temporarily also the official language of Hungary; and Hungarian. It is not by accident that Hungarian is mentioned last. It was more a target than a medium of enlightened thought. The Hungarian word for Enlightenment, 'felvilágosodás', was coined only in 1789[6] and was a product of attempts to standardise Hungarian in order to meet the requirements of a modern state. It was a mirror translation of the German word 'Aufklärung'. This fact is a clear indication that developments within German, themselves a response to the dominance of the French language, triggered off a reaction within Hungarian circles living in the imperial capital. The publication in 1772 of a play in Hungarian (*Ágis tragédiája*) by György Bessenyei, a member of the Hungarian Royal Noble Guard, is traditionally seen as the starting point of the Hungarian Enlightenment. The impulse came from Vienna. Bessenyei consciously sought to follow the example set by Johann Christoph Gottsched and Joseph von Sonnenfels in their attempts to modernise German. Bessenyei, however, and many other noble and non-noble *literati* who tried to emancipate the Hungarian language and formulate a Hungarian cultural policy looked for inspiration beyond Vienna. Besides German novels, plays and poems, they translated other foreign (primarily French) works of international renown into Hungarian. These ranged from plays by Molière to polemic works by Voltaire and from Milton's *Paradise lost* to poems by Edward Young. Bessenyei's own plays were often inspired by foreign authors but he also produced loose translations of works by Voltaire, Molière, Destouches, Pope, Marmontel and Corneille. Another royal noble

5. Ferenc Kazinczy to György Aranka, Kassa (1790), quoted in Miklós Koroda, *A magyar felvilágosodás breviáriuma* [Budapest, 1944], p.101: 'Nagy még a setétség, kedves Barátom! és nékem úgy látszik, hogy mivel némely helyeken napok támadnak, a barlangok setétjei még feketébbekké válnak, mint eddig voltak míg Egünket estveli homály fogta vala bé. Én meg makacsítottam magamat, kicsikarni a Superstitio kezéből a véres tőrt és irtoztató képéről lekapni az álorcát. Voltaire, Rousseau, Helvetius, a Sanssouciban lakott Philosophus s a Kőművesség úgy adnak paist balomba, mint mikor Perseust készítették fel az Istenek Andromeda megszabadítására. Csak attól tartok, hogy lángoló felgyullásom által el ne rontsam igyekezeteimnek boldogulhatásait.'

6. *A magyar nyelv történeti-etimológiai szótára*, vol.1: *A-Gy*, ed. Lajos Kiss and László Papp, 2nd edn (Budapest, 1985), p.882.

guardsman, Sándor Báróczy, stayed closer to the originals in his translation of one of La Calprenède's romances and short stories by Marmontel, while yet other translators came up with a Hungarian version of the above-mentioned works by Milton and Young. In the latter cases, however, the translators used French translations as their source instead of the English originals.[7]

The idea behind these literary enterprises was that Hungary's obvious backwardness could be eliminated only through education and example, and in order to be successful this had to be conducted and conveyed in the mother tongue. Nevertheless, the Hungarian language first had to be improved as a literary medium. Soon calls for 'national' institutions followed, with Bessenyei himself working out a plan for a Royal Academy of Hungary.[8] This primarily literary movement is the one normally emphasised in connection with the Hungarian Enlightenment. The reason for this is the continuation and spectacular success of the language movement well after our period. It produced a modernised Hungarian vernacular in a matter of decades and culminated in 1844 in Hungarian becoming the official language of Hungary. Understandably, it also resulted in a large volume of secondary literature on the topic, which has tilted the Hungarian scholarly interpretation of the Enlightenment one-sidedly in favour of literary output.[9] The case of language and other causes deemed as nationally important wielded increasing support from the politically active part of the Magyar population and, as we will see, remained one of the few political outlets during the time of the French Revolutionary and Napoleonic Wars. In multinational Hungary this strong emphasis on language and culture had long-term implications, but their analysis would lead far beyond the confines of the present chapter.

The Hungarian Enlightenment, however, was far from exclusively cultural. It had political and economic components as well. The economic element even predated the cultural awakening inasmuch as a growing number of nobles established their own enterprises from the 1760s onwards.

---

7. For details, see Domokos Kosáry's impressive survey of eighteenth-century Hungarian culture: *Művelődés a XVIII. századi Magyarországon*, 3rd extented edn (Budapest, 1996), p.663-84. Shortened English edition: D. Kosáry, *Culture and society in eighteenth-century Hungary* (Budapest, 1987).

8. Béla Tóth, 'Bessenyei György: Jámbor szándék (1790)', in *Magyar könyvek – Magyar századok*, ed. István Kollega Tarsoly (Budapest, 2001), p.158-62. For other aspects of Bessenyei's career: *A szétszórt rendszer: Tanulmányok Bessenyei György életművéről*, ed. Sándor Csorba and Klára Margócsy (Nyíregyháza, 1998).

9. It was also due to the readily available sources. Ferenc Kazinczy, the most prominent individual in the language standardisation movement, did not only publish a considerable number of memoirs and other writings but he also left behind a voluminous correspondence. The latter testifies to the literary network he built up during the last thirty years of his life. *Kazinczy Ferenc összes művei: Levelezés*, ed. János Váczy, 1-19 vols (Budapest, 1890-1909).

## The development of an entrepreneurial culture within the Hungarian elite

A handful of aristocrats founded short-lived industrial enterprises on their estates as early as the 1720s and 1730s. These were primarily broadcloth manufactories such as the enterprise of Counts Ferenc and József Esterházy in Tata, and the two independent cloth manufactories of Count János Pálffy and Count Sándor Károlyi in northern Hungary. Incidentally the two latter aristocrats were the main architects of the compromise of 1711. Count Károlyi also had a rudimentary glassworks between 1722 and 1730. This modest flurry of industrial activity among the aristocrats stopped in the late 1730s, only to restart with a vengeance in the early 1760s.[10] One of the triggers again was provided by Vienna, when Maria Theresa's husband, Francis Stephen of Lorraine, founded a substantial cotton enterprise at Sassin in 1736 and a cotton and majolica manufactory at Holics in 1743.[11] Whether by coincidence or as a belated result of the Habsburg–Lorraine example, not to mention the introduction of state subsidies for enterprises in certain branches of industry, a growing number of noble enterprises were set up. There are many examples of smaller- or larger-scale textile manufactories established by noblemen. Count Antal Forgách's broadcloth works (Gács, 1765-1920) proved to be just the most enduring amongst these. Yet it was another aristocrat, Count Károly Batthyány, who founded the first fully mechanised cotton-spinning works in the Habsburg monarchy.[12] Other establishments made use of natural resources such as iron, alum (a material used in dyeing and tanning) and saltpetre, a component of gunpowder. The prominent Andrássy family (the branch holding the title 'count') made its ironworks a financial success. Alum was gained from the ground in Debrő on Baron József Orczy's estate from the 1780s onwards. The best example for refining natural saltpetre was Baron Miklós Vay's saltpetre factory in Nagykálló and later Debrecen that operated from 1800 until 1856.[13] Most aristocrats and noblemen based their enterprises on raw materials provided by their own estates but some branched out further. Count Tódor Batthyány, a serial entrepreneur, tried his hand in enterprises as

---

10. Gusztáv Heckenast, 'Bányászat és ipar', in *Magyarország története, 1686-1790*, ed. Győző Ember and Gusztáv Heckenast, 2 vols (Budapest, 1989), vol.1, p.639-40.

11. Both Sassin and Holics (Holič) were in northern Hungary near the border with Lower Austria. The more important cotton manufactory in Sassin closed down only in 1849, and the majolica manufactory in Holics was also operating until 1825. Heckenast, 'Bányászat és ipar manufaktúra-korszakunk első szakaszában', in *Magyarország története*, ed. Gy. Ember and G. Heckenast, vol.2, p.1018. Unless otherwise stated the other examples in this paragraph are all from this chapter (p.985-1022).

12. His short-lived factory, based in Burgau in the hereditary lands, used machines built on the model of an English carding and spinning machine. Orsolya Szakály, 'A gépesített pamutipar kezdetei a Habsburg birodalomban: A burgaui fonóüzem, 1790-1808', in *Tanulmányok a 18. század történetéből H. Balázs Éva professzor tiszteletére: Sic Itur ad Astra* (Budapest, 2000), p.225-44.

13. For Miklós Vay's saltpetre enterprise, see O. Szakály, 'Hadiipar és nemesi vállalkozás: A Vay-féle salétromtársaság, 1798-1856', *Levéltári Közlemények* (2000), p.129-65.

diverse as needle production and vitriol making.[14] Some of these noble enterprises proved viable and brought in profit, while some, if not most, were costly flops.

Industrial enterprise, however, was just one of the aspects of the entrepreneurial culture that was developing amidst the Hungarian nobility from the 1760s onwards. The Hungarian nobility had been targeting the wider European market with its agricultural produce for centuries before 1760. There was no social stigma for nobles attached to making money from the lucrative cattle trade to the German territories in the early modern period. In the eighteenth century the cattle trade gave way to the equally profitable export of wheat and wine. Some landowning nobles, particularly the aristocrats of western Hungary with huge estates, showed increasing interest in market-orientated agriculture. Considering the importance of agricultural exports, it is not surprising that another manifestation of the emerging entrepreneurial spirit was assessing the market possibilities all over Europe and trying to form trading companies to maximise the chances of success and spread the risks. The nobility of north and northeast Hungary particularly relished such opportunities. In certain parts, such as the Tokaj-Hegyalja wine region, nobles had been trading their Tokaj wine for well over a century. Many of them were Protestants. After the mid 1730s they were not allowed to take up public office, and therefore economic enterprise and involvement in Church policy were their only two outlets. They were the first to propose a joint Hungarian–Polish trade company, mainly with noble shareholders, in the early 1770s. The aim was to revive the flagging wine trade to the traditional markets for Tokaj wine in Poland and Russia. The venture collapsed after a year. Other similar schemes, all unsuccessful, followed suit.[15]

Gradually an influential minority evolved within the Hungarian nobility that realised that a certain degree of change was necessary in order for Hungary to catch up with the more developed parts of the Habsburg monarchy, let alone the rest of Western Europe. Some came to this realisation through their own personal experiences as entrepreneurs, particularly the problems they encountered in the course of setting up their businesses. These ranged from the lack of available credit to the difficulty of finding workers. Others reached the same conclusion thanks to their studies in Vienna or travels abroad, or through working as bureaucrats in the central administrative institutions governing Hungary (the Hungarian Royal Chancery, the Hungarian Royal Treasury and the

---

14. The needle factory in Vas county employed thirty workers, while the vitriol-producing manufactory gave work to a hundred people. This made the latter one of the largest industrial plants in Hungary, an indication of just how underdeveloped Hungarian industry was at the time.

15. A brief footnote deals with this interesting initiative in É. H. Balázs, *Berzeviczy Gergely, a reformpolitikus, 1763-1795* (Budapest, 1967), p.36.

*The development of an entrepreneurial culture within the Hungarian elite*

Royal Lieutenancy), and the administration responsible for the sole Hungarian seaport of Fiume. These were the individuals (exclusively noble) who played an important role in the execution of Maria Theresa's enlightened policies in Hungary – the implementation of the Urbarial Patent (1767), which regulated the conditions of peasants, and the Ratio Educationis (1777), which involved the wholesale reform of the education system. The number of these reform-minded administrators was boosted during Joseph II's reign, after his Edict of Toleration in 1781, when Protestant enlightened nobles flocked to serve the new monarch.

These Hungarian nobles, Catholics and Protestants alike, were the ones best acquainted with political and economic discourse in Europe. Many of them embarked on a version of the Grand Tour and informed themselves at first hand in Britain or France. Others benefited from reading and also from contacts with men at the Habsburg court who devoted their life to the study of economic theories and their potential implementation in the Habsburg monarchy. A good example of such a man was Count Karl von Zinzendorf, who visited all the major European states and the various Habsburg lands in order to learn about all matters economic. On 27 December 1778 Zinzendorf wrote the following entry in his diary: 'I was with Kaunitz [at his residence] and we discussed Adam Smith. He likes certain things about him, and he dislikes other aspects. He agrees with the division of labour but he has a few reservations.'[16] State Chancellor Wenzel Anton von Kaunitz was hugely influential. Together with Maria Theresa and her co-regent Joseph II, this colourful personality was responsible for forming the policy of the Habsburg monarchy at the highest level. He was convinced that studying the economy of Western European states was relevant for the Habsburg monarchy. He gathered able men around him for this very purpose. Zinzendorf was a member of his circle. According to all indications, Chancellor Kaunitz and his protégé, Zinzendorf, were considering the recently published German translation of the *Wealth of nations* on the above-mentioned evening in December. Two Hungarian counts were also present in the company, and on other days many other Hungarians frequented similar events.[17] These Hungarians were keen to learn about the theories discussed and continued debating these issues at home with family members, friends, fellow noble bureaucrats and entrepreneurs. Zinzendorf was especially appreciated by Hungarians, partly because he was convinced that Hungary actually contributed fairly to the Habsburg budget, and

16. Quoted by É. H. Balázs, 'Európai gazdaságpolitika – Magyar válasz', in *Életek és korok: Válogatott írások*, ed. Lilla Krász (Budapest, 2005), p.264-73 (269).

17. The two Hungarian counts present were the maverick Count János Fekete and the future Hungarian chancellor Count Károly Pálffy. For Zinzendorf and Kaunitz's ideas on economic reform, see Grete Klingenstein, 'Between mercantilism and physiocracy: stages, modes, and functions of economic theory in the Habsburg monarchy, 1748-1763', in *State and society in early modern Austria*, ed. Charles W. Ingrao (West Lafayette, IN, 1994), p.181-214.

that its seemingly small share accurately reflected its actual economic backwardness. This view, probably correct, was shared by the members of the Hungarian elite.

It is well known and also borne out by the above quotation that Adam Smith's fame as an authority on political economy, established with the publication of the *Wealth of nations* in 1776, quickly extended to the Habsburg monarchy.[18] His book was regarded as the key text to the understanding of British economic success. In 1778, as we have seen, a German translation of the *Wealth of nations* appeared in two volumes in Leipzig and those who preferred French could read a full French edition after 1781.[19] It comes as no surprise that Adam Smith, among others, featured in the second edition of Joseph von Sonnenfels' *Grundsätze der Polizey, Handlung, und Finanzwissenschaft*, a textbook whose aim was to acquaint future bureaucrats of the monarchy with up-to-date European economic discourse.[20]

The reception of Adam Smith in Hungary, I believe, is symptomatic of the Hungarian Enlightenment. It demonstrates how enlightened Hungarians picked and chose from the large corpus of works associated with the Enlightenment, and it shows that they were almost entirely motivated by practical considerations. Adam Smith's book reached the multilingual Hungarian elite too, which read it either in the original English, or in German or French translation. The outstanding authorities on economic questions in Hungary, such as Count János Szapáry, Pál Almássy, Baron József Podmaniczky and Miklós Skerlecz, were certainly well acquainted with this work.[21] They were all high-ranking bureaucrats in the Hungarian administration. It was one of the noble entrepreneurs, however, Baron Miklós Vay,[22] a well-travelled Hungarian aristocrat from northeastern Hungary, who proposed the translation of the *Wealth of nations* into Hungarian. In November 1791 in a letter to one of the most prominent figures of the Hungarian Enlightenment, Count Ferenc Széchényi, Vay made the following suggestion:

> At present, I am spending my solitary days at Golop [his estate] which is at a charming location. I pass my time partly overseeing my estate and partly by

---

18. This happened despite Smith's protestations against being regarded as an 'oeconomist'.

19. For the different editions of Adam Smith's works in English and in other languages, see *A Critical bibliography of Adam Smith*, ed. Keith Tribe (London, 2002).

20. Klingenstein, 'Between mercantilism and physiocracy', p.197. The second edition of Sonnenfels' *Grundsätze der Polizey, Handlung, und Finanzwissenschaft* was published in Vienna in 1787.

21. É. H. Balázs, 'Economistes d'origine aristocratique: un phénomène hongrois: physiocrates et pseudo-physiocrates en Hongrie à la fin du XVIII$^e$ siècle', in *Intellectuels français, intellectuels hongrois XIII$^e$-XX$^e$ siècle*, ed. Jacques Le Goff and Béla Köpeczi (Budapest and Paris, 1985), p.165-73.

22. For Vay's biography, see O. Szakály, *Egy vállalkozó főnemes: Vay Miklós báró, 1756-1824* (Budapest, 2003).

## The development of an entrepreneurial culture within the Hungarian elite

reading a very good book. It is Adam Smith's *An Inquiry into the nature and causes of the Wealth of nations*. I am truly amazed by this author's depth of argumentation. Your Excellency should take this book to Zenk [Nagyzenk, the centre of the Széchényi estates] next year because it has to be read in the countryside. There one has the time to contemplate the profound meaning of this work.

If Your Excellency will learn to appreciate this book as much as I have done, you will see that it is impossible not to erect a monument amongst the Hungarians to the memory of Adam Smith by having this book translated into the language of our nation. – This outstanding work by the above-mentioned scholar had already been translated by almost all important nations in Europe. And the nations have hugely benefited from this. Why should we fall behind them? This work provides a fundamental analysis of the progress of nations and it is obvious that making it available would render manifold advantages both for our King and for our country. Hence such an undertaking is imperative. – I would embark on the translation today but I do not have either the time or the patience, and I also feel my inadequacy for such a task.

But how much praise would be showered upon the Hungarian scholar who could translate this priceless book in a way that it does not lose any of its value in the translation! It would also further increase Your Excellency's already well-established reputation as a promoter of the Arts and Sciences if you could commission a Hungarian scholar [...] to translate it. By doing so you would make it possible for Hungarians who do not speak any other languages to read this well-structured presentation of insights into human society.[23]

Széchényi's reply to this letter is lost (or was never written) but we can assume that he took an interest in the *Wealth of nations*. He might have read it when he was preparing to visit Adam Smith in Scotland in the mid 1780s. The meeting took place, although Széchényi did not elaborate

---

23. Hungarian National Archives (Budapest), Archives of the Széchenyi family, Core Archive, P 623, 9, 'Correspondentia familiae C. Széchenyi: Familiares'. 'A letter written by Baron Miklós Vay to Count Ferenc Széchényi', Golop, 21 November 1791, f.285-86: 'Most itt töltöm magános napjaimat Golopon, melly is természeti situsára nézve egy igen kies hej [*sic*]. Rész szerint a gazdasággal rész szerint egy igen jó könyv olvasásával töltöm időmet. Adam Smith. An inquiry into the Nature and Causes of the Wealth of Nations. – Nem győzök eléggé bámulni ezen auctor fundamentomos okoskodása Méllységén. Nossza vigye ki ezen könyvet magával Excellentiad, jövő Esztendőn Zenkre, mert ezen könyvet mezőn kell olvasni, ott a hol az észnek, a dolog veleje körűl való rágodásra ideje vagyon. Ha ezen könyvet Excellentiád úgy meg szereti mint én, lehetetlen lészen, hogy ezen Könyvnek nemzetünk nyelvére lejendő forditatásával, Adam Smithnek emlékezetire, Excellentiád a magyarok között is oszlopot ne emellyen. – A fent nevezett Tudósnak ezen remek munkáját, már tsak nem minden Európai fényesebb nemzetek, magok különös hasznára evvel megtisztelték, miért maradnánk ki, mi is közzülök, midőn a nemzetek előmenetele okai illy fundamentumos visgalasának, mind a Királyra mind az országra el terjedő sok féle hasznait – sőt szükséges voltát, nyilván láthattyuk. – Én ma hozzá fognék forditásához, de sem időm sem patientiam a forditáshoz nints, és erre elégtelenségemet világosan érzem is. Be nagy ditsiretet érdemelne az a Magyar tudós, aki ezt úgy tudná forditani, hogy a forditással a könyv érdeme semmit ne veszittsen. – Nevelné Excellentiad, minden tiszta szivekbe önnön maga, a Tudományok elő mozditására mind eddig hasznosan folytatott foglalatosságinak érdemit azzal, ha ezen nagy hasznú könyvet, valamellyik érdemes magyar Tudós által [...] fordittatná, – s ezzel, a más nyelvet nem tudó Magyaroknak, az ezen könyvbe olly szép rendbe szedett, s az emberi társaságba igazságoknak olvasására, utat és módot szolgáltatna.'

in his travel diary on what happened.[24] Miklós Vay, like Ferenc Széchényi, visited Britain. He could ill afford this trip but viewed his long stay there as a splendid investment for the future. In 1788 Vay returned to Hungary with, amongst many others things, the design of a state-of-the-art cotton-spinning machine and an elegant leather-bound edition of the *Wealth of nations* in three volumes.[25] Vay was not only interested in economic theory but also in economic practice. He established his own enterprises. In the early 1790s, around the time when he wrote to Széchényi, he turned his attention to the design of the cotton-spinning machine he had bought in London. He sold it on to one of his friends, Count Károly Batthyány, a fellow aristocrat. As we have seen above, Batthyány founded the first completely mechanised cotton manufacture of the Habsburg monarchy which operated machines built on the British design. Vay took an active part in the initial phase of the enterprise and acted primarily as a consultant.

Vay was a Protestant aristocrat of modest means while Batthyány was a rich Catholic magnate. They were just two examples of the nobles who were directly involved in some type of business enterprise, be it agricultural or industrial. They worked closely with fellow noble bureaucrats and landowners, many of whom supported such enterprises by investing their money in manufactories and companies. Within their circles, especially in Masonic lodges, a new programme of government was taking shape in the 1780s. They all shared the conviction that the Hungarian political, economic and social system was not viable. Moderate reforms, especially in the field of the economy, they hoped, would defuse social tensions and bring economic prosperity. Their model state was the constitutional monarchy of Great Britain, the political structure of which – they believed – had much in common with Hungarian 'parliamentarianism'. They saw Britain as an oligarchy, where aristocrats and the gentry not only benefited from political power and patronage, but also freely enjoyed the fruits of economic enterprise. By the second half of Joseph II's reign in the late 1780s, his reforms were becoming ever less compatible with Hungarian nobles' values, including those of the enlightened minority. The final straw was Joseph's proposed tax reform, which would have put an end to the nobility's tax exemption. Even before this the enlightened nobles resented the Habsburgs' protectionist economic policies, and their own inability to influence economic decisions concerning Hungary. Their pet target for scorn was the Habsburg answer for Hungary's allegedly small contribution to the monarchy's budget – a dual system of tariffs. This system was introduced in the mid 1750s. It penalised Hungarian

---

24. Hungarian National Archives (Budapest), Archives of the Széchenyi family, Core Archive, P 623, 12, 'Descriptio itineris seu peregrinationis C. Francisci Széchényi per Germaniam, Belgium, Galliam et Scotiam'.

25. These volumes today are in the library of the Calvinist College in Sárospatak (Hungary), and Vay's personal papers are kept in the archives of the College.

agricultural products that went to markets outside the monarchy. It also cut off the supply of manufactured goods to Hungary from beyond the monarchy, in the case where goods were produced elsewhere in the Habsburg monarchy, particularly in the 'hereditary lands' of Austria and Bohemia. Such products were, at least in the beginning, more expensive and of worse quality. The dual aim of this tariff system was to protect the budding industry of the hereditary lands and to punish the Hungarian estates economically for their continual lack of co-operation. This system of tariffs, which was riddled with contradictions, went through several modifications but continued to be enforced. The Hungarian estates unanimously resented Hungary's treatment merely as a source of cheap primary products for the hereditary lands. Within their ranks, the enlightened nobles hoped to integrate Hungary into a wider European market, where the country could develop its full potential. What they were hoping for was trade liberalisation on their own terms. This was an important consideration, especially since it affected many of them personally through their enterprises.

The economic demands of these enlightened nobles, like all their other demands, were focused exclusively on Hungary – the only context they ever willingly considered. This antagonism set the former Josephists and Joseph II on a collision course and led to co-operation between the conservative and the reformist nobles that culminated in a conspiracy against Habsburg rule in Hungary in the final year of Joseph's reign. Joseph II's successor, Leopold II, was a shrewd operator, who through international concessions and domestic manoeuvres restored calm in Hungary. The Hungarian estates, however, were offered a chance to have their say when the diet of 1790-1791 set up nine committees, so-called 'deputations', in order to survey the situation in Hungary and propose improvements. One of these was the 'commercial deputation' ('deputatio regnicolaris in commercialibus').[26] In theory, here was a chance for the Hungarian elite to influence economic regulations. The economic committee's deliberations and draft proposals provide a unique snapshot of the state of the Hungarian economy and, from our point of view more importantly, into the mindset of the economic experts within the Hungarian elite. Here we find the former Josephists again. Notable members included high-ranking bureaucrats such as Miklós Skerlecz, Baron József Podmaniczky and Pál Almássy working under the direction of Count

---

26. These committees were composed of high-ranking bureaucrats who were considered experts on the individual committee's field. There was a fine balance between enlightened and conservative noble members in each committee. Apart from the commercial committee, there was a political committee which was to work out a new constitutional framework and an administrative structure for Hungary within the monarchy. The other seven committees covered all aspects of Hungarian life ranging from culture to tax issues and from church matters to the re-regulation of serf–lord obligations. For the diet of 1790-1791, see Henrik Marczali, *Az 1790-1791. országgyűlés*, 2 vols (Budapest, 1907).

Miklós Forgách as president. (He was a close relation of Count Forgách's who had established a textile manufacture on his estate in the early 1760s.) These were the very people who had been urging economic policy to be changed by removing restrictions on Hungarian exports and imports, and who regularly cited Adam Smith as their authority.

The actual committee work took place in two phases between August 1791 and January 1793, and it was accompanied by a public consultation. The committee welcomed proposals and received numerous memoranda from towns, bureaucrats, academies, the Catholic, Calvinist and Lutheran Churches, and many private individuals, including especially nobles.[27] Vay's above-quoted letter wished to contribute to this economic debate by making Adam Smith's *Wealth of nations* available in Hungarian to the wider reading public. Vay's aspirations were primarily economic but by proposing a translation he also wanted to further the standardisation of the Hungarian language. For him this was a natural demand since he came from the purely Hungarian milieu of Borsod county in north-eastern Hungary.

The draft proposal by Miklós Skerlecz that emerged by the end of the committee's existence in 1793 was first and foremost a survey of the situation of the Hungarian economy which included a balance of trade. It was partly a detailed refutation of the Habsburg claim that Hungary contributed to the monarchy's finances below its economic potential. It also condemned the Viennese government for keeping Hungary in a 'colonial state' economically through the system of tariffs. It proposed abolishing that system and giving Hungarian goods access to the best markets (be they within or outside the monarchy). This was a demand for the long-desired trade liberalisation. This trade liberalisation, however, was to be coupled with protectionist measures in order for the Hungarian industry to develop. In fact, the draft proposal hoped to introduce a policy very similar to the one it condemned in the case of the monarchy as a whole. But this policy was entirely centred on the kingdom of Hungary.[28] This shows that, although the Hungarian enlightened nobility was well informed about the economic discourse of contemporary Europe and was in the habit of making references to the economic authorities of its day, its actual proposal for change intended to imitate an example much closer to home, that of Vienna. It was much more relevant to the Hungarian reality on the ground and offered a better chance of success.

27. D. Kosáry, 'Pest-Buda és a Kereskedelmi Bizottság 1791-ben', in *Tanulmányok Budapest Múltjából XI* (Budapest, 1956), p.127-52.

28. The documents relating to the work of the commercial deputation, including the draft proposal, are all in Hungarian National Archives, Archivum Regni, N 104, 'Deputatio regnicolaris in commercialibus, 1790-1793', facsimile 1-12. The draft proposal was published in Hungarian in *Skerlecz Miklós báró művei*, ed. Pál Berényi (Budapest, 1914).

Other thinkers who figured in enlightened discourse also received a special spin in Hungary. Voltaire's anti-clericalism made a strong impact, especially in Protestant circles, although without reference to his praise of strong central royal power.[29] Montesquieu was popular from the start as the champion of noble power who had kind words to say about the Hungarian nobility.[30] Most intriguingly, a modified version of the arguments presented in Rousseau's *Contrat social* caught on in Hungary where the 'people' were equated with the Hungarian nobility. Resistance to Joseph II's rule in 1789 and 1790 was legitimised by stating that Joseph II broke the social contract between the ruler and the people (in this case the Hungarian estates) and called for his successor, Leopold II, to sign a new contract in the form of a coronation diploma.[31]

The Enlightenment in Hungary was marked by a painful awareness of Hungary's relative backwardness within Europe and even within the Habsburg monarchy. The vast majority of the Hungarian nobles believed that all was well and that they lived in the best of all worlds. A small minority, however, was confronted with the fact that the status quo was unsustainable in the long run. It comprised well-positioned individuals searching for models to implement in order for Hungary to maximise its potential without undermining the political, social and economic dominance of the nobility within the kingdom of Hungary. These individuals looked primarily to the most developed parts of Europe, the centre, but also followed developments closely in Prussia and Poland, and were aware of what was going on in Spain and on the Italian peninsula. They found the most relevant example, however, in the much-criticised Habsburg policies.

By the time the committees produced their final reports in early 1793, even the illusory chance of a Hungarian impact on central policy-making had vanished. The reports of the nine committees were shelved. During the French Revolutionary and Napoleonic Wars reform in general – and economic reform in particular – was taken off the agenda. In this period, former Josephists were silenced politically, but those who had enterprises flourished financially. The Napoleonic Wars created an economic boom in Hungary and the noble entrepreneurs were best placed to benefit from

---

29. László Ferenczi, 'Voltaire a XVIII. századi Magyarországon', in '*Sorsotok előre nézzétek': A francia felvilágosodás és a magyar kultúra: Tanulmányok*, ed. Béla Köpeczi and László Sziklay (Budapest, 1975), p.183-200.

30. Bk 8, ch.9 of *De l'esprit des lois* where Montesquieu praised the Hungarian nobility made his book such an instant success in Hungary that it was allegedly translated into Latin and sold in bookshops in Hungary already in the early 1750s. This translation, mentioned in only one source, has not yet been identified. A Hungarian version, however, was published in 1833. Balázs, *Hungary and the Habsburgs*, p.134.

31. Kálmán Benda, 'Rousseau és Magyarország', in *Emberbarát vagy hazafi: Tanulmányok a felvilágosodás korának magyarországi történetéből* (Budapest 1978), p.351-63. Sándor Pukánszky, *Természetjog és politika a XVIII. századi Magyarországon: Batthyány Alajostól Martinovicsig* (Budapest, 2001).

this. The boom marked a shift from interest in economic theory and practice, solely to practical enterprise.[32] Moreover, it temporarily removed the imperative for change and gave a new lease of life to the existing socio-economic system based on privileges. This might have been one of the reasons which removed the urgency of a Hungarian translation of the *Wealth of nations*. In the event, Adam Smith's book appeared in Hungarian in 1891,[33] exactly one hundred years after Vay wrote his letter to Count Széchényi.

32. The sole but important exception to this was Gergely Berzeviczy who kept working in self-imposed internal exile on his estate and published on issues concerning the Hungarian economy. For his career to 1795, see Balázs, *Berzeviczy Gergely* (Budapest, 1967) and most recently also her 'Berzeviczy Gergely: *De Commercio et Industria Hungariae* (1797)', in *Magyar könyvek – Magyar századok*, ed. I. Kollega Tarsoly (Budapest, 2001), p.170-75.
33. Adam Smith, *Vizsgálódás a nemzeti vagyonosság természetéről és okairól* (Budapest, 1891).

MARTIN FITZPATRICK

# The view from Mount Pleasant: Enlightenment in late-eighteenth-century Liverpool

So long as frugal industry prevails,
And punctual honour guides her virtuous sons,
So long as innocence, and modest worth,
Enhance the native beauties of the FAIR,
So long shall LEVERPOLIA'S wealth increase,
Her stately structures and extensive trade;
Still, in the bosom of her crouded port,
Receive the tribute of each foreign clime;
To ev'ry realm unfurl her swelling sails,
And be th' EMPORIUM of the western world.

So wrote George Perry in his poem *The Prophecy of commerce*. Perry had been working on a history of Liverpool, but died before it could be completed. That was left in the capable hands of Reverend William Enfield. He had been a minister at the Benn's Garden chapel, the home of a congregation of liberal Protestant Dissenters in Liverpool, before moving to Warrington to teach at the new Dissenting academy and to be minister at the Sankey Street Dissenting chapel. Enfield shared Perry's enthusiasm for Liverpool. *An Essay towards the history of Leverpool*, the first history of Liverpool, was first published in 1773.[1] Enfield felt he had good reason to regard Liverpool as a town with special potential: it was a salubrious place, enjoying a mild climate with sea breezes dispelling diseases; it had its fair share of impressive buildings, it had the most advanced docks of the time; it was well policed, its people were well looked after and its wealth and population was growing at a rapid pace.[2] His history of Liverpool contributed to perceptions of the town as an enlightened place. The Welshman David Samwell wrote to his friend in Liverpool, Matthew Gregson, that everything in Liverpool was 'on the

---

1. William Enfield, *An Essay towards the history of Leverpool, drawn up from the papers of the late George Perry, and from other materials collected since*, 2nd edn (London, printed for Joseph Johnson, 1774).
2. Enfield estimated the population to be 34,407 and that it had increased by 'considerably above one-third' in the previous twenty years, *History of Leverpool*, p.24-25.

improving plan' and that 'as you have entirely made a new town of it, you are resolved to have a new name.'[3] Enfield had used the spelling Leverpool, following the etymological notes of Perry. The spelling was, however, old rather than new and it did not catch on. In all other respects Samwell could have been echoing Enfield who wrote that 'the extension of commerce, and the consequent increase in wealth, have introduced a taste for ornament and splendour, which has of late appeared in a variety of forms, and particularly in its buildings both public and private.'[4]

Enfield was a modest man and was anxious to credit George Perry with the ambition of creating 'a connected and complete history'. Yet his own contribution was very much that of a man in touch with currents of Enlightenment thought on matters such as health, population and commercial activity. He was not satisfied with anecdotal information but wanted proper empirical evidence.[5] The result is that his history differs from many urban histories of the time. They are often antiquarian in content and/or are descriptive of a particular town or city – listing such elements as parishes, churches, other buildings, manufactures, the liberties of the corporations, charities, clubs and so on.[6] What they do not usually have is genuine narrative history, or detailed information and analysis of the various aspects of life in the town. Enfield has something of both.

One particularly interesting feature of Enfield's history is that, following Perry, he was not content to rely on readily available evidence, but was anxious to collect new data and where necessary draw on research and experimentation. Here he was assisted by a like-minded enquirer after truth for he included in the history contributions on the temperature of the air and the sea at Liverpool by Matthew Dobson, M. D. (1732-1784), physician to Liverpool Infirmary.[7] Dobson exemplified two key features

3. Liverpool Record Office (hereafter cited as LRO), Gregson Papers, Samwell–Gregson Correspondence, MS GRE 2/17/4, David Samwell to Matthew Gregson, 25 March 1774. David Samwell's main claim to fame would be his voyaging as a surgeon with Cook on his third expedition and his influential account of Cook's death. See Martin Fitzpatrick, Nicholas Thomas and Jenny Newell, *David Samwell: the death of Cook and other writings* (Cardiff, 2006).

4. Enfield, *History of Liverpool*, p.20.

5. Enfield, *History of Liverpool*, p.v-vi. Rosemary Sweet argues that Enfield should be described, as he described himself, as the editor. Without Perry's work the history would never have seen the light of day. Enfield was responsible for the arrangement of the work and for adding new materials to it. I have chosen not to describe the history as 'their' history since, although many of my assertions may also apply to Perry, I am confident that all of them apply to Enfield. See Rosemary Sweet, *The Writing of urban histories in eighteenth-century England* (Oxford, 1997), p.129, n.72.

6. The contemporary histories I have searched are of Manchester, Newcastle-upon-Tyne, Bristol and Birmingham. For a systematic study of urban histories, see Sweet, *The Writing of urban histories*.

7. Matthew Dobson, physician and natural philosopher, was the son of Joshua Dobson (c.1692-1767), minister of New Mill, Lydgate, near Todmorden, Yorkshire, from 1715 to

of Enlightenment in Liverpool: the importance of religious Dissent and of the connection with Scottish Universities.

Matthew Dobson came from a Dissenting background in the north of England; his father was a minister and his mother was the daughter of a minister. He studied medicine at Glasgow University where he was inspired by the work of William Cullen, whom he assisted in his experiments on evaporation. After graduating at Glasgow in 1753, Dobson continued his studies at the Edinburgh medical school, becoming a member of the Medical Society and gaining his title of Doctor of Medicine in 1756 with a thesis on menstruation. He settled in Liverpool around 1759 or 1760 and was appointed to the infirmary in 1770. Like Cullen, Dobson was interested in the comparative aspects of his work. He kept in touch with Cullen and other leading practitioners.[8] His own research led him to discover that the urine of diabetic patients contained sugar. He concluded that diabetes was not a disease of the liver or kidneys but was a form of imperfect digestion or assimilation affecting the entire body. As to his observations on the climate and geography of Liverpool, they were somewhat optimistic: 'the dryness of the soil, the purity of the waters, the mildness of the air, the antiseptic effluvia of pitch and tar, the acid exhalations from the sea, the frequent brisk gales of wind, and the daily visitations of the tides, render Leverpool one of the healthiest places in the kingdom, in proportion to the number of the inhabitants.'[9]

Climate was not the only reason why Enfield regarded Liverpool as an advantaged place. There were many examples he could draw on of enlightened philanthropy and civility. As Liverpool grew prosperous its citizens created philanthropic institutions and sought to promote a polite and civilised urban environment.[10] It was a participant in the urban renaissance which appealed both to enlightened charitable instincts and enlightened self-interest. Enfield could find many noteworthy achievements from the founding of the Bluecoat Hospital in 1709 to the building

---

1720, and of Cockey Moor Chapel, Ainsworth, near Bolton, Lancashire, from 1732 to 1767, and Elizabeth Smith (d.1767), daughter of Reverend Matthew Smith, Independent minister of Mixenden, Yorkshire. Margaret DeLacy, 'Dobson, Matthew (1732-1784)', *Oxford Dictionary of National Biography* (hereinafter cited as *ODNB*).

8. Dobson was appointed to the infirmary in same year as another pupil of Cullen, Dr John Bostock. A student at Warrington Academy before training in Edinburgh, Bostock contributed tables of diseases and deaths in Liverpool in 1772 to Enfield's *History of Leverpool* (p.29-32). His son, John Bostock junior, also trained as a doctor and played an important role in Roscoe's programme of enlightened reforms. Norman Moore, 'John Bostock (1744?-1774), revised by Kay Bagshaw, *ODNB*; M. B. Emanuel, 'John Bostock, junior (1772-1846)', *ODNB*.

9. Enfield, *History of Leverpool*, p.38.

10. James Wallace confirms that Liverpool was a well-policed and well-ordered place, noteworthy considering it was a port: *A General and descriptive history of the ancient and present state of the town of Liverpool* (Liverpool, printed for and sold by R. Phillips, sold also by W. Richardson, London, 1795), p.275.

of the Exchange designed by John Wood in 1748[11] and the founding of the Liverpool library in 1758. His history, however, was published at a time when the broad consensus between the various interests within the town was under threat and urban renaissance appeared to be coming to an end. This idea has been examined by Jon Stobart in an impressive paper on 'Culture versus commerce' to which I shall now turn.[12]

The historian of the urban renaissance of the eighteenth century, Peter Borsay, has argued that the movement affected not only towns which catered for the activities of the growing leisured classes, but also commercial and manufacturing centres, notably Birmingham, Manchester and Liverpool. These towns 'far from being obsessed only with the pursuit of work and money, were centres (even pioneers) of fashionable culture'.[13] Stobart endorses and develops Borsay's argument. He agrees that Liverpool exemplified many contemporary trends: 'by the third quarter of the eighteenth century (it) had all the characteristics of cultured urban life', including impressive public spaces, assembly rooms, an active literary, theatrical and musical life, libraries, clubs and learned societies, and philanthropic institutions.[14] It had a wealthy corporation more than willing to spend money on civic improvement, and 'a growing number of middle-ranking merchants, professionals and tradesmen who were happy to subscribe to and patronise its cultural facilities and institutions'. Yet Stobart also suggests that cultural activities suffered in the last two decades of the century when commercial and industrial activities successfully competed for the public spaces enjoyed by the leisured classes.[15]

The notion that commerce was hostile to Enlightenment was expressed by an emerging figure in Liverpool Enlightenment circles at the very time Enfield was prefixing his history with George Perry's poem celebrating commerce. This was William Roscoe, son of a local innkeeper and market gardener. In his poem, 'Mount Pleasant' (Mount Pleasant was on the outskirts of Liverpool, from where one could look down on the town), he argued that commerce initially derived from mutual want; innocent peoples welcomed the trading strangers with open arms. It promised:

---

11. See Tim Mowl and Brian Earnshaw, *John Wood, architect of obsession* (Huddersfield, 1988), p.164-68. Wood was assisted by his son John. The authors note that Wood was 'in his active prime'. The Exchange was completed in 1754 and opened with a 'splendid ball, graced by the presence of three hundred and forty ladies'. See Peter Borsay, *The English urban renaissance: culture and society in the provincial town* (Oxford, 2002; reprint of Oxford, 1989), p.157, 342.

12. Jon Stobart, 'Culture versus commerce: societies and spaces for elites in eighteenth-century Liverpool', *Journal of historical geography* 28:4 (2002), p.471-85.

13. Peter Borsay and Angus McInnes, 'The emergence of a leisure town: or an urban renaissance?', *Past and present* 126 (1990), p.189-202 (192); see also Borsay, *The English urban renaissance*, p.30, 98, 157, 290, 342.

14. Stobart, 'Culture versus commerce', p.473-74.

15. Stobart, 'Culture versus commerce', p.474-75.

once to bind
In leagues of strictest amity, mankind.

But commerce had become a 'bloated monster', had thrown away the olive branch, grasped 'the red sword' and become the means of imperial oppression in Africa and India. The virtues of 'innocence and modest worth' had been lost with the development of commerce.[16] Roscoe did not deny that Liverpool had become an enlightened place. Genuine taste had bloomed, and the arts had 'chosen [...] their blest retreat' there. Gothicism had been eclipsed by classicism and knowledge had progressed:

> Reviving science opes her latent mines,
> The judgment ripens, and the thought refines.

The Muses had softened manners and loosened the 'chains of avarice'. The erection of the Theatre Royal by public subscription made Liverpool attractive to the virtuous, and Liverpool was the home of charitable action which had created a public infirmary, an almshouse next to the infirmary and the Blue Coat Hospital (for orphans).

Thus far Enfield and Roscoe could agree. The view from Mount Pleasant had many pleasing features. Roscoe, however, worried about the consequences of the rapid acquisition of wealth, of 'adding gold to gold' and swelling the 'shining pile'. He was not content with Perry's formula for the prevention of commercial corruption:

> So long as frugal industry prevails,
> And punctual honour guides her virtuous sons,
> So long as innocence, and modest worth,
> Enhance the native beauties of the FAIR.

The wealth that came from commerce undermined the values which had led to that success. Those values could no longer discipline commerce; only the pursuit of cultural Enlightenment could do that. Roscoe suggested that the relentless pursuit of wealth eventually palls, that avarice decays, 'And nobler passions in their turns bear sway'.[17] But the early signs that 'each ruder passion' would be 'banish'd from the breast',[18] that the commercial spirit would be tamed by the further development of the arts, were not good. Roscoe's cultural enterprises from the 1770s through to the 1790s were all relatively short lived. Indeed the

---

16. See George Chandler, *William Roscoe of Liverpool 1753-1831* (London, 1953), p.330-42 for the text of the poem. The poem may also be consulted in eighteenth-century collections online. The version there contains a preface in which Roscoe stressed his hope that his poem would help 'to abate' the 'spirit of enterprise, and thirst of gain'.

17. Chandler, *William Roscoe*, p.334. David Samwell, a friend of Roscoe's, later echoed his lines: 'This fiend, whose breath inflames the spark of strife, / And pays with trivial toys the price of life', and underlined the theme of the 'corruptions of avarice' in 'The Negro boy': 'When Avarice enslaves the mind, / And selfish views alone bear sway, / Man turns a savage to his kind / And blood and rapine mark his way / Alas! for this poor simple toy / I sold a hapless NEGRO BOY.'

18. Chandler, *William Roscoe*, p.341.

view that avaricious commerce was driving out culture received support from James Wallace, historian of Liverpool. Writing in the 1790s he declared: 'Liverpool is the only town in England of any pre-eminence that has not one single erection or endowment, for the advancement of science, the cultivation of the arts, or promotion of useful knowledge' and he blamed this on the single-minded pursuit of commerce.[19] Wallace's history of Liverpool was published in 1795; by then, he suggested, Enfield's history which furnished ample evidence of enlightened activity in contemporary Liverpool work (and which could be seen as an example of it) was out of date and somewhat irrelevant; 'such various alterations and improvements have since arisen, not only in respect of the town, but of its commerce, manufactures, and public erections, that the matter therein contained can afford, at this time, very little amusement or information either to inhabitant or stranger.'[20]

All this fits in with trends which Stobart has noted and with the thesis, which he examines, that there had been a real cultural deterioration in Liverpool in the closing decades of the eighteenth century. Was Wallace right in arguing that Enfield's account of Liverpool could no longer be accepted? The answer will be complex, but I shall examine various strands of the argument, beginning with that which suggested that public spaces were being crowded out by commercial concerns.

In the context of the time when Liverpool's prosperity was growing apace and it was easy to be over-enthusiastic about the town, Enfield's history was quite measured.[21] Although Enfield described some of the splendid buildings in Liverpool, he also noted that the public space was often crowded: 'Leverpool, in common with most other large towns, labours under the inconveniences which arise from the want of a regular plan of building, when it first began to flourish.'[22] The Exchange, designed by John Wood (which included the Assembly room, the Council room and the mayor's office), was a 'handsome edifice' but 'there is no point from which it may be seen to advantage'.[23] Burnt down in 1795, the grand front façade was unaffected and was retained.[24] The new building was a third larger than the old Exchange and contained all the essential facilities for the business of the town and for civic functions. Habit, however, died hard. John Aikin junior noted that the Exchange contained 'ample accommodation for the merchants and public at large', yet the merchants had 'from immemorial custom, always held their 'Change

19. Wallace, *A General and descriptive history*, p.283, cited in Stobart 'Culture versus commerce', p.476.
20. Wallace, *A General and descriptive history*, p.4.
21. Rosemary Sweet suggests that Enfield was taking a 'defensive stance' and that 'although Liverpool was presented in a favourable light, the claims made were far from extravagant and were couched in reasonable language', *The Writing of urban histories*, p.129.
22. Enfield, *History of Leverpool*, p.20.
23. Enfield, *History of Leverpool*, p.58-59.
24. For the rebuilding see Mowl and Earnshaw, *John Wood*, p.165.

in the open space at the top of Castle-street, and were not, even by a shower, driven to shelter elsewhere than in the adjoining shops'.[25] If they failed to make use of the enlightened public space available to them, that would seem to validate Wallace's view that the Liverpudlians were too interested in making money to have time for anything else. This also might well be seen as an endorsement of Roscoe – avarice continued to rule and there is no doubt that towards the end of the century Liverpool's dominance of the slave trade was unassailable. Indeed the *New Bristol guide of 1799* noted with disdain and maybe a touch of envy:

> The ardor for the trade to Africa for men and women, our fellow-creatures and equals, is much abated among the humane and benevolent merchants of Bristol. In 1787 there were but 30 ships employed in this melancholy traffic; while the people of Liverpool in their indiscriminate rage for commerce and for getting money at all events have nearly engrossed this trade, incredibly exceeded London and Bristol in it, employ many thousand tons of shipping for the purpose of buying and enslaving God's rational creatures, and are venders (*horresco referens*) of the souls and bodies of men and women! to almost all the West Indian islands!!![26]

Such an attack on money-grubbing Liverpudlian merchants was a convenient way of deflecting criticism of Bristol's involvement in the trade and of fortifying a view of the Bristolian merchant as one who had gained his wealth steadily over a long period of time through virtuous industry.[27] But maybe Bristol was experiencing similar trends to those suggested for Liverpool.[28] It has been suggested that the urban renaissance of the eighteenth century was coming to an end and that burgeoning centres of commerce and industry ceased to sustain cultural institutions – for such things polite society could migrate to towns which specialised in taste and polite living, Buxton or Harrogate in the north, or, further south, Cheltenham or Bath, or to London which could sustain everything. As Jon Stobart has pointed out, however, there is a problem with the argument that commercial society could not sustain cultural institutions, for had they not developed earlier in the century when commerce was also flourishing?[29]

---

25. John Aikin, *A Description of the country from thirty to forty miles round Manchester* (London, printed for John Stockdale, 1795), p.359-61.

26. Heath, *The New Bristol guide*, p.66. There was a long history of rivalry between Bristol and Liverpool. Liverpool commissioned John Wood to design their Exchange after he had designed one for Bristol; see Mowl and Earnshaw, *John Wood*, p.164-65.

27. The guide was plagiarising Rev. George Heath's *New history: survey and description of the city and suburbs of Bristol* (Bristol, printed, published and sold by W. Matthews, sold by the booksellers of Bristol, Hotwells and Bath, 1794). See Sweet, *The Writing of urban histories*, p.128-29.

28. Stobart, 'Culture versus commerce', p.484, n.50, observes that attacks on Bristol's cultural life had been made for most of the century, and later in the century both Manchester and Birmingham suffered from similar attacks.

29. Stobart, 'Culture versus commerce', p.476-77.

Wallace's argument and that of others who see commercialism triumphing over culture certainly needs modulating. There is no doubt that, due to overcrowding, a fast expanding town like Liverpool suffered housing and associated public-health problems, though apparently not the development of a dangerous criminal underclass. Also not all the health dangers from local industry were recognised.[30] But if commercial success was responsible for many of these problems, it was also responsible for the development of the town in a more positive sense. Even Wallace recognised this. If it is broadly true that, as Stobart notes, Wallace viewed culture 'in terms of art, literature and the sciences, so there are areas of enlightened endeavour which were outside his vision, and those within his vision he viewed with hostility and little discrimination', that is not quite the whole story.[31] Puzzling as it may seem given his bleak final assessment of Liverpudlian culture, Wallace concluded an earlier chapter, chapter 9, in a more positive vein, noting that since 1760 Liverpool 'may be said to have experienced a total resuscitation'. He referred to the 'genius, taste and refinement of the present day'. 'The floating wings of commerce' had enlightened Liverpudlians and 'given them not only the pride of imitation, but the ambition of equality'. He went on: 'during this interval eight new churches and chapels have been erected, three new docks completed, public edifices built, streets enlarged, squares augmented, and one entire improvement and embellishment shews itself in all its varieties, hotels, theatres, assemblies, music-halls, baths, tennis-courts, bowling-greens, archeries, taverns, and a compleat assemblage of the *scavoir vivre* pervades the whole town.'[32] Wallace, who was not a native of Liverpool, found excellent accommodation available in the town. He also drew attention to the amount of civic building, noting 'the influenza for public erections'.[33] Such remarks need to be offset against his concluding dismissal of Liverpool as a philistine town.

Although Wallace claimed that Enfield's history was out of date, in many areas of enlightened culture there was both continuity and development in the late eighteenth century. This is especially noteworthy in relation to philanthropic endeavour, for there was no pause in philanthropic initiatives. Here we may draw particularly on the work of John Aikin junior, whose more famous sister was Anna Laetitia Barbauld.

---

30. Rosemary Sweet regards William Moss's *A Familiar medical survey of Liverpool* (Liverpool, printed by H. Hodgson, and sold by T. and W. Lowndes, London, 1784) as an attempt to defend Liverpool from attacks on the unhealthy and insanitary conditions of the town, *The Writing of urban histories*, p.131, n.77. Arguably, his failures were those of the science of medicine at the time, rather than a result of a deliberate attempt to distort known facts in the town's favour. See Moss, *A Familiar medical survey*, p.21-22n, 23-24, 30-31, 51, 54-58, 70; *Gore's Liverpool directory* (1781), p.63, and *Gore's Liverpool directory* (1796), p.102.

31. Stobart, 'Culture versus commerce', p.477.

32. Wallace, *A General and descriptive history*, p.191-92.

33. Wallace, *A General and descriptive history*, p.184n. This is presumably a reference to the re-building of the Exchange.

Their father taught at the Warrington Academy and was from 1761 until his death in 1780 rector of the academy.[34] Aikin junior was educated there and completed his training as a medical doctor at Edinburgh University. He was one of a group of enlightened doctors from the Liverpool–Manchester–Chester nexus who used to meet monthly at Warrington to compare notes. A rational Dissenter, Aikin junior was well informed about developments in Liverpool and judged them from an enlightened rather than parochial perspective.[35] His *Description of the country from thirty to forty miles round Manchester* (1795) includes a valuable section on Liverpool, and as a doctor he was particularly knowledgeable about philanthropic developments in the period between 1770 and 1800.

In March 1770 the foundation stones were laid for a new workhouse, an impressive edifice to be constructed on the outskirts of the town with enough room for 600. It was completed in August 1771.[36] Over the period further additions were made with the numbers rising to 1197 in 1794.[37] According to Aikin, 'few institutions of the kind have been better managed.'[38] Some six years later, a Bridewell was 'built upon an improved plan'.[39] Aikin had a particular interest in prison reform. In 1777 John Howard chose to come to Warrington to see through the press his *State of the prisons in England and Wales; with preliminary observations, and an account of some foreign prisons*. A Dissenter, Howard had already had considerable help in preparing his manuscript from the distinguished philosopher and Dissenter, Dr Richard Price.[40] Howard came to Warrington because he knew that he would find assistance from the academy in the final preparation and the checking of the proof, and because there was an excellent press there, that of the Eyres. The Eyres' press printed many of the most important works emanating from the academy and including those of Joseph Priestley, and has been likened to a university

---

34. Dianna K. Jones, 'John Aikin (1713-1780)', *ODNB*. Aikin, an ordained minister, tutored in belles-lettres from 1758 to 1761 and thereafter in divinity.

35. Rational Dissenters were those who claimed to espouse a liberal, enlightened form of Christianity, in contrast with enthusiastic evangelical and/or Calvinist forms of Dissent. Particularly through the influence of Joseph Priestley and Theophilus Lindsey, in the late eighteenth century rational Dissent became associated with heterodox Christianity and increasingly Unitarianism.

36. Enfield, *History of Liverpool*, p.48 – the overall cost was £8000, 'Money for this purpose was borrowed under the corporation seal', p.58.

37. Aikin, *Description*, p.351. The number first reached over a thousand in 1788 and fluctuated above and below that mark over the next few years. Aikin notes that there were also almshouses 'erected in various parts of the town' from private donations, particularly for old sailors and their widows.

38. Aikin, *Description*, p.343.

39. Aikin, *Description*, p.345.

40. J. Aikin, *A View of the character and public service of the late John Howard* (London, printed for J. Johnson, 1792), p.43-44; *The Correspondence of Richard Price, 1748-1791*, ed. D. O. Thomas and W. Bernard Peach, 3 vols (Cardiff and Durham, NC, 1983-1994), vol.3, p.138.

press.[41] Along with Joseph Johnson, the Dissenting publisher from Liverpool who had set up shop in London in 1760, the Eyres were the main publishers of enlightened publications from the north-west of England. Their publications included Roscoe's 'Mount Pleasant' and other notable anti-slavery writings.[42] Aikin became thoroughly acquainted with Howard's ideas for he spent three months assisting his work through the press, and would become Howard's literary executor and biographer. Howard's ideas had an impact in Liverpool. Around 1795 a borough gaol was built. It was, as Aikin noted, 'a great and costly structure, containing all the improvements suggested in Mr Howard's works, and introduced into the modern architecture of those buildings'.[43] This was the only significant municipal gaol in Lancashire at the time.[44]

There had been an infirmary in Liverpool since 1748. Enfield noted it was founded on liberal principles and would turn no one away who came within the rule of the trust. Over the years there was a steady increase of inpatients and outpatients. There were 122 inpatients and 72 outpatients in its first year and by the early 1770s the numbers being treated annually had reached 604 and 1095 respectively.[45] In that decade there were nine doctors, thirty-one surgeons and five apothecaries working in Liverpool.[46] In the following year a dispensary was established which took over from the infirmary the care of outpatients. In 1782 it was given a new building in Church Street.[47] Aikin's account is especially instructive:

an institution liberal in its plan. Its avowed object is to afford medical relief to the poor at their own dwellings; but medical relief is in many cases only another phrase for a more cordial or plentiful diet; and hence this charity has often been the means of providing a resource for the unfortunate stranger, when deprived of all other assistance, and without any legal claim for support. It was instituted in the year 1778, chiefly by the interposition of some of the medical gentlemen of Liverpool, on whose recommendation a competent subscription was speedily

---

41. See P. O'Brien, *Eyres' press, Warrington (1756-1803): an embryo university press* (Wigan, 1993).

42. See Helen Braithwaite, *Romanticism, publishing and Dissent* (Basingstoke, 2003), p.76-77. It should be noted that, although Eyres and Johnson were particularly associated with enlightened publications, Liverpool in the late eighteenth century was a hive of activity for printing and associated trades. See *The Book trade in Liverpool to 1805: a directory*, ed. M. R. Perkin (Liverpool, 1981).

43. Aikin, *Description*, p.345.

44. Margaret DeLacy, *Prison reform in Lancashire 1700-1850: a study in local administration* (Stanford, CA, 1986), p.20n.

45. Enfield, *History of Leverpool*, p.50-51. Aikin, *Description*, p.346, says the infirmary was opened in 1749.

46. R. D. Thornton, *James Currie the entire stranger and Robert Burns* (Edinburgh and London, 1963), p.104, citing Thomas H. Bickerton's *Medical history of Liverpool* (London, 1936), p.104. The doctors included Matthew Dobson, John Bostock, Joseph Brandreth and John Rutter, who all had Edinburgh degrees, and James Currie, who was about to join them – he was introduced to them by his cousin Dr William Currie who had an established practice in Chester.

47. Aikin, *Description*, p.347-48.

obtained. It is directed by a president, two auditors, and a committee of the subscribers. The professional duty was originally performed by three physicians and three surgeons, who receive no compensation for their trouble, and an apothecary, who resides on the spot and receives a salary; but the number of physicians was in the year 1791 increased to seven, who visit the patients according to regulations established among themselves. Of the 14,402 patients treated in 1794, 12,880 were cured – 30 were removed to the infirmary, 397 died. [...] The constant visits of the physicians and the surgeons at the dwellings of the sick poor are attended with the most beneficial effects: order and cleanliness are introduced – infectious disorders are opposed in the first stage of their progress – and a sentiment of mutual good-will is excited between the different classes of society, of benevolence on the one hand, and of gratitude on the other, which cannot be too industriously cultivated.

If Wallace had had the vision to include applied science within his notion of science, he would have seen that it was alive and well in Liverpool at this time. Liverpool medics sought to be as up to date as possible – in 1779 a medical library was established with Matthew Dobson as the first president – and they themselves, together with their colleagues in Manchester and Chester, were pioneers in the management of infectious diseases.[48]

Liverpool chalked up a first in 1791 when it established a school for the indigent blind. Funds for the enterprise were raised by the blind anti-slavery poet and campaigner, Edward Rushton, and his friends. According to John Aikin the initiative for the school came from Reverend Henry Dannet, minister of St John's, 'a humane and public spirited clergyman'.[49] In fact the school appears to be the result of a collective concern, but it was Dannet who was largely responsible for managing the school in its early years.[50] It was the first school in the world to take in the blind of almost all ages. Despite early difficulties, partly a result of the novelty of the enterprise and of the exigencies of financing it at a time when public confidence was affected by the war with France, it gradually

---

48. Especially influential was John Haygarth, a Yorkshireman educated at Sedbergh Grammar School, Cambridge University and Edinburgh University (1762-1765) where William Cullen was a major influence. He completed his studies at Leiden, Paris and London. Appointed physician at Chester Infirmary (founded 1755) in 1766, he remained there until 1798. In 1783 he created isolation wards at his infirmary, the first in a general hospital in Britain. See G. H. Weaver, 'John Haygarth, clinical investigator, apostle of sanitation, 1740-1827', *Bulletin of the Society of medical history of Chicago* 4 (1928-1935), p.156-200, and Simon Harrison, 'John Haygarth (1740-1827)', *ODNB*.

49. The early years of the school were difficult. In February 1793, under the weight of ill-informed public criticism, Henry Dannet resigned from the governors of the school. A merchant, and future mayor of Liverpool, Pudsey Dawson (1752-1816), whose father was a doctor practising in London, played a leading role in stabilising its fortunes. The school found suitable occupations for its blind pupils, paying them 'a weekly sum proportioned to the nature of their work', Aikin, *Description*, p.350; Michael W. Royden, *Pioneers and perseverance: a history of the Royal School for the Blind, Liverpool 1791-1991* (Birkenhead, 1991), p.49-53, 72.

50. Royden, *Pioneers and perseverance*, p.30-41.

began to prosper; by 1798 the school had fifty-four attendees and the governors began to look for new premises.[51]

In the area of philanthropic institutions for the poor, sick and needy there was thus no slackening of impetus in the late eighteenth century – quite the reverse. There were new and pioneering enterprises. They may not have been able to cater for all but their scale was impressive, especially in relation to medicine. One particularly notable feature is that the forces for enlightened change were willing to take on public prejudice. In 1789 James Currie wrote two long letters to Gore's *Liverpool and general advertiser* urging the construction of a lunatic asylum and answering the critics of the scheme. Although Currie claimed not to be the originator of the scheme, he was certainly a driving force behind it. The asylum was completed in 1792. It was built close to the infirmary and was incorporated into its administrative structure. Indeed the trustees of the infirmary had to make up the £3000 shortfall in the fund raised by public subscription (£2770 14s. 6d.). The institution made a slow start, but by the end of its first decade had treated 472 patients, of whom 269 were eventually discharged as cured.[52]

The asylum is noteworthy in that, unlike many of the other philanthropic institutions, it was designed for both the poor and the well-to-do. In his first letter to the newspaper Currie explained that, 'Under other diseases the rich may have every assistance at their own homes, but under insanity relief can seldom be obtained but from an establishment for the treatment of this particular disease.' Moreover, the intention was that 'the increased payments made by the rich may serve to diminish, in some degree, the demands on the poor.'[53]

Does this mean that Wallace was entirely wrong, that commerce had not driven out Enlightenment? Not entirely, for the pursuit of commercial gain undoubtedly caused tensions within Enlightenment circles in Liverpool. There is no doubt that the problems caused by commerce were felt more acutely in Liverpool than elsewhere, nor that they were raised within the town by William Roscoe before outsiders voiced their own criticisms. The key issue was that of the slave trade from which Liverpudlians profited hugely, but before discussing that issue, it needs to be placed in the context of other Enlightenment concerns, some of which were also manifest in Liverpool at a relatively early date.

In the late eighteenth century the Enlightenment became more radical. Issues of religious toleration, the rights of communities and of men came to the fore. In Liverpool those concerns were reflected in movements for wider toleration for Dissenters, for borough reform and most contentiously

---

51. Royden, *Pioneers and perseverance*, p.42-63.
52. For all this, see George McLoughlin, *A Short history of the first Liverpool infirmary* (London and Chichester, 1978), p.45-55, and appendix 12, p.106-116; and Thornton, *James Currie*, p.138.
53. McLoughlin, *Liverpool infirmary*, appendix 12, p.108.

*Enlightenment in late-eighteenth-century Liverpool*

for the abolition of the slave trade. Radical Enlightenment thinking would challenge those who preferred change to occur gradually, through the development of enlightened consensual thought. For example William Enfield, a man who cherished consensus and moderation, would find that he would have to make choices. The first challenge to his outlook came from a fellow rational Dissenter, Reverend Joseph Priestley, who had preceded him in teaching belles-lettres at the Warrington Academy. Priestley believed that it was time the rational Dissenters asserted their identity and their own outlook and values. Priestley was in favour of toleration of all religions and for the separation of Church and State. He believed that truth would make rapid progress through free enquiry, and that religious progress was impeded by the established Church and the penalisation of citizens for religious Dissent. Citizenship should be a secular matter and there should be no religious tests for officeholders. In practice that meant supporting reform of the Church of England and the repeal of the Test and Corporation Acts. Enfield was upset by Priestley's assertion of the superiority of rational Dissent over Catholicism and Anglicanism. He argued that Dissenters, too, had their prejudices which they were loath to cast aside.[54] He believed that change should come gradually, and not through adversarial tactics. He recommended Bacon's view that it should be allowed to occur 'quietly, and by degrees scarce to be perceived'.[55] For Enfield it was the best way for enlightened change to take place. Prejudice would be eroded gradually, rather than confronted head on. Priestley's way, he feared, would re-awaken age-old fears of Dissent and make persecution more, not less, likely. His words of caution were prophetic, for Priestley would suffer from the prejudice of the mob – with not a little connivance from the Church and magistrature – in the Birmingham Riots of July 1791.[56]

The ostensible cause of the Birmingham Riots, a dinner to celebrate the anniversary of the fall of the Bastille, is a reminder of the circumstances of the late eighteenth century which made Enlightenment a difficult and contentious matter. Rational Dissenters in particular faced criticism for regarding the French Revolution as the embodiment of Enlightenment values. The attack was headed by Edmund Burke, who came to see Enlightenment as a form of betrayal. Although Enfield belonged to the moderate wing of rational Dissent, he did not abandon Enlightenment as it became more radical and that meant being prepared to support reform in a more active sense than he would no doubt have preferred. That can be seen in his attitude towards the slave trade.

---

54. W. Enfield, *Remarks on several late publications relative to the Dissenters in a letter to Dr Priestley, by a Dissenter* (London, printed for S. Bladon, 1770), p.24.
55. Enfield, *Remarks on several late publications*, p.5.
56. See my *Rousing the sleeping lion: Joseph Priestley and the constitution in Church and state, Occasional publications of the Leeds library* 3 (Leeds, 1993).

Enfield's *History* gave details which showed that more than 10 per cent (10.56 per cent) of ships involved in foreign trade leaving Liverpool were bound for Africa and they accounted for 17.6 per cent of tonnage. Comparable figures for Bristol were 9 per cent of ships and almost 12 per cent of tonnage, but the tonnage from Bristol was 23,548 tons compared with 40,750 from Liverpool.[57] Double the number of slavers sailed from Liverpool as compared with Bristol. Indeed Liverpool was becoming the major slave-trading port of Europe. Enfield did not comment on the figures he had given, although he did note that the development of the African trade was an important stage in the expansion of the town.[58] In marked contrast, when William Roscoe wrote his 'Mount Pleasant', he was not prepared to overlook this dark source of Liverpudlian prosperity. For Roscoe the virtues of 'innocence and modest worth' had been lost with the development of commerce:

> –Blest were the days ere Foreign Climes were known,
> Our wants contracted, and our wealth our own;
> When health could crown, and Innocence endear,
> The temperate meal, that cost no eye a tear:
> Our drink, the beverage of the chrystal flood.
> –Not madly purchas'd by a brother's blood–
> Ere the wide spreading ills of Trade began,
> Or Luxury trampled on the rights of Man.[59]

Roscoe's protest was, moreover, not just an abstract assertion of the rights of man. He dwelt on the hopeless conditions of the life of the slave:

> From morn, to eve, by rigorous hands opprest,
> Dull fly their hours, of every hope unblest.

Only,

> Death, in kindness, from the tortur'd breast
> Calls the free spirit to the realms of rest.[60]

Roscoe's views were not entirely original for around the time he was writing opinion about slavery and the slave trade was beginning to change in enlightened circles in Britain.[61] Yet he was voicing deeply unpopular views in his own home town, and he was doing so before the national anti-slave-trade campaign began.[62] Roscoe's poem was not

---

57. Enfield, *History of Leverpool*, p.70.
58. Enfield, *History of Leverpool*, p.25.
59. Chandler, *William Roscoe*, p.333.
60. Chandler, *William Roscoe*, p.332-33.
61. Porter, *Enlightenment*, p.359-61. Porter argues that, 'if it was the Evangelical lobby which in the event secured in Parliament the abolition of the trade, the groundswell of criticism owed much to enlightened liberalism.'
62. This is not to suggest that Roscoe was unique in his detestation of the slave trade, but that the concerted campaign for its abolition dates from the 1780s, and that he was ahead of opinion even amongst fellow Liverpool Dissenters, many of whom had

published until 1777, but his views would have already been known to his circle.[63] No doubt Enfield, if consulted, would have counselled caution in publishing the poem for Roscoe's opinions threatened to enrage many in Liverpool who lived by the trade. For 'an amiable man in society', as Aikin described Enfield,[64] divisive issues were difficult. Nonetheless, in his *Biographical sermons*, also published in 1777, Enfield condemned slavery. In describing how Joseph was sold by his brothers into slavery, he remarked that 'slavery was a crime scarcely less heinous in its nature' than the fate initially proposed for Joseph of being cast into a pit and left to die. He went on, 'but probably, the frequency of the practice of purchasing and selling slaves might in those days, as it does at present, render men inattentive to the moral nature of the action; and they might perhaps think it a small crime to buy or sell a brother.'[65] Comments made in a sermon in a large tome of sermons were hardly likely to strike a blow against slavery and could be regarded as relatively safe to make. But Enfield was not a craven spirit and he would stick to enlightened causes even when unpopular, despite his distaste for controversy.[66] Later, after he had moved from Warrington to Norwich, in a sermon in 1788 commemorating the centenary of the Glorious Revolution, Enfield declared that the emancipation of the slaves was 'a universal obligation of natural justice'.[67] By then the various issues of the time concerning liberty and equality had joined up.[68] In Liverpool there was a very public debate not just about the slave trade but about the institution of slavery.

connections with the trade. Anne Holt, *Walking together: a study in Liverpool nonconformity* (London, 1938), p.156-57.

63. For the circulation of his poems amongst friends see LRO, MS GRE 2/17/5, David Samwell to Matthew Gregson, 25 June 1774.

64. J. Aikin, *General biography, or Lives, critical and historical, of the most eminent persons of all ages, countries, conditions, and professions*, 10 vols (London, 1799-1815), vol.3, p.571-72.

65. W. Enfield, *Biographical sermons, or a Series of discourses on the principal characters in Scripture* (London, printed for J. Johnson, 1777), p.65-66.

66. See LRO, Nicholson Papers, 920 NIC 9/12/1, Enfield to Reverend Dr Clayton, 2 May 1787. See also W. Enfield, *The History of philosophy from the earliest periods: drawn from Brucker's Historia Critica Philosophiae* (1787; London, 1837), p.v: 'Possibly, the time may not be far distant when an end will be put to fruitless controversy, by distinctly ascertaining the limits of the human understanding.'

67. Holt, *Walking together*, p.128-29; W. Enfield, *A Sermon on the centennial commemoration of the Revolution* (Norwich, 1788), p.17; Oxford, Bodleian Library, Western MS SC 28460, correspondence of Ralph Griffiths, f.63-64, Enfield to Griffiths, 21 February 1792, described the slave trade as 'the most iniquitous of all human transactions', and wanted Griffiths' *Monthly review* to take a firmer line against it.

68. This does not mean that the campaigns for the various reforms amalgamated or that they shared identical support. See G. M. Ditchfield, 'Manchester College and anti-slavery', in *Truth, liberty and religion: essays celebrating two hundred years of Manchester College*, ed. Barbara Smith (Oxford, 1986), p.185-224 (204-207); G. M. Ditchfield 'Repeal, abolition and reform: a study of the interaction of reforming movements in the parliament of 1790-1796', in *Anti-slavery, religion and reform: essays in memory of Roger Anstey*, ed. C. Bolt and S. Drescher (Folkestone, 1980), p.101-18, and Iain Sellers, 'William Roscoe, the Roscoe

Over time the distance between the views and approaches of Roscoe and Enfield concerning slavery had become negligible: Roscoe's approach to abolition was gradualist, and Enfield shared Roscoe's desire to improve society. For Roscoe, however, the abolition of the slave trade was only one step, though a very important one, towards enlightening Liverpool. His indictment of commerce was not just an indictment of the slave trade. What hope then of Enlightenment in Liverpool? Could commerce be civilised – the bloated monster metamorphosed into a benevolent force? Roscoe's answer may not be entirely plausible, but it was based on what he saw around him and what he himself sought to attain. In 'Mount Pleasant', despite his indictment of commerce, he recognised that the pursuit of wealth had already brought cultural benefits to Liverpool,[69] but crucially he did not accept that commercial wealth and Enlightenment were obvious bedfellows and his main hope was that 'nobler passions' would eventually 'bear sway'. Interestingly Roscoe differed from those who thought that the middle station in life was in itself conducive to the cultivation of virtue, a view elaborated upon by one of Liverpool's surgeons, William Moss, who thought that merchants were naturally given to promote enlightened culture.[70] This was not borne out by the recollections of a young visitor to Liverpool, Mary Anne Galton. In later life she recalled the lavish lifestyle of Liverpool's West India merchants, remembering in particular the 'multitude of black servants' and her amazement at the 'sumptuous drawing-rooms [...] in houses where there was no library'.[71] For all the favourable dimensions of Liverpool's urban renaissance there were undoubted limitations from the point of view of Enlightenment. Roscoe's unsuccessful attempts to stimulate the arts in Liverpool in the late eighteenth century seemed to confirm the sombre analysis of 'Mount Pleasant'.[72] Yet, since Roscoe's quest was cultural in

---

circle and radical politics in Liverpool', *Transactions of the Historic society of Lancashire and Cheshire* 120 (1968), p.45-62.

69. One of the paradoxes of the poem is that in praising many aspects of Liverpool's culture, Enfield ignored the fact that some of the money for philanthropic subscriptions came from the profits of avaricious trade, starting with the Bluecoat Hospital, in whose founding and subsequent success the slaver Bryan Blundell was instrumental. His heirs, too, contributed notably to the institution. See Enfield, *History of Leverpool*, p.48-49.

70. Moss, *A Familiar medical survey*, p.61-66.

71. *Life of Mary Anne Schimmelpennick*, ed. C. Christiana Hankin, 3rd edn (London, 1860), p.243-44, cited in Malcom Dick, 'Joseph Priestley, the Lunar Society and anti-slavery', in *Joseph Priestley and Birmingham*, ed. Malcom Dick (Studely, 2005), p.65-80 (74, 80). Mary Anne's recollections were written late in life and there may be some exaggeration in the above account. See Robert E. Schofield, *The Lunar Society of Birmingham: a social history of provincial science and industry in eighteenth-century England* (Oxford, 1963), p.221-23.

72. An attempt in 1769 to set up an Academy of Art on the model of the Royal Academy failed. Roscoe and friends tried unsuccessfully to revive this in 1773. There was a mini revival in the 1780s before activities were suspended in the 1790s. A Literary and Philosophical Society was set up in 1779 and came to an end in 1783. Roscoe and Currie set up a Literary Society in the following year on a smaller scale which met in members'

the widest sense, embracing politics as well as the arts and sciences, it is unsurprising that that quest would go through a bumpy passage in the late eighteenth century. If his circle was increasingly at odds with what had been mainstream enlightened culture in Liverpool, the challenge of late Enlightenment reformism and humanitarianism would have arrived in Liverpool in some form or other. The town, which gained so much from the slave trade, would, of all communities, have to face some awkward questions. If it was the case that many merchants chose not to have their own personal libraries, it was impossible for them to ignore the new ideas. Kay Flavell has written, of the subscribers to the Liverpool Library, that 'no-one could claim ignorance of topical issues or of new developments in literature on the grounds of geographical isolation.'[73] Although there was sometimes hesitation about ordering challenging works, the library maintained a liberal purchasing policy even in the contentious closing decades of the century. It was well stocked with the works of Joseph Priestley. It bought both parts of Paine's *Rights of Man* and Mary Wollstonecraft's *Rights of Woman*. The thirty-six volumes of Voltaire's work were purchased after initial dithering and the *Encyclopédie* found a home there.[74]

If there was a broad consensus about the maintenance of a liberal purchasing policy for the library, there was no such agreement about the contents of provocative works. Just as in national politics the American and French Revolutions and domestic reform issues proved divisive, so too within Liverpool political culture rifts developed. As Stobart notes, these can be portrayed as between the Corporation and commercial interests on one side (the Corporation would for instance commission the publication of a pro-slavery tract in 1788, and in the early 1790s arrange for the free distribution of 10,000 copies of an anti-Jacobin tract),[75] and on the other, Roscoe and a set of 'radical non-conformists' – men like William Rathbone, James Currie, Edward Rushton and the Reverends William Shepherd and John Yates.[76] Since thirty-seven out of forty-one Liverpool councillors in 1787 were slave traders it is not surprising that Roscoe's Literary Society was regarded as an abolitionist club,[77] and was hardly likely to draw support from councillors and their friends. Indeed after the outbreak of the French Revolution it was convenient to make life impossible for Roscoe's society as a potential nest of English Jacobins.

homes. It was disbanded in 1793 under suspicion of Jacobinism. Stobart, 'Culture versus commerce', p.475.

73. M. Kay Flavell, 'The enlightened reader and the new industrial town: a study of the Liverpool library 1758-1790', *British journal for eighteenth-century studies* 8:1 (1985), p.17-36. There were fewer than 500 subscribers but they represented a cross-section of Liverpool's elite, although doctors and Dissenters were particularly prominent (p.25).

74. Flavell, 'The enlightened reader', p.24-25.
75. Flavell, 'The enlightened reader', p.24.
76. Stobart, 'Culture versus commerce', p.479.
77. Stobart, 'Culture versus commerce', p.480.

At the same time the Corporation continued to support philanthropic activities, while, it is argued, few in the Roscoe circle showed such interest. What is clear is that these tensions were resolved more quickly than one might have predicted and Liverpool came to enjoy a remarkable cultural renaissance early in the nineteenth century.[78]

If it is true, as Stobart concedes, that 'the precise role of these rivalries and conflicts remains uncertain and must await further detailed research',[79] there are pointers to suggest that there were cross-currents between the rival groups and that maybe the rifts were not always as deep as they seemed. The influence of Roscoe's friend Dr James Currie in philanthropic activity was immense. He was discreet about his anti-slavery sympathies and was prepared to defend the character of the Liverpool merchants to the national committee for the abolition of the slave trade.[80] He formed one bridge – he was made a freeman of the borough in 1802. Roscoe himself became something of a local hero after the abolition of the slave trade. The fact that Liverpool traders continued to develop and prosper after 1807 no doubt helped in the acceptance of his view.[81] But already before then, the Council had been anxious to retain its enlightened credentials and besides supporting philanthropic activities had encouraged the founding of both the Athenaeum and the Botanic Gardens. Almost all the institutions founded at this time had late-eighteenth-century precursors but this time they put down firm roots. It was increasingly in the Corporation's interest to refurbish the image of the town and to support Roscoe's enlightened vision of creating a 'Florence of the North'. Indeed Roscoe's pioneering biography of *Lorenzo de Medici*, published in 1796, has been regarded as marking a turning point in relations between Roscoe's circle and the Corporation, for it enabled the Liverpool merchants to see themselves as latter-day Florentines, whose city represented the 'apotheosis of the union between culture and commerce'.[82] Roscoe the reform politician and abolitionist could be set aside and Roscoe the cultural icon could be embraced. The rapprochement was immediately evident in the Council's support for the founding of the Athenaeum in 1797, which became 'one of the largest and

---

78. Stobart, 'Culture versus commerce', p.478-81.
79. Stobart, 'Culture versus commerce', p.480.
80. See F. E. Sanderson, 'The Liverpool abolitionists', in *Liverpool, the African slave trade and abolition: essays to illustrate current knowledge and research*, ed. Roger Anstey and P. E. H. Hair, *Historic society of Lancashire and Cheshire*, occasional series 2, enlarged edn (1989), p.196-238 (209-10). There is a large literature on slavery and the slave trade. For Liverpool, this is the best introduction.
81. See Martin Lyon, 'Liverpool and Africa in the nineteenth century: the continuing connection', *Transactions of the Historic society of Lancashire and Cheshire* 147 (1997), p.27-54.
82. Arline Wilson, 'The cultural identity of Liverpool, 1790-1850: the early learned societies', *Transactions of the Historic society of Lancashire and Cheshire* 147 (1997), p.55-80 (62). It is probably true to say that the elites found the rapprochement easier than most of the citizens of Liverpool. See Sellers, 'William Roscoe, the Roscoe circle and radical politics', p.54-56.

most impressive of the urban gentlemen's libraries founded in Britain at this time'. Membership of the library would soon become de rigueur for Liverpool's elite whatever their political colouring.[83]

Such a speedy rapprochement was possible not simply because the Corporation was alert to the need to change its self-image at a time when the anti-slave-trade campaign drew attention to the profits which the trade brought to the premier slaving port in Europe. It was also possible because there had already existed a wide range of enlightened activity enabling co-operation between those with differing outlooks and in certain areas quite different beliefs. R. D. Thornton, in his study of James Currie, divides the elite of Liverpool society into four main sets: the Roscoe circle, the fashionable, the wealthy and commercial, and the Corporative.[84] If we take the example of Matthew Gregson, a member of Roscoe's circle and a friend from the early initiative in setting up an Academy of Art, we find that it was possible for some to move comfortably within all those sets. Gregson was able to do this both through his work and through his many interests. Moreover, he was not all things to all men. Despite his friendship with Roscoe he was prepared to defend the slave trade at least in private, and may have invested in it.[85] He was at one time treasurer of the Bluecoat Hospital; he was a supporter of the School for the Indigent Blind, a supporter and subscriber to the Liverpool Library, and as noted he supported the Academy of Art, and was himself an exhibitor in the first exhibition of 1774. Later, he was an enthusiastic supporter of the Botanic Gardens and of the Liverpool Institution. Many of the fashionable were his clients, and he had a wide network of friends – his hospitality was such that his house was known as Gregson's hotel.[86]

This is not to suggest that Enlightenment in Liverpool was a matter of pick and mix. Although the movement was never homogeneous, it consisted of related impulses. Its very diversity may have helped to give it coherence. Stobart suggests that the broad divisions he noted represented different faces of Liverpool's cultural life.[87] And there were undoubtedly shared values which transcended political differences. There was an underlying belief in improving the life of all within a civic community. The Dissenting concern for independent conscientious action was married to a concern to improve the quality of life in one's own community. Benevolence was not a luxury but a duty, although not an unpleasant one.[88] The humanitarian credo was increasingly felt to be consonant with

83. Wilson, 'Cultural identity of Liverpool', p.63-64.
84. Thornton, *James Currie*, p.161.
85. LRO, Gregson Papers, MS GRE 2/17/41, Gregson to Samwell, 11 October 1788.
86. See H. A. Taylor, 'Matthew Gregson and the pursuit of taste', *Transactions of the Historic society of Lancashire and Cheshire* 110 (1958), p.157-76.
87. Stobart, 'Culture versus commerce', p.479.
88. See my 'Heretical religion and radical politics', in *The Transformation of political culture: England and Germany in the late eighteenth century*, ed. Eckhart Hellmuth (Oxford, 1990), p.339-74 (362).

the utilitarian principle of the happiness of the greatest number. Indeed Jeremy Bentham thought that he had gained the principle of the happiness of the greatest number from reading Joseph Priestley's *Essay on the first principles of government* (1768), although the range of alternatives from Francis Hutcheson to Cesare Beccaria suggests the diffusion of the idea.[89] Science and the arts could all be seen as part of the civilising endeavour and even commerce need not be corrupting.

The Roscoe of the 'Mount Pleasant' poem, who had pointed out that the ceaseless pursuit of wealth, far from securing happiness, undermined it,[90] came to believe that commerce need not be avaricious and corrupting, but properly conducted could be a civilising influence. He had already suggested in his long poem of 1788 against the slave trade, *The Wrongs of Africa*, that a healthy trade could have existed between Africa and Britain, rather than a trade in useless merchandise and men.[91] Honest commerce could have beneficial effects.[92] As Roscoe put it in his discourse celebrating the Royal Institution: 'It is to the union of the pursuit of literature with affairs of the world, that we are to look forwards towards the improvement of both.'[93] Wherever possible, it was felt that individuals should be encouraged to help themselves (something which Aikin commended in the asylum for the blind) but those with particular skills and knowledge had special responsibilities for applying them. Perhaps that was seen most of all in the concern for public health. Here a tradition of local philanthropy and civic pride was built on by men like Matthew Dobson and James Currie. They were not content to apply existing knowledge but they were constantly seeking new medical knowledge in order to make the rapidly expanding town a healthier place. And perhaps it was the nexus of medical expertise in Liverpool, Warrington, Manchester and Chester which gave most character to Enlightenment in this periphery.[94] And if that is so, then one might argue that Scotland rather than England had more influence on Enlightenment

---

89. See Robert E. Schofield, *The Enlightenment of Joseph Priestley: a study of his life and work from 1733 to 1773* (Pennsylvania University Press, PA, 1997), p.207-208. For the importance of Hutcheson's notion of active benevolence in the development of anti-slavery attitudes see Roger Anstey, 'Eighteenth-century thought and anti-slavery', in his *The Atlantic slave trade and British abolition* (Aldershot, 1992; reprint of London, 1975), p.91-125 (102).

90. Chandler, *William Roscoe*, p.331: 'why then to gain the means neglect the end [happiness]?'

91. Chandler, *William Roscoe*, p.349: 'Cou'd not Afric's wealth / Her ivory, and her granulated gold, / To her superfluous, well repay the stores, / [Superfluous too] from distant Europe sent?' In fact such a trade already existed before 1807 and was developed thereafter. See Lyon, 'Liverpool and Africa in the nineteenth century', p.27-54.

92. John Whale, 'The making of a city of culture: William Roscoe's Liverpool', *Eighteenth-century life* 29:2 (2005), p.91-107 (101). Whale argues that Roscoe gained sustenance from Dugald Stewart's notion of the 'man of benevolence'.

93. Whale, 'The making of a city of culture', p.102.

94. The doctors in the area of Manchester, Warrington and Liverpool met quarterly at Warrington to compare notes. M. DeLacey, 'Matthew Dobson', *ODNB*.

## Enlightenment in late-eighteenth-century Liverpool

in Liverpool. Crucial as rational Dissent was, it was the medical dimensions which gave it its local distinction. Such a distinction, however, is somewhat artificial since the rational Dissenters were so prominent in medicine, and their links with the Scottish universities and with metropolitan Dissent were crucial in shaping the nature of Enlightenment in Liverpool.[95] Warrington-educated doctors, moreover, most notably Thomas Percival, played a central role in medical Enlightenment in the north-west, as indeed they did in provincial medicine in England more generally.[96]

The danger of characterising Liverpool's Enlightenment as peripheral in a geographical sense is that it can be confused with the Enlightenment being peripheral in other senses, as for example to the development of Liverpool, or the Enlightenment movement. One solution, that adopted by R. D. Thornton, is to distinguish between local initiatives and broad Enlightenment themes. He suggests a distinction between parochial achievements, which could be described as peripheral Enlightenment accomplishments, and which included pretty well the whole gamut of local initiatives from libraries to help for the indigent, and 'championship of the broadest issues of the day'.[97] Such distinctions are convenient but they simplify complex relationships. If we return to 'Mount Pleasant' which tackled at an early stage the deeply unpopular cause of anti-slavery,[98] we find that Roscoe's stance was based both on local worries and on the wider concern for the rights of humanity. The major issues of the day had a parochial context – not only the most obvious one of anti-slavery, but that of toleration, borough reform and, later, Irish relief, monopoly breaking and peace with France (the broad issues named by Thornton). For such matters distinctions between centre and periphery, between narrow and broad issues, provincial and central, are not always helpful. The broad issues were discussed within a context which was local. War and peace had a special significance to a trading port. The issue of religious toleration also had an interesting local content. Although

---

95. For a valuable analysis of the enlightened nexus of Liverpool, Warrington and Manchester see Flavell, 'The enlightened reader', p.25-32, also n.91.

96. See Charles Webster and Jonathan Barry, 'The Manchester medical revolution', in *Truth, liberty and religion*, ed. B. Smith, p.165-84. Between 1757 and 1777, twenty-one academy students subsequently pursued a medical career. The authors suggest that Dissenters may have 'reached the peak of their influence in medicine and related activities in the second part of the eighteenth century' (p.167-68). Percival was the first president of the college set up in Manchester in 1786 following the closure of the Warrington Academy. Like Warrington it played a pivotal role in Dissenting culture in the north-west of England.

97. Thornton, *James Currie*, p.163.

98. In 1764, before he collaborated in the publication of 'Mount Pleasant' (1777), Johnson had published John Newton's anonymous first-hand account of his experiences on a slaver trading out of Liverpool. Its main impact, however, appears as an account of the relief of Newton's troubled soul from the sins of slave trading. Braithwaite, *Romanticism, publishing and Dissent*, p.76.

Liverpool had an anti-Jacobite history, unlike much of the rest of Lancashire,[99] Roman Catholics, notably the Blundells, contributed towards civic life. The same is true of Protestant Dissenters although their role in corporate politics had diminished since the mid-century.[100] Rational Dissenters made common cause with Roman Catholics in their quest for wider toleration. In the 1807 election when Roscoe failed to defend the seat he had won in the previous year, he was the target of anti-Catholic and pro-slave-trade sentiment.[101]

It would be easy to portray the tensions which existed in late-eighteenth-century Liverpool as between enlightened cosmopolitan forces, pro-universal toleration, Parliamentary reform and peace with France on the one hand, against loyalist, anti-Jacobin, pro-war, anti-Dissent and anti-Catholic forces on the other. But that would be simplistic. Many of Liverpool's concerns may be described as cosmopolitan in the sense given to the term by Franco Venturi. This, as John Robertson has explained, has a 'specific and original quality [...] is receptive to the ideas of others, while respecting the different circumstances of each'.[102] It was a cosmopolitanism which found a place for patriotism, for patriotism gave a specific flavour to its enlightened commitments. In this form, patriotism was committed to enlightened improvement at a local as well as a national level and it found expression in civic-mindedness. However powerful and compelling the general propaganda and promptings from national organisations were for change, those seeking reform and improvement did so with the local situation in mind; in Liverpool those who supported the general case for parliamentary reform did so because they were involved in trying to reform the representation of their own borough. The tension between freemen and the Corporation existed before the development of the movement for parliamentary reform in the early 1780s. Civic politics did not give way to national reformism, rather it became a matter of national concern that civic independence should be ensured.[103] The same sort of relationship, however, did not exist in relation to the campaign for the abolition of the slave trade. There the national patriotic agenda gave strength to the local abolitionists. If the local abolitionists were more circumspect and gradualist in their views, that was not because Liverpool was peripheral but because, as the leading

99. R. Sweet, 'Freemen and independence in English borough politics c.1770-1830', *Past and present* 161 (1998), p.84-115 (112). Liverpool was the only Lancashire borough to remain loyal in 1715 and 1745.
100. The Presbyterian congregation at Benn's Garden which had provided four mayors in the middle decades of the century lost its influence in corporate politics later in the century, and the proportion of Dissenters who were freemen of the borough also appears to have diminished at that time. James E. Bradley, *Religion, revolution and English radicalism: non-conformity in eighteenth-century politics and society* (Cambridge, 1990), p.274-75.
101. Sellers, 'William Roscoe, the Roscoe circle and radical politics', p.60.
102. Robertson, 'Franco Venturi's Enlightenment', p.202.
103. See Sweet, 'Freemen and independence', p.113.

slave-trading port in Europe, it was at the centre of the debate.[104] Moreover, how does one measure in Enlightenment terms a stance taken in the teeth of local opposition and a more radical stand taken where there is little local opposition? On the issue of religious toleration it was the metropolitan committee for procuring the repeal of the Test and Corporation Acts which took the initiative and which orchestrated a national campaign. But the local and regional meetings at Chester and Liverpool indicate that metropolitan initiative was not only welcome, but also reflected dissatisfaction in the country about the legal status of Dissent.[105] In Liverpool this was of long standing. The first campaign for repeal began in the early 1730s partly as a result of a dispute in Liverpool when Dissenters there urged those in the metropolis to conduct a vigorous and open campaign for repeal.[106] The appeal to Enlightenment was even stronger in the campaign later in the century. The Dissenters argued that, 'in every age and country, there appears to be a necessary connection between the progress of knowledge and of freedom.' Universal toleration would be accepted once the mists of prejudice had been lifted. This would benefit everyone – it would be good for the 'order of the community' and it was perfectly consonant with the 'warmest attachment' to country, loyalty to the king and 'deepest reverence' for the constitution.[107]

Perhaps the best example of Enlightenment, civic-mindedness, patriotism and cosmopolitanism can be found in James Currie's appeals to the Liverpool public for the foundation of a lunatic asylum. He begins his letter with an analysis of the national society which would appeal to Liverpudlians:

in forming an idea of the connection between the various ranks of society, we may consider the nation as a great trading company. [...] [E]ach partner in the business is not equally concerned, because every one does not throw the same share of property, talents, and activity into the common stock; but all are interested in the general success, and the welfare of each is connected with that of the whole.[108]

---

104. The situation might have been different if Thomas Clarkson's visit to Liverpool in 1787 had not been so disastrous. See Sanderson, 'The Liverpool abolitionists', p.208-209. It is also worth noting that Liverpool abolitionists were closely associated with the Manchester campaign for abolition which paid a key role in the development of the national campaign. Ditchfield, 'Manchester College and anti-slavery', p.197-200.

105. See G. M. Ditchfield, 'The campaign in Lancashire and Cheshire over the repeal of the Test and Corporation Acts, 1787-1790', *Transactions of the Historic society of Lancashire and Cheshire* 126 (1977), p.109-38, and Sellers, 'William Roscoe, the Roscoe circle and radical politics', p.50.

106. N. C. Hunt, *Two early political associations: the Quakers and Dissenting deputies in the age of Walpole* (Oxford, 1961), p.126, 131, 195-97.

107. These aspirations were encapsulated in the unanimous resolutions of Dissenters 'of all denominations', who met at the Golden Lion, in Dale Street, Liverpool, on 19 January 1790, which were printed in *Gore's Liverpool general advertiser*, vol. xxix, no.1256, 21 January 1790.

108. McLoughlin, *Liverpool infirmary*, appendix 12, p.106.

Currie then went on to note that in this company those who 'labour and execute' were 'by far the most numerous'. They formed the foundation of society, and as such needed special care, for if the foundation 'be too much pressed' it will crumble. This led him to make a general appeal for the enlightened treatment of the labouring poor:

> They demand our constant attention. To inform their minds, to repress their vices, to assist their labours, to invigorate their activity, and to improve their comforts: – these are the noblest offices of enlightened minds in superior stations; offices which are of the very essence of virtue and patriotism, which must attract the approbation of the good and wise, and which will obtain the favour of the Eternal Being, who is the Great Father of us all.[109]

Finally, in appealing for subscriptions from the public and especially 'the magistrature', Currie appealed to the civic pride of his audience:

> It is to be hoped that the public voice will be unanimous in favour of the proposed establishment [...] so shall another evidence be reared, in addition to those which already reflect credit on the munificence of Liverpool. Our public buildings for pleasure, as well as business, are in a high style of elegance and splendour; our institutions for the care of man's perishing body are already, perhaps, brought near to perfection: our honours will be increased, and the system of charities completed, by an institution for the health of his immortal mind.[110]

The Enlightenment, unlike Lockeian ideas, was not written on a *tabula rasa*. It developed out of existing traditions, but gave them new dimensions. Although there was already a tradition of local philanthropy in Liverpool, that came to be infused with Enlightenment ideas, most notably medical in the very broad area of public health, but also concerning prison reform. The Enlightenment is also reflected in the growing belief in the value of helping others to help themselves (something which Aikin commended in the asylum for the blind). It is therefore probably a mistake to distinguish too strongly between peripheral and central issues. Although national issues were ones which would be affected by legislative change at Westminster, those changes, like local initiatives, aimed to improve the world. This reformist spirit of the late eighteenth century has been aptly described by Roy Porter as the 'second enlightenment' or 'Enlightenment within the Enlightenment'.[111] The British *philosophes* were not the abstract calculators as Burke portrayed them in his *Reflections*. They were often men of theory, it is true, but they aimed to apply their theoretical principles to practical questions. Thus Richard Price, the butt

---

109. McLoughlin, *Liverpool infirmary*, appendix 12, p.106-107. Roy Porter draws special attention to this passage as typical of enlightened paternalism, which was anxious to contain lower-class disorder as well as disorders. See R. Porter, 'Was there a medical Enlightenment in England?', *British journal for eighteenth-century studies* 5:1 (1982), p.49-64 (57).

110. McLoughlin, *Liverpool infirmary*, appendix 12, p.108-109.

111. Porter, *Enlightenment*, p.423.

## Enlightenment in late-eighteenth-century Liverpool

of Burke's attack, sought to promote national legislation to enable the poor to provide for their old age. He was concerned to enable the poor to maintain their independence.[112] Similar concerns informed philanthropic activity in Liverpool, including attempts to create a bank for the savings of labourers, and to provide outpatient medical relief for the poor and work for the blind.[113] Certainly such notions could be driven by pragmatic considerations – indeed in mid-century Liverpool there was a scheme taking sixpence a month from seamen's wages to provide for them in their old age, for their widows and children[114] – but they were powerfully reinforced by the Enlightenment notion, as already noted, that benevolence was not a luxury but a duty, and that independence was vital to the dignity of man.[115]

As a final comment on Liverpool's Enlightenment status one can note the distinctive influence which it had. Liverpool's late-flowering Enlightenment seemed to offer a pattern for others on the geographical periphery. John Whale has noted how Jefferson reacted enthusiastically to Roscoe's description of the Royal Institution, seeing it as offering a pattern for 'our new university', and was equally enthusiastic about Roscoe's treatise on penal jurisprudence.[116] Roscoe's transatlantic correspondence was considerable and he has been portrayed by Katherine Lloyd as a participant in a 'transatlantic community of reform' in which penal reform was especially important, and Unitarianism, Quakerism and Scottish Philosophy were key elements.[117] Other institutions were influential, too. The Athenaeum provided a model for emulation abroad; the Boston Athenaeum (1807) was self-consciously founded on the Liverpool pattern.[118] The Botanic Gardens, too, were copied elsewhere – as far afield as Philadelphia and Calcutta – and Tsar Alexander I was an admirer. In 1811 the Liverpool garden group sent John Bradbury and Thomas Nuttall, a future professor of natural history at Harvard, to explore the upper Missouri. On his return six years later, Bradbury published an account of his travels in the interior of North America. Nuttall would eventually publish a three-volume study of North American Sylva. Interest in North America was also displayed by the group when it encouraged the work of the ornithological artist Audubon. Finally the medical achievements in Liverpool were widely acknowledged.

---

112. See D. O. Thomas, 'Francis Maseres, Richard Price and the industrious poor', *Enlightenment and Dissent* 4 (1985), p.65-80.
113. See Thornton, *James Currie*, p.163.
114. Enfield, *History of Leverpool*, p.55.
115. Fitzpatrick, 'Heretical religion and radical politics', p.362.
116. Whale, 'The making of a city of culture', p.102.
117. Katherine M. R. Lloyd, 'Peace, politics, and philanthropy: Henry Brougham, William Roscoe and America 1808-1868', doctoral dissertation, University of Oxford, 1996, p.78-142, cited in Whale, 'The making of a city of culture', p.103 and 107.
118. Wilson, 'Cultural identity of Liverpool', p.64.

James Currie's work for public health attracted a steady stream of visitors including the Portuguese doctor, Anthony Pegado.[119]

It was Roscoe, however, who became the iconic figure. If epicentres need dominant *philosophes* with a tangible influence on affairs, so too do peripheries. Longevity also helps and Roscoe fitted the bill. He came to epitomise what he had considered impossible in his poem 'Mount Pleasant', namely that the vigorous pursuit of wealth could be harmonised with the development of a civilised society. As John Whale has suggested, 'The example of a fast-growing Atlantic port, considered by many to be remote from the polished metropolitan center of London, must have been appealing to developing cities like New York and Boston.'[120] It does give special resonance to the idea of being not simply a Liverpudlian, as we would say today, but of being a 'Liverpolitan', as Roscoe's biographer George Chandler unselfconsciously called inhabitants of the town, a term which might have been coined to describe a cosmopolitan of the periphery.

---

119. Thornton, *James Currie*, p.139-40.
120. Whale, 'The making of a city of culture', p.103.

SIMON BURROWS

# Grub Street revolutionaries: marginal writers at the Enlightenment's periphery?[1]

FROM both geographical and literary perspectives, London's colony of scandal mongering French exile blackmail pamphleteers (*libellistes*) – a motley collection of adventurers, renegade diplomats, defrocked clergy and petty criminals – appears peripheral to the French Enlightenment. Yet through Robert Darnton's so-called 'Grub Street theory', such writers have in recent decades assumed a centrality to Enlightenment and revolutionary studies disproportionate to their numbers and the intellectual fecundity of their works. This essay reappraises their importance.

Darnton's 'Grub Street theory' finds links between the Enlightenment and the French Revolution not in the productions of the great *philosophes*, but in the output of lesser writers excluded from the gravy train of state pensions, academy places and awards.[2] It contends that by the 1770s, in an overstocked literary marketplace, the plum places were monopolised by careerists and timeservers like Jean-Baptiste-Antoine Suard, who followed an entrenched Enlightenment party line and never published a major work. When budding Voltaires such as Jacques-Pierre Brissot found their progress blocked by such non-entities, they rebelled against the *ancien régime* and its system of patronage, censorship and licensing. Nevertheless, in order to survive, Brissot and his ilk were reduced to shameful expedients, such as political pornography, blackmail and spying for the police. Darnton insinuated that Brissot, the pivotal figure in his theory, had probably tried all three activities, and added that 'hacks' such as Brissot never forgave the regime that degraded them, and in their works 'expressed the passion of men who hated the old regime in their

1. Earlier versions of this paper were given at the Voltaire Foundation in Oxford; University of Leeds Eighteenth-Century Studies Group; and the Centre for Eighteenth-Century Studies at the University of York. I am grateful to those who commented on those occasions as well as to Russell Goulbourne, Tom Kaiser, Iain McCalman and Roger Mettam. Grants from the Universities of Waikato and Leeds; a Fellowship at the Humanities Research Centre at the Australian National University; a British Academy Small Research Grant; and a Research Leave Award from the Arts and Humanities Research Board supported my research.
2. Grub Street theory was formulated in Darnton's seminal articles, 'The Grub Street style of revolution: J.-P. Brissot, police spy', *Journal of modern history* 40 (1968), p.301-27, and 'High Enlightenment', p.81-115.

guts'.[3] Curiously, however, Darnton's classic Grub Street pamphlet was written by Brissot's arch-enemy, Charles-Claude Théveneau de Morande, whose *Gazetier cuirassé* (1771), the most notorious pamphlet of the Maupeou crisis of 1771 to 1774, was a characteristically nihilistic tract and virtual prototype of the *libelle* genre. A systematic attack on a vice-ridden establishment, it denounced the sexual depravity of aristocrats and the royal mistress, Mme Du Barry, and linked them to corruption in army, Church and State. According to Darnton, 'Morande [...] and his fellow hacks had no interest in reform. They hated the system in itself: and they expressed that hatred by desanctifying its symbols, destroying the myths that gave it legitimacy in the eyes of the public, and perpetrating the counter-myth of degenerate despotism'.[4] During the Revolution, many of Darnton's hacks – including Jean-Paul Marat, Pierre-Louis Manuel, Antoine-Joseph Gorsas, Jean-Louis Carra and Brissot – emerged to pursue distinguished journalistic and political careers and destroy the monarchy and its institutions.

Darnton's version of revolutionary causation has proven enormously influential among historians. In particular, revisionists and post-revisionists are attracted to his concept of 'desacralisation', which explains the overthrow of monarchy and aristocracy without recourse to class explanations, and offers a credible explanation for revolutionary anti-aristocratic rhetoric. Gender historians, noting that desacralising attacks on Louis XV's mistresses were succeeded by political pornography aimed at Louis XVI's Austrian-born queen, Marie-Antoinette, draw on Darnton's paradigm to investigate the role of such pamphlets in devalidating women's political participation and creating a masculinist public sphere.[5] In consequence, assertions that desacralising pamphlets and pornographic attacks on Louis XVI's queen fatally undermined the monarchy are widespread in recent studies of the Revolution.[6]

Nevertheless, Darnton's beguiling account of a literary underclass leading a rebellion against its oppressors is open to attack. Elizabeth Eisenstein stresses the openness of the late-Enlightenment elite;[7] John Lough finds the notion of an extensive, expanding literary underclass

---

3. Darnton, 'High Enlightenment', p.115.
4. Darnton, 'High Enlightenment', p.109.
5. For a summary bibliography of this extensive literature, see Elizabeth Colwill, 'Pass as a woman, act like a man: Marie-Antoinette as tribade in the pornography of the French Revolution', in *Marie-Antoinette: writings on the body of a queen*, ed. Dena Goodman (New York and London, 2003), p.139-69 (162-63, n.7).
6. For a recent example see Munro Price, *The Fall of the French monarchy: Louis XVI, Marie-Antoinette and the baron de Breteuil* (London, 2002), p.16.
7. Elizabeth L. Eisenstein, 'Bypassing the Enlightenment: taking an underground route to revolution', in *The Darnton debate*, ed. H. T. Mason, p.157-77 (159). See also Eisenstein, *Grub Street abroad: aspects of the French cosmopolitan press from the age of Louis XIV to the Enlightenment* (Oxford, 1992), ch.5.

fanciful;[8] and Daniel Gordon believes that desacralisation theory is 'undertheorised' and ignores the Bourbon monarchy's dynamism and multiple claims to legitimacy.[9] Others, including D. M. G. Sutherland, point to the chronological disjuncture between pamphlet attacks on Louis XV's mistresses and ministers in the early 1770s and a revolution that occured fifteen years later.[10] This point has been reinforced by Vivian Gruder's recent contention that scandalous and pornographic pamphlets against Louis XVI and Marie-Antoinette only began to appear in significant numbers once the Revolution was underway.[11] Similarly Thomas Kaiser has argued that Darnton's work fails to take adequate account of political contingency.[12] Nor, Jeremy Popkin asserts, does it pay sufficient attention to patronage, for those underground pamphleteers who operated inside France relied on powerful figures both to sponsor production of their work and to protect its dissemination.[13]

The case studies on which many of Darnton's claims rest have also been questioned. Daniel Gordon has rehabilitated Suard's intellectual achievement and shown he played a key participatory role 'in the sphere of enlightenment sociability',[14] while other recent studies challenge Darnton's portrayal of Morande, suggesting he was a patriotic reformer.[15] Finally, and most critically, Darnton's depiction of Brissot has been convincingly refuted. Frederick A. de Luna, Dena Goodman and Leonore Loft have shown that he was no 'hack', but a well-connected and respected *philosophe*. His radicalism dates from the beginning of his career, and he used enlightened sociable networks to advance his favourite causes.[16] They find it improbable that Brissot was involved in producing political pornography or spying for the police. Their conviction was partially confirmed in 2003, when the present writer presented new

8. Lough, 'The French literary underground reconsidered', p.471-82.
9. Daniel Gordon, 'The great Enlightenment massacre', in *The Darnton debate*, ed. H. T. Mason, p.129-56.
10. D. M. G. Sutherland, *The French Revolution and empire: the quest for a civic order* (Oxford, 2003), p.14.
11. Vivian R. Gruder, 'The question of Marie-Antoinette: the queen and public opinion before the Revolution', *French history* 16 (2002), p.269-98.
12. See Thomas E. Kaiser, 'Enlightenment, public opinion and politics in the work of Robert Darnton', in *The Darnton debate*, p.189-206 (196, 200).
13. Jeremy D. Popkin, 'Pamphlet journalism at the end of the Old Regime', *Eighteenth-century studies* 22 (1989), p.351-67.
14. D. Gordon, *Citizens without sovereignty: equality and sociability in French thought, 1670-1789* (Princeton, NJ, 1994), p.150.
15. Gunnar and Mavis von Proschwitz, *Beaumarchais et le Courier de l'Europe: documents inédits ou peu connus*, SVEC 273-74 (1990); Simon Burrows, 'A literary low-life reassessed: Charles Théveneau de Morande in London, 1769-1791', *Eighteenth-century life* 22 (1998), p.76-94.
16. Frederick A. de Luna, 'The Dean Street style of revolution: J.-P. Brissot, *jeune philosophe*', *French historical studies* 17 (1991), p.158-90; Goodman, *The Republic of Letters*, p.281-88, 294-300; Leonore Loft, *Passion, politics and philosophie: rediscovering J.-P. Brissot* (Westport, CT, 2002).

archival evidence which strongly suggested that Brissot was neither the author of anti-Bourbon *libelles* nor a police spy. Brissot nevertheless apparently worked for the police in other capacities and forwarded copies of *libelles* written by his friend Anne-Gédeon de Lafitte de Pelleport to contacts in the book trade. Acting as a typical middleman in the book trade, however, or seeking, like many other late-Enlightenment figures, to influence the regime from the inside, would not have appeared morally culpable to most contemporaries.[17]

Given the cogency of these criticisms of Darnton's thesis, some of which Darnton partially accepts,[18] and the lack of a coherent alternative account of *ancien régime* scandalous pamphleteering, this paper re-examines the Grub Street model at what should be its strongest point – the activities of London's French *libellistes* in the final twenty-five years before the revolutionary crisis. It was from pamphlets written and published in London, not Paris, that Darnton drew his classic examples of 'Grub Street' works, both Morande's *Gazetier cuirassé* and those he linked to Brissot. The inhabitants of London's French Grub Street also resemble Darnton's original model closely because of their relative independence. They operated with impunity, lionised by the London mob and sheltered by relaxed libel laws and a blackmail law which only protected British residents.[19] Writing in hope of suppression fees, they were autonomous of factions and patrons, or at least lacked ideological commitment to their causes. The London *libellistes* were, moreover, involved in enterprises that the French government considered criminal, and most observers found morally culpable. These authors hence offer an opportunity to reassess the Grub Street model and determine whether it retains any interpretational value. Consequently, the remainder of this paper explores London's French Grub Street in terms of its denizens and their careers; a sample of their key works; the French government's reactions to their activities; the *libellistes*' responses to the revolution; and their legacies and wider implications.

The most notorious denizens of London's French Grub Street were Morande; the celebrated cross-dressing diplomat, the chevalier d'Eon; the notorious fraudsters, the comte and comtesse de La Motte; and Pelleport (the real author of the pamphlets attributed to Brissot),[20] who collectively provide this paper's focus.[21] Morande (1741-1805), son of a small-town Burgundian *procureur*, was a violent petty crook, pimp and gambler, who

17. S. Burrows, 'The innocence of Jacques-Pierre Brissot', *Historical journal* 46 (2003), p.843-71.
18. Robert Darnton, 'Two paths through the social history of ideas', in *The Darnton debate*, p.251-94.
19. See Burrows, *Blackmail, scandal, and revolution*, ch.3-4.
20. See Burrows, *Blackmail, scandal, and revolution*, ch.4; Burrows, 'Innocence of Brissot', p.855-60.
21. Burrows, *Blackmail, scandal, and revolution*, identifies a further dozen less prominent London-based blackmailer-*libellistes*, some of whom are mentioned below.

made powerful enemies and fled to London in 1770.[22] There, in August 1771, he published the *Gazetier cuirassé*, which he peddled door-to-door in London's fashionable districts.[23] Thereafter, Morande attempted to blackmail many of the *Gazetier*'s targets, threatening to publish new *libelles* against Voltaire; the marquis de Marigny, Mme de Pompadour's brother, whom he accused of pederasty; the duc de Bethune; the comte de Lauraguais, the celebrated parlementary pamphleteer;[24] and Mme Du Barry, whose royal lover eventually capitulated to his demands. Later Morande served as a French spy, and from 1784 until 1791 he edited the *Courier de l'Europe* newspaper. In the 1780s his pen served the court and his newspaper columns slandered several future revolutionaries. He also provided the false testimony which led to Brissot's imprisonment in the Bastille.[25] Morande's success was phenomenal. Darnton lists him as the fifth best-selling author of France's vast underground book trade in the twenty years before 1789.[26] In the 1780s he also earned between 500 and 1000 louis per annum from espionage and 300 pounds as editor of the *Courier de l'Europe*.[27] For Morande, Grub Street was a means of acquiring the riches to support a dissolute, libertine lifestyle.

Another Burgundian, the chevalier d'Eon (1728-1810), also knew spectacular Grub Street success. Son of a high-ranking provincial administrator, d'Eon had a glittering but short diplomatic career, having the misfortune to serve Louis XV's clandestine espionage organisation, the Secret du roi, which, orchestrated by the comte de Broglie, conducted its secret diplomacy without the knowledge of the foreign ministry. In 1763 d'Eon was sent to England ostensibly to help negotiate peace, but also bearing written instructions to explore invasion routes. Shortly thereafter, Louis decided to dismantle the Secret, sacked Broglie and abandoned its agents. To cap it all, d'Eon, already in dispute with the foreign minister, Praslin, over extravagant expense claims, was overlooked for the post of ambassador to Britain in favour of the comte de

---

22. See Charles Théveneau de Morande, *Réplique de Charles Théveneau de Morande à Jacques-Pierre Brissot: sur les erreurs, les infidélités et les calomnies de sa Réponse* (Paris, Froullé, 1791); Paul Robiquet, *Théveneau de Morande, étude sur le XVIII*[e] *siècle* (Paris, 1882), p.10-23; Burrows, 'Literary low-life', p.76.

23. Paris, Archives du Ministère des affaires étrangères, Correspondance politique, Angleterre (hereafter CPA) 502, f.177-79, d'Eon to [Broglie], London, 13 July 1773.

24. [Anne-Gédeon de Lafitte de Pelleport], *Le Diable dans un bénitier et le gazetier cuirassé transformé en mouche* (London, 1783), p.62; *Mémoires secrets*, 9 February 1774; Pierre-Louis Manuel, *La Police de Paris dévoilée*, 2 vols (Paris, Garnery, 1791), vol.2, p.252; CPA 518, f.78-90, [d'Eon], 'Anecdotes du *Gazetier cuirassé*'; Beaumarchais to [?], Paris, 24 January 1781, published in Proschwitz and Proschwitz, *Beaumarchais et le Courier de l'Europe*, vol.1, p.111-15.

25. Burrows, 'Literary low-life'; Burrows, 'Innocence of Brissot', p.854, 858.

26. Darnton, *Forbidden bestsellers*, p.65; R. Darnton, *The Corpus of clandestine literature in France 1769-1789* (New York and London, 1995), p.199-200.

27. CPA 565, f.288-90, [Morande] to [Montmorin], 18 June 1788; London, National Archives, PC1/127, f.210, Swinton to Calonne, undated letter [late May 1791].

Guerchy, a well-connected aristocrat with no diplomatic experience. When d'Eon was recalled in disgrace, he refused and stayed in England hoping to extort rewards from the French government by threatening to reveal all to the British. To ram home his point, in 1764 d'Eon published his *Lettres, mémoires et négociations particulières*, an abridged account of his diplomatic activities which carefully omitted everything which might seriously compromise France.[28] A work of political blackmail, it clearly qualifies d'Eon as a Grub Streeter, as do numerous accusatory pamphlets and newspaper articles against personal enemies, including Guerchy.[29] D'Eon was seldom long out of the public eye, especially after 1770 when rumours that he was really a woman began to circulate.[30] Although legally declared female by a British court in 1777, upon his death in 1810 he was found to be biologically male.[31] His case fascinated both his contemporaries and historians but, although he has inspired numerous biographical studies and fictional works, none focus on his role in Grub Street. Yet d'Eon succeeded in selling his silence and compromising papers to the French several times.[32]

Contemporaries were also fascinated by the comtesse de La Motte Valois, the former street child who masterminded the diamond necklace fraud. According to the accepted version, this elaborate scam involved convincing the lecherous, gullible and out-of-favour cardinal de Rohan that Marie-Antoinette wished him to buy a fabulous diamond necklace clandestinely on her behalf. For this purpose, the comte de La Motte hired a prostitute, Guay d'Oliva, to impersonate the queen in a carefully choreographed fleeting moonlit meeting with Rohan in the Versailles gardens. A credit contract for the necklace was drawn up and the queen's signature forged. The cardinal, duped, handed over the necklace to the comtesse, whose husband broke it up and fenced the jewels around Europe.[33] The crime was only discovered when payment became overdue and the defrauded jewellers approached the king for their money. The comtesse, who had stayed in France, probably banking on a cover-up, was arrested, as were Rohan, d'Oliva and numerous other suspects.

Louis XVI thought a public trial would clear the queen of suspicion, but the competing parties circulated their trial briefs in print, and many readers apparently concluded that the (innocent) queen was somehow

---

28. On d'Eon's career see Gary Kates, *Monsieur d'Eon is a woman: a tale of political intrigue and sexual masquerade* (New York, 1995).
29. The blackmail threat is explicit in CPA supplément 13, f.148-59, d'Eon to [Broglie], London, 23 March 1764.
30. Kates, *Monsieur d'Eon*, p.182-88.
31. Kates, *Monsieur d'Eon*, p.xi-xiii, 247-51.
32. See Burrows, *Blackmail, scandal, and revolution*, ch.1.
33. See, for example, Frances Mossiker, *The Queen's necklace* (London, 1961), p.130-46; Jones, *The Great nation*, p.336-48; Sarah Maza, *Private lives and public affairs: the causes célèbres of prerevolutionary France* (Berkeley, CA, 1993), p.183-85.

culpable.[34] Moreover, the Paris Parlement acquitted Rohan, thereby accepting that he genuinely believed that Marie-Antoinette might arrange a moonlit assignation at Versailles. The comtesse was found guilty, whipped, branded and sentenced to life imprisonment, but in August 1787 she escaped to Britain, rejoined her husband and announced her intention to publish memoirs containing an amorous correspondence between Rohan and the queen.[35] Clearly she hoped both to negotiate a large suppression fee and to whet the public appetite in case negotiations broke down, which duly happened.

The French court probably refused La Motte's demands because of their experience with Pelleport. Pelleport, whose father was a nobleman of moderate means and equerry in the household of Louis XVI's brother, the comte de Provence, was educated at the prestigious Ecole militaire. He was expelled from two regiments, however, for unbecoming behaviour, and his prospects were further blighted by the loss of his wife's small dowry in ill-judged speculations and his father's remarriage. Pelleport travelled to London to restore his fortunes by writing *libelles*,[36] and published *Les Petits Soupers de l'hôtel de Bouillon*, a *libelle* against the duc de Castries and the princesse de Bouillon, which he offered to suppress. Thereafter, Pelleport threatened to print *Les Passe-tems d'Antoinette*, a *libelle* against the queen,[37] and in late 1783, when his extortion attempts failed, published *Le Diable dans un bénitier et le gazetier cuirassé transformé en mouche*, which contained a highly embroidered account of the suppression negotiations. Several months later, he was arrested on a trip to France and spent four years in the Bastille.[38] His pamphlets against the queen never appeared.

The *confrères* of these notorious *libellistes* are catalogued in French diplomatic correspondence and in Pierre-Louis Manuel's *La Police de Paris dévoilée* (1791), a work compiled from police archives. They included Alphonse-Joseph de Serres de La Tour, who absconded with the wife of his employer, a master of requests at Versailles, to London, where he co-founded the *Courier de l'Europe* and served as the comtesse de La Motte's ghostwriter.[39] La Tour's collaborators included Joseph Perkins de

---

34. Edmund Burke certainly believed the *Mémoires* damaging to Marie-Antoinette and sprang to her defence: see Iain McCalman, 'Mad Lord George and Madame La Motte: riot and sexuality in the genesis of Burke's *Reflections on the revolution in France*', *Journal of British studies* 35 (1996), p.343-67.

35. Alphonse-Joseph de Serres de La Tour, *Appel au bon sens* (London, Kearsley, 1788), p.4-5: advertisements were placed in the *Morning post* in late December 1787.

36. Louis Charpentier *et al.*, *La Bastille dévoilée*, 3rd episode (Paris, Desenne, 1789), p.66-67.

37. CPA 542, f.15-16, Pelleport to [Moustier], Little Chelsea, 12 April 1783; f.285-89, Receveur's 'Compte rendu' of his mission, dated 22 May 1783.

38. Charpentier, *Bastille dévoilée*, p.12.

39. CPA 497, f.95, Sartine to d'Aiguillon, Paris, 19 July 1771; CPA supplément 14, f.20, d'Aiguillon to Guines, Compiègne, 22 July 1771 [minute]; Manuel, *Police dévoilée*, vol.2, p.234; London, National Archives, PRO95/631, pieces 247-49.

MacMahon, a priest who fled France with one of his *penitentes* and supplied libellous anecdotes to the British press,[40] and Delatouche, author of a short-lived, rabidly anti-French *Courier de Londres*.[41] The publishing force behind much of London's *libelle* industry was a Genevan, David Boissière, a former lackey who established a bookshop in James Street, having narrowly escaped hanging in Lübeck for stealing from his master.[42] In the early 1770s Boissière worked with Morande, and other members of his coterie included Belson, a charlatan and double agent; the abbé de Séchamp, a suspected poisoner and budding journalist; La Rochette, a former spy and diplomat; the pamphleteer Ange Goudar and Pelleport.[43] French diplomats were also briefly worried by the baron de Linsing, a violent, self-destructive madman who, having escaped from the French prison system, tried to extort compensation for 50,000 livres he claimed to have expended in French service.[44]

The *libelliste* community was not confined within clear social barriers. It included several minor or *soi-disant* nobles and clergymen as well as lackeys, adventurers and clerks. The most successful mixed in British high society and with French diplomats, writers and travellers, serving as advisers, agents and publicists. Because eighteenth-century politics were intensely personal, revolving around connections and reputation, it was impossible for the diplomatic and literary milieu and Grub Street to remain separate. The borders of Grub Street were especially porous to aggrieved diplomatic personnel such as d'Eon and La Rochette who, as *commissaire des prisonniers*, was the main French diplomatic representative in London from 1761 to 1763, but turned coat when his pension was reduced.[45]

Although French government documents seldom associate them directly with political groupings, there are indications of factional connections. D'Eon's links to Broglie, whose fall from grace drove d'Eon to blackmail, are well documented. Indeed d'Eon attributed his misfortunes to a faction based around Mme de Pompadour and the de facto chief minister Choiseul.[46] In contrast, Morande's *Gazetier cuirassé* appears to show Choiseulist and *parlementaire* sympathies. While Morande's only

---

40. Manuel, *Police dévoilée*, vol.2, p.248-49. For sources on MacMahon see McCalman, 'Mad Lord George', p.365, n.97.

41. Manuel, *Police dévoilée*, vol.2, p.263-64.

42. Manuel, *Police dévoilée*, vol.1, p.143-44, 237-38, vol.2, p.236-37; for material on Boissière and his stable of *libellistes* see CPA 541-47 *passim*.

43. CPA 541, f.346-49, Göezman to Vergennes, 4 April 1783; Manuel, *Police dévoilée*, vol.2, p.236-37, 244-46. On Goudar see Jean-Claude Hauc, *Ange Goudar: un aventurier des Lumières* (Paris, 2005).

44. On Linsing see Burrows, *Blackmail, scandal, and revolution*, ch.1, 4.

45. Manuel, *Police dévoilée*, vol.2, p.245-46.

46. See, for example, CPA 511, f.115-20, d'Eon to [Vergennes?], 14 July 1775, at f.118; Leeds, Brotherton Library, Brotherton collection, d'Eon papers (hereafter ULBC), file 19 f.42-43, 45; file 58 f.91.

known connection at court was a Burgundian *grande dame* named Mme de Courcelle – who also had close links to d'Eon – much of Morande's material on Mme Du Barry probably came from the Choiseul faction.[47] According to Pidansat de Mairobert, the Choiseuls, abetted by the lieutenant of police, Sartine, were behind most early pamphlets and songs against the favourite.[48] But if they supplied Morande, his preference for blackmail must be considered a betrayal. Pelleport's links to the comte de Provence's household also appear suspect as Provence, together with the youngest royal brother, d'Artois, probably orchestrated early written attacks on Marie-Antoinette.[49] Moreover, Pelleport's first *libelle*, the *Petits soupers*, was aimed at Castries, an enemy of d'Artois, who is also maligned in his *Diable dans un bénitier*.[50] Marie-Antoinette and Louis XVI may also have dabbled in *libelles* and reputedly commissioned Morande to write a scandalous life of the future Philippe-Egalité, *La Vie privée du serenissime duc de Chartres*.[51] Despite these links, the *libellistes*' frequent resort to blackmail proves that they were essentially loose cannons, dangerously liable to bite the hand that fed them.

The battles of adventurers, diplomats and propagandists also spilt over into Grub Street. Guerchy, for example, hired Pierre-Henri Treyssac de Vergy and Ange Goudar to write pamphlet attacks on d'Eon, while another ambassador, the comte de Guines, struggled vainly to recover from the slanders of his former secretary Barthélemy Tort de La Sonde, who accused him of profiteering on the public funds.[52] Likewise, Beaumarchais used Morande as a freebooting auxiliary in his struggles with d'Eon, and attempts to traffic in wagers on d'Eon's sex in 1775.[53] Two years later, Morande committed perjury in a case involving bets on the chevalier's sex, insisting that he had seen d'Eon's naked breasts.[54]

Others, besides d'Eon, were ensnared in similar webs of lies, perjuries and intrigues. Morande attacked Mirabeau in print repeatedly, initially at Beaumarchais's behest, and having already calumniated the dissident journalist Simon-Nicholas-Henri Linguet, spat in his face in

---

47. CPA 502, f.177-79, d'Eon to [Broglie], London, 13 July 1773.
48. [Mathieu-François Pidansat de Mairobert], *Anecdotes sur Mme la comtesse Du Barri* (London, n.p., 1775), p.74-76. See also Darnton, *Forbidden bestsellers*, p.158-61.
49. Vincent Cronin, *Louis and Antoinette* (London, 1974), p.197, 402-405.
50. [A.-G. de Lafitte de Pelleport], *Les Petits Soupers et nuits de l'hôtel de Bouillon* (Bouillon [London], Boissière, 1783); [Pelleport], *Le Diable dans un bénitier*, p.9-11,16-17, 26.
51. See Robiquet, *Théveneau de Morande*, p.211-12; Marcellin Pellet, *Variétés révolutionnaires* (Paris, 1885), p.49.
52. ULBC, file 58, p.3 and *passim*; for documents concerning the Tort case see CPA 496-526 *passim* and CPA supplément 28, especially CPA 507.
53. See d'Eon, *Pièces relatives aux démêlés entre mademoiselle d'Eon de Beaumont et le Sieur Caron, dit de Beaumarchais* (Paris, 1778), p.10, 16, 46, 51-60 and *passim*; ULBC, file 4, p.46-53; London, British Library (hereafter BL), Add. MS 11, 340-41; CPA 513, f.421-23, d'Eon's testimony against Morande in the King's Bench.
54. ULBC, file 27, p.241-45; *Gazetteer*, 2 July 1777; *Annual register* 20 (1777), p.189-90.

Piccadilly.[55] Likewise he savaged the ex-minister Charles-Alexandre de Calonne after the exposure of his desperately ill-judged attempt to regain royal favour by toning down the manuscript of Mme de La Motte's memoirs.[56] Finally Brissot had his finances and reputation ruined by Morande's machinations and lies. Clearly all these men bore the scars of Grub Street, although not in the sense suggested by Darnton.

London's Grub Street writers were not driven by frustrated ambition. Most were adventurers motivated by hopes of wealth or repairing financial misfortunes. Their works could command high prices in a buoyant market: Morande sold the *Gazetier cuirassé* for a guinea a copy, and produced 3000 copies of the *Mémoires secrets d'une femme publique*, a large print run for the period, before burning them in return for a suppression fee.[57] The secret sale, by which Morande received 32,000 livres in cash and an annuity of 4000 livres, was leaked, advertising the government's vulnerability to blackmail.[58] It was reported by the *Mémoires secrets*, later editions of the *Gazetier cuirassé* and several bestsellers of the Mairobert corpus.[59] Further references appear in the *Diable dans un bénitier*, revolutionary publications such as Manuel's *Police dévoilée*, and British newspaper reports and satirical prints.[60]

Morande justified his blackmail demands by citing previous payments to scandalous biographers of Pompadour and Du Barry, as well as d'Eon's pay-off in the 1760s.[61] Likewise, the French *chargé d'affaires* Garnier

55. See letters of Morande to Beaumarchais dated 3 October 1784, 12 December 1785, 10 and 20 March 1789 in Proschwitz and Proschwitz, *Beaumarchais et le Courier de l'Europe*, vol.2, p.853-55, 915-17, 1037-38, 1041-42; *Mémoires secrets*, 3 April 1785; *Courier de l'Europe*, 18 March 1789.

56. Simon Burrows, *French exile journalism and European politics, 1792-1814* (Woodbridge, 2000), p.88; R. Lacour-Gayet, *Calonne, financier, réformateur, contre-révolutionnaire, 1734-1802* (Paris, 1963), p.247-74.

57. CPA 497, f.111-13, Marin to d'Aiguillon, 3 August 1771; CPA 503, f.308-10, Morande to d'Eon, 21 December 1773; CPA 517, f.242-43, d'Eon to Morande, second message of 8 August 1776 (copy).

58. For copies and translations of the contract see CPA 504, f.207, 197-200; CPA supplément 18, f.36-39.

59. *Mémoires secrets*, 24 August 1775; unpaginated letter dated London 20 May 1774 in the back of the 1777 edition of the *Gazetier cuirassé*; [Mairobert], *Anecdotes*, p.326-28; [Mairobert], *L'Espion anglais*, new edition, 10 vols (London, John Adamson, 1785), vol.2, p.16-17; [Mairobert], *Lettres originales de Mme la comtesse Dubarry* (London, 1779), p.182.

60. [Pelleport], *Le Diable dans un bénitier*, p.29-30; Manuel, *Police dévoilée*, vol.2, p.251; BL, Add. MS 11, 340, f.8, 18, 21, cuttings from *Westminster gazette*, 20-24 August 1776; *Public advertiser*, 3 and 5 September 1776; caricatures entitled 'The French lawyer' and 'The wicked in triumph', described in F. G. Stephens and D. M. George, *Catalogue of political and personal satires preserved in the Department of prints and drawings in the British Museum*, 11 vols (1870-1954), vol.5, p.178-79, no.5246 and 5247.

61. See London, National Archives, SP France 78, f.210-11, Morande to Benevent (undated letter, 1772); BL, Add. MS 11, 340, f.8, 19, 45 and 46, cuttings from *Westminster gazette*, 20-24 August 1776; *Public ledger*, 4 September 1776; *London evening post*, 25-27 November 1776; *Morning post*, 28 November 1776.

blamed d'Eon's success for the rash of subsequent *libelles*,[62] and when d'Eon's dispute with Beaumarchais led to the exposure of his second pay-off, adventurers everywhere learnt that the French court could be extorted repeatedly. No one knew this better than Boissière, who actively sought potential authors among his fellow refugees. In 1773 Boissière was involved in the negotiation for Morande's *Mémoires secrets d'une femme publique*,[63] and in 1781 he was paid 18,600 livres to suppress an illustrated edition of the scurrilous poem *Les Amours de Charlot et Toinette*.[64] Although the French government suspected that their agent, Louis-Valentin Goëzman, was working in cahoots with Boissière,[65] they felt unable to ignore slanders against the queen and her favourites. Thus in March 1783 they sent a police officer, Receveur, to London to investigate, empowering him to pay 350 guineas for the suppression of the illustrated *La Naissance du dauphin dévoilée* and Pelleport's *Petits soupers*.[66] Pelleport, however, held out for 700 louis before panicking and publishing a broadside entitled *An Alarme-bell against French spies* which exposed Receveur and announced two further pamphlets, *Les Passe-tems d'Antoinette* and *Les Amours du vizir Vergennes*.[67] The *Alarme-bell* unnerved Receveur, who soon concluded his mission was futile and departed for Paris. Pelleport, furious, retaliated by publishing *Le Diable dans un bénitier*.

The *Diable* was a potent political *libelle*. It offered an outspoken critique of ministerial despotism and financial corruption in government and exposed many details of France's secret police and spy networks. It also revealed that Receveur and the ambassador had employed Morande as an agent, commissioning him to prepare a memorandum on *libellistes* in which he advised ignoring them as the only effective means to silence them.[68]

In contrast, Morande's *Gazetier cuirassé* adopted a scattergun approach based on malicious anecdotes and sexual slanders against leading society and court figures. Its main targets, however, were Mme Du Barry and the ministerial triumvirate of Maupeou, Terray and d'Aiguillon. Such an august crowd suggests Morande indeed wrote on behalf of either the parlementary opposition or Choiseul, whose fall in December 1770 had been engineered by Maupeou. The truth is not quite so simple. The chevalier d'Eon, who understood its content as insult, identified 258 individuals, groups and institutions defamed in the *Gazetier*, including a

---

62. CPA 497, f.176-82, Garnier to d'Aiguillon, London, 31 August 1771.
63. CPA 541, f.346-49, Goëzman to Vergennes, London, 4 April 1783.
64. CPA 543, f.108-109, Vergennes to Adhémar, 25 June 1783, with copy of Boissière's quittance dated London, 31 July 1781.
65. CPA 541, f.50-51, [Lenoir] to [Vergennes], 24 February 1783; CPA 542, f.285-89, Receveur's 'Compte rendu', 22 May 1783.
66. CPA 542, f.285-89, Receveur's 'Compte rendu', 22 May 1783, at f.285.
67. CPA 541, f.378, *An Alarme-bell against French spies*.
68. [Pelleport], *Le Diable dans un bénitier*, p.61-72, 95 and *passim*. Morande's memoir on *libellistes* is in CPA 542, f.37-42.

handful of prominent Choiseulists and *parlementaires*.[69] They included the princes of the blood, who except for the comte de La Marche backed the *parlements* in their dispute with Maupeou; Praslin, Choiseul's cousin, who, Morande alleged, was rumoured to have died of rabies contracted while biting his own nails; Jarente, bishop of Orléans, accused here, as elsewhere, of improper relations with a dancer at the Opéra; and the chevalier de Choiseul, exposed as a bad debtor and habitual womaniser.[70] The work's overall Choiseulist and *parlementaire* sympathies are evident, however, together with a reformist *patriote* outlook, especially in its praise of Choiseul's policies of economy and opposition to religious orders. It is not the nihilist work Darnton suggests.

The most damaging *libelle* published in London, however, was Mme de La Motte's *Mémoires*, which appeared in February 1789.[71] The *Mémoires* portrayed the comtesse as a naive, innocent victim, seduced and used by a duplicitous, lesbian, libertine queen to acquire the diamond necklace and be revenged on cardinal Rohan, who had informed her mother of the sexual dalliances of her youth. Marie-Antoinette became Rohan's lover only to obtain the necklace and serve Austria by elevating Rohan to the ministry as an imperial agent. When he outlived his usefulness, she would destroy him. Well-informed contemporaries found the comtesse's story absurd, but in the heat of events, certain aspects rang true, and others anticipated familiar revolutionary motifs. Here, in embryo, is the mythical *comité autrichien* and an explanation for the queen's underhand method of acquiring the necklace: the monarchy was tightening its belt prior to revealing the financial crisis. Above all, here is corruption at court – political, sexual and financial – centred on the adulterous, libertine queen, who fuses together the three public roles played by eighteenth-century women: queen, actress and whore. As the predominant political public woman under the late *ancien régime*, both in terms of the influence she wielded and the publicity she attracted, Marie-Antoinette serves as prototype and stereotype of the revolutionary public woman, corrupting everything she touches. After publication, the monarchy reportedly decided to buy up copies of the comtesse's *Mémoires* at source and, in May 1792, Louis XVI purchased a large consignment of a revised two-volume autobiography.[72]

Until 1789, however, suppression fees proved effective at preventing *libelles* against Marie-Antoinette reaching the market, although they were usually a last resort after law and more draconian means failed.[73] The

---

69. CPA 513, f.439-43, 'An alphabetical list [...] of the princes, princesses, lords, ladies and others [...] insulted and abused in [...] [the] *Gazetier cuirassé*'.

70. C. Théveneau de Morande, *Le Gazetier cuirassé* (London, 1771), part 1, p.26-27, 45, 70, 95; part 2, p.23, 42; part 3, p.32.

71. The *Mémoires* were first advertised in *The Times* on 13 February 1789.

72. *The Times*, 18 June 1789; Mossiker, *The Queen's necklace*, p.562-65.

73. See Burrows, *Blackmail, scandal, and revolution*, ch.3-5; Gruder, 'The question of Marie-Antoinette'.

*libellistes* knew they ran risks. D'Eon, no stranger to French covert operations, believed he was courting assassination. When he fell ill on 28 October 1763, after dining at Guerchy's residence, he concluded he had been poisoned.[74] Morande, expecting to be assassinated, included provision for his widow in his pay-off agreement, while Pelleport panicked and exposed Receveur, apparently because he feared he would be abducted or murdered. The comte de La Motte describes several attempts to assassinate him, and his wife died from injuries sustained when she leapt from a window escaping bailiffs she believed to be French agents.[75]

Historians have ignored the reality behind the *libellistes*' fears, stressing instead that the regime softened in its final years. Yet evidence exists for regular plots against the *libellistes*, right up to the Revolution.[76] For example, before Guerchy's arrival in London, Choiseul and Praslin considered kidnapping and arresting d'Eon.[77] D'Eon's fears, moreover, partly derived from the fate of another refugee, the marquis de Fratteaux, who was delivered to French agents by a corrupt bailiff in 1752.[78] D'Eon's allegation that Praslin ordered Guerchy to have him assassinated to weaken Broglie's faction may also be justified, for in October 1764 Vergy, who admittedly had personal resentments against the ambassador, confessed to involvement in the October 1763 poison plot.[79] In April 1764, moreover, after the publication of d'Eon's *Lettres, mémoires et négociations*, Louis XV directly authorised a kidnap, should attempts to gain a libel conviction or extradition fail.[80] Louis XV likewise ordered the silencing of Morande after extradition requests were refused. In January 1774 an expedition sent to kidnap him arrived in London, led by a sieur Bellanger. Unfortunately Morande learnt of their mission, borrowed money from Bellanger's officers (who hoped to get a corrupt bailiff to seize him), and circulated flyers and newspaper advertisements denouncing them to the London mob, forcing them to flee.[81] Another mission, led by the

74. See CPA supplément 13, f.118-31, d'Eon to Broglie and Louis XV, London, 18 November 1763.
75. Jeanne de La Motte, *The Life of Jane de Saint-Remy de Valois*, 2 vols (Dublin, P. Wogan, P. Bryce, J. Moore, and J. Rice, 1792), vol.2, appendix-supplement, p.33-35.
76. See S. Burrows, 'Despotism without bounds: the French secret police and the silencing of dissent in London, 1760-1790', *History* 89 (2004), p.525-48.
77. *Correspondance secrète du comte de Broglie avec Louis XV, 1756-1774*, ed. Didier Ozanam and Michel Antoine, 2 vols (Paris, 1959-1961), vol.1, p.128n.; CPA supplément 13, f.132-33, Guerchy to Louis XV, 6 November 1763 (copy).
78. See ULBC, file 58, p.14, cutting from *Gazetteer*, 28 June 1764 and *passim*. D'Eon and Fratteaux shared the same lawyer, Peter Fountain.
79. See Kates, *Monsieur d'Eon*, p.130-31; Burrows, *Blackmail, scandal, and revolution*, ch.3.
80. Paris, Archives nationales de France (hereafter AN), K157, Louis XV to Tercier, 10 April 1764, published in *Correspondance secrète inédite de Louis XV, sur la politique étrangère*, ed. Edgar Boutaric, 2 vols (Paris, 1866), vol.1, p.320.
81. CPA 503, f.289, 'Soumission du S. (inconnu) [Sr Bellanger?], entre les mains de M. le D. [duc] d'Aig[uillon]', 18 December 1773; CPA 504, f.20, Morande to [d'Eon], 4 January 1774 'à 11 heures du soir'.

chevalier de Fontaine in 1772, also apparently hoped to silence him and is perhaps connected to an alleged attempt on Morande's life by two assailants who attacked him in a cab.[82]

The comte de La Motte claims an unseen swordsman attacked him, too, in a London hackney carriage, and that he was poisoned after he fled to Ireland. After escaping to Scotland to convalesce, he suspected he was being observed and moved to South Shields on Tyneside on the advice of a 'language master' named Benevent, who accompanied him. There, he uncovered a conspiracy to kidnap him, orchestrated by the ambassador d'Adhémar with the connivance of Benevent and two French police officers. A further boatload of police officers, masquerading as coal merchants, would convey La Motte to France.[83] Historians have been understandably reluctant to believe the comte, but recently discovered documents in the Quai d'Orsay confirm that the mission to Tyneside took place.[84] It is possible that assassination attempts in London and Ireland were also arranged by French ministers, their agents or the Rohan clan.

What became of the London *libellistes* in the Revolution? Darnton's argument implies that they became radical revolutionaries. This description may fit some figures peripheral to London's Grub Street, notably Delatouche, who in January 1793 was deported under the provisions of Britain's newly enacted *Alien Act*, and Serres de La Tour, whose surviving newspapers from 1789 betray a 'patriotic' disposition.[85] Neither rose to revolutionary prominence, however, and it is impossible to gauge the extent of their revolutionary commitment. In contrast, the leading Grub Streeters emphatically rejected Jacobin republicanism. D'Eon initially welcomed the Revolution, believing it would regenerate and purify the French political system to which he had fallen victim but, although he volunteered to fight for France in April 1792, he stayed in Britain, probably due to shortage of funds, and turned against the Revolution after the fall of the monarchy.[86] Thereafter, according to Olivier Blanc, he was involved in counter-revolutionary activities including circulating false

---

82. On Fontaine's mission see London, National Archives, SP78/285, f.293, Harcourt to Rochford, Compiègne, 16 July 1772; CPA 503, f.374, Morande to d'Eon, undated letter [3 or 4 January 1774]; CPA 541, f.346-49, Göezman to Vergennes, 4 April 1783. The cab incident is described in César Lavirotte, 'Notice sur M. de Morande', unpublished manuscript. I thank Bernard Leblanc for sending me a transcribed copy of this source.

83. J. de La Motte, *Memoirs of the countess de Valois La Motte* (Dublin, John Archer and William Jones, 1790), p.158-75. This passage was written by the comte, and differs in some details from the narrative in Marc-Antoine-Nicolas de La Motte, *Mémoires inédits du comte de La Motte-Valois sur sa vie et son époque (1754-1830)*, ed. Louis Lacour (Paris, 1858), p.66-119.

84. Paris, Archives du Ministère des affaires étrangères, Mémoires et documents 1400; CPA supplément 18, f.276-77. The plot is discussed in Munro Price, *Preserving the monarchy: the comte de Vergennes, 1774-1787* (Cambridge, 1995), p.178-80.

85. See London, National Archives, FO27/41, f.150, Audibert to Audibert, London, 28 January 1793; *Décade philosophique*, 10 fructidor An X (27 August 1803); copies of Serres de La Tour's *Journal de l'Europe* and *Journal de Londres* in the Bibliothèque Nationale.

86. See Kates, *Monsieur d'Eon*, p.271-76.

*assignats*.[87] Pelleport, ironically, was an early victim of the Revolution, savaged by the mob on 14 July 1789 and left for dead after attempting to intercede with them on behalf of the deputy governor of the Bastille, who had treated him kindly during his detention. He soon recovered, however, and reverted to intrigue.[88] In 1790 he was recruited as a secret agent and sent to London by the royalist-leaning foreign minister, Valdec de Lessart. After the fall of the monarchy he was briefly re-employed by the Dantonist foreign minister Deforgues and in late 1793 was sent to Chimay, masquerading as an émigré. Arrested by the Austrians, he turned coat again. He was condemned (*décrété d'accusation*), declared an émigré and had great difficulty returning to France,[89] not least because his eldest son was a committed counter-revolutionary activist.[90]

Morande originally welcomed the Revolution. From 1787 his newspaper advised Frenchmen – apparently with independence and sincerity – on how to reform the state, drawing on his experience of English customs and institutions. His ideological position was well to the left of his paymasters, but Morande abhorred mob violence and in May 1791 returned to France to defend the monarchy against extremists of both left and right. Loosely allied to the *feuillants*, he defined himself as a 'patriote royaliste', an ideological position consistent with his views since the early 1770s.[91] Arrested several days after the September massacres, probably at Brissot's instigation, Morande was exonerated, released and fled to Burgundy, where he was sheltered during the Terror by his brother, a revolutionary magistrate.[92] Even the La Mottes were apparently chastened by revolution, for in 1791 the comtesse produced revised memoirs which toned down her criticism of Marie-Antoinette. Iain McCalman concludes that her 1791 *Life* portrays Marie-Antoinette as 'less the dissembling pervert, than an essentially good hearted woman who is over impulsive and naïvely susceptible to manipulation by scheming courtiers'.[93] The only significant figure connected with London's Grub Street to pursue a radical revolutionary career was Brissot, who does not fit the blackmailer-*libelliste* model. Thus it is impossible to draw ideological links from London's Grub Street criminal fraternity to revolutionary Jacobinism.

Darnton's theory does not fit even those French writers most narrowly associated with Grub Street. Their activities and career trajectories cannot be explained by frustrated ambition or nihilism, nor did they become radical Jacobins. Their ideological preferences, so far as they can

87. Olivier Blanc, *Les Espions de la Révolution et de l'Empire* (Paris, 1995), p.15.
88. Charpentier, *Bastille dévoilée*, p.69-70.
89. Blanc, *Espions*, p.15-16, 293.
90. AN, F7 4336$^1$.
91. Burrows, 'Literary low-life'.
92. See AN, F7 4774$^{51}$, dossier 3; W251, dossier 27.
93. See Iain McCalman, 'Queen of the gutter: the lives and fictions of Jeanne de La Motte', in *Adventures in identity: European multicultural perspectives*, ed. John Docker and Gerhard Fischer (Tübingen, 2001), p.111-27.

be discerned, tended towards reformist constitutional monarchism. The denizens of London's French Grub Street were essentially creatures of the *ancien régime*, freebooting masterless men and women wavering between parasitic tension and symbiotic harmony with the court. Several of the most prominent – including d'Eon, Linsing, Pelleport, the La Mottes, La Rochette – were impoverished or fallen nobles with a strong sense of personal entitlement. Flesh and blood Figaros, they subverted traditional patronage relationships but were also dependent on them. Above all, they imitated traditional noble behaviour, using all means at their disposal to win favours and pensions from the court and other patrons. Like so much else in the *ancien régime*, by 1792 they disappeared into obscurity or turned to Counter-Revolution.

London's Grub Street *libellistes* nevertheless made significant contributions to French and British political culture. By furnishing images and concrete examples to confirm British prejudices concerning French despotism and their own liberty, they reinforced British nationalist discourses.[94] Grub Street was, moreover, a school for revolutionaries, although not in the way Darnton argued. It taught Brissot how the unreformed monarchy and its agents treated their victims. In 1791 he was given further proof of the regime's baseness when Morande appeared in Paris and disrupted his election campaign by publishing pamphlets accusing him of writing *libelles*, defrauding his business partner and spying for the British. The experience reinforced both his belief in the importance of press freedom in creating transparent government and his tendency towards paranoia.

If Brissot were the only prominent figure to have suffered at the hands of Grub Street hacks and the French police, or police actions had remained secret, this would be of little significance. But Brissot's experience was shared by revolutionaries and publicists like Mirabeau, Lauraguais, Beaumarchais and Linguet, whose paranoid view of the world confused personal enemies and political rivals.[95] Before the Revolution, any reader of the bestsellers of the Mairobert corpus, *chroniques scandaleuses*, the *Diable dans un bénitier* or the *Mémoires secrets* also knew of the activities of French agents in Grub Street. From 1789 they were further exposed by the La Mottes, and documented in sensational works like the *Bastille dévoilée* (1789) and Manuel's *La Police de Paris dévoilée*. These works revealed the despotism and ruthlessness of an otherwise reformist monarchy. No wonder leading revolutionaries did not trust the monarchy and its agents and saw conspiracies behind every political alliance, association or written attack. Thus, contrary to the assertions of some recent commentators, the revolutionary elite's obsession with conspiracy had long-term, rational

94. Burrows, 'Despotism without bounds'; Burrows, *Blackmail, scandal, and revolution*, ch.7.
95. Myriam Yardeni, 'Paradoxes politiques et persuasion dans les *Annales* de Linguet', in *The Press in the French Revolution*, ed. Harvey Chisick, *SVEC* 287 (1991), p.211-19 (214).

causes rooted in the activities of the *ancien régime* court and its agents.[96] Moreover, assuming that their own experience of court politics was universal, many revolutionaries assumed that other European peoples would welcome French armies as liberators. It is thus no coincidence that Brissot was the leading spokesman for war in 1791 and 1792.

Finally Grub Street armed revolutionaries with some of their main modes of journalistic rhetoric. The denunciatory discourse of political *libellistes* which Chisick dismisses as marginal to Enlightenment discourse (which was 'a literature of dialogue' and sought to convince and persuade) became central to revolutionary discourses of self-styled journalistic tribunes of the people.[97] Grub Street texts – notably the *Mémoires* of Mme de La Motte and suppressed works liberated from the Bastille[98] – also provided the pornographic images and associations that revolutionary propagandists wielded to such effect against the aristocracy and public women and made them formulaic. Their tales and images contributed to Austrophobia and were absorbed into revolutionary political pornography, before being recycled at the trial of Marie-Antoinette, who was accused of a variety of sexual crimes, including debauching her own son.

Thus, although it did not operate according to the Darntonian model, Grub Street helped to shape the progress of the French Revolution. While it was certainly not the sole laboratory for revolution, it played a significantly greater role than Darnton's critics allow. Indeed previously peripheral rhetorical styles, images and fears supplied by London's Grub Street became embedded at the heart of the revolutionary script. To argue that Grub Street discourses were marginal to the Enlightenment mainstream misses the point for, during the revolutionary process, previously marginalised or suppressed discourses move to the centre of the historical stage. Indeed Jeremy Popkin has recently defined a revolutionary cycle as the period when 'unruly texts' are able to proliferate in public space, and consequently create new possibilities for the redefinition of social reality.[99] In 1789 such 'unruly' revolutionary texts were more likely to draw on enlightened rationalism. By 1792 and 1793, however, enlightened rationalism had been displaced by Grub Street discourses which denounced monarchy and foreign courts as obscene, faction-ridden despotisms and fanned the flames of revolutionary paranoia. Hence London's French Grub Street is rather more heavily implicated than the mainstream Enlightenment in the genesis of masculinist revolutionary republicanism, war and Terror.

96. See especially Timothy Tackett, 'Conspiracy obsession in a time of revolution: French elites and the origins of the Terror, 1789-1792', *American historical review* 105 (2000), p.691-713.
97. Harvey Chisick, 'Introduction' in *The Press in the French Revolution*, ed. H. Chisick, p. 1-17 (8). E. L. Eisenstein, 'The tribune of the people: a new species of demagogue', in *The Press in the French Revolution*, ed. H. Chisick, p.145-59; Yardeni, 'Paradoxes politiques'.
98. See Burrows, *Blackmail, scandal, and revolution*, ch.5.
99. J. D. Popkin, *Press, revolution and social identities in France, 1830-1835* (University Park, PA, 2002), especially ch.1. Quotation and definition p.3.

ULTÁN GILLEN

# Varieties of Enlightenment: the Enlightenment and Irish political culture in the age of revolutions

ON 29 March 1792 *Faulkner's Dublin journal*, a conservative newspaper sponsored by the Irish Administration, complained that:

Never was there an unhappy Phrase so abused, as, '*we who live in an enlightened age;*' it's the cant term in every whiskey shop, and a fellow who has no intellects to receive any benefits from light, uses it with as much *sang froid* as Mr. Grattan. – Upon this subject Mr. Hobart makes a just remark, speaking of men who had some cause to boast of being enlightened – 'but what is this illumination?' says he, 'an imperfect light that only serves to mislead them!'

This quotation reflects how central the notion of Enlightenment had become in Irish political culture by the early 1790s. Right across the political spectrum, ranging from radicals from the lower orders to the political elite, politicians, pamphleteers and newspapers sought to associate enlightened principles with their own political positions. The meaning of the Enlightenment for Ireland was under discussion from Parliament to the coffee-house. This was especially true when discussing the potential implications of the French Revolution on Ireland, and the question of increasing the civil and political rights enjoyed by Catholics in a Protestant confessional state.

To the modern reader familiar with Ireland's history of sectarian division, and the ongoing problems resulting from it, the prevalence of Enlightenment language in late-eighteenth-century Irish political debate is surprising. Eighteenth-century Ireland is remembered in Irish popular culture as the Penal Age, when Catholics were not only denuded of what land and power remained in their hands in the wake of the Glorious Revolution of 1688 and the Williamite Wars, but their religion was suppressed. The popular image (though not that of historians) remains that of the priest saying mass for his peasant flock outdoors, with only a rock as an altar, and perhaps with the Redcoats hunting the priest marching across the horizon. Nothing could seem further from the religious toleration that lay at the heart of Enlightenment principles.

The influence of the Enlightenment on Irish politics in the 1790s, however, has long been recognised by historians. Discontent at the Anglican Establishment among Catholics and Presbyterians, influenced to a large extent by the French Revolution, and the demands of the Revolutionary Wars led to the emergence of a revolutionary republican organisation known as the Society of United Irishmen. They attempted a failed rebellion in 1798 that led to the British–Irish Union of 1801. The United Irishmen self-consciously described themselves as enlightened, and the influence of the French and Scottish Enlightenment on them has been extensively discussed.[1]

This essay seeks to explain why the language of Enlightenment was so prominent in Irish political culture at the end of the eighteenth century. It argues that the dominant political rhetoric, which was centred on 1688, regarded the British and Irish constitution of King, Lords and Commons and some form of religious toleration as the epitome of enlightened government. In terms of enlightened government, rather than being on the periphery of the Enlightenment, many Irish people regarded themselves as being at its core. This view was held not only by government supporters in Parliament, but also by reformers, who believed that reforms would perfect the constitution. This consensus was shaken by a debate over the Established Church that began in 1786, and was shattered by the impact of the French Revolution. Both supporters and opponents of, for example, Catholic enfranchisement in the early 1790s claimed to represent the truly enlightened position. These debates over the correct application of enlightened principles to politics are best viewed not as battles between Enlightenment and Anti-Enlightenment, but rather as disputes between varieties of interpretations of the implications of the Enlightenment.[2] The deployment of enlightened language in Irish political debates in the late eighteenth century therefore speaks not only to local Irish concerns, but also to wider debates in European historiography about the nature of the Enlightenment.

The Enlightenment in Ireland has been the subject of increasing historiographical attention over recent years.[3] Several important Enlightenment writers were Irish, and the Irish context for the work of authors

---

1. For example, A. T. Q. Stewart, *A Deeper silence: the hidden origins of the United Irishmen* (London, 1993); Peter Tiesch, 'Presbyterian radicalism', in *The United Irishmen: republicanism, radicalism and rebellion*, ed. David Dickson, Dáire Keogh and Kevin Whelan (Dublin, 1993), p.33-48; Ian McBride, 'William Drennan and the dissenting tradition', in *The United Irishmen*, ed. D. Dickson, D. Keogh and K. Whelan, p.49-61; I. McBride, *Scripture politics: Ulster Presbyterians and Irish radicalism in the late eighteenth century* (Oxford, 1998); Kevin Whelan, *The Tree of liberty* (Cork, 1996), especially p.59-96; Simon Davies, 'The *Northern star* and the propagation of enlightened ideas', *Eighteenth-century Ireland: Iris an Dá Cultúr* 5 (1990), p.143-52.

2. For a discussion of the respective merits of the terms 'Anti-Enlightenment' and 'Counter-Enlightenment', see Richard Butterwick's essay in this volume.

3. David Berman, 'Enlightenment and Counter-Enlightenment in Irish philosophy', *Archiv für Geschichte der Philosophie*, 64 (1982), p.148-65, 257-79 is an important starting point; a collection of texts from around 1690 to 1757 is *The Irish Enlightenment and Counter-Enlightenment*, ed. D. Berman and P. O'Riordan. *Ireland and the French Enlightenment*, ed. G. Gargett and G. Sheridan; M. Kennedy, *French books in eighteenth-century Ireland*.

such as John Toland and Francis Hutcheson has come under scrutiny.[4] Given the absence of any major Irish writer in the later half of the eighteenth century, however, attention has concentrated on the dissemination of ideas. Many major Enlightenment works were sold in Ireland and reprinted in Dublin, both in translation and in the original. This trade, and Ireland's relationship with the French Enlightenment, have received detailed consideration. Magazines and newspapers also made the works of the Enlightenment available through reprinting extracts from major works, and discussing them in reviews and letters.

By the late eighteenth century, the audience for such works was considerable. Although the poverty of the Irish peasantry at the end of the century still shocked contemporaries, eighteenth-century Ireland had experienced a great deal of economic growth, with the linen and provisions trades performing especially well. This economic growth, expressed in the magnificent new buildings that sprang up in Dublin and elsewhere, facilitated the development of print culture and the associational aspects of the public sphere. Printers and bookshops could be found in most significant Irish towns, and booksellers had national networks. By 1792 thirty-five newspapers competed for the audience's attention, including several Dublin newspapers which acted as national newspapers. It must be remembered, however, that many newspapers quickly folded, while others were kept afloat only by government advertising. Libraries, readings rooms, reading societies and coffee-houses provided access to the works of the Enlightenment to a broad audience from different social classes, and the opportunity to discuss their themes. Freemasonry had a strong presence in many parts of Ireland, while interest in science, language, literature and history found expression in the foundation of the Royal Irish Academy in 1784. Ireland's well-developed public sphere facilitated debate on enlightened thinking across the country.

Partly arising from the growth in interest in the Scottish Enlightenment, historians have increasingly focused on the importance of political economy and economic improvement to conceptions of the Enlightenment across Europe. John Robertson's recent examination of Enlightenment thought in Scotland and Naples has examined how two different societies sought to employ Enlightenment concepts to overcome poverty.[5] Ireland was faced with similar problems. Ireland may not have produced many major Enlightenment thinkers but constant attempts were made to apply the ideas of the Enlightenment to the problems of Irish society, especially its poverty. Much of Ireland's associational culture was dedicated to improving its economy, which was seen as the

---

4. For example, T. Duddy, 'Toland, Berkeley and the irrational hypothesis', *Eighteenth-century Ireland: Iris an Dá Cultúr*, 14 (1999), p.49-61 and Michael Brown, *Francis Hutcheson in Dublin, 1719-1730* (Dublin, 2001). Brown is currently writing a history of the Irish Enlightenment.

5. Robertson, *The Case for the Enlightenment*.

duty of an enlightened patriot. Ireland had in fact provided the model for many of the economic improvement societies that sprang up across Europe with the foundation in 1731 of the Dublin Society for Improving Husbandry, Manufactures and other Useful Arts.[6] The Society from 1740 awarded prizes to encourage good practice, and received a Charter in 1750 and support from the Irish Parliament thereafter. The Irish Parliament expended large sums of money on subsidising Irish trade and manufacturing, and creating infrastructure. Enlightenment was institutionalised in the many turnpikes, market towns, canals and other public works funded and encouraged by Parliament, other public bodies and landlords in the eighteenth century.

In 1791 one newspaper claimed that 'the enlightened spirit of the present times has led the inhabitants of this kingdom to some undertakings infinitely important to society', particularly canals and the 'improvement of barren land' which reflected the 'dawn of illumination'. 'The force of reason and the influence of patriotism' would effect improvement.[7] The paper echoed French physiocracy by arguing that agriculture was the basis of a state's strength. 'Every power which comes from any other source except land, is artificial and precarious, either in natural or moral philosophy.' It made clear the link between improvement, patriotism and Enlightenment. Toasting Ireland's economic improvement was de rigueur at any meeting or dinner of a public society, further evidence of the enlightened self-image of Irish public opinion. While selfish reasons undoubtedly played a part in the eagerness of many improvers, there can be no doubt that a desire for improvement was widespread amongst the educated classes, and that it formed a key part of Irish patriotism. In the words of one observer as early as the 1760s, 'a man has a figure in his county in proportion to the improvements he makes.'[8]

At the end of the century, however, there remained an awareness that the penetration of Enlightenment ideas was far from complete. 'A Farmer' lamented that 'at this enlightened period, when most of the nations in Europe are improving their arts, manufactures and agriculture' no 'FARMING CLUBS' existed in Ulster.[9] Irish poverty could not be denied, and the majority appeared to have experienced little improvement in wealth or manners. As one pamphlet produced by Dublin radicals put it, while ostensibly discussing France but actually speaking

6. See Jim Livesey, 'The Dublin Society in eighteenth-century Irish political thought', *Historical journal* 47 (2004), p.615-40 for a recent discussion of the Society's impact.

7. *Freeman's journal*, 25 October 1791. The *Freeman's journal* was published in Dublin three times a week. Its editor, Francis Higgins, was one of the government's chief spymasters in its struggle against the United Irishmen in the later 1790s.

8. Quoted in R. B. McDowell, *Ireland in the age of imperialism and revolution, 1760-1801* (Oxford, 1979), p.6-7. I am grateful to David Hayton for his comments on attitudes to improvement and toleration.

9. J. McCully, *Letters by a farmer* (Belfast, J. Magee, 1787), p.1.

about Ireland, the mass of the people remained 'a set of beings, with their females, their young, and their domestic animals, herding together in hovels that are open to the storm and bare of all furniture – the window a hole, and the door a chimney'.[10]

If economic improvement was one major concern of the Irish Parliament throughout the century, the other was Ireland's relationship with Britain. Throughout the century, but especially from around 1750, Irish political culture fixated on independence from Britain. This included not only the desire for legislative independence (not separation from Britain but an end to Westminster's right to legislate for Ireland), but also freedom from British restrictions on Irish trade. This resentment culminated in the successful campaigns for free trade and legislative independence during the American Revolution, the so-called Revolution of 1782. The foundational text of eighteenth-century Irish patriotism, William Molyneux's *The Case of Ireland's being bound by acts of Parliament in England, stated* (1698), had been produced in response to English regulation of the Irish woollen trade. Molyneux sat for the University of Dublin in the Irish Parliament, and he was a friend of John Locke's. His pamphlet aimed to demonstrate that Westminster legislating for Ireland was a violation of Irish rights, and deployed the concept of natural rights, contract theory and theories of international relations in support of his argument.

Molyneux's was a complex, even tortuous, argument, which sought to deny every possible claim that England might have to legislate for Ireland. English claims went against '*the Law of Nature and Reason*'. Westminster legislating for Ireland violated 'the *Freedoms* and *Immunities* to which all *Mankind* have a *Right*', especially the right to be governed only by laws to which they had given their consent.[11] Molyneux wielded the rhetoric and principles of the Glorious Revolution against the elite it had secured in power, citing chapter 16 of Locke's *Two Treatises of Government* in defence of inalienable natural rights.[12] Unsurprisingly, English MPs were unconvinced, but the key text of Irish patriotism spoke the language of the British Enlightenment, of a political culture centred on 1688. Molyneux's pamphlet, and a government modelled on that of Britain, ensured that Irish demands would be asserted in accordance with Enlightenment concepts. The Irish political classes, and broad swathes of public opinion, believed that they partook of the world's most enlightened political system – they believed a government made up of King, Lords

---

10. *Address from the National Assembly of France to the people of Ireland* (Dublin, J. Chambers, 1790), p.11. This *Address* was an Irish fake, designed to promote the cause of Irish radicalism, and produced by the Whigs of the Capital, a Dublin radical group that would form the backbone of the Dublin United Irishmen.
11. Molyneux, *The Case of Ireland's being bound by acts of Parliament in England, stated* (Dublin, published for J. R., 1698), p.18, 21. Emphasis in the original.
12. Molyneux, *The Case of Ireland (1698)*, p.27.

and Commons represented the interests of all the people of Ireland. Up until the French Revolution, reformers in Ireland called for the proper application of the principles of the constitution, not their overhaul. Despite the acknowledgment that Ireland was peripheral to many advances of the Enlightenment, Irish political culture was infused with the belief that Ireland was at the centre of enlightened government in Europe.

Perhaps the core principle of the Enlightenment was religious toleration. Opponents of the Penal Laws used major Enlightenment thinkers to support their cause. Montesquieu's reputation as a lover of the British constitution ensured that, as elsewhere in Europe, he was regarded in Ireland as the greatest thinker of the age, and his works were used to argue for the repeal of the Penal Laws, which had achieved their primary aim of greatly reducing Catholic ownership of land. For example, in April 1757, a pamphlet advocating the removal of the 'Popery Acts' quoted Montesquieu's *Esprit des lois* twice on the opening page. Another from 1762 quoted Montesquieu's argument that the public good consisted in the protection of property to justify giving propertied Catholics fuller rights.[13] A new Catholic elite had emerged during the century, educated abroad, and composed of the remnants of the aristocracy and Catholics who had prospered in trade. The abolition of the Penal Laws gathered momentum with the Land Act of 1778 which allowed Catholics to hold land on terms similar to Protestants. The social divisions between the various denominations, though very strong in some parts, particularly among the lower orders, were also breaking down among an educated public. Catholics were elected members of the Royal Irish Academy; they participated in associational culture across the country, as well as social activities like theatre-going, and they engaged in public debate on a range of issues. By the late eighteenth century, although Penal Laws restricting Catholic and Presbyterian access to political power remained, as did laws prohibiting Catholics from certain careers, the fact that all forms of worship were freely allowed meant that, as with political representation, the Irish elite regarded Ireland as being at the forefront of enlightened practice.

Overall, then, by the late eighteenth century, there was a growing sense that Ireland was in many ways an enlightened country, even if the poverty and religious divisions among the population also created a sense that she was inferior to other countries, and in need of Enlightenment. The term 'enlightened' was much less used in the 1770s and early 1780s than it would be later, but the preoccupations of political culture at this time were Enlightenment concerns. The remainder of this paper will

---

13. *The Protestant interest, considered relative to the operation of the Popery Acts in Ireland* (Dublin, 1757); Edmond Gorges Howard, *Some observations and queries on the present laws of this kingdom, relative to papists*, 2nd edn (Dublin, O. Nelson, 1762), p.17.

examine the impact upon Irish political culture of these simultaneous perceptions of being at both the core and the periphery of the Enlightenment in the last quarter of the eighteenth century, and trace how differing understandings of how enlightened principles should be applied affected Irish politics in the age of the American and French Revolutions.

Charles Francis Sheridan provided the most intellectually sophisticated case for Irish legislative independence, in a pamphlet from 1779 challenging the legal opinions of no less an authority than Sir William Blackstone. Sheridan, an Irish MP, had been part of the British embassy in Sweden, and had written an account of the revolution carried out there by Gustav III and his supporters.[14] Sheridan's pamphlet was in many respects a modern version of Molyneux's *Case of Ireland*, but it also addressed itself to the role of the individual in the polity. Sheridan challenged Blackstone's views of the power of Parliament, which he claimed granted Parliament absolute power, violating Locke's doctrine on the right of resistance, 'the first article in the political creed of every freeman'.[15] Incorrect understandings of the true principles of the constitution threatened not only individual liberty, but they had led to the oppression of Ireland, and the loss of the American colonies.

Sheridan argued that previous discussions had misunderstood the relationship between power and liberty. Liberty lay in the full enjoyment of natural rights (the right to security of life and property, to do what one wished as long as it did not impinge on others, and to enjoy unmolested what was necessary to enjoy such freedom as long as it did not involve violating the rights and property of others), and the purpose of government was to protect those rights. Parliament had no power to violate the rights of any individual, nor any community that had not delegated power to it – and so Britain's power to legislate for Ireland was a violation of the natural rights of the people of Ireland both as individuals and as a nation. Sheridan separated the fourth natural right, that of resistance, from the others. Enjoying the first three took acts of liberty, but defending them was an act of power. Any act that impinged on others was an act of power, and upon entering society, an individual surrendered only to the limitation of acts of power, not of liberty. Government itself was an act of power, entrusted by the people to the authorities. One people could not entrust the rights of another to its own government, hence Westminster had no right to legislate for Ireland. To do so was '*a usurpation of the fourth*

---

14. Charles Francis Sheridan, *A History of the late revolution in Sweden* (Dublin, M. Mills, 1778). Also printed in London, and it ran to two editions. A French edition was printed in 1783, supposedly in London. Sheridan wrote his work as a warning against the subversion of the liberty of a free people.

15. C. F. Sheridan, *Observations on the doctrine laid down by Sir William Blackstone, respecting the extent of the power of the British Parliament, particularly with relation to Ireland, in a letter to Sir William Blackstone, with a postscript addressed to Lord North, upon the affairs of that country* (Dublin, printed for the Company of Booksellers, 1779), p.20. Also printed in London, it ran to two editions there.

*natural right of mankind*.[16] Like Molyneux before him, Sheridan sought to turn the political principles of the British Enlightenment against the pretensions of the British political elite.

Liberty was divided into two types, civil and political. All should have the enjoyment of civil liberty, but not political liberty, which should be limited only to those who had sufficient resources to put them beyond the reach of government bribery. The community of interest these incorruptibles had with the rest of the population would ensure that government operated in the interests of all. Voting was an act of power whose purpose was to limit the lifetime of Parliaments. It had no other intrinsic value – drawing lots for members of the House of Commons would achieve the same goal. As an act of power, its use should be limited to those who would use it responsibly. Sheridan thus provided a fairly typical excuse for the property qualification, but of course in an Irish context he was also implicitly justifying the exclusion of Catholics from the franchise, and of Catholics and Presbyterians from administrative positions and representative bodies.

Sheridan's pamphlet was written in the midst of the campaign for British restrictions on Irish trade to be ended, for free trade. The American War provided the opportunity for the long-term resentment at these restrictions to burst forward. Britain had withdrawn troops from Ireland for America, leaving the defence of Ireland in the hands of Volunteers who grew 80,000 strong. The Volunteers rapidly turned their attention to political matters, to redressing Ireland's grievances. They may not always have expressed their demands with subtlety – famously hanging a placard inscribed 'Free Trade or This' on a cannon at a massive demonstration outside the Irish Parliament – but they were the genuine voice of public opinion, armed and militant. Sheridan made the same demands, in a more sophisticated fashion.

It was an article of faith among the Irish elite of all political hues that Ireland had the population and resources to develop a flourishing commercial society, and such sentiments were regularly expressed in Parliament, pamphlets and newspapers, and other public forums. Irish enlightened thought projected a vision of an improved society similar to that offered by the Scottish Enlightenment, where modern agriculture, trade and industry, and reformed manners would lift Ireland out of poverty and beyond sectarianism, and into the first rank of nations.[17] The differing political circumstances produced differing emphases, however, demonstrating how the mutual concerns of enlightened thinkers in

16. Sheridan, *Observations*, p.55.

17. Richard Lewis' eclectic work, *The Candid philosopher, or Free thoughts on men, morals and manners*, 2 vols (Dublin, Byrn and Son and W. Kidd, 1778), ranged widely across topics, but asserted the importance of reforming manners, of protection of the linen industry and of independence. It was unusual, however, in criticising Bernard Mandeville's *Fable of the bees* and luxury. It also promoted equal rights for Catholics. It was also printed in London.

different societies could be shaped by local political and societal circumstances.

In Sheridan's words, Ireland was a 'country formed by nature, from its situation, its soil, its climate, to be the seat of plenty, wealth, and commerce'. Although enlightened thinkers attributed Ireland's poverty partly to differences in customs, language and religion, as well as resistance to improved agricultural techniques among the peasantry – often attributed to the landholding system which deprived them of security and thus the incentive to invest in improvements – Sheridan was very clear about why Ireland had not developed into a successful commercial society: 'You, our fellow-subjects of England, have deprived us of the use of these [advantages from nature] by conduct as impolitic, as it is unjust.'[18] Britain was blamed for impoverishing Ireland to enrich herself. Sheridan's sentiments were representative of the vast majority of Irish opinion, and explain why the lifting of British restrictions was of such importance to Volunteers, politicians and public alike.

This focus on foreign restrictions as an explanation for Ireland's poverty also explains why Scottish Enlightenment thinkers like Adam Smith do not occupy the prominent place in Irish enlightened economic thought that we might expect. An edition of *Wealth of nations* had been published in Dublin in 1776, and further editions followed in 1785 and 1793. Smith's works and ideas were well known in Ireland, and had been discussed in print culture. While free trade in Irish terms meant freedom for Irish goods from British restrictions, however, it did not mean laissez-faire. Protection and government subsidies remained a vital part of enlightened Irish economic thinking, the aim being to build up those industries like wool which had been damaged by British restrictions, and foster the further development of the linen trade. Not only that, but the Irish elite demanded that Britain allow Irish goods privileged access to the British and imperial markets. While laissez-faire seemed best suited to exploit Scotland's economic strengths, Ireland's poverty, the feeling of economic rivalry with Britain, and a history of struggle for greater independence gave a very different agenda to Irish political economy. Irish enlightened economic thought remained much more closely tied to political culture than its Scottish cousin.

John Robertson has powerfully argued that political economy was the central theme of enlightened writing. The absence of reference to writers such as Smith has sometimes been taken as demonstrating that there was no Irish Enlightenment. The concerns addressed by enlightened thinkers through political economy across Europe, however, took on a peculiarly Irish edge, one shaped by the consciousness of being at the periphery of economic development and of the concerns of Westminster. An independent Irish Parliament was viewed as the only way to achieve economic

18. Sheridan, *Observations*, p.82-83.

development. Different solutions were being arrived at in other countries, but the central issues under discussion were the same. Enlightenment questions found Enlightenment answers consistent with Irish economic and political realities. Irish economic thought, despite its protectionist assumptions and being somewhat stunted by the issue of independence, was a variety of political economy.[19]

Economic thought remained obsessed with the political after legislative independence. Ireland experienced sustained economic growth after 1782, and contemporaries attributed this to legislative independence, reinforcing their assumptions.[20] Moves were made to liberalise trade. The Anglo-French Commercial Treaty of 1786 in fact included Ireland as a signatory as well. This was the first time that Ireland had signed a treaty in its own right. Although the potential economic benefits were much discussed, government propaganda concentrated on its political significance, as an assertion of independence. The Chief Secretary, who represented the administration in Parliament, Thomas Orde, argued for ratification on these grounds, and the Lord Chancellor congratulated the Irish Parliament on its ability to make foreign treaties. William Ogilvie, a government supporter, argued that after ratification 'Ireland will stand on higher ground than ever' in her relations with Britain.[21] The same arguments were heard out of doors. 'Carlos' reminded his audience that the treaty 'fixes the seal of foreign recognition' on Ireland's independence.[22] The opponents of the treaty also concentrated on political arguments, claiming that the treaty actually violated Ireland's independence as certain goods would have to be transported to France through Britain. The *Dublin evening post*, Ireland's most successful newspaper and the voice of opposition, described the addition of Ireland's name to the treaty as a sop 'added to prevent uproar'.[23] Again, it was the question of Ireland's natural rights as a nation as outlined by Molyneux that was at the core of the discussion, not the finer points of economics.

If the free trade and legislative independence campaigns had reasserted traditional economic thinking, they had also seen the beginnings of serious questioning of the confessional state among radicals. The Protestant political nation relied on the British for protection from the perceived threat from Catholics. The price paid was the subordination of Irish interests to those of Britain. A sense that this price was too high and that

19. For an analysis of mid-eighteenth-century Irish economic thought, see Patrick Kelly, 'The politics of political economy in mid-eighteenth-century Ireland', in *Political ideas in eighteenth-century Ireland*, ed. S. J. Connolly (Dublin, 2000), p.105-29.
20. The Irish Marxist James Connolly famously compared the belief that legislative independence had brought economic growth to a fly on a wheel marvelling at its own strength in making the wheel go round.
21. *Freeman's journal*, 27 February, 13 March, 8 March 1787.
22. *Freeman's journal*, 31 July 1787.
23. *Dublin evening post*, 27 January 1787. Thrice-weekly, with a circulation of around 4000 in 1789.

an alliance of all religious groups to secure greater independence was more in Irish interests began to emerge among radicals. Joseph Pollock's *Letters of Owen Roe O'Nial* gave voice to these feelings. Pollock was a Presbyterian radical from the Ulster town of Newry, which was thriving due to the linen industry. Eoghan Rua Ó Néill, or Owen Roe O'Nial, was a seventeenth-century Gaelic chieftain who had rebelled against the English. The fact that Pollock adopted his persona and that, despite this, the pamphlet achieved great popularity itself says something about the depth of hostility towards British interference.

Pollock blamed a British war for starving Irish manufacturers, said that the free British nation had always behaved like a tyrant towards Ireland, and compared the Irish to American Indians and the Spartan helots. He drew on Molyneux's *Case of Ireland* for his argument that Ireland's rights had been violated and commented that what had once taken a Locke to explain – the rights of a people to form its own government – was now learnt by children in schools. It was time for Ireland to break the bonds of slavery and assert these rights. Like many Irish patriots, he therefore based his arguments on the assumptions of enlightened British and Irish political culture.

Pollock transgressed the accepted boundaries of Irish Protestant political culture by suggesting that the threatened French invasion might be a good thing for Irish liberty. But he warned that, 'unless we lay aside all rancour of prejudice on account of distinctions either political or religious', any attempts to achieve greater independence would fail. The new Irish government's 'first ruling principle must be *toleration*. How far this would contribute to the happiness, greatness and stability of the state, as it would afford an asylum and encouragement to arts, industry and virtue' was obvious from the damage France's economy had sustained from the expulsion of the Huguenots, the prosperity of Holland and the virtues of Pennsylvania.[24] Pollock did not argue for extending toleration on the basis of natural rights, nor did he use the term 'enlightened', but he argued for toleration as the sole way to achieve the patriot vision of a strong, modern, commercial society.

Toleration gained wide acceptance at this time, for both practical and principled reasons. Britain needed to draw on Catholic manpower for the American War, and some Penal Laws were abolished to facilitate this and bolster loyalty amongst the Catholic population, and partly as a reward for Catholic loyalty throughout the century. These changes also reflected the growing influence of enlightened ideas and practices which had significantly softened traditional hostilities. One of the changes in the predominant rhetoric of Irish political culture at this time was the idea that bigotry and prejudice had been largely banished. George Ogle, a patriot MP who would later be one of the chief defenders of Protestant

---

24. Joseph Pollock, *Letters of Owen Roe O'Nial* (Dublin, W. Jackson, 1779), p.24, 42.

Ascendancy, was praised as 'The Assertor of Freedom, the Opposer of Tyranny, the Friend of Ireland, the Advocate for the Right of Private Judgment, in all Matters Civil and Ecclesiastical', demonstrating how far religious toleration was an accepted part of Protestant political culture.[25] In 1782 Henry Grattan described how 'by the charter of toleration those intestine divisions [...] have ceased, and with them the domination of Great Britain has departed.'[26] These changing circumstances were also demonstrated by the fact that Belfast's first Catholic church was opened in 1784, with a guard of honour from local Volunteers and paid for mainly by local Protestants. Although the majority of the Protestant political nation believed that Catholics now enjoyed as full a toleration as they could expect, others did assert the rights of Catholics to still fuller inclusion. As elsewhere in the Atlantic world, the right to bear arms was an important badge of citizenship, and had been made more so in Ireland by a Penal Law banning Catholics from bearing arms. Some radical Volunteer units armed Catholics, and the poor, both of whom were outside the political nation. Partly this was a practical measure, and reflected Catholic support, particularly among Catholic merchants, for free trade and legislative independence. It was also a political statement, a rejection of the confessional state, and an assertion of the right of every individual to be considered as part of the polity. It was, therefore, an expression of a radical interpretation of both natural rights and Locke's theories, the radical Enlightenment in action. In the aftermath of 1782 and the end of the American War, however, Volunteer numbers declined, and the shrunken movement split in 1784 over reform and the Catholic question. The differing interpretations reflected in this split over how far natural rights were political rights – over the implications of Enlightenment for politics – provided the motor of much of the political and violent conflict in the 1790s.

The confessional nature of the state was raised again in the 'Dublin paper war' between 1786 and 1788.[27] The Rightboys, a popular protest movement against the fees charged by Catholic priests and against tithe to the Established Church of Ireland produced a panic amongst hard-line supporters of the Protestant Ascendancy, the dominance of the Church of Ireland in religion and politics. Ultra-Protestant opinion was rallied by Richard Woodward, Anglican bishop of Cloyne, who maintained that the constitution was threatened by concessions to Catholics and

25. Lewis, *Candid philosopher*, dedication of the first volume.
26. *An Address to the Right Honourable Henry Grattan, Esq. by the Independent Dublin Volunteers, relative to the simple repeal, and the recent interference of the Earl of Mansfield, in deciding, in an English court, upon an appeal from Ireland; with Mr Grattan's answer: and observations on Mr Grattan's and Mr Y---L---N's conduct, in a letter to Mr Y---L---N, the A---y G---l of Ireland, to which is annexed the resolutions of the Lawyers Committee and Corps* (London, J. Debrett, 1782), p.5.
27. William McCormack, *The Dublin paper war of 1786-1788: a bibliographical and critical enquiry* (Dublin, 1993).

Presbyterians, both of whose bloody histories proved them intolerant of other religions and inherently disloyal to the Hanoverian monarchy. Only the Anglican Church was suited to the moderate and tolerant principles of the British and Irish constitution.[28] Woodward's pamphlet was immensely popular amongst the elite, and the debate that followed, in Parliament, in around one hundred pamphlets and in newspapers, produced an aggressive reassertion of the conservative interpretation of the Glorious Revolution.

On the opposite side, Catholic clergy argued that Catholics were loyal subjects while Presbyterian clergy and political liberals deployed Enlightenment writers and language. Phrases such as 'an enlightened age' became noticeably more common in political debate from around this time.[29] Presbyterian writers mixed history with enlightened philosophy in their arguments. Reverend William Campbell cited the *Lettres persanes* in favour of toleration, while the future United Irishman Reverend Samuel Barber denied that Catholics were unfit for liberty, pointing out that across the ages they had promoted liberty, from Magna Carta to the Italian republics, so fears for the state were groundless.[30] Daniel Thomas, M. D., though 'long accustomed to philosophical apathy', entered the fray because 'infatuated zeal' threatened 'to deluge this island with blood'.[31] He saw his duty as a man of Enlightenment to fight the dangers of religious bigotry. He wielded Montesquieu, 'the first writer on a political subject which Europe ever beheld' against Woodward, and said that anyone applying the 'clear medium of corrected reason' realised his were groundless fears.[32] Thomas applied both the most respected of all the philosophers and a characteristic enlightened way of thinking to oppose Woodward.

John Ferrar, a Limerick newspaper owner and bookseller, also warned of the danger of religious zealotry. Ferrar, who signed himself 'citizen of Limerick' in the manner of Rousseau, said that no man should be troubled because of his 'manner of worshipping the Supreme Being',

---

28. Richard Woodward, *The Present state of the Church of Ireland stated* (Dublin, W. Sleater, 1786).

29. For instance Rusticus, *A Review on the bishop of Cloyne's book, on the present state of the Church of Ireland, addressed to a friend in the city* (Dublin, P. Byrne, 1787), p.6. This work also quoted Rousseau.

30. William Campbell, *An Examination of the bishop of Cloyne's defence of his principles; with observations on some of His Lordship's apologists* (Belfast, H. Joy Senior and Junior, 1788), p.15. In February 1787 Campbell asked the Speaker of the Irish Commons for support in 'a philosophical age' for a Presbyterian-directed college in the north of Ireland open to students of all religions. Campbell MS, Presbyterian Historical Society of Ireland. Samuel Barber, *Remarks on a pamphlet, entitled The Present state of the Church of Ireland* (Dublin, P. Byrne, 1787).

31. Daniel Thomas, *Observations on the pamphlets published by the bishop of Cloyne, Mr Trant, and Theophilus, on one side; and on those by Mr O'Leary, Mr Barber, and Doctor Campbell on the other* (Dublin, printed for the author, 1787), p.3.

32. Thomas, *Observations*, p.4, 9-10.

reminding his audience that 'the great Mr. Locke' had shown religion was between an individual and God.[33] Ferrar was probably influenced by Rousseau's *Contrat social*, but his arguments lay well within the assumptions of Britain's Enlightenment and political culture. His differences with the likes of Woodward were over how the principles recognised as sacred should be applied to the real world. Ferrar's positive attitude to religion reflected the absence of a strong atheist streak in Enlightenment thought in Ireland. Ferrar feared that religious dissension might threaten Ireland's recent great progress – she was 'the most rising country in Europe, considering what freedom of trade, and toleration she has lately obtained', and nothing should be allowed to threaten her progress.[34] In this stress on material progress and independence, his Enlightenment self-image and way of thinking was again in line with the common assumptions of Irish political culture.

Amyas Griffith, an extremely active Freemason and former government official, reproached the attitude of the Established clergy by comparing it unfavourably to that of the French king. Louis XVI had allowed foreigners of all religions to settle in France and opened the French Royal Academy of Sciences to all religions. 'What a contrast in the French King and the Irish Prelates!' who prevented the opening of Catholic seminaries in Ireland.[35] The *Dublin evening post* echoed these sentiments. Louis's actions were 'a very pleasing instance of the happy prevalence of pure religion and philosophy over bigotry and superstition'. A comparison between the ruling powers of France and Ireland in this instance was 'much to the advantage of the former! There prejudice is no more – here she raises her blind deformed head.'[36] Despite the advances in denominational relationships, radicals felt that developments elsewhere in Europe had left Ireland once more at the periphery of enlightened practice. This sense that developments in enlightened thought and practice were not being reflected in Ireland would only accelerate after the French Revolution, and played an important part in the growth of a challenge to the foundational principles of Irish political culture, those of the Glorious Revolution.

The French Revolution was initially welcomed across the Irish political spectrum as a kind of French 1688, as the application of enlightened principles to government in France. Naturally, Irish attention particularly turned to French attitudes to religion and citizenship. On one hand, the *Morning post*, a radical paper popular with the Dublin lower orders, eulogised the new system 'formed on the great base of reason [...] the enlightened system of an enlightened empire; the empire of common sense

---

33. John Ferrar, *History of Limerick* (Limerick, A. Watson and Co., 1787), p.xii.
34. Ferrar, *History of Limerick*, p.xiv.
35. Amyas Griffith, *Miscellaneous tracts* (Dublin, James Mehain, 1788), p.103.
36. *Dublin evening post*, 4 January 1787.

and equal freedom. Let Irishmen mark the essentials of both.'[37] On the other, the newspaper closest to government lavished praise on France's 'spirit of liberality and sentiments of universal toleration. [...] The bigotry of religious distinction no longer waves her gloomy hand in that country, – and in return ENGLAND, as well as Ireland in this enlightened age, should give to Roman Catholics every privilege granted to others of his Majesty's subjects, and derived under our glorious constitution.' A correspondent called for the abolition of the Penal Laws, pointing out that the French patriots would never have succeeded had they not completely tolerated each other's religions. 'Aristides' condemned hypocrites who referred to the Irish people but whose conception of it 'seldom extends beyond the mere Protestant inhabitants of the country'.[38] It would seem that the Revolution persuaded all shades of opinion that toleration should be extended. The statements from both papers could be interpreted as calls for political rights to be extended to all religions. While the *Morning post* would support Catholic emancipation, however, the *Freeman's journal* would bitterly oppose it in the years ahead. The same word – 'enlightened' – meant completely different political arrangements to each.

The Revolution of 1782 had turned out a disappointment for liberals and radicals. Britain retained effective control of the Irish Parliament by means of patronage, and discrimination against Catholics and Presbyterians remained. Many opponents of government now believed that the centre of enlightened political practice had shifted from Britain and Ireland to France, and they agitated for the adoption of similar measures in Ireland. The debate over Enlightenment and politics in Ireland became very closely tied to debate on the Revolution. The Catholic question would most clearly reveal the varieties of Enlightenment in Ireland. In 1791 various commemorations of the second anniversary of the fall of the Bastille were held in Ireland. By far the biggest was in Belfast, where one participant later boasted they celebrated 'with more pomp than it was done in any part of the world, save the *Champ de Mars*'.[39] At this celebration, the biggest gathering in Belfast's history at that time, a resolution was passed stating 'we wish ALL CIVIL and RELIGIOUS INTOLERANCE annihilated in this land.'[40] The Belfast meeting united opposition opinion in approval of the Revolution, but the resolution passed was actually a compromise motion replacing one that called for immediate Catholic enfranchisement. Even radicals could not agree on whether enlightened politics necessitated the end of the confessional state.

37. *Morning post or Dublin courant*, 27 August 1789. Printed thrice weekly in Dublin.
38. *Freeman's journal*, 19 January 1790.
39. Letter to *Belfast newsletter*, 15 May 1792. This was a twice-weekly paper, the voice of northern Whiggery.
40. *Belfast newsletter*, 19 July 1791. The meeting sent a declaration to the National Assembly, which was published in France. Several responses were received, including from the Jacobin clubs of Bordeaux and Nantes.

In response, the Society of United Irishmen was formed the following winter to campaign for reform and equal rights for all religions.

Catholic agitation for equality began in earnest in 1791. The Catholic argument was made most forcefully by the Dublin doctor Theobald McKenna, in his 'Declaration of the Catholic Society of Dublin'. McKenna set his appeal firmly within the context of the seeming march of Enlightenment – in 'the present enlightened and improving period of society', Irish Catholics ought not to be the only people in Europe to remain silent about their grievances but should demand their rights. 'Reason and justice' were on their side, while Irish 'patriotism and self-interest' dictated equality. The Penal Code 'enervated' industry, and it was in the national interest that 'THE ENTIRE CODE SHOULD BE ABOLISHED'.[41] The British and Irish constitution gave property political representation – Catholic property must have 'its natural weight'.[42] While seeking to convince Catholics to become more active, McKenna couched his argument as simply the natural extension of the enlightened principles of the constitution. He was careful to avoid mentioning France to avoid alienating potential supporters.

McKenna's moderate enlightened position still provoked a furious reaction, the most extreme being the aptly titled pamphlet, *Anti-Catholics*. The author wondered if McKenna meant by 'enlightened', 'that *philosophy* [...] which has learned to reason itself into Deism, and not infrequently into Atheism itself'.[43] For the author, the most liberal positions on toleration were not enlightened, but apathetic, or hostile to religion. He denounced McKenna as an example of the '*modern* philosophers' who had caused the French Revolution and whose principles would bring only anarchy. They aimed to 'take the Government by storm, and shew their friends in France' they had a '*right*' to appoint Catholics to the offices of state. In short, 'with Popery in her right-hand, and Toleration in her left, what may not the Genius of Philosophy accomplish!'[44] More moderate and more reflective of conservative opinion, the *Freeman's journal* argued that 'Reason, philosophy and justice are [Catholics'] natural weapons' which alone could secure equal rights. 'A comprehensive modification, if not a radical abolition of the penal code will be found to be nothing more than an act of retributive justice to this meritorious and loyal body of men' who always defended their country when needed. The paper, 'in a less enlightened period than the present' (and before coming under government influence) had supported Catholic relief, and Catholics should listen when it exhorted 'reason and moderation', which would

---

41. *Transactions of the General Committee of the Roman Catholics of Ireland, during the year 1791; and some fugitive pieces on that subject* (Dublin, P. Byrne, 1792), p.10, 13.

42. *Transactions of the General Committee of the Roman Catholics of Ireland*, p.15.

43. *Anti-Catholics: a refutation of the principles contained in the declaration of the Catholic Society* (Dublin, Richard White, 1792), p.10.

44. *Anti-Catholics*, p.15, 18, 24.

bring equality 'progressively'.[45] Conservatives therefore told Catholics that reform would come, but gradually and only when appropriate. As long as Catholics were guaranteed civil equality, they saw no conflict between this discrimination and their enlightened principles. The opposition of many to Catholic emancipation was not the result of bigotry, but was instead a consequence of their vision of how society could best be governed according to enlightened principles.

The linguistic struggle to associate the concept of Enlightenment with particular political programmes was intensifying. Most conservatives refused to surrender Enlightenment to their opponents. Instead, they distinguished true Enlightenment from modern or French philosophy. They praised Montesquieu and Locke, but held Voltaire and Rousseau in contempt. Clearly their thinking was fundamentally different from the Anti-Enlightenment as studied by Didier Masseau or Darrin McMahon, although the Irish Catholic hierarchy did fit McMahon's model to some extent.[46] To describe their thought as Anti-Enlightenment would be to do them a grave injustice, and to return to imposing a modern vision of what Enlightenment represented on contemporaries. It makes sense to speak of these debates only in terms of varieties of Enlightenment thought.

As the French Revolution progressed and became more violent, many of those who had seen France as the new centre of enlightened practice returned to their traditional view of the British and Irish constitutions. Conservative condemnations of the dangers of anarchy inherent in the new philosophy, epitomised by the Irish-born Edmund Burke's *Reflections on the Revolution in France*, seemed to have been borne out. French events formed an important part of the argument against political reform. As with the American War, the French Revolutionary War brought concessions – Catholic enfranchisement was granted in early 1793. These changing circumstances enabled both Charles Francis Sheridan – the radical of the late 1770s who had provided the intellectual justification for Protestant Ascendancy in a speech to Parliament on 18 February 1792 – and Theobald McKenna – the Catholic propagandist – to unite behind the constitution in opposition to the radical Enlightenment, which now

---

45. *Freeman's journal*, 8 December 1791. See *Faulkner's Dublin journal*, 13 December 1791, for similar sentiments, suggesting the Administration may have been using the press to hint to Catholics that loyalty would bring swift rewards, and to avoid a possible Presbyterian–Catholic alliance as advocated by radicals.

46. Masseau, *Les Ennemis des philosophes*; McMahon, *Enemies of the Enlightenment*. John Thomas Troy, *A Pastoral instruction on the duties of Christian citizens, addressed to the Roman Catholics of the archdiocese of Dublin, with an observation on particular passages of a late publication entitled 'The Roman Catholic claim to the elective franchise, in an essay, &c.' by Charles Francis Sheridan, Esq.* (Dublin, P. Wogan, 1793) is a good example of Irish Catholic Anti-Enlightenment thought, but because it accepted the representative institutions of the British and Irish constitutions its politics differed from a great deal of Continental Catholic Anti-Enlightenment thought.

embraced democracy.[47] Joseph Pollock, perhaps the most radical pamphleteer of the Volunteer agitations, found himself dismissed as an aristocrat for his opposition to republican democracy by the next generation of radicals in the United Irishmen.[48] Under the influence of the French Revolution, radical Enlightenment in Ireland had moved far beyond the positions of the previous decade. By 1793 the ideological split that shattered the broad consensus on the meaning of Enlightenment for Irish politics, and ranged conservative and moderate understandings of Enlightenment principles against radical interpretations, was complete. Many other factors were necessary for the 1798 rebellion to take place, but the rebellion was in large part a physical manifestation of the ideological clash between the varieties of Enlightenment in Ireland.

The place of the Enlightenment in Irish political culture in the age of revolutions illustrates wider concerns in Enlightenment historiography. Irish political culture was similar to that of Britain, and the terms in which the British and Irish constitutions were understood give credence to the notion of enlightened practices that separated the British Isles from the rest of Europe, to a British Enlightenment that had found institutional expression in the forms of government. Local Irish conditions, particularly subordination to Britain, poverty and denominational relations gave a distinctive inflection to what were general European concerns. The fact that Irish thought developed different positions to those of canonical figures and movements in Enlightenment historiography should not obscure the reality of a political culture steeped in the assumptions of the Enlightenment as contemporaries understood them. As far as Irish contemporaries were concerned, their political culture placed them at the core of the Enlightenment, even if they acknowledged that in other areas Ireland was very much at the periphery. The challenge to these perceptions provided by the French Revolution led the men of the Irish Enlightenment into violent conflict with one another. The fact that all elements of the political spectrum maintained that they represented the true understanding of the Enlightenment is a challenge to the traditional assumptions of Irish historiography. It can be met only by developing a more flexible understanding of what constituted Enlightenment, better reflecting the complexity of the contemporary reality, the varieties of Enlightenment. The leading United Irishman, Theobald Wolfe Tone, as well as the leading counter-revolutionary, John Foster, have valid claims to our attention as enlightened thinkers. Any analysis of the Enlightenment in Ireland must move beyond the history of ideas to examine how those ideas were viewed as relevant to politics, and how people attempted

---

47. C. F. Sheridan, *Some observations on a late address to the citizens of Dublin, with thoughts on the present crisis* (Dublin, J. Stockdale, 1797); Theobald McKenna, *An Essay on Parliamentary reform, and on the evils likely to ensue from a republican constitution in Ireland* (Dublin, J. Rice, 1793).

48. J. Pollock, *Letters to the inhabitants of Newry* (Dublin, P. Byrne, 1793).

to enact them in civil society, from improving landlords to popular agitators. Such an analysis can be grounded only on a broad range of sources – laws and speeches made in Parliament, learned treatises and debates in the academies, agricultural and industrial practices, the writings of major thinkers, but also arguments in forgotten pamphlets and newspapers, toasts at convivial gatherings, the resolutions of political meetings and societies, and arguments in public houses and in the street. The Enlightenment in Ireland was not the preserve of a handful of thinkers, scientists or improvers. Rather it was, and could not help being, a central part of public and political discussion because of the governmental system, political culture and societal divisions resulting from the Glorious Revolution and Williamite Wars, and from Ireland's connection with Britain. When the Enlightenment is looked at in these more complete terms – looked at as Irish contemporaries understood it – then the boundaries between the periphery and core of the Enlightenment no longer look so clear-cut to the modern observer.

GABRIEL SÁNCHEZ ESPINOSA

# An *ilustrado* in his province: Jovellanos in Asturias

SPAIN as a unified political entity did not exist in 1700. Aragón and Valencia lost their local privileges and autonomous governments in 1707, during the War of Spanish Succession that followed the death of the last Spanish Habsburg, Charles II. Catalonia and Mallorca lost theirs in 1714 and 1715. In 1716 the triumphant Philip V imposed the centralistic model of the French Bourbons with his 'Decretos de Nueva Planta' ('New Plan decrees') that generalised Castilian law and administration in the Spanish peninsula. Until May 1808, with the violent regional uprisings against the French and their supporters, it would seem that all the acute tensions between centre and peripheries in Spain had mellowed, perhaps with the exception of the Esquilache riots of Easter 1766. But, although the capital Madrid was the seat of the royal court and the government, and soon shone with the new cultural institutions characteristic of enlightened despotism, the main economic powerhouses were Bilbao, Barcelona and Cádiz. The culturally lively Seville, Valencia and Zaragoza tried to live up to their own enterprising scientific, literary and artistic traditions. Other regions and cities constituted a more hidden periphery behind these leading peripheral capitals and regions.[1]

Gaspar Melchor de Jovellanos, undoubtedly one of the most important figures of the Spanish Enlightenment, was born on 5 January 1744 in the coastal town of Gijón in the province of Asturias, into a *hidalgo* family which was well connected with the court. The fourth of the male children to survive childhood, he appeared destined at first for the Church, receiving his first tonsure from the bishop of Oviedo in 1757. The same year he began conventional studies of philosophy in the traditionalist university of the same city, the capital of Asturias. In 1760 he moved to the provincial city of Ávila to study canon and civil law. He graduated, however, as a bachelor from an obscure university in the town of Osma in 1761 and then earned a degree in canon law from Ávila in mid 1763. As a result of family influence, he was awarded a scholarship in May 1764 to the exclusive San Ildefonso college of the University of Alcalá de Henares. At the beginning of 1768, when he gave up his initial plan to sit the exams

---

1. For a general introduction to the Spanish eighteenth century, see John Lynch, *Bourbon Spain, 1700-1808* (Oxford, 1989) and Nigel Glendinning, *The Eighteenth century* (London, 1972).

for an ecclesiastical canonry in the city of Tuy in Galicia, his patrons in Madrid guided him into a judicial career, and appointed him a criminal prosecutor in the criminal court of the Real Audiencia in Seville. His modernising attitude was evident both in his efforts to moderate and eradicate the practice of torture, and in being the first magistrate to dispense with a wig.[2] In February 1774 he rose to *oidor* (prosecutor) in the civil court of the Tribunal de Sevilla, where one of his principal roles was to propose new laws to the king and council of Castile.

A decisive influence in those first years in Seville was the *tertulia* (a gathering similar to the French salon) Jovellanos attended in the Palacio del Alcázar, the official residence of the Peruvian creole Pablo de Olavide, governor of Andalusia and director of the New Agrarian Colonies in the fertile but uninhabited hillsides of Sierra Morena, during the periods that Olavide was not occupied in La Carolina.[3] Other participants in this *tertulia* included the naval officer and scientist Antonio de Ulloa, who accompanied La Condamine in the Franco-Hispanic expedition to Quito to measure one degree of the terrestrial meridian around the Equinox, the modernising magistrates Martín de Ulloa, Francisco de Bruna and Miguel Maestre, and the erudite abbé Cándido María Trigueros, a poet and playwright. It was also attended by several women, most notably Gracia de Olavide, sister of Pablo de Olavide, and the translator of *Paulina*, attributed to Madame de Graffigny. Agriculture and political economics, public education and reform of the theatre were all discussed and planned in the freedom afforded by the *tertulia*. Olavide used to quote foreign authors in support of his arguments. In 1768 alone he had twenty-nine boxes of (principally French) books sent through the port of Bilbao, forming a shipment of 2400 volumes in total. For this purpose he possessed a licence permitting him to read forbidden books which had been issued by Pope Benedict XIV and validated by the Holy Office in Seville. A literary polemic, at the beginning of 1773, among the members of the *tertulia* about the *comédie larmoyante*, a recent development in French theatre which constituted a hybrid genre between comedy and tragedy and an expression of the new bourgeois sensibility, resulted in an

---

2. On the life of Jovellanos, see J.-A. Ceán Bermúdez, *Memorias para la vida de Jovellanos* (Madrid, 1814) and J. Varela, *Jovellanos* (Madrid, 1988).

3. At the end of the seventeenth and the beginning of the eighteenth century, some *tertulias* of *novatores* or partisans of the new, meeting in Seville, Madrid and Valencia, played a decisive role in the introduction and dissemination of medical and scientific innovations in Spain, and under Philip V, with royal sanction, they became academies. Out of the *tertulias* came the stimulus for new enterprises, such as the first periodical literary review *Diario de los Literatos*, or the programme of poetic creation and debate which emerged between 1749 and 1751 in the Academia del Buen Gusto. Nevertheless, until the beginning of the 1780s, unlike the French salons, it was the usual thing for men to meet by themselves, perhaps because there were few women able to participate on an equal footing with the men. See Joaquín Àlvarez Barrientos, 'Sociabilidad literaria: tertulias y cafés en el siglo XVIII', in *Espacios de la comunicación literaria*, ed. J. Àlvarez Barrientos (Madrid, 2002), p.131-46.

*An ilustrado in his province: Jovellanos in Asturias*

informal literary competition won by Jovellanos with his *comédie bourgeoise* in prose, *El delincuente honrado*, which was heavily influenced ideologically by Cesare Beccaria's *Dei delitti e delle pene*, a text that was frequently discussed in Spain in the early 1770s.[4] At the same time Olavide and his circle of friends and collaborators, in keeping with the official boost created by the 'white paper' that was Pedro Rodríguez Campomanes' *Discurso sobre el fomento de la industria popular* (1774), founded the Sociedad Económica Sevillana de Amigos del País during the first months of 1775. In April Jovellanos was appointed as a member of this institution, where his zeal in establishing patriotic schools of linen yarn, in which the young women from the working classes could be occupied, was soon evident.[5]

Jovellanos left Seville at the end of the summer of 1778, when he was appointed *alcalde de Casa y Corte*. This gave him responsibility for public order, the detection of crimes and the monitoring of the markets and shows in Madrid, in addition to the obligation of attending protocolary ceremonies in the Royal House. He moved from this continually demanding and thankless post in April 1780 to the Council of Military Orders, for which he had to pass the nobility tests required to be a knight of the Order of Alcántara. On his arrival in Madrid, the doors of the cultural establishment of Enlightenment and reformist Spain, which was centralised there, were opened wide to him. In October 1778 he was appointed a member of the Economic Society of Madrid (of which he would be elected director in December 1784). In April 1779 he entered the Academy of History, and both the Spanish Academy – devoted to the upkeep of the Spanish language and letters – and the San Fernando Academy of Fine Arts in July 1781. He thus became a regular at the evening *tertulia* held by Campomanes, the all-powerful public prosecutor of the Council of Castile and director of the Academy of History, in his home in the Plaza de la Villa. This was attended by, among others, Francisco Cabarrús, a financier of French extraction, Antonio Ponz, the

---

4. Olavide would be denounced to the Holy Office in September 1775 by those who were against his social reforms in the New Colonies of the Sierra Morena, where convents were not allowed. Imprisoned in the cells of the Madrid Inquisition on 14 November 1776, his *autillo*, which was intended to intimidate the enlightened minority, took place two years later. M. Defourneaux, *Pablo de Olavide, ou l'Afrancesado* (Paris, 1959) is still the central study on Olavide.

5. The Sociedades Económicas de Amigos del País (Economic Societies of Friends of the Region) were promoted by the central government beginning in 1774-1775, after the model of the Sociedad Bascongada (Basque Society), which had been formed independently in 1764. Its instigator Campomanes hoped that it would serve as a conduit for enlightened absolutism's policy of reform in the provinces, chiefly in the fields of agriculture, industry and education. By the beginning of the 1790s, a period of incipient decline for these institutions, eighty-one societies had been created. See J. Sempere y Guarinos, *Ensayo de una biblioteca española de los mejores escritores del reinado de Carlos III*, 6 vols (Madrid, Imprenta Real, 1789), vol.5, p.135-228 and vol.6, p.1-43, and Paula de Demerson and Francisco Aguilar Piñal, *Las Sociedades Económicas de Amigos del País en el siglo XVIII* (San Sebastián, 1974).

secretary of the Academy of San Fernando, the engineer Carlos Lemaur and the architect Ventura Rodríguez.

In spring 1782, after presiding over the election of a new prior in the convent of San Marcos in León, which belonged to the Military Order of Santiago, Jovellanos returned to Asturias after an absence of fourteen years. He was given the official commission of plotting and building a road from Oviedo to Gijón, which would form the first section of the planned road to connect Asturias with León and the rest of Castile. His friend Antonio Ponz (1725-1792) was publishing an eighteen-volume epistolary *Viaje de España* (1772-1794), in which he chronicled in detail the artistic heritage of the towns, cities and provinces of Spain. In addition, he highlighted signs of the reforms being promoted by the Bourbon governments and the enlightened minority, all from an enlightened perspective and with a neo-Classical focus. Ponz asked Jovellanos to write some *Cartas del Viaje de Asturias*, which would subsequently be included in the book. Asturias was one of the few regions that Ponz had not had the opportunity to visit, and it was intended that Jovellanos' collaboration be incorporated into the book exactly as written by its author and under his real name, if he so decided, since Ponz believed such collaborations complemented and strengthened his work.[6]

There were ten *Cartas del Viaje de Asturias*. Letters 2, 4 and 10 consider artistic themes (the description of the San Marcos de León convent, the cathedral of Oviedo and Jovellanos' findings on an obscure seventeenth-century Asturian sculptor, Luis Fernández de la Vega). Letters 6 and 7 chronicle the state of agriculture and the beginnings of industry in Asturias. Both questions received a general introduction and discussion in letter 5, which is now lost. The tone was generally denunciatory. Agriculture in Asturias was blocked by the overwhelming concentration of land ownership in the hands of the nobility and ecclesiastical institutions in a system of entailment and mortmain, with the result that there was very little exchange of lands. Land was not worked by its owners, but let to tenants, which created 'minifundia' (excessive fragmentation), and did not provide adequately for a growing population, with many poor farmers being forced to emigrate to other provinces or overseas. Industry in Asturias was entirely rural in nature. Given the slovenliness of the landowning classes in Asturias, Jovellanos saw encouraging industrialisation as the solution to the lack of work in some rural areas. Letter 1 takes the journey from Madrid to León as its theme, and letter 3 the journey from León to Oviedo. Once he had crossed the fields of Castile

---

6. Thus, for example, Antonio Ponz includes in vol.14 of his *Viaje de España*, 18 vols (Madrid, Joaquín Ibarra, 1772-1794), a 'Carta de cierta persona a un amigo suyo sobre la erección de Cementerios' (letter 5, paragraphs 13-63), the authorship of which Jovellanos would recognise in a letter to his friend Posada on 29 March 1794. This 'Carta' was based on the *Informe dado al Consejo por la Real Academia de la Historia en 10 de junio de 1783 sobre la disciplina eclesiástica antigua y moderna relativa al lugar de las sepulturas* (Madrid, 1786).

'de inmensas llanuras, de horizontes interminables, sin montes ni colinas, sin pueblos ni alquerías, sin árboles ni matas, sin un objeto siquiera que señale y divida sus espacios', Jovellanos gives free rein to a new sensitivity to the landscape in his description of the rugged mountains that separate and isolate Asturias from León: 'Aquellas elevadísimas rocas, monumentos venerables del tiempo que recuerdan las primeras edades del mundo, al paso que ofrecen a la vista un espectáculo grande, raro y en cierto modo magnífico, llenan el espíritu de ideas sublimes y profundas, le ensanchan, le engrandecen y le arrebatan a la contemplación de las maravillas de la creación.'[7] Letters 8 and 9, dedicated to the pilgrimages in Asturias and to the *vaqueiros* – a socially marginalised group of itinerant herdsmen – are of particular interest due to the detail with which they describe this aspect of popular Asturian culture and their attempt to question, through objective examination, the basis on which a group perceived as ethnically different becomes subject to social discrimination. Jovellanos wrote his letters between 1782 and 1788, but only the second of them was published in Ponz's *Viaje de España*,[8] possibly a result of Jovellanos' resistance to publishing at that time a piece of work that had gone beyond Ponz's original purpose and framework, and about which he was not entirely convinced. Jovellanos was still correcting and polishing his letters in the mid 1790s, when he considered the possibility of publishing them independently, although he would never actually do this in his lifetime.[9]

In May 1782 Jovellanos was elected director of the Economic Society of Asturias, founded two years earlier at the initiative of Campomanes, a native Asturian. As the members of the society were overwhelmingly nobles and churchmen, the bourgeois element was missing. From the

---

7. Gaspar Melchor de Jovellanos, *Cartas del viaje de Asturias*, ed. José Miguel Caso González (Gijón, 1981), letter 1, paragraph 10: 'immense plains, horizons without end, with no mountains or hills, with no towns or farmsteads, with no trees or bushes, with not a single object to signal and divide its spaces'; and letter 3, paragraph 16: 'Those most elevated rocks, venerable monuments to time that recall the first ages of the world, at the same time as they offer a great, rare and somewhat magnificent spectacle, fill the spirit with sublime and profound ideas, broaden, increase and captivate it for the contemplation of the wonders of Creation.'

8. Ponz, *Viaje de España*, vol.11, letter 6, paragraphs 63-87.

9. Jovellanos was never certain of his appreciation of this work, and writes in his diary on 19 April 1794: 'Bella mañana; a repasar las *Cartas del viaje de Asturias* por si me resolviere a publicarlas. No me desagrada la primera, que tiene algo que corregir, que añadir nada La segunda necesita mejorarse con noticias históricas adquiridas después' ('A beautiful morning; I shall review the *Cartas del viaje de Asturias* to see if I can decide whether to publish them. The first does not displease me, though it has something to be corrected, though nothing to be added. The second needs to be improved with historical information acquired later'), while in the entry corresponding to 7 April 1796, he notes: 'Repaso las *Cartas del viaje de Asturias*: no me gustan; acaso las abandonaré y quemaré' ('I reviewed the *Cartas del viaje de Asturias*: I do not like them; I may abandon and burn them') (see *Diario 1*, p.572-73 and *Diario 2*, p.528). For Jovellanos' diaries, see Jovellanos, *Obras completas*, ed. José Miguel Caso González *et al.*, 7 vols (Oviedo, 1984-1999), vol.6 and 7 (1994 and 1999).

beginning, there were clashes between those who, like Campomanes, Jovellanos or the Count of Toreno, were in favour of promoting the economic development of the region through mining and industry, and the large landowners, who were more interested in preserving their rents and privileges, and only willing to make improvements in agriculture. The emblem of the society, significantly, makes no reference to mining or coal. Under its motto, 'Disce sapientiam', we see represented two rows of ants entering and leaving their nest, some of them loaded and others searching for a new load, while a small group remains at the entrance to help those returning with something useful, all inside an architectural frame adorned with fruit and instruments typical of regional agriculture as well as the characteristic linen spool, the symbol of popular small industry.[10]

In October 1782, after an absence of six months, Jovellanos returned to Madrid, where he was appointed as a member of the influential Board of Commerce, Exchange and Mines the following year. As regards his literary activity during these years, the two satires *A Arnesto* are worthy of note: these targeted the sexual scandals, excessive luxury and poor education of the nobility, many of whose youngest members, with no sense of social responsibility, were adopting either libertine and Frenchified lifestyles or lower-class mannerisms in an attempt to pass themselves off as *majos*. The satires were first published, anonymously, in issues 99 and 155 of *El Censor*, the most radical and critical periodical of Charles III's reign, which, despite enjoying significant official support, was closed in August 1787. During these years Jovellanos began two of his most important works, both of which were originally reports requested by the Council of Castile from two enlightened advisory institutions. Thus, he accepted the assignments to write a memoir on theatre and public shows and entertainments on behalf of the Academy of History, and to prepare a report on the forthcoming Agrarian Law for the Economic Society of Madrid, a society in which his defence of the admission of women, against the views of other members – among them his friend Cabarrús – led to the creation of the Junta de Damas, the women's branch of that society in February 1787.

When, in 1789, Lerena, the new minister of the Treasury, began a vicious investigation into the role of Cabarrús as the director of the Banco Nacional de San Carlos, Jovellanos openly defended his friend in the boards of the bank. When he discovered that Cabarrús had been arrested, his loyalty led him to return hurriedly to Madrid in August 1790, as soon as he had finished his inspection of Calatrava Imperial College in Salamanca, where he was to set up a new plan of study. Jovellanos' arrival

---

10. Jovellanos outlined his ideal programme for the Asturian Society in his *Discurso dirigido a la Real Sociedad de Amigos del País de Asturias, sobre los medios de promover la felicidad de aquel Principado*, dated Madrid, 22 April 1781. See J. M. Caso González, 'La Sociedad Económica de Asturias desde su fundación hasta 1808', *BOCES* 18:1 (1973), p.21-67.

was a source of considerable discomfort in certain court and government circles, and he was ordered to leave Madrid immediately for Asturias in order to carry out the coal-mine assignments that the minister of the navy had previously requested from him, while the rumour spread in Madrid that he had been exiled. Powerful figures of state, such as the Count of Campomanes, abandoned him: 'que seré observado; que estaré en la lista de los proscritos; que quiero ser heroico; que él [Campomanes] no puede serlo', Jovellanos noted in his diary.[11] Gradually the implementation of reforms by Floridablanca's conservative government under the new king Charles IV began to slow down significantly, as the uncertainty created by events in France spread.

Gaspar Melchor de Jovellanos resided in Gijón between mid September 1790 and mid-November 1797, when he left for Madrid, following his appointment as minister of justice. Dismissed suddenly from this position after just nine months, he was banished again to Asturias, where he would remain between the end of October 1798 and his arrest as a prisoner of state in the early morning of 13 March 1801, when he was sent to the island of Mallorca, where he was imprisoned, first in the Cartuja and then in Bellver Castle, in conditions which were often extremely harsh. The details of his daily routine during this period of almost eleven years' residence in Asturias can be discovered through his diaries, which he began to write when he was first banished and wrote regularly until his final arrest. He chose not to cover the period when he was minister, and these diaries can be supplemented with his correspondence with a great variety of addressees, a total of 850 letters.[12]

In his diaries, which were written on a regular basis for private use and without any thought to their possible publication, Jovellanos' sensibility and his Enlightenment enthusiasm are revealed without any regard or subjection to political interests. Only tangentially can they be considered a personal diary: they are rather the record and logbook of his rigorous and indefatigable everyday activity on behalf of the transformation of Spanish reality on either a small or large scale. Jovellanos' diaries are one of the documents that best synthesise the symbiotic relationship between utilitarianism and utopian thought which is characteristic of the best of the Spanish Enlightenment. They also show that the politician's pragmatism, placed at the service of a monarchy of enlightened despotism, at no time silenced the radical thinker who was always conscious of the ultimate goals of human emancipation.[13]

---

11. 'that I will be observed; that I will be in the list of persons proscribed; that I want to be a hero; which he [Campomanes] cannot be.' In Jovellanos, *Diario 1*, p.79, corresponding to 24 August 1790.

12. On the correspondence maintained by Jovellanos during this period, see Jovellanos, *Obras completas*, vol.2 and 3 (1985 and 1986).

13. Francisco Sánchez-Blanco's polemical books *La Mentalidad ilustrada* (Madrid, 1999) and *El Absolutismo y las Luces en el reinado de Carlos III* (Madrid, 2002), written from the

The town of Gijón had some 6300 inhabitants at the beginning of the 1790s. It was one of the most prosperous localities in a mostly rural Asturias, isolated from Castile owing to a lack of roads along which to trade, and had one of the best ports on the Cantabrian coast through which to trade with northern Europe and even with both Americas, particularly after the liberalisation of trade with Spanish America in 1765 and 1778. It was located close to the proud capital Oviedo, only five leagues away (twenty-five kilometres) by the road built at Jovellanos' initiative during the 1780s. Gijón lacked both Oviedo's cathedral clergy and its friaries and convents.[14]

Jovellanos returned to Asturias to carry out the official mission of producing a report on the viability of exploiting the coal mines which until then had not been used or else had been worked unsystematically. In this, the interest both of the navy, in building up its stocks of this fuel which it needed to run the new steam-based machinery, and of the most progressive enlightened thinkers in Asturias to begin the industrial development of the region, came together. In September and October 1790 Jovellanos undertook several expeditions on horseback to the various coal deposits of which he was aware (Llanes, Avilés, Valdesoto), which allowed him to prepare a report in May and June 1790 for the minister of the navy, Valdés. In his report he proposed, in addition to protecting private initiative in exploiting and trading the mineral, the construction of a road between the Langreo deposit and the nearest port – Gijón – and the establishment in that city of a nautical and mineralogy school, which would be necessary to train technicians. While the government accepted some of his proposals, it rejected the coal road, and embraced instead the plan by military engineer Casado de Torres to make the river Nalón navigable between Langreo and the port of Pravia, with the mineral being transported on barges. In the end the navigation project, which concealed dark private interests and jealousy about the pre-eminence that Gijón could come to enjoy, would prove to be unworkable in practice, even after enormous investments had been made.

---

perspective of the history of ideas, aimed to distinguish between concepts which in the past two decades have been applied indistinguishably in the Spanish context, those of 'Despotismo ilustrado' and 'ilustración'. In *La Mentalidad ilustrada*, devoted to the reigns of Philip V and Ferdinand VI, Sánchez-Blanco situates the true Enlightenment more on the side of the *novatores* and Feijoo than on the eclectic current of thought headed by the Valencian erudite Mayans. In the latter work, he dismisses the almost automatic identification of 'las Luces' with Charles III's technocratic realisations and 'Despotismo ilustrado'. Still, Jovellanos' enlightened activism during the period of his banishment in Asturias shows that, notwithstanding contradictions, his role and collaboration with the economic and social reformism of the central government never distracted him from his more radical goals.

14. M. Cuartas Rivero, 'Gijón: carretera de Asturias y obras en la villa de Jovellanos', in *Jovellanos, ministro de Gracia y Justicia* (Barcelona, 1998), p.100-103.

*An ilustrado in his province: Jovellanos in Asturias*

On 1 February 1792 the minister Floridablanca added a new assignment to Jovellanos' mine-related work when he appointed him director for roads in Asturias. His road from Gijón to Oviedo, which was completed relatively quickly, was considered one of the best in Spain. It was now a question of connecting Oviedo with León, and improving the poor quality road that connected Asturias with Castile, because until that time horses could pass through the Pajares mountain pass, but not carriages; it was thus only possible to operate a limited goods trade based on chains of horses, with a consequent rise in price of products. Starting from Oviedo, some 3.5 leagues (20 kilometres) of the projected road had already been built, with 17 leagues (95 kilometres) remaining to reach León. If the road were finished, Gijón could become the entry and exit point for trade from the provinces bordering Asturias with the rest of the coastal provinces in Spain and also with the colonies in America, a trade which up to then had been very limited or practically non-existent. It is striking that Jovellanos not only worked in support of the road from his study, planning the works and proposing agreements to defray its construction costs, or through his prominence in the boards, but was also able to personally direct the measuring and land-levelling work during the worst weather of the season. This is demonstrated by his expedition between La Perruca and Puente de Olloniego in November 1793: 'Resuélvese el viaje para mañana [...] todo el mundo lo tiene por locura, y el tiempo a la verdad es nebuloso, húmedo y de muy triste apariencia; pero la empresa pide ánimo, y yo le tengo. Se trata de prevenciones. [...] Por la noche viene un capote de camino, que mandé hacer: costó 331 reales.'[15] While what was achieved in the coal commissions and the León road, however, only partly reflected the plans and effort Jovellanos had devoted to them, his Nautical and Mineralogical Institute of Gijón had become, even then, one of the most original creations of Enlightenment Spain and is, without doubt, the principal achievement of his years in Asturias.

In his speech to the Asturian Economic Society on 7 May 1782, on the need to develop the study of natural sciences in the region, Jovellanos had proposed sending two boarding students to the Vergara seminary for four years to study mathematics, physics, chemistry and mineralogy. They would then spend two years visiting factories in France and England. A subscription was opened for this purpose, but the plan came to nothing. Years later, wishing to combine the need to teach mineralogy in Asturias, which was necessary for the future exploitation of the coal mines, with the request from the port of Gijón to establish a nautical school, he received the support of the minister of the navy, Antonio Valdés, to set up a centre to train specialists who would be able to pilot a boat or exploit a mine.

15. 'Tomorrow has been decided for the journey [...] everyone thinks it is madness, and the weather is indeed misty, damp and of sad countenance; but the task requires courage, which I have. It is a matter of taking precautions. [...] This evening a travel cape will arrive, which I have had made: it cost 331 reales', *Diario 1*, p.478.

The aim was to train technicians who would have some basic scientific knowledge. The dependence of this establishment on the naval ministry was due not only to administrative reasons, but also to the intellectual openness demonstrated by navy officers to the new sciences and teaching methods throughout the century. Once government approval for the project had been granted, the opposition of Oviedo, the capital and university seat, to the new institute being set up in Gijón became clear. In his reply to the City Council of Oviedo, Jovellanos defended himself by alluding to the practical nature of the institute and to the difficulty in reconciling the geometric spirit necessary for practical sciences with the scholastic and speculative spirit dominant in the university. Although the Royal Asturian Nautical and Mineralogical Institute of Gijón regulations were confirmed by the government on 15 November 1793, local suspicions in the municipality of Oviedo, feelings of insulted dignity by its university faced with a new institution outside its control, and the mistrust on the part of the Bishop of Oviedo, Juan de Llano Ponte, about a centre focused on teaching new scientific knowledge, would only increase.[16]

Courses began on 7 January 1794. Sixty students were registered that first year, each of whom was to be at least thirteen years old. Jovellanos relied on being able to attract, in the longer term, a section of the children of the principality's nobility and bourgeoisie, as was occurring in the case of the Vergara seminary in the Basque Country. In addition to studying the theory of navigation and mineralogy, to which the mornings were dedicated, students received afternoon classes in drawing, languages and practical mineralogy. Jovellanos considered the study of English and French to be more useful than Latin, but he also included, from 1800, a course in Castilian humanities in the study plan, because:

¿No es un dolor ver hombres de gran mérito científico que apenas saben hablar su lengua ni escribir con orden y método desde el punto que se los saca de sus áridas fórmulas? Pues yo deseo que mis matemáticos contraigan los principios y el uso de un buen estilo didáctico, para que, consultando, informando, proponiendo, escribiendo, puedan dar orden y claridad a sus ideas.[17]

The ecclesiastical wariness towards this enlightened foundation would be translated into the categorical refusal of the archbishop of Toledo and

---

16. See J. M. Caso González, *El Pensamiento pedagógico de Jovellanos y su Real Instituto Asturiano* (Oviedo, 1980) and A. Ruiz de la Peña Solar, 'El Instituto de Gijón: un paraíso perdido', in *Jovellanos, ministro de Gracia y Justicia*, p.80-89.
17. 'Is it not a sadness to see men of great scientific merit that are barely able to speak their own tongue nor to write with order and method from the moment they are removed from their arid formulae? I wish that my mathematicians would contract the principles and use of a good didactic style, so that, when consulting, reporting, proposing, writing, they may be able to give order and clarity to their ideas.' Letter from Jovellanos to C. González de Posada, 7 May 1800, in *Obras completas*, vol.3, p.534.

inquisitor general, Cardinal Lorenzana, to grant a permit to the institute's library allowing forbidden books to be read:

El tonto del cardenal Lorenzana insiste en negar la licencia de tener libros prohibidos en la biblioteca del Instituto, aunque circunscrita a jefes y maestros. Dice que hay en castellano muy buenas obras para la instrucción particular y enseñanza pública, cita el *Curso* de Lucuce, el de Bails y la *Náutica* de don Jorge Juan, y añade en postdata que los libros prohibidos corrompieron a jóvenes y maestros en Vergara, Ocaña y Ávila; pero ¿serían los libros de física y mineralogía para que pedíamos la licencia? Y ¿se hará sistema de perpetuar nuestra ignorancia? Este monumento de barbarie debe quedar unido al *Diario*. ¿Qué dirá de él la generación que nos aguarda, y que, a pesar del despotismo y la ignorancia que la oprimen, será más ilustrada, más libre y feliz que la presente? ¿Qué barreras podrán cerrar las avenidas de la luz y la ilustración?[18]

After Jovellanos' summary dismissal from his ministry which coincided with the traditionalist offensive against real or suspected Jansenists and the fall of the Urquijo government in December 1800, persecution of the institute became more severe, and in Asturias and Madrid the absence of the nobility among students and the institute's supposed inattention to religious practices were both denounced. After its promoter was jailed in 1801, the institute began to decline when all official economic support was removed, and it became merely a nautical school in March 1804. Jovellanos summarised this news to his friend canon González de Posada as follows: 'Dieron por fin al huérfano el golpe que le amenazaba desde que perdió su padre.'[19]

The ambivalent relations of central power with cultural institutions in the periphery are evident in the obstacle course and final suffocation that

---

18. 'The foolish Cardinal Lorenzana insists in refusing a licence to allow forbidden books in the library of the institute, even if it were confined to lecturers and teachers. He says that in Castilian there are very good works for private instruction and public education, he cites the *Curso*s by Lucuce and Bails, and don Jorge Juan's *Náutica*, and adds as a postscript that the forbidden books corrupted young people and teachers in Vergara, Ocaña y Ávila; but would they be the same physics and mineralogy books for which we are requesting the licence? And will a system be made of perpetuating our ignorance? This monument of barbarity should be linked to the *Diario*. What will be made of it by the generation that awaits us, and that, despite the despotism and ignorance which oppress it, will be more enlightened, more free and more happy than the present one? Which barriers can block the avenues of light and Enlightenment?' Entry corresponding to 6 August 1795, *Diario 2*, p.415, 417. On the history of the library of the Asturian Institute and the inventory of its books, see L. Domergue, *Les Démêlés de Jovellanos avec l'Inquisition* (Oviedo, 1971).

19. 'In the end they gave the orphan the blow that had been threatening since it lost its father.' Letter from Jovellanos to González de Posada, 27 March 1804, in *Obras completas*, vol.4 (1988), p.39. The Nautical and Mineralogical Institute was not the only pedagogical institution founded by Jovellanos in Gijón, since in January 1797 he contributed to the opening of a school that provided rudimentary education to eighty children from the city and its surrounding area, in which, contrary to the usual practice at that time, all corporal punishment was banned. His widowed sister, gathering together other family property, also established a school for poor girls, in which they were taught to read and write, among other tasks. See Ceán Bermúdez, *Memorias*, p.228-29.

was the short life of the Nautical and Mineralogical Institute of Gijón. Bourbon centralism, once taken into consideration that Spain was out of step with Europe, established the main scientific and cultural institutions in the capital of the kingdom (royal academies, libraries, the Royal Press, semi-official newspapers and so on), or promoted them administratively from Madrid (economic societies and the like) in a radial structure similar to the communications system being imposed in the peninsula at that time. Nothing was to escape the patronage and control of the governments of enlightened absolutism, which continued to keep watch on the new institutions created in the provinces. For their part, institutions that developed as a result of peripheral initiatives or interests, once they had been slotted into this cultural structure in some way, were always more likely to suffer the consequences of changes in government or alterations in the balance of power in the court.[20]

In spite of the ambiguity of his position during the years he was exiled in Asturias before his call to the ministry of justice, Jovellanos was continually linked to significant projects generated by some of the most relevant cultural institutions of the state. In this respect, he continued writing during those years both the *Memoria para el arreglo de la policía de los espectáculos y diversiones públicas, y sobre su origen en España*, requested by the Academy of History, and the *Informe en el expediente de ley agraria*, entrusted to him by the Madrid Economic Society. He concluded a first version of the *Memoria* in December 1790, and completed a second in 1796, both of which were read successfully in public board meetings of the Madrid Academy. The *Informe* was sent on 28 May 1794 to the secretary of the Economic Society of Madrid, which printed it in 1795.

Each day in his diaries, Jovellanos kept detailed records of his private readings during his years of exile in Gijón, both those which were more directly utilitarian, undertaken because of his literary work or his teaching in the institute, and those he made out of curiosity or pleasure.[21] Between February 1794 and July 1797 he read a number of authors one after the other: Edward Gibbon, Conyers Middleton, Bernardin de Saint-Pierre, William Ogilvie, Jean-Jacques Rousseau, Thomas Paine, Count Buffon, John Gillies, James Bruce, the abbé Barruel, Jacques Necker, Adam Smith, William Young, Captain Cook, Commodore Byron, Adam

---

20. J. Àlvarez Barrientos, 'La República Literaria en Europa: centro y periferia', in *1802: España entre dos siglos, sociedad y cultura*, ed. Antonio Morales Moya (Madrid, 2003), p.223-44.

21. On the inventory of the books and editions mentioned by Jovellanos, see J.-P. Clément, *Las Lecturas de Jovellanos (ensayo de reconstitución de su biblioteca)* (Oviedo, 1980); for a comprehensive discussion of his ways of reading, Gabriel Sánchez Espinosa, 'Gaspar Melchor de Jovellanos: un paradigma de lectura ilustrada', in *El Libro ilustrado: Jovellanos lector y educador*, ed. Nigel Glendinning and G. Sánchez Espinosa (Madrid, 1994), p.33-59; on his use of some of these readings in literary works written in those years, J. H. R. Polt, *Jovellanos and his English sources: economic, philosophical and political writings*, Transactions of the American Philosophical Society 54:7 (Philadelphia, PA, 1964).

Ferguson, Captain Wallis and William Godwin; most of these he read in the original English or French, languages he spoke well and which he liked to translate.[22] It was characteristic of Jovellanos that he read many texts simultaneously – thus, for example, on 9 January 1796, he noted: 'Lectura en Bruce y en Barruel: el primero deleita; el segundo horroriza'[23] – and re-read them habitually – 'Acebedo [his secretary], el día 23, acabó la lectura del Necker y empezó a leerme el Smith [*Wealth of Nations*]: va para mí de tercera vez; leí primero la traducción anónima francesa [of 1778-1779]; después el original inglés [perhaps in an edition of 1793], que regalé a Pedrayes; ahora la traducción de Boucher, hecha para las notas de Condorcet [1790-1791].'[24]

The frequency of the commercial contacts between the port of Gijón and England allowed Jovellanos to obtain English and French books in London with no difficulty, either through Spaniards living there or through occasional travellers. Thus, in the entry corresponding to 14 May 1794, he noted: 'Reconocimiento de cuatro catálogos de libros de Londres, para escoger para el Instituto y para mí. ¡Ojalá estuviera rico uno y otro bolsillo! Por la tarde largo paseo; por la noche repaso del primer catálogo.'[25] In other cases Jovellanos benefited from the mediation of his friend Alexander Jardine, British consul in La Coruña: 'carta del cónsul con otra inclusa del librero White: la cuenta de libros importa 155 esterlinas, pero vienen muchos no pedidos y faltan las *Transacciones* y otros pedidos. Veremos *quid faciendum*.'[26] Significantly, his exile in Gijón

---

22. Thus, already at the end of the summer of 1777, Jovellanos translated the first canto of Milton's *Paradise lost*, to which his friend the poet Meléndez Valdés made major corrections the following year. In May 1794 he translated a letter from English by W. Ogilvie, the author of *An Essay on the right of property in land* (London, 1781), which he sent to his friend, the consul Jardine; in June 1796 he translated the *Decline and fall of the English system of finance* of Thomas Paine. Furthermore, at the beginning of April 1794, he translated J.-H. Bernardin de Saint-Pierre's *Paul et Virginie* for entertainment, which 'pudiera, a salir bien, imprimirse en beneficio del Instituto' ('may, if it turns out well, be printed for the benefit of the Institute'), in *Diario 1*, p.568.

23. 'Reading in Bruce and in Barruel: the first is delightful; the second horrific', in *Diario 2*, p.503.

24. 'Acebedo, on the 23rd, finished reading Necker and began to read Smith to me: this is the third time for me; I read first the anonymous French translation; then the English original, that I gave to Pedrayes; now Boucher's translation, made for Condorcet's notes', entry corresponding to 25 May 1796, *Diario 2*, p.543. In some cases, such as with the *History of Athens* by W. Young, he started re-reading as soon as he had finished his first reading. See *Diario 2*, p.635-36, 640.

25. 'Perusal of four catalogues of books from London, to choose for the Institute and for myself. If only one and the other pocket were rich! In the afternoon, a long walk; in the evening, reviewed the first catalogue', in *Diario 1*, p.580.

26. 'Letter from the consul with another from the bookseller White: the bill for the books comes to 155 pounds sterling, but many have arrived that were not requested and the *Transactions* and others requested are missing. We shall see *quid faciendum*', entry corresponding to 6 February 1794, *Diario 2*, p.78-79. Alexander Jardine, a former artillery officer who was married to a Spanish woman, had travelled extensively through the peninsula between 1776 and 1779 in a military spying mission, and subsequently gathered

enabled Jovellanos to stock up on foreign books which would have been more difficult to acquire in Madrid or Salamanca given their scarcity and higher price, in such cases where the public sale of a given work was not forbidden. Furthermore, Gijón's peripheral location in pro-Enlightenment Spain proved also to be advantageous when it came to more direct contact with other peripheries:

> Por la mañana se despidió don Lorenzo García Jove (de *La Farruca*); se va a embarcar a Baltimore; irá a Filadelfia; doyle carta para el señor Irujo [the Spanish diplomatic representative], recomendándole, y que le dirija el encargo que lleva de comprar cualquiera obra buena y nueva que haya producido aquella nueva Academia de Ciencias, o los sabios del país, y el nuevo código constitucional de la República.[27]

This is the situation in respect of books Jovellanos purchased. Other works that were either difficult to obtain or forbidden were lent to him; such is the case of Rousseau's *Confessions*, among others, which was lent to him by Jardine, or Paine's *Rights of Man*, owned by an acquaintance in Gijón itself.[28]

During the years of the War of the First Coalition against the French Republic, in which Great Britain was an ally of Spain, the publication in the Spanish press of news relating to revolutionary events in France and her influence in peninsular politics was still, in theory, outlawed or was tightly controlled by the government, all of which favoured the propagation of all sorts of rumours. Jovellanos, however, had access to English newspapers in Gijón, among them *The Craftsman* and the *London courier*, although this access was intermittent and usually had a two- or three-week delay; these newspapers were usually sent to him by the consul Jardine attached to his private correspondence.[29] From the Peace of Basel

---

his experiences and impressions in *Letters from Barbarie, France, Spain, Portugal &c.* (London, T. Cadell, 1788). In the early 1790s he moved in London in the circle of William Godwin and the Philomathian Society. Between 1793 and 1796, he served in the post of consul in La Coruña. The London book-keeper, John White, had his shop on Fleet Street, beside Horace's head.

27. 'In the morning, don Lorenzo García Jove (from *La Farruca*) took his leave; he will sail to Baltimore; he will go to Philadelphia; I gave him a letter of recommendation for señor Irujo, and requested him to purchase good new works that may have been produced by that new Academy of Sciences, or by the wise men of that country, and the new constitutional code of the Republic', in note made 9 April 1797, *Diario 2*, p.708.

28. Entries corresponding to 13 October and 19 November 1794, *Diario 2*, p.30 and 47.

29. Thus, for example, in the entry corresponding to 13 July 1795, he noted: 'Correo: carta de Jardine. Tres *Craftsmanes*. Confirman la toma de Luxemburgo, el triunfo de los moderados, la muerte del inocente Luis XVII, de escrófulas, y el mal estado de la salud de su hermana; malas noticias del ejército de Navarra, retirado a Irurzun, dejando descubiertas las fronteras de Guipúzcoa y Vizcaya; esto hace más probable la noticia de ayer.' ('Post: letter from Jardine. Three copies of the *Craftsman*. They confirm that Luxembourg has been taken, the triumph of the moderate camp, the death of the innocent Louis XVII, from scrofula, and the poor state of health of his sister; dark news of the army of Navarra, which has withdrawn to Irurzun, leaving the borders of Guipúzcoa and Vizcaya exposed; this makes yesterday's news more likely.') In *Diario 2*, p.394.

and the Treaty of San Ildefonso onwards, which made Spain an ally of the French Republic and placed her in confrontation with Great Britain, Jovellanos would receive press from France through that country's new consul in Gijón: 'El cónsul de Francia [Louis Mornard] en casa; me trae unos *Monitores*; [...] Lectura en los *Monitores*: excelentes discursos de [Jean-Baptiste] Louvet contra la libertad de prensa; de [Pierre] Pastoret y [François-Antoine] Boissy d'Anglas, por ella, de 19 y 20 de marzo.'[30] Having read them, Jovellanos usually sent these foreign newspapers to other *ilustrados* close by,[31] creating in this way a network of shared information, which was always of superior quality to that available to those who only had the official *Gaceta de Madrid* within reach.

Alongside his private reading in the room in the tower, or while walking, Jovellanos organised shared reading, which was one of the founding elements of the *tertulia* that met daily in his house in the drawing room with the fireplace: 'Nos acompaña don Ramón de Jove, y es muy concurrida la tertulia. Poca lectura por lo mismo, y ésa en el tomo XXXVIII de Risco; se ha hecho tan pesado como Flórez.'[32] Public readings, conversation on what has been read and on other topics of the day, and card games cemented the social links between family, close friends, acquaintances and collaborators. The didactic purpose of this reading, which was chosen and directed by Jovellanos, is clear; perhaps remembering his passage in other times through *tertulias* that spearheaded the debate on the Enlightenment in Spain, he sought to establish in peripheral Gijón also a modest space for debate and criticism: 'Paseo por la tarde, que es bellísima. Por la noche mucha concurrencia. Conversación con Caveda sobre la obra de Mr. de Saint-Pierre y sobre *Las épocas de la naturaleza*, del conde de Buffon. Entra Isla en ella y conoce la última obra.'[33] The *tertulia* in his house, whose membership was somewhat restricted in its social make-up, might have had a parallel space for reading and sociability in the subscription reading society that Jovellanos attempted to set up in Gijón during these years.[34]

---

30. 'The French consul visited me here; he brought me some *Moniteurs*; [...] I read in the *Moniteurs*: excellent speeches by Louvet against the freedom of the press; by Pastoret and Boissy d'Anglas, in favour, on 19 and 20 March', in the entries in his diary on 10 and 12 April 1796, *Diario 2*, p.529.

31. As he does with José Cornide and Agustín Pedrayes, *Diario 1*, p.587 and *Diario 2*, p.26.

32. 'Don Ramón de Jove accompanied us, and the *tertulia* is very well attended. Little reading for that reason; what I did read was in volume XXXVIII of Risco; it has become as tedious as Flórez', in the entry corresponding to 24 March 1794, *Diario 1*, p.562.

33. 'I walk in the afternoon, which is beautiful. In the evening many visits. Conversation with Caveda about the work of Mr. de Saint-Pierre and on the *Épocas de la Naturaleza*, by the Count of Buffon. Isla takes part in it, as he has read this work', in the entry corresponding to 11 January 1794, *Diario 1*, p.526.

34. According to his secretary and first biographer J.-A. Ceán Bermúdez, Jovellanos wrote the constitution for a reading society that he wished to establish in a villa in Gijón, where a maximum of forty members would meet, 'de los más señalados por su educacion,

It was, however, through his frequent correspondences that Jovellanos developed a space for dialogue and debate with intellectuals of his stature. It may be useful here to remember the three-way discussion he held, in May and June 1794, with Jardine and Cabarrús on the right of property and the ideas of William Godwin, always with the reservation that his correspondence may be monitored by the government or might at some point fall into the hands of the Inquisition.[35] Dialogues such as this allowed him to overcome his sense of isolation in the somewhat limited cultural environment of Gijón, described accurately in notes in his diary such as the following:

> A la iglesia: predicó don Félix de Bobes, cura de San Julián de los Prados (Santullano), no de san Antonio, sino contra los espíritus fuertes. Parecíase al que predicó a unas monjas contra los desafíos, o al que a los aguadores de la Puerta del Sol contra las escofietas. ¿A qué combatir los vicios de la sabiduría en un país de ignorancia? ¿Es esto más que adularla? ¡Y qué cosas no dijo! ¡Y cuán groseramente! Pero siguió la moda, y acaso otro impulso.[36]

Months before his return to Madrid to take charge of the ministry of justice, after he had repeatedly requested for years a signal from his contacts in government circles and in the court that he was not in disgrace, Jovellanos began to realise that his exile in the politically peripheral Gijón had allowed him to develop, despite his marginalisation, an intense intellectual and public activity which would benefit the nation as much as the province, and which his previous rhythm of life in Madrid, with all its institutional brilliance, would not have allowed him:

> Según Arias, es tiempo de pensar en volver a Madrid; no lo deseo, lo repugno; concibo que allí no gozaré la más pequeña parte de felicidad que aquí gusto. No negaré que deseo alguna pública señal del aprecio del gobierno, para ganar en ella aquella especie de sanción que necesita el mérito en la opinión de algunos necios... Si por suerte viniese de América para el Instituto algún considerable

---

clase y conducta á conversar, á leer la gazeta de Madrid, mercurio y demás periódicos que se publicasen en el reyno, á jugar al villar y á los naypes con arreglo á las pragmáticas de juegos, y á tomar café' (those most qualified by their education, class and conduct, would meet to converse, to read the *Gazeta de Madrid*, *Mercurio* and other newspapers that are published in the kingdom, to play billiards and cards according to the pragmatics of games, and to take coffee.) See Ceán Bermúdez, *Memorias*, p.225-26.

35. *Diario 1*, p.581 and 587-88. In the entry corresponding to 24 April 1794, Jovellanos notes: '[Letter] A Jardine, prevenciones sobre nuestra correspondencia: que no se puede tratar de todo; que sólo privada y confidencial se deben exponer libremente las ideas' (To Jardine, warnings about our correspondence: we cannot speak of everything; ideas must only be expressed freely in private and in confidence), p.584.

36. 'To Church: don Félix de Bobes, priest of San Julián de los Prados (Santullano), preached, not about Saint Anthony, but against freethinkers. It was similar to the one he preached to some nuns against duelling, or the one to the water carriers of the Puerta del Sol against fashionable headwear. Why combat the vices of wisdom in a country of ignorance? Is this anything more than flattering it? And what things he did not say! And how rudely! But he followed the fashion, and perhaps another force', annotation corresponding to 13 June 1797, in *Diario 2*, p.738.

fondo, emprenderé su nueva casa y procuraré construirla con el mayor calor. Los nuevos establecimientos se cimentan con la opinión, y la opinión también se alimenta por los ojos. Además, estamos muy estrechos para la enseñanza, y la comodidad contribuye a ella. Nos falta el juego de pelota y la mesa de trucos, tan convenientes para el entretenimiento, para el ejercicio y para la educación de los niños. Nos falta una pieza para juntas públicas, que sirva de teatro para los certámenes y aun para representaciones, que deben formar una parte de la educación y que, bien dirigidas, concurrirán en gran manera a su perfección y progresos. [...] Revuelvo en mi ánimo una obrita sobre la instrucción pública, para la cual tengo hechos algunos apuntamientos y observaciones. He meditado mucho sobre esta importante materia y pienso empezar a escribir este año, si la salud y el tiempo lo permitieren. Pero si volviere a Madrid, debo renunciar a ella. Allí ni habrá gusto ni vagar, y cuando ningún encargo extraordinario lo estorbase, los ordinarios del Consejo de Órdenes y Junta de Comercio, los que no pudiera evitar de Academias y Juntas, ¿cuánto no estorbarían? Todo bien combinado, ¿no debo concluir que continuando aquí puedo ser más útil al público que allá? Y, siendo así, ¿no es mi primera obligación prolongar cuanto pueda esta residencia? Así lo haré, sin importunar a nadie, aunque tampoco puedo atar las manos a mi buen amigo Arias, pues que desde el principio me resigné en las suyas. Favor, influjo, amistad, opinión, si algo tuviere, quiero consagrarlo todo al bien de este nuevo establecimiento que está a mi cargo, a la mejora de esta provincia en que nací y cuento morir, y al consuelo de los infelices y de los hombres de bien.[37]

37. 'According to Arias, it is time to think of returning to Madrid; I do not wish it, I find it repugnant; I conceive that I will not enjoy there the smallest part of the happiness I enjoy here. I will not deny that I wish some public signal of the government's esteem, in order to gain with it that type of sanction that, in the opinion of some fools, merit requires... If by chance there should come from America some considerable funds for the institute, I will undertake the building of its new home and will endeavour to construct it with the greatest enthusiasm. New establishments are sustained by opinion, and opinion is also fed by what the eyes see. Furthermore, we lack sufficient funds for education, and comfort contributes so crucially to this. We have neither a *pelota* court nor a billiards table, which are so useful for the entertainment, exercise and education of the pupils. We lack a room for public board meetings, which would double as a theatre for school contests and even for those performances that must form part of children's education and which, if well directed, will contribute greatly to their perfection and progress. [...] I am considering writing a short work about public education, for which I have made some notes and observations. I have meditated much on this important subject and I intend to begin writing it this year, if health and time should permit it. But if I should return to Madrid, I would have to abandon this. There will be neither pleasure nor time to wander, and when no extraordinary duty obstructs my plan, how much will ordinary business in the Council of Orders and Board of Commerce, and those matters that I will not be able to avoid in academies and *juntas*, how much will they not obstruct my intention? All things taken together, should I not conclude that by continuing here I might be more useful to the public than there? And, if this should be the case, is not my first obligation to prolong this residence as much as possible? This I will do, without inconveniencing anyone, although neither can I tie the hands of my good friend Arias, since from the very beginning I have trusted all my affairs to him. Favour, influence, friendship, opinion, if I should have a little of these, I want to dedicate them all to the good of this new establishment that is in my charge, to the improvement of this province in which I was born and intend to die, and to the consolation of unhappy mankind and of the *hombres de bien*', entry corresponding to 31 December 1796, in *Diario 2*, p.643-44.

The long-awaited 'signal' that he enjoyed royal favour came on 16 October 1797, when Jovellanos was appointed ambassador to Russia, which felt to him, in the midst of the congratulations of relatives, friends and fellow-Asturians, as a 'pistol shot': 'cuanto más lo pienso, más crece mi desolación. De un lado lo que dejo; de otro, el destino al que voy; mi edad, mi pobreza, mi inexperiencia en negocios políticos, mis hábitos de vida dulce y tranquila. La noche, cruel.'[38] One month later, Godoy would prefer to make use of him as part of a marked change in political direction, which aimed to resolve the crisis of the Spanish monarchy through a 'monarchic directorate' that would ensure, at the same time, the very position of the Prince of the Peace (Godoy) himself. The painter Goya, a protégé of Jovellanos', has given us a portrait of the enlightened thinker during his short period in the ministry. It has become, over time, one of the iconic images of the Spanish Enlightenment, in addition to being an undoubted precedent – only formal? – for Capricho 43, *El sueño de la razón produce monstruos*. On the table in his ministerial office is Minerva, the symbolic deity of the Spanish Enlightenment;[39] significantly, the shield the goddess is holding is the shield of the Nautical and Mineralogical Institute of Gijón, Jovellanos' most beloved creation.

38. 'The more I think about it, the more my desolation grows. On the one hand, what I leave; on the other, the destination to which I must go; my age, my poverty, my inexperience in political negotiations, my habit of a gentle, quiet life. The night was cruel', in Jovellanos, *Diarios 2*, ed. J. Somoza (Oviedo, 1954), p.449. For this date in Jovellanos' diaries, not covered yet by Caso González's edition, see Jovellanos, *Diarios de Jovellanos*, ed. Julio Somoza, 3 vols (Oviedo, 1953-1955).

39. On the symbolic use of Minerva by the Spanish Enlightenment, see P. Ilie, *The Age of Minerva*, vol.1: *Counter-rational reason in the eighteenth century* (Philadelphia, PA, 1995), especially chapters 1 and 2.

RICHARD BUTTERWICK

# Between Anti-Enlightenment and enlightened Catholicism: provincial preachers in late-eighteenth-century Poland-Lithuania

THE peripheries of the Enlightenment can be pursued spatially and temporally, but also in medium and message. This essay focuses upon discourses – in the older as well as the newer sense of the word – whose location, time, form and content place them in the borderlands of Enlightenment and Anti-Enlightenment. I make these remarks within the context of the Polish-Lithuanian Commonwealth, concentrating on the Grand Duchy of Lithuania. I focus on the 'Polish Revolution' of 1788-1792 – the Four Years' Sejm (or Diet), whose enduring memory, the Constitution of 3 May 1791, gave Poles their claim to have emerged from the Enlightenment's periphery.[1] The medium to which I devote most attention is not the portable dictionary, the novel or the pamphlet, but the sermon, while much of the message is characterised by warnings against the so-called 'enlightened age'. Yet what emerges is evidence that the priorities, assumptions and language of what may fairly be called the Enlightenment permeated the discourse of provincial clergymen, whence it helped to persuade provincial noblemen to support the enlightened Constitution.

## i. Enlightenment, Anti-Enlightenment and enlightened Catholicism

'The expression "our enlightened age" constantly reaches my ears from those who speak, and my eyes from those who write.' So wrote one of the Polish-Lithuanian Commonwealth's most radical writers on social and political questions, Reverend Franciszek Salezy Jezierski.[2] This illustrates

---

1. I justify the usage and introduce the phenomenon in 'Political discourses of the Polish Revolution, 1788-1792', *English historical review* 120 (2005), p.695-731. I thank Dr Martyna Deszczyńska and Dr Ultán Gillen for stimulating discussions on Counter-Enlightenment and Anti-Enlightenment.
2. [Franciszek Salezy Jezierski], *Ktoś piszący z Warszawy dnia 11 lutego 1790 r.*, in *Wybór Pism*, ed. Zdzisław Skwarczyński and Jerzy Ziomek (Warsaw, 1952), p.122: 'Wyraz ten: "wiek nasz oświecony", ustawicznie potyka usze moje od mówiących, a oczy od piszących.'

my view that towards the end of the eighteenth century, the expression 'wiek oświecony', the 'enlightened age' or the 'enlightened century', was ubiquitous. Its meaning, moreover, was fairly clear to educated Poles, regardless of the extent to which they considered their age to be genuinely 'enlightened'. Although, in the first half of the eighteenth century, 'enlightenment' had been employed almost exclusively as a religious metaphor, between the 1760s and the 1790s the noun 'oświecenie', 'enlightenment', was, to a substantial degree, secularised. It was often used as a synonym for 'education', and it connoted an informed, rational and true understanding of things. This is how another priest, Wojciech Skarszewski, used the adjective: 'In this, our excessively rotten century, he who best quips about and mocks religion or the clergy is taken by many to be a wise man. [...] A reasonable and thoroughly enlightened public judges completely differently, knowing full well, that the wittiest jokes and the sharpest cuts never prove anything at all.'[3]

'Nieoświecenie' (unenlightenment) was a synonym for 'ciemnota' – literally darkness, meaning ignorance. Associated with 'enlightenment' were 'tolerancja' (toleration), 'rozum' (reason) and 'polor' (polish or politeness). Associated with 'unenlightenment' were 'fanatyzm' (fanaticism), 'zabobon' (superstition) and 'grubość' (coarseness). Even those authors who criticised the 'enlightened eighteenth century' had to operate within the linguistic and cultural context of those connotations. Some critics attempted to show that the Catholic Church, especially in Poland-Lithuania, had contributed much to the education of the nation, the driving out of pagan superstitions, and had always been characterised by mildness and love towards the heterodox, not by a spirit of persecution. Even the ringing declarations made by some clerical authors that true enlightenment meant divine revelation admitted –explicitly or implicitly – that some had been deceived by a false and godless 'enlightenment', based on exaggerated pride in human reason.[4]

The phenomenon of a 'Counter-Enlightenment' or 'Anti-Enlightenment' in later eighteenth-century Europe has aroused attention in recent years.[5] The trend has been noted among Polish historians of ideas.[6] There is a danger, however, of extending the polarisation of opinion

---

3. [Wojeciech Skarszewski], *Odpowiedź plebana na nowe zarzuty przeciwko duchowieństwu polskiemu* ([Warsaw], 1789), p.8-9: 'W tym aż nadto zepsutym wieku Naszym, kto lepiey żartuie i śmieie się z Religii, albo z Duchowieństwa, ten od wielu poczytany bywa za mądrego człowieka. [...] Inaczey wcale rozumie o takich Powszechność rozsądna i gruntownie oświecona, wiedząc o tym dobrze, iż naydowcipnieysze żarty, nayostrzeysze ucinki nic nigdy nie dowodzą.'

4. Kostkiewiczowa, *Polski wiek świateł*, p.399-432. Butterwick, 'What is Enlightenment?', p.19-37.

5. Masseau, *Les Ennemis des philosophes*; McMahon, *Enemies of the Enlightenment*.

6. Martyna Deszczyńska, review of 'Darrin M. McMahon, *Enemies of the Enlightenment: the French Counter-Enlightenment and the making of modernity*', *Wiek Oświecenia* 21 (2005), p.266-80.

characteristic of the early nineteenth century backwards to the polemics of the later eighteenth century.[7] The term 'Counter-Enlightenment' seems most applicable to the post-revolutionary, and perhaps even the post-Napoleonic era. The 'Counter-Reformation' evokes a vigorous campaign to win back souls and territories lost to the Protestant Reformation, such as that which took place in seventeenth-century Bohemia.[8] Analogously, the revival of monasticism and Mariology in many parts of nineteenth-century Europe, with the associated literary and artistic currents called Romanticism, signal not only a reaction against the Enlightenment but a response to it, with tangible results, for example in terms of the numbers of pilgrims and vocations.[9] But before and during the revolutionary era, the hostile reaction to 'the enlightened age' was largely confined to jeremiads. At least this was so in Catholic Europe and, it seems, Orthodox Russia, for the eighteenth century brought the British Isles and North America evangelical Protestant revivals, which offered positive alternatives to rationalist and latitudinarian tendencies, associated with radical and moderate Enlightenment respectively.[10]

'Anti-Enlightenment' is a less problematic term before the French Revolution. It simply means a hostile reaction to an age that considered itself 'enlightened', and need not exclude critical reactions that were formulated within the mental and linguistic horizons of that age. It can also be argued that critics of the eighteenth century and all it stood for established a coherent image of a 'philosophic', rationalist, sceptical, godless and anti-clerical so-called 'enlightened age', which helped the Enlightenment to become self-conscious.[11]

The notion of 'Anti-Enlightenment' also helps us avoid entanglement between 'Counter-Enlightenment' and 'Catholic Enlightenment'. Again, we could refer to the arguments between those who write 'Counter-Reformation' and those who prefer 'Catholic Reform'. The latter argue that even before Luther's theses, the Roman Catholic Church was engaged in a broadly conceived reform or renewal, and also that the decrees of the Council of Trent (1545-1563) set out a rolling programme

---

7. M Deszczyńska, *'Historia sacra' i dzieje narodowe: Refleksja lat 1795-1830 nad rolą religii i Kościoła w przeszłości Polski* (Warsaw, 2003) is essential to understanding the late Enlightenment and its critics in the former Polish-Lithuanian lands.

8. On the Habsburg Counter-Reformation see R. J. W. Evans, *The Making of the Habsburg monarchy 1550-1700: an interpretation* (Oxford, 1979), especially chapter 12.

9. See Nigel Aston, *Christianity and revolutionary Europe c.1750-1830* (Cambridge, 2002), especially chapter 8, and Hugh McLeod, *Religion and the people of Western Europe 1789-1970* (Oxford, 1981).

10. W. R. Ward, *Christianity under the ancien régime, 1648-1789* (Cambridge, 1999). Russian Orthodox reflections on the century, as Simon Dixon's essay in this volume shows, were often critical, but the propagation of a radical alternative was hardly possible for a Church so subordinate to the state.

11. McMahon, *Enemies of the Enlightenment*, p.11-14. The alternative of 'antiphilosophie', advocated by Masseau, *Les Ennemis des philosophes*, perhaps even more than 'Anti-Enlightenment', conveys a hostile reaction to a ubiquitous catchphrase.

of reform, which was still being implemented in the mid eighteenth century.[12] By that time, reminders of the Tridentine decrees were being issued to the clergy and laity by bishops in language that already showed the impact of Enlightenment assumptions. Thus there is a case for a degree of continuity between 'Catholic Reform' and 'Catholic Enlightenment', summed up in the chosen phrase of historians of the Habsburg monarchy: 'Enlightened Reform Catholicism'.[13]

Here we enter the debates on 'Catholic Enlightenment' and 'enlightened Catholicism'. A semantic observation may help – the adjective conveys a subset of the noun. 'Enlightened Catholicism' is one species of the Catholic genus, whereas 'Catholic Enlightenment' signifies the reverse. In other words, 'enlightened Catholicism' is substantively Catholicism, whereas the substance of Catholic Enlightenment is Enlightenment. Much that has been written about '(the) Catholic Enlightenment' would be better classified under 'enlightened Catholicism'.[14]

The Jesuit Mark O'Connor, for example, defines the Catholic Enlightenment as a confrontation with the theological implications of the scientific revolution. It involved the difficult task of choosing the useful ideas and rejecting the harmful. It was motivated by a desire to understand God's creation better – especially in astronomy, which was seen as a means of overthrowing astrology. The Church should analogously be cleansed from superstitious ideas and rituals. This involved adapting, rather than rejecting, the post-Tridentine renewal. O'Connor holds up Marcin Poczobut, the rector of Wilno University, as an exemplar of this stance. To me this is better called enlightened Catholicism.[15] A similar verdict should be passed on the eclectic approach practised by the reformed Piarist and Jesuit colleges of the 1750s and 1760s, which permitted developments in *philosophia recentiorum* to be absorbed by subjecting them to the criteria of revelation.[16]

If, on the other hand, the principles of Enlightenment take first place, and the Catholic Church is seen principally as a means to their dissemination and implementation, if the context is that of a Catholic state and culture, and especially if the proponent is a Catholic clergyman or

---

12. See Robert Bireley, *The Refashioning of Catholicism, 1450-1700* (Basingstoke, 1999), and R. Po-chia Hsia, *The World of Catholic renewal, 1540-1770* (Cambridge, 1998), and regarding the mid-eighteenth century, Aston, *Christianity and revolutionary Europe*, p.14.

13. Peter Hersche, quoted in T. C. W. Blanning, *Joseph II* (Harlow, 1994), p.44.

14. I follow the usage of Irena Stasiewicz-Jasiukowa, 'Der aufgeklärte Katholizismus im Polen der Frühaufklärung', in *Europa in der Frühen Neuzeit: Festschrift für Günter Mühlpfordt, vol.3: Aufbruch zur Moderne*, ed. Erich Donnert (Weimar, Cologne and Vienna, 1997), p.555-64.

15. Mark O'Connor, 'Oświecenie katolickie i Marcin Poczobut SJ', in *Jezuici a kultura polska*, ed. Ludwik Grzebień and Stanisław Obirek (Cracow, 1993), p.41-49.

16. See Stanisław Janeczek, *Oświecenie chrześcijańskie: Z dziejów polskiej kultury filozoficznej* (Lublin, 1994) and 'Czym była oświeceniowa *philosophia recentiorum*?', *Kwartalnik Filozoficzny* 26:1 (1998), p.115-28.

practising Catholic layperson, then we may speak of a Catholic Enlightenment. Here Reverend Hugo Kołłątaj, rector of Cracow University, politician and pamphleteer, seems to fit the bill.[17] To go one step further, if 'the Enlightenment' is considered a foreign seed planted in Catholic Polish soil, then we have 'the Enlightenment in Catholic Poland'.[18] Many foes and some friends of 'the enlightened eighteenth century', as we shall see, treated Enlightenment as an import, usually from France. Some still do.

If Enlightenment in Poland was at least partially of French provenance (or mediation, via French translations of English and Italian works), so was Anti-Enlightenment. Refutations such as the Jesuit Claude-François Nonnotte's *Les Erreurs de Voltaire* were avidly translated.[19] This reflected the continuing prestige of French Catholicism. Emanuel Rostworowski counted 160 French religious works (80 authors, 300 editions) translated into Polish in the eighteenth century. The trend peaked in the 1770s, when five times as many religious as secular books translated from French were published. Although the 1780s saw a fall-off of strictly religious works in favour of refutations and lay moralists, the number of wholly secular translations rose only slightly.[20]

It was possible, and in the circumstances perhaps advisable, to refute anti-Catholic manifestations of Enlightenment in an 'enlightened' manner. Secular learning, rational and utilitarian arguments, and quotations from the age's favourite philosophical writers involved fighting the cause of the Church on the territory of the foe. And whatever did not explicitly contradict Catholic orthodoxy might be wielded as a defensive

17. See Emanuel Rostworowski, 'Ksiądz pleban Kołłątaj', in *Wiek XIX: Prace ofiarowane Stefanowi Kieniewiczowi w 60 rocznicę urodzin*, ed. Barbara Grochulska, Bogusław Leśnodorski and Andrzej Zahorski (Warsaw, 1967), p.49-63 (49-50). Further on the 'Catholic Enlightenment' see, for example, Zofia Libiszowska, 'L'Eglise et les Lumières en Pologne au XVIII$^e$ siècle', in *Les Contacts religieux franco-polonais du moyen âge à nos jours: relations, influences, images d'un pays vu par l'autre* (Paris, 1985), p.199-203; Ludwik Bieńkowski, 'Le siècle des Lumières catholiques en Pologne', in *Les Contacts religieux*, p.203-10; Barbara Grochulska, 'Miejsce Kościoła w polskim Oświeceniu', *Mówią Wieki* 11 (1990), p.19-22.

18. This is posited as an alternative in *Katholische Aufklärung – Aufklärung im katholischen Deutschland*, ed. Harm Klueting (Hamburg, 1993).

19. Jerzy Snopek, *Objawienie i oświecenie: Z dziejów libertynizmu w Polsce* (Wrocław, 1986), p.218-19, 229-36; McMahon, *Enemies of the Enlightenment*, p.109; Masseau, *Les Ennemis des philosophes*, p.246-47; Claude-François Nonnotte, *Les Erreurs de Voltaire*, revised edn, 2 vols (Lyon, V. Reguilliat, 1770); *Błędy Woltera wybrane z księgi francuskiey pod tymże tytułem Les Erreurs de Voltaire napisaney przez X: Franciszka Nonnotta, á zaleconey listem Klemensa XIII papieża z odpowiedzią na nie y życiem tegoż Woltera* (Łowicz, Drukarnia J. O. Xcia Prymasa, 1780). Other translations were published in 1779 and 1781. Władysław Smoleński, *Przewrót umysłowy w Polsce wieku XVIII: Studia historyczne*, 4th edn (Warsaw, 1979), p.187. For what was gained and lost in the French mediation to Poland of Soame Jenyns' *A View of the internal evidence of the Christian religion* (1776), see R. Butterwick, 'Stanisław August Poniatowski jako latitudynarysta religijny', *Wiek Oświecenia* 14 (1998), p.179-91 (186-87).

20. E. Rostworowski, 'Les auteurs de la littérature religieuse française traduite en Pologne au XVIII$^e$ siècle', in *Les Contacts religieux*, p.211-14 (see also his contribution to the discussion on p.261).

or offensive weapon. 'Enlightened Anti-Enlightenment' is not a contradiction in terms. 'Catholic Enlightenment' and 'Anti-Enlightenment' cannot overlap; 'enlightened Catholicism' and 'Anti-Enlightenment' can. One danger, from an orthodox Catholic point of view, was that secular discourses of 'enlightenment' might by degrees permeate theology.

Historians of ideas might consider a wide spectrum of attitudes towards the 'enlightened age', ranging from enthusiastic propagation of Voltairean anti-clericalism or even Holbachian materialism at one extreme, to eager anticipations of the Last Judgement, often expressed in conjunction with the exposure of Masonic plots, at the other. In the Polish-Lithuanian Commonwealth, among the writers most hostile to Catholicism were the poets Kajetan Węgierski and Stanisław Trembecki, the pamphleteer Jan Baudouin de Courtenay and the polymath Stanisław Staszic, a reluctant clergyman in lower orders.[21]

Their polar opposite was the Reformed Franciscan friar, Karol Surowiecki (1750-1824), who fulminated bitterly against the age in pamphlets and from Warsaw pulpits.[22] He gladly quoted Nonnotte: 'the philosophical spirit is pride, [...] it is the desire of debauchery.'[23] Enraged by an anonymous pamphleteer's praise of Voltaire's *Saul*, which appeared in Polish translation in 1789, he wrote a counterblast. He set the first act of his play in Heaven, with God, Archangel Michael and Saints Peter and Paul anticipating the approaching Apocalypse, 6000 years after the Creation. God explained the present age to Paul: 'Anything, which in your time broke the pride of sinners and brought them to penance, it calls stupidity, barbarity, or enthusiasm. Tell it about Heaven, and it will laugh at you; mention Hell, and it will call you a fanatic; make a miracle for it, and it will say that you are a fraudster, or else a witty physicist.'[24]

Michael was then despatched on a mission to hell. Having arrived there for the second act, he was met by Lucifer riding a horse: 'Voltaire'. 'Voltaire''s tail contained many glistening nits: his pupils, including

---

21. On the religiously and philosophically more radical proponents of Enlightenment in Poland-Lithuania, see Snopek, *Objawienie i oświecenie*; and Smoleński, *Przewrót umysłowy*, p.167-70, 177-94; also R. Butterwick, 'Progress and violence in the thought of the Polish Enlightenment', in *Progrès et violence au XVIII<sup>e</sup> siècle*, ed. Valérie Cossy and Deirdre Dawson, p.17-34.

22. See Smoleński, *Przewrót umysłowy*, p.368-73, and Agnieszka Kwiatkowska, *Piórowe wojny: Polemiki literackie polskiego oświecenia* (Poznań, 2001), p.148-51 and *passim*.

23. [Karol Surowiecki], *Gora rodząca, bayka sprawdzona w osiemnastym wieku na schyłku onegoż wyiaśniona* (n.p., [1792]), p.50-51: 'Duch Filozoficzny iest to pycha [...] iest to chęć rozwiązłości.'

24. [K. Surowiecki], *Python lipsko-warszawski diabeł: Kontr-tragedya na tragedyą Saul wyjętą z Pisma Świętego, grana przez aktorów tamtego świata w roku 1789; a w roku 1792, światu ziemskiemu obiawiona* (n.p., 1792), p.31-32: 'On wszystko głupstwem, barbarzyństwem, enthuzyazmem zowie, cożkolwiek twego czasu grzesznikow do pokuty kruszyło. Powiedz mu o Niebie; to cię wyśmieie: wspomniy o piekle; to cię fanatykiem przezwie: uczyń mu cud; powie żeś oszust, abo dowcipny fizyk.'

pamphleteers who had clashed with Surowiecki. Beelzebub was riding 'Rousseau', who bit and kicked at 'Voltaire', continuing their earthly feud. They were duly thrashed. Lesser devils rode 'Montesquieu' and 'Mirabeau'. Lucifer responded to Michael's complaints of excessive recruitment by explaining that the devils were on vacation, because the inhabitants of Earth now needed no diabolical assistance, and laughed at devils, just as they did at angels. Indeed, they might set his devils a bad example of insubordination.

After one devil delivered a report from Paris, where priests were being compelled to marry, another reported from Warsaw. Although the 'heads of the nation still keep with Rome', the devil could laugh:

> because I have plenty of newly educated youngsters, who think in the French way and they have already done enough: they have founded Freemasonic clubs, they have opened printhouses for propagandists: fight and kill clergymen[, they cry]; there is a heightened appetite for ecclesiastical lands. They sing that the monasteries should be dissolved; they even whisper in Warsaw about priests' wives and citizenship for Jews. And what else is needed? Are these not French steps?

When asked if priests did not preach against all this, the devil answered that they could not even denounce ordinary sins, let alone the Freemasons, from the pulpit — an allusion to Surowiecki's own experience.[25] The rest of the play becomes increasingly sadistic and scatological, probably reflecting Surowiecki's own psyche.

In a pamphlet comparing the eighteenth century to Aesop's fable, 'Mons parturiebat, natus est ridiculus mus', Surowiecki denounced the Freemasons for their alternative religion: suitable, he claimed, for bestial natures. Its god was liberty, which meant unlimited licence, was worshipped with cocards, laurels and trees, and had its own catechism. In a Masonic lodge, he alleged, pictures of Bacchus and Venus took the place of Jesus and Mary, and the Antichrist's emissaries Voltaire and Rousseau took those of Christ's apostles. In place of Catholic relics, there were bricks from the Bastille. Instead of crosses and rosaries, there were trowels and hammers. Fanaticism and intolerance were far more characteristic of the Jacobins, he claimed, than the Spanish Inquisition, which was a 'paternal power, made milder by Christian love', which only reached for the whip when all 'enlightenment' and persuasion had been exhausted. But the

---

25. [Surowiecki], *Python*, p.104-105: 'Prawda, że Głowy Narodu ieszcze z Rzymem trzymaią: Król gorliwy Katolik, i panom seymuiącym nie wadzi. Ale ia śmieię się z tego; bo mam po sobie pełno młokosow edukacyi dzisieyszey, którzy po Francuzku myślą i iuż dosyć zrobili: pozakładali Farmazońskie kluby, Drukarnie po otwierali dla Propagandystow: na Duchownych biy za biy [an old-Polish battle cry]: na dobra Kościelne wytężony apetyt. O Klasztorach śpiewaią że ie trzeba skassować: nawet o Xiężych Zonach i Zydowskim Obywatelstwie iuż tam szepcą w Warszawie. I czegoś ieszcze brakuie? Zali to nie Francuzkie kroki?'

violence of his assaults on the temper of the times led to Surowiecki being banned from the pulpit by his bishop.[26]

In between anti-clerical and rationalist Enlightenment, and splenetic, apocalyptic Anti-Enlightenment were many authors, for whom 'enlightenment' in its secularised sense was a positive value, who were supportive of various political and social reforms, and yet referred critically, sometimes extremely critically, to the 'enlightened age'. The episcopal ranks contained many such pastoral administrators. The ecclesiastical history and dogmatic theology taught in their reformed seminaries were intended to help priests refute 'philosophic' critics of the Church and the Faith in a rational manner.[27] The aforementioned Wojciech Skarszewski (1742-1827), bishop of Chełm and Lublin from 1790, and at the end of his life archbishop of Warsaw, may be considered a model. In his pastoral letters and instructions he forbade the lower clergy 'the least persecution' ('naymnieysze prześladowanie') of those of another religion, any 'novelties' ('nowości') and 'superstitions' ('zabobony') in their parishes, and enjoined them to lead the 'dark and simple common folk' ('ciemne i proste pospólstwo') out of error.[28] In his many pamphlets, written between the 1770s and the 1810s to defend ecclesiastical temporalities, he cited the likes of Montesquieu and Hume, supposedly in order to convince readers, who could not be convinced by Scripture or the teaching of the Church, but his own theology tended to the legalistic and utilitarian, with little transcendent spirituality.[29]

Clergymen dominated the ranks of recognisably 'enlightened' writers before the First Partition in 1772 and continued to make up a majority in the two decades that followed.[30] With such a substantial ecclesiastical presence, 'enlightened' Polish opinion generally took a moderate line towards the Church, and strongly upheld the need for socially useful

26. [Surowiecki], *Gora rodząca*, p.53-61 (60): 'to władzy Oycowskiey, władzy ułagodzoney affektem miłości Chrześciańskiey'.
27. For three examples, see Józef Wysocki, *Józef Ignacy Rybiński biskup włocławski i pomorski 1777-1806: Zarys biograficzny na tle rządów diecezji* (Rome, 1967); Michał Grzybowski, 'Kościelna działalność Michała Jerzego Poniatowskiego biskupa płockiego', *Studia z Historii Kościoła w Polsce* 7 (1983), p.5-225; Tadeusz Kasabuła, *Ignacy Massalski, biskup wileński* (Lublin, 1998).
28. W. Skarszewski, *Rozporządzenie pasterskie na diecezyą hełmską i lubelską roku 1792*, dated Warsaw, 16 July 1792, p.45-55. The instruction illustrates the arguments of Magdalena Ślusarska, 'Les modèles d'évêque, de curé et de paroisse au siècle des Lumières: continuation ou changement de tradition?', in *Proceedings of the Commission internationale d'histoire ecclésiastique comparée, Lublin 1996*, vol.3: *Churches – states – nations in the Enlightenment and in the nineteenth century*, ed. Mirosław Filipowicz (Lublin, 2000), p.23-35. Expanded version: 'Oświeceniowe modele biskupa, plebana i parafii: Kontynuacja czy zmiana tradycji?', in *Dwór, plebania, rodzina chłopska: Szkice z dziejów wsi polskiej XVII i XVIII wieku*, ed. M. Ślusarska (Warsaw, 1998), p.37-53.
29. M. Deszczyńska and Ewa Zielińska, 'Skarszewski, Wojciech Leszczyc', *Polski Słownik Biograficzny*, 43 vols. to date (Cracow, Wrocław and Warsaw, 1935-), vol. 38 (Warsaw and Cracow, 1997), p.50-61. Butterwick, 'What is Enlightenment?', p.23-24, 29.
30. Bieńkowski, 'Le siècle des Lumières catholiques en Pologne', p.202.

religion. Only after the French Revolution turned down the path of terror and dechristianisation, and when the final dismemberment of the Commonwealth in 1795 could be used as evidence of divine displeasure, did the 'enlightened' positions in the marchlands between Enlightenment and Anti-Enlightenment become increasingly untenable for the Polish-Lithuanian clergy.

## ii. Periphery and province

Before the French Revolution and the Second and Third Partitions, it was easier for Polish clergymen to applaud the 'enlightened age'. The principal cheerleader was Piotr Świtkowski, the ex-Jesuit editor of the monthly periodical, the *Historical and political recorder*. In a programmatic review of the progress of 'enlightenment', which he linked closely with toleration, he claimed that its source was the 'cleansing of philosophy', so that it was now 'the daughter of experience, and of the keen observation of all Nature'. He traced the improvement of learning from Italy in the sixteenth century, through France, England, Germany, Poland, and even Sweden and Russia: 'So nations which were first enlightened now learn together with those which they had taught. Exquisite taste spreads ever wider, and almost all the nations of Europe contribute to their mutual enlightenment.' In other words, the centres and peripheries of 'enlightenment', which Świtkowski saw as continuous with what we might call the Renaissance and the scientific revolution, had shifted – he concurred with Voltaire that *lumières* now shone brightly in the north.[31]

Others remained convinced that Poland lagged behind other nations. The most dramatic articulation of her peripherality came from Stanisław Staszic in 1790: 'Elsewhere despotism is falling. In Poland there is still a noble oligarchy. Poland is still in the fifteenth century. All Europe is finishing the eighteenth!'[32] King Stanisław August Poniatowski repeatedly expressed a strong sense of his country's junior status in letters to the Tuscan veteran of the American War of Independence, Filippo Mazzei,

---

31. *Pamiętnik Historyczny i Polityczny Przypadkow Ustaw, Osób, Mieysc i Pism Wiek Nasz Szczegulniey Interessuiących*, January 1783, p.1-31 (p.6-7). Reprinted in Irena Łossowska, 'Piotr Świtkowski (1744-1793)', in *Pisarze polskiego Oświecenia*, ed. Teresa Kostkiewiczowa and Zbigniew Goliński, 3 vols (Warsaw, 1992-1996), vol.2, p.305-31 (320-22): 'oczyszczenia filozofii'; 'corką doświadczenia, i pilnego uważania natury całey'; 'Tak że wprzód już oświecone narody uczą się razem z tymi, których przedtem pouczały. Smak wyborny szerzy się coraz, i wszystkie prawie Europy narody przykładają się do wzajemnego oświecenia sobie.' I cover Świtkowski's concepts of progress and enlightenment in my articles 'Progress and violence' and 'What is Enlightenment?' See Simon Davies, 'Whither/wither France: Voltaire's view from Ferney', in this volume.

32. [Stanisław Staszic], *Przestrogi dla Polski*, in S. Staszic, *Pisma filozoficzne i społeczne*, ed. Bogdan Suchodolski, 2 vols (Warsaw, 1954), vol.1, p.303: 'Gdzie indziej już despotyzm upada. W Polsce jeszcze oligarchia szlachecka. Polska dopiero w wieku piętnastym. Cała Europa już wiek osiemnasty kończy!'

his agent in revolutionary France. We find verdicts such as 'depuis qu'on a beaucoup lu en Pologne les Encyclopédistes, et les Economistes, et surtout qu'on lit de ce que l'on fait et écrit en France depuis un an, bien des gens commencent à secouer le préjugé anti-roturier';[33] 'la masse des lumières est encore infiniment moins répandue ici et que le petit nombre de gens qui ont commencé à s'instruire depuis 20 ans, se sont laissés aller à trop de bonnes opinions d'eux-mêmes';[34] and 'gens, qui se regardent encore comme d'un siècle ou deux plus jeunes, qu'on ne l'est en France'.[35] But the monarch was keen to convince his correspondent of the advances made in Poland, as well as the analogies between the two revolutions. Later, he too would shudder in horror at events in France.

This is not the place to discuss the reasons why so many self-consciously 'enlightened' Poles believed that their 'nation' had fallen far behind others in economic, social, cultural and intellectual development, and had only recently begun to catch up with 'more enlightened nations'.[36] A word or two of explanation, however, may be welcome about the Polish-Lithuanian polity and its 'provinces'. The word 'prowincja' was used in both constitutional and geo-cultural senses.

At Lublin in 1569, after nearly two centuries of uneasy personal union under the Gediminid-Jagiellon dynasty, the Kingdom (or Crown) of Poland and the Grand Duchy of Lithuania were joined into a federal polity, the Commonwealth of the Two Nations, Polish and Lithuanian, with a common elective monarch, and a common *sejm*. The polity was nicely balanced between dualism and trialism. The dualism, between the Polish Crown and the Grand Duchy of Lithuania, included laws, armies, ministries and other offices, which remained largely separate until the end of the Commonwealth. The trialism did not reflect adequately the Commonwealth's Ruthenian component. Most of the Grand Duchy and the south-eastern expanses of the Polish Crown were inhabited predominantly by Ruthenians (non-Great Russian eastern Slavs), rather than by ethnic Balts and Poles. The Polish language was spreading among the Lithuanian elite even before the Union of Lublin, and the official language of the Grand Duchy, Chancery Ruthenian, known to modern linguists as Old Belarusan, was, at the request of the nobility,

---

33. Stanisław August [hereafter S.A.] to Filippo Mazzei, Warsaw, 3 October 1789, Warsaw, Biblioteka Narodowa Akc. 11,356, vol.1, f.139. Further references to this correspondence will give only date and folio. See Fabre, *Stanislas-Auguste Poniatowski et l'Europe des Lumières*, p.509-22, and Jerzy Michalski, 'La Révolution française aux yeux d'un roi', *Acta Poloniae Historica* 66 (1992), p.75-91.

34. 21 November 1789, f.161-62.

35. 6 January 1790, f.188.

36. See Jerzy Lukowski, *Liberty's folly: the Polish-Lithuanian Commonwealth in the eighteenth century* (London, 1991); for an 'optimist' rejoinder, see Józef Andrzej Gierowski, *The Polish-Lithuanian Commonwealth in the XVIIIth century: from anarchy to well-organised state* (Cracow, 1996). I offer my own views in *Poland's last king and English culture: Stanisław August Poniatowski 1732-1798* (Oxford, 1998).

finally abandoned for Polish in official records in 1697. Instead of a Polish-Lithuanian-Ruthenian federation, it was held – especially in the Crown, but increasingly accepted (in certain contexts) by noble citizens of the Grand Duchy – that the Commonwealth was composed of three provinces: Lithuania, and in the Crown, Great Poland ('Wielkopolska') to the north-west, and Little Poland ('Małopolska') to the south-east. This division corresponded more accurately, but still imperfectly, to the distribution of population and wealth, and tended to be reflected in taxes and soldiers, although of course Lithuania voted her own taxes and maintained her own military establishment.

In the course of the seventeenth and eighteenth centuries, the Commonwealth increasingly came to be known unofficially as 'Poland', and spokesmen for the Grand Duchy proudly proclaimed themselves Poles. This Polonophone nobility, however, also retained a strong sense of Lithuanian identity until well after the partitions. The Grand Duchy was always something more than either of the two Crown provinces. 'La Lithuanie est pour nous à peu près ce qu'est l'Ecosse pour l'Angleterre', Stanisław August tried to explain to Mazzei, after the *sejm* had endorsed a local government reform for the Grand Duchy agreed at a Lithuanian 'provincial session', and as he worked 'à engager les deux provinces de Grande et Petite Pologne (ce qu'on appelle chez nous la Couronne) à imiter l'exemple de Lithuanie'.[37]

Only about half of Poland's present territory was part of the Commonwealth in its 1772 to 1793 borders, whereas roughly three-quarters of those lands now lie in Lithuania, Latvia, Belarus and Ukraine. About two-thirds of the population of 10 to 11 million lived in the Grand Duchy of Lithuania and the Ruthenian regions of the Polish Crown. Here, the great majority of the peasantry spoke dialects of either Ruthenian, or, in the north-western parts of the Grand Duchy, Lithuanian. Polish was the first language of slightly less than half of the Commonwealth's population. There were also 750,000 Yiddish-speaking Jews, settled most densely in the towns of Ruthenia.[38]

'Prowincja' was also the preferred term to evoke the traditional opposition, familiar since classical antiquity, between the 'country' on the one hand and the 'court' and 'city' on the other. The provinces were the nursery of republican 'patriotism' (understood as the defence of liberties) and 'old-Polish' ('staropolskie') virtues. Warsaw was irredeemably polluted by every kind of vice, including the subservience that might allow the establishment of monarchical *absolutyzm*.[39] Such profoundly embedded

37. 18 November 1789, f.158.
38. The point is made forcefully by E. Rostworowski, 'Miasta i mieszczanie w ustroju Trzeciego Maja', in *Sejm Czteroletni i jego tradycje*, ed. Jerzy Kowecki (Warsaw, 1991), p.138-51 (138, 144).
39. For examples of this usage, which largely replaced the older *absolutum dominium*, and confounds the belief that 'absolutism' was coined in the nineteenth century, see Butterwick,

suspicion of the metropolis made the task of reformers in all aspects of life more difficult. Yet, if we are to believe the moralists, fashionable Warsaw and Paris exercised their corrupting influences on provincial manor houses.[40]

Such convictions meant that even those who advocated change to established beliefs and patterns of behaviour usually adopted an anti-metropolitan discourse. A prime example is Bishop Ignacy Krasicki's didactic novel of 1778, *Pan podstoli* (*Mr Pantler*). The hero, an idealised nobleman who weighs up all novelties strictly on their merits, is cast as the fount of true wisdom, whereas the Varsovian narrator is its recipient. When humane treatment of serfs is advocated by one whose motto is 'Moribus antiquis', it seems less threatening. Besides, as Teresa Kostkiewiczowa has shown, Krasicki's works and correspondence reveal a writer critical of his age, who reacted ironically to its claims to 'enlightenment'.[41] *Pan podstoli* also featured a sensibly conservative model parish priest, as did a novel published in 1786 by Bishop Józef Kossakowski of Livonia.[42]

The moderate ideals promoted in novels were echoed in pastoral letters. In a letter to his parish clergy in 1775, Bishop Ignacy Massalski of Wilno set out his hopes, 'that in you, my beloved, [...] our flock should have teachers of truth and not falsehood, interpreters of the essential precepts of religion, and not superstition, an example of genuine virtue, and not just its appearance; the image of a decent lifestyle and management, and not miserliness or extravagance'.[43] With this programme we have moved into the Lithuanian province, in both the political and cultural senses (although Massalski did not fulfil his ambition to become archbishop of a separate Lithuanian ecclesiastical province).

### iii. The provincial context: the diocese of Wilno

Most of the Grand Duchy was covered by the enormous Latin-rite diocese of Wilno (in Lithuanian, Vilnius; in Yiddish, Vilne; in Belarusan, Vilnia). Overall it probably contained more Uniate (Ruthenian-rite) than Latin-rite Catholics. Ignacy Massalski, bishop of Wilno from 1762 until his hanging in Warsaw in 1794, remains a divisive figure. Lithuanian historiography partially recasts both him and the other bishop hanged as a

---

'Political discourses', p.713, 725. The king used 'absolutisme' to Mazzei on 22 July 1789, f.112, printed in *Lettres de Philippe Mazzei et du roi Stanislas-Auguste de Pologne*, ed. J. Michalski et al. (Rome, 1982), vol.1, p.324. Only this volume has appeared. Most of the king's letters to Mazzei remain unpublished.

40. See J. Michalski, '"Warszawa" czyli o antystołecznych nastrojach w czasach Stanisława Augusta', *Studia warszawskie* 12 (1972), p.9-78.

41. Teresa Kostkiewiczowa, 'Krasicki a oświecenie', in *Studia o Krasickim* (Warsaw, 1997), p.138-62.

42. [Józef Kossakowski], *Xiądz pleban* (Warsaw, Gröll, 1786).

43. Kasabuła, *Ignacy Massalski*, p.338.

traitor, Józef Kossakowski of Livonia, as defenders of the separate status of the Grand Duchy. Undoubtedly, however, Massalski's long pontificate had tremendous significance for the diffusion of Enlightenment – and the critical reaction to it – into provincial corners of Eastern Europe.[44]

Having encountered leading physiocrats in France in 1767, Massalski became a proponent of their ideas.[45] He gathered a group of like-minded priests around him, notably Michał Karpowicz, Wilhelm Kaliński and Jan Nepomucen Kossakowski (no relation of Bishop Józef's). Kaliński recorded in his diary the intellectually stimulating, rather worldly atmosphere at Massalski's palace, until his death in 1788.[46] It was in this milieu that Ludovico Muratori's seminal *Della regolata devozione dei cristiani* appeared in Polish translation. Although Massalski was not averse to liturgical ceremony and music, like many of his colleagues he encouraged a religiosity pruned of baroque excrescences and what he regarded as disruptive and superstitious practices, in line with Muratori's recommendations.[47] In 1787 he reproved a rural priest for stirring up belief in witchcraft: 'it is a strange thing, that in this substantially enlightened age, such superstitions reign, but a still stranger one, that the clergy in this century, more enlightened than formerly, do not clear up these superstitions, and frequently they are responsible for them, and imbue the lightheaded common folk with them.'[48]

In 1773 Massalski became the first chairman of the Commission for National Education, established in the wake of the suppression of the Jesuits. On the one hand he helped himself to some of the commission's funds, leading to his exclusion after his malefactions were publicised in 1778. On the other hand, he seems genuinely to have desired the 'enlightenment' of the rural population. With his imagination fired by physiocratic ideas, he initiated a campaign to found parish schools in his diocese. He was assisted by the likes of Kaliński and Karpowicz. During the autumn and winter, children were taught to read and write – in Polish and either Lithuanian or Ruthenian, depending on the area – and sometimes arithmetic. Unsurprisingly, it was not possible to teach peasant children crop rotations and other agricultural improvements. Most

44. Ramunė Šmigelskytė-Stukienė, 'Livonijos vyskupo Juozapo Kazimiero Kosakovskio LDK vizija antropo valstybės padalijimo akivaizdoje', *Lietuvos Istorijos Metraštis* 2001:1 (Vilnius, 2002), p.73-86. Eligijus Raila, 'Vilniaus vyskupas Ignotas Masalskis ir katališka apšvieta: edukacijos ir pastoracijos simbiozė', in *Kultūros istorijos tyrenėjimai*, 5 vols (Vilnius, 1997), vol.3, p.92-146.

45. Ambroise Jobert, *Magnats polonais et physiocrates français (1767-1774)* (Paris, 1941).

46. Wilhelm Kaliński, *Dziennik 1787-1788*, ed. Łukasz Kurdybacha (Wrocław, 1968).

47. Ludovico Muratori, *O porządnym nabożeństwie chrześcian*, translated by M. Tukałło (Wilno, Drukarnia J.K.Mci i Rzeczypospolitey u XX. Scholarum Piarum, 1787).

48. Letter to the dean of Wilkomierz, Reverend Józef Wieliczko, quoted after Kasabuła, *Ignacy Massalski*, p.422-23: 'rzecz dziwna, że w tym wieku znacznie oświeconym podobne panują przesądy, ale dziwniejsza, że duchowni w tymże wieku więcej jak dawniej oświeceni tych przesądów nie uprzątają, a częstokroć są onych sprawcami i pospólstwu lekkomyślnemu wrażają.'

Latin-rite parishes were huge, but in most places, the number of pupils in school did not exceed twenty. Many schools were fragile blooms. Qualified teachers were few, and only rarely were they paid a living wage. Nobles were usually suspicious and sometimes hostile, peasants often reluctant and clergymen mostly unenthusiastic. The commission failed to provide adequate financial, administrative and even moral support.[49]

Prominent preachers in the Polish-Lithuanian Commonwealth sometimes called on lords not to oppress and exploit their serfs, in the tradition of Piotr Skarga and other Jesuits at the turn of the sixteenth century. But during the papal jubilee year of 1776 in the diocese of Wilno, Michał Karpowicz and Wilhelm Kaliński also deployed physiocratic theories of the natural rights of all men to property, their persons and the fruits of their labour, in order to persuade nobles that it was in their own and the Commonwealth's interests to have well-fed, well-housed, well-educated and well-disposed peasants. In doing so, they undermined the ideological foundations of serfdom, although not of paternalism. Peasants were also expected to know their duties: to God, their lords and their fatherland.[50]

Alongside, and partly in opposition to Massalski's palace, the intellectual hub of Wilno, the Commonwealth's second city, with a population of about 25,000, was the university, which had been a wholly Jesuit institution until 1773. The Commonwealth was in its own way the most Jesuitical state in Europe. Poles comprised almost an eighth of European Jesuits before the expulsions of 1759 to 1767, whereas the overall Polish monastic population (of the Latin-rite area) was about one-twentieth of that of Europe.[51] Elsewhere, Jesuits were confessors to monarchs; in the Commonwealth they brought up generations of nobles as republicans. Since the 1750s, Jesuit schooling had been brought firmly into the eighteenth century, as reflected in the inculcation of civic values and experimental science, and the moving away from the literal interpretation of Scripture. In Lithuania, due to the stimulation from Wilno, the decline in standards during the later seventeenth century had been less severe than in the Crown, and recovery had begun earlier. Marcin Poczobut, a fellow of the Royal Society, was renowned for his astronomy throughout Europe. None of this should surprise those familiar with work on Jesuits in eighteenth-century France. Indeed French Jesuits taught modern languages in the Commonwealth from the early eighteenth century; more

---

49. Kasabuła, *Ignacy Massalski*, p.561-83. Raila, 'Vilniaus vyskupas Ignotas Masalskis'. See A. Jobert, *La Commission d'Education Nationale: son œuvre d'instruction civique* (Paris, 1941), p.203-10, and Irena Szybiak, *Szkolnictwo Komisji Edukacji Narodowej w Wielkim Księstwie Litewskim* (Wrocław, 1973), p.97-116, 230-39.

50. M. Ślusarska, '*Powinność i należytość*: Wzajemne relacje między właścicielami dóbr a społecznością wiejską w świetle kazań z epoki stanisławowskiej', in *Dwór, plebania, rodzina chłopska*, ed. M. Ślusarska, p.69-102.

51. Statistics from Stanisław Litak, *Od Reformacji do Oświecenia: Kościół katolicki w Polsce nowożytnej* (Lublin, 1994), p.185, and D. Beales, *Prosperity and plunder: European Catholic monasteries in the age of revolution, 1650-1815* (Cambridge, 2003), p.2, 147.

came following their expulsion from France. By 1772 or 1773 Poland-Lithuania had sixty-six Jesuit colleges with 417 Jesuit professors, about three times more than the Piarists.[52]

The reform of Wilno University has long been compared unfavourably with that of Cracow. Much of the responsibility for this tradition rests with Reverend Kołłątaj, whose dislike of the Jesuits became typical of the 'enlightened' Polish laity in the early nineteenth century. It was at this point that Kołłątaj's ally Jan Śniadecki moved to Wilno, where with his brother Jędrzej he presided over the university's golden age.[53] Undoubtedly, the suppression was morally and materially debilitating. The academy remained in a kind of limbo for seven years. After Poczobut was appointed rector in 1780, however, matters improved more rapidly than has usually been acknowledged. Ex-Jesuits and Piarists worked together reasonably harmoniously. Karpowicz, a secular priest, became professor of dogmatic theology, although Poczobut accused him of missing lectures and siding with Massalski. The rector recruited foreigners of the calibre of Georg Forster (who had sailed with James Cook) to teach natural history, although when they left, they were hard to replace. Visitations of secondary schools were carried out efficiently, facilitated by contacts between former Jesuits, most of whom remained at their posts. As they died or retired, they were generally replaced by lay teachers trained at the two universities.[54] By 1788 Wilno had arguably surpassed Cracow as the leading intellectual centre of the Commonwealth's provinces.[55]

---

52. The renaissance of Jesuit schooling is covered by Stanisław Bednarski, *Upadek i odrodzenie szkół jezuickich w Polsce: Studium z dziejów kultury i szkolnictwa polskiego* (Cracow, 2003; reprint of Cracow, 1933), and Ludwik Piechnik's monumental *Dzieje Akademii Wileńskiej*, 4 vols (Rome, 1983-1990), as well as by many contributions to *Jezuici a kultura polska*, ed. Ludwik Grzebień and Stanisław Obirek (Cracow, 1993); *Z dziejów szkolnictwa jezuickiego w Polsce: Wybór artykułów*, ed. Jerzy Paszenda (Cracow, 1994); *Wkład Jezuitów do nauki i kultury w Rzeczyspospolitej Obojga Narodów i pod zaborami*, ed. I. Stasiewicz-Jasiukowa (Cracow and Warsaw, 2004). Compare, for France, R. R. Palmer, *Catholics and unbelievers in eighteenth-century France* (Princeton, NJ, 1939) and C. B. O'Keefe, *Contemporary reactions to the Enlightenment (1728-1762)* (Paris, 1974).

53. For instance Jobert, *La Commission d'Education Nationale*, p.253-61.

54 Janina Kamińska, *Universitas Vilnensis: Akademia Wileńska i Szkoła Główna Wielkiego Księstwa Litewskiego 1773-1792* (Pułtusk and Warsaw, 2004); Szybiak, *Szkolnictwo*, p.44-67, 117-94; I. Szybiak, 'Portret zbiorowy nauczycieli szkół średnich Komisji Edukacji Narodowej', *Wiek Oświecenia* 5 (1989), p.55-68; Jan Popłatek, *Komisja Edukacji Narodowej: Udział byłych Jezuitów w pracach Komisji Edukacji Narodowej* (Cracow, 1974), p.388-89 and passim.

55. On 'provincial' 'literary culture' see J. Snopek, *Prowincja oświecona: Kultura literacka ziemi krakowskiej w dobie Oświecenia* (Warsaw, 1992), and M. Ślusarska, 'Kultura literacka Wilna w dobie stanisławowskiej: Zarys wybranych zagadnień', *Wiek Oświecenia* 14 (1998), p.95-129.

*Richard Butterwick*

## iv. Michał Karpowicz, Jan Nepomucen Kossakowski and the Revolution of 1788-1792

Following a period of intense 'fermentation' and against the king's advice, the *sejm* of 1788 took advantage of the Russo-Turkish war to repudiate the Russian 'guarantee' of the Commonwealth's institutions, and prolong itself. By the summer of 1792, when Catherine II's armies had installed her counter-revolutionary supporters (including Bishops Józef Kossakowski, Ignacy Massalski and Wojciech Skarszewski) in power, public life in Poland-Lithuania had been transformed. Besides new institutions of central and local government, and greatly increased revenues and armed forces, contemporaries were struck by the outpouring of political pamphlets, poems and plays, while demand for less politicised forms of literary output fell sharply.[56]

The Warsaw *sejm* sought to win the support of the provincial nobility for its policies through various media, including proclamations, pamphlets and pastoral letters. Sermons had a crucial place in the thanksgiving ordained by the *sejm*, especially after the Constitution of 3 May 1791. Even at an earlier stage, however, sermons mediated between the metropolis and the provinces and vice versa. The *sejm* was often called 'enlightened'. Initially this was part of a persuasive strategy to put provincial pressure on the *sejm* to act wisely; later the emphasis shifted to persuading provincial audiences to put their trust in the wisdom of the *sejm*.

Politically charged sermons were an integral part of ceremonies traditionally held to mark occasions such as the king's nameday. These were especially prominent in Warsaw, as well as the four cities which hosted the supreme legal tribunals, and the two seats of universities. Wilno had both. For all the political and social content that might be carried by a sermon, however, predication remained a form of rhetorical communication dedicated to the salvation of souls. The 'physiocratic priests' criticised by most nineteenth- and twentieth-century historians of the Polish Church did not, in fact, forget their primary vocation.[57]

One difference between metropolitan and provincial political culture seems to have been in the relative impacts of pamphlets and sermons. When Michał Karpowicz published a sermon preached on the feast of Saints Peter and Paul in 1789, he began his dedication (to Bishop Józef Kossakowski) thus:

Among so many writings which have been thrown out about the clergy, against the clergy, and for the clergy, it also fell to me to present the teaching [of the

---

56. See Jan IJ. van der Meer, *Literary activities and attitudes in the Stanislavian age in Poland (1764-1795): a social system?*, Studies in Slavic literature and poetics 36 (Amsterdam and New York, 2002).

57. See M. Ślusarska, 'Problematyka polityczno-społeczna w polskim kaznodziejstwie okolicznościowym w latach 1775-1795', doctoral dissertation, University of Warsaw, 1992.

Church] on this subject, for the enlightenment of the faithful, who for the most part probably do not read, and have not read those writings, while even the speeches on behalf of the clergy, at this memorable *sejm* by the most virtuous and enlightened patriots, beginning with the throne, so zealously standing by the house of God and the altar, are probably known to and read by a small number [of persons] in the provinces.

He recognised that provincial citizens were more likely to hear sermons, or even to read them, than to read the latest pamphlets and orations.[58] Wishing to demonstrate the salutary effects of ecclesiastical authority and property at a time when they were under attack from 'the blind enlightenment of supposed wiseacres'[59] and 'libertyni' who until now had only dared to blaspheme in foreign languages, he used some of Skarszewski's pamphlets, praising him in the footnotes as an 'enlightened author' ('oświecony Autor'), and in places following him almost word for word:

These unbelieving debauchees sow their opinions, infected with the venom of debauchery, under the appearance of enlightenment, they undermine virtue, they inflame and unchain all the passions of hearts, they set alight the most dreadful intentions and crimes, they break the bonds of human society, they bring honest souls to fear and despair, and covering all this with the mask of zeal for the public good, they place the flattering perspective of the happiness of the Fatherland in the overthrow of the authority of the Church, in the dissolution and oppression of the altar, and in the absorption of the properties and estates of the clergy![60]

The keynote was unmasking the purveyors of a false 'enlightenment'.

58. Michał Karpowicz, *Kazanie o władzy Kościoła, jak jest narodom zbawienna, i o majątkach Kościołów, jak narodom są użyteczne w dzień SS. Apostołów Piotra y Pawła w Wilnie na Antokolu w Kościele Kanoników Laterańskich miane 1789* [...] *Józefowi z Korwinów Kossakowskiemu biskupowi inflantskiemu* [...] *w dzień imienin jego offiarowane* (Wilno, 1790): 'W pośrzód tylu Pism teraz o Duchownych, przeciw Duchownym, i za Duchownemi rozrzuconych, zdało mi się w Duchu Religii także, z mieysca poświęconego, Naukę o tym ku oświeceniu Wiernych przełożyć, których większa część pewnie, Pism tamtych ani czyta, ani czytała, a Mowy nawet za Duchowieństwem, na tym Wiekopomnym Seymie Naycnotliwszych Patriotow i oświeconych, poczowszy od Tronu za Domem Boskim i Ołtarzem tak gorliwie obstawaiącego, pewnie od małey liczby po Prowinciach są znane i czytywane.' Karpowicz and Józef Kossakowski had been contemporaries at the renowned seminary run by the Lazarist order in Warsaw. As we shall see, they fell out in 1791-1792.

59. Karpowicz, *Kazanie o władzy Kościoła*, p.4: 'slepe mniemanych mędrkow oświecenie'.

60. Karpowicz, *Kazanie o władzy Kościoła*, p.9-10: 'Rozsiewaią ci rozpustnicy bezwierni pod pozorem oświecenia, zarażone jadem rozpusty zdania, podkopuią cnotę z Fundamentow; rozniecaią i rozwiązuią wszelkich serc namiętności, zapalaią w sercach nayszkaradnieysze ułożenia i zbrodnie, zrywaią ogniwa Towarzystwa ludzkiego, wprowadzaią w bojaźń i rozpacz Dusze poczciwe, a to wszystko pokrywaiąc gorliwości o dobro publiczne Maską, a w obaleniu władzy Kościoła, w rozsypaniu i uciemiężeniu Ołtarza, w pochłonieniu Maiątkow i Dóbr Duchownych zakładaią perspektywę podchlebną szczęśliwości Oyczyzny!' See Skarszewski, *Odpowiedź plebana*, p.3; M. Ślusarska, 'Sejm Czteroletni w okolicznościowym kaznodziejstwie lat 1788-1790', in *Ku reformie państwa i odrodzeniu moralnemu człowieka: Zbiór artykułów i rozpraw poświęconych rocznicy ustanowienia Konstytucji 3 Maja 1791 roku*, ed. Piotr Żbikowski (Rzeszów, 1992), p.65-80 (69-70). Karpowicz also quoted F. S. Jezierski's sermon, preached to the *sejm* on 7 October 1788: see Karpowicz, *Kazanie o władzy Kościoła*, p.25-26.

Karpowicz emphasised that the greatness of the 'Lithuanian nation' ('Naród Litewski') had come at a time of generous endowments from magnate families – not least the magnificently stuccoed church on the outskirts of Wilno, in which he preached. But those who were fiercest in their attacks had never given anything, although they had received their education, advance and even their property from their clerical brethren.[61] At the same time, Karpowicz stressed that the purpose of the temporal power was to make nations happy ('uszczęśliwienie narodów'), and that the clergy was bound to support it in that endeavour by enlightening minds.[62]

A similar emphasis on the temporal utility of religion emerged a few weeks earlier, on 8 May 1789, from Prelate Jan Nepomucen Kossakowski's St Stanisław's Day sermon in Wilno, preached in the university church. The sermon's dedication, 'To the Fatherland' ('Do Oyczyzny'), reveals a defensive frame of mind: 'Let sacrilegious blasphemers say and write whatever corrupted reason and the most dreadful crimes put into their lips and pens, this truth shall always be unshaken: that our holy religion not only in no way harms the [general] good, but most efficaciously contributes to it.'[63] This paean to love of country was justified, when some ingrate sons concealed their full incomes in order to avoid taxation, and the clergy was accused of teaching nobles to neglect their civic duties for eternal salvation. Yet Poles owed the clergy their upbringing and 'enlightenment'.[64] Most of the sermon consisted of uplifting historical and Biblical examples.

Karpowicz and Kossakowski had to tailor their arguments to their audience, who could in turn exercise pressure upon the *sejm*. That is not to say that they were insincere. Most of the published sermons preached on public occasions during the first year or so of the Revolution expressed generalised support for the 'enlightened' *sejm*, while defending the clergy's rights and property, as well as revealed religion.

In Wilno on St Stanisław's Day in 1790, Jan Kossakowski preached a sunnier sermon on 'the keeping of the laws of the nation'. In advocating an amelioration in the condition of the enserfed peasantry, he cited

---

61. Karpowicz, *Kazanie o władzy Kościoła*, p.30-36.
62. Karpowicz, *Kazanie o władzy Kościoła*, p.12-19.
63. Jan Nepomucen Kossakowski, *Kazanie o miłości oyczyzny w dzień S. Stanisława biskupa krakowskiego pamiątką jego męczeństwa, y dorocznym obchodzeniem imienin J. Krolew: Mosci uroczysty w Kościele S. Jana Akademickim* (Wilno, 1789), reprinted in J. N. Kossakowski, *Kazania* (Wilno, Drukarnia J.K.Mci przy Akademii, 1793), p.1-39: 'Co tylko poda do ust i pióra zepsuty rozum i nayskaradnieysza zbrodnia, niech mówią i piszą świętokradzcy bluźnierce, nigdy niewzruszoná zostanie zawsze ta Prawda: że S. Religia nasza nie tylko w niczém powszechnégo nieuszkadza Dobra, ale nadto naydzielniéy i nayskuteczniéy przykłada się do niego.' See M. Ślusarska, 'Królewskie kaznodziejstwo okolicznościowe czasów Stanisława Augusta Poniatowskiego', *Napis: Tom poświęcony literaturze okolicznościowej i użytkowej* 1 (1994), p.135-52 (147-48).
64. J. N. Kossakowski, *Kazanie o miłości oyczyzny*, p.3-15.

neglected statutes, the laws of Denmark, the Renaissance political theorist Andrzej Frycz Modrzewski, as well as Piotr Skarga. He anticipated the admission to the protection of the law of 'all those, in proportion to their enlightenment, whom until now we have paid for their useful efforts and bloody labour with contempt and burdens, and who have a just hope at the end of the eighteenth century'.[65] Implicitly, as the serfs became 'enlightened', so they could gradually be emancipated. Such optimism was closer to Karpowicz's and Kaliński's sermons of the 1770s than the clouded tone of 1789, in which the rhetoric of Anti-Enlightenment predominated. The peasant question was marginal or absent in most sermons published during the Revolution.[66]

On 3 May 1791, in circumstances resembling a coup d'état, the *sejm* passed the Law on Government, which made the monarchy hereditary, strengthened both the executive and legislative powers, extended the protection of the law in general terms to peasants and confirmed the concessions to the burghers made on 18 April. On 5 May the *sejm* unanimously endorsed the Constitution of 3 May, and announced that a votive church dedicated to Divine Providence would be built.

On 8 May Karpowicz was due to preach to the Lithuanian tribunal in Grodno, but he improvised, after the news of the Constitution arrived the previous day. Karpowicz reached for the rhetoric of Enlightenment to build trust in the monarch: 'The rights of humanity and reasonable liberty are resurrected, [...] prejudices and barbarity have vanished, the light of reason and citizenship rises up, the paternal goodness of the best of kings wins the complete trust of an honest nation.'[67] But, he asked, could they flatter themselves that their morals and piety had won God's

65. J. N. Kossakowski, *Kazanie o zachowaniu praw narodowych w dzień uroczystości S. Stanisława biskupa i męczennika jmienin N. P. N. M. Stanisława Augusta i pamiątki ustanowionego orderu pod imieniem tegoż Świętego dorocznie obchodzoney w Kościele S. Jana Akademickim przez X. Jana Nepomucena Kossakowskiego prałata kated: i administratora dyecezyi wileń: miane* (Wilno, 1790), reprinted in J. N. Kossakowski, *Kazania*, p.40-73 (52-53): 'A do téy Księgi że będą i ci przypuszczeni w miarę swojego Oświecenia, którym za użyteczne zabiegi i krwawé ich prace, dotąd nayczęściey wzgardą i uciążliwościa wypłacaliśmy się, sprawiedliwą maią nadzieję przy końcu osiemnastego wieku.' See Ślusarska, 'Królewskie kaznodziejstwo', p.148-49.
66. Ślusarska, *'Powinność i należytość'*, p.94-99. Jean-Jacques Rousseau also counselled a gradual emancipation of the worthiest and most enlightened serfs: *Considérations sur le gouvernement de Pologne et sur sa réformation projetée*, ed. Jean Fabre, in *Œuvres complètes*, vol.3, p.1024-27. But several writers, including Staszic and Kołłątaj, insisted on 'liberty' and 'property' preceding 'enlightenment'. For a thorough examination of the subject, see J. Michalski, ' "Wolność" i "własność" chłopska w polskiej myśli reformatorskiej XVIII wieku', *Kwartalnik Historyczny* 110:4 (2003), p.5-45, and 111:1 (2004), p.69-103.
67. M. Karpowicz, *Kazanie w uroczystość imienin J. K. Mci y pamiątkę ustanowienia Orderu S. Stanisława biskupa i męczennika do Trybunału Głł: W. X. Litt: w dzień doszłey wiadomości do Grodna o Konstytucyi rządowey szczęśliwie na wiekopomnym seymie warszawskim ustanowioney, miane dnia 8. maia 1791. roku* (Grodno, Drukarnia J. K. Mci i P.K.E.N., 1791), not paginated: 'Prawa ludzkości i rozumney Wolności wskrzeszone, [...] Przesądy i Barbarzyństwa zginęły, Swiatło rozumu i Obywatelstwa się wznosi, Dobroć Oycowska naylepszego z Królów, zupełne Pocżciwego Narodu zaufanie zyskuie.'

favour? Without an improvement in mores, Providence would have raised them up, only to cast them down again later from a greater height. First came the jeremiad:

> Clergymen upbraid laymen for their debauchery and coolness in Faith, laymen reproach clergymen for greed, incompetence, laziness, and neglect of the House of God; oh God! Was *Jerusalem* more guilty in your eyes at that time? [...] The Most Holy Saviour would find among us flagrant adultery respected, extortion by offices legitimised, debaucheries honoured by the example of great lords, the Son of God would find among us offices for sale, courts and justice at a price, officers' oaths treated as jokes, the public treasury robbed without scruple [...] he would find pastors without zeal, priests without holiness, clergymen without the spirit of faith and piety, he would find learning neglected, altars despised, sacred things insulted, churches abandoned, and hypocrisy in the vows of the holiest monastic rules.[68]

But while reproving in general, he flattered individuals. He named a string of legislators as Phocions and Demosthenes, Washingtons and Franklins, Vergennes and Turgots. Stanisław Małachowski, the marshal of the *sejm*, was an Aristides, its financial experts were Neckers, while the author of *Letters of an anonymous correspondent* (Kołłątaj) was Locke and Montesquieu rolled into one. No longer should Poles 'envy other nations their enlightenment': a claim that they were no longer on the intellectual periphery of the European and Atlantic world.[69]

Karpowicz trod a fine line between praising the Poles' 'enlightenment' and suggesting that 'enlightenment' could become savage fanaticism if, as in France, it was unrestrained by religion:

> Oh! what happiness in our *Revolution*, in comparison with the almost barbaric savagery and slaughters of those almost too enlightened French – even unto the abandonment of the sentiments of humanity and religion. They, having overthrown the throne and altar, made savage *fanatics* of riotous licence out of enlightened people. Whereas the honest Pole has confirmed the dominant religion, has reasonably secured civil toleration for all, has not oppressed the conscience of any person, has made the liberty of millions of useful people eternal through their rights and freedoms, has not forgotten to improve the fate of villagers and peasants, taking them under the protection of the laws, strengthened the throne of his kings, curtailed the influence of hostile spirits, waiting for the

---

68. Karpowicz, *Kazanie w uroczystość imienin J. K. Mci*: 'Duchowni wyrzucaią Swieckim ich rozwiązłość i oziembłość w Wierze, Swieccy wymawiaią Duchownym ich łakomstwo, nieumieiętność, gnuśność i Domu Boskiego zaniedbanie; o Boże! Czyliż winnieysze w twych oczach było na ten czas *Jeruzalem*? [...] Znalazłby pomiędzy nami ten Nayświętszy Zbawiciel: Cudzołostwa jawne i szanowane, zdzierstwa Urzędami upoważnione, rozpusty przykładami wielkich Panow zaszczycone, znalazłby Syn Boski pomiędzy nami Urzędy przedayne, Sądy i sprawiedliwości płatne, przysięgi Urzędnikow w żart obrócone, Skarb Publiczny bez skrupułu kradziony [...] znalazłby Pasterzow bez gorliwości, Kapłanow bez Swiątobliwości, Duchownych bez ducha wiary i pobożności, znalazłby zaniedbane nauki, pogardzone Ołtarze, znieważone Swiątości, opuszczone Kościoły, obłudę w Nayświętszych Zakonności zaprzysiężeniach.'

69. Karpowicz, *Kazanie w uroczystość imienin J. K. Mci*, 'Nie zazdrośćmy iuż innym Narodom ich oświecenia!'

ruin of the Fatherland; has dedicated the day of this law for eternal solemn commemoration, for thanksgiving to God; has obliged himself by a vow to build a Divine sanctuary to everlasting Providence, in gratitude for the miraculous defence of the Fatherland.[70]

In the dedication Karpowicz recalled 'how much joy and tearful feeling with astonishment it had produced among many thousands listening, and the entire enlightened public'.[71]

The news reached Wilno during the St Stanisław's Day dinner for the professors of the university. Rector Poczobut wrote of how it:

led us all joyfully to admire and ponder the work and miracle of the Divine hand, delivering us from ultimate calamity and disaster. Our joy was inexpressible. It roused us to a public thanksgiving to God, which we are to celebrate solemnly, and ask, that His omnipotent hand would guide the steps of such an enlightened and active *sejm* well.[72]

As the peal of church bells echoed across Lithuania (reaching Mozyrz in the far south-east on 21 May), the repertoire of salutes, banquets with patriotic toasts, illuminations, votive masses, sermons and the *Te Deum laudamus* was repeated.[73]

The celebrations at Wilno on 1 July featured one of Jan Kossakowski's most eloquent sermons. He asserted that the same omnipotent right hand had cast down the French, and raised up the Poles. Psalms and prophets evoked God's anger with a sinful nation, and His grace in answering its prayers. But while Kossakowski denounced the corruption of morals, he did not join the chorus against the eighteenth century. He lauded the

70. Karpowicz, *Kazanie w uroczystość imienin J. K. Mci*: 'O! cóż za szczęśliwość *Rewolucyi* naszey, w porównaniu dziczy prawie Barbarzyńskiey i rzezi nazbyt oświeconych, aż do wyzucia się z sentymentu ludzkości i Religii owych Francuzow? Oni Tron obaliwszy i Ołtarz, z oświeconych ludzi, uczynili dzikich rozhukaney swywoli *Fanatykow*. Poczciwy zaś Polak Religią Panującą utwierdził; Tolerancyą Cywilną dla wszystkich rozumnie zabeśpieczył, sumnienia żadnego z ludzi nie ucisnął, Wolność Milionom ludu użytecznego przy Prawach i Swobodach uwiecznił, Rolnikow i Kmieci polepszenia losow, pod Opieką Praw nie zapomniał, Tron Królów swoich umocnił, wpływ Duchom nieprzyiaznym na zgubę Oyczyzny czuwaiącym zamknął; dzień tey ustawy na Wieczną pamiątkę, ku dziękczynieniu Bogu, Uroczystym poświęcił; Świątnicę Boską, Świętą Opatrzności Przedwieczney, na wdzięczność za Cudowną Oyczyzny obronę, zbudować, Szlubem obowiązał się.'

71. Karpowicz, *Kazanie w uroczystość imienin J. K. Mci*: 'ile radości i rozrzewnienia w kilkotysiącznego Ludu słuchaczach i całey Oświeconey Powszechności'. See also W. Smoleński, *Ostatni rok Sejmu Wielkiego*, 2nd edn (Cracow, 1897), p.12-13, and M. Ślusarska, 'Konstytucja 3 Maja w kaznodziejstwie okolicznościowym lat 1791-1792', in '*Rok Monarchii Konstytucyjnej*': *Piśmiennictwo polskie lat 1791-1792 wobec Konstytucji 3 Maja*, ed. Teresa Kostkiewiczowa (Warsaw, 1992), p.153-75 (158-59).

72. Poczobut to Śniadecki, 12 May 1791, quoted after Smoleński, *Ostatni rok*, p.10-11: 'wprawił nas wszystkich w radosne zachwycenie i zadumienie nad dziełem i cudem ręki boskiej, wyrywającej nas z ostatniego nieszczęścia i zguby. Trudno mi wyrazić, jaka to była radość. Zagrzała nas ona do publicznego dziękczynienia Bogu, które mamy uroczyście odprawić, a prosić, ażeby taż wszechmocna ręka Jego kierowała dobrze kroki tak oświeconego i czynnego sejmu.'

73. Smoleński, *Ostatni rok*, p.5-21.

century's voices of wisdom, resanctifying the secular discourse of enlightenment:

> Various voices were raised on behalf of humanity in enlightened writings, the Pole finally felt his rights and honours, and began to think of making all his brothers happy. But the time had not yet come for this oppressed land, the eighteenth century had not yet shone for her in its full light, the clouds of prejudice and delusions still covered her too thickly; in a word, Divine justice still punished our Fatherland for the offences of her sons.[74]

But when the 'rays of grace' shone, all changed:

> All Europe is astonished by such a splendid transformation of our Fatherland, enlightened nations take her as an example to follow, and when in almost all countries sudden and great changes have spilt human blood, only Poland may pride herself that her new government, established calmly and mildly, is the most beautiful fruit of love of the Fatherland and fraternal unity, the honour of enlightened humanity, and the crowning glory of the eighteenth century as it nears its close.

Thus Kossakowski also claimed that Poland's peripheral status among 'enlightened nations' had come to an end.[75]

In February 1792 the assemblies of the provincial nobility, the *sejmiki*, were asked to endorse the Revolution. Twenty-seven out of thirty-three *sejmiki* in the Grand Duchy of Lithuania chose to do so in the strongest possible form, by swearing an oath to defend the Constitution, a much higher proportion than in the Polish Crown.[76] The clearest example of clerical influence on the nobility comes from the *sejmik* of Preny, held

---

74. J. N. Kossakowski, *Kazanie w dzień uroczystego nabożeństwa w Wilnie odprawionego na podziękowanie Bogu za całość i szczęśliwość Oyczyzny naszey ustanowieniem dobrego Rządu dnia 3. maja roku 1791 zabeśpieczoną, miane przez X. Jana Nepomucena Kossakowskiego prałata kated: i administratora dyecezyi wileń* (Wilno, 1791), reprinted in Kossakowski, *Kazania*, p.106-34 (120): 'odzywały się w oświeconych Pismach rozmaite za ludzkością głosy, uczuł nareszcie prawa swoje i zaszczyty Polak, i myśleć o powszechném Braci swoich uszczęśliwieniem zaczął. Ale ieszcze nie przyszła pora dla téy uciśnioney ziemi, ieszcze wiek ośmnasty nie zajaśniał był dla niéy w całem swoiém świetle, ieszcze zbyt grube okrywały ią chmury przesądow, i omamienia, słowem, ieszcze sprawiedliwość Boska, karała naszę Oyczyznę za nieprawości iey Synów.'

75. J. N. Kossakowski, *Kazanie w dzień uroczystego nabożeństwa*, p.126: 'Zdumiewa się cała Europa nad tak świetną Oyczyzny naszéy odmianą, biorą ią oświecone Narody za wzór do naśladowania, i kiedy we wszystkich prawie krajach nagłe, a wielkie odmiany krew ludzka oblała, Polska sama chlubić się może że Jey Rząd nowy spokoynie i łagodnie ustanowiony iest naypięknieyszym miłości Oyczyzny i iedności braterskiey owocem, iest zaszczytem oświeconey ludzkości, iest chwałą i wieńcem kończącego się wieku ośmnastego.' Ślusarska, 'Konstytucja 3 Maja w kaznodziejstwie', p.163-65, uses the Biblical character of this sermon to refute nineteenth-century charges of rationalism and secularity levelled against the leading preachers of this period, but she does not note Kossakowski's more positive attitude towards the eighteenth century, compared to Karpowicz, nor the extent to which, especially in his sermon of 3 May 1792, Enlightenment discourse permeated his theology. See below.

76. Wojciech Szczygielski, *Referendum trzeciomajowe: Sejmiki lutowe 1792 roku* (Łódź, 1994), p.394-96.

in the capacious wooden parish church, picturesquely situated on the wooded banks of the River Niemen. Karpowicz, the parish priest, preached on Deuteronomy 6.6-9, quoting Moses' command to the Israelites to obey the law and in doing so to demonstrate their wisdom and understanding to other nations. The themes of the nation's newly acquired reputation in Europe (he cited 'that zealous English republican, Mr *Burke*'), enlightened legislation and the need to execute it, resonated throughout.[77] First he defended his right and duty to speak as a citizen:

> I do not know (thanks be to my God!) that prejudice, which debauched philosophy hurls at the clerical estate, that a priest cannot be a good citizen: that a clergyman should not mix teachings about the government of the country into the *catechism* of faith. The well-founded teaching of the Gospel enlightens me otherwise; the true teaching of Christ's faith, true and essential *theology*, teaches me otherwise. I was first born as a man, before I entered the clerical estate; I was first a citizen, before I became a priest; and the duties of my estate obliged me all the more strictly to serve citizens usefully, as the surest foundation of the happiness of all governments, is religion, the Gospel, and the teaching of Christ.[78]

The sermon was anti-aristocratic and anti-anarchic: 'The intrigue and cabal of the aristocrats ruled everywhere, and honesty, when poor, was despised. Proud violence was everything, and the poor nobility had to prostrate itself before rich lords.' Karpowicz also attacked 'political errors canonised by antiquity', in a secular application of religious language. He struck a Rousseauesque emotional note in exclaiming: 'O Fatherland! Free Fatherland! Apart from religion, the holiest word in nature!' He saw the hand of Providence in the overthrow of the Russian yoke.[79]

---

77. M. Karpowicz, *Kazanie X. Karpowicza archidiakona smoleńskiego, proboszcza preńskiego, theologii y pisma ś. w Szkole Gł: Lit: professora, na pierwszym ufundowaniu powiatu preńskiego i rozpoczęciu pierwszych seymików w kościele parafialnym preńskim 14 lutego, 1792. roku* (Wilno, Drukarnia XX. Bazylianów, 1792), p.22: 'Ow Angielski republikant gorliwy P. *Burke*'. There was also a Warsaw edition. He referred to 'Hume Anglik', when citing him to show the advantages of ecclesiastical unity: Karpowicz, *Kazanie o władzy Kościoła*, p.15.
78. Karpowicz, *Kazanie X. Karpowicza*, p.4: 'Nie znam ja (Bogu moiemu dzięki!) nie znam tego uprzedzenia, które stanowi Duchownemu rozwiązła zarzuca filozofia: iż Xiądz bydź nie może dobrym obywatelem: iż Duchowny mieszać nie powinien do *Katechizmu* wiary, nauki o rządzie kraiowym. Inaczey mnie oświeca gruntowna nauka Ewangelii: inaczey mnie przekonywa skład rządu szlachetnego Polskiego narodu; inaczey mię uczy prawdziwa nauka Chrystusowey wiary, prawdziwa i istotna *Teologia*. Wpierweyiem się urodził człowiekiem, nimem się umieścił w stanie Duchownym; wprzód byłem Obywatelem, niżelim został Kapłanem; a powinności moiego stanu, tym ściśley mię obowiązały, do użyteczney Obywatelom posługi, im pewnieyszym gruntem szczęśliwości wszelkich rządów, jest Religia, Ewangelia, i nauka Chrystusowa.'
79. Karpowicz, *Kazanie X. Karpowicza*, p.31: 'Intryga i kabała możnowładzcow, panowała wszędzie; a pocczciwość przy ubóstwie była wzgardzona. Przemoc dumna dokazywała wszystkiego: a Szlachta uboga płaszczyć się musiała przed bogatemi Panami'; p.33: 'kanonizowanych starożytnością politycznych błędów'; p.34: 'O! Oyczyzno! wolna Oyczyzno! jedno tylko prócz Religii nayświętsze słowo w naturze!'

The celebrated preacher sought to impress, when he told his congregation:

> There was never yet such an age in our nation, in which enlightenment reached such a level among citizens, as we now see in the persons composing the current sejm and legislature; so far, that no *political, statistical, civil,* or *economic* matter is not considered in the clearest, and most thorough manner, for the enlightenment of the nation, in the speeches of the patriot legislators.[80]

He named a substantial part of the united 'patriot' party, including Kołłątaj. There was nothing to add to their voices, but he reiterated that it 'would be the duty of teachers of the people to repeat it from the pulpit to distant provinces; to say the same, would be a praiseworthy imitation of incomparable men; it would be the most useful persuasion of the most illustrious nobles in the provinces, of how thoroughly they could trust such enlightened men'.[81] It is striking how Karpowicz felt confident enough to adopt a top-down discourse, encouraging his provincial flock to trust the enlightened metropolis. Preaching from his own pulpit (a minor rococo gem), his authority and plausibility were enhanced.

The *sejmik* of Preny duly took an oath to defend the Constitution.[82] The nobles were followed by the municipality and burghers. Although the latter had not formally taken part in the *sejmik*, they were present in a show of inter-estate solidarity. The resolution was signed by about a hundred nobles, including Karpowicz, while about fifty more, illiterates, affixed the sign of the cross to their names. This *sejmik* shows how the Church could bring its influence to bear most effectively. Of course, few clergymen were as persuasive as Karpowicz.

On 15 March 1792 the *sejm* voted to celebrate the first anniversary of the Constitution with great pomp. Simultaneously the Lithuanian tribunal in Wilno swore an oath to uphold it. From the pulpit of the university church, Karpowicz turned in another bravura performance. He denounced the 'sacrilegious insolence against the nation' of the Constitution's opponents, perhaps unconsciously echoing the French concept of 'lèse-nation'.[83] He stated that the Constitution was the work of God's

---

80. Karpowicz, *Kazanie X. Karpowicza*, p.7: 'Nie był jeszcze wiek taki nigdy w naszym narodzie, gdzieby do tego punktu oświecenie dochodziło w Obywatelach, jako widziemy go teraz w osobach Seym ninieyszy i prawodawstwo składaiących; tak dalece, że żadney naywyższey *Polityczney, Statystyczney, Cywilney, Ekonomiczney* materyi nie masz, któraby w mowach *Patryotow* prawodawcow, w nayiaśnieyszym, a naygruntownieyszym sposobie roztrząsioną ku oświeceniu narodu nie została.'

81. Karpowicz, *Kazanie X. Karpowicza*, p.8: 'powtarzać to odległym prowincyom, byłoby powinnością nauczycielow ludu z ambony; mówić to samo, byłoby naśladowaniem chwalebnym nieporównanych mężów, byłoby naypotężnieyszym przekonaniem przezacney Szlachty na prowincyach: jak gruntownie tak oświeconym mężom można zaufać'.

82. Cracow, Biblioteka Czartoryskich (hereafter BCz.) 886, p.795-96. Szczygielski, *Referendum,* p.314.

83. M. Karpowicz, *Na zaprzysiężeniu uroczystym Ustawy Rządowey 3. i 5. maja od Trybunału G. W. X. L. jego palestry, kancellaryi, y chorągwi trybunalskiey w dniu 15. marca roku 1792. w Kościele Akademickim S. Jana w Wilnie Kazanie Xiędza Karpowicza prałata archidiak: smoleń:*

right hand, a covenant between God and the nation. He looked to the future: 'Enlightened *education* under the supervision of the nation, then, is confirmed by our happy Constitution; what happy posterity does it promise to future centuries? That happy next *generation* shall not know the repulsive anarchy of interregna! It shall not know the dreadful *despotism* of overmighty aristocrats over king and commons.'[84] Lauding the 'immortal writings' of Kołłątaj and other 'enlightened citizens, which are capable of enlightening the prejudiced, and bringing lost ones back to the way', Karpowicz contended that 'virtue' ('cnota') could not outlast 'enlightenment' ('oświecenie'). Just as in his sermon to the *sejmik* of Preny, the 'enlightenment' of the legislators was a key persuasive strategy. But on this occasion, his attack on the magnates was worded even more strongly – appropriately for the tribunal.[85]

On the Constitution's anniversary, 3 May 1792, Jan Kossakowski again preached amidst the sinuous late baroque and rococo splendour of Wilno's university church. Taking 'one shepherd, and one flock' as his text, he told the congregation that 'the whole of Christ's divine teaching tended to this end, that among all people, unity of hearts and minds, unity of belief and deed should cause people, bonded more strongly by this link, to live happily in harmony and peace.'[86] Indeed, 'Our holiest legislator, Christ, who for the enlightenment of people, and to make them happy, came down to Earth from Heaven, commands us nothing more clearly and strongly than to maintain mutual love and harmony, without which he does not accept our offering, or forgive us our offences, or permit us to call ourselves his followers.'[87] Enlightened Christology

---

*Pisma Ś. i Teologii w Szkole Głow: W. X. Lit: Professora* (Wilno, Drukarnia XX. Bazylianów, 1792), p.3:'świętokradzką przeciw Narodowi zuchwałością'.

84. Karpowicz, *Na zaprzysiężeniu uroczystym*, p.19: '*Edukacya* zatym światła szczęsliwą Konstytucyą naszą utwierdzona pod dozorem Narodu, jakże szczęśliwa przyszłym Wiekom obiecują potomność? Nie będzie znała *Generacya* ta szczęśliwa następna obrzydłych bezkrólewia nierządow! nie będzie znała przemożnych Możnowładcow nad Królem i Gminem okropnego *Despotyzmu*'.

85. Karpowicz, *Na zaprzysiężeniu uroczystym*, p.17-19: 'Pisma nieśmiertelne *Kołłątaia, Trębickiego, Stroynowskiego, Potockiego* i innych światłych Obywatelow zdolne są oświecić uprzedzonych, i na drogę naprowadzić obłąkanych'. See also Ślusarska, 'Konstytucja 3 Maja w kaznodziejstwie', p.167.

86. J. N. Kossakowski, *Kazanie o jedności, zgodzie i pokoiu, w dzień przeniesioney Stanisława S. uroczystości jmienin Nayiaśnieyszego Pana i pierwszéy obchodu Ustawy Rządowéy rocznicy przez X. Jana Nepomucena Kossakowskiego prałata kated: i administratora dyecezyi wileń: roku 1792 miane* (Wilno, 1792), reprinted in J. N. Kossakowski, *Kazania*, p.169-94 (170): 'Cała Boska Chrystusa Nauka do tego zmierzała celu, ażeby we wszystkich Ludziach jedność serc i umysłow jedność wierzenia i czynienia sprawiła, ażeby Ludzie tym naymocnieyszym spoieni węzłem, w zgodzie i pokoiu żyli szczęśliwi.'

87. Kossakowski, *Kazanie o jedności, zgodzie i pokoiu*, p.178: 'Nayświętszy Prawodawca nasz Chrystus, który dla oświecenia i uszczęśliwienia ludzi stąpił z Nieba na ziemię, nic nam wyraznéy i mocniéy nienakazuie nad zachowanie wspolnéy miłości i zgody, bez któréy ani Ofiary Naszéy przyiąć, ani odpuścić nam przewinienia, ani się nam nazywać swemi Uczniami dozwala.'

apart,[88] Kossakowski voiced the conviction at the heart of the celebrations: that Poles 'by unity and harmony alone could keep and save the rescued Fatherland'.[89] It was not to be.

When the counter-revolutionary confederates, led by the preacher's namesakes, the brothers General Szymon and Bishop Józef Kossakowski, arrived in Wilno in mid June 1792, they staged ceremonies which were mirror images of the celebrations of the Constitution.[90] The preamble to the General Confederacy of the Grand Duchy of Lithuania proclaimed the equal privileges of the Lithuanian and Polish nations. This appeal to Lithuanian national feeling accompanied slogans setting virtuous province against enlightened metropolis. The preamble anathematised those 'heated enemies of government and human society, who from cursed philosophical maxims, under the painted figure of patriotism, equality, culpable liberty, and the Rights of Man newly and basely made into concepts, with the overthrow of altar and government, with the destruction of the noble estate and the ruin of the long and hard-won fame and properties of virtuous citizens'.[91]

Troops surrounded Wilno University in an attempt to catch Karpowicz. He was pursued to Preny but he had already left. He went to Warsaw, seeking the king's protection, who in turn appealed to Massalski. Bishop Kossakowski threatened to put Karpowicz on trial for allegedly inciting peasants to rebellion, before finding other fish to fry.[92] The Lithuanian confederacy soon issued a warning to politicking priests. Having declared that religion and 'liberty' were each other's strongest supports, it lamented that 'in some places not apostles, but politicians and commentators were seen in the pulpits of churches; in cathedrals, not teachers of morals and old-Polish virtue, but commandants and partisans;

---

88. Skarszewski, *Odpowiedź plebana*, p.65-66, also described Christ's mission in terms of enlightening humans for their temporal benefit.

89. Kossakowski, *Kazanie o jedności, zgodzie i pokoiu*, p.172: 'samą tylko iednością i zgodą ocaloną zachować mogą Oyczyznę'. He sent a copy to the king, who complimented him warmly. J. N. Kossakowski to SA, 7 May 1792; SA to J. N. Kossakowski, 23 May 1792, BCz. 922, p.792-805.

90. W. Smoleński, *Konfederacya targowicka* (Cracow, 1903), p.108-26, 191-94. R. Šmigelskytė-Stukienė, *Lietuvos Didžiosios Kunigaikštystes konfederacijos susidarymas ir veikla 1792-1793* (Vilnius, 2003), p.78-80, 83.

91. Text of the Lithuanian act of confederation in *Zbiur wszystkich druków Konfederacyi Targowickiey y Wileńskiey* (Warsaw, Drukarnia na Krakowskim Przedmieściu nr 427, 1792), p.3-16 (15-16): 'własney zaciętości i fanatyzmu biorącemu okropne początki, z przeklętych Maxym Filozoficznych, zagorzałych nieprzyiacioł Rządu i społeczności Ludzkiey, pod ubarwioną postącią Patriotyzmu, równości, wolności szkaradney, i Praw nowo z głowy podłey w koncepta utworzonych Człowieka, z wywróceniem Ołtarza i Rządu, z wyniszczeniem Stanu Szlacheckiego i zgubą zapracowany wiekiem Sławy i maiątków Cnotliwych Obywateli.' See Šmigelskytė-Stukienė, *Lietuvos Didžiosios Kunigaikštystes konfederacijos*, p.80-85, 265-69.

92. Karpowicz to SA, Grażyszki, 11 August 1792, Warsaw, 5 October 1792; SA to Karpowicz, 18 August 1792, BCz. 924, p.155-63. SA to Massalski, 8 October 1792; Massalski to SA, 7 November 1792, BCz. 927, p.343, 345.

in some parsonages, not pastors, but rebels.' Yet Bishop Kossakowski's old maxims surfaced in the request to priests to report 'malicious tyrants' ('złośliwi tyrani') who treated their serfs inhumanely.[93]

The confederates failed to bring stability to the Commonwealth. It suited Catherine II to partition Poland-Lithuania with Prussia in 1793, and with Austria and Prussia in 1795, as her contribution to the anti-Jacobin crusade. Both Michał Karpowicz (1744-1803) and Jan Nepomucen Kossakowski (1755-1808) ended their careers in episcopal mitres under the new regimes. Karpowicz became the first bishop of Wigry in 'New East Prussia', whereas Kossakowski became bishop of Wilno in the Russian Empire. He had to do without Massalski's palace and substantial revenues. But he oversaw the completion of the Grecian cathedral, and continued to promote an optimistic strain of 'enlightenment'.[94]

## v. Conclusion

The Constitution of 3 May 1791 was hailed by opinion-formers across Western Europe and beyond the Atlantic.[95] Jan Kossakowski and Michał Karpowicz, along with many of their ecclesiastical colleagues, proclaimed Poland's equality with other nations in terms of 'enlightenment'. If one of the criteria of belonging to the centre of Enlightenment is an original intellectual contribution, then the Commonwealth's came in constitutional legislation. The law of 3 May 1791 was a felicitous balance between Polish, French and American republicanism, and British limited monarchy, between the Montesquieuvian separation of powers and the Rousseauvian sovereignty of the nation, between toleration and the universally perceived need for a dominant religion, and between the rights of all inhabitants of the country to security of person and property, and the inescapable reality of a society and polity dominated by the landowning nobility.[96] The clergy helped convince the provincial nobility that the Constitution was both the work of an 'enlightened *sejm*' and a miracle of Divine Providence. They were helped to do so by the obvious contrast

---

93. Proclamation 27 August 1792, quoted by Smoleński, *Przewrót umysłowy*, p.408-409: 'widziano po niektórych miejscach na ambonach kościelnych nie apostołów, ale statystów i polityków; w katedrach nie nauczycieli obyczajnej nauki i cnoty staropolskiej, ale komendantów i partyzantów; po plebaniach niektórych nie pasterzów, ale buntowników.' See also W. Smoleński, *Konfederacya targowicka* (Warsaw, 1903), p.272, 274-75.

94. M. Ślusarska, 'Michał Franciszek Karpowicz (1744-1803)', in *Pisarze polskiego oświecenia*, ed. T. Kostkiewiczowa and Z. Goliński, vol.2, p.74-98. Deszczyńska, '*Historia sacra*', p.70.

95. Z. Libiszowska, 'Odgłosy Konstytucji 3 Maja na Zachodzie', in *Konstytucja 3 Maja w tradycji i kulturze polskiej*, ed. Alina Barszczewska-Krupa, 2 vols (Łódź, 1991), vol.1, p.70-81.

96. Well-informed analyses of the Constitution include J. Michalski, 'The meaning of the Constitution of 3 May', in *Constitution and reform in eighteenth-century Poland: the Constitution of 3 May 1791*, ed. Samuel Fiszman (Bloomington, IN, 1997), p.251-86, and J. Lukowski, 'Recasting utopia: Montesquieu, Rousseau and the Polish Constitution of 3 May 1791', *Historical journal* 37 (1994), p.65-87.

to be drawn with revolutionary France. The Anti-Enlightenment and anti-metropolitan slogans of the confederates failed to erase the memory of Lithuanian support for the Constitution:

> But of the old men everyone remembers
> That Third of May, when senators and members
> In that assembly hall with joy went wild,
> That king and nation had been reconciled;
> 'Long live the king! Long live the sejm!' they sang,
> 'Long live the nation!' through the concourse rang.

So testified the exiled Adam Mickiewicz in the epic poem he devoted to his lost Lithuanian fatherland, *Pan Tadeusz*.[97]

Clergymen such as Karpowicz and Jan Kossakowski were by no means uncritical admirers of 'the enlightened age' but they testified to others who were. In many respects they were sharply critical of the tendencies of their century, especially after the outbreak of the French Revolution. Both they and their provincial congregations and readers had a clear sense of what the eighteenth century stood for. While both Karpowicz and Kossakowski were undoubtedly representatives of enlightened Catholicism, Karpowicz was the closer to Anti-Enlightenment. Criteria of reason, utility, toleration and earthly happiness were instantly recognisable points of reference and defined the battlefield on which they fought for souls. But the language in which these and other priests couched their arguments in defence of the clergy and religion helped to insinuate the secular and temporal priorities of the 'enlightened age' into spheres hitherto regarded as transcendental.

The peripheries of the Enlightenment may be pursued far, even into late-eighteenth-century Lithuanian ecclesiastical discourses. I would suggest that these provincial pulpits offer notably clear vistas over the Enlightenment as a whole.

---

97. Adam Mickiewicz, *Pan Tadeusz* [1834], book 12, l.685-90. The standard translation by Kenneth R. MacKenzie, 3rd (bilingual) edn (New York, 2000), p.564, does not note the social dimension – the local celebrations took place in the town hall ('ratusz') and the toasts included all estates ('wszystkie stany'): 'Lecz starców myśli z dzwiękiem w przeszłość się uniosły, / W owe lata szczęśliwe, gdy senat i posły / Po dniu Trzeciego Maja w ratuszowej Sali / Zgodzonego z narodem króla fetowali; / Gdy przy tańcu śpiewano: 'Wiwat Król kochany! / Wiwat Sejm! wiwat Naród, wiwat wszystkie Stany!''

SIMON DIXON

# 'Prosveshchenie': Enlightenment in eighteenth-century Russia

IN 1816 the poet Konstantin Batiushkov published an imaginary conversation between an anonymous abbé V., Montesquieu and Prince Antiokh Kantemir, the satirist who served as Russian ambassador to the court of Versailles between 1738 and his death in 1744.[1] Kantemir, Batiushkov explained to his reader, 'loved scholarship for scholarship's sake and poetry for poetry's: a rare quality, and a true sign of a great mind and a fine, strong soul!' But he wrote at a time 'when our language was barely capable of expressing the ideas of an enlightened man' and when Russian society was too immature to appreciate them. This was Montesquieu's starting point in the conversation: 'You write in Russian, but your language and nation are still in swaddling clothes.' Acknowledging that the Russian language was 'still in its youth', Kantemir countered that it was nevertheless 'rich and expressive, like Latin' and would 'in time become precise and clear like the language of the witty Fontenelle and the profound Montesquieu'. By introducing new vocabulary into his translations of both these authors, he had 'cleared the way' for his successors (the Russian carries connotations of purification).[2] Mocking the notion that Kantemir's version of the *Lettres persanes* was being read 'at this very minute on the banks of the Arctic Ocean, on the banks of the Lena and the Ob, and in the wastelands of Tatary', the abbé insisted that Peter the Great's 'titanic' efforts to enlighten Russia were ultimately bound to be in vain. 'Nature, ancient customs, superstition, [and] incurable barbarity will gain the upper hand over weak and superficial enlightenment, and the whole of semi-savage Muscovy will once again become savage.' Montesquieu concurred: even if the government somehow managed to 'open the way to enlightenment', the climate would surely block it again. But Kantemir remained adamant. The 'immeasurable space' of the Russian empire covered many different climatic zones. And, as Montesquieu himself had pointed out in his 'immortal book' (*De l'esprit des lois*), 'the influence of the climate might be reduced or restricted by governments, morals and society.' Peter had not

1. Konstantin Batiushkov, 'Vecher u Kantemira', in *Sochineniia K. N. Batiushkova*, 5th edn (St Petersburg, 1887), p.347-62.
2. Kantemir translated both Fontenelle and the *Lettres persanes*, though the latter work has not survived and it remains uncertain whether he met Montesquieu.

so much 'created' people as 'cured them of their ignorance, and the Russians, under the leadership of a great man, had proved in a short time that talents are *peculiar to humanity*'. 'With the successes of population and enlightenment the north is constantly changing and, if I may say so, expanding towards enlightened Europe.' How much more might be expected from Russians in the future! 'Maybe in two or three hundred years' time, perhaps even earlier, the gracious heavens will grant us a genius who will fully comprehend Peter's great idea, and the largest land on earth will become the repository of laws, of the freedom founded upon them, and of the morals that give the laws their permanence – in a word, the repository of enlightenment.' Proud of his nation's achievements, Kantemir was equally proud of his own. His name, he claimed, would be remembered more for the fact that he had been 'the first who dared to speak the language of the muse and of philosophy' than because of his status at the court of Versailles. 'Magnificent!' the abbé exclaimed. 'You speak like a true philosopher.'

Batiushkov's thinly disguised plea to Tsar Alexander I to permit writers of his own generation to perfect the civilising process in Russia exemplifies the prevailing view that enlightenment there remained unfinished business in the early nineteenth century. Batiushkov also shared the widespread sense that the *philosophes*, for all their learning and wit, had proved to be perfidious mentors. Already in 1794 Catherine II had approved Grimm's decision to stand apart from *philosophes* whose work had led only to 'destruction'.[3] This was precisely the sort of facile interpretation that Karamzin had sought to counter in his 'Essay on the sciences, arts and enlightenment', a defence of 'true' enlightenment written in 1793 and published in the first issue of his journal *Aglaia* in January of the following year. Though he dismissed Rousseau's *First discourse* as 'a logical chaos' in which 'only a *false* sun shines', Karamzin defended Catherine's least favourite *philosophe* as a 'great man, never to be forgotten in the annals of philosophy'.[4] Yet it proved impossible to prevent suspicions from growing as part of a broader reaction against Gallomania impelled by international politics. By 1807 a sustained course of reading on Voltaire had

---

3. *Sbornik imperatorskago russkago istoricheskago obshchestva*, 148 vols (St Petersburg, 1867-1916), vol.23, p.593, Catherine to Grimm, 11 February 1794.

4. 'Nechto o naukakh, iskusstvakh i prosveshchenii', in N. M. Karamzin, *Izbrannye sochinenii*, ed. G. P. Makogonenko, 2 vols (Moscow and Leningrad, 1964), vol.2, p.122: 'Был человек – и человек великий, незабвенный в летописях философии [...] Я чту великие твои дарования, красноречивый Руссо!' But compare p.123: 'Вообще рассуждение его о науках есть, так сказать, логический хаос, в котором виден только обманчивый порядок или призрак порядка; в котором сияет только ложное солнце.' See also Anthony G. Cross, *N. M. Karamzin: a study of his literary career 1783-1803* (Carbondale, IL, 1971), p.146-47. On Karamzin's attitude to Rousseau and Voltaire, see Andrew Kahn, 'Nikolai Karamzin's discourses of Enlightenment', in Nikolai Karamzin, *Letters of a Russian traveller*, ed. Andrew Kahn, *SVEC* 2003:04 (henceforth, *Letters*), p.459-551 (515-27).

persuaded N. I. Turgenev that it was 'entirely possible' that he and Rousseau had been responsible for the French Revolution: 'At any rate, I have noticed much in Voltaire's works that contributed to it.'[5] The Napoleonic invasion understandably made such anxieties more urgent. Ascribing 'all our mistakes' to 'the French alone', Ivan Murav'ev-Apostol blamed the *philosophes* for the decline of French morals from the time of Louis XIV. It is then, he declares, that 'the light of true enlightenment begins to fade; talents are employed as a weapon of depravity, and that most dangerous of sophists, the false-sage of Ferney, strains every nerve of his extraordinary mind over the course of half a century to strew with flowers the cup of hemlock he prepared to poison future generations'.[6] Batiushkov could only watch in horror as the fall of Moscow set the seal on a catalogue of French treachery: 'And this nation of monsters dared to speak of freedom, of philosophy, of humanity! And we were so blind that we imitated them like apes! How well they have repaid us!'[7]

The vision of enlightenment in Russia as a pale reflection of all things French dominated the field until the imposition of a Soviet-style regime in East Germany unexpectedly prompted detailed investigation of the contacts between the eighteenth-century Academies of Science in St Petersburg and Berlin.[8] Subsequent research into regional divergences within the Enlightenment prompted scholars in the second half of the twentieth century not only to debate the rival influences of French and German thought on Russian intellectual life, but also to claim that the Enlightenment in Russia should be seen as 'a local phenomenon in its own right'.[9] Since fluctuating assumptions about the essence of the Enlightenment inevitably influenced successive attempts to define a Russian

---

5. *Dnevniki i pis'ma Nikolaia Ivanovicha Turgeneva za 1806-1811 goda*, ed. E. I. Tarasov, 4 vols (St Petersburg, 1911), vol.1, p.54, 5 April 1807; P. R. Zaborov, *Russkaia literatura i Vol'ter: XVIII – pervaia tret' XIX veka* (Leningrad, 1978), p.172-73.

6. I M. Murav'ev-Apostol, *Pis'ma iz Moskvy v Nizhnii Novgorod*, ed. V. A. Koshelev (St Petersburg, 2002), p.39-40, letter 6: 'Меркнет свет истинного просвещения; дарования употребляются, как орудия разврата, и опаснейший из софистов лжемудрец Фернейский, в течение полвека напрягает все силы необыкновенного ума своего на то, чтобы осыпать цветами чашу с ядом, уготованную им для отравления грядущих поколений.'

7. *Sochineniia Batiushkova*, p.470, to N. I. Gnedich [October 1812], from Nizhnii Novgorod. See also p.529, to P. A. Viazemskii, 3 October 1812.

8. Marc Raeff, 'Les Slaves, les Allemands et les Lumières', *Canadian-American Slavic studies* 1 (1967), p.521-51(523).

9. Paul Dukes, 'The Russian Enlightenment', in *The Enlightenment in national context*, ed. R. Porter and M. Teich, p.176-91 (179). While the Germans were championed by M. Raeff, 'The Enlightenment in Russia and Russian thought in the Enlightenment', in *The Eighteenth century in Russia*, ed. J. G. Garrard (Oxford, 1973), p.25-47, the *philosophes* found a more sympathetic commentator in Isabel de Madariaga, *Politics and culture in eighteenth-century Russia* (London, 1998) p.215-83, especially p.273-74, than in Albert Lortholary, *Le Mirage russe en France au XVIII$^e$ siècle* (Paris, [1951]). For more recent reflections, see *Le Mirage russe au XVIII$^e$ siècle*, ed. Serguei Karp and Larry Wolff (Ferney-Voltaire, 2001).

Enlightenment in objective terms (or deny its existence altogether),[10] I shall take a more subjective approach by examining contemporary Russian usages of the word 'enlightenment' ('prosveshchenie' / 'просвещение') and its associated adjectives. Although I cannot claim that my sample is either comprehensive or representative, I hope to compensate by ranging widely over both time and genre, drawing in the process on most types of writing from the sermon to satirical verse and from published journalism to private correspondence. The essay explores themes highlighted by Batiushkov: the infinite variety of the multinational Russian empire; the fragility of enlightenment in Russia; and the inspirational role of the tsars in its diffusion. The 1760s - 'a decisive time for the whole of Europe'[11] - will be pivotal to the discussion, and nowhere more so than in relation to my first topic: the linguistic underdevelopment that helped to underpin persistent anxieties about Russian inferiority.

In 1767 - the year in which Catherine II's *Nakaz* proclaimed that 'La Russie est une puissance Européenne'[12] - Diderot warned the empress that 'whatever its progress in the sciences and the arts, a nation must remain ignorant and almost barbarous as long as its language is imperfect'.[13] Russian writers hardly needed to be told, having spent the middle decades of the century debating the best way to formulate a cultivated literary style capable of preserving the Church Slavonic legacy in a natural balance with new foreign loanwords and the living spoken language.[14] The 1760s marked a significant breakthrough. Even as a new generation of men educated at Moscow's nascent university (f.1755) threatened to overwhelm the Church's contribution to Russian intellectual life,[15] secular and ecclesiastical learning converged towards a unitary culture, owing much to Western models, in which secular and spiritual writers agreed a common conception of a single 'literature' encompassing everything from the Bible to contemporary poetry. Each side felt able to

10. For the contortions that resulted from attempts to transform cosmopolitan nobles capable of reconciling Orthodoxy and Enlightenment into atheists imbued with bourgeois values, see David M. Griffiths, 'In search of Enlightenment: recent Soviet interpretation of eighteenth-century Russian intellectual history', *Canadian-American Slavic studies* 16 (1982) p.317-56.
11. Venturi, *Utopia and reform*, p.127.
12. *Nakaz Imperatritsy Ekateriny II, dannyi kommissii o sochinenii proekta novago Ulozheniia*, ed. N. D. Chechulin (St Petersburg, 1907), p.2, article 6: 'Россия есть Европейская держава'.
13. Quoted in W. Gareth Jones, *Nikolay Novikov: enlightener of Russia* (Cambridge, 1984), p.83.
14. Ioakhim [Joachim] Klein, *Puti kul'turnogo importa: Trudy po russkoi literature XVIII veka* (Moscow, 2005), part 2.
15. As the total number of books published rose from an annual average of 52.4 between 1756 and 1760 to 191.6 between 1771 and 1775, the proportion of religious works dropped from 46 per cent in the second quarter of the century to just over 20 per cent between 1755 and 1775. See Gary Marker, *Publishing, printing and the origins of intellectual life in Russia, 1700-1800* (Princeton, NJ, 1985), p.71-73, tables 3.1 and 3.2, and p.60, table 2.2.

criticise the other on the basis of shared stylistic criteria, and leading clerics collaborated with secular scholars to compile a dictionary under the auspices of the new Russian Academy, whose statute proclaimed in 1783 that the Russian language deserved praise for comprising 'so to speak, two languages, i.e. the ancient [Church] Slavonic and the language in current use that is descended from it'.[16] In view of these developments, it is no surprise to find that those described as 'learned and enlightened' ('uchenyi i prosveshchennyi' / 'ученый и просвещенный') in N. I. Novikov's *Historical dictionary of Russian writers* (1772) included not only M. M. Kheraskov and V. E. Adodurov, successive curators of Moscow University, and A. A. Nartov, the son of Peter the Great's master-carpenter who went on to become secretary of the Academy of Sciences having studied at Leipzig and translated Voltaire, but also no fewer than nine contemporary bishops, including the Ukrainian Samuil (Mislavskii), to whom Novikov dedicated an issue of his *Moscow monthly publication* in 1781.[17] The translation of *Bélisaire* produced by Catherine and her entourage on their Volga cruise fourteen years earlier was dedicated to another of her favourite churchmen, Archbishop Gavriil (Petrov), whose virtues, listed in the inscription by Voltaire's Russian correspondent, Count A. P. Shuvalov, were said to include 'gentleness, humility, moderation, [and] enlightened devotion'.[18]

Whereas many of the ideas that they borrowed from the West required a vocabulary as novel as the concepts themselves,[19] the Russians already had a word of their own for 'enlightenment': 'prosveshchenie' ('просвещение'). Its religious associations – ranging from illumination ('osiianie' / 'осияние'), through the restoration of sight, to mental and spiritual perfection, to the ceremony of baptism itself – still dominated the Russian Academy dictionary's definitions in the 1820s.[20] By then, however, the word had long since acquired secular meanings as an antonym for ignorance ('nevezhestvo' / 'невежество') and a synonym for education ('obrazovanie' / 'образование'). By 1760 it was natural to

16. V. M. Zhivov, *Iazyk i kul'tura v Rossii XVIII veka* (Moscow, 1996), p.402-407. Statute quoted at p.412: 'Таковым обилием язык российский преимущественно хвалиться может, будучи составлен, так сказать, из двух языков, т.е. древняго, или словенскаго и от сего происшедшаго – ныне употребляемаго.'

17. Nikolai Novikov, *Opyt istoricheskago slovaria o rossiiskikh pisateliakh* (St Petersburg, 1772), p.2, 30, 48, 112, 142, 145, 170, 172, 199, 203, 205, 227, 236, 264; Jones, *Nikolay Novikov*, p.172.

18. Quoted in V. M. Zhivov, 'Gosudarstvennyi mif v epokhu Prosveshcheniia i ego razrushenie v Rossii kontsa XVIII veka', in *Razyskaniia v oblasti istorii i predystorii russkoi kul'tury* (Moscow, 2002), p.439-60 (449): 'Добродетели ваши известны; а особливо кротость, смирение, умеренность, просвещенное набожество.'

19. See James Cracraft, *The Petrine revolution in Russian culture* (Cambridge, MA, 2004), especially p.256-300, 377-485.

20. *Slovar' russkogo iazyka XI-XVII vv.*, 27 vols (Moscow, 1995-), vol.20, p.213-14; *Slovar' akademii rossiiskoi po azbuchnomu poriadku raspolozhennyi*, 6 vols (St Petersburg, 1822), vol.5, p.624.

refer to Russia's nascent readership of secular books as the 'educated public' ('prosveshchennaia publika' / 'просвещенная публика');[21] by the early 1780s the phrase 'popular enlightenment' ('narodnoe prosveshchenie' / 'народное образование') had been adopted to mean 'elementary education' in the sense enshrined in the title of the new ministry formed in 1802.[22] As in Poland, 'one of the most universally accepted meanings of "enlightenment" was its opposition to "superstition"': Novikov, for example, referred to metropolitan Arsenii (Mogilianskii)'s 'enlightened intelligence' ('prosveshchennyi razum' / 'просвещенный разум') to signal that his mind was 'alien to superstition and hypocrisy'.[23] In the aftermath of Peter the Great's ecclesiastical reforms, no prelate was likely to prosper without a degree of political acumen, and this too came to be counted among the attributes of the enlightened. The archbishop of Novgorod, Dmitrii (Sechenov), a tacit supporter of Catherine II's coup, offered a classic case in point: 'Ses lumières', as Princess Dashkova later put it, 'lui faisaient voir encore plus clairement, combien sous un souverain comme Pierre III l'église devait perdre de son poids.'[24] Since the notion of enlightenment was never wholly secularised in the eighteenth century, etymological ambiguities offered fertile opportunities to those who sought to reconcile traditional religious beliefs with new ideas.[25] By referring to the members of the Holy Synod as 'enlightened men' ('prosveshchennye liudi' / 'просвещенные люди') no fewer than three times in her short speech to mark the secularisation of the Church lands, a measure they could hardly have been expected to applaud, Catherine implied that her bishops were not only intelligent enough to grasp the need for reform but also sufficiently enlightened to appreciate its benefits.[26] Two could play at this game. Platon (Levshin), having initially impressed the empress with a sermon on 'The uses of piety' (1 Timothy 4.8) in May 1763, was convinced that he

---

21. *Arkhiv kniazia Vorontsova*, ed. P. I. Bartenev, 40 vols (Moscow, 1870-1895), vol.6, p.312, M. L. Vorontsov to I. I. Shuvalov, 7 May 1761. Paul Keenan, 'Creating a "public" in St Petersburg, 1703-1761', doctoral dissertation, University of London, 2005, shows how little this 'public' had in common with some putative Habermasian 'public sphere'.

22. *Opisanie del arkhiva Ministerstva narodnogo prosveshcheniia*, ed. S. F. Platonov, A. S. Nikolaev and S. A. Pereselenkov, 2 vols (Petrograd, 1917), vol.1 contains materials dating from 1783-1802.

23. Butterwick, 'What is Enlightenment?', p.23-24, offers a number of instructive parallels to the subject of this essay, though the chronology it suggests is rather different. Novikov, *Opyt istoricheskago slovaria*, p.10.

24. 'Mémoires de la Princesse Dashkaw, d'après le manuscrit revu et corrigé par l'auteur', *Arkhiv kniazia Vorontsova*, ed. Bartenev, vol.21, p.61. Novikov, *Opyt istoricheskago slovaria*, p.210, praises Dmitrii for his 'deep and enlightened theological learning'.

25. At the most sophisticated literary level, see the profusion of light imagery that suffuses Derzhavin's ode, 'God' ('Bog') (1784): Klein, *Puti kul'turnogo importa*, p.489-97.

26. 'Rech' Gosudaryni Imperatritsy Ekateriny II, govorennaia eiu k Sinodu, po sluchaiu otchuzhdeniia tserkovnykh imushchestv v Rossii', in *Chteniia v Imperatorskom Obshchestve Istorii Drevnostei Rossiiskikh pri Moskovskom Universitete* (1862), vol.2, p.187-88.

owed his subsequent appointment as tutor to her son to an interview in which he ascribed his monastic vocation to a quest for 'enlightenment'.[27]

No play on words could fully bridge the gap between secular and religious world views. The sheer novelty of secular scholarship in Russia guaranteed that its challenge to the Church's cultural monopoly was bound to be keenly felt long after ecclesiastical suspicions had prompted Kantemir to mock episcopal pomposity and obscurantism in a satire of 1729, steeped in references to Horace and Boileau,[28] and Tatishchev to defend secular learning in a more pedestrian 'Dialogue between two friends on the usefulness of scholarship and schools', whose first draft in 1733 was modelled closely on a German philosophical dictionary.[29] The first appearance in print of Kantemir's satire in 1762 speaks of the longevity of detractors of secular learning. Indeed, long after the Enlightenment ideal of the 'temple of sciences' had been more securely established,[30] a sense of the distinction between rational thought and contemplative piety was shared not only among lay writers attracted by sentimentalist vocabulary, but even by bishops sympathetic to enlightened reform. Looking back on her teenage years on an estate near Ekaterinburg in the late 1760s and early 1770s, Anna Labzina recalled her regular morning swim, followed by prayers before breakfast, as she knelt with her nanny, facing east: 'How sweet it was to pray then with an innocent heart! And then I loved my Creator more, though I knew less of [his] enlightenment.'[31] The potential for harmony between man's intellectual, physical and spiritual capacities is a recurrent theme in the sermons of Platon (Levshin). But to one convinced of the divine origins of enlightenment, the hierarchy was clear. While an educated man might be expected to prevail over an uneducated one, knowledge could never guarantee true enlightenment: 'Knowledge puffs up, but love builds up' (1 Corinthians 8.1). 'All forms of knowledge are fruitless when morals are defective', Platon insisted. 'An upright conscience is more than enough to make up for shortcomings of education. Besides, there is nothing more dangerous than education itself when it is not governed

---

27. *Zhizn' moskovskago mitropolita Platona* (Moscow, 1890), p.213. Revealingly, Platon's modern biographer translates this use of 'prosveshchenie' as 'knowledge': K. A. Papmehl, *Metropolitan Platon of Moscow (Petr Levshin, 1737-1812): the enlightened prelate, scholar and educator* (Newtonville, MA, 1983), p.9.

28. Antiokh Kantemir, *Sobranie stikhotvorenii*, ed. F. Ia. Priima and Z. I. Gershovich (Leningrad, 1956), p.57-62, 'Na khuliashchikh uchenii'.

29. V. N. Tatishchev, *Izbrannye proizvedeniia*, ed. S. N. Valk (Leningrad, 1979), p.51-132, 'Razgovor dvu priiatelei o pol'ze nauki i uchilishchakh'.

30. For example, N. N. Popovskii, 'Pis'mo o pol'ze nauk i o vospitanii vo onykh iunoshestva', in *Poety XVIII veka*, ed. G. P. Makogonenko and I. Z. Serman, 2 vols (Leningrad, 1972), vol.1, p.108-14 (114), first published in Novikov's journal, *The Painter* (*Zhivopisets*), in 1772; E. R. Dashkova, *O smysle slova 'vospitanie'*, ed. G. I. Smagina (St Petersburg, 2001), p.120-27 (125).

31. Anna Labzina, *Vospominaniia Anny Evdokimovny Labzinoi 1758-1828*, ed. B. L. Modzalevskii (St Petersburg, 1914), p.5-6.

by good behaviour.'[32] So although he found no contradiction between 'true reason' and 'true faith', Platon was nevertheless anxious to distinguish between 'learning' ("uchenost" / 'ученость') and 'enlightenment' ('prosveshchenie' / 'просвещение'):

A virtuous man may not know the movements of the stars, the dimensions of the earth, multiplication and division, the arts and sciences of cunning and delicacy; but he knows what virtue is, knowledge of the simplest sort, and that it is pleasant and useful both for him and for others, and pleasing to God, and he knows how to distinguish it from vice. Blessed is such a man through his lack of learning; unhappy the scholar who has no such enlightenment.[33]

Having established a reputation for toleration with his 1765 *Exhortation*, in which he argued that the Old Believers were more likely to be influenced by kindness and persuasion than by the sort of persecution sponsored by both Church and state under Empress Elizabeth, Platon was allegedly regarded by Joseph II as 'plus philosophe que prêtre'.[34] But he remained appalled by the 'terrible wound' inflicted on the Church by 'the ruinous schism' and limits to his tolerance emerged in his interview with John Parkinson in December 1793. In addition to charging Voltaire with responsibility for Catherine's ecclesiastical policy, he seemed 'to have a great antipathy to the Pope and was sorry that we had begun to relax in England in regard to the Roman Catholics'.[35]

Although Karamzin thought Russian superior to German in its 'harmonie' and 'souplesse',[36] he acknowledged in a letter to Bonnet in 1790 that 'notre langue, quoique fort riche, n'est pas assez cultivée, et nous avons encore très peu de livres de philosophie et de physique écrits ou

32. 'Все науки суть безплодны: когда нравы неисправны. Честная же совесть весьма довольна дополнить недостаток просвещения. Но притом и нет опаснее самаго просвещения когда оно неисправляемо благонравием', *Pouchitel'nyia slova* [...] *s 1763. goda po 1780. god Skazyvannyia* [...] *Preosviashchenneishim Platonom*, 6 vols (Moscow, 1780), vol.5, p.49. See also, inter alia, vol.3, p.69 (divine origins of enlightenment); vol.4, p.107-108 (Corinthians); vol.4, p.36 and vol.5, p.81 (the Church as a spiritual school of virtue).

33. Quoted in O. A. Tsapina, 'Pravoslavnoe prosveshchenie – oksiumoron ili istoricheskaia real'nost'?', in *Evropeiskoe Prosveshchenie i tsivilizatsii Rossii*, ed. S. Ia. Karp and S. A. Mezin (Moscow, 2004), p.301-13 (304): 'Добродетельный может не знать течения звезд, измерения земли, сложения и разделения чисел, художеств и наук хитростей и тонкостей; но знает что есть добродетель, знанием простейшим, что она есть и приятна и полезна и для него и для других и угодна Богу, и оную от порока отличить умеет. Блажен таковый при не учености своей; нещастлив ученый не имея такового просвещения.'

34. Papmehl, *Metropolitan Platon*, p.15; Georgii Florovskii, *Puti russkogo bogosloviia*, 2nd edn (Paris, 1981), p.109.

35. 'Не говорю уже о погибельном расколе: сколь тяжка сія для церкви рана, знает тот, кто понимает души погибающия', Platon, *Pouchitel'nye slova*, vol.5, p.112. John Parkinson, *A Tour of Russia, Siberia and the Crimea 1792-1794*, ed. William Collier (London, 1971), p.218, 9 December 1793.

36. Charges of Teutonic inflexibility were commonplace: see Eric A. Blackall, *The Emergence of German as a literary language* (Cambridge, 1959), p.201 and *passim*.

traduits en russe'.[37] One might think that there had been little progress in Russia since Semen Poroshin, then tutor in mathematics to Grand Duke Paul, responded in 1764 to the appearance of a French edition of Krashenninikov's history of Kamchatka by wishing for more such translations of original Russian works: 'That would bear true witness to the flourishing state of [our] scholarship! That way, the age of enlightenment would indisputably shine its light directly in Russia.'[38] Karamzin, however, consoled himself with the thought that there had been no alternative to Russia's intellectual dependence on Western Europe: 'There is only *one* path of education or enlightenment for peoples; they all follow it one after another. Foreigners were more intelligent than Russians: and so it was necessary to borrow from them, to learn, to use their experiences.'[39] The past tense is significant. No longer the wide-eyed innocents who had ventured to the West under Peter the Great, Russian travellers in Catherine's time appealed to universal standards as a way of justifying Russian claims to moral superiority. Criticising Parisian society's devotion to gambling and *'le beau sexe'* in 1778, Fonvizin famously found 'little that is human' in French literary debates: 'It is said authors waged war in antiquity only by criticising each other's works, whereas now they not only trespass upon honour with caustic abuse, but destroy each other completely, like animals.'[40] Subtler in tone, richer in content and infinitely more allusive in style, Karamzin's *Letters of a Russian traveller* left the reader to infer for himself most of the author's implied comparisons between Russia and the West. Yet he echoed Fonvizin's distaste for intemperate scholarship in his remarks on the Berlin *Aufklärer*:

Where can we seek tolerance if the very Philosophers, the very enlighteners – as they call themselves – demonstrate such hatred toward all those who do not think as they do? He is a true Philosopher who is able to live with everyone in this world, who will even look kindly on ideas that are not in harmony with his own way of thinking. It is a duty to point out the delusions of human reason with noble zeal but without malice.[41]

37. Karamzin, *Letters*, p.204, attached to letter 82. Further quotations are from Kahn's translation, though I have restored capitals and italics from the definitive Russian text in Karamzin, *Pis'ma*, here p.170. Subsequent references are to both editions.

38. *Semena Poroshina Zapiski, sluzhashchiia k istorii Ego Imperatorskago Vysochestva Blagovernago Gosudaria Tsesarevicha i Velikago Kniazia Pavla Petrovicha, naslednika prestolu rossiiskago*, ed. V. S. Poroshin (St Petersburg, 1844), p.87, 20 October 1764: 'Сие было бы уже не ложное свидетельство цветущаго наук состояния! Тем-то бы неоспоримо возсиял прямо просвещенный век в России.'

39. Karamzin, *Letters*, p.293, letter 103; Karamzin, *Pis'ma*, p.253: 'Путь образования или просвещения *один* для народов: все они идут им в след друг за другом. Иностранцы были умнее Руских: и так надлежало от них заимствовать, учиться, пользоваться их опытами' (italics in the original).

40. D. I. Fonvizin, *Sobranie sochinenii*, ed. G. P. Makogonenko, 2 vols (Moscow and Leningrad, 1959), 'Pis'ma iz vtorogo zagranichnogo puteshestviia', vol.2, p.439, 11/12 March 1778, vol.2, p.443, April 1778.

41. Karamzin, *Letters*, p.61, letter 15, Berlin, 1 July 1789; Karamzin, *Pis'ma*, p.38: 'Где искать терпимости, естьли самые Философы, самые просветители – а они так

If no Russian journal published the sort of formal debate over the meaning of 'enlightenment' that prompted the appearance of Kant's essay 'Was ist Aufklärung?' in the *Berlinische Monatsschrift* in 1784, then the failure evidently owed something to temperamental conviction as well as to censorship. By the end of Catherine II's reign, however, the chill of official disapproval was clearly felt in the minds of younger writers such as P. N. Slovtsov:

> While Russia has long been reading freethinkers,
> She soon scared off her own native wits;
> She gives thanks to the Montaignes and the Rousseaus,
> But her son is her enemy when he is a *philosophe*.[42]

Even in the earlier years of her reign, the empress' consistent stress on the need for obedience – revealed at its most explicit in the elementary school primer, *Book on the duties of man and citizen*, published in 1783 – limited the possibility of sustained public debate.[43]

Discussion of a more fragmentary kind nevertheless flourished as their shared confidence in a unitary process of enlightenment drew Europeans from across the continent to study the expanding Russian empire as a laboratory of civilisation.[44] Believing that the Russian lands encompassed 'all the stages of transformation from the ancient, simple World very close to its natural condition to the present World, refined and enriched by needs', the ethnographer Johann Gottlieb Georgi hoped in the 1780s that the introduction of uniform administrative measures could lead 'our rude Peoples by giant steps towards the common goal of general Enlightenment in Russia'.[45] It was a daunting ambition. As Catherine herself acknowledged at the former Tatar stronghold of Kazan' in 1767, contemplating the elaboration of her own 'general principles' at the forthcoming Legislative Commission, 's'est presque un monde à créer, à unir, à conserver etc'.[46] Indeed it was. In the Baltic lands, *Aufklärer* such as

---

себя называют – оказывают сколько ненависти к тем которые думают не так как они? Тот есть для меня истинный Философ, кто со всеми может учиться в мире; кто любит и несогласных сего образом мыслей. Должно показывать заблуждения разума человеческого с благородным жаром, но без злобы.' See also, *Letters*, p.70-71, letter 20; *Pis'ma*, p.47; and Kahn's discussion of Karamzin's attitude to cultural differentiation in *Letters*, p.504-507.

42. 'Россия хоть давно читает вольнодумов, / Но рано ей своих отважить остроумов; / Она благодарит Монтениев, Руссов, / Но сын ее ей враг, когда он филосов', *Poety 1790-1810-kh godov*, ed. Iu. M. Lotman (Leningrad, 1971), p.208, 'Poslanie M. M. Speranskomu'.

43. An English translation by Elizabeth Gorky is published as an appendix to J. L. Black, *Citizens for the fatherland: education, educators and pedagogical ideals in eighteenth-century Russia* (Boulder, CO, 1979), p.209-66.

44. Gianluigi Goggi, 'The philosophes and the debate over Russian civilization', in *A Window on Russia*, ed. Maria di Salvo and Lindsey Hughes (Rome, 1996), p.299-305.

45. Quoted in Yuri Slezkine, 'Naturalists versus nations: eighteenth-century Russian scholars confront ethnic diversity', *Representations* 47 (1994), p.170-95 (187, 179).

46. D14219, 29 May/9 June 1767.

Johann Georg Eisen and Peter Ernst Wilde extended their improving activity from the peasantry to the population of Livonia as a whole.[47] Though Wilde had founded his own printing press some seventeen years before Catherine's decree of 1783, both men were published in Riga by Johann Friedrich Hartknoch, whose more celebrated authors included not only Herder and Kant, but also Rousseau and Diderot (*La Religieuse* appeared in German translation in 1797).[48] In the New Russian lands in the south, enlightenment radiating out from St Petersburg intersected with ideas disseminated from Greece.[49] Such a complex web of overlapping cultural influences makes it hard to conceive of any simple linear transmission of enlightenment between centre and periphery in Russia. It was even risky for Russians to condescend to exotic African savages:

> The unenlightened Negro, Turon and Hottentot,
> Ignorant of the true virtues of cohabitation.[50]

Contrasting the iniquities of Russia's servile regime with the emancipationist movement in 'enlightened England', I. P. Pnin reminded readers in his *Essay on Enlightenment as it relates to Russia* (1804) how 'pitiful' it was 'for a Russian who loves his fatherland to see there things that happen only in the native land of the negroes'.[51]

So long as the Enlightenment's classical preoccupations with decline and fall held its more optimistic anthropology in check, anxieties about the fragility of progress in Russia were bound to persist. Like Karamzin, Herder had regarded the Russians' desire to imitate as 'nothing but the healthy disposition of a developing nation – a tendency in the right direction'. But he was equally sure in 1769 that 'the great work of "civilizing a nation to perfection"' was 'yet to be accomplished' because

---

47. J. G. Eisen, *Ausgewählte Schrifte: Deutsche Volksaufklärung und Leibeigenschaft im Russischen Reich*, ed. Roger Bartlett and Erich Donnert (Marburg, 1998); Roger Bartlett, 'German popular enlightenment in the Russian Empire: Peter Ernst Wilde and Catherine II', *Slavonic and East European review* 84 (2006), p.256-78 (260-73).

48. *Svodnyi katalog knig na inostrannykh iazykakh, izdannykh v Rossii v XVIII veke, 1701-1800*, ed. A. I. Kopanev et al., 3 vols (Leningrad, 1984-1986), no. 755 (Diderot); 840-46 (Eisen); 1271-93 (Herder); 1491-1507 (Kant); 2403-405 (Rousseau); 3082-86 (Wilde).

49. Stephen K. Batalden, *Catherine II's Greek prelate: Eugenious Voulgaris in Russia 1771-1806* (Boulder, CO, 1982); Gregory L. Bruess, *Religion, identity and empire: a Greek archbishop in the Russia of Catherine the Great* (Boulder, CO, 1997).

50. 'Непросвещенный Негр, Турон и Готтентот / Не зная истинных сожитія доброт', *Sochineniia V. Petrova*, 3 vols, 2nd edn (St Petersburg, 1811), vol.1, p.47, 'Ego Prevoskhoditel'stvu Grigor'iu Aleksandrovichu Potemkinu'.

51. Ivan Pnin, *Sochineniia*, ed. I. K. Luppol (Moscow, 1934), p.139: 'Горестно, весьма горестно для россіянина, свое отечество любящего, видеть в нем дела совершающіеся только в отечестве негров, коих, однакож, несчастную часть просвещенная Англія, несмотря на прибыльный им торг, лучше желает облегчить, лучше желает лишиться всех получаемых ею чрез то выгод, нежели итти против природы, противу прав человечества, столько ею почитаемых и приемлемых ею в основаніе всех ее постановленій.'

the Russians had thus far remained 'bunglers' in the adoption of everything they had taken from Western Europe, from the art of navigation to French manners.[52] Catherine's triumphs at the expense of Poland and the Ottoman Empire in the early 1770s seemed to herald an equally significant shift in the intellectual balance of power. 'The sciences, the arts, taste and wisdom climb to the North,' as Diderot put it to Falconet in April 1772, 'and barbarism with its train comes southwards.'[53] Yet demand from Russian readers proved too weak to sustain the unparalleled burst of intellectual activity unleashed by the publication of the *Nakaz* and exemplified by the Society for the Translation of Foreign Books, founded and financed by the empress in 1768, and the plethora of short-lived satirical journals launched in 1769. By the 1780s, Russian society's retreat into private clubs, frowned upon by both the empress and her critics, seemed more likely to restrict than to encourage the wider propagation of enlightenment. The Freemasons' quest for self-knowledge was explicitly sectarian: the lodge of the Rising Sun in Kazan' reserved its highest fine – a punitive twenty-five roubles – for any brother who forgot himself sufficiently to reveal the craft's secrets to a 'false brother or to a completely unenlightened individual'.[54] Karamzin caught a sense of the wider dangers by making his traveller reflect in the cathedral at Königsberg after a conversation with Kant: 'Where are you, I thought, where are you, dark ages of barbarism and heroism? Your pale shadows unnerve the timid enlightenment of our days.'[55] A generation further on, by the time of Karamzin's own death in 1826, Russian intellectual life seemed to have fallen between two stools. On the one hand, as Pushkin put it in *Evgenii Onegin*, 'enlightenment' had never 'stuck' to the Russians, having left them 'with nothing but mincing airs and graces'.[56] On the other hand, the persistent fascination for foreign ideas had made it harder for native traditions to take root, so that as Viazemskii noted in his pioneering study of Fonvizin, written between 1828 and 1830, Russian society was 'not brought up on Russian books: you cannot find people who share Derzhavin's sensibility or think like Kniazhnin.'[57] From here,

52. 'Journal of my voyage in 1769', in *Herder on social and political culture*, ed. F. M. Barnard (Cambridge, 1969), p.87.
53. Quoted in Jones, *Nikolay Novikov*, p.83.
54. Douglas Smith, *Working the rough stone: Freemasonry and society in eighteenth-century Russia* (DeKalb, IL, 1999), p.193, n.85.
55. Karamzin, *Letters*, letter 8, Königsberg, 19 June 1789, p.41; Karamzin, *Pis'ma*, p.21: 'Где вы – думал я – где вы мрачные веки, веки варварства и героизма? Бледные тени ваши ужасают робкое просвещение наших дней.'
56. A. S. Pushkin, *Polnoe sobranie sochinenii*, 17 vols (Moscow and Leningrad, 1937-1959), vol.6, p.42, stanza 24: 'Нам просвещенье не пристало, / И нам досталось от него / Жеманство – больше ничего.'
57. P. A. Viazemskii, *Polnoe sobranie sochinenii*, 12 vols (St Petersburg, 1878-1896), vol.5, p.3: 'Русское общество не воспитано на чтении отечественных книг: вы не можете найти людей которые чуствовали-бы по Державину, мыслили-бы по Княжнину.'

it was but a short step to the apocalyptic conclusion of Chaadaev's first philosophical letter, written in 1829, that Russian thinkers belonged neither at Europe's intellectual core nor on its periphery, but instead occupied some ghastly vacuum all of their own: 'Solitaires dans le monde, nous n'avons rien donné au monde, nous n'avons rien appris au monde; nous n'avons pas versé une seule idée dans la masse des idées humaines; nous n'avons en rien contribué au progrès de l'esprit humain, et tout ce qui nous est revenu de ce progrès, nous l'avons défiguré.'[58]

Viktor Zhivov ascribes the Russian Enlightenment's failure to take root to the fact that it was merely 'a Petersburg mirage. Only the leading figures of the Russian Enlightenment truly believed in its reality: others may unwittingly have participated in it, but that did not alter its mythological essence.'[59] Although the modern ear soon tires of panegyric praise for Peter the Great's superhuman attempts to cast light into Muscovite gloom,[60] the contemporary power of such myths can hardly be exaggerated. If anything, it grew over time, as Karamzin's comparison between Peter and Louis XIV suggests: 'His subjects glorified Louis; Peter glorified his subjects. The former *partly* facilitated the successes of enlightenment; the latter, like a radiant god of light, appeared on the horizon of humanity and illuminated the deep darkness around himself.'[61] The further diffusion of enlightenment was one of the most significant ways in which contemporaries believed that Catherine II could complete Peter's work. Her 'pocket poet' Vasilii Petrov duly proclaimed that his mind had been 'enlightened' by an empress whose provincial reform of 1775 ultimately helped to reshape 'a crowd of the unenlightened' into a realm of 'courageous, lively and enlightened souls'.[62] No one, however, hymned Catherine more carefully than Derzhavin. Having established the image of a truth-loving philanthropist who enlightened all mortals in his ode *Felitsa* in 1782, Derzhavin went on in 1789, while under

---

58. *Sochineniia i pis'ma P. Ia. Chaadaeva*, ed. M. Gershenkron, 2 vols (Moscow, 1913-1914), vol.1, p.84.

59. Zhivov, *Iazyk i kul'tura*, p.424: 'Русское Просвещение – это петербургский мираж. Одни деятели русского Просвещения искренне верили в его реальность, другие были его невольными участниками, но это не меняло его мифологического существа.'

60. See, for example, A. A. Rzhevskii, 'Oda blazhennyia i vechno dostoinyia pamiati istinnomu otsu otechestva, imperatoru pervomu, gosudariu Petru Velikomu', in *Poety XVIII veka*, vol.1, p.245-49.

61. Karamzin, *Letters*, p.232, letter 89, Lyons, 9 March 1790 (I have removed the translator's definite article from 'enlightenment'); Karamzin, *Pis'ma*, p.198: 'Подданные прославили Людовика: Петр прославил своих подданных – первый *отчасти* способствовал успехи просвещения: второй, как лузечарный бог света, явился на горизонте человечества, и осветил глубокую тьму вокруг себя.'

62. *Sochineniia V. Petrova*, vol.3, p.7: 'Na podnosimuiu Eia Velichestvu, vysokuiu titlu, Velikiia Ekateriny, premudryia materi otechestvam, 1767 goda'; vol.1, p.133: 'Na novyia uchrezhdeniia dlia upravleniia guberniiami, 1776'; vol.2, p.201: 'Plach' i utеshenie Rossii i Ego Imperatorskomu Velichestvu Pavlu Pervomu Dekabria 1796 goda'.

investigation by the Senate, to emphasise the spirit of critical self-reflection embodied by his goddess:

> I give you the freedom to think
> And learn to value yourselves,
> To count yourselves subjects rather than slaves,
> And not to humble yourselves before me.
> I give you the right to present me
> With your needs without impediment,
> To read and understand my laws
> And to point out mistakes in them.[63]

While some critics have found it hard to stomach close links between government and enlightenment,[64] the state's vanguard role in its diffusion was both a necessary substitute for the universities that Russia lacked and a natural legacy of German enlightened influences. Like 'Aufklärung', 'prosveshchenie' signified an active process.[65] And it left a more permanent institutional imprint than Zhivov's verdict might imply. It was squarely in the spirit of improvement that Karamzin urged his fellow countrymen to:

Achieve something lasting and useful: establish a school, a hospital. Be fathers to the poor, and convert the feeling of envy in them to a feeling of gratitude. Invigorate agriculture, trade, industry; facilitate easy communication between the people and the state. Let this be the new channel that unites two rivers [...] Then will the foreigner who sees such wise use of wealth, say: 'Russians are able to make use of their life and take pleasure in their wealth.'[66]

Though ambitions naturally exceeded achievements, some followed his example even when their motives were not explicitly humanitarian.[67] While Novikov bemoaned the reading public's lasting preference for trivial novels over serious books, the compatibility of utility and enjoyment to which Karamzin referred had been a central motif of Russian publications since the 1740s. Kheraskov's landmark journal, *Useful*

---

63. 'Я вам даю свободу мыслить / И разуметь себя ценить, / Не в рабстве а в подданстве числить, / И в ноги мне челом не бить. / Даю вам право без препоны / Мне ваши нужды представлять, / Читать и знать мои законы / И в них ошибки замечать', G. R. Derzhavin, *Stikhotvoreniia*, ed. D. D. Blagoi (Leningrad, 1957), p.136, 'Izobrazhenie Felitsy', stanza 13. Compare p.100, 103, 'Felitsa', stanzas 13 and 22.

64. Dismissing Novikov as 'a small man with a small mind', Shpet complained in 1922 that when the government arrogated to itself the role of the intelligentsia, '"Enlightenment" barricaded itself off from serious scholarship and philosophy.' G. G. Shpet, 'Ocherk razvitiia russkoi filosofii', reprinted in his *Sochineniia* (Moscow, 1989) p.75, 40.

65. V. N. Vsevolodskii-Gerngross, 'O terminakh "prosveshchenie" i "prosvetitel'stvo"', in *Problemy russkogo Prosveshcheniia v literature XVIII veka*, ed. P. N. Berkov (Moscow and Leningrad, 1961) p.141.

66. Karamzin, *Letters*, p.10, introduction by Andrew Kahn.

67. Janet M. Hartley, 'Philanthropy in the reign of Catherine the Great: aims and realities', in *Russia in the age of the Enlightenment*, ed. Roger Bartlett and Janet M. Hartley (London, 1990), p.167-202.

*entertainment* (*Poleznoe uveselenie*), launched in Moscow in 1760, was followed nine years later by *The Pleasant and useful* (*Poleznoe s priiatnym*).[68] By writing some twenty-five plays herself, Catherine II both acknowledged and enhanced the edificatory power of dramatic entertainment, even allowing for contemporary objections that Moscow's allegedly 'enlightened' audiences were made up of 'Russian orangutans', unable to discriminate between impressive and worthless productions.[69] The study of the past might serve the same exemplary purpose, though the empress's sometime favourite P. V. Zavadovskii warned that history was 'pleasant and useful' only when written by philosophers or politicians.[70]

Although Catherine II's travels through her empire took the form of a medieval progress attended by countless priests, monks and nuns, their purpose by the 1780s was increasingly to publicise modern social and economic developments. On her journey to inspect the new locks at Vyshnii Volochek in May 1785, Catherine characteristically ascribed the improved villages she saw to her subjects' precise fulfilment of her own edicts. Tver' province had indeed prospered under its energetic Protestant governor, J. J. Sievers. But the degree of economic vitality witnessed by numerous travellers along the main road between Moscow and St Petersburg in the decade after the Provincial Reform could hardly have been sustained without a vigorous response from the local merchantry.[71] V. V. Krestinin's *Short history of the town of archangel* (1792) suggests that such a response could be found even in the most inhospitable northern outposts of the empire. Krestinin evidently shared the aspiration projected in the Charter to the Towns (1785) of a prosperous civic society protected by law.[72] Even Radishchev's friend Pnin, concerned, like most Russian political thinkers, more with attitudes than institutions, assumed that it would be possible to achieve social justice without increasing social mobility provided that Russians accepted their god-given place in life. Equating 'the lamp of enlightenment' with the 'hand of the wise monarch', Pnin defined 'prosveshchenie' in far from radical terms:

Enlightenment, in the sense that I am currently using it, consists in every member of society, whatever rank he may occupy, knowing and fulfilling his duties to perfection: that is, those in command ['nachal'stvo'] for their part fulfil the

---

68. P. N. Berkov, *Istorii russkoi zhurnalistiki XVIII veka* (Moscow and Leningrad, 1952), p.129-39, 239-42.

69. Elise Kimerling Wirtschafter, *The Play of ideas in Russian Enlightenment theatre* (DeKalb, IL, 2003), p.45. The critic was N. P. Nikolev: see below, n.76.

70. T. V. Artem'eva, *Ideia istorii v Rossii XVIII veka* (St Petersburg, 1998), p.66.

71. 'Zhurnal'naia vsednevnaia zapiska, vo vremia Vysochaishago Eia Imperatorskago Velichestva puteshestviia iz Tsarskago sela do Vyshniago Volochka, i ottuda do Moskvy i obratno', *Kamer-fur'erskii zhurnal 1785 goda* (St Petersburg), p.279-390; Robert E. Jones, *Provincial development in Russia: Catherine II and Jakob Sievers* (New Brunswick, NJ, 1984); N. V. Sereda, *Reformy upravleniia Ekateriny Vtoroi* (Moscow, 2004).

72. Adrian Jones, 'A Russian bourgeois's Arctic Enlightenment', *Historical journal* 48 (2005), p.623-46.

obligations entrusted to them by the authorities ['vlasti'], while people of the lower orders perform the sacred duties of their obedience. Provided that these two categories of people do not obstruct one another, and maintain the necessary balance in their relationship, then enlightenment has achieved its desired aims.[73]

Looking back in a memoir written around 1811, G. S. Vinskii defied cries of 'Crucify the French!' to date the 'precise onset' of enlightenment in Russia to the 1770s. While Russia laboured under 'the German rod of iron' imposed by Peter the Great, it had 'failed to manifest even the [barest] signs of enlightenment': 'To the reign of Catherine belongs the entire honour of the introduction to our fatherland of useful scholarship which began to influence morality in the most striking way.'[74] The publication of the *Nakaz* led the empress' admirers to make similar claims at the time. However, successive Russian translations of Rousseau's *First discourse* also prompted associations of *prosveshchenie* with immorality.[75] The 1772 'Satire on the morals of the present century' by Princess Dashkova's teenage protégé, N. P. Nikolev, offered a clear case in point:

> What is to be gained? ... Teachers' depravities,
> The husk of prostrations and lack of regulations,
> Atheism and lies – that's their enlightenment![76]

This line of argument proved particularly attractive to Catherine's emergent critics. In his 1783 play *The Minor* (*Nedorosl'* / *Недоросль*), Fonvizin, a writer associated with the circle of Grand Duke Paul, allows Starodum, a character representing old-fashioned moral virtue, to recommend Fénelon to the reader. The contemporary *philosophes* were a different matter: 'I have been able to read everything of theirs that has been translated into Russian. It's true that they zealously root out

---

73. Pnin, *Sochineniia*, p.121, 123-24: 'Просвещение, в настоящем смысле приемлемое, состоит в том, когда каждый член общества, в каком бы звании ни находился, совершенно знает и исполняет свои должности: то есть когда начальство с своей стороны свято исполняет обязанности вверенной оному власти, а нижнего разряда люди ненарушимо исполняет обязанности своей повиновения. Если сий два состояния не переступают своих мер, сохраняя должное в отношениях своих равновесие, тогда просвещение достигла желаемой цели.' See also Samuel C. Ramer, 'The traditional and the modern in the writings of Ivan Pnin', *Slavic review* 35 (1975), p.539-59 (546).

74. G. S. Vinsky, *Moe vremya, Zapiski*, reprinted with an introduction by Isabel de Madariaga (Cambridge, MA, 1974), p.16: 'Царствованию Екатерины принадлежит вся честь водворение в нашем отечестве полезных наук, которыя разнительнейшим образом начали иметь влияние на нравственность.'

75. Iu. M. Lotman, 'Russo i russkaia kul'tura', in *Epokha Prosveshcheniia: iz istorii mezhdunarodnykh sviazei russkoi literatury*, ed. M. P. Alekseev (Leningrad, 1967), p.215-19; N. D. Kochetkova, *Literatura russkogo sentimentalizma (Esteticheskie i khudozhestvennye iskaniia)* (St Petersburg, 1994), p.44-45.

76. 'Что может приобресть? ... Учительски развраты, / Поклоны с выжимкой, а правил никаких, / Безбожие и ложь – вот просвещенье их!', N. P. Nikolev, 'Satira na razvrashchennye nravy nyneshnego veka', *Poety XVIII veka*, vol.2, p.21-28 (25).

prejudice, but they uproot virtue at the same time.'[77] In a similar vein, the aristocratic constitutionalist Prince M. M. Shcherbatov, himself acknowledged by Novikov as 'enlightened and deserving of great respect',[78] stressed the costs of Russia's civilising process at the start of his confidential treatise *On the corruption of morals in Russia* (1786-1787):

> I can truly say that if, after entering later than other nations upon the path of enlightenment, nothing more remained for us than to follow prudently in the steps of nations previously enlightened, then indeed, in sociability and in various other things, it may be said that we have made wonderful progress and have taken gigantic steps to correct our outward appearance. But at the same time, with much greater speed, we have hastened to corrupt our morals, and have even come to this: that faith and God's Law have been extinguished in our hearts, Divine mysteries have fallen into disrepute and civil laws have become objects of scorn.[79]

'See the fruits of our moral depravity,' echoed N. N. Bantysh-Kamenskii in 1791, 'a profusion of luxury and an enlightened upbringing that lead children away from their devotion to religion and seek to separate man from God.'[80]

More positive images of enlightenment are to be found in the self-consciously literary correspondences in which young nobles complimented one another on their growing cosmopolitanism, their manners and style polished by a burgeoning advice literature that saw more than twenty times as many conduct books published in Russia in total between 1762 and 1800 as between 1700 and 1762.[81] 'Reading your letters,' remarked Zavadovskii to Count S. R. Vorontsov in the mid 1770s, 'I imagine that I am in conversation with Cicero, whose words have been supplemented by Horatian jokes.' 'Surely to bring a man to reason and foster the

---

77. Fonvizin, *Sobranie sochinenii*, vol.1, p.149-50, 'Nedorosl'', act IV. For the values personified by Starodum, see David L. Ransel, *The Politics of Catherinian Russia: the Panin party* (New Haven, CT, 1975), p.269-77.

78. Novikov, *Opyt istoricheskago slovaria*, p.250.

79. Prince M. M. Shcherbatov, *On the corruption of morals in Russia*, ed. Antony Lentin (Cambridge, 1969), p.112-13: 'Воистину могу я сказать что естли вступя позже других народов в путь просвещения нам ничего не оставалось более как благоразумно последовать стезям прежде просвещенных народов, – мы подлинно в людкости и в некоторых других вещах можно сказать удивительные имели успехи и исполинскими шагами шествовали к поправлению наших внешностей. Но тогда же гораздо с вящшей скоростию бежали к повреждению наших нравов и достигли даже до того, что Вера и Божественный закон в сердцах наших истребились, тайны Божественныя в презрение впали, гражданския узаконения презираемы стали.'

80. *Russkii arkhiv* (1876), vol.3, p.259, N. N. Bantysh-Kamenskii to A. B. Kurakin, January 1791.

81. Catriona Kelly, *Refining Russia: advice literature, polite culture, and gender from Catherine to Yeltsin* (Oxford, 2001), p.3-22, 32-42 (20). E. N. Marasinova, *Psikhologiia elity rossiiskogo dvorianstva poslednei treti XVIII veka* (Moscow, 1999), p.281, table 21, found references to 'the semantic concept of "*prosveshchennost*"' in eight of the forty-five sets of noble correspondence she studied.

enlightenment of his mind', he wrote later, 'is the greatest of all talents?'[82] Nor were such ambitions confined to the metropolis. In 1785, the year that Vorontsov began forty years of almost uninterrupted residence in England on his appointment as ambassador to the Court of St James', the Moscow Freemason A. A. Petrov heaped praise on another budding Anglophile, the nineteen-year-old Karamzin:

'Glory to the enlightenment of the current century, which illuminates even the Simbirsk region!' That's what I exclaimed on reading your Epistles – (I do not dare to use a Russian name to describe such scholarly writings), which anyone would have thought had come from England or Germany. What is missing from them in relation to Literature? Everything is there. You write about translations, about your own works, about Shakespeare, about tragic Characters, about unjust criticism of Voltaire, just as about coffee and tobacco.[83]

Contemporary Russian usages of 'prosveshchenie' make it hard to agree with Derek Beales that 'in the eighteenth century German was the only language to possess an abstract noun which can be directly translated as "Enlightenment"'.[84] Indeed, if we take Beales' own definition of Enlightenment as 'a term denoting critical, rationalist, reformist opinion',[85] then it is clear that 'prosveshchenie' was used in precisely this way, even if only rarely. The thirteenth issue of Novikov's journal *The Drone* in 1769 gives a clear example. It mocked corrupt judges who had unaccountably failed to read Beccaria's *On crimes and punishments* and understood as little of their own duties as they did of the Syrian and Khaldean languages. 'O enlightenment,' the writer urges, 'heavenly gift, lift the veil of ignorance and cruelty swiftly for the defence of humanity!'[86] In a no less obvious reference to the *Nakaz*, Platon (Levshin) proclaimed

---

82. *Arkhiv kniazia Vorontsova*, ed. Bartenev, vol.24, p.150 (undated, 1775-1776?): 'Читая твои письма, мне кажется, что я собеседую с Цицероном, к котораго словам еще присоединены Горациевы шутки.' See also p.152, 16 March 1777: 'разве вразумлять человека и пещись о просвещении его ума не есть добротворения и не больше всех даров?'

83. Karamzin, *Pis'ma*, p.502, A. A. Petrov to N. M. Karamzin, 11 June 1785: '"Слава просвещению нынешняго столетия и краи Симбирские озарившему." Так воскликнул я при чтении твоих Епистол – (не смею назвать Руским именем столь ученыя писания), окоторых всякой подумал бы что оне получены из Англии или Германии. Чего нет в них касающегося до Литтературы? Все есть. Ты пишешь о переводах, о собственных сочинениях, о Шакеспере, о трагических Характерах, о несправедливой Волтеровой критике, равно как о кофе и табаке'. Though Karamzin's letters are missing, the correspondence has been reconstructed as a literary artifice by R. M. Lazarchuk, 'Perepiska N. M. Karamzina s A. A. Petrovym. (K probleme rekonstruktsii "romana v pis'makh")', *XVIII vek* 20 (1996), p.135-43. On Petrov's tutelary relationship with his protégé, see Cross, *N. M. Karamzin*, p.7-9.

84. Derek Beales, *Enlightenment and reform in eighteenth-century Europe* (London, 2005), p.43.

85. Beales, *Enlightenment and reform*, p.264.

86. *Satiricheskie zhurnaly N. I. Novikova*, ed. P. N. Berkov (Moscow and Leningrad, 1951), p.92: 'О просвещение, дар небесной, расторгни скорее завесу незнания и жестокости для защищения человечества!'

*'Prosveshchenie': Enlightenment in eighteenth-century Russia*

in his New Year sermon for 1771 that 'Our age is the age of enlightenment'. Given in Catherine's presence, this oration marks Platon's most fulsome acknowledgement of secular reform. Praising impartial judges for bringing clarity to Russian legislation (in words which echoed the empress' own), he went on to laud her emphasis on the need for moderate punishments: the aim was to destroy vice itself, and not the unhappy criminal. 'Never, indeed, has a government incorporated so abundantly the spirit of guardianship and philanthropy.'[87]

Yet, however determined Novikov and Platon may have been to disperse the clouds of prejudice and injustice, they never self-consciously subscribed to an intellectual movement that we could call 'the Russian Enlightenment'. In a seminal essay published in 1961, P. N. Berkov sought to situate 'the Enlightenment' – 'Prosveshchenie' with a capital 'P' – as a specific cultural-historical phenomenon around 1760 to 1790 within a longer Russian tradition of 'enlightening' – 'prosvetitel'stvo' ('просветительство') – stretching from the late seventeenth to the mid nineteenth century.[88] Although this formulation has been found useful as a way of distinguishing between Petrine utilitarianism and Catherine II's broader, cultural concerns,[89] it would not have been easily recognisable to contemporary writers. Their references to a philosophical or an enlightened age ('filosofskii' / 'prosveshchennyi vek' / **философский** / **просвещенный век**) in the 1790s and beyond owed more to sentimentalist than to rationalist vocabulary and their intentions were usually pejorative.[90] In the disillusion of his twilight years, even Novikov himself was moved to complain that 'the current enlightened age rejects all miracles, [which] modern philosophers call superstition: I wish that some grammarian of the etymology of the word superstition would show them that the superstitious ones are not those who believe in miracles, but those who do not believe in them.'[91] Advocates of humanitarian reform in the

---

87. 'Наш век, есть век просвещения [...] никогда поистинне правительство не заключало в себе столь обильно попечительнаго и человеколюбиваго духа', Platon, *Pouchitel'nye slova*, vol.2, p.310-11.

88. P. N. Berkov, 'Osnovnye voprosy izucheniia russkogo prosvetitel'stva', in *Problemy russkogo Prosveshcheniia*, p.5-27.

89. Madariaga, *Politics and culture*, p.273. Iu. A. Bubnov, *Drevnerusskii sekuliarizm i formirovanie ideologii prosvetitel'stva: Ot kreshcheniia Rusi do nachala petrovskikh preobrazovanii* (St Petersburg, 1999) envisages a still broader timescale.

90. Irina Reyfman, *Vasilii Trediakovsky: the fool of the 'new' Russian literature* (Stanford, CA, 1990), p.66-67, offers a salutary warning about the perils of rigid terminological distinctions in literary scholarship.

91. *Pis'ma N. I. Novikova*, ed. A. I. Serkov (St Petersburg, 1994), p.165, to Kh. A. Chebotarev, 22 June 1813: 'Нынешней просвещенной век все чудеса отметает, новые философы называют это суеверием, я бы желал, чтобы какой грамматик этимологию слова суеверие доказал им что суеверные, не те которые веруют чудесам: но те которые не веруют.' For a critical reference to '*filosofskii vek*', see Slovtsov's 1794 'Epistle', above, n.42.

247

early nineteenth century were more likely to hark back to 'the age of Catherine' ('vek Ekateriny' / 'век Екатерины') in the hope of persuading Alexander I to emulate his grandmother.[92] In marked contrast to 'Providence' ('Providenie' / 'Провидение'), 'prosveshchenie' was given a capital letter in the eighteenth century only when it formed the first word of a sentence. No sooner had it been dignified by upper case at the beginning of the nineteenth, in the title of Count D.I. Khvostov's Moscow journal *Friend of Enlightenment* (*Drug Prosveshcheniia* / *Друг Просвещения*), than the editor felt obliged to quash any notion that he might harbour reformist ambitions:

> To be a *Friend of Enlightenment*
> Means to love the light of scholarship
> And there is no wish or aspiration in this title
> To instruct and enlighten everyone.[93]

By then, as we saw at the start of this essay, the Enlightenment had fallen under suspicion as an alien source of temptation in the manner of Kapnist's epigram, 'The *philosophe*':

> Everyone praises enlightenment,
> But ask them: 'What is it?' – and rarely
> Can anyone answer,
> Or they will say: 'Knowledge, or learning'.
> Unfortunately this false opinion,
> Is accepted by everyone.
> But, good people! Have you forgotten the tree,
> Plucked by Eve?[94]

Even after the savage resentments of the Napoleonic era had faded, the continued association of enlightenment with Western Europe prompted renewed insecurities about Russia's peripheral status (Viazemskii warned that Russia's suppression of the Polish revolt in 1830 would 'set us back from European enlightenment by 50 years').[95] As late as 1890, when the Brockhaus and Efron encyclopedia finally defined 'Prosveshchenie' as

---

92. Simon Dixon, 'The posthumous reputation of Catherine the Great in Russia, 1797-1837', *Slavonic and East European review* 77 (1999), p.646-79.

93. 'Быть Другом Просвещенья. / Есть тоже самое что свет наук любить / И нет в названье сем желания стремленья / Чтоб всех наставить, просветить', *Drug Prosveshcheniia* (1806), part 1, p.83. For the context, see *Drug Prosveshcheniia*, part 2, p.211-13, 'Pis'mo k izdateliam Druga Prosveschheniia'.

94. 'Все хвалят просвещенье; / Спроси их: "Что оно такое?" – редко кто / Умеет дать ответ на то, / Иль скажет: "Знание, ученье". / Так, это ложно мненье, / К несчастью всеми принято. / Но, люди добрые! Иль вы забыли древо, / Ощипанное Евой?' V. V. Kapnist, 'Filozof', in *Sobranie sochinenii*, ed. D. S. Babkin, 2 vols (Moscow and Leningrad, 1960), vol.1, p.219-27 (226), stanza 41, part of a cycle written no earlier than the first decade of the nineteenth century and collected in this form in 1814-1815 (p.736).

95. P. A. Viazemskii, *Zapisnye knizhki (1813-1848)*, ed. V. S. Nechaeva (Moscow, 1963), p.213, 14 September 1831: 'Наши действии в Польше откинут нас на 50 лет от просвещения Европейского.'

synonymous with 'Aufklärung', Russia was nowhere mentioned in an article that glossed 'Enlightenment' as 'a cultural-historical term which predominantly signifies the intellectual movement in western Europe in the XVIII century (*siècle des lumières*)'.[96]

---

96. F. A. Brokgauz and I. A. Efron, *Entsiklopedicheskii slovar'*, 82 vols (St Petersburg, 1890-1904), vol.49,'Praiaga-Prosrochka otpuska', p.469.

FIONA CLARK

# The *Gazeta de Literatura de México* and the edge of reason: when is a periphery not a periphery?

Ah, qué extraña habrás sido Europa sin América,
Europa sin saber que América esperaba.

Silvina Ocampo

In recent years, particularly among scholars of the history of science, the terms 'peripheral' and 'central' or 'core', whilst still being frequently discussed, have been put to one side in order to find new avenues of understanding. In their stead we find references to 'spaces', 'localities', 'local frames of awareness' and even 'vectors of assemblage',[1] to mention but a few. It is increasingly clear, however, that care must be taken when using the terms 'periphery' and 'centre'. These terms have become part of a variety of theoretical approaches and debates that are not always compatible or helpful in every context. This includes the slant towards a Marxist critique, never mind negotiating the choppy waters of postcolonial and subaltern studies. The present work does not seek to venture into these discussions, limiting itself instead to a framework that is closer to the ideas espoused by David Wade Chambers and Antonio Lafuente in their studies of centre and periphery in colonial science.[2] As such, it is seeking to explore one area within the network of individuals, institutions and practices active towards the end of the eighteenth century in their particular socio-economic and political realities. It thus recognises that for the Spanish American context, the local scientific structure was very much subject to the interests of cultural and economic imperialism and was played out against the imposition of Spanish metropolitan interests.

---

1. The term 'vectors of assemblage' appears with reference to the usage made by David Turnbull to denote an 'amalgam of places, bodies, voices, skills, practices, technical devices, theories, social strategies and collective work that together constitute technoscientific knowledge/practices', in David Wade Chambers and Richard Gillespie, 'Locality in the history of science: colonial science, technoscience, and indigenous knowledge', in *Nature and empire: science and colonial enterprise*, ed. Roy MacLeod (Chicago, IL, 2001), p.221-40 (230).

2. D. W. Chambers, 'Locality and science: myths of centre and periphery', in *Mundialización de la ciencia y cultura nacional: actas del congreso internacional ciencia, descubrimiento y mundo colonial*, ed. Antonio Lafuente, A. Elena and M. L. Ortega (Madrid, 1993), p.605-17; Antonio Lafuente, 'Enlightenment in an imperial context: local science in the late eighteenth-century Hispanic world', *Osiris* (2001), p.155-73.

In what follows we shall explore some of the ideas and comments printed in one of Mexico's earliest and most important periodical publications, the *Gazeta de Literatura de México*.[3] We shall examine how they form part of a network of exchange and a control of authority on a local and an international level.[4] The arguments put forward are based on an understanding that for the editor of the periodical, José Antonio Alzate y Ramírez, there existed multiple centres of authority (geographical, social and intellectual) with regard to the generation, appropriation and rejection of ideas. His depiction of 'enlightenment' and his role within the community of knowledge created interface situations with the established centres of authority both in New Spain, that is, Mexico, and in Europe. In seeking to address these differences, Alzate attempted to find what may be called a third way, through the publication of his periodicals and by reaching out to a readership that he hoped would span the breadth of literate society.

## i. Alzate and the periodical press

Born in 1737, son of a native Spanish father and Mexican-born mother, the secular priest José Antonio Alzate y Ramírez stands as one of the most illustrious figures of eighteenth-century New Spain. This fact refers not only to his prolific career but also to his insatiable desire for scientific investigation and the propagation of new ideas. In terms of character he attracted admiration and anger in equal measure. A controversial polemicist, even in terms of his relationship with the various viceroys of New Spain, Alzate was a formidable adversary.[5] Whilst expressive in his praise of those people or ideas he felt deserving, he was also inclined to interpret opposing views as personal affronts, and react accordingly with mockery, ridicule and sarcasm. Trained in the Royal Pontifical University of Mexico in the 1760s, Alzate was to serve under some of the most illustrious state and ecclesiastical authorities of late-colonial Mexico. In this capacity, he performed a series of administrative roles communicating directly with various archbishops and viceroys, undertaking a wide

---

3. *La Gazeta de Literatura de México*, 3 vols (Mexico, Zúñiga y Ontiveros, 1788-1795), henceforward *GLM*. Two later editions appeared in 1831 and 1892. All references in this study are to the original publication and follow the format of volume, issue, page number and date of publication. The two subscription runs of vol.1 begin with issue 1 and run to 24, rather than 1 to 48. In order to differentiate between the two subscriptions within the same volume I have chosen to number each issue of this second subscription run as 1b, 2b and so on to 24b.

4. Prior to the commencement of the *GLA*, Alzate had published three periodicals: *El Diario Literario de México* (1768); *Asuntos varios sobre ciencias y artes* (1772-1773); *Observaciones sobre la física, historia natural y artes útiles* (1787-1788).

5. See Roberto Moreno, 'José Antonio de Alzate y los Virreyes', in *Cahiers du monde hispanique et luso-brézilien* 12 (1969), p.97-114, and by the same author, *Un Eclesiástico criollo frente al estado Borbón: discurso* (Mexico, 1980).

variety of reports into subjects as diverse as topography, cartography, meteorology, statistics, agriculture, technology and mining.[6]

During the course of these duties, Alzate also played a role in several of the scientific expeditions sent from Europe to the Americas. Already a member of the Basque Society of Friends of the Country,[7] he was elected in 1771 as a corresponding member to the Paris Royal Academy of Sciences as a result of his report on the passage of Venus over the solar disc, a report ensuing from his contact with the ill-fated Chappe d'Auteroche expedition.[8] As the only Mexican to hold such a position during that period it was indeed a mark of esteem.[9] The importance derived from his membership of these widely recognised and acclaimed societies, along with his later incorporation as correspondent of the Royal Botanical Gardens in Madrid, would play a key part in his presentation of ideas in the *Gazeta de Literatura*.

The *Gazeta de Literatura* was the last and greatest of Alzate's periodical publications, ending a career that spanned almost thirty years.[10] Published between 1788 and 1795 it consisted, on average, of two issues every month, each consisting of at least eight pages, sometimes as many as twelve.

6. For more detail see Roberto Moreno's introduction to, and collection of, Alzate's early works in José Antonio Alzate y Ramírez, *Memorias y ensayos*, ed. R. Moreno (Mexico, 1985).

7. The Sociedad Bascongada de los Amigos del País (Basque Society of Friends of the Country) founded in 1763 was a precursor to many such societies across Spain and Spanish America in the eighteenth century. They were established to stimulate progress in agriculture, industry and commerce, also publishing a breadth of information on scientific, technological and economic topics. No society was ever established in Mexico City, yet there were a considerable number of members, such as Alzate, across Mexico. Alzate's father had been a member of the same society. See Robert J. Schafer, *The Economic societies in the Spanish world (1763-1821)* (Syracuse, NY, 1958).

8. Chappe d'Auteroche died of typhus alongside many of his expedition team during the expedition to map the transit of Venus in 1769. His reports were returned to the Paris Royal Academy of Sciences along with a report on the transit written by Alzate. After 1786 Alzate's name no longer appeared on the list of correspondents for the Academy, although he does not seem to have become aware of this fact until some years later. Patrice Bret, 'Alzate y Ramírez et l'Académie Royale des Sciences de Paris: la réception des travaux d'un savant du Nouveau Monde', in *Periodismo Científico en el siglo XVIII: José Antonio de Alzate y Ramírez*, ed. Aceves Pastrana (Mexico, 2001), p.123-206.

9. In the footnotes added to the published version of Alzate's report Cassini remarks: 'Le zèle de Don Alzate y Ramyrez à nous communiquer tout ce qui peut se trouver d'intéressant dans un pays si nouveau pour nous, ses qualités personnelles, ses connaissances particulières, ont mérité & excité la reconnaissance de l'Académie, qui s'est empressée de le lui témoigner, en l'admettant au nombre de ses Correspondants.' Quoted in Rafael Aguilar y Santillán, 'Una carta interesante de Alzate' in *Memorias de la Sociedad Científica 'Antonio Alzate'* 23 (Mexico 1905), p.74-87 (87).

10. Alberto Saladino García has written extensively on the role of the periodical press and science in colonial Spanish America, including the *Gazeta de Literatura de México*: see *Ciencia y prensa durante la ilustración latinoamericana* (Mexico, 1996). For a more in-depth discussion of the *Gazeta de Literatura de México*, especially the links with the *Gazeta de México* and European periodical publications, see Fiona Clark, 'The *Gazeta de Literatura de México* (1788-1795): the formation of a literary-scientific periodical in late-viceregal Mexico', *Dieciocho: Hispanic Enlightenment* 28:1 (2005), p.7-30.

Supplements were occasionally added, but these were few. As one of only two periodicals published in Mexico City in the final decades of the eighteenth century, the *Gazeta de Literatura* acted in a complementary role to the *Gazeta de México*, which concentrated on news relating to more official or governmental and commercial interests. Alzate had also, however, contributed numerous articles relating to the natural sciences to the *Gazeta de México* from its commencement in 1784 under Manuel Antonio Valdés, and continued to do so, although on a less regular basis, almost to his death in 1799.

The periodical publications were further linked by two factors. First, after the first ten issues, the *Gazeta de Literatura* changed printing houses, moving from the office of Gerardo Flores to that of Zúñiga y Ontiveros under the direction of Manuel Antonio Valdés, editor of the *Gazeta de México*. Second, and perhaps due to this ongoing collaboration between the two editors, the *Gazeta de México* came to serve as the repository for critical articles responding to work published in the *Gazeta de Literatura*. Indeed, Alzate encouraged such an avenue of response, stressing how on various occasions he had offered the public a ready means through which they could publish articles for the *utilidad pública*.[11] Although indicating that such an open offer left room for negative consequences, he was adamant that the process should be seen to be impartial and in accordance with the ethos of the Republic of Letters.[12] However inconsistent this method was in actual practice, it remains an important indicator of Alzate's concern to engage his readers in debate, to awaken inquisitive minds, and to foster engagement with the 'useful arts' and sciences deemed of greatest value to the public.[13] As a result, the *Gazeta de Literatura* must be considered as one of the leading early examples of the tradition of periodical publications in Spanish America that would forge a role as a tool of dissemination of useful and practical information.

For many Spanish-American authors such publications constituted a means of serving their country, *la patria*, by recognising the importance of promoting useful public knowledge. The periodicals acted as a bridge

---

11. 'Utilidad pública', or public good/public usefulness, was the recurrent theme throughout the *GLM*. While on occasion space was created within its pages for themes dealing with literary criticism and limited discussion over philosophical and educational ideas, these are rare and infrequent. Even in his dealing with issues of a scientific, medical and technological nature (the useful arts), Alzate showed that he was not interested as much in discussing theory as in providing concrete ways to benefit the public by indicating how ideas can be put into practical application.

12. *GLM*, vol.2, issue 15, p.117 (22 March 1791). Quotations remain as in the original text without any attempts at modernisation or correction of accentuation or spelling.

13. Although Alzate's original intention was to open the *GLM* to publish articles and contributions submitted by the readers, by the end of the second subscription run, he was already lamenting the lack of response (*GLM*, vol.1, issue 24b, p.192, 16 August 1790). Despite this fact, Alzate continued in his belief that the reading public constitutes the best final judge when both sides of a polemic are published for all to read *GLM* (vol.2, issue 2, p.18, 21 September 1790).

between charting the road towards scientific and technological developments, and criticism of the shortcomings of the social and educational systems as they stood at the time. Many adopted an encyclopedic character in order to address the many and various needs within the country, while at the same time struggling with practical limitations, such as printing costs or lack of material resources. For Alzate, the *Gazeta*, as well as being a tool of instruction, was symbolic of a weapon in the battle for literary and scientific truth and the minds of the Mexican public. He frequently argued that he had not studied to write, but rather wrote because of what he had studied and observed. As such, the writing process served an end and means greater than itself.

## ii. The *Gazeta de Literatura*: voice of a nation?

Many diverse approaches have been adopted, as has already been mentioned, within the larger debate concerning centres and peripheries in an attempt to understand the breadth of issues involved in the use of such lines of argument. The identification of centre or periphery in geographical terms has raised as many, if not more, questions as answers. For the purpose of our study of the *Gazeta de Literatura*, however, it is necessary to start with the geographical in order to understand the basis from which Alzate was working, and the premise that underlies his entire work. Within the first two pages of volume 1, Alzate used three phrases that place his periodical and its contents firmly on the map in terms of geography and nationhood: 'la Metrópoli del Nuevo Mundo' ('the Metropolis of the New World'), 'la voz México' ('the voice of Mexico') and 'nuestra Nación Hispano Americana' ('our Hispanic American nation'):

La Série de producciones literarias Periódicas, es en tan grande número, que si se coordinan respecto á las Ciudades en que se publican, el simple Alfabeto no puede comprehenderlas. ¿En tanta abundancia, no es de estrañar que la Metrópoli del Nuevo mundo (en el que se hallan raros talentos, particulares producciones de los tres Reynos) se verifique un vacío que pudiera ocupar con lustre la voz México?[14]

These statements in themselves are full of ambiguities, for New Spain, like any other geographical region or society, did not consist of one homogeneous group of people. For whom, therefore, was Alzate speaking as the 'voz México' and to whom was his Hispano-American nation referring? These are questions which Alzate did not attempt to clarify. Whilst he is a frequent advocate of indigenous knowledge and methods,

---

14. *GLM*, vol.1, issue 1, p.1 (15 January 1788): 'The series of literary periodical productions is of such a great quantity that if they were to be organised according to the cities in which they are published, the simple alphabet would not be sufficient to contain them. In the midst of such abundance, is it not strange that in the Metropolis of the New World [...] there should be a vacuum that the voice of Mexico could fill with distinction?'

often favouring their techniques over and above that of his European contemporaries, Alzate clearly identifies himself with the educated elite of Mexican society. As a Mexican-born descendant of a European father and Mexican mother, he did not reject the Iberian aspect of his identity (socially, politically or historically).[15] Yet his interchangeable use of terminology (Spanish, American, Hispanic-American and Mexican) is indicative of a period in which national identity and the focus of national interests were slowly being transformed by an increasing sense of separateness from the Iberian metropolis. The central point of his position is, however, made abundantly clear: the metropolis was no longer the privileged site within a European nation; it was also a reality of the Americas.

Having stated that Alzate placed himself firmly within an exact geographical location and wrote directly from his knowledge and understanding of this reality, we must also recognise that, above and beyond the national context, various layers of relationship existed between the institutions, ideas and people featured or referenced in his publications. Any incorporation of the changing axes of relationship must therefore also step beyond the merely geographical to consider the fluctuating points of reference. And, as a consequence, examine the role that Alzate carved for himself within these.

### iii. Shils: a thesis of centre and periphery

In the remainder of this study, the ideas proposed in the *Gazeta de Literatura* will be explored through the use of a framework based on some initial ideas published by the sociologist Edward Shils.[16] There are, of course, inherent dangers involved in the partial adoption of a broad theoretical framework and its application to a much narrower context than that for which it was originally intended. Such risks notwithstanding, it is hoped that this approach will add some new angles to our understanding of Alzate's relationship with what he perceived to be the centres of power and knowledge both in New Spain and in Europe. It will thus highlight some of the tensions existent in the flow of scientific ideas in an international setting.

The central zone, according to Shils, has 'nothing to do with geometry and little with geography', but is, instead, a phenomenon of both the realm of values and beliefs, and that of action. It is, therefore, not

---

15. For more biographical detail on Alzate, see: *José Antonio Alzate y Ramírez: homenaje en el bicentenario de su fallecimiento*, ed. Alberto Saladino García and Juan José Saldaña (Mexico, 1999); Moreno, *Un Eclesiástico criollo frente*; Juan Hernández Luna, *José Antonio de Alzate* (Mexico, 1945); Agustin Aragón y Leiva, *Elogio a Alzate* (Mexico, 1942); Francisco Fernández del Castillo, *Apuntes para la bibliografía del Presbítero bachiller José Antonio Félix de Alzate y Ramírez Cantilla* (Mexico, 1927).

16. Shils, *Center and periphery*.

necessarily a spatial phenomenon. Shils further indicates that the latter was a structure of activities, roles and persons that exist within a network of institutions that embody and propound the values and beliefs within a society. These same structures consist of interdependent subsystems, 'which have in their special custody the cultivation of cultural values'.[17] This encapsulates a variety of groupings, such as the economy, the status system, the polity and those institutions governing cultural values, for example, universities and ecclesiastical bodies. The subsystems, furthermore, are built upon a network of organisations connected with varying degrees of affirmation, such as through a common authority, personal relationships, perceived identities of interest or 'a sense of affinity within a transcendent whole', to name but a few.[18] Each organisation is overseen by an elite, or some form of authority, that makes decisions that will maintain the organisation and control the conduct of members. Their decisions are based on general standards of judgement and action, and concrete values, that is, the 'central value system'. As such, they interlink that which the society holds to be sacred and that which the ruling authorities espouse.[19] Shils argues that authority thereby 'enjoys appreciation because it arouses sentiments of sacredness', including, to some extent, those persons or offices indirectly or remotely linked to it.[20] In addition to the appreciation of the institutions through which this authority works, one finds an appreciation of the qualities (secondary values) that qualify or characterise a person for the exercise of authority, be they educational, economic, professional or familial. These may be acquired through relationship but also through study or experience. Such a person, therefore, enjoys the 'appreciation of the central value system' simply through the connection with the exercise of authority. Finally, the 'central value system' legitimises the distribution of roles and rewards to those possessing the appropriate qualities symbolising their proximity to authority.[21]

## iv. Alzate and the centre/periphery thesis

Shils' argument that the central zone lies within the realm of values and beliefs that is supported by a series of interconnected subsystems is a particularly constructive means of approaching Alzate's work. The 'transcendent whole' to which Shils refers is, for Alzate, the Republic of Letters, the community and network of scientific knowledge that superseded geographical and political interests and was aimed at benefiting man.

17. Shils, *Center and periphery*, p.3.
18. Shils, *Center and periphery*, p.4.
19. Shils, *Center and periphery*, p.4.
20. Shils, *Center and periphery*, p.5.
21. Shils, *Center and periphery*, p.6.

This is particularly apparent in his comments on the role of the *Gazeta* and the promotion of the understanding of physics:[22]

> La Gazeta de Literatura debe comunicar al pais las novedades utiles que se publican en otros muy distantes de la América, y tambien debe participar las prácticas ventajosas que se palpan aquí, para que los hombres de todo pais se utlizen de ellas. La Física es una Ciencia en que no debe verificarse rivalidad; la envidia, el monopolio le son desconocidos. Procuremos hacer felices á nuestros semejantes, ya sean nacidos en los climas ardientes de la Africa, ó en los helados del Norte: todo hombre debia tener presente á la vista esta máxima: *Soy hombre: debo coadyuvar á la felicidad de mis hermanos.*[23]

And again: 'La Física, esta ciencia tan útil como deleytosa, en la que, como en el mas delicado espejo, aun los rústicos registran las maravillas de la Omnipotencia, no puede ampliarse y difundirse si no se unen los Aplicados de todo el Orbe á exponer lo que diariamente observan en sus respectivos Paises.'[24]

If, then, following this pattern within the context of the *Gazeta de Literatura*, we consider the realm of values and beliefs to consist of those themes that most occupied Alzate and that were also central to Enlightenment concerns, we encounter ideas and discoveries relating to the natural sciences and technology. The realm of action, therefore, signifies those individuals, and at times institutions, that undertake observations and experimentation, publishing their findings and testing the veracity of the statements made by others within the public sphere. In the same way, by pursuing his observations and presenting his own findings, especially when they are corrections of the European modes of thought, Alzate created for himself and for his readers perceived identities of interest within the wider scientific world. The *Gazeta de Literatura* formed a space wherein all those contributing studies, reports and criticism became part of the network of interdependent subsystems embodying and cultivating the new ideas.

---

22. Although the more commonly used term at the time was 'natural philosophy', Alzate frequently spoke of physics. This early use should not, of course, be confused with the modern-day understanding of the discipline.

23. *GLM*, vol.2, issue 14, p.112, 8 March 1791: 'The Gazeta de Literatura should communicate to the country all the useful new discoveries that are published in lands far from America as well as demonstrating the beneficial practices that are experienced here, so that all men in all nations should use them. Physics is a science in which there should be no rivalry; envy and monopoly are unknown to it. We endeavour to make our neighbour happy, whether they are born in the burning climates of Africa, or the freezing atmosphere of the North: everyone should have before them this injunction: *I am human: I should look to my brothers' happiness.*'

24. *GLM*, vol.2, issue 46, p.369, 11 September 1792: 'Physics, this science that is as useful as it is delightful, in which, as in the most delicate mirror, even the rustics become aware of the wonders of the Omnipotent, cannot increase and be disseminated if all the diligent workers throughout the world do not join together in displaying what they are daily observing in each of their countries.'

That said, perhaps one of the most problematic areas of Shils' argument for the generally quite nationalistic reading of Alzate's work that has existed until now is his assertion that this action takes place within the network of institutions, the custodians of the cultivation of cultural values. If we are to understand that such institutions must at some level refer to the centres of education existent in Mexico City, such as the Real y Pontificia Universidad de México, we must also recognise one of the great areas of tension present in the periodical. On the one hand, Alzate formed part of the central Creole educated elite in Mexico City and played an important role within the ecclesiastical institutions, particularly under Archbishop Francisco Antonio Lorenzana (1722-1804), who served in Mexico City between 1766 and 1772. He was, therefore, connected with the circles of authority in his administrative and report-writing capacities for Church and government.[25] With regard to the natural sciences, however, he was largely self-taught, a factor that seems to have weighed heavily for him in his dealings with his contemporaries, especially in New Spain. He had no professional affiliation to the Pontifical University, which he considered largely a bulwark of scholasticism, or any other institutions in New Spain. In fact he was in open disagreement with the recently arrived Spanish scientists who were responsible for the newly established Botanical Garden and the introduction of the Linnean taxonomical system.[26] His lack of official position and recognised scientific qualifications within the viceroyalty were potential sources of weakness that he felt the need to defend constantly when faced with the jibes of his critics. The institutional backing which he lacked in New Spain, however, was gained from his European connections. His position within the Paris Royal Academy of Sciences became the launch-pad from which he claimed authority over his critics in New Spain, while at the same time creating a platform from which he could criticise European ideas almost from within their own ranks:

Yo, es cierto, no he cursado las Academias; pero tampoco se me puede negar que por una inclinación innata al estudio, lo he hecho muy prolixo en lo que propongo; y últimamente quando un individuo ya sea por sus producciones, ó por

25. Alzate's correspondence with the various viceroys serving the Spanish Crown in Mexico, particularly the Second Count of Revillagigedo (1789 to 1792), testifies to a relationship with authority that struggled to remain respectful and yet questioned methods and ideas espoused among the highest ranks. It is possible that this attitude and the recriminatory tone of his later letters to the Marquis of Branciforte (1794 to 1798) were the cause of the eventual demise of the *GLM*. See documents in Mexico City, Archivo General de la Nación de México, 'Correspondencia de los Virreyes', vol.32, f.99r, 282r-83v, 347r-49r and 'Historia', f.1r-133r.

26. For further detail on this exchange see particularly Patricia Aceves Pastrana, *Química, Botánica y Farmacia en la Nueva España a finales del siglo XVIII* (México, 1993). We should also recognise, however, that Alzate had unsuccessfully petitioned to become Director of the Real Tribunal de Minería, and so was not averse to participating in all the local institutions.

otro cualquier motivo, consigue que algun cuerpo literario lo asocie al número de los que lo componen, es acreedor á que por lo menos se le escuche. Conozco en Nueva España á muchos condecorados con varios títulos, los supongo literatos, y lo son en efecto, pero hasta el dia ninguno de ellos pueda presentar Título de mayor esfera que el mio porque se sabe que la Real Academia de las Ciencias de París no confiere el Título de Correspondiente, sino al que lo merece: y esta (es el primer Tribunal en las Ciencias naturales) por aclamacion en 22 Abril de 1771 me asoció á su Cuerpo. Este Título, que me abochornó al saber lo había obtenido sin empeño, sin otro mérito que haber remetido á ese Ilustre Cuerpo algunas Memorias de Física y de Geometría; precisamente me pone en estado de examinar á lo menos como a qualquier otro literato, las ideas ridículas, y pretensiones infundadas de los que sin los requísitos necesarios quieren emprenderlo todo.[27]

We find the reason for this strongly defended position on the following page when he writes:

En el catálogo de Académicos que anualmente imprime la Real Academia, observé que estos últimos años se omitia mi nombre: en defensa de mi honor hize el correspondiente reclamo, y resultó que un cierto ... escribió á la Academia que mi vida habia llegado á su termino. Pero no es así: vivo y viviré (lo que Dios quiera) para trabajar lo que me resta de vida en beneficio del Público: siempre me reputaré feliz por haber sido el primero y hasta el día único habitante de Nueva España que logra ser de la Real Academia de las Ciencias de París.[28]

Linked to his membership of these groups, moreover, is the fact that the majority of examples used in defence of the form and content of the *Gazeta* were based upon three important factors. The first that he had access to the long-established European periodicals, particularly the French[29];

27. *GLM*, vol.2, issue 38, p.301, 24 April 1792: 'It is certainly the case that I have not completed any courses in the Academies; but it cannot be denied that through my natural inclination to studies, I have been very prolific in my suggestions; and lately when an individual, whether it be as a result of his work, or for whatever other reason, attains acceptance as a member of some literary body, he deserves to at least be heard. I know many individuals in New Spain who are awarded with various titles, I presume they are literary men, and they are in effect, but to this day none of them can attest to holding a greater title than mine because it is a well-known fact that the Royal Academy of Sciences in Paris only confers the title of Correspondent to those who merit it: and this body (the greatest Tribunal in the natural sciences) by a declaration of 22 April 1771 made me an associate to its ranks. I was embarrassed to realise that I had been given this title without exerting any effort, without any other merit than to have sent this Illustrious body some reports on Physics and Geometry: this title places me, as much as any other literary figure, precisely in the position of being able to judge ridiculous ideas and the unfounded claims of those without the necessary requirements who wish to undertake all kinds of projects.'

28. *GLM*, vol.2, issue 38, p.302: 'I have noticed that my name has been missing from the catalogue of academicians published yearly by the Royal Academy: in defence of my honour I made an enquiry and it appears that a certain ... wrote to the Academy to tell them that my life had reached its end. But this is not so: I am alive and will continue to live (as long as God wishes) in order to spend the rest of my life working for the public good: I own that I have always been happy to have been, and continue being to this day, the only inhabitant of New Spain who has achieved membership of the Royal Academy of Sciences in Paris.' The omission of the name and the use of suspension marks appear in the original.

29. Alzate's articles appeared mostly in the early 1770s soon after he succeeded in becoming a corresponding member of the Paris Royal Academy of Science: *Journal de*

second, that his experience had shown that they followed similar formats; and third, he carried the practical authority of one who had successfully published within the pages of the leading French scientific journals:[30]

Varios Lectores se quejan de que en mis Periódicos trato de asuntos que en su dictamen no corresponden al Título de *Gazeta de Literatura*. [...] Mas permitaseme decir, que estos Señores están muy distantes de conocer lo que comprende una Gazeta de Literatura, y si se tomasen el trabajo de registrar las Obras periódicas que se han impreso con semejante título en la sabia Europa, hubieran visto como estas son unas especies de colecciones en que se proponen ideas de todas clases de asuntos.[31]

On the one hand then, Alzate rejected the institutional authority of New Spain, yet at the same time, he embraced the opportunities opened to him through his introduction into the scientific networks of the European institutions. By this means, he was qualified for inclusion within what Shils describes as the authority or elite of the sub-systems, setting the standards of judgement for the concrete value system. He enjoyed the 'appreciation of the central value system simply through his connection with the exercise of authority'.[32] His connection with exercise of authority in the European scientific circles was then a weapon used to substantiate his work and his claims on his own home ground.

This said, should we presume that Alzate's form of enlightenment-thinking led him to privilege Europe over and above America? As is clear from the prologue to the *Gazeta de Literatura*, there is no theme that does not refer directly back to the *patria* or *nación* with the intention of encouraging and inspiring advancement, directed at concrete problems and demands within the viceroyalty:

Uno de los fines con que me dediqué á publicar la *Gazeta de Literatura*, fue el comunicar á la Patria aquellos descubrimientos útiles que se ejecutaban en Europa, y participar á esta ciertos conocimientos relativos á las artes que se ven establecidos por los Indios, ó que les dieron á conocer los Sabios Españoles que

---

*physique* (February 1773), p.221-23; *Journal des sçavans* (October 1771), p.117-38; *Journal des sçavans* (June 1773), p.238-44. A further article appeared in Spain, *Memorial Literario* 62 (May 1788), p.87-98, the original of which appeared in the *GLM*, vol.1, issue 2, p.9-20 (31 January 1788). Alzate commented on the Spanish publication in *GLM*, vol.1, issue 7b, p.53 (9 December 1789).

30. For further discussion on the connections between the *GLM* and the non-Mexican periodical press see F. Clark, 'Read all about it: science, translation, adaptation and confrontation in the *Gazeta de Literatura de México* (1788-1795)', in *Science and medicine in the Spanish and Portuguese empires*, ed. Daniela Bleichmar, Paula de Vos, Kristin Huffine and Kevin Sheehan (Stanford, CA, forthcoming).

31. *GLM*, vol.2, issue 24, p.187 (26 July 1791): 'Various readers complain that in my periodicals I deal with subjects that, in their opinion, do not correspond to the title *Gazeta de Literatura*. [...] But let me say this, these men are very far from understanding of what a literary gazette should consist, and had they made the effort to observe the periodical works that have been printed with a similar title in wise Europe, they would have noticed that they are a form of collection in which ideas are proposed on all class of subjects.'

32. Shils, *Center and periphery*, p.5.

introdujeron aquí [...] se verá con sorpresa lo que en Nueva España se sabe, tocante á algunas Artes.[33]

Not only was Alzate to engage in the positive promotion of those ideas originating in Europe, he was also to undertake an active resistance when ideas or discoveries were either inapplicable to the Mexican reality or already existed in an improved form to that used in Europe. He did this by dealing with subjects as varied as the production of varnish for covering cooking utensils, the architectural styles used for building houses, the use of steam cooking and the production of dye, to name but a few. His underlying belief was strongly based on the recognition that the native or ancient knowledge held in New Spain had long been overlooked due to the lack of a written record:

> Lo cierto es que en Nueva España es necesarísimo una Obra periódica para dar á conocer las riquezas que encierra este País privilegiado por la Naturaleza, para corregir los muchos errores acerca de la Historia natural, que se reimprimen y reimprimirán interin desde aquí no ministremos noticias seguras, observaciones completas. [...] Si en alguna ocasión se expresa que algunas Artes estan mas perfeccionadas aquí que en Europa, se mira semejante asercion como un delirio; pero en honor de la Nacion, y en obsequio de la verdad y utilidad del Genero humano, ya se hará ver como el Arte del Salitrero se halla en Nueva España en un estado de perfeccion á que no llega la práctica estrangera. Lo mismo se puede decir respecto al Arte del Ladrillero y de otros muchos: lo que se profiere en virtud de haber leído con reflexa la exacta descripción de las Artes publicada por la Real Academia de las Ciencias de París, y observado las prácticas del País.[34]

## v. Concluding remarks

The Mexican historian of science, Roberto Moreno, has remarked that: 'Cualquier página de los periódicos deja la impresión de que la Nueva

---

33. *GLM*, vol.2, issue 34, p.273-74 (31 January 1792): 'One of the ends to which I dedicated myself in publishing the *Gazeta de Literatura*, was that of communicating to the nation the useful discoveries taking place in Europe, and in sharing certain knowledge relating to the arts established by the Indians, or that were established by the first wise Spaniards who arrived here [...] just how much New Spain already knows regarding the certain Arts will prove to be surprising.'

34. *GLM*, vol.1, issue 24b, p.192, 195 (16 July 1790): 'What is certain is that in New Spain a periodical publication is absolutely necessary in order to make known the riches held within the country that is so privileged by Nature, and to correct the many errors that are printed and will continue to be re-printed regarding Natural history whilst from here we do not publish definite facts, complete observations. [...] If on some occasion certain Arts here are found to be in a greater state of perfection to those in Europe, such an assertion will no doubt be looked upon as a delusion; but in honour of the Nation, and in deference to the truth and the utility of humanity I will demonstrate how the Art of producing saltpetre is in a state of much greater perfection in New Spain than any foreign practice. The same could be said of the Art of brick making and of many others: a fact that can be vouchsafed as a result of what I have read in the exact description of these Arts published by the Royal Academy of Sciences in Paris, and having observed the practices of this country.'

España es una comunidad material y espiritual, una unidad geográfica y mental, pese a las diferencias de razas, a las separaciones impuestas por la geografía y la lengua, a las diversas concepciones políticas y religiosas.'[35] As we know, such apparent unity in public representation can often cover underlying discontent on many levels, yet these issues, perhaps because they verge on the political, did not occupy Alzate, who instead was dedicated to the defence and promotion of the Americas.[36] The imperial unity of the Spanish nation was maintained throughout, demonstrating Alzate's belief that the Spanish so-called peripheries were an integral part of this organic whole of the Spanish kingdom and functioned as parts of it.[37] This fact, when added to Shils' framework of affinity to the transcendent whole discussed above, demonstrates why, despite his great respect for the European institutions, Alzate had no qualms about setting New Spain as the centre point for the promotion of new scientific and technological ideas. He did not consider New Spain to be in any way peripheral to the established European institutions, just as New Spain was not peripheral to Spain. On the contrary, he considered himself to be working alongside the European elite, correcting poor scholarship where necessary, demonstrating where the Americas were in advance of Europe when possible, and adapting those new ideas that were of use to the public or the colonial institutional systems as he considered profitable.

Roy MacLeod in his introduction to *Nation and empire* argues that science occurs locally but it is recognised universally.[38] His injunction to 'think globally, but act locally' is a fitting expression of Alzate's work within the eighteenth-century Republic of Letters and the global community of science to which he aspired from the vantage point of the Valley of Mexico. Alzate's true contributions originated with his local observations and the comparison of his findings with those of scientists in other countries across Europe, and at times in English-speaking America. One might argue, indeed, that Alzate, by studying, adapting and correcting European ideas was, in many ways, returning the 'structured gaze

---

35. Rafael Moreno, 'Creación de la nacionalidad mexicana', *Historia Mexicana* 12 (1963), p.531-51 (535): 'Any page of the periodical leaves the impression that New Spain is a material and spiritual community, a geographical and mental unity, despite the differences in race and the separations on the diverse perceptions of politics and religion, imposed by geography and language.'

36. Alzate had, moreover, experienced the wrath of the colonial authorities as a result of articles printed in his previous periodical publications, two of which were terminated as a result of viceregal censorship. In the pages of the *Gazeta de Literatura* he clearly and continually stated that he had no interest in pursuing topics of a political nature.

37. John Jay TePaske, 'Integral to empire: the vital peripheries of colonial Spanish America', in *Negotiated empires: centers and peripheries in the Americas, 1500-1870*, ed. Christine Daniels and Michael V. Kennedy (London, 2002), p.29-41.

38. Roy MacLeod, 'Introduction', in *Nature and empire: science and colonial enterprise*, ed. Roy MacLeod (Chicago, IL, 2000), p.1-13.

of power'.[39] He did this on two levels: first, by creating a legitimising space for new ideas outside of the established institutions in New Spain, and second, by turning back on Europe those ideas and misrepresentations that were not valid for the American experience and reclaiming the knowledge that had long been held within that culture and disregarded in Europe. It may not have been the 'strategic reversal of the process of domination' to which Bhabha refers, but it was a claim to some form of equality, albeit equality based upon acceptance within the 'transcendent whole', that community of knowledge that he recognised to be governed by the elite of the established European institutions. The fact remains, therefore, as Alzate was clearly aware, that the effective return of the 'structured gaze of power' necessitates on some level the participation and recognition of the one who originally gazed, a validation of the action/ reaction. This validation, as Shils similarly argued, was legitimised by the central value system. In the *Gazeta de Literatura*, Alzate attempted to show that, if he was at the 'edge of reason', his was not a distant, backward, peripheral location, but rather at the cutting edge in the development and advancement of understanding, specifically of the non-European natural world.

---

39. Homi Bhabha quoted in Peter Beardsell, *Europe and Latin America: returning the gaze* (Manchester, 2000), p.17-18.

LYNDA PRATT

# Tea and national history? Ann Yearsley, John Thelwall and the late-eighteenth-century provincial English epic

IN 1806 Francis Jeffrey, editor of the influential Whig periodical the *Edinburgh review*, launched the latest in a series of broadsides against the pretensions of English provincial culture. His pretext for doing so was a review of the *Memoirs* of the scientist, philosopher and political reformer Joseph Priestley.[1] Although Priestley had died in Pennsylvania in 1804, most of his life had been spent in the English provinces, culminating in his flight from a Birmingham mob in 1791. For Jeffrey, it was 'quite evident' to any reader that Priestley had entertained no doubts about his posthumous reputation, 'confidently expect[ing] his name to go down to posterity' and to take his place next to Luther and Newton in the 'Temple of Immortality'. To the *Edinburgh* reviewer, this was evidence of his limitations, proof that: 'there is universally something presumptuous in provincial genius, and that it is a very rare felicity to meet with a man of talents out of the metropolis, who does not overrate himself and his *coterie* prodigiously.'[2] For Jeffrey such regional pretension – whilst equally reprehensible everywhere and anywhere – characterised one English locality in particular: 'In the West of England [...] there has been a succession of authors, who seem to have laid claim to a sort of omnipotence, and to have fancied that they were born to effect some mighty revolution in the different departments to which they applied themselves.'[3] In fact Jeffrey's polemics help to draw attention to the dynamic nature of English regional culture in what some might label the late Enlightenment, others the early Romantic period, but which perhaps needs no label at all. This is, of course, a vitality that the canonisation of

1. *Memoirs of Dr Joseph Priestley, to the year 1795, written by himself: with a continuation to the time of his decease, by his son Joseph Priestley; and observations on his writings, by Thomas Cooper, president judge of the fourth district of Pennsylvania, and the Reverend William Christie* (London, 1805).
2. *Edinburgh review* 9 (1806), p.136-61 (147). Jeffrey was sole editor of the *Edinburgh* from 1803 to 1829, apart from a brief gap in the winter of 1813-1814. His attacks on what he perceived as provincial cliques had begun with his review of Robert Southey's oriental romance *Thalaba the Destroyer* (1801), in *Edinburgh review* 1 (1802), p.63-83. The most recent study of the *Edinburgh*'s significance is *British Romanticism and the 'Edinburgh review': bicentenary essays*, ed. Massimiliano Demata and Duncan Wu (Basingstoke, 2002).
3. *Edinburgh review* 9 (1806), p.147.

authors such as Samuel Taylor Coleridge and William Wordsworth seems at first to confirm. Both men were – after all – very much the product of the English regions and of English regionalism: Coleridge was born at Ottery St Mary in Devon and Wordsworth at Cockermouth in Cumberland. Their most celebrated joint poetical production, the 1798 collection *Lyrical ballads* – for a long time seen as a foundational work of British Romanticism – was initially published in Bristol by the local publisher Joseph Cottle. Later in their careers, contemporaries labelled them as key members of the 'Lake School', a tag both poets equally vigorously resisted.[4]

Yet, whilst the literary canon might seem to undermine Jeffrey's ridiculing of regional pretension, its own tendency towards centralising and homogenising culture in the late eighteenth and early nineteenth centuries has led it firstly to overlook (even discount) the contribution of provincial culture to one of the most dynamic periods of English literary history, and secondly to ignore the conflict between regional and centralised metropolitan and national identities which Jeffrey's review expresses. In other words, cutting Coleridge and Wordsworth off from their non-canonical contemporaries, even from fellow 'Lake' writers such as Robert Southey, has artificially removed them from the complex, frequently non-metropolitan, contexts that both produced them and helped to define them for their peers.[5]

This essay will demonstrate that the rehabilitation of provincial culture is an essential part of any examination of the construction of literary and national identities in the late eighteenth and early nineteenth centuries. Indeed, as documents such as Jeffrey's review illustrate, it was impossible for contemporaries to ignore. In spite of all its boasts that metropolitan sophisticates (presumably even metropolitan Scottish sophisticates such as Jeffrey himself) could – and would – laugh the pretensions of the provinces to scorn, Jeffrey's essay does in fact disclose an underlying anxiety over the nature and increasing influence of what it seeks to condemn. For example, its employment of a quasi-Burkean rhetoric of inheritance and 'succession' only draws attention to the growing, and by implication, unstoppable, number of provincial authors competing for attention in the literary marketplace. The essay's lack of discrimination between different centres of regional activity – in the course of the essay Jeffrey confuses (possibly deliberately) Midlanders such as Thomas Day and Erasmus Darwin (both members of the Lunar Society) with West Country writers such as Coleridge and his brother-in-law Robert Southey – also suggests

---

4. For a recent study see David Chandler, 'The early development of the "Lake School" idea', *Notes and queries* 250 (2005), p.35-37.

5. The diversity and vitality of English regional culture in the eighteenth century is explored in John Brewer, *The Pleasures of the imagination: English culture in the eighteenth century* (London, 1997), p.493-612. See also C. R. Johnson, *Provincial poetry 1789-1839: British verse printed in the provinces: the Romantic background* (Otley, 1992).

not so much Jeffrey's ignorance of English regional geography as his nervousness about the interconnectedness he detected in such non-metropolitan cultural groups.[6] Indeed such interlinking was demonstrated by the inclusion in his list of presumptuous 'provincial philosophers' of 'Beddoes' – a reference to Thomas Beddoes, the radical physician, scientist and poet who connected the Midlands with Bristol, the Lunar Society with the Coleridge circle.[7] Most revealingly of all, Jeffrey's rhetoric of 'revolution' exposes the potentially subversive nature of provincial enterprise.[8] What seems most troubling to him is not the existence of provincial culture per se but the capacities of its most prominent members to challenge and destabilise the certainties supposedly embodied by the metropolitan centre. Jeffrey is, then, concerned not so much by the existence of provincial culture but by its refusal to remain on the periphery. His remarks both portray and envisage a society menaced by the threat of a provincial revolution – a society in which the peripheries increasingly challenge the authority of the centre, in which the margins dare to assume the role of defining the nation as a whole. In so doing they imply the instability and vulnerability of the centre itself. Jeffrey's words draw attention to a nation characterised by competing cultures and uncertain languages of self-definition, a nation needing to define itself but equally far from united about how – and by whom and from where – such definition could best be accomplished.

## i. Defining the nation

The necessity in a period of international revolution, war and crisis, like that witnessed in late-eighteenth- and early-nineteenth-century Britain, to define the nation is a historical and critical commonplace.[9]

6. For the Lunar Society see Schofield, *The Lunar Society of Birmingham*, and Jenny Uglow, *The Lunar men: the friends who made the future* (London, 2002).

7. *Edinburgh review* 9 (1806), p.147. Jeffrey echoes the concerns about provincial radicalism felt by conservatives in the 1790s; see Albert Goodwin, *The Friends of liberty: the English democratic movement in the age of the French Revolution* (London, 1979), *passim*.

8. Compare with his review of Robert Southey, *Madoc* (London, 1805) in *Edinburgh review* 7 (1805-1806), p.[1]-28. This characterised Southey's literary 'ambition' as 'of a more undisciplined and revolutionary character. He affects to follow the footsteps of no predecessor, and to acknowledge the supremacy of no chief or tribunal: he rather looks [...] with a jealous and contemptuous eye on the old aristocracy of the literary world, and refused the jurisdiction of its constituted authorities. He [...] seems to aim at dethroning the old dynasty of genius, in behalf of an unaccredited generation', p.[1].

9. See, for example, Colley, *Britons*, and Katie Trumpener, *Bardic nationalism: the Romantic novel and the British Empire* (Princeton, NJ, 1997). Recent studies of the cultural identities of the constituent nations of the United Kingdom include: Murray G. H. Pittock, *Celtic identity and the British image* (Manchester, 1999); Ina Ferris, *The Romantic national tale and Ireland* (Cambridge, 2002); *English Romanticism and the Celtic world*, ed. Gerard Carruthers and Alan Rawes (Cambridge, 2003); *Scotland and the borders of Romanticism*, ed. Leith Davis, Ian Duncan and Janet Sorensen (Cambridge, 2004); and *Wales and the Romantic imagination* (Cardiff, 2007) ed. Damian Walford Davies and Lynda Pratt.

National definition could take many different forms: for example, the establishment in 1791 of the Ordnance Survey; the alternative versions of the nation proffered by writers such as Burke and Paine; government celebrations of success in war against external enemies (for example the great Naval Thanksgiving of 19 December 1797);[10] and the establishment in 1795 of a government committee to oversee the commissioning and erection of public monuments to recent national heroes, an idea which saw the conversion of St Paul's Cathedral into a British version of the French Pantheon (and the use of a French comparison here suggests the instability involved), thus creating a public space in which national heroics and identity could be commemorated, celebrated, defined and invoked.[11] National definition could also involve the assertion of regional identity. For example, James Gillray's 1793 satirical print 'The French invasion; – or – John Bull, bombarding the Bum-Boats' does, as Linda Colley notes, depict the defecating monarch 'as being in the most intimate sense possible entirely at one with England and Wales'.[12] Yet it is also an illustration of the regional distinctiveness that lay within those same national boundaries. National identity is, as Gillray reminds us, characterised not merely by the coastline (the border between land and sea that separates England from revolutionary France) but also by internal borders, the lines that divide one English or Welsh county from its neighbours.

As John Brewer has demonstrated, creative writers from both the metropolis and the regions played important parts in the process of shaping national identities. Indeed, in an age increasingly concerned with what Nathan Drake (in a volume of essays first published in Sudbury in Suffolk in 1798) defined as the 'national advantages [...] [to] be derived from perpetuating the memory of any remarkable event or deed', writing and reading about the national character (whether in the metropolis or the provinces) assumed especial significance.[13] Drake was a particularly astute and up-to-date critic, whose speciality was literary form. The remainder of this essay will focus on one particular genre – the national epic – and look at the way in which two English provincial writers of the 1790s and early 1800s made use of it.

---

10. For two politically opposed interpretations of the Naval Thanksgiving see the accounts in the loyalist *Anti-Jacobin, or Weekly examiner* 7 (25 December 1797), p.49-51 and the radical *Cambridge intelligencer* (23 December 1797), unpaginated. See also L. Pratt, 'Naval contemplation: poetry, politics and the navy 1797-1799', *Journal for maritime research* (December 2000), accessed from http://www.jmr.nmm.ac.uk/server/show/conJmrArticle.22/viewPage/1.

11. See Alison Yarrington, *The Commemoration of the hero 1800-1864: monuments to British victors of the Napoleonic wars* (London and New York, 1988), p.61-78.

12. Colley, *Britons*, p.210. The print is reproduced on p.[211].

13. Nathan Drake, *Literary hours, or Essays literary and critical* (Sudbury, printed by J. Burkitt, 1798), p.81.

## ii. The national epic in the late eighteenth century

Why epic? Epic is a word much misused in our culture – we might talk about 'epic' films, 'epic' football games or even an 'epic' Ashes series. But in the late eighteenth century things were different. By the 1790s, the epic was acknowledged by most writers (a notable exception being a curmudgeonly Horace Walpole) as the highest of all literary forms.[14] The national epic – an epic poem about an explicitly national subject – offered ambitious poets a suitable means (to paraphrase Drake) of 'perpetuat[ing] the memory of any remarkable [national] event or deed' and in so doing of attempting to define the nation.[15] The epic, moreover, was suitable to the demands of the period in other – less obvious – ways. As the responses of writers, reviewers and readers of the numerous epic poems produced in Britain in the late eighteenth and early nineteenth centuries reveal, in spite – or possibly as a result – of its high status and considerable lineage, the epic was also an essentially unstable form.[16] Recapitulating and reiterating earlier debates, producers and consumers of the genre were unable (amongst other things) to agree on what an epic was, on what subject matter was most suitable for it, or on the appropriateness or inappropriateness of epic machinery (such as gods and goddesses and supernatural interventions in the actions of the human characters). Such lack of unanimity may reflect what David Quint has described as the dual tradition of the epic (its position as a narrative written by both winners and losers), but it also indicates the complex state and complex affiliations of literary and political culture.[17] Both national identity and the epic were beset by a fundamental instability – in the case of the national epics produced in Britain in this period, formal instability echoes the contested nature of what they (as national poems) were attempting to inscribe. As Hugh Cunningham has suggested in relation to late-eighteenth- and early-nineteenth-century writings on the vexed issue of patriotism, it is fair to say that the 'outpourings [of epics] from the presses are not so much a celebration of national unity as an exercise in persuasion'.[18] The national epic – whether written from the metropolis or the provinces – is therefore the ideal literary form to encapsulate the nation. In terms of writing epics about the nation,

---

14. For the debate about the nature of epic see H. T. Swedenberg, *The Theory of the epic in England 1650-1800* (Berkeley and Los Angeles, CA, 1944).

15. Drake, *Literary hours*, p.81.

16. The best surveys of epic writing in this period are Stuart Curran, *Poetic form and British Romanticism* (Oxford, 1986), p.158-79 and Brian Wilkie, *Romantic poets and epic tradition* (Madison, WI, 1965).

17. David Quint, *Epic and empire: politics and generic form from Virgil to Milton* (Princeton, NJ, 1993).

18. Hugh Cunningham, 'The languages of patriotism', *History workshop journal* 12 (1981), p.8-33 (14).

moreover, this double instability (poetic form and national identity) is potentially both the poet's greatest asset and greatest challenge.

One fact about this period that is not in doubt is that poets from the metropolis and the provinces took up the challenge. Contemporaries reported on the 'singular phaenomenon', as the *Anti-Jacobin review* called it, 'that [in the late eighteenth century] [...] the number of candidates for epic fame [...] exceed[ed] [...] those of the early and middle ages of the world'.[19] Although, as Stuart Curran has noted, the production of national epics intensified in the last decade of the eighteenth and opening decades of the nineteenth centuries, especially in the years surrounding the 1801 Act of Union, this profusion of newly composed national poems implied neither certainty about how the nation should be defined nor agreement about the kind of poetry best suited to record so-called national virtues.[20] Literary culture in this period was a battlefield, with warfare raging in local and national contexts, and nowhere was the conflict fiercer – or of potentially greater significance – than in the field of the national epic, the genre that of its very nature (Milton after all had described epic as 'doctrinal and exemplary to a Nation') sought to define both the nation's identity and the type of poet and poetry best suited to enshrine this.[21]

At its most basic – though also most neglected – level, in the 1790s and early 1800s the contest for the soul of the national epic occurred between loyalist and radical, Anti-Jacobin and Jacobin practitioners and consumers. Its dynamics can, for example, be seen in the response to the 'handsomest book that Bristol had ever yet sent forth', Robert Southey's radically anti-national *Joan of Arc*, first published by Joseph Cottle in late 1795.[22] Those with radical sympathies saw much to admire in *Joan* and its author; Coleridge for example described Southey as 'the Poet [...] for the Patriot' (using the word in its radical sense).[23] Conservative readers found little – if anything – to approve of, deploring the poem's

---

19. *Anti-Jacobin review* 11 (1802), p.272, review of John Ogilvie, *Britannia* (1801). For further evidence of this proliferation see Curran, *Poetic form*, p.158-59. For a more sobering account of the 'two years' deep study, toil, and application; friendless, unnoticed, unassisted, and without ten useful books to consult' that was experienced by a would-be epic poet see [J. F. Pennie], *The Tale of a modern genius, or the Miseries of Parnassus, in a series of letters*, 3 vols (London, 1827), vol.3, p.[1].

20. Curran, *Poetic form*, p.161.

21. John Milton, 'The reason of Church government', quoted in Curran, *Poetic form*, p.159. For the relationship between eighteenth- and early-nineteenth-century writers and Milton see Dustin H. Griffin, *Regaining paradise: Milton and the eighteenth century* (Cambridge, 1986); Lucy Newlyn, *Paradise lost and the Romantic reader* (Oxford, 1993); and *Milton, the metaphysicals and Romanticism*, ed. Anthony J. Harding and Lisa Low (Cambridge, 1994).

22. Robert Southey, *Joan of Arc*, ed. Lynda Pratt, in *Poetical works, 1793-1810*, 5 vols (London, 2004), vol.1 (201). Southey himself claimed that he 'much wish[ed] to write an English epic could I find a subject, but, after beating over all the ground, can start no game', to William Taylor, 11 April 1804, *A Memoir of the life and writings of the late William Taylor of Norwich*, ed. J. W. Robberds, 2 vols (London, 1843), vol.1, p.499.

23. Coleridge to John Thelwall, 19 November [1796], *The Collected letters of Samuel Taylor Coleridge*, ed. E. L. Griggs, 6 vols (Oxford, 1956-1971), vol.1, p.258.

anti-British politics and its revisionist poetics. The *Anti-Jacobin review* (founded in late 1797), for example, was not around to criticise the first edition of *Joan*, but it got its claws into the second, revised version (published in 1798), accusing it of displaying a seditious spirit and supporting the nation's enemies – the French.[24] Other readers, such as the poet laureate Henry James Pye, a political appointee of Prime Minister William Pitt, also took up literary cudgels on behalf of the government. In 1801 Pye published his own national epic on the subject of Alfred the Great, a poem which stated its opposition to the radical productions of 'some poets of the day' (and by this he meant Southey) and which attempted to reclaim the genre for the loyalist cause.[25]

It is important, however, to realise that the debate on the nature of the national epic (and the production and publications of poems that contributed to that debate) occurred in both metropolitan and provincial contexts. In 1808, for example, the *Edinburgh review* published a letter from one of its readers. The letter described a recent event – a 'tea-drinking in the West of England at which there assisted no fewer than six epic poets'.[26] It was intended to offer another snide commentary on pretentious provincials, but its author was (in his/her cataloguing of those six poets) forced to acknowledge (no matter how ironically) the ability of that same provincial culture to contribute to the nation's well-being in what it described as these 'disastrous times'.[27] What I want to do in the final two sections of this essay is to look at the work of two writers of national epic: Ann Yearsley and John Thelwall. Both were connected through birth or residence with the 'West of England' (Bristol and the English-Welsh borders) and both might have been at the *Edinburgh*'s infamous tea-party – though neither of them actually was.

## iii. Ann Yearsley

By the time she came to publish her final collection – *The Rural lyre* – in 1796, Yearsley was a local and national celebrity.[28] Brought to public

---

24. *Anti-Jacobin review* 3 (1799), p.120-28. Southey had been one of the chief targets of the *Anti-Jacobin* since its foundation; for examples of its earlier attacks on him see *Robert Southey: the critical heritage*, ed. Lionel Madden (London, 1972), p.55-60.

25. Henry James Pye, *Alfred; an epic poem, in six books* (London, 1801), 'Dedication' (unpaginated). Pye's choice of subject was not unique: a year earlier Joseph Cottle, Southey and Coleridge's publisher and friend, had published his own *Alfred, an epic poem in twenty-four books* (London, 1800). See Lynda Pratt, 'Anglo-Saxon attitudes? Alfred the Great and the Romantic national epic', in *Literary appropriations of the Anglo-Saxons from the thirteenth to the twentieth century*, ed. Donald G. Scragg and Carole Weinberg (Cambridge, 2000), p.138-56.

26. *Edinburgh review* 11 (1808), p.362.

27. *Edinburgh review* 11 (1808), p.362.

28. See Mary Waldron, *Lactilla, milkwoman of Clifton: the life and writings of Ann Yearsley, 1753-1806* (Athens, GA, 1996).

attention in the 1780s as 'Lactilla', the poetical milk-woman and an example of provincial labouring-class genius, Yearsley's increasingly acrimonious relationship with her early patron Hannah More had earned her fame and notoriety in equal measure.[29] *The Rural lyre* was anything but an uncontroversial coda to a controversial public career. Yearsley's 'upwardly mobile' ambitions had already led to her publishing poems on public subjects such as Louis XVI, Marie-Antoinette and Stanislaw August Poniatowski, the last king of Poland.[30] *The Rural lyre* was no different. Indeed, the pastoralism invoked in the volume's title and its epigraphical confession that its author was now 'to rural scenes resigned' masked a collection that was equally polemical, political and public.[31] *The Rural lyre* encapsulated Yearsley's determination to comment on local and national affairs and to claim civic and state recognition for this. The result is a collection that is both eclectic and ambitious: regional and topographically precise poems, such as the sonnet written 'On St Vincent's rock, Bristol Hot-Wells', are juxtaposed with works on national themes, such as 'The genius of England, *On the rock of ages*, recommending order, commerce and union to the Britons'.[32] Local politics (including the Bristol Bridge Riots of 1793) are addressed in the 'Bristol elegy' and personal, patronal politics in the 'Address to friendship', pointedly dedicated to Yearsley's new patron Frederick Hervey, earl of Bristol and bishop of Derry.[33] Subjects that might seem typically female, such as motherhood, are in turn given national inflections: the long poem 'To Mira, on the care of her infant' describes the ideal mother as involved in work of national importance, educating her son for his future role in the public sphere.[34] The most direct statement of Yearsley's desire to be seen as a writer of national significance is, however, found in the poem condemned by the *Critical review* as the 'least' admirable of the entire collection – the fragmentary national epic 'Brutus'.[35]

'Brutus' is based on the legend of the descendants of the survivors of Troy coming to Britain and founding a dynasty of kings. It was the opening poem in *The Rural lyre* and was prefaced with a two-paragraph 'Argument'.[36] This began with a reminder of Brutus' early history – his

---

29. For an account of the relationship see Anne Stott, *Hannah More: the first Victorian* (Oxford, 2003), p.70-78.

30. Stott, *Hannah More*, p.77. See Yearsley's *Reflections on the death of Louis XVI* (Bristol, printed for the author, 1793), *Sequel to reflections on the death of Louis XVI* (Bristol, printed for the author, 1793) and *An Elegy on Marie Antoinette, of Austria, ci-devant queen of France: with a poem on the last interview between the king of Poland and Loraski* (Bristol, printed by J. Rudhall for the author, [1796]).

31. A. Yearsley, *The Rural lyre; a volume of poems* (London, G. G. and J. Robinson, 1796), title page.

32. Yearsley, *The Rural lyre*, p.93, 94-99.

33. Yearsley, *The Rural lyre*, p.100-109, 74-81.

34. Yearsley, *The Rural lyre*, p.113-24.

35. *Critical review*, new series 19 (1797), p.462-63 (462).

36. Yearsley, *The Rural lyre*, p.[unpaginated]-27.

Trojan ancestry and adventures prior to arriving on the shores of Britain. It then turned into a series of more personal reflections as Yearsley set out her reasons for writing and publishing her fragmentary epic:

> The Author offers this humble specimen as a spark, from whence she wishes a body of fire may arise in the imagination of some more able Poet. The Aeneid is not so eventful, nor so interesting, but that an Epic Poem from the History of England might vie with it. If the Author may presume to offer an opinion, her opinion will be, that some of the greatest geniuses of this island neglect the choice of subjects best suited to their learning and their natural powers.[37]

Late-eighteenth- and early-nineteenth-century critical opinion was more likely than not scornful of the pretensions of a female (let alone a labouring-class female) who attempted the highest of all literary forms.[38] Yearsley's 'effort' met with a different but equally disconcerting fate – almost total neglect. The *Critical review*, for example, dismissed it with a condemnatory half-sentence and passed over its 'Argument' without comment.[39] Yet, in spite of such contemporary indifference and despite its politic humility, the 'Argument' to 'Brutus' is a compelling testimony both to Yearsley's literary ambitions (even in the twilight of her literary career) and to her confidence in theorising on and for her own culture. Her brief statement on the necessity for writers of the late eighteenth century to get writing and to produce national epics affirms the provincial Yearsley's claim to the roles of epic poet, muse and cultural critic.[40]

Yearsley was, however, not as original or trail-blazing as her 'Argument' asserted. Her demand for the revitalisation of national epic came some fourteen years after William Hayley's *Essay on epic poetry* (1782) had noted the dearth of national heroic poems:

> Our gen'rous Isle, with far superior claim,
> Asks for her Chiefs the palm of Epic fame.
> In every realm where'er th' Heroic Muse
> Has deign'd her glowing spirit to infuse,
> Her tuneful Sons with civic splendor blaze,
> The honour'd Heralds of their country's praise,
> Save in our land, the nation of the earth
> Ordain'd to give the brightest Heroes birth! –

---

37. Yearsley, *The Rural lyre*, 'Argument' to 'Brutus: a fragment' (unpaginated).

38. *British critic* 18 (1802), p.518. For women writers and the epic see Adeline Johns-Putra, *Heroes and housewives: women's epic poetry and domestic ideology in the Romantic age (1770-1835)* (Bern, 2001).

39. *Critical review* 19 (1797), p.462.

40. An indication of Yearsley's knowledge of epic is shown in the catalogue of the circulating library she ran at Hotwells. The library contained editions of Dryden's translation of Virgil, Pope's translation of Homer's *Iliad* and *Odyssey* and Rowe's translation of Lucan's *Pharsalia*, alongside an edition of Milton. See *Catalogue of the books, tracts &c contained in Ann Yearsley's public library, No.4, Crescent, Hotwells* (Bristol, printed for the proprietor, 1793), p.27-28.

> By some strange fate, which rul'd each Poet's tongue,
> Her dearest Worthies yet remain unsung.[41]

By the time 'Brutus' appeared in 1796, Hayley's call for British poets to 'devote' their talents 'To Patriot Chiefs unsung' had been answered.[42] Late-eighteenth-century epic poets included James Ogden, Richard Cumberland and Robert Southey, and by the turn of the century a period of 'epomania' was well under way.[43] If Yearsley's engagement with epic was not unique, her choice of subject matter was also far from innovative. Brutus had been much used by earlier seventeenth- and eighteenth-century writers of different political persuasions, and both John Milton and Hildebrand Jacob had toyed with the idea of making him the subject of epic poems.[44] Alexander Pope had gone further, producing eight lines of verse, a 'Fragment of Brutus, an epic', that revealed his desire to use a poem on the

> Patient Chief, who lab'ring long, arriv'd
> On Britain's Shore

as the vehicle for advancing his claims to the title of 'My Countrys Poet'.[45] Brutus remained a popular subject for later eighteenth-century poets. For some would-be writers, he led to 'despondency and madness'. As Southey explained, the poet John Brown (1715-1766) had as 'a young man [...] projected an epic poem upon the story of Brutus, the Trojan, considerable fragments of which are supposed to exist. His father was of opinion that the intense earnestness with which he applied to this favourite object occasioned the derangement of intellect, which even then began to shew itself.'[46]

---

41. William Hayley, *An Essay on epic poetry; in five epistles to the Revd. Mr. Mason, with notes* (London, J. Dodsley, 1782), p.110. His influence on later writers is discussed in Curran, *Poetic form*, p.160-61.

42. Curran, *Poetic form*, p.114.

43. The term was Southey's, used by him in a letter to John Rickman (October 1800), in *The Life and correspondence of Robert Southey*, ed. Charles Cuthbert Southey, 6 vols (London, 1849-1850), vol.2, p.121. The Manchester poet James Ogden's works included *Emanuel, or Paradise regained, an epic poem* (Manchester, Sowler and Russell, 1797); a prolific dramatist, Richard Cumberland was also the author of the epics *Calvary, or the Death of Christ* (London, C. Dilly, 1792) and (with James Bland Burges) *The Exodiad* (London, 1807).

44. For Brutus' use by earlier eighteenth-century writers see Gerrard, *The Patriot opposition to Walpole*. For Brutus' importance in arguments for the heterogeneity of the British, see Howard D. Weinbrot, *Britannia's issue: the rise of British literature from Dryden to Ossian* (Cambridge, 1993), p.559-60.

45. 'Fragment of Brutus, an epic', lines 1, 8, in Alexander Pope, *Poems*, ed. John Butt (London, 1963; corrected reprint 1989), p.836.

46. Southey to Grosvenor Charles Bedford, 12 May 1805, *New letters of Robert Southey*, ed. Kenneth Curry, 2 vols (New York, 1965), vol.1, p.383. Southey's account of Browne's derangement and death was intended for the brief sketch of the poet's life and works that appeared in *Specimens of the later English poets*, ed. Robert Southey and Grosvenor Charles Bedford, 3 vols (London, 1807), but it was not used.

*The late-eighteenth-century provincial English epic*

Brown 'cut his throat 1766'.[47] Others were more fortunate. The scientist and poet Humphry Davy toyed with the idea of writing on Brutus, and the Scot John Ogilvie actually did so, in his 1801 *Britannia*.[48] Shared thematic preoccupation aside, there were other, potentially more significant, connections (though not necessarily similarities) between Yearsley and her fellow British poets of the 1790s.

The fragment of 'Brutus' published by Yearsley in 1796 is concerned with the founding of Britain. It also discloses a preoccupation with the origins of what Yearsley saw as the distinctive qualities of Britishness, an interest in the constituent parts of national identity. The poem offers a vision of Britain as ordered, successful and commercial. This state is achieved not through Brutus invading and subjugating the native Britons, but through his following the advice of Britannia's tutelary genius loci 'Liberty' and establishing a compact with the peoples he conquers. As Liberty advises him, the victor should remember:

> To yield is to deserve a throne.
> Let fall thy spear: my Britons are not slaves.[49]

(Liberty is, of course, paraphrasing the section of James Thomson's patriotic masque *Alfred* which had been set to music by Thomas Arne and become known as 'Rule Britannia'.) Yearsley's poem suggests that as well as founding a line of British rulers, Brutus also establishes a relationship between the monarch and his subject that is essentially British and that lies behind the new nation's later success. Indeed it is possible to argue that Yearsley connects Brutus (a Trojan prince married to a Trojan wife, Hermia) with his genetic (or mythologically genetic) descendant George III (who, despite his pride in being 'Briton born', was a member of the foreign house of Hanover and married to a foreign princess, Charlotte of Mecklenberg-Strelitz). Her use of national myth/history thus reaffirms both dynastic imperatives (a Protestant, Hanoverian succession) and the body politic.

---

47. *New letters*, ed. K. Curry, vol.1, p.383. Southey himself rejected the idea of writing an epic on Brutus but noted that 'The British Brutus has been too often thought upon, to remain for ever without his fame', in R. Southey, *Common-place book*, ed. John Wood Warter, 4 series (London, 1849-1850), vol.4, p.11.

48. See John Ogilvie, *Britannia: an national epic poem* (Aberdeen, 1801). Davy's interest in Brutus was encouraged by Southey, who drew attention to the legend's provincial associations, noting that although 'There is little merit or originality in it from its utter obscurity: the story is good, and it suits a Cornish man [like Davy] from the rank Corinaeus must necessarily hold', Southey to Davy, 18 October 1799, in *Fragmentary remains, literary and scientific, of Sir Humphry Davy, Bart.*, ed. John Davy (London, 1858), p.40-41. Corinaeus was Brutus' faithful follower, often compared to Achates in Virgil's *Aeneid*. Southey had previously tried to interest Davy in writing a revisionist heroic poem on Manco Capac, the legendary founder of Incan Peru, Southey to Davy, 3 August 1799, *Fragmentary remains*, ed. J. Davy, p.37.

49. Yearsley, *The Rural lyre*, p.16. The same connection between Liberty, British identity and the epic had been put forward in Hayley's *Essay*, p.114, where the national poet was advised to 'swell to Liberty the lofty note!'

## iv. John Thelwall

'Brutus' envisages a polyglot state in which potential differences are reconciled by the realisation of communal, national interest. Its vision of a Britain united and made prosperous by a benevolent constitutional monarch was, however, one that was not shared by all of Yearsley's provincially based, epic-writing contemporaries. The multifaceted nature of the national epic emerges very clearly in the work of one of the leading British radicals of the 1790s, the writer and lecturer John Thelwall. Yearsley's epic is testimony to her belief that a provincial writer had the ability and the right to comment on national affairs. Thelwall shared her preoccupation with defining the centre, but the background to the writing of his own national epic was radically different. Yearsley's career had followed a trajectory that led from provincial impoverishment and obscurity to local and then national fame, and (finally) back to provincial obscurity. By the late 1790s Thelwall, a Londoner by birth, was forced, by government legislation and the activities of a network of spies and informers, out of the metropolis and into temporary provincial exile in the 'obscure and romantic' village of Llyswen on the border between England and Wales.[50] Although he described the idyllic possibilities of his new retreat, his 'enchanted dormitory, where the agitations of political feeling might be cradled to forgetfulness' soon revealed itself to be anything but paradisal.[51] As he observed in the 'Prefatory memoir' attached to the volume that was the product of his exile in the borders, the 1801 collection *Poems, chiefly written in retirement*, the persecution that had dogged Thelwall during his public, metropolitan career followed him into provincial exile. In Llyswen, the 'Recluse [Thelwall] and his family were again exposed to all the bitterness of vulgar insult'. His farm failed, his eldest daughter died and under such intolerable pressures 'the calm enthusiasm of poetic meditation was [...] effectually dissipated.'[52] Although the closing pages of his 'Memoir' give an increasingly grim picture of Thelwall's life in the provinces, they also reveal his future, national literary ambitions and the problems that his re-entry into some semblance of public, publishing life (signalled by the publication of the 1801 collection *Poems*) created for him:

On the renewal of his intercourse with the profession of Literature, he finds, also, the press teeming, and, perhaps, the public already satiated with NATIONAL HEROICS, which, when his principal work was first projected, was *a desideratum* in English Poesy: and, what is more than all, he has to encounter prejudice and hostility in those classes of society, who alone can be expected to have a taste for such compositions, or to give them extensive encouragement. From the most advantageous field of poetical cultivation [...] he is effectually excluded.[53]

50. J. Thelwall, *Poems, chiefly written in retirement* (Hereford, 1801), p.xxxv.
51. Thelwall, *Poems*, p.xxxvi.
52. Thelwall, *Poems*, p.xxxix.
53. Thelwall, *Poems*, p.xliii.

Thelwall here presents himself as multiply disadvantaged. His enforced removal from public cultural life due to his politics has made him a latecomer to a field (the national epic) in which he would under more favourable circumstances have been an originator. The future reception of his poems, moreover, especially of his epic poem, will be affected by his personal notoriety.

The poem Thelwall is thinking about here is his national epic 'The hope of Albion, or Edwin of Northumbria', 'Specimens' of which appeared at the end of his 1801 collection.[54] The 'Memoir' tried to distance 'The hope of Albion' from the radical Thelwall of the 1790s, claiming that the 'first rough sketch' of the poem 'had been drawn up before the commencement of his political career'.[55] Yet this attempt to abstract his national epic from the personal, political and cultural conflicts of the 1790s was, at best, half-hearted. Anxious though he was about the hostile propensities of the British reading public, Thelwall was equally acutely conscious of the epic's potential as a propagandistic vehicle – its ability to effect national change. As early as 1793 his generically diverse *The Peripatetic* had included a debate (*pace* Hayley) on who, 'Of all the illustrious names in British story, [was] the character best calculated for the hero of a national epic poem'.[56] In the mid to late 1790s, moreover, Thelwall's burgeoning friendship with Coleridge guaranteed his acquaintance with one of the most infamous revisionist political epics of the time – Southey's *Joan of Arc*.[57]

Thelwall was uneasy with Southey's poem and, outwardly at least, his own attempt at an epic is more conformist and conservative.[58] It employs conventionally elevated language, supernatural machinery and great set pieces such as councils and debates. As Thelwall later acknowledged, 'Epic poetry [...] is nothing without machinery. – Mere mortal agency cannot support its dignity.'[59] Above all the subject of his poem – in direct opposition to Southey's – is avowedly national. Indeed 'The hope of Albion' engages with an Anglo-Saxon history that was increasingly

---

54. Thelwall, *Poems*, p.[175]-202.
55. Thelwall, *Poems*, p.xxxviii.
56. Thelwall, *The Peripatetic, or Sketches of the heart, of nature and society; in a series of politico-sentimental journals, in verse and prose, of the eccentric excursions of Sylvanus Theophrastus; supposed to be written by himself*, 3 vols (Southwark, printed for the author, 1793), vol 3, p.48.
57. For *Joan*'s impact on contemporary readers see Lynda Pratt, 'Patriot poetics and the Romantic national epic: placing and displacing Southey's *Joan of Arc*', in *Placing and displacing Romanticism*, ed. Peter J. Kitson (Aldershot, 2001), p.88-105.
58. Thelwall's correspondence about *Joan* does not survive, but his critique can be reconstructed from letters sent to him by Coleridge. See Coleridge's letter of 17 December [1796] sending Thelwall a mutilated copy of *Joan* 'with [...] the passage of my writing cut out', *Collected letters*, ed. E. Griggs, vol.1, p.285. By 31 December 1796 Coleridge was in 'entire accord' with him, noting 'the 9th book [Joan's descent to the underworld and vision of the future] is execrable – and the poem tho' it frequently reach the *sentimental*, does not display, the *poetical, Sublime*', *Collected letters*, ed. E. Griggs, vol.1, p.293.
59. J. Thelwall, 'Lucan's Pharsalia', *The Renovator* 21 (21 July 1821), p.208.

familiar to educated readers. Drawing upon David Hume's *History of England* (1762), it tells the story of Edwin, 'the greatest prince of the Heptarchy', who 'distinguished himself, both by his influence over the other kingdoms, and by the strict execution of justice in his own dominions'.[60] The poem's eponymous hero is the Anglo-Saxon ruler who 'reclaimed his subjects from the licentious life, to which they had been accustomed' and whose marriage to a Kentish princess led to his and his peoples' conversion to Christianity.[61] Thelwall claimed that his national epic would celebrate Edwin's 'emancipation of Northumbria [...] and consequent establishment of English liberty, and the Christian faith'.[62] It would portray how

> [Edwin] from the strife
> Of feuds and deadly factions, haply wrought
> A nation's bliss: whence union, wisdom, power,
> Spread thro' The Seven-fold Isle; and cheering lights
> Of Holy Truth – and Liberty, and Laws.[63]

Beneath its superficial conformity, however, the fragment of the poem published by Thelwall in 1801 is both extremely personal and extremely subversive, portraying a society at war with the man who is potentially its most important member. Exiled from his rightful inheritance of the kingdom of Northumbria through the machinations of his evil sister and brother-in-law, Edwin, like the hero of William Godwin's novel *Caleb Williams, or things as they* (1794), is relentlessly pursued by his enemies and forced to flee

> the fratricidal rage
> That sought his life, insatiate.[64]

The connections between Thelwall's experiences (detailed in the 'Memoir') and those of his hero were inescapable to the volume's readers. Indeed, 'The hope of Albion' translated Anglo-Saxon history into epic autobiography, as Edwin's struggles to survive parallel Thelwall's own battles in 1790s Britain with what he felt to be an illicit regime. Edwin – 'Freedom's first prototype' – has a modern double in Thelwall.[65] Just as Edwin, a true patriot and ideal national hero, opposes the false patriotism promoted by the illegal rulers of Northumbria and their cohorts (some of whom are quite literally devils in disguise), so Thelwall presents himself as an alternative to the fake, war-mongering version of 'national pride' and

---

60. David Hume, *The History of England, from the invasion of Julius Caesar to the accession of Henry VII*, 2 vols (London, A. Millar, 1762), vol.1, p.29. Thelwall's use of Hume is discussed in Michael Scrivener, *Seditious allegories: John Thelwall and Jacobin writing* (University Park, PA, 2001), p.251-52.
61. Hume, *History*, vol.1, p.29-30.
62. Thelwall, *Poems*, p.177.
63. Thelwall, *Poems*, p.[179].
64. Thelwall, *Poems*, p.[179].
65. Thelwall, *Poems*, p.183.

identity fostered by William Pitt and his supporters. In contrast to 'Brutus', where Yearsley links the Trojan prince with George III, Thelwall suggests an alternative line of descent in which true concern for the

> nation's weal
> For Albion's glory

pass from Edwin, via Alfred the Great, not to the king or ruling classes but to that most misunderstood of figures – the true patriot John Thelwall. In a similar fashion 'The hope of Albion's' sub-Miltonic allusions and versification construct an implicit epic canon, a literary genealogy in which the mantle of national bard is transferred from the seventeenth-century republican to his late-eighteenth-century counterpart – Thelwall.[66]

What can be learned from Yearsley and Thelwall's epics, or rather, epic fragments? Both are proof of the revitalisation of the epic as a key literary genre during the closing years of the eighteenth century, and both demonstrate the participation of male and female poets in contemporary debates about cultural, political and national identities.[67] They prove that Francis Jeffrey was in some ways right to be concerned about (or at least to recognise) the ambitions of provincial writers, and that in this period poets writing from the geographical margins (whether through choice or personal expediency) were asserting their abilities and rights to comment upon the centre. This essay has concentrated on two non-canonical authors, writers whom conventional literary history has placed on the margins of criticism. Moving them to the centre of the debate not only allows for a reconsideration of cultural priorities (that is, 'marginal' writers and genres being seen as central), but also highlights the (literary) historical instability, malleability and changeability of terms such as centre and periphery.

---

66. Thelwall's interest in 'The hope of Albion' continued, see Scrivener, *Seditious allegories*, p.252, n.39. The complete version (if it ever existed) does not survive. Sections appeared in *The Renovator* 23 (29 September 1821), p.235-40. Thelwall also incorporated readings from it into his public lectures on the significance of elocution in forming the national character. Francis Jeffrey described how one such recitation in Edinburgh reduced the audience to fits of laughter, in *Observations on Mr Thelwall's letter to the editor of the Edinburgh review* (Edinburgh, 1804), p.5. For Thelwall's public quarrel with Jeffrey, see Scrivener, *Seditious allegories*, p.278-80.

67. Thelwall's continued interest in the epic as a vehicle for national regeneration – and his promotion of this message in the provinces – is shown in his *The Trident of Albion, an epic effusion; and an oration on the influence of elocution on martial enthusiasm; with an address to the shade of Nelson [...] to which is prefixed, an introductory discourse on the nature and objects of elocutionary science; and the studies and accomplishments connected with the faculty of oral expression* (Liverpool, 1805).

PETER HANNS REILL

# The Enlightenment from the German periphery: Johann Herder's reinterpretation of the Enlightenment

THE theme of the Enlightenment and its peripheries raises a number of perplexing problems that this volume addresses: what is a periphery and, more importantly, what is Enlightenment? What reactions to the Enlightenment core were available to those we now judge as peripheral to it, or who at the time considered themselves at the Enlightenment's periphery? What interactions between the Enlightenment core and the periphery were possible and how did they play out? A look at Johann Gottfried Herder can help us investigate these questions. Herder certainly can be considered a peripheral figure in both of the above senses, as someone we see as coming from the periphery and as one who considered his early education backward and misplaced. Born of extremely modest means, without easy access to advanced education, Herder spent his youth and early manhood in the easternmost regions of Central Europe, the area in which German, Russian and Baltic culture met and interacted. Trained at Königsberg (itself a provincial university), he found his first position as a pastor and schoolteacher in Riga, then controlled by Russia. Though he experienced some success there, Herder quickly made enemies and in 1769 abruptly quit his position and boarded a ship bound for France, beguiled by the prospect of enriching his view of the world by experiencing firsthand the most advanced intellectual forces of the time. Herder charted his confrontation with, and reaction to, the Enlightenment core in his fascinating *Journal meiner Reise im Jahr 1769*, written for himself and only published after his death.

The *Journal* begins with a long lament about how Herder had misspent his youth grubbing in books and writing learned, dull and contentious pieces that did little to change the world: 'Ich hätte meine Jahre geniessen, gründliche, reelle Wißenschaft kennen, und Alles anwenden gelernt, was ich lernte. Ich wäre nicht ein Tintenfaß von gelehrter Schriftstellerei, nicht ein Wörterbuch von Künsten und Wißenschaften geworden, die ich nicht gesehen habe und nicht verstehe: ich wäre nicht ein Repositorium voll Papier und Bücher geworden, das nur in die

Studierstube gehört.'[1] His voyage to the West would, he believed, rectify these early mistakes. Rather than wallow in abstruse knowledge as he had done in the East, he would learn about and appreciate life in France and in the West. There, he could concentrate upon 'real subjects': he would learn to speak French, study history, natural history, mathematics, drawing, acquire the ability to mix with people and, in the process, enrich his talent by developing a lively and engaging mode of representation.[2] This voyage would enable him to capture the correct understanding of life in all of its manifestations and to use this new understanding to act in the world, to change it: 'Zu thun, um die Barberei zu zerstören, die Unwißenheit auszurotten, die Cultur und Freiheit auszubreiten, ein zweiter Zwinglius, Calvin und Luther, dieser Provinz zu werden?' Armed with these new insights, Herder thought he could emerge as Livonia's legislator.[3] In so doing, he believed he would demonstrate 'welch ein Großes Thema zu zeigen, daß man, um zu seyn, was man seyn soll, weder Jude, noch Araber, noch Grieche, noch Wilder, noch Märtrer, noch Wallfahrter seyn müsse; sondern eben der aufgeklärte, unterrichtete, feine, vernünfttige, gebildete, Tugendhafte, geniessende Mensch, den Gott auf der Stuffe unsrer Cultur fördert'.[4]

Obviously, Herder considered this voyage essential to prepare him for this enormous task. The question is: how did he react to the challenge posed by his confrontation with the Enlightenment core? One can envision at least two types of possible response. The first and often most obvious would be to imitate what he saw, heard and read. That is, to become a 'German' Voltaire, Montesquieu or Rousseau. An example of such a response was given by Prince Leopold III Friedrich Franz von Anhalt-Dessau (commonly referred to as Franz), Herder's contemporary, who after an intensive visit to England sought to recreate English culture in Wörlitz. There Franz constructed a Palladian country house and an English garden modelled after the leading English gardens of the period, and attempted to introduce the type of advanced husbandry one associated with England. Visiting Wörlitz, one felt as though one had been magically transported to an English country manor looked over by

---

1. Herder, *Journal*, p.9-10: 'I would have benefited from my years of study, acquiring solid, real knowledge and applying everything that I learned. I would not have become an inkwell filled with learned writings, not an encyclopedia of arts and sciences that I haven't seen and don't understand, a repository stuffed with papers and books that belongs only in the study.'

2. Herder, *Journal*, p.9, 121-22.

3. Herder, *Journal*, p.28: his goal was 'to destroy barbarism, to eradicate ignorance, and expand culture and freedom to become a second Zwingli, Calvin and Luther to this province'.

4. Herder, *Journal*, p.31: 'that one in order to be what one should be, did not have to be a Jew, or an Arab, a Greek, or a primitive, a martyr or a pilgrim, but rather the enlightened, informed, fine, rational, educated, virtuous and passionate person that God demands for our level of culture'.

an English high aristocrat.[5] Herder's disdain for such imitative responses was expressed in his evaluation of Russia in the *Journal*. No nation, he claimed, was more adept at imitation than the Russians. Because of that, however, after successfully imitating Western models, they believe they know everything and go no further. For that reason they always remain bunglers in all things, incapable of discovering and cultivating their own original genius.[6] This disdain for 'mere' imitation also explains Herder's later ambivalent stance towards Weimar neo-Classicism with its thorough-going adulation of Greek models.

The second and more difficult response to the core's challenge would be critically and creatively to confront what one experienced and attempt to reconceptualise it in a manner more in line with one's own lived experience. This was Herder's response. The *Journal*, written after his journey,[7] makes it clear that Herder, after his initial confrontation with French culture, rejected imitation and chose the second path. Though composed after the event, the *Journal* clearly reveals the tension Herder felt between admiration and inferiority as he confronted French culture. In many places he clearly expressed his admiration for the leading figures of the French Enlightenment; he wished to see the world with Montesquieu's eyes, to understand nature as did Buffon, to write with Rousseau's fire and to institutionalise Rousseau's love for liberty.[8] Herder desired to acquire 'Von allem, was zum Jahrhundert Frankreichs gehört, lebedinge Begriffe zu haben, um z.E. einen Clement, einen de La Place, einen Freron recht verstehen zu können!'[9] At the same time, each new experience with French culture increased Herder's feeling of being unappreciated and by extension intensified his critique of what he thought was the French penchant to minimise the achievements of others and set up French culture as a universal model for Europe.[10] For the young Herder, French culture had become a hollow shell; despite its marvellously fluid and capable language it had disintegrated into a mere

5. On Leopold III Friedrich Franz see Maiken Umbach, 'Visual culture, scientific images and German small-state politics in the late Enlightenment', *Past and present* 158 (1998), p.110-45 and her 'Franz of Anhalt-Dessau and England: the Wörlitz landscape garden and anti-Prussian politics in the late Enlightenment', doctoral dissertation, University of Cambridge, 1996.

6. Herder, *Journal*, p.20.

7. The *Journal* was written after the event; it was a reflection of what the whole trip meant rather than a traditional journal. Hence, it serves as an important document charting Herder's intellectual development. It is fascinating because in it he outlined in rough form most of the literary projects he later undertook during his lifetime, clearly an indication of the central importance his personal confrontation with the 'core' had for him.

8. Herder, *Journal*, p.79: 'da muß man aber mit dem Geist eines Montesquieu sehen; mit der feurigen Feder Roußeaus schreiben...'

9. Herder, *Journal*, p.121-22: 'Above all, to acquire living ideas of what belongs to the French century in order, for example, to be able to understand correctly a Clement, a de La Place, a Freron!'

10. Rainer Wisbert, *Das Bildungsdenken des Jungen Herder: Interpretationen der Schrift 'Journal meiner Reise im Jahr 1769'* (Frankfurt, 1987), p.407.

concern for gallantry, taste and egoism, where truth was sacrificed for novelty, sound logic for superficiality, and genius ignored, in fact even scorned.[11] France had become a nation of compilers, textbook writers, encyclopedists. In this sense, France was no better than the east-central Europe from which Herder had fled, with the major exception that the French knew how to express and enact good taste. The *Encyclopédie*, considered by many to be France's triumphal achievement, was nothing, Herder proclaimed, but a sign of its degeneration. Instead of composing original works, the French, including D'Alembert and Diderot, only concern themselves with excerpts: 'Jetzt macht man schon Encyklopädien: ein D'Alembert und Diderot selbst lassen sich dazu herunter: und eben dies Buch was den Franzosen ihr Triumph ist, ist für mich das erste Zeichen zu ihrem Verfall. Sie haben nichts zu schreiben und machen also *Abregés, Dictionaires, Histoires, Vocabulaires, Esprits, Encyclopedieen*, u.s.w. Die Originalwerke fallen weg.'[12] Herder's alienation was mirrored in his remarks concerning his own failure to establish close relations with the French, many of whom, Herder believed, considered him a barbarian because of his German ways. His attempts at forging viable relations were a disaster, plunging him into an abyss: 'Und in welche Kluft stürzest du dich alsdenn von Beschämungen, Mißvergnügen, unaufgeräumten Stunden, verfehlten Visiten, müssigen Tagen?'[13]

Herder's *Journal* contains a long indictment of France and French culture, but it goes beyond a merely negative evaluation. Herder internalised his feelings of inferiority and made them part of his attempt to restate and reinterpret basic Enlightenment positions. Guiding this endeavour were Herder's twin assumptions that every nation, every way of living, every class of people had its own genius, its own set of values, and his idea that the Enlightenment was not a set of fixed doctrines but rather a process, a means of discovery: 'Alle Aufklärung ist nie Zweck, sondern immer Mittel; wird sie jenes so ists Zeichen daß sie aufgehört hat, dieses zu seyn.'[14] Individuality and process were crucial to a correct understanding of life and the world, necessary for acting in the world. These two guiding principles led Herder to propose an epistemology and programme that drew their nourishment from thinkers as diverse as

11. The extensive critique of France and French culture is advanced in the *Journal* on p.91-121. It far exceeds in breadth and vehemence any of Herder's critical commentaries on other cultures, such as Holland, Russia and England.

12. Herder, *Journal*, p.91: 'Now everybody is writing Encyclopaedias; even D'Alembert and Diderot demeaned themselves with this activity. And this work, that for the French is a success, is for me the first sign of their decadence. They have nothing to say, and that is why they just write *Abregés, Dictionnaires, Histoires, Vocabulaires, Esprits, Encyclopédies*... There are no more original works.'

13. Herder, *Journal*, p.120: 'And in what kind of an abyss of blame, displeasure, wasted time, forgotten appointments, and lost days do you fall?'

14. Herder, *Journal*, p.91: 'Enlightenment is never an end but always a means. If it becomes the former it is a sign that it has ceased.'

Bacon, Spinoza, Hume, Montesquieu, Maupertuis, the pre-critical Kant and Buffon, to name but a few. His position incorporated and developed the important shifts – symbolised by these major figures – that were taking place in Enlightenment thought during the second half of the century.

Herder's goal was to chart the way in which life in all of its manifestations could be apprehended, which would lead to a better understanding of humanity and its needs. In articulating this programme, Herder believed that nature formed the basic analogue for understanding culture and humanity. What operated in nature was similar to what operated in culture. Thus, Herder would proclaim: 'Die ganze Menschengeschichte ist eine reine Naturgeschichte menschlicher Kräfte, Handlungen und Triebe nach Ort und Zeit.'[15] This analogy was founded on Herder's idea that everything in the world was ordered by eternal principles. Though first proclaiming it in the *Journal*, Herder continued to develop this idea, leading him during his lifetime to a long and painstaking study of the major natural philosophers of the period, especially those who concerned themselves with living nature. Driven by this assumption, Herder sought to elevate the study of humanity to what we today would call a science. This meant that one should steer between the twin shoals of mere fact collection and overly speculative reason, combining elements of both in 'lebendigen Känntnißen', and producing 'eine Experimental Seelenlehre der obern Kräfte'.[16]

But what did this new science or philosophy look like? Herder was drawn to the type of thought I have elsewhere described as Enlightenment Vitalism,[17] which, as formulated in the second half of the eighteenth century, posited the existence of active or self-activating forces in living nature. Herder, as his Vitalist guides, envisioned nature as a teeming interaction of drives, sympathies and elective affinities, revolving around each other in a developmental dance. With the re-introduction of active forces in nature, Herder, as others, was drawn to reassess the basic methodological and analytic categories of scientific investigation and explanation. The new conception of matter dissolved the strict distinction between observer and observed, since both were related in a much larger conjunction of living nature. Relation or elective affinity ('Verwandschaft') replaced mechanical aggregation as one of the defining principles of matter. In the world of living nature, each constituent part

---

15. J. Herder, *Ideen zur Philosophie der Geschichte des Menschheit, Sämmtliche Werke*, ed. Bernhard Suphan, 33 vols (Berlin, 1877-1913), vol.14, p.145, henceforward *SWS*: 'The whole of human history is a pure natural history of powers, actions and drives according to place and time.'

16. Herder, *Journal*, p.42, 55: 'living knowledge', leading to 'an experimental psychology of the higher powers'.

17. Peter Hanns Reill, *Vitalizing nature in the Enlightenment* (Berkeley, CA, and Los Angeles, CA, 2005).

of an organised body was both cause and effect of the other parts. All were symbiotically linked. Further, with the re-introduction of telos onto living nature, Herder and Enlightenment Vitalists made it the efficient cause of development. An explanation for something's existence took the form of a narrative modelled upon the concept of 'genesis', in which a body evolves through stages from a point of creation. Unique creation and true qualitative transformation were central to Herder's vision of nature: hence his constant concern with growth and decay, images and metaphors with which he constantly populated his works. In them all, he constantly strove to locate individual existence within the continuum of growth and decay, trying to decipher how and when 'original' cultures were born and what led to their decay and death.

This shift in natural philosophy challenged Herder to construct an epistemology capable of justifying and validating it. Herder assumed that active life forces could not be seen directly. They were similar to Newton's idea of gravity – basically occult forces. At best such forces could only be detected by their effects, by signs whose meaning could only be grasped indirectly. This language of nature re-introduced the topos of locating essential reality as something hidden within a body. That which was immediately observable was superficial: hence Herder's critique of the transparency of the French language and its expositional clarity. For him no one can describe with better clarity than the French, but their descriptions only touch the surface, only show 'daß sie Erziehung haben'. What they miss is the portrayal of 'des Sturms der Wahrheit und Empfindung'.[18] For Herder, understanding entailed a progressive descent into the shadowy depths of observed reality, using signs as the markers to chart the way.

The basic epistemological problem, therefore, was to understand the meaning of these signs and how to perceive the interaction of the individual yet linked forces without collapsing one in the other. Herder in confronting this problem called for a form of understanding that combined the individualised elements of nature's variety into a harmonic conjunction that recognised nature's unity and diversity. The methods he proposed to accomplish this were analogical reasoning and comparative analysis. Analogical reasoning became the functional replacement for mathematical analysis. With it, one could discover similar properties or tendencies between dissimilar things that approximated natural laws, without dissolving the particular in the general. Herder's use of analogical reasoning was mind-boggling, ranging over the whole of creation. Already in the *Journal*, his fascination with analogical reasoning was apparent. In it he expressed the desire that consumed him during his whole life, that of comprehending the vast sweep of human history, the 'Universalgeschichte der Bildung der Welt',[19] which, he believed, could only be comprehended

---

18. Herder, *Journal*, p.108: 'they are educated'; 'the storm of truth and sensation'.
19. Herder, *Journal*, p.17: 'universal history of the formation of humanity'.

through analogies.[20] Comparative analysis reinforced the concentration upon analogical reasoning. It allowed one to consider nature as composed of systems having their own character and dynamics, yet demonstrating similarities not revealed by the concentration upon outward form. Thus, for example, in the *Journal*, Herder employed a comparison with the migration of herrings to highlight the history of the barbarian invasions,[21] or, to cite another example, he drew a comparison and an analogy between life on a ship and forms of government.[22]

In pursuing this programme, Herder believed one could produce a higher form of understanding by continually nourishing a concentration upon the particular with a concern for the general. He called this form of understanding *Anschauung* and employed the image of mediation to characterise its operation, letting each element reinforce and modify the other. In this operation, however, understanding passed through a third, hidden and informing agent that was, in effect, the ground upon which all reality rested. Herder characterised this middle element, opaque, yet essential, as the *Haupttypus*, which harmonically united the polarities of life in the middle, the place where both extremes enhance and reinforce each other.

It is for this reason that the image of the middle and its correlates play such a central role in Herder's thought. The middle served as centre of reality and the place from which true action flowed. He inscribed it upon the earth's history, defining it and its human inhabitants as a 'Mittelgeschöpf'.[23] For him, the turn towards the middle was part of nature's law, the place where everything good and beautiful was produced, either in the geographical sense as the middle realm, or more importantly in the realm of freedom, in which freedom is attained only by the juxtaposition of opposites. But every attained level of freedom contained within itself its own negation for, given the relativity of all cultures, nothing absolute could be achieved. Each age or nation had to work to realise its own form of freedom, which was always threatened with degeneration, as he believed France now was. Hence the progress of culture, which, he affirmed, took place in fits and starts, the achieved maxima never totally transferred to other cultures, but capable of serving as analogues to that which later can be achieved. However difficult progress may be, Herder, in good Enlightenment fashion, assumed the goal of all development to be the expansion of freedom and humanity. Freedom meant individual self-determination and personal autonomy, which Herder defined as 'nichts als Humanität d.i. Vernunft und Billigkeit in allen Classen, in allen Geschäften der Menschen'.[24] Herder believed this goal to be dictated by

20. Herder, *Journal*, p.19.
21. Herder, *Journal*, p.15.
22. Herder, *Journal*, p.19.
23. *SWS*, vol.12, p.65: 'a middle creature'.
24. *SWS*, vol.14, p.230: 'as humanity, that is reason and justice in all classes, in all human activities'.

nature, for 'Zu diesem offenbaren Zweck, sahen wir, ist unsre Natur organisiert.'[25] Thus freedom's expansion was possible because it constituted an implicit part of our natural condition, but it could only be achieved by action, by consciously pursuing the desire to expand reason and justice, according to one's time and place.

Herder has often been stereotyped as a major critic of the Enlightenment, as a leading proponent of what Isaiah Berlin has called the 'Counter-Enlightenment'.[26] This position can only be maintained if Enlightenment is defined as an end, as a single set of positive beliefs. When seen as an investigative imperative, however, as a means rather than an end, then it should be obvious that Herder's reaction to France and French culture was not a denial of the Enlightenment but an intense reformulation of its basic elements carried out within its general boundaries by a peripheral figure whose alienation resulted in a rethinking of positions that had acquired the status of received wisdom. In this sense, Herder provides a classic example of the creative process by which outsiders mastered, transformed and advanced the Enlightenment.

---

25. *SWS*, vol.14, p.208: 'To this manifest purpose, we have seen, is our nature organized.'

26. See Berlin, 'The Counter-Enlightenment', and *Three critics of the Enlightenment*, p.168-242.

# Summaries

## SIMON DAVIES
Whither/wither France: Voltaire's view from Ferney

Voltaire was an adventurer. He travelled both the physical and intellectual highways of Europe. In addition to inventing his own name of Voltaire, he also sought to invent a new destiny for a re-invigorated France. Paradoxically, France contributed to the Enlightenment through being unenlightened. It was from the geographical periphery of his homeland that Voltaire, a Parisian in exile at Ferney, conducted his campaign to enlighten his compatriots and humanity in general. He recognised that France had benefited from advances in various fields abroad and could profit equally from the enlightened regimes of rulers elsewhere.

## GRAHAM GARGETT
French periphery, European centre: eighteenth-century Geneva and its contribution to the Enlightenment

Despite its tiny size, eighteenth-century Geneva's role in the French Enlightenment was seminal. Inflamed by D'Alembert's *Encyclopédie* article 'Genève', political dissension there eventually (in 1766) necessitated political intervention by France, Bern and Zurich, the outside resonance of this increased by the fact that Jean-Jacques Rousseau was closely associated with one of the city's opposing groups, the *bourgeois* or *représentants*. In religious terms, Calvin's city had paradoxically become theologically 'liberal', though its pastors – including the most prominent at the time of the Enlightenment, Jacob Vernet – denied this. Above all, the presence of Voltaire and the connection with Rousseau focused European attention on the minuscule city's ambiguous contribution to progressive thought, in both politics and religion.

## MICHAEL BROWN
Was there an Irish Enlightenment? The case of the Anglicans

According to the historiography, the Irish Enlightenment does not exist. Ireland has remained outside the purview of the students of the movement. Yet this article proposes that an Irish variation on the European Enlightenment did exist. By configuring Enlightenment as a set of intellectual methods, rather than as a cluster of practical conclusions, Irish thinkers and writers are seen as fully engaged in exploring the possibilities of the Enlightenment for understanding Ireland's peculiar confessional circumstances. Taking the Anglican community as a case study, the essay maps the attitudes taken towards the Enlightenment, from Jonathan Swift's trenchant disavowal to John Toland's subversive playful acceptance. In doing so the essay reflects on the reach of the Enlightenment into cultural peripheries, and the limits of the category's application in comprehending cultural and intellectual developments in the eighteenth century.

## JOHN ROBERTSON
Political economy and the 'feudal system' in Enlightenment Naples: outline of a problem

Neapolitan participation in the Enlightenment may have been too strong to be called 'peripheral', but at least one feature of Neapolitan society, the persistence of 'feudal' relations between lords and peasantry, confronted its thinkers with problems at the outer reaches of their analytical range. This essay examines the efforts of Neapolitan political economists to come to terms with the 'feudal system', which they sought to do by adapting concepts drawn from French economic writing. The essay concludes that the resulting conceptual resources were ill adapted to grasping and identifying solutions to the problems.

## MARIE-CHRISTINE SKUNCKE
Jean-Jacques Rousseau in Swedish eyes around 1760

Geographical peripheries were not passive receivers of ideas; as Robert Darnton writes, 'the foreigners talked back'. In mid-eighteenth-century Sweden, Rousseau's early works were largely rejected by the elites. His critique of civilisation in the two discourses collided head-on with the prevailing ideology in Sweden, which combined a belief in science and progress with an adherence to established religion. The scientist Linneaus, the top politician C. F. Scheffer and the publicist C. C. Gjörwell dismissed Rousseau's discourses. The woman poet H. C. Nordenflycht attacked his view of women in the *Lettre à D'Alembert*. In their eyes, Enlightenment was on their side, not on Rousseau's.

## ORSOLYA SZAKÁLY
Enlightened self-interest: the development of an entrepreneurial culture within the Hungarian elite

It is clear from the late-eighteenth-century Hungarian discourse that 'enlightenment', although never clearly defined, was seen as a weapon against superstition, which was identified as the main cause of Hungary's relative backwardness within Europe. The Hungarian Enlightenment is normally presented as a primarily literary movement. The reason for this is the continuation and spectacular success of the language movement well after our period, culminating in 1844 when Hungarian became the official language of Hungary. Understandably, this success also resulted in a large volume of secondary literature on the topic, which has tilted the Hungarian scholarly interpretation of the Enlightenment one-sidedly in favour of literary output. The present chapter attempts to set the balance right by examining enlightened economic discourse in Hungary. By doing so it aims to demonstrate how enlightened Hungarians picked and chose from the large corpus of works associated with the Enlightenment, and to show that they were almost entirely motivated by practical considerations.

## MARTIN FITZPATRICK

The view from Mount Pleasant: Enlightenment in late-eighteenth-century Liverpool

This article examines the relationship between commerce, fashionable culture and Enlightenment in the rapidly growing port of Liverpool. In the later eighteenth century, Enlightenment ideas placed strains on what had been a relatively harmonious civic polity. They were particularly manifest amongst a nexus of religious dissenters and medical practitioners, who presented a challenge to the local establishment in politics, religion and commerce. In William Roscoe they found a champion of fashionable culture and enlightened reform. By the time the slave trade was abolished in 1807 many of the tensions were resolved. Local pride in a remarkable range of civic endeavours enabled Liverpudlians to regard themselves as citizens both of the world and of their own distinctive community.

## SIMON BURROWS

Grub Street revolutionaries: marginal writers at the Enlightenment's periphery?

Although some scholars dismiss London's colony of scandal-mongering French exile blackmail pamphleteers (*libellistes*) – a motley collection of adventurers, renegade diplomats, defrocked clergy and petty criminals – as peripheral to the French Enlightenment, they have in recent decades through Robert Darnton's 'Grub Street theory' assumed a centrality to Enlightenment and revolutionary studies disproportionate to their numbers and the intellectual fecundity of their works. This essay reappraises their importance, suggesting that although their pre-revolutionary role has been misunderstood and exaggerated, after 1789 rhetorical styles, images and fears supplied by London's Grub Street became embedded at the heart of the revolutionary script.

## ULTÁN GILLEN
Varieties of Enlightenment: the Enlightenment and Irish political culture in the age of revolutions

Poverty and the lack of great Enlightenment thinkers in the last quarter of the eighteenth century produced a feeling that Ireland languished on the periphery of the Enlightenment among contemporaries and historians. Irish political culture, however, simultaneously proclaimed Ireland's constitution, derived from the principles of 1688, Europe's most enlightened. Enlightenment ideas, language and practice permeated Ireland's political thought and public sphere. Differing interpretations of Enlightenment principles justified a range of political positions, reactionary as well as revolutionary. The role of the Enlightenment in Irish political culture challenges assumptions about where contemporaries situated centre and periphery in the Enlightenment.

## GABRIEL SÁNCHEZ ESPINOSA
An *ilustrado* in his province: Jovellanos in Asturias

Jovellanos, perhaps the leading figure of the Spanish Enlightenment, returned briefly to his home region of Asturias, geographically isolated and economically backward, in the spring of 1782, after an absence of fourteen years. Subsequently, he resided in Gijón during his two periods of exile from the court between the summer of 1790 and the autumn of 1797, and the autumn of 1798 and the winter of 1801. Through his private diaries and correspondence, we can follow both his indefatigable activity to fulfil his official commissions to reform Asturian infrastructure and his unstoppable and enthusiastic efforts to foster and create enlightened institutions on a regional scale that would awaken consciences to both the utilitarian and the utopian goals of the Enlightenment.

## RICHARD BUTTERWICK
Between Anti-Enlightenment and enlightened Catholicism: provincial preachers in late-eighteenth-century Poland-Lithuania

The peripheries of the Enlightenment may be pursued not only spatially and temporally, but also in medium and message. This essay explores the borderlands between Enlightenment and Anti-Enlightenment, exemplified by the discourse of two preachers in the late-eighteenth-century Grand Duchy of Lithuania. These sermons testify to the permeation of Enlightenment priorities, assumptions and discourse even into trenchant critiques of the 'enlightened age' and hitherto transcendental spheres, in the provincial setting of the diocese of Wilno. In hailing the Constitution of 3 May 1791 Michał Karpowicz and Jan Nepomucen Kossakowski proclaimed Poland's equality with other nations in terms of 'enlightenment' ('oświecenie'), and thus her emergence from Europe's intellectual periphery.

## SIMON DIXON

'Prosveshchenie': Enlightenment in eighteenth-century Russia

Whereas others have attempted to define the Russian Enlightenment in objective terms, this essay takes a subjective approach by examining contemporary Russian usages of the word 'enlightenment' ('prosveshchenie' / просвещение) in a variety of texts ranging from the sermon to satirical verse, and from published journalism to private correspondence. It suggests that, although the word was occasionally used to denote critical, rationalist, reformist opinion, such usages were rare. Russian writers never self-consciously subscribed to a movement we could call 'the Russian Enlightenment', and by the time they began more frequently to refer to a philosophical or an enlightened age, in the 1790s and beyond, their intentions were usually pejorative.

## FIONA CLARK

The *Gazeta de Literatura de México* and the edge of reason: when is a periphery not a periphery?

This study examines the role and work of the Mexican priest and polymath, José Antonio Alzate y Ramírez (1733-1799), focusing particularly on his final periodical publication, the *Gazeta de Literatura de México* (1788-1795). The work begins by briefly exploring the question of national identity in Alzate's publications, as well as outlining his involvement in eighteenth-century scientific networks in Mexico and in Europe. In an attempt to find a new approach to our understanding of Alzate within this international republic of learning, the author adopts the 'centre/periphery' framework outlined by the sociologist Edward Shils. Through this process the article highlights how the changing axes of relationship dictated the ambiguous perception of concepts such as centre and periphery.

## LYNDA PRATT

Tea and national history? Ann Yearsley, John Thelwall and the late-eighteenth-century provincial English epic

The rehabilitation of English provincial culture is an essential part of any examination of the construction of literary and national identities in the late eighteenth and early nineteenth centuries. Using two fragmentary epic poems – one by Ann Yearsley, the other by John Thelwall – this essay argues that contemporary critics such as Francis Jeffrey were right to be concerned about (or at least to recognise) the ambitions of provincial writers, and that in this period poets writing from the geographical margins (whether through choice or personal expediency) were asserting their abilities and rights to comment upon the centre. The examples of Yearsley and Thelwall, moreover, also demonstrate that moving writers whom conventional literary history has placed on the margins of criticism to the centre of the debate not only allows for a reconsideration of cultural priorities (that is 'marginal' writers and genres being seen as central) – but also highlights the (literary) historical instability, malleability and changeability of terms such as centre and periphery.

## PETER HANNS REILL

The Enlightenment from the German periphery: Johann Herder's reinterpretation of the Enlightenment

The theme of the Enlightenment and its peripheries raises the question of what a periphery is and, more importantly, what Enlightenment is. An evaluation of the evolving thought of Herder, someone raised in the east of Central Europe with modest means, provides a useful case study for addressing this question. Herder set out for France to encounter what he took to be the advanced thinking of his day and recorded his reactions in a journal. While appreciating aspects of French culture, he refused to follow it slavishly as it tended to disregard the achievements of other cultures, setting itself up as a universal model. Herder saw Enlightenment as a process, rather than a product, and stressed the value of analogical reasoning.

# Bibliography

## General works and collections (including France and Geneva)

Adams, Geoffrey, *The Huguenots and French opinion 1685-1787* (Waterloo and Ontario, 1991).

Alembert, Jean D', *Mélanges de littérature, d'histoire, et de philosophie*, 5 vols (Amsterdam, Zacharie Chatelain & fils, 1763-1767).

Aston, Nigel, *Christianity and revolutionary Europe c.1750-1830* (Cambridge, 2002).

Baczko, Bronisław, 'Enlightenment', in *A Critical dictionary of the French Revolution*, ed. François Furet and Mona Ozouf (English translation: Cambridge, MA, 1988), p.659-68.

Barber, William H., 'Voltaire and Quakerism: Enlightenment and the inner light', *SVEC* 24 (1963), p.81-109.

Beales, Derek, *Enlightenment and reform in eighteenth-century Europe* (London, 2005).

—, 'Philosophical kingship and enlightened despotism', in *Enlightenment and reform in eighteenth-century Europe* (London and New York, 2005), p.28-59.

—, *Prosperity and plunder: European Catholic monasteries in the age of revolution, 1650-1815* (Cambridge, 2003).

—, 'Religion and culture', in *The Eighteenth century*, ed. T. C. W. Blanning, *Short Oxford history of Europe*, 12 vols (Oxford, 2000), vol.8, p.131-77.

Benoît, Daniel, *L'Etat religieux du protestantisme français dans la seconde moitié du XVIII*ᵉ *siècle* (Montauban, 1909).

Berlin, Isaiah, 'The Counter-Enlightenment' (1973), reprinted in I. Berlin, *Against the current: essays in the history of ideas*, ed. Henry Hardy (London, 1997), p.1-24.

—, *Three critics of the Enlightenment: Vico, Hamaan, Herder*, ed. Henry Hardy (Princeton, NJ, 2000).

Bertrand, Pierre, *Genève et la Révocation de l'Edit de Nantes* (Geneva, 1935).

Besterman, Theodore, *Voltaire* (London and Harlow, 1969).

Bireley, Robert, *The Refashioning of Catholicism, 1450-1700* (Basingstoke, 1999).

Blanc, Olivier, *Les Espions de la Révolution et de l'Empire* (Paris, 1995).

Blanning, T. C. W., *The Culture of power and the power of culture: Old Regime Europe 1660-1789* (Oxford, 2002).

Boncerf, Pierre-François, *Les Inconvénients des droits féodeaux* (London, 1776).

Boucher, Gwenaëlle, 'La poésie philosophique de Voltaire', *SVEC* 2003:05, p.1-286.

Boutaric, Edgar (ed.), *Correspondance secrète inédite de Louis XV, sur la politique étrangère*, 2 vols (Paris, 1866).

Brandli, Fabrice, 'Le résident de France à Genève (1679-1798): institution et pratiques de la diplomatie', *Dix-huitième siècle* 37 (2005), p.49-68.

Brockliss, L. W. B., *Calvet's web: Enlightenment and the Republic of Letters in eighteenth-century France* (Oxford, 2002).

Brown, Andrew, and Ulla Kölving, 'Voltaire and Cramer?', in *Le Siècle de Voltaire: hommage à René Pomeau*, ed. Christiane Mervaud and Sylvain Menant (Oxford, 1987), p.149-83.

Burnand, Léonard, *Necker et l'opinion publique* (Paris, 2004).

295

Burrows, Simon, *Blackmail, scandal, and revolution: London's French libellistes, 1758-1792* (Manchester, 2006).

–, 'Despotism without bounds: the French secret police and the silencing of dissent in London, 1760-1790', *History* 89 (2004), p.525-48.

–, *French exile journalism and European politics, 1792-1814* (Woodbridge, 2000).

–, 'The innocence of Jacques-Pierre Brissot', *Historical journal* 46 (2003), p.843-71.

–, 'A literary low-life reassessed: Charles Théveneau de Morande in London, 1769-1791', *Eighteenth-century life* 22 (1998), p.76-94.

Candaux, Jean-Daniel, et al. (ed.), *Deux astronomes genevois dans la Russie de Catherine II: journaux de voyage en Laponie russe de Jean-Louis Pictet et Jacques-André Mallet pour observer le passage de Vénus devant le disque solaire, 1768-1769* (Geneva, 2005).

Candolle, Augustin-Pyramus de, *Mémoires et souvenirs (1778-1841)*, ed. Jean-Daniel Candaux and Jean-Marc Drouin (Geneva and Paris, 2004).

Cassirer, Ernst, *The Philosophy of the Enlightenment* (1932; English translation: Cambridge, 1953).

Ceitac, Jane, *Voltaire et l'affaire des Natifs: un aspect de la carrière humanitaire du patriarche de Ferney* (Geneva, 1956).

Cellerier, J.-E., *L'Académie de Genève* (Geneva, 1872).

Chadwick, Owen, *The Reformation*, The Pelican history of the Church 3 (Harmondsworth, 1964; reprinted 1970).

Charpentier, Louis, et al., *La Bastille dévoilée*, 3rd episode (Paris, Desenne, 1789).

Chenevrière, Marc-Edouard, *La Pensée politique de Calvin* (Paris and Geneva, 1937).

Cherbuliez, Emilie (ed.), *Mémoires de Isaac Cornuaud, sur Genève et la Révolution de 1770 à 1795* (Geneva, 1912).

Colwill, Elizabeth, 'Pass as a woman, act like a man: Marie-Antoinette as tribade in the pornography of the French Revolution', in *Marie-Antoinette: writings on the body of a queen*, ed. Dena Goodman (New York and London, 2003), p.139-69.

Coquerel, Charles, *Histoire des églises du désert*, 2 vols (Paris, 1841).

Cossy, Valérie, and Deirdre Dawson (ed.), *Progrès et violence au XVIII$^e$ siècle*, Etudes internationales sur le dix-huitième siècle 3 (Paris, 2001).

Cramer, Lucien, *Une Famille genevoise, les Cramer: leurs relations avec Voltaire, Rousseau et Benjamin Franklin-Bache* (Geneva, 1952).

Cronin, Vincent, *Louis and Antoinette* (London, 1974).

Darnton, Robert, *The Corpus of clandestine literature in France 1769-1789* (New York and London, 1995).

–, *The Forbidden bestsellers of pre-Revolutionary France* (New York and London, 1996).

–, 'George Washington's false teeth: a civic sermon', in *La Recherche dix-huitiémiste: objets, méthodes et institutions (1945-1995)*, Etudes internationales sur le dix-huitième siècle 1, ed. Michel Delon and Jochen Schlobach (Paris, 1998), p.149-65.

–, 'The Grub Street style of revolution: J.-P. Brissot, police spy', *Journal of modern history* 40 (1968), p.301-27.

–, 'The High Enlightenment and the low-life of literature in pre-revolutionary France', *Past and present* 51 (1971), p.81-115.

–, *The Literary underground of the Old Regime* (Cambridge, MA, 1982).

–, 'Two paths through the social history of ideas', in *The Darnton debate: books and revolution in the eighteenth century*, ed. Haydn T. Mason (Oxford, 1998), p.251-94.

Davies, Simon, 'Poetry and propaganda: 1760-1778', in *Voltaire et ses combats*, ed. Ulla Kölving and Christiane Mervaud, 2 vols (Oxford, 1997), vol.1 p.181-88.

–, 'Reflections on Voltaire and his idea of colonies', *SVEC* 332 (1995), p.61-69.

–, 'Voltaire's *Les Lois de Minos*: text and context', in *The Enterprise of Enlightenment*, ed. Terry Pratt and David McCallum (Bern, 2004), p.245-64.

Dedieu, Joseph, *Histoire politique des protestants français (1715-1794)*, 2 vols (Paris, 1925).

Delon, Michel, and Jochen Schlobach (ed.), *La Recherche dix-huitiémiste: objets, méthodes et institutions (1945-1995)*, Etudes internationales sur le dix-huitième siècle 1 (Paris, 1998).

Desgraves, Louis, *Montesquieu* (Paris, 1981).

Diderot, Denis, *Correspondance*, ed. Georges Roth, 16 vols (Paris, 1955-1970).

–, *Le Neveu de Rameau*, ed. Jean Fabre (Genève, 1963).

Doyle, William, 'Voltaire and venality: the ambiguities of an abuse', in *The Secular city*, ed. T. M. Hemming, E. Freeman and D. Meakin (Exeter, 1994), p.102-11.

Dziembowski, Edmond, *Un Nouveau Patriotisme français, 1750-1770: la France face à la puissance anglaise à l'époque de la guerre de sept ans*, SVEC 365 (1998).

Eisenstein, Elizabeth L., 'Bypassing the Enlightenment: taking an underground route to revolution', in *The Darnton debate: books and revolution in the eighteenth century*, ed. Haydn T. Mason (Oxford, 1998), p.157-77.

–, *Grub Street abroad: aspects of the French cosmopolitan press from the age of Louis XIV to the Enlightenment* (Oxford, 1992).

–, 'The tribune of the people: a new species of demagogue', in *The Press in the French Revolution*, ed. Harvey Chisick, SVEC 287 (1991), p.145-59.

Eon de Beaumont, Charles-Geneviève, chevalier d', *Pièces relatives aux démélés entre mademoiselle d'Eon de Beaumont et le Sieur Caron, dit de Beaumarchais* (Paris, 1778).

Fahmy, Jean Mohsen, *Voltaire et Paris*, SVEC 195 (1981).

Falletti, N.-C., *Jacob Vernet, théologien genevois (1698-1789)* (Geneva, 1885).

Foucault, Michel, *Discipline and punish* (New York, 1977).

Gaberel, Jean-Pierre, *Voltaire et les Genevois* (Paris and Geneva, 1857).

Gargett, Graham, 'Genève au dix-huitième siècle: de la cité de Calvin au foyer des Lumières', in *The City in French writing, the eighteenth-century experience/Ecrire la ville au dix-huitième siècle*, ed. Síofra Pierse (Dublin, 2004), p.136-61.

–, 'Jacob Vernet éditeur de Montesquieu: la première édition de *L'Esprit des lois*', *Revue d'histoire littéraire de la France* 90 (1990), p.890-900.

–, *Jacob Vernet, Geneva and the 'philosophes'*, SVEC 321 (1994).

–, *Voltaire and Protestantism*, SVEC 188 (1980).

Gay, Peter, *The Enlightenment: an interpretation*, 2 vols (New York, 1966-1969).

–, *The Party of humanity: studies in the French Enlightenment* (London, 1964).

–, *Voltaire's politics: the poet as realist* (New York, 1965).

Gébelin, François, 'La publication de l'*Esprit des lois*', *Revue des bibliothèques* 34 (1924), p.125-58.

Geisendorf, P.-F., 'Quelques notes sur une maison d'édition genevoise du XVIII$^e$ siècle: les Barrillot', *Genava* 22 (1924), p. 203-10.

Goldgar, Anne, *Impolite learning: conduct and community in the Republic of Letters, 1680-1750* (London, 1995).

Goodman, Dena, *The Republic of Letters: a cultural history of the French Enlightenment* (Ithaca, NY, and London, 1994).

Gordon, Daniel, *Citizens without sovereignty: equality and sociability in French*

thought, *1670-1789* (Princeton, NJ, 1994).
–, 'The great Enlightenment massacre', in *The Darnton debate: books and revolution in the eighteenth century*, ed. Haydn T. Mason (Oxford, 1998), p.129-56.
Goulemot, Jean, André Magnan and Didier Masseau (ed.), *Inventaire Voltaire* (Paris, 1995).
Grimsley, Ronald, *Jean D'Alembert (1717-1783)* (Oxford, 1963).
Gruder, Vivian R., 'The question of Marie-Antoinette: the queen and public opinion before the Revolution', *French history* 16 (2002), p.269-98.
Gür, André, 'Un précédent à la condamnation du *Contrat social*: l'affaire George-Louis Le Sage (1752)', *Bulletin de la société d'histoire et d'archéologie de Genève* 14 (1968), p.77-94.

Habermas, Jürgen, *The Structural transformation of the public sphere: an inquiry into a category of bourgeois society* (1962; English translation: Cambridge, MA, 1989).
Hampson, Norman, *The Enlightenment* (London, 1968).
Hauc, Jean-Claude, *Ange Goudar: un aventurier des Lumières* (Paris, 2005).
Hazard, Paul, *La Crise de la conscience européenne* (Paris, 1935).
–, *La Pensée européenne au XVIII$^e$ siècle: de Montesquieu à Lessing* (Paris, 1946).
Hine, Ellen McNiven, *Jean-Jacques Dortous de Mairan and the Geneva connection: scientific networking in the eighteenth century*, SVEC 340 (1996).
Hochstrasser, T. J., 'Physiocracy and the politics of *laissez-faire*', in *The Cambridge history of eighteenth-century political thought*, ed. Mark Goldie and Robert Wokler (Cambridge, 2006), p.419-42.
Hof, Ulrich im, *The Enlightenment* (1993; English translation: Oxford, 1994).
Hont, István, *Jealousy of trade: international competition and the nation-state in historical perspective* (Cambridge, MA, 2005).
Horkheimer, Max, and Theodor Adorno, *Dialectic of Enlightenment* (1947; English translation: New York, 1972).
Hsia, R. Po-chia, *The World of Catholic renewal, 1540-1770* (Cambridge, 1998).

Ihalainen, Pasi, *Protestant nations redefined* (Leiden and Boston, 2005).
Ilie, P., *The Age of Minerva*, vol.1: *Counter-rational reason in the eighteenth century* (Philadelphia, PA, 1995).
Israel, Jonathan, *Enlightenment contested: philosophy, modernity and the emancipation of man, 1670-1752* (Oxford, 2006).
–, *Radical Enlightenment: philosophy and the making of modernity, 1650-1750* (Oxford, 2001).

Jacob, Margaret C., *Living the Enlightenment: Freemasonry and politics in eighteenth-century Europe* (Oxford, 1991).
–, *The Radical Enlightenment: pantheists, Freemasons and republicans* (London, 1981).
Jones, Colin, *The Great nation: France from Louis XV to Napoleon, 1715-1799* (London, 2002).

Kaiser, Thomas E., 'Enlightenment, public opinion and politics in the work of Robert Darnton', in *The Darnton debate: books and revolution in the eighteenth century*, ed. Haydn T. Mason (Oxford, 1998), p.189-206.
Kates, Gary, *Monsieur d'Eon is a woman: a tale of political intrigue and sexual masquerade* (New York, 1995).
Koselleck, Reinhart, *Critique and crisis: the Enlightenment and the pathogenesis of modern society* (1973; English translation: Oxford, 1988).

Lacour-Gayet, R., *Calonne, financier, réformateur, contre-révolutionnaire, 1734-1802* (Paris, 1963).
La Motte, Jeanne de, *The Life of Jane de Saint-Remy de Valois*, 2 vols

(Dublin, P. Wogan, P. Bryce, J. Moore, and J. Rice, 1792).

–, *Memoirs of the countess de Valois La Motte* (Dublin, John Archer and William Jones, 1790).

La Motte, Marc-Antoine-Nicolas de, *Mémoires inédits du comte de La Motte-Valois sur sa vie et son époque (1754-1830)*, ed. Louis Lacour (Paris, 1858).

Larrère, Catherine, 'Une philosophie de la propriété: les physiocrates entre droit naturel et économie', *Studi settecenteschi* 24 (2004), *Fisiocrazia e proprietà terriera*, special number ed. Maria Albertone, p.49-70.

La Tour, Alphonse-Joseph de Serres de, *Appel au bon sens* (London, Kearsley, 1788).

Launay, Michel, 'Jean-Jacques Rousseau, écrivain politique', in *Au siècle des Lumières* (Moscow, 1970), p. 77-136.

–, *Jean-Jacques Rousseau, écrivain politique (1712-1762)* (Grenoble, 1971).

Lauriol, Claude, *La Beaumelle: un protestant cévenol entre Montesquieu et Voltaire* (Paris, 1978).

Leigh, R. A. (ed.), *Correspondance complète de Jean-Jacques Rousseau* (Geneva, Banbury and Oxford, 1965-1995).

Léonard, E.-G., *Histoire générale du protestantisme*, 3 vols (Paris, 1961-1964).

Litchfield, R. Burr (trans.), *The End of the Old Regime in Europe, 1776-1789*, 2 vols (Princeton, NJ, 1991).

–, *The End of the Old Regime in Europe, 1768-1776: the first crisis* (Princeton, NJ, 1989).

Livingstone, David, and Charles W. J. Withers (ed.), *Geography and Enlightenment* (Chicago and London, 1999).

Loft, Leonore, *Passion, politics and philosophie: rediscovering J.-P. Brissot* (Westport, CT, 2002).

Lough, John (ed.), *The Encyclopédie of Diderot and D'Alembert* (Cambridge, 1954).

–, 'The French literary underground reconsidered', *SVEC* 329 (1995), p.471-82.

Luna, Frederick A. de, 'The Dean Street style of revolution: J.-P. Brissot, *jeune philosophe*', *French historical studies* 17 (1991), p.158-90.

Lüthy, Herbert, *La Banque protestante en France de la Révocation de l'Edit de Nantes à la Révolution*, 2 vols (Paris, 1959-1961).

McCalman, Iain, 'Mad Lord George and Madame La Motte: riot and sexuality in the genesis of Burke's *Reflections on the revolution in France*', *Journal of British studies* 35 (1996), p.343-67.

–, 'Queen of the gutter: the lives and fictions of Jeanne de La Motte', in *Adventures in identity: European multicultural perspectives*, ed. John Docker and Gerhard Fischer (Tübingen, 2001), p.111-27.

Mackrell, J. Q. C., *The Attack on 'feudalism' in eighteenth-century France* (London and Toronto, 1973).

McLeod, Hugh, *Religion and the people of Western Europe 1789-1970* (Oxford, 1981).

McMahon, Darrin M., *Enemies of the Enlightenment: the French Counter-Enlightenment and the making of modernity* (New York, 2001).

[Mairobert, Mathieu-François Pidansat de], *Anecdotes sur Mme la comtesse Du Barri* (London, n.p., 1775).

, *L'Espion anglais*, new edition, 10 vols (London, John Adamson, 1785).

–, *Lettres originales de Mme la comtesse Dubarry* (London, 1779).

Manuel, Pierre-Louis, *La Police de Paris dévoilée*, 2 vols (Paris, Garnery, 1791).

Mason, Haydn T. (ed.), *The Darnton debate: books and revolution in the eighteenth century* (Oxford, 1998).

–, 'Voltaire européen naissant et l'Europe', in *Voltaire en Europe, hommage à Christiane Mervaud*, ed. Michel Delon and Catriona Seth (Oxford, 2000), p.23-31.

## Bibliography

Masseau, Didier, *Les Ennemis des philosophes: l'antiphilosophie au temps des Lumières* (Paris, 2000).

Masson, André (ed.), *Œuvres complètes de Montesquieu*, 3 vols (Paris, 1950-1955).

Maury, Léon, *Le Réveil religieux dans l'église réformée à Genève et en France (1810-1850)* (Paris, 1892).

Maza, Sarah, *Private lives and public affairs: the causes célèbres of prerevolutionary France* (Berkeley, CA, 1993).

Mazzolini, Renato G., and Shirley A. Roe, *Science against the unbelievers: the correspondence of Bonnet and Needham, 1760-1780*, SVEC 243 (1986).

Melon, Jean-François, *Essai politique sur le commerce* (1734; Amsterdam, François Changuion, 1754).

–, *Saggio politico sul commercio del Signor Melon, tradotto dal Francese, nuova edizione con note* (Naples, Nicola Russo, 1795).

–, *Saggio politico sul commercio, tradotto dal Francese colle annotazioni dell' Ab. Longano*, 2 vols (Naples, Vincenzo Flauto, 1778).

Michalski, Krzysztof (ed.), *Oświecenie dzisiaj: Rozmowy w Castelgandolfo* (Cracow, 1999).

Micheli, Léopold, *Les Institutions municipales de Genève au XV$^e$ siècle* (Geneva, 1912).

Mijnhardt, Wijnand W., 'The Dutch Enlightenment: problems and definitions', in *Centre(s) et périphérie(s): les Lumières de Belfast à Beijing*, ed. Marie-Christine Skuncke (Paris, 2003), p.169-83.

Morande, Charles Théveneau de, *Le Gazetier cuirassé* (London, 1771).

–, *Mémoires secrets d'une femme publique*, [volumes burnt through bribery] 9 February 1774.

–, *Réplique de Charles Théveneau de Morande à Jacques-Pierre Brissot: sur les erreurs, les infidélités et les calomnies de sa Réponse* (Paris, Froullé, 1791).

Mossiker, Frances, *The Queen's necklace* (London, 1961).

Munck, Thomas, *The Enlightenment: a comparative social history, 1721-1794* (London, 2000).

Muthu, Sankar, *Enlightenment against Empire* (Princeton, 2003).

Naves, Raymond, *Voltaire et l'Encyclopédie* (Paris, 1938).

Nonnotte, Claude-François, *Les Erreurs de Voltaire*, revised edn, 2 vols (Lyon, V. Reguilliat, 1770).

O'Keefe, C. B., *Contemporary reactions to the Enlightenment (1728-1762)* (Paris, 1974).

Outram, Dorinda, *The Enlightenment* (Cambridge, 1995).

Ozanam, Didier, and Michel Antoine (ed.), *Correspondance secrète du comte de Broglie avec Louis XV, 1756-1774*, 2 vols (Paris, 1959-1961).

Palmer, R. R., *Catholics and unbelievers in eighteenth-century France* (Princeton, NJ, 1939).

Pelleport, Anne-Gédeon de Lafitte de, *Le Diable dans un bénitier et le gazetier cuirassé transformé en mouche* (London, 1783).

–, *Les Petits Soupers et nuits de l'hôtel de Bouillon* (Bouillon [London], Boissière, 1783).

Pellet, Marcellin, *Variétés révolutionnaires* (Paris, 1885).

Petrusewicz, Marta, *Latifundium: moral economy and material life in a European periphery* (Ann Arbor, MI, 1996).

Pitassi, Maria-Cristina, *De l'orthodoxie aux Lumières: Genève 1670-1737* (Geneva, 1992).

Pocock, J. G. A., *Barbarism and religion: the Enlightenments of Edward Gibbon, 1737-1764* (Cambridge, 1999).

Pomeau, René, *D'Arouet à Voltaire* (Oxford, 1988).

– (ed.), *Voltaire en son temps*, 2nd edn, 2 vols (Oxford, 1995).

–, Christine Mervaud et al., *De la cour au jardin* (Oxford, 1991).

Popkin, Jeremy D., 'Pamphlet journalism at the end of the Old

# Bibliography

Regime', *Eighteenth-century studies* 22 (1989), p.351-67.
–, *Press, revolution and social identities in France, 1830-1835* (University Park, PA, 2002).
Porter, Roy, and Mikuláš Teich (ed.), *The Enlightenment in national context* (Cambridge, 1981).
Pratt, Mary Louise, *Imperial eyes: travel writing and transculturation* (London and New York, 1992).
Price, Munro, *The Fall of the French monarchy: Louis XVI, Marie-Antoinette and the baron de Breteuil* (London, 2002).
–, *Preserving the monarchy: the comte de Vergennes, 1774-1787* (Cambridge, 1995).
Proschwitz, Gunnar and Mavis von, *Beaumarchais et le Courier de l'Europe: documents inédits ou peu connus*, SVEC 273-74 (1990).

Quastana, François, *Voltaire et l'absolutisme éclairé (1736-1778)* (Aix and Marseille, 2003).

Raeff, Marc, 'Les Slaves, les Allemands et les Lumières', *Canadian-American Slavic studies* 1 (1967), p. 521-51.
Reill, Peter Hanns, *Vitalizing nature in the Enlightenment* (Berkeley, CA, and Los Angeles, CA, 2005).
Rivoire, Emile, *Bibliographie historique de Genève au XVIII$^e$ siècle, vol.1 (1701-1792)* (Geneva, 1897).
Robertson, John, 'Franco Venturi's Enlightenment', *Past and present* 137 (1992), p.183-206.
Robiquet, Paul, *Théveneau de Morande, étude sur le XVIII$^e$ siècle* (Paris, 1882).
Roche, Daniel, *France in the Enlightenment* (1993; English translation: Cambridge, MA, 1998).
Rosenblatt, Helena, *Rousseau and Geneva: from the First discourse to the Social contract, 1749-1762* (Cambridge, 1997).
Rousseau, Jean-Jacques, *Œuvres complètes*, ed. Bernard Gagnebin and Marcel Raymond, 4 vols (Paris, 1964).

–, *Œuvres complètes*, ed. Bernard Gagnebin and Marcel Raymond, 5 vols, Pléiade edn (Paris, 1995).

Schmid d'Avenstein, Georg-Ludwig, *Principes de la législation universelle* (Amsterdam, Marc-Michel Rey, 1776).
–, *Principj della legislazione universale [...] ed in questa prima edizione Napoletana rivedute e corretta sull'originale, ed accresciuta di più note dell'autore medesimo non ancora pubblicate*, 4 vols (Naples, Michele Stasi, 1791).
Schmidt, James (ed.), *What is Enlightenment? Eighteenth-century answers and twentieth-century questions* (Berkeley, CA, 1996).
Sheehan, Jonathan, 'Enlightenment, religion, and the enigma of secularization: a review essay', *American historical review* 108 (2003), p.1061-80.
Shils, Edward, *Center and periphery: essays in macrosociology* (Chicago, IL, 1975).
Skuncke, Marie-Christine (ed.), *Centre(s) et périphérie(s): les Lumières de Belfast à Beijing* (Paris, 2003).
Smith, D. W., *Helvétius: a study in persecution* (Oxford, 1965).
Sonenscher, Michael, 'Physiocracy as a theodicy', *History of political thought* 23 (2002), p.326-39.
Sordet, Louis, *Histoire des résidents de France à Genève* (Geneva, 1854).
Sorkin, David, 'Reform Catholicism and religious Enlightenment', with commentary by T. C. W. Blanning and R. J. W. Evans, *Austrian history yearbook* 30 (1999), p.187-235.
Steiner, Philippe, 'Les propriétaires dans la philosophie économique', *Studi settecenteschi* 24 (2004), *Fisiocrazia e proprietà terriera*, special number ed. Maria Albertone, p.23-47.
Stephens, F. G., and D. M. George, *Catalogue of political and personal satires preserved in the Department of prints and drawings in the British Museum*, 11 vols (1870-1954).

Sutherland, D. M. G., *The French Revolution and empire: the quest for a civic order* (Oxford, 2003).

Tackett, Timothy, 'Conspiracy obsession in a time of revolution: French elites and the origins of the Terror, 1789-1792', *American historical review* 105 (2000), p.691-713.

Trousson, Raymond, *Jean-Jacques Rousseau jugé par ses contemporains: du Discours sur les sciences et les arts aux Confessions* (Paris, 2000).

Vallette, Louis, *L'Eglise de Genève à la fin du XVIII$^e$ siècle* (Geneva, 1892).

Van Kley, Dale K., 'Christianity as casualty and chrysalis of modernity: the problem of dechristianization in the French Revolution', *American historical review* 108 (2003), p.1081-104.

Venturi, Franco, *The End of the Old Regime in Europe, 1768-1776: the first crisis* (Princeton, NJ, 1989).

–, *The End of the Old Regime in Europe, 1776-1789*, 2 vols (Princeton, NJ, 1991).

–, *Utopia and reform in the Enlightenment* (Cambridge, 1971).

Vernet, Jacob, *Instruction chrétienne*, 2nd edn, 5 vols (Geneva, Henri-Albert Gosse & Comp., 1756).

Ward, W. R., *Christianity under the ancien régime, 1648-1789* (Cambridge, 1999).

Withers, Charles W. J., and David Livingstone, 'Introduction: on geography and Enlightenment', in *Geography and Enlightenment*, ed. D. Livingstone and C. W. J. Withers (Chicago and London, 1999), p.1-28.

Wolff, Larry, *Inventing Eastern Europe: the map of civilization on the mind of the Enlightenment* (Stanford, CA, 1994).

Yardeni, Myriam, 'Paradoxes politiques et persuasion dans les *Annales de Linguet*', in *The Press in the French Revolution*, ed. Harvey Chisick, *SVEC* 287 (1991), p.211-19.

# England, Scotland, Wales and Great Britain

Aikin, John, *A Description of the country from thirty to forty miles round Manchester* (London, printed for John Stockdale, 1795).

–, *General biography, or Lives, critical and historical, of the most eminent persons of all ages, countries, conditions, and professions*, 10 vols (London, 1799-1815).

–, *A View of the character and public service of the late John Howard* (London, printed for J. Johnson, 1792).

Anstey, Roger, 'Eighteenth-century thought and anti-slavery', in *The Atlantic slave trade and British abolition* (Aldershot, 1992; reprint of London, 1975), p.91-125.

–, and P. E. H. Hair (ed.), *Liverpool, the African slave trade and abolition: essays to illustrate current knowledge and research*, Historic society of Lancashire and Cheshire, occasional series 2, enlarged edn (1989).

Bolt, C., and S. Drescher (ed.), *Anti-slavery, religion and reform: essays in memory of Roger Anstey* (Folkestone, 1980).

Borsay, Peter, *The English urban renaissance: culture and society in the provincial town* (Oxford, 2002; reprint of Oxford, 1989).

–, and Angus McInnes, 'The emergence of a leisure town: or an urban renaissance?', *Past and present* 126 (1990), p.189-202.

Bradley, James E., *Religion, revolution and English radicalism: non-conformity* in eighteenth-century politics and society (Cambridge, 1990).

Braithwaite, Helen, Romanticism, publishing and Dissent (Basingstoke, 2003).

Brewer, John, The Pleasures of the imagination: English culture in the eighteenth century (London, 1997).

Carruthers, Gerard, and Alan Rawes (ed.), English Romanticism and the Celtic world (Cambridge, 2003).

Catalogue of the books, tracts &c contained in Ann Yearsley's public library, No.4, Crescent, Hotwells (Bristol, printed for the proprietor, 1793).

Chandler, David, 'The early development of the "Lake School" idea', Notes and queries 250 (2005), p.35-37.

Chandler, George, William Roscoe of Liverpool 1753-1831 (London, 1953).

Clark, J. C. D., English society 1660-1832: religion, ideology and politics during the ancien régime (Cambridge, 2000).

Colley, Linda, Britons: forging the nation 1707-1837 (New Haven, CT, and London, 1992).

Cottle, Joseph, Alfred, an epic poem in twenty-four books (London, 1800).

Cumberland, Richard, Calvary, or the Death of Christ (London, C. Dilly, 1792).

–, and James Bland Burges, The Exodiad (London, 1807).

Cunningham, Hugh, 'The languages of patriotism', History workshop journal 12 (1981), p.8-33.

Curran, Stuart, Poetic form and British Romanticism (Oxford, 1986).

Curry, Kenneth (ed.), New letters of Robert Southey, 2 vols (New York, 1965).

Davies, Damian Walford, Presences that disturb: models of Romantic identity in the literature and culture of the 1790s (Cardiff, 2002).

–, and Lynda Pratt (ed.), Wales and the Romantic imagination (Cardiff, 2007).

Davis, Leith, Ian Duncan and Janet Sorensen (ed.), Scotland and the borders of Romanticism (Cambridge, 2004).

Davy, John (ed.), Fragmentary remains, literary and scientific, of Sir Humphry Davy, Bart. (London, 1858).

DeLacy, Margaret, Prison reform in Lancashire 1700-1850: a study in local administration (Stanford, CA, 1986).

Demata, Massimiliano, and Duncan Wu (ed.), British Romanticism and the 'Edinburgh review': bicentenary essays (Basingstoke, 2002).

Dick, Malcom, 'Joseph Priestley, the Lunar Society and anti-slavery', in Joseph Priestley and Birmingham, ed. Malcom Dick (Studely, 2005), p.65-80.

Ditchfield, G. M., 'The campaign in Lancashire and Cheshire over the repeal of the Test and Corporation Acts, 1787-1790', Transactions of the Historic society of Lancashire and Cheshire 126 (1977), p.109-38.

–, 'Manchester College and anti-slavery', in Truth, liberty and religion: essays celebrating two hundred years of Manchester College, ed. Barbara Smith (Oxford, 1986), p.185-224.

–, 'Repeal, abolition and reform: a study of the interaction of reforming movements in the parliament of 1790-1796', in Anti-slavery, religion and reform: essays in memory of Roger Anstey, ed. C. Bolt and S. Drescher (Folkestone, 1980), p.101-18.

Drake, Nathan, Literary hours, or Essays literary and critical (Sudbury, printed by J. Burkitt, 1798).

Enfield, William, Biographical sermons, or a Series of discourses on the principal characters in Scripture (London, printed for J. Johnson, 1777).

–, An Essay towards the history of Leverpool, drawn up from the papers of the late George Perry, and from other materials collected since, 2nd edn (London, printed for Joseph Johnson, 1774).

–, The History of philosophy from the earliest periods: drawn from Brucker's

*Historia Critica Philosophiae* (1787; London, 1837).

—, *Remarks on several late publications relative to the Dissenters in a letter to Dr Priestley, by a Dissenter* (London, printed for S. Bladon, 1770).

—, *A Sermon on the centennial commemoration of the Revolution* (Norwich, London, 1788).

Evans, R. J. W., 'Was there a Welsh Enlightenment?', in *From medieval to modern Wales: historical essays in honour of Kenneth O. Morgan and Ralph A. Griffiths*, ed. R. R. Davies and Geraint H. Jenkins (Cardiff, 2004), p.142-59.

Fitzpatrick, Martin, 'Heretical religion and radical politics', in *The Transformation of political culture: England and Germany in the late eighteenth century*, ed. Eckhart Hellmuth (Oxford, 1990), p.339-74.

—, *Rousing the sleeping lion: Joseph Priestley and the constitution in Church and state*, Occasional publications of the Leeds library 3 (Leeds, 1993).

—, Nicholas Thomas and Jenny Newell, *David Samwell: the death of Cook and other writings* (Cardiff, 2006).

Flavell, M. Kay, 'The enlightened reader and the new industrial town: a study of the Liverpool library 1758-1790', *British journal for eighteenth-century studies* 8:1 (1985), p.17-36.

Gerrard, Christine, *The Patriot opposition to Walpole: politics, poetry and national myth, 1725-1742* (Oxford, 1994).

Goodwin, Albert, *The Friends of liberty: the English democratic movement in the age of the French Revolution* (London, 1979).

Griffin, Dustin H., *Regaining paradise: Milton and the eighteenth century* (Cambridge, 1986).

Griggs, E. L. (ed.), *The Collected letters of Samuel Taylor Coleridge*, 6 vols (Oxford, 1956-1971).

Hankin, C. Christiana (ed.), *Life of Mary Anne Schimmelpennick*, 3rd edn (London, 1860).

Harding, Anthony J., and Lisa Low (ed.), *Milton, the metaphysicals and Romanticism* (Cambridge, 1994).

Harris, Tim, *Revolution: the great crisis of the British monarchy, 1685-1720* (London, 2006).

Hayley, William, *An Essay on epic poetry; in five epistles to the Revd. Mr. Mason, with notes* (London, J. Dodsley, 1782).

Holt, Anne, *Walking together: a study in Liverpool nonconformity* (London, 1938).

Hume, David, *The History of England, from the invasion of Julius Caesar to the accession of Henry VII*, 2 vols (London, A. Millar, 1762).

Hunt, N. C., *Two early political associations: the Quakers and Dissenting deputies in the age of Walpole* (Oxford, 1961).

Jeffrey, Francis, *Observations on Mr Thelwall's letter to the editor of the Edinburgh review* (Edinburgh, 1804).

Johnson, C. R., *Provincial poetry 1789-1839: British verse printed in the provinces: the Romantic background* (Otley, 1992).

Johns-Putra, Adeline, *Heroes and housewives: women's epic poetry and domestic ideology in the Romantic age (1770-1835)* (Bern, 2001).

Lloyd, Katherine M. R., 'Peace, politics, and philanthropy: Henry Brougham, William Roscoe and America 1808-1868', doctoral dissertation, University of Oxford, 1996.

Lyon, Martin, 'Liverpool and Africa in the nineteenth century: the continuing connection', *Transactions of the Historic society of Lancashire and Cheshire* 147 (1997), p.27-54.

McElroy, D. D., *Scotland's age of improvement: a survey of eighteenth-century literary clubs and societies* (Washington State, 1969).

McLoughlin, George, *A Short history of the first Liverpool infirmary* (London and Chichester, 1978).

Madden, Lionel (ed.), *Robert Southey: the critical heritage* (London, 1972).

Mason, Haydn, 'Voltaire versus Shakespeare: the *Lettre à l'Académie Française* (1776)', *British Journal for eighteenth-century studies* 18:2 (1995), p.173-84.

Matthews, William, *New history: survey and description of the city and suburbs of Bristol* (Bristol, printed, published and sold by W. Matthews, sold by the booksellers of Bristol, Hotwells and Bath, 1794).

Moss, William, *A Familiar medical survey of Liverpool* (Liverpool, printed by H. Hodgson, and sold by T. and W. Lowndes, London, 1784).

Mowl, Tim, and Brian Earnshaw, *John Wood, architect of obsession* (Huddersfield, 1988).

Murdoch, Alexander, *British history, 1660-1832: national identity and local culture* (Basingstoke, 2001).

Newlyn, Lucy, *Paradise lost and the Romantic reader* (Oxford, 1993).

O'Brien, P., *Eyres' press, Warrington (1756-1803): an embryo university press* (Wigan, 1993).

Ogden, James, *Emanuel, or Paradise regained, an epic poem* (Manchester, Sowler and Russell, 1797).

Ogilvie, John, *Britannia: an national epic poem* (Aberdeen, 1801).

Oz-Salzberger, Fania, *Translating the Enlightenment: Scottish civic discourse in eighteenth-century Germany* (Oxford, 1995).

[Pennie, J. F.], *The Tale of a modern genius, or the Miseries of Parnassus, in a series of letters*, 3 vols (London, 1827).

Perkin, M. R. (ed.), *The Book trade in Liverpool to 1805: a directory* (Liverpool, 1981).

Pittock, Murray G. H., *Celtic identity and the British image* (Manchester, 1999).

Pope, Alexander, *Poems*, ed. John Butt (London, 1963; corrected reprint 1989).

Porter, Roy, *Enlightenment: Britain and the creation of the modern world* (Harmondsworth, 2000).

–, 'Was there a medical Enlightenment in England?', *British Journal for eighteenth-century studies* 5:1 (1982), p.49-64.

Pratt, Lynda, 'Anglo-Saxon attitudes? Alfred the Great and the Romantic national epic', in *Literary appropriations of the Anglo-Saxons from the thirteenth to the twentieth century*, ed. Donald G. Scragg and Carole Weinberg (Cambridge, 2000), p.138-56.

–, 'Naval contemplation: poetry, politics and the navy 1797-1799', *Journal for maritime research* (December 2000), accessed from http://www.jmr.nmm.ac.uk/server/show/conJmrArticle.22/viewPage/1.

–, 'Patriot poetics and the Romantic national epic: placing and displacing Southey's *Joan of Arc*', in *Placing and displacing Romanticism*, ed. Peter J. Kitson (Aldershot, 2001), p.88-105.

Priestley, Joseph, *Memoirs of Dr Joseph Priestley, to the year 1795, written by himself: with a continuation to the time of his decease, by his son Joseph Priestley; and observations on his writings, by Thomas Cooper, president judge of the fourth district of Pennsylvania, and the Reverend William Christie* (London, 1805).

Pye, Henry James, *Alfred; an epic poem, in six books* (London, 1801).

Quint, David, *Epic and empire: politics and generic form from Virgil to Milton* (Princeton, NJ, 1993).

Robberds, J. W. (ed.), *A Memoir of the life and writings of the late William Taylor of Norwich*, 2 vols (London, 1843).

Roberts, Adam, *Romantic and Victorian long poems* (Aldershot, 1999).

305

Robertson, John, *The Case for the Enlightenment: Scotland and Naples 1680-1760* (Cambridge, 2005).

–, 'The Enlightenment above national context: political economy in eighteenth-century Scotland and Naples', *Historical journal* 40 (1997), p.667-97.

Rousseau, André Michel, *L'Angleterre et Voltaire*, SVEC 145-47 (1976).

Royden, Michael W., *Pioneers and perseverance: a history of the Royal School for the Blind, Liverpool 1791-1991* (Birkenhead, 1991).

Sanderson, F. E., 'The Liverpool abolitionists', in *Liverpool, the African slave trade and abolition: essays to illustrate current knowledge and research*, ed. Roger Anstey and P. E. H. Hair, Historic society of Lancashire and Cheshire, occasional series 2, enlarged edn (1989), p.196-238.

Schaffer, Simon, and Stephen Shapin, *Leviathan and the airpump: Hobbes, Boyle and the experimental life* (Princeton, NJ, 1985).

Schofield, Robert E., *The Enlightenment of Joseph Priestley: a study of his life and work from 1733 to 1773* (Pennsylvania University Press, PA, 1997).

–, *The Lunar Society of Birmingham: a social history of provincial science and industry in eighteenth-century England* (Oxford, 1963).

Scrivener, Michael, *Seditious allegories: John Thelwall and Jacobin writing* (University Park, PA, 2001).

Sellers, Iain, 'William Roscoe, the Roscoe circle and radical politics in Liverpool', *Transactions of the Historic society of Lancashire and Cheshire* 120 (1968), p.45-62.

Sewall, R. B., 'Rousseau's second discourse in England from 1755 to 1762', *Philological quarterly* (April 1938), p.99-114.

Shapin, Stephen, *A Social history of truth: civility and science in seventeenth-century England* (London, 1994).

Southey, Charles Cuthbert (ed.), *The Life and correspondence of Robert Southey*, 6 vols (London, 1849-1850).

Southey, Robert, *Common-place book*, ed. John Wood Warter, 4 series (London, 1849-1850).

–, *Joan of Arc*, ed. Lynda Pratt, in *Poetical works, 1793-1810*, 5 vols (London, 2004), vol.1.

–, and Grosvenor Charles Bedford (ed.), *Specimens of the later English poets*, 3 vols (London, 1807).

Stobart, Jon, 'Culture versus commerce: societies and spaces for elites in eighteenth-century Liverpool', *Journal of historical geography* 28:4 (2002), p.471-85.

Stott, Anne, *Hannah More: the first Victorian* (Oxford, 2003).

Swedenberg, H. T., *The Theory of the epic in England 1650-1800* (Berkeley, CA, and Los Angeles, CA, 1944).

Sweet, Rosemary, 'Freemen and independence in English borough politics c.1770-1830', *Past and present* 161 (1998), p.84-115.

–, *The Writing of urban histories in eighteenth-century England* (Oxford, 1997).

Sykes, Norman, *Church and state in England in the 18th century* (Cambridge, 1934).

Taylor, H. A., 'Matthew Gregson and the pursuit of taste', *Transactions of the Historic society of Lancashire and Cheshire* 110 (1958), p.157-76.

Thelwall, John, *The Peripatetic, or Sketches of the heart, of nature and society; in a series of politico-sentimental journals, in verse and prose, of the eccentric excursions of Sylvanus Theophrastus; supposed to be written by himself*, 3 vols (Southwark, printed for the author, 1793).

–, *Poems, chiefly written in retirement* (Hereford, 1801).

–, *The Trident of Albion, an epic effusion; and an oration on the influence of elocution on martial enthusiasm; with an address to the shade of Nelson [...] to which is prefixed, an introductory discourse on the nature and objects of elocutionary science; and the studies and accomplishments connected with the faculty of oral expression* (Liverpool, 1805).

Thomas, D. O., 'Francis Maseres, Richard Price and the industrious poor', *Enlightenment and dissent* 4 (1985), p.65-80.

–, and W. Bernard Peach (ed.), *The Correspondence of Richard Price, 1748-1791*, 3 vols (Cardiff and Durham, NC, 1983-1994).

Thornton, R. D., *James Currie the entire stranger and Robert Burns* (Edinburgh and London, 1963).

Tribe, Keith (ed.), *A Critical bibliography of Adam Smith* (London, 2002).

Trumpener, Katie, *Bardic nationalism: the Romantic novel and the British Empire* (Princeton, NJ, 1997).

Uglow, Jenny, *The Lunar men: the friends who made the future* (London, 2002).

Voltaire, *Letters concerning the English nation*, ed. Nicholas Cronk (Oxford, 1994).

Waldron, Mary, *Lactilla, milkwoman of Clifton: the life and writings of Ann Yearsley, 1753-1806* (Athens, GA, 1996).

Wallace, James, *A General and descriptive history of the ancient and present state of the town of Liverpool* (Liverpool, printed for and sold by R. Phillips, sold also by W. Richardson, London, 1795).

Weaver, G. H., 'John Haygarth, clinical investigator, apostle of sanitation, 1740-1827', *Bulletin of the Society of medical history of Chicago* 4 (1928-1935), p.156-200.

Webster, Charles, and Jonathan Barry, 'The Manchester medical revolution', in *Truth, liberty and religion: essays celebrating two hundred years of Manchester College*, ed. Barbara Smith (Oxford, 1986), p.165-84.

Weinbrot, Howard D., *Britannia's issue: the rise of British literature from Dryden to Ossian* (Cambridge, 1993).

Whale, John, 'The making of a city of culture: William Roscoe's Liverpool', *Eighteenth-century life* 29:2 (2005), p.91-107.

Wilkie, Brian, *Romantic poets and epic tradition* (Madison, WI, 1965).

Wilson, Arline, 'The cultural identity of Liverpool, 1790-1850: the early learned societies', *Transactions of the Historic society of Lancashire and Cheshire* 147 (1997), p.55-80.

Yarrington, Alison, *The Commemoration of the hero 1800-1864: monuments to British victors of the Napoleonic wars* (London and New York, 1988).

Yearsley, Ann, *An Elegy on Marie Antoinette, of Austria, ci-devant queen of France: with a poem on the last interview between the king of Poland and Loraski* (Bristol, printed by J.Rudhall for the author, [1796]).

–, *Reflections on the death of Louis XVI* (Bristol, printed for the author, 1793).

–, *The Rural lyre; a volume of poems* (London, G. G. and J. Robinson, 1796).

–, *Sequel to reflections on the death of Louis XVI* (Bristol, printed for the author, 1793).

Young, B. W., *Religion and Enlightenment in eighteenth-century England* (Oxford, 1998).

# Ireland

*Address from the National Assembly of France to the people of Ireland* (Dublin, J. Chambers, 1790).

*An Address to the Right Honourable Henry Grattan, Esq. by the Independent Dublin Volunteers, relative to the simple repeal,* and the recent interference of the Earl of Mansfield, in deciding, in an English court, upon an appeal from Ireland; with Mr Grattan's answer: and observations on Mr Grattan's and Mr Y---L---N's conduct, in a letter to Mr Y---L---N, the A---y G---l of Ireland, to which is annexed the resolutions of the Lawyers Committee and Corps (London, J. Debrett, 1782).

Anti-Catholics: a refutation of the principles contained in the declaration of the Catholic Society (Dublin, Richard White, 1792).

Asgill, John, An Argument proving, that according to the covenant of eternal life revealed in the Scriptures, man may be translated from hence into that eternal life, without passing through death (1700; London, 1715).

Barber, Samuel, Remarks on a pamphlet, entitled The Present state of the Church of Ireland (Dublin, P. Byrne, 1787).

Barnard, Toby, The Kingdom of Ireland, 1641-1760 (Basingstoke, 2004).

Berkeley, George, Philosophical works, ed. Michael R. Ayers (London, 1993).

Berman, David, Berkeley and Irish philosophy (London, 2005).

–, 'Enlightenment and Counter-Enlightenment in Irish philosophy', Archiv für Geschichte der Philosophie 64 (1982), p.148-65, 257-79.

–, George Berkeley: idealism and the man (Oxford, 1996).

–, 'The Irish Counter-Enlightenment', in The Irish mind: exploring intellectual traditions, ed. Richard Kearney (Dublin 1985), p.119-40.

–, 'Irish philosophy and the American Enlightenment during the eighteenth century', Eire-Ireland 24 (1989), p.28-39.

–, and Patricia O'Riordan (ed.), The Irish Enlightenment and Counter-Enlightenment, 6 vols (Bristol, 2002).

Brown, Michael, Francis Hutcheson in Dublin, 1719-1730 (Dublin, 2001).

Caffentzis, George C., 'Why did Berkeley's bank fail? Money and libertinism in eighteenth-century Ireland', Eighteenth-century Ireland 12 (1997), p.100-15.

Campbell, William, An Examination of the bishop of Cloyne's defence of his principles; with observations on some of His Lordship's apologists (Belfast, H. Joy Senior and Junior, 1788).

Champion, Justin, Republican learning: John Toland and the crisis of Christian culture, 1696-1722 (Manchester, 2003).

Clayton, Robert, A Vindication of the histories of the Old and New Testament, part III, containing some observations on the nature of angels and the scriptural account of the fall and redemption of mankind (Dublin, George Faulkner, 1757).

Connolly, S. J., 'The Glorious Revolution in Irish Protestant political thinking', in Political ideas in eighteenth-century Ireland, ed. S. J. Connolly (Dublin, 2000), p.27-63.

Conway, Tim, and Graham Gargett, 'Voltaire's La Voix du sage et du peuple in Ireland, or enlightened anticlericalism in two jurisdictions', Eighteenth-century Ireland 20 (2005), p.79-90.

Davies, Simon, 'L'Irlande et les Lumières', Dix-huitième siècle 30 (1998), p.17-35.

–, 'The Northern star and the propagation of enlightened ideas', Eighteenth-century Ireland: Iris an Dá Cultúr 5 (1990), p.143-52.

DePorte, Michael, 'Swift, God and power', in Walking Naboth's vineyard: new studies in Swift, ed. Christopher Fox and Brenda Tooley (Notre Dame, IN, 1995), p.73-97.

Doody, Thomas (ed.), The Dictionary of Irish philosophers (Bristol, 2004).

Eccleshall, Robert, 'The political ideas of Anglican Ireland in the 1690s', in Political discourse in seventeenth- and eighteenth-century Ireland, ed.

D. George Boyse, Robert Eccleshall and Vincent Geoghegan (Basingstoke, 2001), p.62-80.

Fauske, Christopher, *Jonathan Swift and the Church of Ireland* (Dublin, 2002).

Ferrar, John, *History of Limerick* (Limerick, A. Watson and Co, 1787).

Ferris, Ina, *The Romantic national tale and Ireland* (Cambridge, 2002).

Fox, Christopher, and Brenda Tooley, *Walking Naboth's vineyard: new studies in Swift* (Notre Dame, IN, 1995).

Gargett, Graham, 'Jean-Pierre Droz, *A Literary journal*, and francophone influence on the "Irish Enlightenment"', in *France-Ireland: anatomy of a relationship: studies in history, literature and politics*, ed. Eamon Maher and Grace Neville (Frankfurt, Berlin, New York and Oxford, 2004), p.177-90.

–, 'Voltaire's *Lettres philosophiques* in eighteenth-century Ireland', *Eighteenth-century Ireland* 14 (1999), p.77-98.

–, and Geraldine Sheridan (ed.), *Ireland and the French Enlightenment, 1700-1800* (Basingstoke, 1999).

Gillespie, Ray (ed.), *Scholar bishop: the recollections and diary of Narcissus Marsh, 1628-1696* (Cork, 2003).

Griffith, Amyas, *Miscellaneous tracts* (Dublin, James Mehain, 1788).

Hoppen, K. T., 'Early science in Ireland: a study of the Dublin Philosophical Society, 1683-1709', MA dissertation, University College Dublin, 1963.

[Howard, Edmond Gorges], A True Church of England-Man, *Some observations and queries on the present laws of this kingdom, relative to papists*, 2nd edn (Dublin, O. Nelson, 1762).

Kelly, Patrick, 'The politics of political economy in mid-eighteenth-century Ireland', in *Political ideas in eighteenth-century Ireland*, ed. S. J. Connolly (Dublin, 2000), p.105-29.

Kennedy, Máire, *French books in eighteenth-century Ireland*, SVEC 2001:07.

Lewis, Richard, *The Candid philosopher, or Free thoughts on men, morals and manners*, 2 vols (Dublin, Byrn and Son and W. Kidd, 1778).

Livesey, Jim, 'The Dublin Society in eighteenth-century Irish political thought', *Historical journal* 47 (2004), p.615-40.

Luce, A. A., *Berkeley and Malebranche: a study in the origins of Berkeley's thought* (Oxford, 1967).

–, and T. E. Jessop (ed.), *The Works of George Berkeley*, 9 vols (Nendel, 1979).

McBride, Ian, *Scripture politics: Ulster Presbyterians and Irish radicalism in the late eighteenth century* (Oxford, 1998).

–, 'William Drennan and the dissenting tradition', in *The United Irishmen: republicanism, radicalism and rebellion*, ed. David Dickson, Dáire Keogh and Kevin Whelan (Dublin, 1993), p.49-61.

McCormack, William, *The Dublin paper war of 1786-1788: a bibliographical and critical enquiry* (Dublin, 1993).

McCully, J., *Letters by a farmer* (Belfast, J. Magee, 1787).

McDowell, R. B., *Ireland in the age of imperialism and revolution, 1760-1801* (Oxford, 1979).

McKenna, Theobald, *An Essay on Parliamentary reform, and on the evils likely to ensue from a republican constitution in Ireland* (Dublin, J. Rice, 1793).

Molyneux, William, *The Case of Ireland's being bound by acts of Parliament in England, stated* (1698), ed. J. G. Simms (Dublin, 1977).

Pollock, Joseph, *Letters of Owen Roe O'Nial* (Dublin, W. Jackson, 1779).

–, *Letters to the inhabitants of Newry* (Dublin, P. Byrne, 1793).

*The Protestant interest, considered relative to the operation of the Popery Acts in Ireland* (Dublin, 1757).

Rusticus, *A Review on the bishop of Cloyne's book, on the present state of the Church of Ireland, addressed to a friend in the city* (Dublin, P. Byrne, 1787).

Sheridan, Charles Francis, *Observations on the doctrine laid down by Sir William Blackstone, respecting the extent of the power of the British Parliament, particularly with relation to Ireland, in a letter to Sir William Blackstone, with a postscript addressed to Lord North, upon the affairs of that country* (Dublin, printed for the Company of Booksellers, 1779).
–, *Some observations on a late address to the citizens of Dublin, with thoughts on the present crisis* (Dublin, J. Stockdale, 1797).
Sheridan, Geraldine, 'Warring translations: Prévost's *Doyen de Killerine* in the Irish press', *Eighteenth-century Ireland* 14 (1999), p.99-115.
Simms, J. G., *Jacobite Ireland, 1685-1691* (Dublin, 2000).
Stewart, A. T. Q., *A Deeper silence: the hidden origins of the United Irishmen* (London, 1993).
–, *The Shape of Irish history* (Belfast, 2001).
Swift, Jonathan, *Gulliver's travels*, ed. Robert Demaria Jr (London, 2001).
–, *Major works*, ed. Angus Ross and David Wooley (Oxford, 2003).

–, *The Works of Jonathan Swift*, ed. Herbert Davis and Louis Landa (Oxford, 1968).

Thomas, Daniel, *Observations on the pamphlets published by the bishop of Cloyne, Mr Trant, and Theophilus, on one side; and on those by Mr O'Leary, Mr Barber, and Doctor Campbell on the other* (Dublin, printed for the Author, 1787).
Tiesch, Peter, 'Presbyterian radicalism', in *The United Irishmen: republicanism, radicalism and rebellion*, ed. David Dickson, Dáire Keogh and Kevin Whelan (Dublin, 1993), p.33-48.
*Transactions of the General Committee of the Roman Catholics of Ireland, during the year 1791; and some fugitive pieces on that subject* (Dublin, P. Byrne, 1792).
Troy, John Thomas, *A Pastoral instruction on the duties of Christian citizens, addressed to the Roman Catholics of the archdiocese of Dublin, with an observation on particular passages of a late publication entitled 'The Roman Catholic claim to the elective franchise, in an essay, &c.' by Charles Francis Sheridan, Esq.* (Dublin, P. Wogan, 1793).

Whelan, Kevin, *The Tree of liberty* (Cork, 1996).
Woodward, Richard, *The Present state of the Church of Ireland stated* (Dublin, W. Sleater, 1786).

# Germany

Blackall, Eric A., *The Emergence of German as a literary language* (Cambridge, 1959).

Hellmuth, Eckhart (ed.), *The Transformation of political culture: England and Germany in the late eighteenth century* (Oxford, 1990).
Herder, Johann, *Ideen zur Philosophie der Geschichte der Menschheit, Sämmtliche Werke*, ed. Bernhard Suphan, 33 vols (Berlin, 1877-1913).

–, *Journal meiner Reise im Jahr 1769: Historisch-Kritische Ausgabe*, ed. Katherina Mommsen (Stuttgart, 1976).

Jaumann, Herbert (ed.), *Rousseau in Deutschland: neue Beiträge zur Erforschung seiner Rezeption* (Berlin and New York, 1995).

Kant, Immanuel, *An Answer to the question 'What is Enlightenment?'* (1784), in I. Kant, *Political writings*, ed. Hans

Reiss, 2nd edn (Cambridge, 1991), p.55-61.

Klueting, Harm (ed.), *Katholische Aufklärung – Aufklärung im katholischen Deutschland* (Hamburg, 1993).

Knabe, Peter-Eckhard, *Die Rezeption der französischen Aufklärung in den 'Göttingischen gelehrten Anzeigen' (1739-1779)* (Frankfurt am Main, 1978).

Mervaud, Christiane, *Voltaire et Frédéric II: une dramaturgie des Lumières, 1736-1778*, SVEC 234 (1985).

Nisbet, H. B., 'Was ist Aufklärung? The concept of Enlightenment in eighteenth-century Germany', *Journal of European studies* 12 (1982), p.77-95.

Oz-Salzberger, Fania, *Translating the Enlightenment: Scottish civic discourse in eighteenth-century Germany* (Oxford, 1995).

Reill, Peter Hanns, *The German Enlightenment and the rise of historicism* (Berkeley, CA, and Los Angeles, CA, 1975).

Schleich, Thomas, *Aufklärung and revolution* (Stuttgart, 1981).

Sorkin, David, *Moses Mendelssohn and the religious Enlightenment* (Berkeley, CA, 1996).

Trousson, Raymond, 'J.-J. Rousseau et son œuvre dans la presse périodique allemande de 1750 à 1800', part 1, *Dix-huitième siècle* 1 (1969), p.289-310, part 2, *Dix-huitième siècle* 2 (1970), p.227-64.

Umbach, Maiken, *Federalism and Enlightenment in Germany, 1740-1806* (London, 2000).

–, 'Franz of Anhalt-Dessau and England: the Wörlitz landscape garden and anti-Prussian politics in the late Enlightenment', doctoral dissertation, University of Cambridge, 1996.

–, 'Visual culture, scientific images and German small-state politics in the late Enlightenment', *Past and present* 158 (1998), p.110-45.

Wisbert, Rainer, *Das Bildungsdenken des Jungen Herder: Interpretationen der Schrift 'Journal meiner Reise im Jahr 1769'* (Frankfurt, 1987).

## Hungary and the Habsburg monarchy

Balázs, Éva H., *Berzeviczy Gergely, a reformpolitikus, 1763-1795* (Budapest, 1967).

–, 'Berzeviczy Gergely: De Commercio et Industria Hungariae (1797)', in *Magyar könyvek – Magyar századok*, ed. István Kollega Tarsoly (Budapest, 2001), p.170-75.

–, 'Economistes d'origine aristocratique: un phénomène hongrois: physiocrates et pseudo-physiocrates en Hongrie à la fin du XVIII$^e$ siècle', in *Intellectuels français, intellectuels hongrois XIII$^e$-XX$^e$ siècle*, ed. Jacques Le Goff and Béla Köpeczi (Budapest and Paris, 1985), p.165-73.

–, 'Európai gazdaságpolitika – Magyar válasz', in *Életek és korok: Válogatott írások*, ed. Lilla Krász (Budapest, 2005), p. 264-73.

–, *Hungary and the Habsburgs, 1765-1800: an experiment in enlightened absolutism* (Budapest, 1997).

Beales, Derek, 'Christians and *philosophes*: the case of the Austrian Enlightenment', in *History, society and the Churches: essays in honour of Owen Chadwick*, ed. Derek Beales and Geoffrey Best (Cambridge, 1985), p.169-94, reprinted in D. Beales, *Enlightenment and reform in eighteenth-century Europe* (London, 2005), p.60-89.

311

–, Enlightenment and reform in eighteenth-century Europe (London, 2005).
Benda, Kálmán, 'Rousseau és Magyarország', in Emberbarát vagy hazafi: Tanulmányok a felvilágosodás korának magyarországi történetéből (Budapest, 1978), p.351-63.
Berényi, Pál (ed.), Skerlecz Miklós báró művei (Budapest, 1914).
Bíró, Ferenc, A felvilágosodás korának magyar irodalma (Budapest, 1994).
Blanning, T. C. W., Joseph II (Harlow, 1994).

Csorba, Sándor, and Klára Margócsy (ed.), A szétszórt rendszer: Tanulmányok Bessenyei György életművéről (Nyíregyháza, 1998).

Ember, Győző, and Gusztáv Heckenast (ed.), Magyarország története, 1686-1790, 2 vols (Budapest, 1989).
Evans, R. J. W., Austria, Hungary, and the Habsburgs: essays on Central Europe, c.1683-1867 (Oxford, 2006).
–, 'Joseph II and nationality in the Habsburg lands', in R. J. W. Evans, Austria, Hungary, and the Habsburgs: essays on Central Europe, c.1683-1867 (Oxford, 2006), p.134-46.
–, The Making of the Habsburg monarchy 1550-1700: an interpretation (Oxford, 1979).
–, 'The origins of Enlightenment in the Habsburg lands', in R. J. W. Evans, Austria, Hungary, and the Habsburgs: essays on Central Europe, c.1683-1867 (Oxford, 2006), p.36-55.

Ferenczi, László, 'Voltaire a XVIII. századi Magyarországon', in 'Sorsotok előre nézzétek': A francia felvilágosodás és a magyar kultúra: Tanulmányok, ed. Béla Köpeczi and László Sziklay (Budapest, 1975), p.183-200.

Kiss, Lajos, and László Papp (ed.), A magyar nyelv történeti-etimológiai szótára, vol.1: A-Gy, 2nd edn (Budapest, 1985).

Klingenstein, Grete, 'Between mercantilism and physiocracy: stages, modes, and functions of economic theory in the Habsburg monarchy, 1748-1763', in State and society in early modern Austria, ed. Charles W. Ingrao (West Lafayette, IN, 1994), p.181-214.
Koroda, Miklós, A magyar felvilágosodás breviáriuma [Budapest, 1944].
Kosáry, Domokos, Művelődés a XVIII. századi Magyarországon, 3rd extended edn (Budapest, 1996); shortened English edn: Culture and society in eighteenth-century Hungary (Budapest, 1987).
–, 'Pest-Buda és a Kereskedelmi Bizottság 1791-ben', in Tanulmányok Budapest Múltjából XI (Budapest, 1956), p.127-52.
Kovács, Elisabeth (ed.), Katholische Aufklärung und Josephinismus (Vienna, 1979).

Marczali, Henrik, Az 1790-1791. országgyűlés, 2 vols (Budapest, 1907).

Pálffy, Géza, A tizenhatodik század története, Magyar Századok (Budapest, 2000).
Pukánszky, Sándor, Természetjog és politika a XVIII. századi Magyarországon: Batthyány Alajostól Martinovicsig (Budapest, 2001).

Smith, Adam, Vizsgálódás a nemzeti vagyonosság természetéről és okairól (Budapest, 1891).
Szakály, Orsolya, 'A gépesített pamutipar kezdetei a Habsburg birodalomban: A burgaui fonóüzem, 1790-1808', in Tanulmányok a 18. század történetéből H. Balázs Éva professzor tiszteletére: Sic Itur ad Astra (Budapest, 2000), p.225-44.
–, Egy vállalkozó főnemes: Vay Miklós báró, 1756-1824 (Budapest, 2003).
–, 'Hadiipar és nemesi vállalkozás: A Vay-féle salétromtársaság, 1798-1856', Levéltári Közlemények (2000), p.129-65.

*Bibliography*

Tóth, Béla, 'Bessenyei György: Jámbor szándék (1790)', in *Magyar könyvek – Magyar századok*, ed. István Kollega Tarsoly (Budapest, 2001), p.158-62.

Váczy, János (ed.), *Kazinczy Ferenc összes művei: Levelezés*, 19 vols (Budapest, 1890-1909).

## Naples and Italy

Ajello, Raffaele, *Una Società anomala: il programma e la sconfitta della nobiltà napoletana in due memoriali cinquecenteschi* (Naples, 1996).

Astarita, Tommaso, *Between salt water and holy water: a history of southern Italy* (New York and London, 2005).

–, *The Continuity of feudal power: the Caracciolo of Brienza in Spanish Naples* (Cambridge, 1992).

Becagli, Vieri, 'Georg-Ludwig Schmid d'Avenstein e i suoi *Principes de la législation universelle*: oltre la fisiocrazia', in *Studi settecenteschi* 24 (2004), *Fisiocrazia e proprietà terriera*, special number ed. Maria Albertone, p.215-52.

Burnet, Gilbert, *Some letters containing an account of what seemed most remarkable in Switzerland, Italy &c* (Amsterdam, Abraham Acher, 1686).

Carpanetto, Dino, and Giuseppe Ricuperati, *Italy in the age of reason 1685-1789* (London, 1987).

Chiosi, Elivira, 'Il regno dal 1734 al 1799', in *Storia del Mezzogiorno, vol.4: il regno dagli Angioini ai Borboni*, ed. Giuseppe Galasso and Rosario Romeo (Naples, 1986), p. 373-467.

Chorley, Patrick, *Oil, silk, and Enlightenment: economic problems in XVIII<sup>th</sup>-century Naples* (Naples, 1965).

Conti, Vittorio, *Paolo Mattia Doria: dalla repubblica dei togati alla repubblica dei notabili* (Florence, 1978).

Corona, Gabriella, *Demani ed individualismo agrario nel regno di Napoli* (Naples, 1995).

Croce, Benedetto, *History of the kingdom of Naples* (first Italian edition: 1925; English edition by H. Stuart Hughes: Chicago and London, 1970).

Davis, John A., *Naples and Napoleon: southern Italy and the European revolutions 1780-1860* (Oxford, 2006).

Diaz, Furio, and Luciano Guerci (ed.), *Opere di Ferdinando Galiani, Illuministi italiani* 6 (Milan and Naples, 1975).

Donati, Claudio, 'The Italian nobilities in the seventeenth and eighteenth centuries', in *The European nobilities in the seventeenth and eighteenth centuries*, vol.1: *Western Europe*, ed. H. M. Scott (London and New York, 1995), p.237-68.

Doria, Paolo Mattia, 'Del commercio del regno di Napoli [...] lettera [...] diretta al Signor D. Francesco Ventura, degnissimo Presidente del Magistrato di Commercio, Napoli, 2 Aprile dell'anno 1740', in *Il Pensiero civile di Paolo Mattia Doria negli scritti inediti*, ed. Enrico Vidal (Milan, 1953), p.161-206.

–, *Massime del governo spagnolo a Napoli*, ed. G. Galasso and V. Conti (Naples, 1973).

Fabrizio, Pasquale di (ed.), *Manoscritti Napoletani di Paolo Mattia Doria, vol.4* (Galatina, 1981).

Filangieri, Gaetano, *La Scienza della legislazione*, ed. Vincenzo Ferrone, 7 vols (Venice, 2003-2004).

Galanti, Giuseppe Maria, *Descrizione dello stato antico ed attuale del contado di Molise, con un saggio storico sulla costituzione del Regno*, 2 vols (Naples, Società Letteraria e Tipografica, 1781).

–, *Elogio storico del Signor Abate Antonio Genovesi* (Naples, 1772).
–, *Nuova descrizione storica e geografica delle Sicilie* (1786-1794), ed. F. Assante and D. Demarco, 2 vols (Naples, 1969).
Galasso, Giuseppe, *La Filosofia in soccorso de' governi: la cultura napoletana del settecento* (Naples, 1989).
–, *Il Mezzogiorno nella storia d'Italia* (Florence, 1977).
Giannone, Pietro, *Storia civile del regno di Napoli*, 4 vols (Naples, Niccol Naso, 1723).
Grimaldi, Domenico, *Piano di riforma per la pubblica economia delle provincie del regno di Napoli, e per l'agricoltura delle due Sicilie* (Naples, Giuseppe-Maria Porcelli, 1780).

Imbruglia, Girolamo (ed.), *Naples in the eighteenth century: the birth and death of a nation state* (Cambridge, 2000).

Longano, Francesco, *Viaggi per lo regno di Napoli*, ed. Giulio Gentile (Naples, 2002).

Muto, Giovanni, 'The structure of aristocratic patrimonies in the kingdom of Naples: management strategies and regional economic development: 16th-18th centuries', in *European aristocracies and colonial elites: patrimonial management strategies and economic development 15th-18th centuries*, ed. P. Janssens and B. Yun-Casalilla (Aldershot, 2005), p.115-33.

Pagano, Francesco Mario, *Saggi politici: de' principii, progressi e decadenza delle società* (1791-1792), ed. Luigi and Laura Salvetti Firpo (Naples, 1993).
Palmieri, Giuseppe, *Della ricchezza nazionale* (Naples, Vincenzo Flauto and Michele Stasi, 1792).
–, *Osservazioni su varj articoli riguardanti il pubblica economia* (Naples, Vincenzo Flauto and Michele Stasi, 1790).

–, *Pensieri economici relativi al regno di Napoli* (Naples, Vincenzo Flauto, 1789).
–, *Riflessioni sulla pubblica felicità relativamente al regno di Napoli* (Naples, the brothers Raimondi, 1787; 2nd edn 1788).
Perna, Maria Luisa, *Antonio Genovesi: Delle Lezioni di commercio o sia di economia civile, con Elementi del commercio* (Naples, 2005).
– (ed.) *Antonio Genovesi: scritti economici*, 2 vols (Naples, 1984).
–, 'Giuseppe Galanti editore', in *Miscellanea Walter Maturi* (Turin, 1966), p.221-58.
Petrusewicz, Marta, *Come il meridione divenne una questione: rappresentazioni del sud prima e dopo il quarantotto* (Catanzaro, 1998).

Rao, Anna Maria, *L'"Amaro della feudalità": la devoluzione di Arnone e la questione feudale a Napoli alla fine del' 700* (Naples, 1984).
–, 'The feudal question, judicial systems, and the Enlightenment', in *Naples in the eighteenth century: the birth and death of a nation state*, ed. Girolamo Imbruglia (Cambridge, 2000), p.95-117.
–, 'La questione feudale nell'età tanucciana', *Archivio Storico per la Sicilia Orientale* 84:2-3 (1988), special number on *Bernardo Tanucci: la corte, il paese 1730-1780*, p.77-162.
Reinert, Sophus A., 'Blaming the Medici: footnotes, falsification, and the fate of the "English model" in eighteenth-century Italy', *History of European ideas* 32:4 (2006), special issue on *Commerce and morality in eighteenth-century Italy*, ed. Koen Stapelbroek, p.430-55.
Ricuperati, Giuseppe, 'Définir les Lumières: centres et périphéries du point de vue européen, cosmopolite et italien', *SVEC* 2005:10, p.303-21.
Robertson, John, 'The Enlightenment above national context: political

economy in eighteenth-century Scotland and Naples', *Historical journal* 40 (1997), p.667-97.
Rovito, Pier Luigi, *Respublica dei togati: giuristi e società nella Napoli del Seicento* (Naples, 1981).

Silvestrini, Maria Teresa, 'Free trade, feudal remnants and international equilibrium in Gaetano Filangieri's *Science of legislation*', *History of European ideas* 32 (2006), p.502-24.

Venturi, Franco (ed.), *Riformatori napoletani, Illuministi italiani* 5 (Milan and Naples, 1962).
–, *Settecento riformatore*, 5 parts, 7 vols (Turin, 1969-1991).
–, *Settecento riformatore*, vol.1: *Da Muratori a Beccaria 1730-1760* (Turin, 1969).
–, *Settecento riformatore*, vol.2: *La chiesa e le repubblica dentro i loro limiti* (Turin, 1976).
–, *Settecento riformatore*, vol.5: *L'Italia dei lumi 1764-1790: i. la rivoluzione di Corsica; le grande carestie degli anni sessanta; la Lombardia delle riforme* (Turin, 1987).
–, 'Su alcune pagine di antologia', *Rivista storica Italiana* 71 (1959), p.321-25.
Villani, Pasquale, 'Il dibattito sulla feudalità nel regno di Napoli dal Genovesi al Canosa', in *Saggi e ricerche sul Settecento*, ed. E. Sestan (Naples, 1968), p.252-331.
Villari, Lucio, 'Note sulla fisiocrazia e sugli economisti napoletani del '700', in *Saggi e ricerche sul Settecento*, ed. E. Sestan (Naples, 1968), p.224-51.
Villari, Rosario, *Mezzogiorno e contadini nell'età moderna* (Bari, 1961).
–, *The Revolt of Naples*, translated by James Newell (Cambridge, 1993).
Visceglia, Maria Antonietta, 'Un groupe social ambigu: organisation, stratégies et représentations de la noblesse napolitaine XVI-XVIII$^e$ siècles', *Annales ESC* 48 (1993), p.819-51.

Winspeare, David, *Storia degli abusi feudali* (Naples, 1811).

# Poland-Lithuania

Bednarski, Stanisław, *Upadek a odrodzenie szkół jezuickich w Polsce: Studium z dziejów kultury i szkolnictwa polskiego* (Cracow, 2003; reprint of Cracow, 1933).
Bieńkowski, Ludwik, 'Le siècle des Lumières catholiques en Pologne', in *Les Contacts religieux franco-polonais du moyen âge à nos jours: relations, influences, images d'un pays vu par l'autre* (Paris, 1985), p.203-10.
*Błędy Woltera wybrane z księgi francuskiey pod tymże tytułem Les Erreurs de Voltaire napisaney przez X: Franciszka Nonnotta, á zaleconey listem Klemensa XIII papieża z odpowiedzią na nie y życiem tegoż Woltera* (Łowicz, Drukarnia J.O. Xcia Prymasa, 1780).

Butterwick, Richard, *Poland's last king and English culture: Stanisław August Poniatowski 1732-1798* (Oxford, 1998).
–, 'Polite liberty or *l'esprit monarchique*? Stanisław August Poniatowski, Jean-Jacques Rousseau and *politesse* in England', *SVEC* 2003:07, p.249-70.
–, 'Political discourses of the Polish Revolution, 1788-1792', *English historical review* 120 (2005), p.695-731.
–, 'Progress and violence in the thought of the Polish Enlightenment', in *Progrès et violence au XVIII$^e$ siècle*, ed. Valérie Cossy and Deirdre Dawson, *Etudes internationales sur le dix-huitième siècle* 3 (Paris, 2001), p.17-34.

–, 'Stanisław August Poniatowski jako latitudynarysta religijny', *Wiek Oświecenia* 14 (1998), p.179-91.
–, 'What is Enlightenment (*oświecenie*)? Some Polish answers, 1765-1820', *Central Europe* 3:1 (2005), p.19-37.

Deszczyńska, Martyna, '*Historia sacra*' i *dzieje narodowe: Refleksja lat 1795-1830 nad rolą religii i Kościoła w przeszłości Polski* (Warsaw, 2003).
–, and Ewa Zielińska, 'Skarszewski, Wojciech Leszczyc', *Polski Słownik Biograficzny*, 43 vols (Warsaw and Cracow, 1997), vol.38, p.50-61.

Fabre, Jean, *Stanislas-Auguste Poniatowski et l'Europe des Lumières: étude de cosmopolitisme* (Paris and Strasbourg, 1952).

Gierowski, Józef Andrzej, *The Polish-Lithuanian Commonwealth in the XVIIIth century: from anarchy to well-organised state* (Cracow, 1996).
Grochulska, Barbara, 'Miejsce Kościoła w polskim Oświeceniu', *Mówią Wieki* 11 (1990), p.19-22.
Grzebień, Ludwik, and Stanisław Obirek (ed.), *Jezuici a kultura polska* (Cracow, 1993).
Grzybowski, Michał, 'Kościelna działalność Michała Jerzego Poniatowskiego biskupa płockiego', *Studia z Historii Kościoła w Polsce* 7 (1983), p.5-225.

Janeczek, Stanisław, 'Czym była oświeceniowa *philosophia recentiorum*?', *Kwartalnik Filozoficzny* 26:1 (1998), p.115-28.
–, *Oświecenie chrześcijańskie: Z dziejów polskiej kultury filozoficznej* (Lublin, 1994).
[Jezierski, Franciszek Salezy], *Ktoś piszący z Warszawy dnia 11 lutego 1790 r.*, in *Wybór Pism*, ed. Zdzisław Skwarczyński and Jerzy Ziomek (Warsaw, 1952).
Jobert, Ambroise, *La Commission d'Education Nationale: son œuvre d'instruction civique* (Paris, 1941).

–, *Magnats polonais et physiocrates français (1767-1774)* (Paris, 1941).

Kaliński, Wilhelm, *Dziennik 1787-1788*, ed. Łukasz Kurdybacha (Wrocław, 1968).
Kamińska, Janina, *Universitas Vilnensis: Akademia Wileńska i Szkoła Główna Wielkiego Księstwa Litewskiego 1773-1792* (Pułtusk and Warsaw, 2004).
Karpowicz, Michał, *Kazanie o władzy Kościoła, jak jest narodom zbawienna, i o majątkach Kościołów, jak narodom są użyteczne w dzień SS. Apostołów Piotra y Pawła w Wilnie na Antokolu w Kościele Kanoników Laterańskich miane 1789 [...] Józefowi z Korwinów Kossakowskiemu biskupowi inflantskiemu [...] w dzień imienin jego offiarowane* (Wilno, 1790).
–, *Kazanie w uroczystość imienin J. K. Mci y pamiątkę ustanowienia Orderu S. Stanisława biskupa i męczennika do Trybunału Głł: W.X. Litt: w dzień doszłey wiadomości do Grodna o Konstytycyi rządowey szczęśliwie na wiekopomnym seymie warszawskim ustanowioney, miane dnia 8. maia 1791. roku* (Grodno, Drukarnia J.K. Mci i P.K.E.N., 1791).
–, *Kazanie X. Karpowicza archidiakona smoleńskiego, proboszcza preńskiego, theologii y pisma ś. w Szkole Gł: Lit: professora, na pierwszym ufundowaniu powiatu preńskiego i rozpoczęciu pierwszych seymików w kościele parafialnym preńskim 14 lutego, 1792. roku* (Wilno, Drukarnia XX. Bazylianów, 1792).
–, *Na zaprzysiężeniu uroczystym Ustawy Rządowey 3. i 5. maja od Trybunału G. W. X. L. jego palestry, kancellaryi, y chorągwi trybunalskiey w dniu 15. marca roku 1792. w Kościele Akademickim S. Jana w Wilnie Kazanie Xiędza Karpowicza prałata archidiak: smoleń: Pisma Ś. i Teologii w Szkole Głow: W. X. Lit: Professora* (Wilno, Drukarnia XX. Bazylianów, 1792).
Kasabuła, Tadeusz, *Ignacy Massalski, biskup wileński* (Lublin, 1998).

Kossakowski, Jan Nepomucen, *Kazanie o jedności, zgodzie i pokoiu, w dzień przeniesioney Stanisława S. uroczystości jmienin Nayiaśnieyszego Pana i pierwszéy obchodu Ustawy Rządowéy rocznicy przez X. Jana Nepomucena Kossakowskiego prałata kated: i administratora dyecezyi wileń: roku 1792 miane* (Wilno, 1792), reprinted in J. N. Kossakowski, *Kazania* (Wilno, Drukarnia J.K.Mci przy Akademii, 1793), p.169-94.

–, *Kazanie o miłości oyczyzny w dzień S. Stanisława biskupa krakowskiego pamiątką jego męczeństwa, y dorocznym obchodzeniem imienin J. Krolew: Mosci uroczysty w Kościele S. Jana Akademickim* (Wilno, 1789), reprinted in J. N. Kossakowski, *Kazania* (Wilno, Drukarnia J.K.Mci przy Akademii, 1793), p.1-39.

–, *Kazanie o zachowaniu praw narodowych w dzień uroczystości S. Stanisława biskupa i męczennika jmienin N. P. N. M. Stanisława Augusta i pamiątki ustanowionego orderu pod imieniem tegoż Świętego dorocznie obchodzoney w Kościele S. Jana Akademickim przez X. Jana Nepomucena Kossakowskiego prałata kated: i administratora dyecezyi wileń: miane* (Wilno, 1790), reprinted in J. N. Kossakowski, *Kazania* (Wilno, Drukarnia J.K.Mci przy Akademii, 1793), p.40-73.

–, *Kazanie w dzień uroczystego nabożeństwa w Wilnie odprawionego na podziękowanie Bogu za całość i szczęśliwość Oyczyzny naszey ustanowieniem dobrego Rządu dnia 3. maja roku 1791 zabeśpieczoną, miane przez X. Jana Nepomucena Kossakowskiego prałata kated: i administratora dyecezyi wileń* (Wilno, 1791), reprinted in Kossakowski, *Kazania* (Wilno, Drukarnia J.K.Mci przy Akademii, 1793), p.106-34.

[Kossakowski, Józef], *Xiądz pleban* (Warsaw, Gröll, 1786).

Kostkiewiczowa, Teresa, 'Krasicki a oświecenie', in *Studia o Krasickim* (Warsaw, 1997), p.138-62.

–, *Polski wiek świateł: Obszary swoistości* (Wrocław, 2002).

–, *Studia o Krasickim* (Warsaw, 1997).

Kwiatkowska, Agnieszka, *Piórowe wojny: Polemiki literackie polskiego oświecenia* (Poznań, 2001).

Libiszowska, Zofia, 'L'Eglise et les Lumières en Pologne au XVIII$^e$ siècle', in *Les Contacts religieux franco-polonais du moyen âge à nos jours: relations, influences, images d'un pays vu par l'autre* (Paris, 1985), p.199-203.

–, 'Odgłosy Konstytucji 3 Maja na Zachodzie', in *Konstytucja 3 Maja w tradycji i kulturze polskiej*, ed. Alina Barszczewska-Krupa, 2 vols (Łódź, 1991), vol.1, p.70-81.

Litak, Stanisław, *Od Reformacji do Oświecenia: Kościół katolicki w Polsce nowożytnej* (Lublin, 1994).

Łossowska, Irena, 'Piotr Świtkowski (1744-1793)', in *Pisarze polskiego Oświecenia*, ed. Teresa Kostkiewiczowa and Zbigniew Goliński, 3 vols (Warsaw, 1992-1996), vol.2, p.305-31.

Lukowski, Jerzy, *Liberty's folly: the Polish-Lithuanian Commonwealth in the eighteenth century* (London, 1991).

–, 'Recasting utopia: Montesquieu, Rousseau and the Polish Constitution of 3 May 1791', *Historical journal* 37 (1994), p.65-87.

Meer, Jan IJ. van der, *Literary activities and attitudes in the Stanislavian age in Poland (1764-1795): a social system?*, Studies in Slavic literature and poetics 36 (Amsterdam and New York, 2002).

Michalski, Jerzy, 'The meaning of the Constitution of 3 May', in *Constitution and reform in eighteenth-century Poland: the Constitution of 3 May 1791*, ed. Samuel Fiszman (Bloomington, IN, 1997), p.251-86.

–, 'La Révolution française aux yeux d'un roi', *Acta Poloniae Historica* 66 (1992), p.75-91.

–, '"Warszawa" czyli o antystołecznych nastrojach w czasach

Stanisława Augusta', *Studia warszawskie* 12 (1972), p.9-78.

—, '"Wolność" i "własność" chłopska w polskiej myśli reformatorskiej XVIII wieku', *Kwartalnik Historyczny* 110:4 (2003), p.5-45, and 111:1 (2004), p.69-103.

—, et al. (ed.), *Lettres de Philippe Mazzei et du roi Stanislas-Auguste de Pologne* (Rome, 1982).

Mickiewicz, Adam, *Pan Tadeusz* [1834], translated by Kenneth R. MacKenzie, 3rd (bilingual) edn (New York, 2000).

Muratori, Ludovico, *O porządnym nabożeństwie chrześcian*, translated by M. Tukałło (Wilno, Drukarnia J.K.Mci i Rzeczypospolitey u XX. Scholarum Piarum, 1787).

O'Connor, Mark, 'Oświecenie katolickie i Marcin Poczobut SJ', in *Jezuici a kultura polska*, ed. Ludwik Grzebień and Stanisław Obirek (Cracow, 1993), p.41-49.

Paszenda, Jerzy (ed.), *Z dziejów szkolnictwa jezuickiego w Polsce: Wybór artykułów* (Cracow, 1994).

Piechnik, Ludwik, *Dzieje Akademii Wileńskiej*, 4 vols (Rome, 1983-1990).

Popłatek, Jan, *Komisja Edukacji Narodowej: Udział byłych Jezuitów w pracach Komisji Edukacji Narodowej* (Cracow, 1974).

Raila, Eligijus, 'Vilniaus vyskupas Ignotas Masalskis ir katališka apšvieta: edukacijos ir pastoracijos simbiozė', in *Kultūros istorijos tyrenėjimai*, 5 vols (Vilnius, 1997), vol.3, p.92-146.

Rostworowski, Emanuel, 'Les auteurs de la littérature religieuse française traduite en Pologne au XVIIIe siècle', in *Les Contacts religieux franco-polonais du moyen âge à nos jours: relations, influences, images d'un pays vu par l'autre* (Paris, 1985), p. 211-14.

—, 'Ksiądz pleban Kołłątaj', in *Wiek XIX: Prace ofiarowane Stefanowi Kieniewiczowi w 60 rocznicę urodzin*, ed. Barbara Grochulska, Bogusław Leśnodorski and Andrzej Zahorski (Warsaw, 1967), p.49-63.

—, 'Miasta i mieszczanie w ustroju Trzeciego Maja', in *Sejm Czteroletni i jego tradycje*, ed. Jerzy Kowecki (Warsaw, 1991), p.138-51.

[Skarszewski, Wojeciech], *Odpowiedź plebana na nowe zarzuty przeciwko duchowieństwu polskiemu* ([Warsaw], 1789).

Ślusarska, Magdalena, 'Konstytucja 3 Maja w kaznodziejstwie okolicznościowym lat 1791-1792', in '*Rok Monarchii Konstytucyjnej': Piśmiennictwo polskie lat 1791-1792 wobec Konstytucji 3 Maja*, ed. Teresa Kostkiewiczowa (Warsaw, 1992), p.153-75.

—, 'Królewskie kaznodziejstwo okolicznościowe czasów Stanisława Augusta Poniatowskiego', *Napis: Tom poświęcony literaturze okolicznościowej i użytkowej* 1 (1994), p.135-52.

—, 'Kultura literacka Wilna w dobie stanisławowskiej: Zarys wybranych zagadnień', *Wiek Oświecenia* 14 (1998), p.95-129.

—, 'Michał Franciszek Karpowicz (1744-1803)', in *Pisarze polskiego oświecenia*, ed. Teresa Kostkiewiczowa and Zbigniew Goliński, 3 vols (Warsaw, 1992-1996), vol.2, p.74-98.

—, 'Les modèles d'évêque, de curé et de paroisse au siècle des Lumières: continuation ou changement de tradition?', in *Proceedings of the Commission internationale d'histoire ecclésiastique comparée, Lublin 1996*, vol.3: *Churches – states – nations in the Enlightenment and in the nineteenth century*, ed. Mirosław Filipowicz (Lublin, 2000), p.23-35.

— (ed.), 'Oświeceniowe modele biskupa, plebana i parafii: Kontynuacja czy zmiana tradycji?', in *Dwór*, *plebania, rodzina chłopska: Szkice z dziejów wsi polskiej XVII i XVIII wieku* (Warsaw, 1998), p.37-53.

– (ed.), '*Powinność i należytość*: Wzajemne relacje między właścicielami dóbr a społecznością wiejską w świetle kazań z epoki stanisławowskiej', in *Dwór, plebania, rodzina chłopska: Szkice z dziejów wsi polskiej XVII i XVIII wieku* (Warsaw, 1998), p.69-102.

–, 'Problematyka politycznospołeczna w polskim kaznodziejstwie okolicznościowym w latach 1775-1795', doctoral dissertation, University of Warsaw, 1992.

–, 'Sejm Czteroletni w okolicznościowym kaznodziejstwie lat 1788-1790', in *Ku reformie państwa i odrodzeniu moralnemu człowieka: Zbiór artykułów i rozpraw poświęconych rocznicy ustanowienia Konstytucji 3 Maja 1791 roku*, ed. Piotr Żbikowski (Rzeszów, 1992), p.65-80.

Šmigelskytė-Stukienė, Ramunė, *Lietuvos Didžiosios Kunigaikštystes konfederacijos susidarymas ir veikla 1792-1793* (Vilnius, 2003).

–, 'Livonijos vyskupo Juozapo Kazimiero Kosakovskio LDK vizija antropo valstybės padalijimo akivaizdoje', *Lietuvos Istorijos Metraštis* 2001:1 (Vilnius, 2002), p.73-86.

Smoleński, Władysław, *Konfederacya targowicka* (Cracow, 1903).

–, *Konfederacya targowicka* (Warsaw, 1903).

–, *Ostatni rok Sejmu Wielkiego*, 2nd edn (Cracow, 1897).

–, *Przewrót umysłowy w Polsce wieku XVIII: Studia historyczne*, 4th edn (Warsaw, 1979).

Snopek, Jerzy, *Objawienie i oświecenie: Z dziejów libertynizmu w Polsce* (Wrocław, 1986).

–, *Prowincja oświecona: Kultura literacka ziemi krakowskiej w dobie Oświecenia* (Warsaw, 1992).

Stasiewicz-Jasiukowa, Irena, 'Der aufgeklärte Katholizismus im Polen der Frühaufklärung', in *Europa in der Frühen Neuzeit: Festschrift für Günter Mühlpfordt, vol.3: Aufbruch zur Moderne*, ed. Erich Donnert (Weimar, Cologne and Vienna, 1997), p.555-64.

– (ed.), *Wkład Jezuitów do nauki i kultury w Rzeczyspospolitej Obojga Narodów i pod zaborami* (Cracow and Warsaw, 2004).

[Staszic, Stanisław], *Przestrogi dla Polski*, in S. Staszic, *Pisma filozoficzne i społeczne*, ed. Bogdan Suchodolski, 2 vols (Warsaw, 1954).

[Surowiecki, Karol], *Gora rodząca, bayka sprawdzona w osiemnastym wieku na schyłku onegoż wyiaśniona* (n.p., 1792).

–, *Python lipsko-warszawski diabeł: Kontr-tragedya na tragedyą Saul wyjęta z Pisma Świętego, grana przez aktorów tamtego świata w roku 1789; a w roku 1792, światu ziemskiemu obiawiona* (n.p., 1792).

Szczygielski, Wojciech, *Referendum trzeciomajowe: Sejmiki lutowe 1792 roku* (Łódź, 1994).

Szybiak, Irena, 'Portret zbiorowy nauczycieli szkół średnich Komisji Edukacji Narodowej', *Wiek Oświecenia* 5 (1989), p.55-68.

–, *Szkolnictwo Komisji Edukacji Narodowej w Wielkim Księstwie Litewskim* (Wrocław, 1973).

Wysocki, Józef, *Józef Ignacy Rybiński biskup włocławski i pomorski 1777-1806: Zarys biograficzny na tle rządów diecezji* (Rome, 1967).

*Zbiur wszystkich druków Konfederacyi Targowickiey y Wileńskiey* (Warsaw, Drukarnia na Krakowskim Przedmieściu nr 427, 1792).

# Russia

Artem'eva, T. V., *Ideia istorii v Rossii XVIII veka* (St Petersburg, 1998).

Barnard, F. M. (ed.), *Herder on social and political culture* (Cambridge, 1969).

Bartenev, P. I. (ed.), *Arkhiv kniazia Vorontsova*, 40 vols (Moscow, 1870-1895).

Bartlett, Roger, 'German popular enlightenment in the Russian Empire: Peter Ernst Wilde and Catherine II', *Slavonic and East European review* 84 (2006), p.256-78.

Batalden, Stephen K., *Catherine II's Greek prelate: Eugenious Voulgaris in Russia 1771-1806* (Boulder, CO, 1982).

Batiushkov, Konstantin, 'Vecher u Kantemira', in *Sochineniia K. N. Batiushkova*, 5th edn (St Petersburg, 1887).

Berkov, P. N., *Istorii russkoi zhurnalistiki XVIII veka* (Moscow and Leningrad, 1952).

– (ed.), 'Osnovnye voprosy izucheniia russkogo prosvetitel'stva', in *Problemy russkogo Prosveshcheniia v literature XVIII veka* (Moscow and Leningrad, 1961), p.5-27.

– (ed.), *Satiricheskie zhurnaly N. I. Novikova* (Moscow and Leningrad, 1951).

Black, J. L., *Citizens for the fatherland: education, educators and pedagogical ideals in eighteenth-century Russia* (Boulder, CO, 1979).

Brokgauz, F. A., and I. A. Efron, *Entsiklopedicheskii slovar'*, 82 vols (St Petersburg, 1890-1904).

Bruess, Gregory L., *Religion, identity and empire: a Greek archbishop in the Russia of Catherine the Great* (Boulder, CO, 1997).

Bubnov, Iu. A., *Drevnerusskii sekuliarizm i formirovanie ideologii prosvetitel'stva: Ot kreshcheniia Rusi do nachala petrovskikh preobrazovanii* (St Petersburg, 1999).

Chechulin, N. D. (ed.), *Nakaz Imperatritsy Ekateriny II, dannyi kommissii o sochinenii proekta novago Ulozheniia* (St Petersburg, 1907).

Cracraft, James, *The Petrine revolution in Russian culture* (Cambridge, MA, 2004).

Cross, Anthony G., *N. M. Karamzin: a study of his literary career 1783-1803* (Carbondale, IL, 1971).

Dashkova, E. R., *O smysle slova 'vospitanie'*, ed. G. I. Smagina (St Petersburg, 2001).

Derzhavin, G. R., *Stikhotvoreniia*, ed. D. D. Blagoi (Leningrad, 1957).

Dixon, Simon, *Catherine the Great* (Harlow, 2001).

–, *The Modernisation of Russia, 1676-1825* (Cambridge, 1999).

–, 'The posthumous reputation of Catherine the Great in Russia, 1797-1837', *Slavonic and East European review* 77 (1999), p.646-79.

Dukes, Paul, 'The Russian Enlightenment', in *The Enlightenment in national context*, ed. Roy Porter and Mikuláš Teich (Cambridge, 1981), p.176-91.

Eisen, J. G., *Ausgewählte Schrifte: Deutsche Volksaufklärung und Leibeigenschaft im Russischen Reich*, ed. Roger Bartlett and Erich Donnert (Marburg, 1998).

Florovskii, Georgii, *Puti russkogo bogosloviia*, 2nd edn (Paris, 1981).

Fonvizin, D. I., *Sobranie sochinenii*, ed. G. P. Makogonenko, 2 vols (Moscow and Leningrad, 1959).

Gershenkron, M. (ed.), *Sochineniia i pis'ma P. Ia. Chaadaeva*, 2 vols (Moscow, 1913-1914).

Goggi, Gianluigi, 'The philosophes and the debate over Russian civilization', in *A Window on Russia*, ed. Maria di Salvo and Lindsey Hughes (Rome, 1996), p.299-305.

Griffiths, David M., 'In search of Enlightenment: recent Soviet interpretation of eighteenth-century Russian intellectual history', *Canadian-American Slavic studies* 16 (1982) p.317-56.

Hartley, Janet M., 'Philanthropy in the reign of Catherine the Great: aims and realities', in *Russia in the age of the Enlightenment*, ed. Roger Bartlett and Janet M. Hartley (London, 1990), p.167-202.

Jones, Adrian, 'A Russian bourgeois's Arctic Enlightenment', *Historical journal* 48 (2005), p.623-46.

Jones, Robert E., *Provincial development in Russia: Catherine II and Jakob Sievers* (New Brunswick, NJ, 1984).

Jones, W. Gareth, *Nikolay Novikov: enlightener of Russia* (Cambridge, 1984).

Kahn, Andrew, 'Nikolai Karamzin's discourses of Enlightenment', in Nikolai Karamzin, *Letters of a Russian traveller*, ed. Andrew Kahn, SVEC 2003:04, p.459-551.

Kantemir, Antiokh, *Sobranie stikhotvorenii*, ed. F. Ia. Priima and Z. I. Gershovich (Leningrad, 1956).

Kapnist, V. V., 'Filozof', in *Sobranie sochinenii*, ed. D. S. Babkin, 2 vols (Moscow and Leningrad, 1960), vol.1, p. 219-27.

Karamzin, Nikolai M., *Izbrannye sochinenii*, ed. G. P. Makogonenko, 2 vols (Moscow and Leningrad, 1964).

–, *Pis'ma russkogo puteshestvennika*, ed. Iu. M. Lotman, N. A. Marchenko and B. A. Uspenskii (Leningrad, 1984).

Karp, Serguëi, and Larry Wolff (ed.), *Le Mirage russe au XVIII$^e$ siècle* (Ferney-Voltaire, 2001).

Keenan, Paul, 'Creating a "public" in St Petersburg, 1703-1761', doctoral dissertation, University of London, 2005.

Kelly, Catriona, *Refining Russia: advice literature, polite culture, and gender from Catherine to Yelstin* (Oxford, 2001).

Klein, Ioakhim [Joachim], *Puti kul'turnogo importa: Trudy po russkoi literature XVIII veka* (Moscow, 2005).

Kochetkova, N. D., *Literatura russkogo sentimentalizma (Esteticheskie i khudozhestvennye iskaniia)* (St Petersburg, 1994).

Kopanev, A. I., et al. (ed.), *Svodnyi katalog knig na inostrannykh iazykakh, izdannykh v Rossii v XVIII veke, 1701-1800*, 3 vols (Leningrad, 1984-1986).

Labzina, Anna, *Vospominaniia Anny Evdokimovny Labzinoi 1758-1828*, ed. B. L. Modzalevskii (St Petersburg, 1914).

Lazarchuk, R. M., 'Perepiska N. M. Karamzina s A. A. Petrovym. (K probleme rekonstruktsii "romana v pis'makh")', *XVIII vek* 20 (1996), p.135-43.

Lortholary, Albert, *Le Mirage russe en France au XVIII$^e$ siècle* (Paris, [1951]).

Lotman, Iu. M. (ed.), *Poety 1790-1810-kh godov* (Leningrad, 1971).

–, 'Russo i russkaia kul'tura', in *Epokha Prosveshcheniia: iz istorii mezhdunarodnykh sviazei russkoi literatury*, ed. M. P. Alekseev (Leningrad, 1967), p. 208-81.

Madariaga, Isabel de, *Politics and culture in eighteenth-century Russia* (London, 1998).

–, *Russia in the age of Catherine the Great* (New Haven, CT, 1981).

Marasinova, E. N., *Psikhologiia elity rossiiskogo dvorianstva poslednei treti XVIII veka* (Moscow, 1999).

Marker, Gary, *Publishing, printing and the origins of intellectual life in Russia, 1700-1800* (Princeton, NJ, 1985).

Murav'ev-Apostol, I. M., *Pis'ma iz Moskvy v Nizhnii Novgorod*, ed. V. A. Koshelev (St Petersburg, 2002).

Nikolev, N. P., 'Satira na razvrashchennye nravy nyneshnego veka', in *Poety XVIII veka*, vol.2, p. 21-28.

Novikov, Nikolai, *Opyt istoricheskago slovaria o rossiiskikh pisateliakh* (St Petersburg, 1772).

Papmehl, K. A., *Metropolitan Platon of Moscow (Petr Levshin, 1737-1812): the enlightened prelate, scholar and educator* (Newtonville, MA, 1983).

Parkinson, John, *A Tour of Russia, Siberia and the Crimea 1792-1794*, ed. William Collier (London, 1971).

Peters, D. I., *Nagradnye medali Rossii vtoroi poloviny XVIII stoletiia* (Moscow, 1999).

Platon, *Pouchitel'nye slova*, 6 vols (Moscow, 1780).

—, *Zhizn' moskovskago mitropolita Platona* (Moscow, 1890).

Platonov, S. F., A. S. Nikolaev and S. A. Pereselenkov (ed.), *Opisanie del arkhiva Ministerstva narodnogo prosveshcheniia*, 2 vols (Petrograd, 1917).

Pnin, Ivan, *Sochineniia*, ed. I. K. Luppol (Moscow, 1934).

Popovskii, N. N., 'Pis'mo o pol'ze nauk i o vospitanii vo onykh iunoshestva', in *Poety XVIII veka*, ed. G. P. Makogonenko and I. Z. Serman, 2 vols (Leningrad, 1972), vol.1, p.108-14.

Poroshin, V. S. (ed.), *Semena Poroshina Zapiski, sluzhashchiia k istorii Ego Imperatorskago Vysochestva Blagovernago Gosudaria Tsesarevicha i Velikago Kniazia Pavla Petrovicha, naslednika prestolu rossiiskago* (St Petersburg, 1844).

Pushkin, A. S., *Polnoe sobranie sochinenii*, 17 vols (Moscow and Leningrad, 1937-1959).

Raeff, Marc, 'The Enlightenment in Russia and Russian thought in the Enlightenment', in *The Eighteenth century in Russia*, ed. J. G. Garrard (Oxford, 1973), p.25-47.

Ramer, Samuel C., 'The traditional and the modern in the writings of Ivan Pnin', *Slavic review* 35 (1975), p.539-59.

Ransel, David L., *The Politics of Catherinian Russia: the Panin party* (New Haven, CT, 1975).

Reyfman, Irina, *Vasilii Trediakovsky: the fool of the 'new' Russian literature* (Stanford, CA, 1990).

Rzhevskii, A. A., 'Oda blazhennyia i vechno dostoinyia pamiati istinnomu otsu otechestva, imperatoru pervomu, gosudariu Petru Velikomu', in *Poety XVIII veka*, vol.1, p.245-49.

*Sbornik imperatorskago russkago istoricheskago obshchestva*, 148 vols (St Petersburg, 1867-1916).

Scott, Hamish M., *The Emergence of the eastern powers 1756-1775* (Cambridge, 2001).

Sereda, N. V., *Reformy upravleniia Ekateriny Vtoroi* (Moscow, 2004).

Serkov, A. I. (ed.), *Pis'ma N. I. Novikova* (St Petersburg, 1994).

Shcherbatov, M. M., *On the corruption of morals in Russia*, ed. Antony Lentin (Cambridge, 1969).

Shpet, G. G., 'Ocherk razvitiia russkoi filosofii' (1922), reprinted in *Sochineniia* (Moscow, 1989).

Slezkine, Yuri, 'Naturalists versus nations: eighteenth-century Russian scholars confront ethnic diversity', *Representations* 47 (1994), p.170-95.

*Slovar' akademii rossiiskoi po azbuchnomu poriadku raspolozhennyi*, 6 vols (St Petersburg, 1822).

*Slovar' russkogo iazyka XI-XVII vv.*, 27 vols (Moscow, 1995-).

Smith, Douglas, *Working the rough stone: Freemasonry and society in eighteenth-century Russia* (DeKalb, IL, 1999).

*Sochineniia V. Petrova*, 3 vols, 2nd edn (St Petersburg, 1811).

Tarasov, E. I. (ed.), *Dnevniki i pis'ma Nikolaia Ivanovicha Turgeneva za 1806-1811 goda*, 4 vols (St Petersburg, 1911).

Tatishchev, V. N., *Izbrannye proizvedeniia*, ed. S. N. Valk (Leningrad, 1979).

Tsapina, O. A., 'Pravoslavnoe prosveshchenie – oksiumoron ili istoricheskaia real'nost'?', in *Evropeiskoe Prosveshchenie i tsivilizatsii Rossii*, ed. S. Ia. Karp and S. A. Mezin (Moscow, 2004), p.301-13.

Viazemskii, P. A., *Polnoe sobranie sochininenii*, 12 vols (St Petersburg, 1878-1896).

–, *Zapisnye knizhki (1813-1848)*, ed. V. S. Nechaeva (Moscow, 1963).

Vinsky, G. S., *Moe vremya, Zapiski*, reprinted with an introduction by Isabel de Madariaga (Cambridge, MA, 1974).

Vsevolodskii-Gerngross, V. N., 'O terminakh "prosveshchenie" i "prosvetitel'stvo"', in *Problemy russkogo Prosveshcheniia v literature XVIII veka*, ed. P. N. Berkov (Moscow and Leningrad, 1961).

Wirtschafter, Elise Kimerling, *The Play of ideas in Russian Enlightenment theatre* (DeKalb, IL, 2003).

Zaborov, P. R., *Russkaia literatura i Vol'ter: XVIII – pervaia tret' XIX veka* (Leningrad, 1978).

Zhivov, V. M., 'Gosudarstvennyi mif v epokhu Prosveshcheniia i ego razrushenie v Rossii kontsa XVIII veka', in *Razyskaniia v oblasti istorii i predystorii russkoi kul'tury* (Moscow, 2002), p. 439-60.

–, *Iazyk i kul'tura v Rossii XVIII veka* (Moscow, 1996).

## Spain and the Spanish Empire

Álvarez Barrientos, Joaquín, 'La República Literaria en Europa: centro y periferia', in *1802: España entre dos siglos, sociedad y cultura*, ed. Antonio Morales Moya (Madrid, 2003), p.223-44.

–, 'Sociabilidad literaria: tertulias y cafés en el siglo XVIII', in *Espacios de la comunicación literaria*, ed. J. Álvarez Barrientos (Madrid, 2002), p.131-46.

Alzate y Ramírez, José Antonio, *Memorias y ensayos*, ed. R. Moreno (Mexico, 1985).

Aragón y Leiva, Agustin, *Elogio a Alzate* (Mexico, 1942).

Barrera-Osorio, Antonio, *Experiencing Nature. The Spanish American Empire and the Early Scientific Revolution* (Austin, TX, 2006).

Beardsell, Peter, *Europe and Latin America: returning the gaze* (Manchester, 2000).

Bret, Patrice, 'Alzate y Ramírez et l'Académie Royale des Sciences de Paris: la réception des travaux d'un savant du Nouveau Monde', in *Periodismo Científico en el siglo XVIII: José Antonio de Alzate y Ramírez*, ed. Aceves Pastrana (Mexico, 2001), p.123-206.

Calderón España, María Consolación, *Las reales sociedades económicas de amigos del país y el espíritu ilustrado: análisis de sus realizaciones* (Seville, 2001).

Cañizares-Esguerra, Jorge, *Nature, Empire, and Nation. Explorations of the History of Science in the Iberian World* (Stanford, CA, 2006).

–, *Puritan Conquistadors. Iberianizing the Atlantic, 1550-1700* (Stanford, CA, 2006).

–, 'Whose Centers and Whose Peripheries? Eighteenth-Century Intellectual History in Atlantic Perspective', in *History and Nation* ed. Julia Rudolph (Lewisburg, PA, 2005), p.71-95.

Caso González, José Miguel (ed.), *Asturias y la Ilustración* (Oviedo, 1996).

–, *El Pensamiento pedagógico de Jovellanos y su Real Instituto Asturiano* (Oviedo, 1980).

–, 'La Sociedad Económica de Asturias desde su fundación hasta 1808', *BOCES* 18:1 (1973), p.21-67.

Ceán Bermúdez, J.-A., *Memorias para la vida de Jovellanos* (Madrid, 1814).

Chambers, David Wade, 'Locality and science: myths of centre and periphery', in *Mundialización de la ciencia y cultura nacional: actas del Congreso Internacional Ciencia, descubrimiento y mundo colonial*, ed. Antonio Lafuente, A. Elena and M. L. Ortega (Madrid, 1993), p.605-17.

–, and Richard Gillespie, 'Locality in the history of science: colonial science, technoscience, and indigenous knowledge', in *Nature and empire: science and colonial enterprise*, ed. Roy MacLeod (Chicago, IL, 2001), p.221-40.

Chen Sham, Jorge, *La comunidad nacional "deseada": la polémica imparcialidad de las Cartas marruecas* (San José, 2004).

Clark, Fiona, 'The *Gazeta de Literatura de México* (1788-1795): the formation of a literary-scientific periodical in late-viceregal Mexico', *Dieciocho: Hispanic Enlightenment* 28:1 (2005), p.7-30.

–, 'Read all about it: science, translation, adaptation and confrontation in the *Gazeta de Literatura de México* (1788-1795)', in *Science and medicine in the Spanish and Portuguese empires*, ed. Daniela Bleichmar, Paula de Vos, Kristin Huffine and Kevin Sheehan (Stanford, CA, forthcoming).

Clément, J.-P., *Las Lecturas de Jovellanos (ensayo de reconstitución de su biblioteca)* (Oviedo, 1980).

Cuartas Rivero, M., 'Gijón: carretera de Asturias y obras en la villa de Jovellanos', in *Jovellanos, ministro de Gracia y Justicia* (Barcelona, 1998), p.100-103.

Defourneaux, M., *Pablo de Olavide, ou l'Afrancesado* (Paris, 1959).

Demerson, Paula de, and Francisco Aguilar Piñal, *Las Sociedades Económicas de Amigos del País en el siglo XVIII* (San Sebastián, 1974).

Domergue, L., *Les Démêlés de Jovellanos avec l'Inquisition* (Oviedo, 1971).

Fernández Alvadalejo, Pablo (ed.), *Fénix de España: modernidad y cultura propia en la España del siglo XVIII (1737-1766)* (Madrid, 2006).

Fernández Clemente, Eloy, *Estudios sobre la Ilustración aragonesa* (Zaragoza, 2004).

Fernández del Castillo, Francisco, *Apuntes para la bibliografía del Presbítero bachiller José Antonio Félix de Alzate y Ramírez Cantilla* (Mexico, 1927).

García, Alberto Saladino, *Ciencia y prensa durante la ilustración latinoamericana* (Mexico, 1996).

–, and Juan José Saldaña (ed.), *José Antonio Alzate y Ramírez: homenaje en el bicentenario de su fallecimiento* (Mexico, 1999).

*La Gazeta de Literatura de México*, 3 vols (Mexico, 1788-1795).

Glendinning, Nigel, *The Eighteenth century* (London, 1972).

Guerrero, Carolina, *Súbditos ciudadanos: antinomias en la Ilustración de América Andina* (Caracas, 2006).

Hill, Ruth, *Hierarchy, commerce and fraud in Bourbon Spanish America: a postal inspector's exposé* (Nashville, TN, 2005).

–, *Sceptres and sciences in the Spains* (Liverpool, 2000).

Jardine, Alexander, *Letters from Barbarie, France, Spain, Portugal &c.* (London, T.Cadell, 1788).

Jovellanos, Gaspar Melchor de, *Cartas del viaje de Asturias*, ed. José Miguel Caso González (Gijón, 1981).

–, *Obras completas*, ed. José Miguel Caso González *et al.*, 7 vols (Oviedo, 1984-1999).

## Bibliography

Jüttner, Siegfried, 'España, ¿un país sin ilustración? Hacia la recuperación de una herencia reprimida', in *La Ilustración en España y Alemania*, ed. Reyes Mate and Friedrich Niewöhner (Barcelona, 1989), p.121-37.

Krauss, Werner, *Die Aufklärung in Spanien, Portugal und Lateinamerika* (Munich, 1973).

Lafuente, Antonio, 'Enlightenment in an imperial context: local science in the late eighteenth-century Hispanic world', *Osiris* (2001), p.155-73.

Lluch, Ernest, *Las Españas vencidas del siglo XVIII* (Barcelona, 1999).

Luna, Juan Hernández, *José Antonio de Alzate* (Mexico, 1945).

Lynch, John, *Bourbon Spain, 1700-1808* (Oxford, 1989).

MacLeod, Roy, 'Introduction', in *Nature and empire: science and colonial enterprise*, ed. Roy MacLeod (Chicago, IL, 2000), p.1-13.

Moreno, Roberto, 'Creación de la nacionalidad mexicana', *Historia Mexicana* 12 (1963), p.531-51.

–, *Un Eclesiástico criollo frente al estado Borbón: discurso* (Mexico, 1980).

–, 'José Antonio de Alzate y los Virreyes', in *Cahiers du monde hispanique et luso-brézilien* 12 (1969), p.97-114.

Polt, J. H. R., *Jovellanos and his English sources: economic, philosophical and political writings*, Transactions of the American philosophical society 54:7 (Philadelphia, PA, 1964).

Ponz, Antonio, *Viaje de España*, 18 vols (Madrid, Joaquín Ibarra, 1772-1794).

Ruiz de la Peña Solar, A., 'El Instituto de Gijón: un paraíso perdido', in *Jovellanos, ministro de Gracia y Justicia* (Barcelona, 1998), p.80-89.

Sánchez-Blanco, Francisco, *El Absolutismo y las Luces en el reinado de Carlos III* (Madrid, 2002).

–, *Europa y el pensamiento español del siglo XVIII* (Madrid, 1991).

–, *La Mentalidad ilustrada* (Madrid, 1999).

Sánchez Espinosa, Gabriel, 'Gaspar Melchor de Jovellanos: un paradigma de lectura ilustrada', in *El Libro ilustrado: Jovellanos lector y educador*, ed. Nigel Glendinning and G. Sánchez Espinosa (Madrid, 1994), p.33-59.

Sarrailh, Jean, *L'Espagne éclairée de la seconde moitié du XVIII$^e$ siècle* (Paris, 1954).

Schafer, Robert J., *The Economic societies in the Spanish world (1763-1821)* (Syracuse, NY, 1958).

Sempere y Guarinos, J., *Ensayo de una biblioteca española de los mejores escritores del reinado de Carlos III*, 6 vols (Madrid, Imprenta Real, 1789).

TePaske, John Jay, 'Integral to empire: the vital peripheries of colonial Spanish America', in *Negotiated empires: centers and peripheries in the Americas, 1500-1870*, ed. Christine Daniels and Michael V. Kennedy (London, 2002), p.29-41.

Tietz, Manfred (ed.), *Los jesuitas españoles expulsos: su imagen y su contribución al saber sobre el mundo hispánico en la Europa del siglo XVIII* (Madrid, 2001).

Torrecilla, Jesús, *España Exótica: la formación de la identidad española moderna* (Boulder, CO, 2004).

Varela, J., *Jovellanos* (Madrid, 1988).

# Sweden

Annerstedt, Claes, *Uppsala universitets historia*, 3 vols (Uppsala and Stockholm, 1914), vol.3, part 2.

Bergström, Carin, *Lantprästen: Prästens funktion i det agrara samhället 1720-1800* (Stockholm, 1991).

Broberg, Gunnar, *Homo sapiens L. Studier i Carl von Linnés naturuppfattning och människolära* (Uppsala, 1975).

Burman, Lars and Carina (ed.), *Poetiskt och prosaiskt: texter från svenskt 1600- och 1700-tal* (Lund, 1992).

Dalin, Olof von, *Svea Rikes Historia*, 4 vols (Stockholm, Lars Salvius, 1747-1761).

Frängsmyr, Tore, 'The Enlightenment in Sweden', in *The Enlightenment in national context*, ed. Roy Porter and Mikuláš Teich (Cambridge, 1981), p.164-75.
– (ed.), *Science in Sweden: the Royal Swedish Academy of Sciences 1739-1989* (Canton, MA, 1989).
–, *Sökandet efter Upplysningen* (Höganäs, 1993); revised edn (Stockholm, 2006); French translation by Jean-François and Marianne Battail: *A la recherche des Lumières: une perspective suédoise* (Bordeaux, 1999).

Hansson, Sven G., *Satir och kvinnokamp i Hedvig Charlotta Nordenflychts diktning* (Stockholm, 1991).

Helander, Hans, *Neo-Latin literature in Sweden in the period 1620-1720* (Uppsala, 2004).

Högnäs, Sten, *Människans nöjen och elände: Gyllenborg och upplysningen* (Lund, 1988).

Ihre, Johannes, / Petrus Svedelius, *Dissertatio in quaestionem, an studia litterarum contulerint ad emendationem morum?* (Arosiae, n.d.).

Johannisson, Karin, *Det mätbara samhället: Statistik och samhällsdröm i 1700-talets Europa* (Stockholm, 1988).
–, 'Society in numbers: the debate over quantification in 18th-century political economy', in *The Quantifying spirit in the 18th century*, ed. Tore Frängsmyr et al. (Berkeley, CA, and Los Angeles, CA, 1990), p.353-61.

Koerner, Lisbet, *Linnaeus: nature and nation* (Cambridge, MA, 1999).

Lamm, Martin, *Upplysningstidens romantik*, vol.1 (Stockholm, 1918).

Lindroth, Sten, *Svensk lärdomshistoria: Frihetstiden* (Stockholm, 1978).

Linnaeus, Carl, *Tal, vid Deras Kongl. Majesteters Höga Närvaru [...] den 25 Septemb. 1759* (Uppsala, n.d.).

Metcalf, Michael F., 'Parliamentary sovereignty and royal reaction, 1719-1809', in *The Riksdag: a history of the Swedish parliament*, ed. M. F. Metcalf (Stockholm and New York, 1987), p.109-64.

Nilzén, Göran, 'Scheffer, Carl Fredrik', *Svenskt biografiskt lexikon* (Stockholm, 2001), vol.154, p.520-26.

Nordenflycht, Hedvig Charlotta, *Witterhets Arbeten*, 2 vols (1762; facsimile edition, Stockholm, 1992).

Öhrberg, Ann, *Vittra fruntimmer: Författarroll och retorik hos frihetstidens kvinnliga författare* (Hedemora, 2001).

Oscarsson, Ingemar, 'Med tryckfrihet som tidig tradition (1732-1809)', in *Den svenska pressens historia*, ed. Karl Erik Gustafsson and Per Rydén, 5 vols (Stockholm, 2000), vol.1, p.114-16.

Östlund, Krister, *Johan Ihre on the origins and history of the runes: three Latin dissertations from the mid-18th century* (Uppsala, 2000).

Proschwitz, Gunnar von (ed.), *Gustave III par ses lettres* (Stockholm and Paris, 1986).

Roberts, Michael, *The Age of liberty: Sweden 1719-1772* (Cambridge, 1986).

Scheffer, Carl Fredrik, *Commerce épistolaire entre un jeune prince et son gouverneur* (Stockholm, 1771).

–, *Lettres particulières à Carl Gustaf Tessin 1744-1752*, ed. Jan Heidner (Stockholm, 1982).

Sheridan, Charles Francis, *A History of the late revolution in Sweden* (Dublin, 1778).

Skuncke, Marie-Christine, *Gustaf III _ Det offentliga barnet: en prins retoriska och politiska fostran* (Stockholm, 1993).

–, 'Press and political culture in Sweden at the end of the age of liberty', in *Enlightenment, revolution and the periodical press*, ed. Hans-Jürgen Lüsebrink and Jeremy D. Popkin, *SVEC* 2004:06, p.81-86.

–, 'Un prince suédois auteur français: l'éducation de Gustave III, 1756-1762', *SVEC* 296 (1992), p.123-63.

–, 'Was there a Swedish Enlightenment?', in *Norden och Europa 1700-1830: Synvinklar på ömsedigt kulturellt inflytande*, ed. Svavar Sigmundsson (Reykjavik, 2003), p.25-41.

Stålmarck, Torkel, 'Hedvig Charlotta Nordenflychts brev till Albrecht von Haller och Johan Arckenholtz', *Samlaren* 1959 (16 January 1756), p.106-21.

–, *Hedvig Charlotta Nordenflycht – Ett porträtt* (Stockholm, 1997).

Sylwan, Otto, *Svenska pressens historia till statshvälfningen 1772* (Lund, 1896).

Wolff, Charlotta, *Vänskap och makt: den svenska politiska eliten och upplysningstidens Frankrike* (Helsingfors, 2005).

# Index

Academies, *see* universities and academies, and learned societies
Adodurov, Vasily Evdokimovich, 233
Adolf Frederick, king of Sweden, 95, 96
agriculture, 67-68, 72-86, 110, 114, 115, 166, 171, 181, 184, 185, 186, 188
Africa, 5, 7, 14, 18, 20, 239, 258
Aikin, John, Rev., 126
Aikin Jr, John, Dr, 124-29, 133, 138
Alembert, Jean D', 2, 7, 15, 24, 31-36, 38, 43, 45, 87, 94, 95, 99, 101, 284
Alexander I, emperor of Russia, 143, 230, 248
Alfred the Great, king of Wessex, 271, 279
Allamand, François-Louis, 44
Almássy, Pál, 112, 115
Alsace, 30
Alzate y Ramírez, José Antonio, 8, 10, 252-64 *passim*
America, thirteen colonies, and United States of, 3, 4, 49, 167, 169, 173, 174, 203, 209, 223
Amsterdam, 3, 6
Andrássy family, 109
Anglicanism, 16, 52, 53, 60, 131, 163, 164, 172, 173, 174, 175, 177, 179
Anglophilia, 7, 12, 38, 74, 107, 108, 112, 113, 114, 246, 282
Anti-Enlightenment, or Counter-Enlightenment, 13-16, 47, 50, 164, 179, 201-209, 216-28, 286
anti-Trinitarians, anti-Trinitarianism, 2, 15, 32, 34, 36, 44, 45, 60, 61, 127
antiquity, 12, 92, 173, 272-73
Aragón, 183
archangel, 243
Arctic Ocean, 229
Argental, Marc Pierre de Voyer, comte d', 22
Argental, Jeanne-Grâce Bosc Du Bouchet, comtesse d', 22
Aristides, 220

Arne, Thomas, 275
Arnone, 81
Artois, Charles, comte de, later Charles X, 153
Asgill, John, 61
Asturias, 183-200 *passim*
Audubon, John James, 143
Austria, 109, 115, 156
  *see also* Habsburg monarchy
Aurivillius, Carl, 97
Auzière, Georges, 40
Ávila, 183, 193

Bacon, Francis, Lord Chancellor, 131, 285
Badin, 103
Baggot, Mark, 56
Bantysh-Kamenskii, Nikolai Nikolaevich, 245
Barbauld, Anna Laetitia, 126
Barber, Rev. Samuel, 175
Barbeyrac, Jean, 41
Barcelona, 183, 190
Barrillot, Jacques, 42
Báróczy, Sándor, 108
Barruel, abbé Augustin, 194, 195
Basque country, Basques, 11, 185, 192, 253
Bastille, 151, 159, 161, 177, 207
Bath, 125
Batiushkov, Konstantin, 229, 230, 231, 232
Batthyány, Count Károly, 109, 114
Batthyány, Count Tódor, 109
Baudouin de Courtenay, Jan, 206
Baynard, John, 56
Beaumarchais, Pierre-Augustin Caron de, 153, 155, 160
Beauteville, Pierre de Puisson, chevalier de, 40
Beccaria, Cesare, 138, 246
Beddoes, Thomas, 267
Belarus, 210, 211
Bellanger, 157
Belfast, 174, 177

329

Belson, 152
Benedict XIV, pope, 184
Benevent, François, 158
Bentham, Jeremy, 138
Berch, Anders, 89
Berkeley, George, bishop of Cloyne, 14, 49, 58, 59, 60, 61, 62
Berlin, 6, 231, 237, 238
Bern, 30, 35, 41, 42, 44, 77
Bertrand, Elie, 39, 44
Berzeviczy, Gergely, 118
Bessenyei, György, 107, 108
Bethune d'Orval, Maximilien-Antoine-Armand de, 7th duc de Sully, 149
Bilbao, 183, 184
Birmingham, 9, 122, 125, 131, 265, 267
Blackstone, Sir William, 169
Blundell family, 134, 140
Bobes, Félix de, 198
Bohemia, 203
Boileau, Nicolas, 235
Boissière, David, 152, 155
Boncerf, Pierre-François, 75
Bonnet, Charles, 42, 236
Bordeaux, 17
Bostock, John, 121, 128
Bostock Jr., 121
Boston (MA), 143-44
botany, 89, 98, 136-37, 143, 253, 259
Bouillon, Louise-Henriette-Gabrielle de Lorraine, princesse de, 151
Boulainvilliers, Henri, comte de, 75
Boyle, Robert, 56
Bradbury, John, 143
Branciforte, Miguel de la Grúa Talamanca, marquis of, 259
Brandreth, Joseph, 128
Brissot de Warville, Jacques-Pierre, 145, 146, 147-8, 149, 154, 159, 160, 161
Bristol, 125, 132, 266-67, 270-72
Britain, 3, 12, 14, 22, 29, 42, 49, 80, 111, 114, 148, 149, 150, 151, 152, 158, 160, 164, 167, 169, 170, 171, 172, 173, 175, 176, 177, 179, 180, 196, 197, 203, 227, 265-79 *passim* see also England, Ireland, Scotland, Wales,
Broglie, Charles-François, comte de, 149, 152, 157

Browallius, Johan, bishop of Åbo (Turku), 89
Brown, John, 274
Bruce, James, 194, 195
Bruna, Francisco de, 184
Brutus the Trojan, 272-76
Brutus, Lucius Junius, 10
Buffon, Georges-Louis Leclerc, comte de, 194, 197, 283, 285
Burke, Edmund, 15, 131, 142-143, 179, 223, 266, 268
Burlamaqui, Jean-Jacques, 41
Burnet, Gilbert, 68
Burgundy, 148, 149, 153, 159
Butel-Dumont, Georges Marie, 74
Buxton, 125
Byron, John, Commodore, 194

Cabarrús, Francisco, 185, 188, 198
Cádiz, 183
Caesar, Julius, 22
Calabria, 69, 80
Calas, Jean, 19, 21, 26
Calcutta (Kolkata), 143
Calonne, Charles-Alexandre de, 154
Calvin, Jean, 29, 39
Calvinism, 30, 31-36, 44-47, 116, 163, 168, 170, 173, 175, 177
Campbell, Rev. William, 175
Campomanes, Pedro Rodríguez, 185, 187, 188, 189
Candolle, Augustin-Pyramus de, 42
Capitanata (northern Puglia), 80
Carra, Jean-Louis, 146
Cary, John, 74
Casado de Torres, Fernando, 190
Cassini, Jacques Dominique, 253
Castile, 184, 185, 186, 188, 190, 191
Castries, Charles-Eugène-Gabriel, duc de, 151, 153
Catalonia, Catalans, 183
Catherine II, empress of Russia, 8, 9, 20, 23, 24, 25, 216, 227, 230, 232, 233, 234, 236, 237, 238, 239, 240, 241, 242, 243, 244, 245, 247, 248
Celsius, Anders, 89
Chaadaev, Petr Iakovlevich, 241
Chappe D'Auteroche, Jean, 253
Charles II, king of Spain, 183
Charles III, king of Spain, formerly king of Naples, 69, 71, 188, 190

## Index

Charles IV, king of Spain, 189
Charles XII, king of Sweden, 88
Charlotte, queen of Great Britain and Ireland, 275
Chartres, Philippe, duc de, later called Philippe-Egalité, 153
Chatenay, 17
Cheltenham, 125
Chester, 127, 128, 129, 138, 141
Chimay, 159
Choiseul, chevalier de, 156
Choiseul, Etienne-François de Choiseul-Stainville, duc de, 40, 152, 153, 155-56, 157
Christian VII, king of Denmark, 23, 24
Christianity, 3, 5, 14-16, 29-39, 42-47
 see also anti-Trinitarianism, Anglicanism, Calvinism, Dissent, Lutheranism, Old Believers, Orthodoxy, Protestantism, Roman Catholicism
Cicero, 245
Clarke, Rev. Samuel, 45
Clarkson, Thomas, 141
Clayton, Robert, bishop of Clogher, 60, 61
Cleves, 26
Cockermouth, 266
Coleridge, Samuel Taylor, 266-67, 270-71, 277
commerce, 8, 11, 52, 71-77, 79, 82, 85-86, 100, 110, 115, 116, 119-26, 130, 132, 134, 138, 171, 172, 173, 174, 176, 178, 188, 195, 199, 272
Condorcet, Jean-Antoine-Nicolas de Caritat, marquis de, 195
Cook, Captain James, 194, 215
Corinaeus, follower of Brutus, 275
Corneille, Pierre, 99, 107
cosmopolitanism, 10-12, 43, 140-141, 144, 232, 245
Cottle, Joseph, 266, 270-71
Counter-Enlightenment, see Anti-Enlightenment
Courcelle, Mme de, 153
Cox, Sir Richard, 56
Cracow, 205, 215
Cramer, Gabriel, 42
Cromwell, Oliver, 53
Cullen, William, 121, 129
Cumberland, Richard, 274

Currie, James, 128, 130, 134, 135-38, 144
Currie, William, 128
Czechs, 11

D'Adhémar, Jean-Balthazar, comte de, 158
D'Aiguillon, Armand du Plessis, duc de, 155
Damilaville, Etienne Noël, 21
Danviken, 94
Damiens, Pierre, 33
Dannet, Rev. Henry, 129
Darwin, Erasmus, 266
Dashkova, Ekaterina, Princess, 234, 244
Davy, Humphry, 275
Dawson, Pudsey, 129
Day, Thomas, 266
Debrecen, 109
Debrő, 109
Deforgues, François-Louis-Michel Chemin, 159
Delatouche, 152, 158
Delfico, Melchiorre, 80, 83
D'Eon de Beaumont, Charles-Geneviève-Louis-Auguste-André-Timothée, chevalier de, 148, 149-150, 152, 153, 154-59, 160
Derzhavin, Gavrila Romanovich, 234, 240, 241, 242
Descartes, René, 50
Destouches, Philippe Néricault, 107
Demosthenes, 220
Denmark, 23, 219
Derry (Londonderry), 56
Diderot, Denis, 2, 3, 9-10, 17, 22, 23, 26, 232, 239, 240, 284
Diodorus, 92
Dissent, Dissenters, 119, 121, 127, 128, 130, 131, 132, 135, 137, 139, 140-41
 see also anti-Trinitarians
Dobson, Matthew, 120-21, 128, 129, 138
D'Oliva, Guay, see Guay, Nicole
Doria, Paolo Mattia, 71-72, 73
Drake, Nathan, 268-69
Droz, Jean-Pierre, 45
Dryden, John, 273
Du Barry, Jeanne Bécu, Mme, 146, 149, 153, 154, 155

331

Du Châtelet, Gabrielle-Emilie Le Tonnelier de Breteuil, marquise de, 103
Du Deffand, Marie de Vichy-Chamrond, marquise, 21, 95
Du Pan, Jean, 35
Dublin, 56, 58, 80, 81, 165, 166, 167, 171, 174, 176, 178
Dupaty, Charles Marguerite Jean Baptiste Mercier, 19
Dutch Republic, *see* the Netherlands

East Indies, 22
*Economistes, see* Physiocrats
Edinburgh, 80, 121, 127, 128, 129, 279
education, *see* schools, and universities and academies
Edwin, king of Northumbria, 277-79
Eisen, Johann Georg, 239
*Encyclopédie, encyclopédistes,* 15, 31-36, 43, 45, 87, 90, 135, 210, 284
Elizabeth, empress of Russia, 236
Enfield, Rev. William, 119-24, 126, 128, 131-34
England, 2-3, 4, 9, 10, 15, 17, 18, 38, 43, 57, 74, 82, 84, 111, 114, 124, 127, 128, 138, 139, 149, 150, 167, 171, 177, 191, 195, 209, 223, 236, 239, 246, 265-79 *passim*
*see also* Britain
enlightened absolutism, or enlightened despotism, 9-10, 20, 51, 97, 99, 106, 109, 111, 115, 185, 189, 194, 211-12, 235, 241
Enlightenment,
  historiography, 1-16, 49, 50, 51, 52, 62, 63, 106, 145-48, 149, 154, 156, 158-61, 164, 179, 202-205, 230, 231, 249
  in the 'North', 7, 9, 23, 25, 209, 230, 237, 238, 239, 241, 243, 247
  'project', 1, 3, 20, 29, 31, 33, 35, 37, 42-47, 51, 87, 90, 103
  word, 5-6, 14-16, 65, 66, 71, 78, 79, 85-86, 87, 90, 163-181 *passim,* 201-210, 213, 216-28, 232, 233, 234, 236, 242, 243, 246, 247, 284, 288
Esterházy, Count Ferenc, 109
Esterházy, Count József, 109
Eyres' press, 127-28

Farel, Guillaume, 29
Farnese, Elizabeth, 71
Fawkener, Sir Everard, 17
Fekete, count János, 111
Fénelon, François de Salignac de La Mothe, 72
Ferdinand VI, king of Spain, 190
Ferguson, Adam, 195
Fernández de la Vega, Luis, 186
Ferney, 16, 17-27 *passim*
Ferrar, John, 175, 176
feudalism, 66-71, 74-75, 77-86
Filangieri, Gaetano, 65, 76-79, 81, 82, 84
Finland, Finns, 11, 87, 89
Florence, 71, 136
Flores, Gerardo, 254
Floridablanca, count of, 189, 191
Fontaine, chevalier de, 157-58
Fontenelle, Bernard Le Bovier de, 35-36
Fonvizin, Denis Ivanovich, 237, 240, 244, 245
Forgách, count Antal, 109, 116
Forgách, count Miklós, 116
Forster, Georg, 215
Foster, John, 180
Fountain, Peter, 157
France, 2-5, 7-10, 12-16, 17-27 *passim,* 29-47 *passim,* 62, 65, 74, 75, 76, 85, 147, 148, 149, 150, 151, 159, 164, 165, 166, 172, 173, 176, 177, 178, 179, 205, 207, 209-210, 213, 214-15, 227, 231, 237, 240, 244, 284, 287, 288
Francis I Stephen, Holy Roman Emperor, 109
Franklin, Benjamin, 220
Fratteaux, Louis-Mathieu Bertin, marquis de, 157
Frederick, prince of Hesse-Cassel, 41
Frederick II, king of Prussia, 20, 23, 24, 31, 106
freemasonry, 3, 52, 61, 107, 114, 165, 176, 207, 240, 246
French language, 3, 93, 95, 97, 98, 99, 205, 282, 286
French Revolution, 3, 131, 135, 145-46, 147, 156, 157, 158-61, 163, 164, 168, 169, 176, 179, 180, 207, 209-210, 220-21, 224, 225, 227, 231, 267-68

332

## Index

French Revolutionary and Napoleonic Wars, 12, 85, 108, 117, 160, 161, 164, 179, 183, 196, 197, 231, 267
Fréron, Elie-Catherine, 21, 95, 283
Freudenreich, Abram, 35

Gács, 109
Galanti, Giuseppe Maria, 75, 77, 79-81, 83, 84, 85
Galiani, Celestino, 72, 73
Galiani, Ferdinando, 65, 73, 75, 76, 85
Galicia (Spain), 184
Galileo Galilei, 102
Galton, Mary Anne, 134
Garnier, Charles Jean, 154-55
Gassendi, Pierre, 72
gazettes, *see* periodicals
Geneva, 9, 11, 14, 15, 16, 17, 29-47 *passim*, 152
Gennaro, Domenico, Duca di Cantalupo, 81, 83
Genoa, 71
Genovesi, Antonio, 65, 73-75, 76, 77, 78, 79, 82, 85-86
George III, king of Great Britain and Ireland, 275, 279
Georgi, Johann Gottlieb, 238
Germany, 4, 5, 16, 42-43, 62, 209, 231, 235, 236, 239, 242, 246, 281
Giannone, Pietro, 43, 65, 69, 71
Gibbon, Edward, 194
Gijón, 183-200 *passim*
Gillray, James, 268
Gjörwell, Carl Christoffer, 93-94, 99, 100, 101
Godoy, Manuel, Prince of the Peace of Basel, 200
Godwin, William, 195, 196, 198
Goëzman, Louis-Valentin, 155
González de Posada, Carlos, 192, 193
Gorsas, Antoine-Joseph, 146
Gotha, 92, 98
Gothenburg, 100, 103
Gottsched, Johann Christoph, 107
Goudar, Ange, 152, 153
Gournay, Vincent de, 73-74
Goya, Francisco de, 200
Graffigny, Françoise d'Issembourg d'Happoncourt de, 184
Grattan, Henry, 174
Great Britain, *see* Britain
Greece, 239

Gregson, Matthew, 119, 133, 137
Greifswald, 99
Grimm, Frederich Melchior, 230
Griffith, Amyas, 176
Grimaldi, Domenico, 80, 85
Grodno (Harodna), 219
Guay, Nicole, *known as* baronne d'Oliva, 150
Guerchy, Claude-Louis-François, comte de, 149-150, 157
Guines, Adrian-Louis de Bonnières de Souastres, comte de, 153
Gustavus III, king of Sweden, 9, 12, 21, 23, 24, 25, 87, 103, 169

Habsburg monarchy, 71, 105-118 *passim*, 156, 159, 161
*see also* Austria, Bohemia, Hungary
Haller, Albrecht von, 101-102
Harrogate, 125
Hartknoch, Johann Friedrich, 239
*Haskalah*, 15
Haygarth, John, 129
Hayley, William, 273-75, 277
Helvétius, Claude Adrien, 2, 20, 23, 33, 95, 100, 102, 107
Hénault, Charles-Jean-François, 95
Henri IV, king of France, 25
Henry VIII, king of England and Ireland, 57
Herder, Johann Gottfried, 5-6, 14, 16, 239, 240, 281-88 *passim*
Hermia, wife of Brutus, 275
Herodotus, 92
Hervey, Frederick, earl of Bristol and bishop of Derry, 272
Holbach, Paul-Henri Thiry, baron d', 2, 206
Holics (Holič), 109
Holland, *see* the Netherlands,
Höpken, count Anders Johan von, 89
Homer, 273
Horace, 235
Howard, John, 127-128
Huguenots, 2-3, 52, 173
Huguetan, Jean, 42
Hume, David, 13, 79, 85, 208, 223, 278, 285
Hungary, 4, 6, 7, 10, 16, 105-18 *passim* *see also* Habsburg Monarchy
Hutcheson, Francis, 49, 138, 165

333

Ihre, Johan, 91-92, 94
India, 123
Intieri, Bartolomeo, 72, 73, 85
Ireland, 7, 9, 10, 13, 16, 49, 50, 52, 53, 56, 57, 58, 61, 62, 63, 158, 163-81 *passim*
Italy, 6, 22, 30, 43, 65-86 *passim*, 165, 209

Jacob, Hildebrand, 274
Jacobites, 53, 60
Jallabert, Jean, 42
James II and VII, king of England, Scotland and Ireland, 53
James VI and I, king of Scotland, England and Ireland, 53
Jansenists, 193
Jarente de La Bruyère, Louis-Sextius de, bishop of Orléans, 156
Jardine, Alexander, 195, 196, 198
Jaucourt, chevalier Louis de, 87, 90
Jefferson, Thomas, 143
Jeffrey, Francis, 265-67, 279
Jenyns, Soame, 205
Jesuits, 35, 69, 204, 205, 209, 213, 214-15
Jews, 15, 51, 60, 207, 211
Jezierski, Franciszek Salezy, 201, 217
John, king of England and Ireland, 57
John Paul II, pope, 2
Johnson, Joseph, 128, 139
Joseph II, Holy Roman Emperor, king of Hungary, 111, 114, 115, 117, 236
Jove, Ramón de, 197
Jovellanos, Gaspar Melchor de, 10, 183-200 *passim*

Kapnist, Vasilii Vasil'evich, 248
Kazinczy, Ferenc, 106, 107, 108
Kaliński, Wilhelm, 213-14, 219
Kamchatka, 237
Kant, Immanuel, 5-6, 239, 240, 285
Kantemir, prince Antiokh, 229, 230, 235,
Karamzin, Nikolai M., 1, 7, 13, 230, 236, 237, 238, 239, 240, 241, 242, 246
Károlyi, count Sándor, 109
Karpowicz, Michał Franciszek, later bishop of Wigry, 213-14, 216-28
Kaunitz, prince Wenzel Anton von, 111

Kazan, 238, 240
Kheraskov, Mikhail Matveyevich, 233, 242
Kołłątaj, Hugo, 205, 215, 220, 224, 225
Königsberg (Kaliningrad), 6, 240, 281
Kossakowski, Jan Nepomucen, later bishop of Wilno, 213, 216, 218-19, 221-22, 225-28
Kossakowski, Józef Kazimierz, bishop of Livonia, 213, 216, 226-27
Kossakowski, Szymon, 226
Krashenninikov, Stepan Petrovich, 237
Krasicki, Ignacy, bishop of Warmia, 212
Krestinin, Vasilii, 243

La Barre, Jean François Antoine Lefebvre, chevalier de, 21
La Beaumelle, Laurent-Angliviel de, 34, 39, 47
Labzina, Anna, 235
La Calprenède, Gautier de Costes de, 108
La Condamine, Charles-Marie de, 184
La Coruña, 195, 196
La Marche, Louis-François-Joseph de Bourbon, comte de, later prince de Conti, 156
La Motte Valois, Jeanne de Saint-Rémy, comtesse de, 148, 150-51, 154, 156, 157, 158, 159, 160, 161
La Motte Valois, Marc-Antoine-Nicolas, comte de, 148, 150-51, 157, 158, 159, 160
Langreo, 190
Langres, 17
La Rochette, 152, 160
La Sonde, Barthélemy Tort de, 153
La Tour, Alphonse-Joseph de Serres de, 151, 158
Latvia, 211, 281
Lauraguais, Louis-Léon-Félicité de Brancas, comte de, 149, 160
Le Sage, George-Louis, 39
learned societies, 41, 52, 56, 58, 80, 82, 89, 185, 122, 136, 165, 166, 168, 176, 194, 214, 240, 253, 259, 260, 262, 266-67
Leipzig, 99, 233
Lemaur, Carlos, 186

Lena, river, 229
Lens, Peter, 61
León, 186, 187, 191
Leopold II, Holy Roman Emperor, king of Hungary, 115, 117
Leopold III Friedrich Franz, prince of Anhalt-Dessau, 282, 283
Lerena, Count of, 188
Lessart, Claude-Antoine de Valdec de, 159
Letourneur, Pierre, 26
Lewis, Richard, 170
liberty, 4, 10, 169, 170, 173, 175, 211, 219, 220, 226, 275, 278
Limerick, 175
Lindsey, Theophilus, 127
Linguet, Simon-Nicholas-Henri, 153-54, 160
Linnaeus, Carl, 89, 91, 94, 97-98, 103, 259
Linsing (or Linsingen), baron de, 152, 160
Lithuania, see Polish-Lithuanian Commonwealth
Liverpool, 8, 10, 119-44 passim
Livonia, 16, 213, 239, 282
Llano Ponte, Juan de, bishop of Oviedo, 192
Llyswen, 276
Locke, John, 17, 50, 142, 167, 173, 174, 176, 179, 220
Longano, Francesco, 76, 80, 82, 85
London, 3, 6, 10, 11, 148, 149, 151, 154, 155, 157, 158, 159, 195, 196, 276
Lorenzana, Francisco Antonio, archbishop of Mexico City and later of Toledo, 193, 259
Louis XIV, king of France, 25, 231, 241
Louis XV, king of France, 20, 21, 24, 25, 149, 157
Louis XVI, king of France, 147, 150, 156, 176, 272
Louis XVII, acknowledged by some as king of France, 196
Lovisa Ulrika, queen of Sweden, 95, 96, 102, 103
Lübeck, 152
Lucan, 273, 277
Luther, Martin, 203, 265
Lutheranism, 30, 90, 116

McKenna, Theobald, 178, 179
MacMahon, Joseph Perkins de, 151-52
Madrid, 183-99 passim
Maestre, Miguel, 184
Mairobert, Pidansat de, 153, 154, 160
Małachowski, Stanisław, 220
Malebranche, Nicolas, 59
Mallorca, 183, 189
Manchester, 122, 125, 127, 129, 138, 139, 141
Manco Capac, legendary Inca, 275
Mandeville, Bernard, 170
Manuel, Pierre-Louis, 146, 151, 154, 160
Marat, Jean-Paul, 146
Maria Theresa, queen of Hungary and Bohemia, archduchess of Austria, 106, 109, 111
Marie-Antoinette, queen of France, 146, 147, 150-151, 153, 156, 159, 161, 272
Marigny, Abel-François Poisson, marquis de, 149
Marmontel, Jean-François, 107, 108
Marsh, Narcissus, archbishop of Dublin, 56
Massalski, Ignacy, bishop of Wilno, 212-16, 226-27
Maupeou, René-Nicolas-Charles-Augustin de, 21, 146, 155, 156
Maupertuis, Pierre-Louis Moreau de, 285
Mazzei, Filippo, 7, 209-10, 211
Meléndez Valdés, Juan, 195
Melon, Jean-François, 72-74, 76, 79, 80, 85
Mexico, 8, 10, 11, 251-64 passim
Mexico City, 253, 254, 259
Mickiewicz, Adam, 228
Middleton, Conyers, 194
Milan, 71
Milton, John, 11, 107, 108, 195, 270, 273-74, 279
Minerva, 200
Mirabeau, Victor Riqueti, marquis de, 2
Mirabeau, Honoré-Gabriel de Riqueti, marquis de, 160, 207
Mislavskii, Bishop Samuil, 233
Missouri river, 143
Modrzewski, Andrzej Frycz, 219

335

*Index*

Molière, Jean-Baptiste Poquelin *known as*, 107
Molise, 75, 80
Molyneux, William, 56, 57, 58, 62, 167, 169, 172, 173
monarchy, monarchism, 10, 25, 51, 66-70, 71, 81, 84, 146-47, 156, 159, 160-61, 164, 167, 175, 189, 200, 210-11, 214, 219-20, 227-28, 243, 268, 275-76
Montaigne, Michel de, 238
Montesquieu, Charles de Secondat de la Brède et de, 2, 4, 10, 13, 17, 37-38, 63, 78, 98, 117, 168, 175, 179, 207, 208, 220, 227, 229, 282, 283, 285
Morande, Charles-Claude Théveneau de, *see* Théveneau de Morande
More, Hannah, 16, 272
Moscow, 230, 231, 232, 233, 243, 246, 248
Moss, William, 126, 134
Moultou, Paul, 44
Mozyrz (Mozyr), 221
Murav'ev-Apostol, Ivan, 231
Muratori, Ludovico, 213

Nagykálló, 109
Naples, 7-8, 65-86 *passim*, 165
Nartov, Andrei, 233
nations, nationalism, 6, 7, 9-12, 49, 50, 62, 63, 66, 71, 79-80, 160, 161, 167, 170, 171, 172, 209-10, 218-28, 232, 238, 239, 245, 255, 256, 258, 259, 260, 262, 263, 265-79 *passim*, 283, 284, 287
Necker, Jacques, 42, 194, 220
Netherlands, 2-3, 30, 43, 65
New Spain, *see* Mexico
New York, 144
newspapers, *see* periodicals
Newton, Sir Isaac, 17, 265, 286
Nikolev, Nikolay Petrovich, 243, 244
nobility, 66-70, 74, 76, 78-79, 80, 81, 83-84, 85, 109-12, 114-17, 185, 186, 188, 192, 193, 209-12, 214, 217-28 *passim*, 232, 245
Nonnotte, abbé Claude-François, 205, 206
Nordenflycht, Hedvig Charlotta, 7, 101, 102, 103
Norwich, 133

Novikov, Nikolai Ivanovich, 232, 233, 234, 235, 240, 242, 245, 246, 247
Nuttal, Thomas, 143

Ó Néill, Eoghan Rua (Owen Roe O'Nial), 173
Ob, river, 229
Ogden, James, 274
Ogilvie, John, 270, 275
Ogilvie, William, 172, 194, 195
Ogle, George, 173
Olavide, Pablo de, 184, 185
Olavide, Gracia de, 184
Old Believers, 236
Orczy, Baron József, 109
Orde, Thomas, 172
orthodoxy, 16, 203, 232
Osma, 183
Ottoman Empire, 105, 216, 240
Ottery St Mary, 266
Oviedo, 183-200 *passim*

Pagano, Francesco Mario, 65, 80, 84
Paine, Thomas, 135, 194, 195, 196, 268
Pálffy, count János, 109
Pálffy, count Károly, 111
Palmieri, Giuseppe, 77, 81-85
Paris, 6, 7, 14, 17, 24, 35, 36, 37, 94, 95, 100, 160, 207, 212, 253, 259, 260, 262
Parlements, 100, 151, 155-56
parliaments (diets, Estates, *Riksdag, sejm*), 57, 60, 61, 88, 90, 95, 105, 106, 114, 115, 164, 166, 167, 169, 170, 171, 172, 175, 177, 181, 201, 210-11, 216-28
patriotism, 7-13, 33, 80-81, 82, 93, 112, 113, 115, 140-42, 147, 156, 158, 159, 166, 167, 178, 185, 209-13, 217-28 *passim*, 265-79 *passim*
Paul, Grand Duke, later Paul I, emperor of Russia, 237, 244
peasants, 68, 80-81, 83-84, 111, 165, 171, 186, 211-14, 218-19, 227
Pedrayes, Agustín, 195
Pegado, Anthony, 144
Pelleport, Anne-Gédeon de Lafitte de, 148, 151, 152, 153, 155, 157, 159, 160
Pellet, Pierre, 42
Pennie, John F., 270

*Index*

Pennsylvania, 173, 265
Percival, Thomas, 139
periodicals, 4, 6, 8, 128, 149, 151, 152, 154, 159, 163, 165, 166, 172, 176, 177, 184, 188, 196, 197, 209, 230, 238, 240, 242, 246, 248, 251-64 *passim*, 265-73, 279
Perry, George, 119-20, 122-23
Peter I, emperor of Russia, 229, 230, 233, 234, 237, 241, 244
Peter III, emperor of Russia, 234
Petrov, A. A., 1, 246
Petrov, archbishop Gavriil, 233
Petrov, Vasilii, 241
Petty, William, 56
Philadelphia, 143
Philibert, Claude, 42
Philip V, king of Spain, 183, 184, 190
*philosophes*, 2-3, 8, 12, 15, 17, 29-47 *passim*, 205-10, 230, 231, 236, 238, 244, 248
Phocion, 220
physiocrats, physiocracy, 2, 7-8, 75-77, 83, 84, 166
Piarists, 204, 215
Pictet, Charles, 41
Pitt the Younger, William, 271, 279
Platon, metropolitan (Petr Levshin), 246, 247, 234, 235, 236
Pnin, Ivan P., 239, 243, 244
Poczobut, Marcin, 204, 214-15, 221
Podmaniczky, Baron József, 112, 115
Polish-Lithuanian Commonwealth, 4, 6-16 *passim*, 110, 117, 201-28
Political economy, 5, 7-8, 65-86 *passim*, 112, 165, 171, 184
Pollock, Joseph, 173, 180
Pompadour, Jeanne, marquise de, 149, 152, 154
Ponz, Antonio, 185, 186, 187
Pope, Alexander, 107, 273-74
Poroshin, Semen, 237
Praslin, Gabriel de Choiseul-Chevigny, duc de, 149, 156, 157
Pravia, 190
Preny (Prieniai), 222-24
Presbyterianism, 52, 53
 *see* Calvinism, Protestantism
Price, Rev. Richard, 11, 127, 142-43
Priestley, Rev. Joseph, 9, 127, 131, 135, 138, 265

Provence, Louis-Stanislas, comte de, later Louis XVIII, 151, 153
province, provincialism, 9-12, 185, 186, 191, 192, 201, 209-17, 222-24, 226, 228, 265-79 *passim*
Providentialism, 53, 96, 219-28
Protestantism, 11, 16, 29-47 *passim*, 53, 119, 140, 203, 243, 275
 *see also* Anglicanism, anti-Trinitarianism, Calvinism, Christianity, Lutheranism, Presbyterianism
Prussia, 50, 106, 117, 227, 283
Prussophilia, 12
public sphere, public opinion, 'the public', 4, 10, 52, 61, 65, 78, 84, 146, 156, 161, 165, 166, 167, 170, 202, 216-17, 221, 254, 255, 258, 260, 263
public good, public utility, 10, 166, 167, 168, 184, 185, 193, 199, 218, 254, 255, 258, 260, 263
Puglia, 82
Pushkin, Aleksandr, 240
Pye, Henry James, 271

Quercy, 22
Quesnay, François, 2, 76, 84
Quito, 184

Radishchev, Aleksandr, 243
Rathbone, William, 135
Receveur de Livermont, 155, 157
republics, republicanism, 10, 11, 16, 29-47 *passim*, 180
Republic of Letters, 4, 8, 10, 52, 65, 254, 257, 263
Rickman, John, 274
Riga, 239, 281
Rivarol, Antoine de, 26
Roberts, Francis, 56
Robertson, Rev. William, 51, 79
Rochement, Daniel, 33
Rodríguez, Ventura, 186
Rohan, Louis, cardinal, 150, 156
Roman Catholicism, Catholics, 14-16, 29, 30, 32, 33, 34, 35, 41, 42, 52, 53, 62, 68-69, 74, 111, 114, 116, 131, 140, 163, 168, 170, 172, 173, 174, 175, 177, 178, 179, 192, 201-28, 236, 251-64 *passim*
Romanticism, 10-12, 42, 203, 265-66
Rome, republic and empire, 79-80
 *see also* antiquity

337

## Index

Roscoe, William, 119-144
Rosén, Johan, 100-102, 103
Rousseau, Jean-Jacques, 2, 7, 11-12, 17, 21, 31, 33, 37, 38, 39-41, 42-44, 87-103 *passim*, 107, 117, 175, 176, 179, 207, 223, 227, 230, 231 238, 239, 244, 282, 283
Roustan, Antoine-Jacques, 33
Rowe, Nicholas, 273
Rushton, Edward, 129, 135
Russia, 1, 4, 6, 7, 12, 49, 200, 210, 216, 227, 229-49 *passim*, 281, 283, 284
Rutter, John, 128

Salamanca, 188, 196
Salfi, Francesco Saverio, 77
Saint-Pierre, Jacques-Henri Bernardin de, 194, 195, 197
Salvius, Lars, 93, 94,
Samwell, David, 119-120, 123
Sappho, 103
Sartine, Antoine-Gabriel de, 153
Savoy, 30
Schaumburg-Lippe, counts of, 41
Scheffer, Baron Carl Fredrik, 87, 94-96, 98, 99, 100, 103
Schmid d'Avenstein, Georg-Ludwig, 76-77, 79, 82, 83
schools, 89, 192, 193, 195, 198, 204, 213-15, 225
Scotland, 5, 7, 30, 51, 79, 113, 138, 158, 164, 165, 170, 171, 211, 266-67
Séchamp, abbé de, 152
Sechenov, Dmitrii, archbishop of Novgorod, 234
sermons, 9, 60, 133, 201, 214, 216-28
Seven Years War (1756-1763), 12, 18, 22, 33
Sévigné, Marie de Rabutin-Chantal de, 103
Seville, 183, 184, 185
Shcherbatov, prince Mikhailo Mikhailovich, 245
Shakespeare, William, 26
Shepherd, Rev. William, 135
Sheridan, Charles Francis, 169, 170, 171, 179
Shuvalov, count Andrei Petrovich, 233
Siena, 77
Sierra Morena, 184, 185
Sievers, Jakob Johann, 243
Simbirsk, 1, 13, 246

Skarga, Piotr, 214
Skarszewski, Wojciech, bishop of Chełm and Lublin, 202, 208, 216, 217
Skerlecz, Miklós, 112, 115, 116
slave trade, 125, 128-29, 130-41, 173
Slovaks, 11
Slovenes, 11
Slovtsov, P. N., 238, 247
Smith, Adam, 7, 85, 113, 116, 118, 171, 194, 195
Śniadecki, Jan, 215, 221
Śniadecki, Jędrzej, 215
Socrates, 102
Sofia Albertina, princess of Sweden, 96
Sonnenfels, Joseph von, 107, 112
Sorbs, 11
South Shields, Tyneside, 158
Southey, Robert, 265-66, 270-71, 274-75, 277
Spain, 8, 10, 66, 68, 69, 71, 117, 183-200 *passim*, 253, 261, 263
*see also* Mexico
Spanish Inquisition, 184, 185, 193, 198, 207
Spinoza, Baruch, 3, 285
St Petersburg, 10, 229-49 *passim*
Staël, Germaine Necker, baronne de, 42
Stanisław I Leszczyński, king of Poland and duke of Lorraine, 98
Stanisław II August Poniatowski, king of Poland, 7, 20, 21, 23, 24, 209-10, 211, 216-17, 219, 226, 228, 272
Staszic, Stanisław, 206, 209
Stockholm, 93, 94, 98, 99, 103
Strasbourg, 43
Suard, Jean-Baptiste-Antoine, 145, 157
Sudbury, 268
superstition, 13, 15, 202, 204, 208, 212, 213, 229, 234, 247
Surowiecki, Karol, 206-208
Svedelius, Petrus, 91-92
Sweden, 7, 12, 15, 87-103 *passim*, 209
Swift, Jonathan, 13, 14, 49, 53, 54, 55, 56, 63
Swiss cantons, Switzerland, 30, 41, 43, 77
Świtkowski, Rev. Piotr, 9, 209
Szapáry, count János, 112
Széchényi, count Ferenc, 112, 113, 114, 118

338

*Index*

Tanucci, Bernardo, 69-70, 75
'Tartary', 229, 238
Tata, 109
Tatishchev, Vasily Nikitich, 235
Terray, Joseph-Marie, abbé, 155
theatre, 99, 102, 123, 126, 184, 188, 199
Thelwall, John, 9, 270-71, 276-79
Théveneau de Morande, Charles-Claude, 146-49, 152-60
Thomas, Daniel, 175
Thomson, James, 275
Tokaj, 110
Toland, John, 49, 61, 165
toleration, 3, 13, 15, 16, 20, 29, 31-33, 34, 35, 36, 43-47, 111, 130-31, 139-41, 168, 173, 176, 177, 178, 202, 207-208, 220, 227, 228
Tollot, Jean-Baptiste, 35
Tone, Theobald Wolfe, 180
Toreno, count of, 188
Tort de La Sonde, Barthélemy, 153
Tournemine, René-Joseph, 35
Towne, Robert, 18
translations, 4, 7, 74, 76, 77, 79, 82, 85, 93, 103, 107, 108, 111, 112, 113, 116, 117, 118, 205, 213, 229, 233, 237, 239, 240, 244, 246
Trembecki, Stanisław, 206
Trent, Council of (1545-1563), 203-204
Trigueros, abbé Cándido María, 184
Trinci, Cosimo, 75
Tronchin, Théodore, 34
Turrettini, François, 35
Turrettini, Jean-Alphonse, 35, 43
Turgenev, Nikolai Ivanovich, 231
Turgot, Anne-Robert-Jacques, 220
Turks, *see* Ottoman Empire
Tuy, 184
Tver', 243

Ukraine, 211
Ulloa, Antonio de, 184
Ulloa, Martín de, 184
Ulster, 38, 166, 173
universities and academies, 56, 62, 72, 87, 89, 90, 91, 94, 96, 97, 98, 100, 119, 121, 127-28, 131, 134, 137, 139, 143, 183, 184, 192, 194, 199, 204-205, 214-15, 218, 231, 232, 233, 252, 253, 259, 260, 262, 281

United Provinces, *see* the Netherlands,
Uppsala, 89, 90, 91, 93, 94, 96, 97, 98, 100, 103

Valdés, Antonio, 190, 191, 195
Valdés, Manuel Antonio, 254
Valencia, 183
Vannes, 22
Vay, Baron Miklós, 7, 109, 112, 113, 114, 116, 118
Venice, 71, 99
Vergara, 191, 192, 193
Vergennes, Charles Gravier, comte de, 155, 220
Vergy, Pierre-Henri Treyssac de, 153, 157
Vernes, Jacob, 44
Vernet, Isaac, 41
Vernet, Jacob, 31, 35-38, 41-46
Versailles, 150, 151, 229, 230
Vesey, John, archbishop of Tuam, 56
Viazemskii, Petr Andreevich, prince, 231, 240, 248
Vico, Giambattista, 65, 70, 80
Vienna, 10, 106, 107, 110, 112
*see also* Habsburg Monarchy
Vinskii, G. S., 244
Virgil, 273, 275
Volland, Sophie, 22
Voltaire, François-Marie Arouet de, 2, 9-10, 17-27 *passim*, 29-31, 34-38, 40-47, 51, 107, 117, 135, 149, 179, 205-207, 230, 231, 233, 236, 246, 282
Vorontsov, count Simon R., 245, 246
Vyshnii Volochek, 243

Wales, 11, 267-68, 276
Wallace, James, 121, 124-26, 129-30
Wallerius, Johan Gottschalk, 89
Wallis, Captain Samuel, 195
Walpole, Horace, 269
War of the Austrian Succession (1740-1748), 106
War of the Spanish Succession (1701-1714), 183
War of the Two Kings (1688-1691), 53, 62
Wargentin, Pehr Wilhelm, 89
Warrington, 119, 121, 127, 131, 133, 138-39
Warsaw, 206-207, 211-12, 216, 224, 226

339

*Index*

Washington, George, 220
Węgierski, Kajetan, 206
Weimar, 283
West Indies, 103, 125
Westphalia, Treaty of (1648), 30
White, John, 195, 196
Wilde, Peter Ernst, 239
William III, king of England, Scotland and Ireland, 53, 56, 163, 181
Wilno (Vilnius), 204
Wollstonecraft, Mary, 135
Wood, John, 122, 124, 125
Woodward, Richard, bishop of Cloyne, 174

Wordsworth, William, 266
Wörlitz, 282, 283

Yates, Rev. John, 135
Yearsley, Ann, 9, 271-76, 279
Young, Edward, 107, 108
Young, William, 194

Zaragoza, 183
Zavadovskii, Petr V., prince, 243, 245
Zinzendorf, count Karl von, 111
Zúñiga y Ontiveros, Felipe de, 252, 254
Zurich, 41